A Day in a Working Life

A Day in a Working Life

300 TRADES AND PROFESSIONS THROUGH HISTORY

VOLUME 1: PREHISTORY, BEGINNINGS– 1000 BCE THROUGH THE ISLAMIC WORLD, 600–1500

GARY WESTFAHL

An Imprint of ABC-CLIO, LLC
Santa Barbara, California • Denver, Colorado

Library of Congress Cataloging-in-Publication Data

Westfahl, Gary.
　A day in a working life : 300 trades and professions through history / Gary Westfahl.
　　volumes cm
　Includes bibliographical references and index.
　ISBN 978-1-61069-402-5 (alk. paper) — ISBN 978-1-61069-403-2 (ebk)
　1. Occupations—History.　2. Professions—History.　I. Title.
　GT5910.W47 2015
　331.709—dc23　　　2014035771

ISBN: 978-1-61069-402-5
EISBN: 978-1-61069-403-2

19　18　17　16　15　　　1　2　3　4　5

This book is also available on the World Wide Web as an eBook.
Visit www.abc-clio.com for details.

ABC-CLIO, LLC
130 Cremona Drive, P.O. Box 1911
Santa Barbara, California 93116–1911

This book is printed on acid-free paper ∞
Manufactured in the United States of America

To my granddaughter, Serena Michelle Kong, who I am sure will work very hard, and work very well, in whatever profession she chooses to enter.

Contents

Preface xv

VOLUME 1
Prehistory, Beginnings–1000 BCE 1

Introduction 1
Animal Herders 1
Cave Painters 5
Chieftains 8
Farmers 11
Fishers 14
Food Preparers 18
Gatherers 22
Healers 26
Hunters 30
Metalworkers 34
Potters 37
Shamans 40
Textile Workers 45
Toolmakers 48
Warriors 51

Ancient Egypt and the Near East, 3200–500 BCE 57

Introduction 57
Architects 57
Boat Builders 61
Carpenters 65
Embalmers 68
Farmers 71
Food Preparers 75
Miners 80
Officials 83
Painters 87
Pharaohs 90
Priests and Priestesses 95
Prophets 98
Scribes 101
Slaves 104
Soldiers 108
Stonemasons 113
Storytellers 117

Ancient Asia, 3000 BCE–500 CE   121

Introduction   121
Acrobats   121
Architects   125
Calligraphers   129
Emperors   133
Farmers   137
Hydraulic Engineers   142
Jewelers   146
Merchants   150
Musicians   153
Philosophers   157
Poets   162
Scholars   166
Sculptors   169
Shamans   172
Warriors   176
Weavers   180

Ancient Greece, 2000–30 BCE   185

Introduction   185
Actors   185
Architects   189
Athletes   193
Farmers   197
Historians   200
Household Managers   203
Mathematicians   206
Merchants   210
Metalworkers   214
Orators   217
Philosophers   220
Physicians   224
Playwrights   228
Poets   231
Priests and Priestesses   236
Sailors   240
Sculptors   244
Slaves   248
Soldiers   251
Tyrants   255

Ancient Rome, 1000 BCE–500 CE   259

Introduction   259
Barbers and Hairdressers   259
Cooks   263
Couriers   268
Emperors   271
Farmers   276
Gladiators   281

Glassblowers   285
Historians   289
Household Managers   293
Orators   296
Popes   300
Priests   303
Prostitutes   306
Satirists   310
Senators   314
Slaves   317
Soldiers   321
Tutors and Teachers   326
Vestal Virgins   329
Winemakers   333

The Byzantine Empire and Russia, 300–1500   337

Introduction   337
Actors and Dancers   337
Architects   341
Bishops   346
Emperors and Empresses   349
Eunuchs   354
Farmers   357
Goldsmiths   361
Jewelers   365
Merchants   369
Physicians   373
Sailors   377
Soldiers   381

The Islamic World, 600–1500   387

Introduction   387
Alchemists   387
Caliphs   391
Cooks   396
Farmers   399
Hunters   403
Imams   406
Mathematicians   409
Merchants   413
Poets   416
Soldiers   421
Weavers   426

VOLUME 2
Africa, 3000 BCE–1500 CE   431

Introduction   431
Blacksmiths   431
Farmers   435
Fishers   438

Food Preparers   441
Hunters   445
Kings and Queens   448
Musicians and Singers   453
Pastoralists   457
Potters   459
Shamans   462
Warriors   466

The Americas, 3000 BCE–1500 CE   471

Introduction   471
Architects   471
Astronomers   475
Farmers   480
Fishers   485
Food Preparers   489
Goldsmiths   493
Hunters   498
Kings and Emperors   500
Merchants   506
Musicians and Dancers   508
Potters   512
Priests and Priestesses   516
Shamans   519
Warriors   523
Weavers   527

Central and East Asia, 500–1500   531

Introduction   531
Actors   531
Acupuncturists   535
Astrologers   539
Cooks   542
Emperors   546
Farmers   550
Gunsmiths   554
Monks and Nuns   557
Painters   561
Printers   565
Sailors   568
Samurai   571
Soldiers   575
Storytellers   580

Medieval Europe, 500–1500   585

Introduction   585
Architects   585
Blacksmiths   589
Cooks   592
Crusaders   596

Farmers   601
Innkeepers   606
Kings and Queens   610
Knights   614
Lawyers   618
Lords and Ladies   621
Merchants   625
Millers   630
Monks and Nuns   633
Poets   636
Priests   641
Shoemakers   645
Stonemasons   648
Students   651
Troubadours   656

The Emergence of Modern Europe, 1500–1700   661

Introduction   661
Actors   661
Bankers   666
Clockmakers   670
Cooks   673
Courtiers   677
Farmers   680
Jesters   684
Kings and Queens   689
Ministers (Protestant)   692
Painters   696
Playwrights   701
Poets   706
Printers   710
Scientists   714
Soldiers   719

The World beyond Europe, 1500–1776   723

Introduction   723
Architects   723
Conquistadors   728
Explorers   733
Farmers   737
Geishas   740
Governors   744
Mapmakers   747
Missionaries   751
Pirates   755
Silversmiths   759
Slave Traders   762
Sumo Wrestlers   766
Traders   769
Travel Writers   773

The Age of Reason, 1700–1800   779

Introduction   779
Chemists   779
Composers   783
Cossacks   787
Dancers   791
Economists   795
Encyclopedists   799
Farmers   804
Grammarians   808
Highwaymen and Highwaywomen   811
Kings and Queens   815
Mathematicians   819
Novelists   823
Tailors and Seamstresses   827
Theologians   831

A Time of Revolutions, 1776–1825   835

Introduction   835
Balloonists   835
Candle Makers   839
Executioners   842
Farmers   847
Generals   852
Journalists   856
Militiamen   860
Painters   865
Presidents   869
Priests   874
Schoolteachers   878
Vice Presidents   881

VOLUME 3
Spheres of Influence, 1776–1914   887

Introduction   887
Anthropologists   887
Big Game Hunters   892
Bureaucrats   896
Explorers   899
Farmers   903
Guides   908
Missionaries   911
Naturalists   916
Rajahs   920
Sailors   924
Soldiers   928
Taxidermists   932

The Rise of Nationalism, 1815–1914   937

Introduction   937
Cowboys   937
Diplomats   943
Evangelists   947
Geologists   952
Lecturers   957
Librarians   961
Paleontologists   965
Photographers   969
Poets   974
Postal Workers   979
Prime Ministers   982
Professors   986
Sociologists   989
Songwriters   993

The Power of the Industrial Revolution, 1800–1914   999

Introduction   999
Biologists   999
Charity Workers   1004
Chimney Sweeps   1009
Detectives   1013
Factory Workers   1017
Farmers   1021
Fire Fighters   1024
Magicians   1030
Maids and Butlers   1035
Mayors   1040
Miners   1043
Morticians   1047
Nurses   1052
Office Workers   1055
Police Officers   1059
Railroad Engineers   1064
Tycoons   1067
Union Leaders   1071
Vaudevillians   1076
Whalers   1080

The World at War, 1914–1945   1087

Introduction   1087
Airplane Pilots   1087
Chaplains   1091
Comedians   1096
Cryptographers   1100
Deep-Sea Divers   1104

Dictators   1110
Efficiency Experts   1114
Physicians   1119
Physicists   1124
Psychologists   1129
Singers   1134
Soldiers   1137

The Cold War, 1945–1991   1143

Introduction   1143
Ambassadors   1143
Astronauts   1148
Broadcast Journalists   1153
Computer Scientists   1158
Legislators   1163
Peace Corps Volunteers   1168
Popes   1173
Presidents   1178
Soldiers   1181
Spies   1186
Translators and Interpreters   1190
Vice Presidents   1195

A Global World, 1914–Present   1201

Introduction   1201
Athletes   1202
Chefs   1206
Farmers   1212
Fashion Designers   1216
Film Actors   1221
Film Directors   1226
Flight Attendants   1230
Grocers   1233
Lawyers   1237
Plumbers and Electricians   1242
Real Estate Agents   1247
Rock Musicians   1250
Screenwriters   1255
Social Workers   1260
Teachers   1265
Television Evangelists   1270
Travel Agents   1274
Veterinarians   1278
Video Game Designers   1282
Web Site Designers   1285

Afterword: The Future of Work   1291

Recommended Print Resources   1295

Recommended Online Resources   1303

Index   1311

Preface

Throughout human history, people have needed to work in order to stay alive. In prehistoric cultures, men and women in small groups had to find and prepare their own food, craft their own tools and utensils, make their own clothing, and construct their own shelters. As civilizations emerged all over the world, people began to specialize in one profession, which enabled them to earn an income and purchase the goods and services provided by workers in other professions. All too often, though, a person's job was not a matter of choice: sons were expected to learn and practice the trades of their fathers, and women were generally forced to work solely as wives and mothers, with few other occupations open to them. But gradually, though ancient practices still prevail in some areas, there emerged the belief that men and women should have the right to choose the activity that will occupy much of their lives.

Scope and Purpose

A Day in a Working Life: 300 Trades and Professions through History surveys some of the common occupations of people who lived in various civilizations and at various times, from human prehistory to the present day. Its coverage is necessarily selective, since no work of this size could possibly examine every single occupation in every single culture, although the book exceeds the promise of its title by actually covering 315 professions, not 300. This three-volume reference work spans twenty-one eras, from prehistoric times to the present, and ranges from cave painters to online game designers. Some of the eras, such as Ancient Asia, 3000 BCE–500 CE, are limited by geography as well as by time period. The eras are arranged chronologically. In examining each of the twenty-one eras, the book will generally focus its attention on workers in six categories that seem to represent universal human occupations:

Leaders, who control governments that seek to benefit their citizens;
Farmers, who provide most of the food in people's diets;
Artisans, who make the utensils, tools, furniture, and structures needed in everyday life;
Warriors, who defend their compatriots from domestic and foreign threats;
Religious leaders, who guide people in understanding spiritual matters and engaging in moral behavior; and
Entertainers, who offer citizens necessary diversions from their everyday worries and concerns.

Granted, other sorts of workers might be regarded as equally indispensable, such as the businessmen and businesswomen who strive to provide what people want in an efficient and economical manner and the officials who implement their leaders' decisions, and these professions are also well documented here, if not in every section. Beyond occupations taken from the six categories, other professions in each era were selected because they seemed especially important or interesting, like the clockmakers of the European Renaissance or the cowboys of nineteenth-century America, or because they are widely perceived as emblematic of their cultures, such as the embalmers of ancient Egypt or the geishas of Japan.

There are several reasons why readers will benefit from reading or browsing through *A Day in a Working Life: 300 Trades and Professions through History*. Whether one speaks of the chores of the Stone Age or the careers of the Information Age, occupations are central to world history. This book will help readers learn about occupations in different times and places and compare occupations across periods and cultures, and it will help them use occupational history to learn more about daily life. These facts and personal accounts of how people lived will help to provide a better understanding of world history.

It can simply be interesting to read detailed accounts, for example, of how ancient Asian acrobats performed for their audiences or how eighteenth-century balloonists mastered the art of flying through the sky. People who are already sure about their career goals will want to learn what it was like to be a part of this profession in other times and other places, while those still pondering a variety of future occupations might garner some insight into which one would be best for them by considering the histories of several potential choices. Since such historical information is rarely provided in references aimed exclusively at future jobseekers, individuals who have learned something about the history of their future profession might have an edge over others who lack this background knowledge. Finally, this work will remind readers that everyone entering a profession is also joining a long tradition of dedicated effort, and though these are traditions that demand respect, they are also traditions that new practitioners may have to change and improve in order to adapt to new technologies and new societal norms, just as their predecessors were constantly required to create new techniques and new approaches to their work.

Structure and Special Features

Each section, after a brief introduction, will provide from eleven to twenty essays about particular professions in each era. All of the essays endeavor to focus on the daily lives and routines of each sort of worker, although some attention is also given to the various products of their labors, which in many cases are better documented than the activities of their creators.

The recommended further readings after each essay include only recent books of interest (most of them published in the last twenty-five years), primarily because one can now assume that today's students and readers are familiar with the processes of finding reliable information online, but may be less skilled in locating valuable resources in print. (All of the books listed here should always be available without charge to any student and to most public library users with access to an interlibrary loan service.) For readers who prefer to rely more on online sources, the Recommended List of Online Resources at the end of Volume Three, arranged by eras, will guide users to helpful sites offering information about various professions through history.

Each discussion of an occupation will also offer two sidebars that make some interesting connection between the workers who are discussed and their counterparts in other periods or in contemporary times. They may offer key facts, interesting trivia, or connections to popular culture. In some cases, photographs and illustrations will provide images of people at work or their products.

Every occupation description is also accompanied by one or two documents that provide detailed, and often fascinating, looks at certain aspects of the profession. Whenever possible, these were written by the actual workers or holders of the positions, though the writings of contemporary observers and later scholars are featured as well. In some cases the documents will help readers understand what historical sources thought of the occupations. Document examples include Plato writing about Socrates teaching mathematics in ancient Greece; a nineteenth-century English executioner discussing his hope to make his job more humane; and the twentieth-century naturalist William Beebe's own notes, as he descended to what were record-setting oceanic depths in 1934.

If some readers are disappointed because their favorite occupation seems to be underrepresented, the bibliographies following each entry and the general bibliographies at the end of Volume Three will guide them to additional resources that can satisfy their curiosity.

An afterword offers some general thoughts about the probable future of human labor. Volume Three concludes with general recommended print and online sources to provide users with more ideas for information. In addition to the detailed table of contents listing all the eras and occupations surveyed, a comprehensive index offers more access to the three volumes.

Like all reference works, *A Day in a Working Life: 300 Trades and Professions through History* is primarily designed to be a book to consult, not a book to read all the way through. Nonetheless, the rare individual who chooses to read every single entry will gain a special appreciation for the remarkable energy and ingenuity that countless people have displayed throughout human history in developing and mastering all of the complex and demanding professions that have always been, and will always be, a central aspect of the human experience.

Prehistory, Beginnings–1000 BCE

Introduction

As those who work in the difficult field of paleoanthropology know, there is no fossil behavior, and since our distant ancestors did no writing, there are also no written records of their daily activities. All that we know about life in very ancient times, then, must be based solely on careful examination of human skeletons, which offer evidence of recurring actions, injuries, and diseases; preserved tools, weapons, and utensils, which were visibly utilized for certain purposes; and anthropological observations of remote twentieth-century cultures that, until in regular contact with the developed world, seemingly maintained lifestyles that were similar to those of ancient humans. For fully rendered accounts of their daily lives, all we can rely on are the skillful modern writers, fascinated by our prehistory, who have built upon the best research of their day to eloquently describe prehistoric humans in works like H. G. Wells's "A Story of the Stone Age" (1897), Jack London's *Before Adam* (1907), J.-H. Rosny's *La Guerre du Feu* (*Quest for Fire*) (1911), and William Golding's *The Inheritors* (1955).

Even if our understanding of many specific aspects of their lives remains conjectural, some general truths are starkly clear: living nomadically in small groups, the earliest humans had to work very hard, every single day, to obtain the food, water, and shelter that they constantly required to stay alive, with survival as their only reward. Necessarily, they applied their burgeoning intelligence with desperate energy to the business of devising technologies and techniques that would enable them to maintain and improve their lives in a harsh and threatening environment. Thus, over a long period of time ranging from almost 200,000 years ago—when the species *homo sapiens* first emerged—to the beginnings of recorded history several thousand years ago, our ancestors mastered fire, learned how to hunt and fish, constructed basic tools, crafted pottery, and covered their unprotected bodies with furs. In the forms of decorated pots, small statues, and cave paintings, they further demonstrated these creative impulses in a less utilitarian manner, also providing signs of their embryonic religious and philosophical beliefs, and as their numbers and knowledge grew, they mastered new arts like agriculture and metalworking. As all of their many innovations were gradually perfected and passed on from generation to generation by means of their greatest invention, spoken language, humanity was gradually able to forge its first true civilizations.

Animal Herders

Soon after humans began experimenting with agriculture, around 10,000 years ago, they started to domesticate and herd animals for the same reason: to provide people with a controlled, steady supply of a resource that had previously been available only in the wild. Animals kept in herds could be more easily slaughtered and eaten than hunted animals, and they represented an indirect way for people to feed off of wild plants that they could not directly consume: the animals could eat the shrubs and weeds, and humans could eat the animals. Furthermore, humans found that certain animals could be exploited in several other ways. Cows and goats offered nourishing milk; animal skins could be made into clothing; the wool from sheep produced a fabric with multiple uses; animal manure was an effective fertilizer for crops; and large animals could be trained to pull plows and transport goods.

While herding generally accompanied the rise of agriculture, the practice may have been a necessary precursor to farming in some regions, as a way to provide people with needed protein that their crops did not offer. There were also some people who maintained herds while continuing to lead a generally nomadic life without ever turning to farming, taking their animals with them as they traveled. Thus, for example, in prehistoric Mesopotamia, people would move with their sheep and goats to the highlands during the summer, when temperatures in lower regions were unsuitable for the animals and the vegetation they feasted on, and they would migrate back to the plains in the fall and winter. This style of life, termed pastoralism, long remained commonplace in some regions of Africa. More often than not, however, herding was carried out as an adjunct to farming; while one man tended the crops, another member of his family, perhaps the oldest son, would be assigned to take a group of animals out to graze all day and return at night. Dogs, already domesticated, were trained to assist their human masters in keeping the animals close together at all times.

In different areas of the world, it can be difficult to determine precisely when the prehistoric humans there first began to herd animals, but archaeologists can sometimes deduce the practice of herding by discovering a large number of animal remains outside their normal habitats, or detecting a sudden increase in an animal population that cannot be explained by a change in climate. In addition, domestication can sometimes modify the appearance of animals; for wild goats and sheep, for example, there is an evolutionary pressure to grow large horns to protect themselves and battle for mates, but domesticated goats and sheep, not facing these problems, tend to have smaller horns. In a few cases, ancient art might provide a clue; in the deserts of North Africa, for instance, cave paintings showing large numbers of oxen suggest that the animal was being kept in herds by people around 6,000 years ago.

This ancient rock art, believed to have been created about 4000–2000 BCE, from the Tassili n' Ajjer mountain range in present-day Algeria, demonstrates that prehistoric humans herded oxen as well as smaller animals. (Patrick Gruban)

Based on such evidence, scientists believe that the first animals to be herded were goats and sheep, and this makes sense, since they are by nature herding animals; prehistoric humans might have observed them together and speculated about taking control of the group. Managing these animals would not have been difficult, since goats and sheep bond with their parents at an early age, and in the absence of animal parents, they would readily bond with a human instead. Thus, a human goatherd or shepherd could establish himself as the master of a herd, watching over and guiding the animals as they wandered through the countryside, grazing on the vegetation. It is also likely that some herders deliberately engaged in selective breeding in order to produce animals with more favorable traits, like smaller goats and sheep with more suitable wool.

When humans turned their attention to other candidates for domestication, such breeding became a necessity. Sedate pigs were interbred with wild boars to produce larger animals with more meat, which were kept in herds within forests. To master a more challenging animal, the large and dangerous aurochs, or wild cattle, people first lured them with food and captured them individually; those that adapted well to human control would be bred with other docile cattle to gradually produce a more desirable domesticated breed. Over time, humans were able to achieve smaller aurochs with smaller horns, suitable for herding—a long process that must have been the work of settled farmers, not nomads. Initially, these were herded like other animals, guided to grazing grounds near forests and bodies of fresh water, but as these animals grew more valuable as a source of milk and cheese, they may have been the first to be kept in fixed enclosures and fed with grain.

In certain areas of the world, people herded many other animals. As noted, oxen were herded in the ancient Sahara Desert; near the Arctic, prehistoric people in present-day Scandinavia, Siberia, and Alaska herded reindeer; in sub-Saharan Africa, gazelles were a common choice; and ancient Peruvians formed herds of llamas and alpacas. The pattern in all cases is clear: humans focused their attention on large, generally docile animals that could provide an abundance of meat and milk. Over time, under human supervision, the animals tended to become smaller and tamer.

In the pastoral poetry of ancient Greece and Rome, the lifestyle of animal herders was highly romanticized; with nothing else to do but to watch placid animals as they chewed on plants, the poets imagined, the shepherd or goatherd had plenty of time to play his pipes, write songs, chat with companions, and woo any young woman who wandered into his purview. The reality of the herders' life was considerably different. They had to constantly watch for approaching predators, like wolves or bears, which might suddenly attack and kill one animal while driving the other panicked animals to scatter in all directions. Herded animals with horns, if suddenly enraged or maddened for some reason, might become a menace to the people watching them. Herders effectively functioned as the world's first veterinarians, as the health of the animals was their responsibility; they were the ones who would have to tend to the animals' wounds, remove thorns from their paws or hooves, and isolate apparently diseased animals from the others so that they would not all get infected. Even if no problems arose, herders faced the unending pressure of keeping large numbers of animals under their careful supervision, and even the calmest of animals might wander away and get lost if its overseer was momentarily distracted. When a young shepherd left the farm with forty sheep and returned with only thirty-eight, he would surely be chastised by the master of the farm, and perhaps even instructed to go back out into the twilight to search for the missing sheep.

Herding also led to adventures of another kind: the colonization of remote islands, which are often home to only a limited number of small animals. People need a steady source of protein, and when humans first tried to live on islands, they usually tended to hunt and kill all of their resident wildlife rather quickly; then, they were forced to abandon their new homes when there were no more animals there to be hunted. However, once people had learned to domesticate animals, they could bring them along in their boats and breed them in their new island communities. Thus, in the Mediterranean Sea, the evidence indicates that its islands were not inhabited until several thousand years ago, when people had domesticated animals that they could bring with them; much later, the islands of the South Pacific were finally colonized when the people of Southeast Asia belatedly started domesticating animals like pigs

ANIMALS HERDING ANIMALS

Since dogs had already been domesticated when humans began to herd animals, it was only natural for them to enlist these trusted companions to assist in the business of keeping animals together in groups. Later, they began to breed dogs especially for this purpose. This ancient role is still recognized in the names of several dog breeds, including the sheepdog, the German shepherd, and the Australian cattle dog, and even though these dogs are now better known to most people as pets, some continue to perform their ancestral duties in pastures throughout the world.

GOOD SHEPHERDS

Throughout Western culture, shepherds have long been celebrated for the wisdom and benevolence they display in watching over their animals. In Christianity, for example, the twenty-third Psalm of the Bible famously likened the Lord to a kindly shepherd; stories of the Nativity emphasize that humble shepherds were among the first to worship the newborn Jesus Christ; and in the Gospel of John, Jesus described himself as "the good shepherd" of Earth's people. Building upon the positive connotations of this profession, the English language allows "shepherd" to be used as a verb, meaning to guide or oversee a project.

and chickens. Paradoxically, though, the skill of herding became less important on these islands, since the animals could no longer wander far from their homes.

On the world's continents, herding animals is one of the few professions that has largely remained the same from prehistoric times to the present day; contemporary shepherds may wear the latest styles and carry a cell phone, but their routine of accompanying groups of animals while they graze on hillsides is more or less similar to what their counterparts were doing thousands of years ago. For these people, the kinship forged long ago with friendly, useful animals has endured as an important aspect of their daily lives.

Further Reading

Karega-Mŭnene. 2002. *Holocene Foragers, Fishers and Herders of Western Kenya*. Oxford: Archaeopress.

Kuznar, Lawrence A. 1995. *Awatimarka: The Ethnoarchaeology of an Andean Herding Community*. Fort Worth, Texas: Harcourt Brace College Publishers.

Russell, Nerissa. 2012. *Social Zooarchaeology: Humans and Animals in Prehistory*. Cambridge and New York: Cambridge University Press.

Serjeantson, Dale, and David Field, editors. 2006. *Animals in the Neolithic of Britain and Europe*. Oxford: Oxbow Books.

Shirai, Noriyuki. 2010. *The Archaeology of the First Farmer-Herders in Egypt: New Insights into the Fayum Epipalaeolithic and Neolithic*. Leiden, The Netherlands: Leiden University Press.

Smith, Andrew B. 2005. *African Herders: Emergence of Pastoral Traditions*. Walnut Creek, CA: AltaMira Press.

Document

From Berthet, Elie Bertrand. 1876. *The Pre-Historic World*. Translated by Mary J. Stafford. 1879. Philadelphia: Porter & Coates.

In this passage, the author provides an overview of a prehistoric community that herds animals and describes one shepherd.

The village of Argenteuil was not protected by any kind of fortifications, but its inhabitants doubtless possessed, either on the knoll of Orgemont or the hill afterward called Mont Valerien, one of the fortified enclosures where the Gauls took refuge with their families and herds in case of invasion. Around were cultivated fields that extended to the Seine; they produced wheat, barley, flax, hemp, and were bordered with fruit-trees. There were also meadows whose verdant carpets intersected the yellow gold of the harvests; but the sheep and oxen, horses and asses, of the hamlet seemed more accustomed to live in the woods under the care of shepherds than in regular pastures. It does not appear that there were any stables at this remote period; the domestic animals were shut up for the night in pens in the open air. The swine, whose flesh was of considerable importance in supplying the Gauls with food, were allowed to roam in the forests, after having doubtless been marked by their owners. . . .

Dumorix soon distinguished the person who had uttered the cry standing on the opposite bank. He was an old shepherd, who had no garments except a pair of goat-skin breeches, and stood leaning on a spear with a flint head. The man with whom he wished to communicate, and who had answered in the usual manner, was invisible, but doubtless he too was a shepherd.

Cave Painters

Prehistoric humans, for the most part, have spoken to their descendants solely through bones and tools, forcing paleoanthropologists to make deductions about their lifestyles from these scattered bits of data. However, paintings found in numerous caves, dating from 40,000 to 30,000 BCE, seem like direct messages from the past to the present, conveying information about the general lives of ancient peoples and the thoughts of the artists who executed them. It is little wonder, then, that they have attracted the attention of both scientists and laypersons.

We cannot be sure why our ancestors worked so hard to produce these paintings, but the most common theory is that they represented a form of sympathetic magic: if artists painted a successful hunt, they believed, it would bring about this desirable outcome. Evidence for this comes from many paintings, which often display spears penetrating animals, or depict the heart of the hunted animal with lines drawn toward it, as if to guide hunters' arrows to this vital organ; in addition, there are numerous depictions of pregnant animals, conveying the hope that in times when sparse, game animals would be replenished by many new births. It is also significant that artists generally chose deep and almost inaccessible caves for their paintings, indicating that they were not designed to be viewed and admired by all members of the tribe, but rather served some religious purpose best achieved by artists and shamans working in isolation. Perhaps they felt that the magic would not work if people without the proper background observed the paintings. (Today, of course, they can be observed by anyone at various websites, such as the Art of the Chauvet Cave [http://www.bradshawfoundation.com/chauvet/chauvet_cave_art.php] and Gallery: Amazing Cave Art [http://www.livescience.com/20966-gallery-cave-art-paintings.html].) In some places, the same wall was painted over several times, even though other empty spaces were available, indicating that certain areas might have been considered "lucky": that is, if a painting of a bountiful hunt apparently produced that result, people would paint there again hoping to achieve similar success. As a final indication of the art's sacred purpose, some caves, like the Tuc d'Audoubert cave in southern France, contain dancers' footprints, and images of men dressed in strange, elaborate costumes, suggesting that a ritual or ceremony was performed when the images were completed.

We also know that these cave paintings were considered important because of the strenuous efforts that went into their creation. First, the artists would seek out dark, distant caves that were unpleasantly cold and damp. Then, using torches to provide light, they would prepare their paints, using materials they had brought. Certain minerals would provide a limited range of colors: iron oxide (rust) made various shades of yellow, orange, red, and brown; magnesium oxide made darker browns and blues; and blacks were produced with burned bones. The minerals or bones were ground into powder, using the mortars and pestles that are sometimes found in these caves; the powder was then mixed with clay and animal blood to produce the paint. The rocky canvasses they chose for their paintings demanded additional labor; some images are found on very high walls, which must have required the artists to stand precariously on others' shoulders while they worked, while others could only be accessed if the artists painfully contorted their bodies. When they chose to paint on ceilings, they must have built some sort of wooden scaffolding to support the artists while they painted. Artists did not work hastily: a large rock discovered in India with etchings of multiple animals suggests that they made preliminary sketches before beginning to paint; they would start by drawing outlines of figures using charcoal or a stone; and finally, they would fill the outlines with colorful paint, by either applying it with their fingers, using a brush made of animal fur, or blowing paint into the spaces using a hollow bone.

Because hunting was an almost exclusively male activity, and because the vast majority of cave paintings depicted hunts, it was long supposed that all of the artists were men as well; however, one piece of recent evidence suggests otherwise. Many cave paintings included palmprints, perhaps intended to function

A stencil image of a human hand, found in the Chauvet cave of southern France, may represent the first form of cave painting, though such images also accompany later, more elaborate paintings, perhaps functioning as a sort of artists' signature. (French Ministry of Culture and Communication, Regional Direction for Cultural Affairs–Rhône-Alpes Region, Regional Department of Archaeology)

as an artist's signature, and a recent analysis of the palmprints in eight caves in France and Spain revealed that about seventy-five percent of them were female. This indicates that at least some women were present during the process of painting and strongly suggests that they also assisted in painting the images. In fact, the large number of female palmprints has led some experts to theorize that a majority of the cave painters may have actually been women. Another way that artists immortalized their hands was by making stencils, placing one hand on the wall and painting around it with the other hand. Such images provide the information that a majority of the cave painters were right-handed, since most of the stencils are of left hands; clearly, the artist would have put the weaker

hand into position and used the stronger hand to do the painting.

For modern artists, what is most interesting to note about the cave paintings is the way that the artists changed and refined their techniques over time, conveying an intense desire to improve the ways that they rendered their hunters and animals. This was first shown by Henri Breiul, a French priest who, in 1901, discovered cave paintings in southern France and northern Spain, executed by members of the Upper Paleolithic culture called the Aurignacians, and devoted the rest of his life to their study. He found that the earliest images of animals resembled crude stick figures shown in profile; not knowing how to show their antlers from the side, the artists had the animals awkwardly turn their heads to face the observers. But over time, the artists learned how to use shading and proper perspective to make their animals seem more realistic, sometimes conveying the texture of their fur and the bulges of their muscles. Their desire to accurately portray animals as they truly appeared has been recently vindicated: observing numerous images of horses with leopard spots, experts long believed that the artists were being imaginative, but DNA analysis of ancient horses now demonstrates that such spotted horses actually existed in prehistoric times. To enhance the realism of their work, some artists would cleverly make use of natural bumps and shallow areas to make animals appear three-dimensional, perhaps engaging in some deliberate carving as well so that the images stand out. Some paintings were so expertly executed that early scientists insisted that they had to be frauds, produced by modern artists who were familiar with Renaissance painters; yet it was eventually demonstrated that, in fact, these ancient artists had anticipated their techniques. In their final stage of development, the cave painters even experimented with abstract art: to show a herd of reindeer, for example, they might fully portray the first and last animal but show only legs or antlers to represent all the others. Later paintings also include what appear to be purely geometric figures that were not intended to represent humans or animals.

This progress in artistic development, along with the sheer numbers of images discovered to date, further suggests that painting was becoming a true profession for ancient humans, as tribes must have assigned certain members to work full-time on cave paintings, valuing the magical assistance that they could provide. Artists probably brought their children with them to the caves to teach them all the necessary skills, effectively establishing an hereditary guild of artists, though other youngsters with obvious talent might have been recruited as well; the occasional presence of young artists is proved by some palmprints made by children. Artistic training may have begun at a very young age by having children run their fingers through soft clay to produce lines, a process known as fluting; a study of France's Cave of One Hundred Mammoths, which contains many such lines, showed

ANCIENT ARTISTRY

As the world's first artists, one might imagine that the prehistoric cave painters would be vastly inferior to their modern counterparts, who can draw upon thousands of years of accumulated expertise. Yet, when they depicted animals in motion, they were generally superior to contemporary artists. According to research conducted by Gabor Horvath, a professor of biological physics at Hungary's Eotvos University, a large majority of ancient cave painters correctly illustrated the way that animals moved their limbs, while many modern artists have depicted their limbs in positions that they would never actually assume. Clearly, the cave painters observed their animal subjects thoroughly and carefully before they completed their works.

CAVEMAN CINEMA

Prehistoric cave art is impressive in itself, but to ancient observers it may have represented a multimedia experience. Seen in a torch's flickering light, images may have appeared to move, and researcher Steven Waller believes that they were also designed to have a soundtrack. Theorizing that paintings were carefully placed where certain echoes could be heard, he claims that making sounds near one picture of herding animals produced the sound of hooves striking the ground, while echoes near a picture of a person seemed to come from that figure. With such movements and sounds, then, visiting a decorated cave may have been the ancient equivalent of watching a movie.

that some were made by children between the ages of three and seven.

The introduction of agriculture effectively ended the tradition of cave paintings, as humans were no longer dependent upon successful hunting and stopped spending their time in caves. It is fortunate, then, that the artists selected very remote places for their paintings, so their work was protected from the elements and preserved for modern viewers. Ironically, though, the discovery of the Lascaux paintings in southwestern France almost destroyed them, as accommodation for numerous tourists brought improved ventilation and lighting that spawned damaging lichen and mold, requiring that the caves be closed in 1963, with access now limited to a handful of visitors. But scientists are working hard to maintain the paintings in Lascaux and elsewhere, so that the masterful art of our distant ancestors will remain available to new generations of admirers.

Further Reading

Bahn, Paul G. 1998. *The Cambridge Illustrated History of Prehistoric Art*. Cambridge and New York: Cambridge University Press.

Chauvet, Jean-Marie, Éliette Brunel Deschamps, and Christian Hillaire. 1996. *Dawn of Art: The Chauvet Cave: The Oldest Known Paintings in the World*. New York: H. N. Abrams.

Clottes, Jean. 2008. *Cave Art*. London and New York: Phaidon Press.

Curtis, Gregory. 2006. *The Cave Painters: Probing the Mysteries of the World's First Artists*. New York: Alfred A. Knopf.

Guthrie, R. Dale. 2005. *The Nature of Paleolithic Art*. Chicago: University of Chicago Press.

Whitley, David S. 2009. *Cave Painters and the Human Spirit: The Origin of Creativity and Belief*. Amherst, NY: Prometheus Books.

Document

From Renard, Georges François. 1929. *Life and Work in Prehistoric Times*. Translated by R. T. Clark. 1929. New York: Alfred A. Knopf.

In this passage, the French author provides an overview of prehistoric art and its techniques.

Drawing with charcoal, chalk, and ochre was no doubt the first way in which man endeavoured to express his vision of the world around him. On horn, bone, soft stone, and then on ivory and on the horns of stag and reindeer, man adorned his weapons with pictures in relief of animals, worked for the most art with the saw. In the caves appear bas-reliefs which represent in little big animals and hunting scenes, while in full relief we find statues of men and women, clay bisons which were only sketches and are small in size, and were then executed in natural size.

On the other hand, drawing gave birth to engraving, which is seen on the rocks in the open air, on the walls of the caves, and, in America, on shells, or, elsewhere, on bone. The first of these have practically all disappeared as a result of the elements, although here and there it is still possible to recognize on a rock a herd of horses or the outline of a lioness. The second still remain but are covered over with drawing upon drawing, probably because the surface which presented itself as suitable to the early artists was so small, or because they disliked their first attempts and persistently emended them, or because a layer of paint which later scaled off showed up the contours of the last work and concealed all the earlier ones.

Lines begin to be used to indicate shadow on the hairs on the skins of animals. Then engraving is combined with painting. On the walls of the inner galleries of the caves are visible prints of hands of which the fingers are mutilated or bent back. Sometimes the hands were dipped in red liquid and then pressed on the rocks; sometimes they were simply sketched round with red or black on the smooth surface of the rock, such hands as one finds imprinted on the Australian rocks and which perhaps were believed to ward off the evil eye. Tubes of ochre have been found in the caves and the painter's brushes and the smooth slabs of stone that served as palettes. Even when painting in which at first only one colour was used, became many colored, the colours do not vary much. There is little more than red and yellow, which mixed with black give brown. But it is quite possible that other colours were used, but having been of vegetable origin the sun or the damp destroyed them. Red is the dominant colour. The colour of blood, it was the emblem of life and perhaps of survival.

Chieftains

As best we can determine, human beings have always lived in groups, beginning with small nomadic bands and later settling into larger communities. The daily lives of such groups require constant decisions, and since a consensus cannot always be reached, there must be some sort of leader to resolve conflicts and choose the next course of action. What sorts of people the earliest tribal leaders were, and how they were chosen, is necessarily a matter of conjecture. Some authors have suggested that early human communities were structured like the communities of chimpanzees observed today: that is, they were led by an alpha male, who had previously proved himself to be the strongest of his peers, and he retained his position until he was successfully challenged by another male who defeated him in a personal battle and then took charge. Popular depictions of prehistoric life have seized upon this idea to present tales of virtuous young cavemen who successfully overcome aging leaders and assume their positions. However, humans value knowledge and wisdom as much as strength, and since so many prehistoric people died at an early age, a man who survived into his thirties or forties might be entrusted with authority because of his long experience, even if he was no longer an effective fighter. Further, despite the traditional assumption that all prehistoric chieftains were male, we cannot discount the possibility that, in some cases, an older woman would be the one in control, though most experts are skeptical about modern theories that prehistoric societies were characteristically matriarchal.

Based on their observations of contemporary peoples of the underdeveloped world, paleoanthropologists once accepted a four-stage pattern of political development, though this has been recently criticized as overly simplistic and haunted by antiquated notions of human "progress." According to this model, the earliest human groups were *band societies*; these may have included only about fifteen to forty members and were governed informally by an older or respected man, though his authority was not absolute. When such groups grew larger and became *tribes*, an official leader would be designated, but although he managed the distribution of food and presided over ceremonies, he generally had no other special privileges. When tribes expanded to have hundreds or thousands of members, they evolved into *chiefdoms*; now, entrenched rulers claimed to govern by divine authority, enjoyed great wealth, wore special garments and carried symbols of their authority, and were often succeeded by their sons when they died, like hereditary kings. Finally, chiefdoms would expand and combine to become true *states*, or nations, large territories ruled by a central government.

Whatever its flaws, this traditional theory does help to explain the growing importance of leaders during human prehistory, as larger political units brought more power and prestige to their leaders, and the model is also backed by some archaeological evidence gleaned from burial sites. The most ancient graves tend to be simple and uniform in character, indicating a basically egalitarian society, but in later graves, some individuals are buried with nothing while others are accompanied by a wide range of rich goods, indicating their high social rank. One also finds juveniles buried with wealthy items that must be the result of an inherited status, since they could not have accumulated such treasures by their own efforts; these children must have been the cherished children of leaders who sadly died at a young age. Early archaeologists, well aware that historic kings held scepters to represent their power, were also excited to find prehistoric scepters made of stone, antlers, or gold in tombs, believing that these proved that the buried men were once chieftains, though the scepters may have also had religious significance.

The recent research into ancient chiefs has tended to focus on the ways that these men were able to obtain and retain their power. Scholar Timothy Earle, who has written a book on this subject, observes three major forces that might elevate a person to a position of authority. The first, and most obvious, is military skill; a man who can fight well as an individual, and who has success in leading others to win battles, is likely to gain mastery over his society. The second is an economic edge; the man who comes to own more possessions than others will have natural influence due to his wealth. The third is a compelling ideology: a person might rally a group to his side by appealing to their patriotic fervor or announcing that he has

been the recipient of a divine vision instructing him to lead his people in performing some action. In smaller tribes, however, more personal factors may have come into play: the biblical story of Saul suggests that, in some cases, a man's unusual height and imposing appearance might have inspired people to choose him as their commander, and the man buried in ancient England with extensive possessions, sometimes called the "King of Stonehenge," also happened to be very tall. Family connections—in particular, being the oldest son of a popular chieftain—might elevate a man to power, and an individual might also possess that indefinable quality known as personal charisma, making him a popular candidate for a leadership role.

Once they became leaders, chiefs undoubtedly sought to solidify their control in various ways. They might have appealed to religion, arguing that they should rule because they were blessed by the gods, or even because they were living gods themselves; they could establish sacred places that only they had access to as a way to emphasize their special relationship to the divine. Chieftains began to wear elaborate costumes, and carry special objects, to visually convey their superiority to the people below them. To garner support, they would strive to appear as benefactors to their people, and they might offer them gifts on certain holidays or address any problems that their subjects complain about. However, demonstrating their sterner side, they would harshly punish anyone who dared to question their authority, as a warning to others to remain obedient. When agrarian societies came to depend upon stored food for much of the year, chiefs could find it especially easy to govern their subjects by controlling access to those essential supplies. Needless to say, none of these strategies were guaranteed to work all of the time, and many chiefs undoubtedly experienced a great deal of stress, fearing that one bad harvest or one mistake on their part might provide an opening for other men to assassinate the leader and seize power themselves.

Even if their positions involved some tension and uncertainty, no one can doubt that being a chieftain, in general, was a very desirable profession. Again, the evidence comes from examinations of their tombs. One apparent leader was buried next to the bodies of several women, suggesting that he enjoyed the privilege

LUCRATIVE LEADERSHIP

As prehistoric chieftains were always able to garner considerable wealth from their position, one could argue that they were the first workers to receive a regular salary. Throughout the ages, rulers of all kinds have similarly been able to enrich themselves, and several twentieth-century dictators were driven from power with billions of dollars in their foreign bank accounts. Even in the United States, where presidents receive a relatively modest salary and are not allowed to keep expensive gifts, all presidents eventually become multi-millionaires after leaving office, earning huge sums by writing their memoirs and accepting fees for speaking engagements.

CLOTHING FIT FOR A KING

The early chieftains were the first to wear special clothing, jewelry, and other colorful accoutrements to symbolize their superiority to the people they commanded, a practice followed by innumerable hereditary rulers and dictators in historical times, who appeared before their subjects wearing golden crowns, thick robes, arrays of medals, and other striking decorations. Today, however, preferring to emphasize their kinship with those that they govern, most modern leaders wear ordinary business suits and subdued dresses. Even Great Britain's Queen Elizabeth II usually meets with her subjects wearing only a nice dress and fancy hat, though she still wears her bejeweled crown and lavish clothing for official ceremonies.

of multiple wives (who may have been ritually slaughtered at the moment of his own death). The bodies of chieftains were often covered with jewelry made of precious gems and accompanied with large objects made of gold and silver, demonstrating that they were very wealthy. The carcasses of large animals, probably sacrificed as part of the funeral ceremony, indicate that they feasted on similar fare during their lifetimes. The very size and elaborateness of certain burial sites testify to the great esteem that people felt for their leaders, who must have been granted many special privileges. This great affection did not necessarily endure, however, since like the great tombs of ancient Egypt, some prehistoric burial chambers also show signs that they were visited by grave robbers who took away their most valuable goods.

Pondering the rich and luxurious lifestyles of ancient chieftains, and the harsh conditions endured by their subjects, contemporary observers may wonder why people, in both prehistoric and historic times, tolerated such inequality and failed to demand a more just society. But it must be recognized that prehistoric humans viewed themselves as weak beings beset by a world of powerful forces, and being governed by a harsh and unpredictable ruler would seem a natural extension of living in a harsh and unpredictable world. It would require millennia of civilization before people, having developed the science and technology to control their worlds, would begin to imagine that they might collectively control their own governments as well, inspiring the first stirrings of true democracy and heralding the decline of a system of absolute rule that was forged when humanity was young and endured for thousands of years thereafter.

Further Reading

Earle, Timothy K. 1997. *How Chiefs Come to Power: The Political Economy in Prehistory*. Stanford, CA: Stanford University Press.

Eller, Cynthia. 2000. *The Myth of Matriarchal Prehistory: Why an Invented Past Won't Give Women a Future*. Boston: Beacon Press.

Hass, Jonathan, editor. 2001. *From Leaders to Rulers*. New York: Kluwer Academic/Plenum Publishers.

Pauketat, Timothy R. 1994. *The Ascent of Chiefs: Cahokia and Mississippian Politics in Native North America*. Tuscaloosa: University of Alabama Press.

Scarry, John F., editor. 1996. *Political Structure and Change in the Prehistoric Southeastern United States*. Gainesville: University Press of Florida.

Stein, Gil, and Mitchell S. Rothman, editors. 1994. *Chiefdoms and Early States in the Near East: The Organizational Dynamics of Complexity*. Madison, WI: Prehistory Press.

Document

From Berthet, Elie Bertrand. 1876. *The Pre-Historic World*. Translated by Mary J. Stafford. 1879. Philadelphia: Porter & Coates.

This passage describes a young man's father, who serves as the leader of his small tribe.

[Fair-Hair] had gone to the abode of his own family, on the other side of the mountain, to make arrangements for his father-in-law's funeral [because] the ceremonies of a funeral were the only occasions on which these rude hunters met, and the custom of assembling all the invited guests at a banquet had perhaps contributed to the establishment of such a usage.

Fair-Hair's relatives were of the same type as himself, though they had not his frank and almost intelligent face. The shape of their skin garments varied according to the convenience of each individual; fashion did not appear to be very tyrannical. The women, like the men, were armed with bows, lances, or clubs.

Fair-Hair's father, still a strong, vigorous man, exerted a certain degree of authority over all the members of his family. He held in his hand one of those singular insignia of office several specimens of which have been found in the strata of the Quaternary period, and which, from their resemblance to those savage chiefs still carry, have been recognized as "rulers' batons." This one, the work of Fair-Hair, was a piece of reindeer's horn pierced with two holes, on which the hunter had carved the figures of animals. Still, it may be doubted whether these batons gave the head of a family or tribe undisputed power when age had deprived him of the strength necessary to make himself respected: veneration for the old is a virtue of later times.

Farmers

During most of their history on Earth, people lived on the food that they hunted and gathered, traveling as needed to have access to these resources. Then, about 10,000 years ago, humans began to engage in agriculture, planting and raising crops as their principal means of sustenance. As this led them to live in one place, near their fields, people were eventually inspired to create the first human civilizations. We may never know precisely why humans made this transition, but one theory is that nomadic peoples would periodically return to a few familiar sites, which were filled with garbage and leftovers from previous visits, and find that some of their favorite plants had grown out of the

debris. This gave them the idea to purposefully plant food in these places and linger there while it grew. Some recent evidence indicates, however, that ancient people first decided to settle down in one place while they continued to rely on hunting and gathering, then decided later to start farming as well.

As best we can determine, farming began about 10,000 years ago in present-day Syria, Palestine, and Iraq and gradually spread throughout the world. The earliest farming was generally done by individual families, who lived beside a small field. If most of the land was covered by forests, as in prehistoric Europe, the prospective farmers would first have to clear the land by cutting down trees and burning the remaining stumps and brush. This removal of forests often drove away the animals that hunters depended on, a further incentive to engage in farming. The other preliminary work of farmers involved building some sort of permanent home out of wood or stone where they could live while they tended their crops.

At first, the technology that farmers employed was fairly basic: hoes and spades to dig up the soil for planting, and knives and axes to cut down the grown crops. A key innovation was the plow, which at first was only a pointed stick attached to another stick that was pulled by a pair of domesticated animals, such as oxen. This could quickly make gouges in the ground where seeds could be planted, leading to the long, straight rows of crops that still characterize farming today. Farmers also developed sickles and pruning knives for harvesting their crops. While the men probably handled the business of plowing, both men and women would participate in the harvest, since there were many plants that needed to be cut down in a short period of time.

Further improvements in agricultural techniques emerged in different parts of the world. As European farmers noticed that repeatedly using the same fields produced more and more meager results, they devised systems of crop rotation to keep their fields fertile. In Africa, where more land was available, farmers practiced a variant method termed slash-and-burn agriculture: a forest is cleared and burned down, leaving fertile soil which can be planted for a few years; then, farmers move on to clear and burn another field. In prehistoric America, farmers figured out how to make use of hillsides by constructing terraces on them, supported by stone walls, that provided narrow strips of flat land for crops; and in regions subject to flooding, they built raised fields to protect the crops. Ancient American farmers also engaged in selective breeding of a wild grass named teosinte to eventually create modern corn. In both ancient America and ancient Iran, where conditions were often dry, farmers began to practice irrigation, digging ditches to bring water to their crops. Since this was necessarily a collective enterprise, requiring the cooperative efforts of many farmers, some theorize that irrigation in particular may have served as an important impetus for the formation of larger communities. Also, perhaps noticing that areas frequented by animals tended to have more plants, European farmers discovered that manure would function as an effective fertilizer, readily available from their animals, while early American farmers added fish to the soil; both products were filled with nitrogen, which has remained a basic element in fertilizers to this day.

Because plant materials generally disintegrate over time, we cannot always be sure what the first farmers were growing, but in ancient Europe, the main priority was cereals like wheat, oats, rye, barley, and millet, which could be ground into flour and used to make a variety of foods. There are occasional indications that they also planted cabbage, green peas, lentils, and carrots. Near the Mediterranean Sea, fruits like olives, pomegranates, figs, and grapes were a common choice. While food was the farmer's principal goal, some plants were grown for other purposes: linseed or flax could make oil and linen, hemp and poppies were probably used as narcotics, and saffron flavored foods and produced a yellow dye. Elsewhere, in sub-Saharan Africa, farmers planted peanuts, yams, and the ensete or "false banana"; in the Americas, the first farmers cultivated a variety of plants that were unique to their region, including avocados, squash, and potatoes; and in eastern Asia, cabbages, soybeans, and hazelnuts were among the staple crops. This is also where rice was first cultivated, a grain that required special treatment since it flourished best with submerged roots; so farmers had to figure out how to first grow rice seedlings on dry land, then transplant them into specially created pools of water called paddies, and pull them out when they had matured.

While their harvests would provide an abundance of food, farmers also needed to master new forms of technology to preserve their harvests so they would have enough to eat during the winter. Grains were cooked in special ovens, or placed on frames over hearths, to dry them so they would last longer; before storage, farmers or their cattle crushed the grains on a threshing floor to separate the seeds from the straw; and grains and other crops were initially stored by digging a large pit, filling it with crops, and covering it with clay and soil. Hay was gathered into bundles to be fed to animals. Later, European farmers built special buildings to store crops, also using them to shelter their animals, though they also built granaries on elevated platforms to store grain where rodents could not reach them.

While focused on raising their crops, farmers practiced other professions as well. Before they figured out how to build fences to keep their animals from straying, farmers or people in their employ had to work regularly as animal herders. To augment their diets, farmers' wives continued to engage in gathering, venturing into forests to pick nuts, berries, and mushrooms, and if they were near bodies of water, farmers might also collect shellfish or do some fishing. Because they needed to know exactly when to plant and harvest crops, farmers kept a keen eye on the sky, tracking the movements of stars and planets and mastering a form of practical astronomy; it is telling that some ancient people regarded the constellation of Ursa Major as a plow being pulled by oxen. Seeking variety in meals dominated by a few crops, farmers' wives created many new ways to prepare their food, as suggested by the names of dishes like farmer's stew, harvest soup, and shepherd's pie; settled homes were also well suited for potter's wheels and kilns, so that significantly larger numbers of pots are found in agricultural communities. More broadly, since the profession of farming offered more leisure time than a nomadic life, it is believed that farmers played important roles in the development of many artistic pursuits like art and music.

Overall, while agriculture contributed greatly to human progress in innumerable ways, it also brought new problems: eating a limited range of crops often caused malnutrition, and living close to animals

ACCIDENTAL FARMING

By one theory, farming emerged as the accidental by-product of the garbage left behind by nomadic tribes; when they noticed that places they returned to had many of their favorite plants growing, they figured out the cause and began to plant them deliberately. Such unplanned farms can still be found today: for example, since the seeds in consumed tomatoes have a protective coating, they can pass through the human digestive system intact, and as a result, landfills of garbage and fields irrigated with waste water will often be filled with tomato plants.

AGRICULTURAL ASTRONOMERS

Farmers were probably the world's first astronomers, since they had to carefully observe the movements of the stars in order to know precisely when to plant and harvest their crops. Some later farmers who watched the sky also developed an interest in this subject. One prominent example is an eighteenth-century African American, Benjamin Banneker, who spent most of his life working as a farmer in Maryland; however, he eventually taught himself astronomy and used this knowledge to successfully publish a series of almanacs. His astronomical background also led to an assignment to assist in the first survey of the land used for the nation's capital, Washington, D.C.

brought virulent new diseases to human populations. Also, while a more dependable source of food than hunting and gathering, crops could be devastated by drought and decimated by animal and insect predators, so that uncertainty about steady food supplies was not entirely eliminated. Still, the ancient farmers persevered through these and other problems, continually seeking ways to improve their work and increase their yields, and forged a tradition that remains an important aspect of all human civilizations to this day.

Further Reading

Anderson, Patricia C., editor. 1999. *Prehistory of Agriculture: New Experimental and Ethnographic Approaches.* Los Angeles: Institute of Agriculture, University of California Press.

Barker, Graeme. 2006. *The Agricultural Revolution in Prehistory: Why Did Foragers Become Farmers?* Oxford and New York: Oxford University Press.

Denham, Tim, José Iriarte, and Luc Vrydaghs, editors. 2007. *Rethinking Agriculture: Archaeological and Ethnoarchaeological Perspectives.* Walnut Creek, CA: Left Coast Press.

Killion, Thomas W. 1992. *Gardens of Prehistory: The Archaeology of Settlement Agriculture in Greater Mesoamerica.* Tuscaloosa: University of Alabama Press.

Price, T. Douglas, and Anne Birgitte Gebauer, editors. 1995. *Last Hunters, First Farmers: New Perspectives on the Prehistoric Transition to Agriculture.* Santa Fe, NM: School of American Research Press.

Pryor, Francis. 1998. *Farmers in Prehistoric Britain.* Stroud, England: Tempus.

Documents

From Abbott, Charles T. 1899. *The Cliff-Dweller's Daughter, or, How He Loved Her: An Indian Romance of Prehistoric Times.* London and New York: F. Tennyson Neely.

This passage describes a group of prehistoric Native Americans who migrate to a new region where they plan to farm its fertile ground.

The plain, inclosed by high cliffs, could be seen to its full extent from the rising ground, and Wisdom said: "We shall stay here, Thundercloud"; for gazing upon the verdant plain, his eyes grew prophetic, and he saw in his mind's eye the fields green with corn, and the ditches carrying water, with groups of his people stooping over the rich black soil. . .

The grain they had they would keep until the spring, for with this they hoped to sow the fields, which some of the men had cleared of the mesquite and cacti that cumbered the soil. The scorching sun had dried the ground, until the slightest movement raised the dust in clouds, and glad indeed were the men to wash the sand from their mouths in the stream which, in spite of the heat, ran bubbling by.

No want of water here—the hottest summer would still spare it to them, and the quivering sky could not draw it into their embrace. Around the level ground ditches were dug to lead the treasured moisture, and across some waste the hollow trees were laid to carry the water to the other side; all was in readiness for the spring. . . .

[Later] A number of men were gathering the ears of corn which they had deposited in the new ground, and though few the grains they planted the crop exceeded their fondest hope and the quantity of deep red ears laid aside by the women to plant in the spring was very large, while still larger the quantity they strung up to the ceiling in the rooms of the castle. Good and wholesome it was, but not so pure as the red corn so much valued by the farmers for planting in the field and therefore laid aside to be crushed into meal for the bread of life. . . .

From Renard, Georges François. 1929. *Life and Work in Prehistoric Times*. Translated by R.T. Clark. 1929. New York: Alfred A. Knopf.

This passage explains both the great difficulties, and the great rewards, of the human transition to a life dependent on agriculture.

When he placed the grain in the soil he had to wait till a mysterious process was accomplished beneath it. He had to make frost and heat, rain, snow, and sun his allies. He had to show great patience and see far ahead. He had to observe the periodicity of the seasons and fit his work to it.

It requires no great effort of imagination to understand how miraculous it must have been for man to be able to take regular nourishment from the land. It meant the permanent leaving of a mode of life which was always precarious, the escape from the perpetual recurrence of famine, from desperate expedients in the struggle for food. Agriculture was an inestimable boon to man, and its first result was to make him sedentary.

A new civilization arose with the growth of agriculture. The peoples who adopted it, submitted to endure disciplined, regular, daily work accomplished often by a co-operative effort according to the seasons. They had a hearth, a home lit up at night by the oil lamps, surrounded by a stockade. They took root where they were born, where their dead were buried. Eaters of bread, they had gentler manners. . . . Every change of environment causes a change in habits, ideas, beliefs, and the change that wedded man to the soil, fixed him on the land and for the first time gave him a country, was an enormous one.

Fishers

Humans have always been attracted to large bodies of water, and a controversial theory even claims that our ancestors were once on a path toward evolving into aquatic creatures, as evidenced by our lack of fur and our webbed fingers. Yet in other respects, humans are ill-equipped for life in the water, with legs that are better adapted for walking than paddling and lungs that must breathe in some air every few minutes. Even if water was never their home, though, humans had many reasons to spend much of their time near rivers, lakes, and oceans: bodies of water could serve as a refuge to escape predators who avoided getting wet; fresh water was needed for drinking and washing clothes; bodies of water attracted game animals for hunters; and most importantly, the water was filled with creatures to nourish beings who often struggled to find enough food on the land. As a matter of necessity, beginning in most places around 30,000 years ago, humans gradually mastered the art of fishing.

In the beginning, fishing was a matter of improvisation: the fish that were isolated in shallow pools could be picked up without much effort, and with a quick, well-aimed grab a person might be able to catch fish as they swam in rivers. The spears that humans had crafted to kill animals on land could be used to impale the larger, more active fish when they came close to the surface. In addition, some sedentary forms of sea life, such as shellfish and oysters, could be easily harvested by wading into shallow waters, a task probably assigned to children and elderly people. Excavations of coastal settlements in ancient Europe often uncover huge piles of shells, indicating that shellfish was at one time a major part of the human diet. Finally, even when humans lacked the technology to catch or kill them, larger sea animals, like seals, dolphins, and whales, would die and be occasionally washed on shore, providing people with a hearty meal that may have whetted their appetite for similar prizes.

Recognizing the value of seafood, humans soon developed specialized technologies for catching fish. One of these was the net, which could be cast into the water and pulled in with captured fish inside; only a few remnants of such nets, often made of fibers from willow trees, have been preserved, but the small, cylindrical stones used as weights to hold the nets in position are commonly found, indicating that their use was widespread. In ancient Australia, people developed a device called the fish gorge, a sharpened piece of wood or bone that was attached to a strip of leather or muscle and cast into the water. If a fish happened to swallow the gorge, it would lodge in its throat, and the fisher could pull it to shore. But most prehistoric fishers came to rely upon a line attached to a hook and bait, the method most frequently employed in modern times. The hooks found in ancient sites reveal a wide variety of designs, indicating that a considerable amount of ingenuity and craftsmanship went into their creation; especially noteworthy was the use of compound blades to ensure that the fish who consumed the bait could not escape. In Europe, around 14,000 years ago, fishers set up weirs, barriers made of stone, in the rivers to force the innumerable salmon that annually migrated upstream into narrow channels where they could be killed with a three-pronged spear called a leister, an early form of the trident. In North America, early fishers employed another method of catching fish, grinding up the husks of hickory nuts, which contained a chemical that was poisonous to fish, and pouring the powder into nearby lakes to kill numerous fish, which could then be easily gathered as they floated on the water.

For a while, fishers were content to work on the shores, but a desire for more and larger fish surely became the driving force behind the invention of simple boats, such as canoes and kayaks, which could provide access to those species of fish that preferred deep waters. Excavations at a site in East Timor suggest that humans may have successfully engaged in deep-sea fishing as early as 42,000 years ago. From their boats, fishers could use the same nets and lines that were effective on shore, but catching large fish in the open seas eventually required the invention of a new sort of spear, the harpoon; this device had a hook at its end, which firmly implanted itself into the body of the fish, while a rope attached to the other end allowed fishers to pull their catches into their boats. Such harpoons could not be employed against the very largest sea creatures, the whales, since the boats were too small and their crewmen too few to handle such massive objects; however, around 3,000 BCE, some people would use several boats to surround a whale and try to steer it toward the shore, hoping to immobilize and kill the behemoth in shallow water. The ancient Aleutians of North America, however, eventually learned how to hunt and kill whales.

While food remained the main reason for fishing, humans also discovered other uses for the increasing numbers of fish that they were catching. Fish provided an oil that could be used in oil lamps, and small fish bones and fish scales were ideal material for decorative bracelets and necklaces. Parts of the fish that humans did not want to eat, such as fish heads, could be fed to their domesticated animals.

As ancient people increasingly exploited maritime resources, they also came to realize that many sea creatures were abundant only at certain times of the year, and they adjusted their activities accordingly. For example, near the Santa Barbara Channel in present-day California, prehistoric Native Americans survived during the winter, when fish were scarce, by relying upon stored food and shellfish found on the shore, like mussels; in the spring, they would gather edible plants. But the summer brought many warm-water fish, like tuna, to the ocean, so they would get into their canoes and catch as many fish as they could. As their numbers declined in the fall, they would again begin to focus on collecting shellfish; and at all times of the year, they would keep an eye out for stranded whales on the shore. They did, however, face one problem that they could not anticipate: the occasional and unpredictable weather condition known as El Niño, which would dramatically reduce the population of fish and force them to rely upon hunting and gathering.

When fishing developed into a genuine profession, with its own tools and techniques, it was surely dominated by men, who might need to use all of their strength to pull in a large harpooned fish or a net filled with smaller fish. Women, however, continued to assist by gathering shellfish and weaving and repairing the nets. As in many communities today, boys probably learned the craft by accompanying their fathers or older relatives to the shore, entrusted with increasingly important tasks as they matured. On days when the weather did not permit any fishing, the fishers made productive use of their time by crafting new hooks and

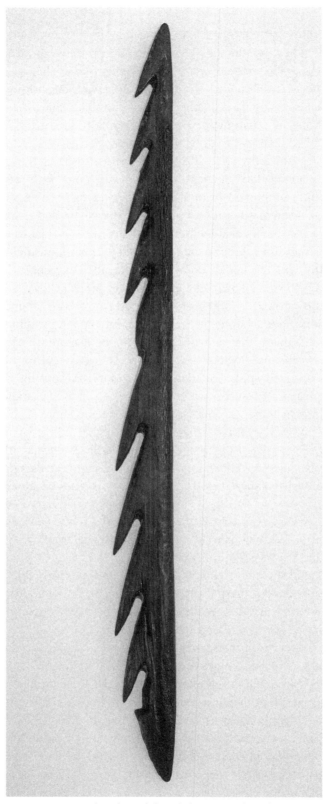

Having not yet developed the ability to craft tools out of metal, prehistoric fishers from approximately 3000 BCE carved the earliest harpoons out of bones, like this 6-inch one discovered in a river in present-day Ljubljana, Slovenia. (Arne Hodalic/Corbis)

OLD-FASHIONED FISHING

The earliest form of fishing—catching fish with one's bare hands—was soon abandoned by prehistoric fishers in favor of more efficient techniques involving the use of nets, lines with bait, and harpoons. Strangely enough, however, this difficult approach to fishing has enjoyed a recent revival as a challenging sport. In 2011, a briefly popular reality show, *Hillbilly Handfishin'*, recounted the adventures of two fishers from Oklahoma, Skipper Bivins and Trent Jackson, who regularly lead groups of tourists to lakes and rivers to teach them the art of "noodling"—catching large catfish with their bare hands.

WRANGLING OVER WHALING

The Inuit people of Alaska and northwest Canada long ago mastered the ultimate form of fishing by hunting the bowhead whale, and both the activity and the useful products taken from whale carcasses became integral parts of their culture. This ancient tradition is now at odds with modern concerns about preserving the species from extinction, leading to ongoing conflicts between environmentalists seeking to ban such whaling and cultural activists endeavoring to preserve the practice while observing strict quotas on the numbers of whales killed. As of today, these Native Americans are still allowed to hunt a limited number of whales each year, though the whalers frequently attract hostile protesters.

harpoons and making sure their boats and equipment were in good repair. Fishing could be a dangerous job, as sudden storms could sink vessels or push men overboard to drown in icy waters, and there were other hazards ranging from shark attacks to the bites of poisonous fish. Yet fishers might also live for many years, sustained by a healthy diet rich in protein and fish oil.

Overall, while agriculture is correctly regarded as the main reason why humans began to live in fixed communities, fishing played a role in this transition as well, as evidenced by the numerous ancient settlements found on the shores of oceans, seas, lakes, and rivers. Indeed, along the coast of ancient Chile, some evidence suggests that food from the ocean was the initial reason that people settled down in that region, as they only developed agriculture in later times. Fishing also provided an important outlet for men who preferred the sort of adventurous life that farming could not offer, and they certainly provided their peers with many interesting anecdotes about the exotic creatures that they observed, launching a literary tradition of sea stories that endures to this day.

Further Reading

Bekker-Nielsen, Tønnes. 2006. *Ancient Fishing and Fish Processing in the Black Sea Region.* Aarhus, Denmark, and Oakville, CT: Aarhus University Press.

Leach, Foss. 2006. *Fishing in Pre-European New Zealand.* Kilbirnie, Wellington, New Zealand: New Zealand Journal of Archaeology.

Menotti, Francesco, editor. 2004. *Living on the Lake in Prehistoric Europe: 150 Years of Lake-Dwelling Research.* London and New York: Routledge.

Plew, Mark G., editor. 1996. *Prehistoric Hunter-Gatherer Fishing Strategies.* Boise, ID: Department of Anthropology, Boise State University.

Powell, Judith. 1996. *Fishing in the Prehistoric Aegean.* Jonsered, Sweden: Astrom Editions.

Rick, Torben C., and Jon Erlandson, editors. 2008. *Human Impacts on Ancient Marine Ecosystems: A Global Perspective.* Berkeley: University of California Press.

Documents

From Berthet, Elie Bertrand. 1876. *The Pre-Historic World.* Translated by Mary J. Stafford. 1879. Philadelphia: Porter & Coates.

In this passage, the novelist describes the chief of a tribe that lives beside a lake, who is returning from a day of fishing with his catch and his equipment.

Sea-Eagle, holding in his hand a magnificent fish, and followed by two stout lads carrying nets, entered the hut.

The chief of the tribe of Cormorants was a man about sixty years old, but who as yet seemed to feel none of the weakness of age. His clothing was a sort of robe of wolf-skin, which revealed his chest with its prominent muscles and his black, hairy, sinewy limbs. His long, tangled gray beard reminded one of the beard of Polyphemus. His reddened eyes, sun-burnt cheeks, and aquiline nose formed a by no means genial countenance, which betrayed cunning and greed of gain. A flint axe in a deer-horn handle hung at his belt, and he leaned on a harpoon of barbed bone as if it were a cane. No one rose when he entered, but all eyes turned eagerly toward him. Without taking any notice of his guests, he gave orders to the young men who accompanied him, and who seemed to be in his special service. Then, while they were arranging the fishing-gear in one corner of the hut, he threw his fish on the floor and advanced toward the strangers. . . .

"Chief," said Hurricane in his turn, "I've been hunting, and have brought you my game." "Very well," replied Sea-Eagle; "let us eat it. Light-Foot shall stay to the feast, for he probably has had no opportunity to treat himself during his journey. Come," he added, raising his voice, "daughters and lads, to work. Fishing on the lake has made me hungry."

Instantly all present, even the guests, set to work to prepare the meal. While the two sisters were hurrying the baking of the cakes, one of the young men threw dry wood on the fireplace to make embers; the others busied themselves in skinning and cutting up the roe. . . .

The banquet was enjoyable because it was abundant. The roe having been devoured to the bones, they attacked the fish, which had been stretched on the embers in its turn, and was served half raw, as usual. The fish was succeeded by fresh or dried fruits, which the young housekeepers produced from their stores, together with a little hard cheese covered with mould from the dampness of the lake, and the dinner was considered one of the most elegant ever remembered in the Lacustrian city of the Cormorants.

From Bandelier, Adolph Francis Alphonse. 1890. *The Delight-Makers: A Novel of Prehistoric Pueblo Indians.* New York: Dodd, Mead, and Co.

This passage describes a prehistoric Native American child of the American Southwest who practices the most ancient form of fishing—catching a fish with one's bare hands.

Like a statue of light-coloured bronze decked with scanty drapery, and adorned with crude trinkets, holding a bow in the right hand, while the left clenched a few untipped arrows, the youth stood on the boulder outlined against the shrubbery, immovable above the running brook. His gaze was fixed on the opposite bank, where a youngster was kneeling.

The latter was a boy of perhaps nine years. A dirty wrap hung loosely over shoulders and back, and no necklace or ear-pendants decorated his body. But the childish features were enlivened by a broad grin of satisfaction, and his eyes sparkled like coals just igniting, while he pointed to a large mountain trout which he pressed against a stone with both hands. He looked at the older youth with an expression not merely of pleasure, but of familiar intimacy also. It was clear that both boys were children of the same parents.

The younger one spoke first,—

"See here, Okoya," he began, grinning; "while you are older than I, and bigger and stronger, I am more cunning than you. Ever since the sun came out you have followed the turkeys, and what have you? Nothing! Your hands are empty! I have just come down from the field, and look! I caught this fish in the water. Shall we fry and eat it here, or carry it home to the mother?"

The older brother did not relish the taunt; his lips curled. He replied scornfully,—

"Any child may catch a fish, but only men can follow turkeys. The tzina is shy and wary; it knows how sure my aim is, therefore it hides when I go out to hunt. . . . Come, take your fish, and let us go home."

With this Okoya leaped over the brook. . . . Proudly the little boy tossed his fish from one hand to the other.

Food Preparers

In the beginning, humans simply ate whatever they found in its original form, as long as it was nutritious and reasonably palatable. But eventually, they began experimenting with different ways to prepare their food, as this provided more variety in their diet and made certain foods tastier and more digestible. As this often involved heating foods over a fire, one can speak of this development as the invention of cooking, but the more general term food preparation also includes other methods of making food edible and pleasurable that did not involve the use of fire. From the beginning, almost certainly, this was primarily the responsibility of women, as the male hunters who had been rapidly moving all day in search of game were doubtless in no mood to chop or cook food when they returned to their camps.

The art of making and controlling fires had been mastered by human species long before the rise of *homo sapiens*, and while a desire for warmth and protection against predators may have been the initial motive, they undoubtedly began to cook the animals that they hunted, since cooked meat was easier to chew. According to one common theory, some ancient human found the charred remains of an animal killed in a forest fire and discovered that burned meat made a better meal; people may have also placed slabs of meat in their fires simply to see what would happen. However the process began, we can be reasonably sure that humans were cooking meat hundreds of thousands of years ago, as their jaws and teeth gradually grew smaller, evidence that they were no longer engaged in the arduous business of chewing raw meat. Cooking meat also contributed to the health of ancient humans without their knowledge, as it killed the poisonous parasites and bacteria that often lurked within pieces of raw meat.

At first, humans may have simply thrown large animals into their fires to be cooked, but they would also cut pieces of meat, place them on sticks, and hold them over the fire—a method of cooking still observed at modern campfires. Another technique involved positioning stones over a fire and placing slabs of meat wrapped in plants on them, effectively the first form of pan frying. Some ancient people used crude spits, as they impaled animals on poles that were held up by sticks over a fire. Cooking fish was more of a challenge, since they tended to char and become too blackened to eat, but some prehistoric cooks learned to cover them with clay and lay them in the fire; when they were fully baked, the clay was chipped away.

Much later, when prehistoric humans mastered pottery, they began using clay pots for cooking; around 10,000 years ago in Japan, for example, women were using such pots to cook mollusks in boiling water. Such pots could be placed directly on a fire, held in an elevated position by stones, and they allowed for the creation of new dishes like stews and soups, so cooks could feed more people with a limited amount of meat by chopping it up and combining it with vegetables. When humans learned to do some metalworking, metal pots came into use, and in prehistoric Europe, some cooking was also done by heating stones and dropping them into leather pouches filled with water to boil and cook food items.

Archaeologists long assumed that humans mostly cooked animals, since burned bones were often found at ancient sites while the plant remains had long vanished. However, we now know that after learning how to cook animals, people quickly began cooking plants as well, perhaps simply seeking greater variety in their diets. But sometimes, such cooking was a matter of necessity; about 19,000 years ago, when ancient people living near the Nile River faced arid conditions and needed new sources of food, they began to grind up and cook plants like club rush tubers and nut grass, having learned through experience that this was the only way to neutralize their toxic ingredients and make them more edible. Cooking also softened hard plants that grew underground, like carrots and potatoes, so they could be eaten by small children or elderly people who had lost their teeth. In prehistoric Asia, people learned to grow and cook rice, which was central to their diet, although this food long remained unknown in other parts of the world.

As their greatest achievement, perhaps, prehistoric people discovered that, by grinding grains like wheat and barley into flour and adding key ingredients, they could produce a very palatable food, bread, which became a staple of the human diet; such flour could also be cooked in a pot to make gruel. But grinding up these plant fibers, using large pieces of stone called querns, may have represented the most laborious task that ancient women faced; examinations of skeletons from ancient Syria have shown that many women suffered from forms of arthritis caused by kneeling and grinding grain against a quern. Archaeologists have also found a wide variety of grinding tools at ancient sites, indicating that this was a regular activity.

After the food had been cooked, food preparers faced two additional tasks: serving the food, and storing unneeded food so it could be eaten later. The former business was probably a matter of little ceremony;

pieces of meat, plants, and bread were placed on wooden plates or bowls and handed to the hungry onlookers, who would eat the food with their hands. Storing food involved more labor, since some items would spoil rapidly unless special steps were taken. Pieces of meat or fish could be dried and pounded into strips to be eaten later, and around 10,000 years ago, when agriculture was beginning in the Middle East, there are signs that people had begun to preserve meat with salt. However, storing plants and grains, usually in pits or special buildings, was usually the task of farmers, not food preparers.

The settled life of agriculture brought many refinements to the art of cooking: women who lived in one home could build up a collection of varied pots and implements designed for special purposes, and they could construct hearths and primitive stoves to replace open fires. Many of them undoubtedly became

accomplished chefs, and two women—Jane Renfrew and Jacqui Wood—have attempted to employ archaeological evidence to reconstruct ancient recipes. One of these called for chopping up nettles, dandelions, sorrel, and watercress; adding salt and flour; placing the mixture on a piece of cloth; tying the cloth into a watertight bag; and placing the bag in a pot of boiling water with bits of meat. When all the items have been cooked, the water is drained, the bag is untied, and the vegetable mixture and meat are combined to make a stew. To make some bread to accompany the stew, the cook could combine oatmeal, barley flour, butter, milk, and salt and apply the dough to a heated stone, producing two bowl-shaped loaves. Many such recipes were developed, passed on to daughters, or shared with neighbors, who sometimes devised their own improvements, gradually building up a rich body of cooking lore that enhanced many eaters' lives.

To use this ancient quern, first used at least 10,000 years ago, prehistoric food preparers would place grains on the flat surface of the larger rock, and pound them with the smaller rock to grind the grains into flour. (SSPL via Getty Images)

To accompany their meals, prehistoric people also learned how to make alcoholic beverages like beer and wine—one form of food preparation that was probably handled by the men. Some speculate that humans first learned of alcohol's intoxicating effects by eating some rotting fruit, then resolving to produce something similar in a more systematic fashion. In ancient Europe, people learned how to boil malt and hops and allow the mixture to ferment, producing beers and ales, and a site in Armenia appears to represent the world's first winery, with a press to crush grapes and vessels for fermenting. Chinese people used rice and saliva to make their alcohol, while prehistoric people in Mexico fermented pieces of pineapple to produce an alcoholic beverage called *tepache*. Indeed, according one controversial theory, humans may have first turned to agriculture in order to have a steady supply of the grains needed to produce such beverages, and only later did they learn to use the same plants to make bread.

Compared to achievements like making tools, raising crops, and taming animals, mastering methods of preparing food might seem a minor matter, but no humans could have made any discoveries if they had not been adequately fed, and one strong motivation for the people who hunted, farmed, and crafted objects was surely the prospect of a warm, nourishing meal at the end of a hard day. The many accomplishments of prehistoric cooks, then, merit more attention than they have so far received.

CAVEMAN CUISINE

Today, many enthusiasts advocate a "Paleolithic diet," or "Paleo diet," urging people to eat only the foods that prehistoric humans ate, prepared in the ways they prepared them. They argue that this is the diet we are evolutionarily adapted for. Yet nutritionists criticize this diet, recognizing its flawed logic: since humans have evolved since ancient times, ancient diets are no longer ideal. For example, prehistoric adults could not digest dairy products and avoided them, yet most Northern Europeans developed a gene allowing them to consume milk, making the Paleo diet's prohibition of dairy products unnecessary. Environmentalists also note that, in an increasingly populated world, producing the foods required for this diet requires an unsustainable amount of resources.

A TIME-TESTED RECIPE

Jean Auel's best-selling novel *The Clan of the Cave Bear* (1980) includes several descriptions of Neanderthal cooking, based upon the author's extensive research. One dish, using a pot made of animal skins placed over a fire, involved dropping pieces of bison meat into boiling water with other ingredients, including "wild onion, salty coltsfoot . . . peeled thistle stalks, mushrooms, lily buds and roots, watercress, milkweed buds, small immature yams, cranberries carried from the other cave, and wilted flowers." Based on her language, modern cooks have created a recipe for "Neanderthal stew" with some omissions and modern substitutions.

Further Reading

Gosdin, Chris, and Jon G. Hather, editors. 1999. *The Prehistory of Food: Appetites for Change*. London and New York: Routledge.

Graff, Sarah R., and Enrique Rodríguez-Alegría, editors. 2012. *The Menial Art of Cooking: Archaeological Studies of Cooking and Food Preparation*. Boulder: University of Colorado Press.

Halstead, Paul, and John C. Barrett, editors. 2004. *Food, Cuisine, and Society in Prehistoric Greece*. Oxford: Oxbow Books.

Renfrew, Jane M. 2005. *Prehistoric Cookery: Recipes and History*. Revised edition. London: English Heritage.

Wood, Jacqui. 2001. *Prehistoric Cooking*. Stroud, England: Tempus.

Wrangham, Richard W. 2009. *Catching Fire: How Cooking Made Us Human*. New York: Basic Books.

Documents

From Hippocrates. C. 380 BCE. *The Genuine Works of Hippocrates, Volume 1*. Translated by Francis Adams. 1849. London: Sydenham Society.

In this passage from On Ancient Medicine, *the Greek physician Hippocrates explains the ancients developed methods of preparing food in order to provide the most healthy diet.*

For the art of Medicine would not have been invented at first, nor would it have been made a subject of investigation (for there would have been no need of it), if when men are indisposed, the same food and other articles of regimen which they eat and drink when in good health were proper for them, and if no others were preferable to these. But now necessity itself made medicine to be sought out and discovered by men, since the same things when administered to the sick, which agreed with them when in good health, neither did nor do agree with them. But to go still further back, I hold that the diet and food which people in health now use would not have been discovered, provided it had suited with man to eat and drink in like manner as the ox, the horse, and all other animals, except man, do of the productions of the earth, such as fruits, weeds, and grass; for from such things these animals grow, live free of disease, and require no other kind of food. And, at first, I am of opinion that man used the same sort of food, and that the present articles of diet had been discovered and invented only after a long lapse of time, for when they suffered much and severely from strong and brutish diet, swallowing things which were raw, unmixed, and possessing great strength, they became exposed to strong pains and diseases, and to early deaths. It is likely, indeed, that from habit they would suffer less from these things then than we would now, but still they would suffer severely even then; and it is likely that the greater number, and those who had weaker constitutions, would all perish; whereas the stronger would hold out for a longer time, as even nowadays some, in consequence of using strong articles of food, get off with little trouble, but others with much pain and suffering. From this necessity it appears to me that they would search out the food befitting their nature, and thus discover that which we now use: and that from wheat, by macerating it, stripping it of its hull, grinding it all down, sifting, toasting, and baking it, they formed bread; and from barley they formed cake (maza), performing many operations in regard to it; they boiled, they roasted, they mixed, they diluted those things which are strong and of intense qualities with weaker things, fashioning them to the nature and powers of man, and considering that the stronger things Nature would not be able to manage if administered, and that from such things pains, diseases, and death would arise, but such as Nature could manage, that from them food, growth, and health, would arise. To such a discovery and investigation what more suitable name could one give than that of Medicine? since it was discovered for the health of man, for his nourishment and safety, as a substitute for that kind of diet by which pains, diseases, and deaths were occasioned.

From Abbott, Charles T. 1899. *The Cliff-Dweller's Daughter, or, How He Loved Her: An Indian Romance of Prehistoric Times*. London and New York: F. Tennyson Neely.

In this passage, the author describes how the prehistoric Native American women would prepare meals for their tribe.

Few words were spoken and many were the grunts of contentment, as the men threw themselves beside the blazing fires and watched the women draw hot embers over the mesquite cakes, or waited while the smaller animals brought in by the huntsmen were smeared with clay, and cooked beneath the roasting charcoal. Here some belated housekeeper was still using the matato with skill and energy, cracking the nuts with the well-worn manos, and crushing the whole into a pasty flour. This required skill and care, for often did some chance blow scatter near and far the flour that was ground with so much labor.

Gazelle was seated at a fire built close to some branches which made a covering for the sleepers, listening to the talk and laughter of the women as they cooked. The deep, guttural replies of the men or the cry of some child ready for its meal and sleep intervening. This served to soften the more strident voices of the women, but soon her father's step awoke her from her reverie, and, hot and tired, he stretched himself beside the fire to obtain his well-earned rest.

"How goes the castle?" questioned Gazelle, as having eaten of the cake and bear steak and drunk from the *ojah* of the cool clear water from the stream, he bent back in contentment and gazed into the starlit heavens. . . .

Gatherers

In the name that we apply to ancient cultures—"hunter-gatherer societies"—there is an implicit bias in placing the "hunter" first, suggesting that tracking down and killing wild animals represented their most important activity. Hunting may also attract more attention because it is a mostly male activity, and tracking down and attacking large animals is surely more glamorous and exciting than picking up plants. Yet hunting, by its very nature, is a hit-or-miss affair: sometimes the game is abundant; sometimes it is sparse. Sometimes, a well-aimed spear strikes its rapidly moving target; sometimes, an equally well-aimed spear misses the mark. Even the most skillful hunters would regularly return to their camps empty-handed, so that for their day-to-day survival, prehistoric humans were undoubtedly more dependent upon the steady supply of food that was brought in by their gatherers. As one valuable piece of evidence to support this claim, scientists have been able to analyze ancient human feces, and they consistently show that most of the human diet consisted of plants. Only in the Arctic regions, where plant life could be extremely difficult to find, did hunting provide the bulk of people's food.

To understand the strategies employed by gatherers, anthropologists employ what is known as optimal foraging theory, which assumes that people will seek certain foods to obtain the maximum amount of energy from the minimal amount of time. Thus, fruits that grow on high tree branches might be highly desirable as food sources, but it would require a lot of time and effort to climb up trees and pick them, so gatherers will instead concentrate on berries that grow close to the ground, even if they are not as nutritious. The theory can help to explain certain changes in the patterns of gathering over time. At certain times of the year, for example, there are abundant amount of acorns on the ground in many regions, but it requires a lot of work to consume them: they are toxic unless they are cooked, and easier to digest if they are ground into meal. For that reason, early gatherers tended to ignore them in favor of plants that could be immediately eaten. Later in human history, as populations increased and food was more difficult to find, the extra energy needed to eat acorns became justifiable, and the evidence indicates that they became an important part of the human diet in some parts of the world.

Based on observations of twentieth-century cultures that still depended on hunting and gathering, we can be confident that gathering was primarily a female activity—although some boys deemed too young to accompany their hunter fathers, or elderly men no longer capable of hunting, may have assisted at times. The men also did a little bit of their own gathering, as they would search for the right sorts of stones to be chiseled into spear points or arrowheads and suitable branches to make spears and arrows. It is sometimes assumed that the work of the gatherers began in the early morning and extended until the late afternoon, but one study suggests that they should have been able to obtain enough food for the day in about three hours, providing plenty of time for the women to return home and address other chores, such as food preparation and making and repairing clothes. Since no one else was available to watch them, they would have to bring their babies along, probably in carriers attached to their backs or chests to keep their hands free for picking up the needed items; in arid regions, they would also have to carry some drinking water. As they became familiar with the regions that their nomadic tribes inhabited, they would learn to focus their attention on the areas that were most likely to offer desirable food at various times of the year, and they would encourage their groups to migrate to certain places where the food would be most abundant.

In the beginning, gatherers worked exclusively with their hands, holding on to their finds and carrying them back to their camps. But like hunters, they also developed special tools to improve their effectiveness. Knives and sickles were designed especially to cut plants and tree branches, and digging sticks helped women to obtain underground roots and bulbs. To carry the items that they gathered, women initially used pieces of tree bark or pouches of animal skin, and later they weaved nets and baskets to bring back even more plants, berries, and nuts without dropping them. Animal hides were employed as crude sleds, as women would place very large finds on the hides and drag them home.

Because plants, unlike animal bones, are rarely preserved, we are not always sure what sorts of plants our ancestors were gathering on their daily expeditions. Presumably, the science of gathering resulted from a lengthy process of trial and error, as people gradually determined which items were safe and nutritious, and which items were poisonous or indigestible, and passed this hard-earned knowledge on to their children. We do know that ancient people frequently made use of trees, which offered many edible fruits—like apples, pears, cherries, plums, and figs—and nuts—like almonds, walnuts, beechnuts, and acorns. On the ground, they looked for smaller plants that offered several varieties of berries, as well as wild rice, lentils, water chestnuts, and watercress. A site in Switzerland suggests that people harvested and ate mushrooms; in ancient Australia, women dug wild yams out of the ground; and in prehistoric America's western desert, popular items to gather included cactuses, sunflower seeds, and yucca seeds.

In some areas, gatherers searching for food also focused their attention on small animals and animal products. The eggs of birds and reptiles, for example, could be an excellent source of protein. In ancient Australia, gatherers collected insects, snails, and small reptiles, and if they happened upon an animal that had recently died, they would bring the carcass back to their camps to make use of its meat and fur.

While food was the main priority of the gatherers, some materials were collected for other uses. Reeds and rushes, for example, could be woven into cords, baskets, and mats, and when snakes molted, their discarded snakeskins would be picked up and used to make small items of clothing. The bark of trees was carved to make containers, and when burned, the bark of birch trees produced a black tar that functioned as an adhesive, employed to attach pointed stones to arrows. Branches lying on the ground would be gathered to be used as firewood. When people were ill, the women would look for the plants and herbs that were believed would help cure the ailment; for example, chaga, a fungus that grows on birch trees, was found on the body of the Iceman, the prehistoric human found frozen in the Alps, and since it is now used as a folk remedy, gatherers may have collected it for him as a medicine. Finally, beyond any utilitarian goals, they might have gathered attractive flowers solely to decorate themselves or their surroundings; for while the flowers found in Neanderthal graves are often thought to be present for their medicinal properties, it is also possible that they served the same purpose as the flowers on modern graves, to honor the deceased with colorful embellishments.

A SICKENING STEW

To this day, some cooks believe that their dishes will taste best if they gather fresh wild herbs instead of relying on powdered herbs sold in stores. Yet these well-meaning women do not always bring the keen eyes of their ancient counterparts to this task. One television documentary, for example, told the story of an emergency room filled with family members suffering from mysterious symptoms. It turned out that they had recently eaten a stew prepared by their grandmother, who had gathered wild herbs for the stew; but she mistakenly picked up and used some leaves of tobacco, which is toxic if eaten, causing her family's medical problems.

INFANT FORAGERS

As parents learn, babies at a certain stage obsessively pick up things and put them in their mouths—an instinct that may stem from the actions of ancient gatherers. Women would necessarily bring children on their daily expeditions, and if preoccupied with other business, they would place babies on the ground, leaving them to forage for themselves. Babies who made poor decisions and consumed poisonous plants would die, while those who chose nourishing food would survive. Over time, evolution would produce babies who made intelligent decisions—which might explain why contemporary babies generally manage to survive, despite their seemingly dangerous habit of putting unsanitary objects in their mouths.

Overall, gathering functioned as an effective way to obtain plant food until rising populations, and changing climates, made it more and more difficult for nomadic groups to find all the plant life they needed, leading them to rely upon agriculture instead. Yet because it provided a nourishing and variegated diet, gathering might have actually been a superior method to feed one's people, as signs of malnutrition are typically not detected in human remains until the rise of farming, which forced people to depend on a more limited range of plant foods. And the tradition of gathering has never entirely vanished, as even today, some people enjoy occasionally leaving their civilized homes to search for edible berries, nuts, and mushrooms in the wild, much like their ancient ancestors.

Further Reading

Bower, John R. F., and Michal Kobusiewicz. 2002. *A Comparative Study of Prehistoric Foragers in Europe and North America: Cultural Responses to the End of the Ice Age.* Lewiston, NY: Edwin Mellen Press.

Johnson, Allen W., and Timothy Earle. 2000. *The Evolution of Human Societies: From Foraging Group to Agrarian State.* Second edition. Stanford, CA: Stanford University Press.

Kobayashi, Tatsuo. 2004. *Jomon Reflections: Forager Life and Culture in the Prehistoric Japanese Archipelago.* Edited by Simon Kaner with Oki Nakamura. Oxford: Oxbow Books.

Lee, Richard B., and Richard Daly, editors. 1999. *The Cambridge Encyclopedia of Hunters and Gatherers.* Cambridge: Cambridge University Press.

Mithen, Stephen J. 2000. *Thoughtful Foragers: A Study of Prehistoric Decision Making.* Cambridge and New York: Cambridge University Press.

Scarry, C. Margaret, editor. 1993. *Foraging and Farming in the Eastern Woodlands.* Gainesville: University Press of Florida.

Documents

From Waterloo, Stanley. 1897. *The Story of Ab: A Tale of the Time of the Cave Man.* Chicago: Way & Williams.

Here, the novelist describes the woman's role in gathering food and the way that her findings were carried back to the home.

There came no new alarm, and soon the cave was reached, though on the way there was a momentary deviation from the path, to gather up the nuts and berries the woman had found in the afternoon while the babe was lying sleeping. The fruitage was held in a great leaf, a pliant thing pulled together at the edges, tied stoutly with a strand of tough grass, and making a handy pouch containing a quart or two of the food, which was the woman's contribution to the evening meal. As for the father, he had more to offer, as was evident when the cave was reached. . . .

There was a certain regularity in the daily program of the household, although, with reference to what was liable to occur outside, it can hardly be said to have partaken of the element of monotony. The work of the day consisted merely in getting something to eat, and in this work father and mother alike took an active part, their individual duties being somewhat varied. In a general way [the father] relied upon himself for the provision of flesh, but there were roots and nuts and fruits, in their season, and in the gathering of these [the mother] was an admitted expert. Not that all her efforts were confined to the fruits of the soil and forest, for she could, if need be, assist her husband in the pursuit or capture of any animal. She was not less clever than he in that animal's subsequent dissection, and was far more expert in its cooking. In the tanning of skins she was an adept. . . .

From Bandelier, Adolph Francis Alphonse. 1890. *The Delight-Makers: A Novel of Prehistoric Pueblo Indians.* New York: Dodd, Mead, and Co.

After devoting eight years to the study of New Mexico's Pueblo Indians, archaeologist Adolph Francis Alphonse Bandelier (1840–1914) wrote a novel based on his research about their ancient ancestors, the Queres. He focused on a woman named Shotaye who regularly gathered herbs, plants, and nuts, and on one occasion also obtained the valuable feather of an owl, believed to have magical properties. Bandelier National Monument, a U.S. National Monument, is named after Bandelier. A beautiful area of 33,000 acres, it was the home of the ancient Pueblo Indians, and is located near Los Alamos, New Mexico.

Shotaye was in the habit of strolling alone all around the Rito, over the timbered mesa as well as through the gorges which descend from the mountains. . . . Of what is called to-day the mesa del Rito, the high table-land bordering the Tyuonyi on the south, Shotaye knew every inch of ground, every tree and shrub.

On a clear, cool November day she strolled again in that direction, climbing the heights and penetrating into the scrubby timber, interspersed with tall pines, which covers the plateau for miles. To her delight she discovered the remains of an owl at no great distance from the declivity of the Rito beneath a rotten pine. Instead of picking up the carcass she kicked it aside disdainfully, but took good care to notice whither so as to remember the place. It landed on a juniper-bush and remained suspended from its branches. Shotaye went onward carelessly. She looked for herbs and plants, picking up a handful here, pulling out a root there, until she had made a long circuit, which however brought her back to the place where the dead owl was. Here she stopped, listening, all the while looking out for plants. As if by accident she neared the bush on which the carcass was still hanging, and after assuring herself that the body had not been disturbed, she brushed past so as to cause it to drop to the ground. She hastily plucked a few feathers, put them with the herbs and roots already gathered, and turned homeward. . . .

[Later] Shotaye left her cave in quest of vegetable medicaments. . . . She simply took a walk on the mesa of the Bird, Ziro kauash. She hoped also to gather some useful plants,—such as the shkoa, a spinach-like vegetable; asclepias; apotz, a fever-medicine of the genus *artemesia*, and many other medicinal herbs known to the Indian and used by him. For it had sprinkled if not rained every day of late, and last night's rain was still visible in the drops that covered the leaves. . . . She gathered a few leaves of the dark-green shiutui, sauntered from juniper-bush to juniper-bush, glanced from time to time upward into the tops of pines to see whether they bore edible nuts of the kind now called piñons, or threw stones at the noisy birds that fluttered about.

Healers

Prehistoric humans, as a rule, did not live very long; based on examinations of skeletal remains, scientists estimate that the average life expectancy may have been as low as twenty-five to thirty years. This was largely because our ancestors had very few ways to deal effectively with the injuries and diseases that regularly afflicted them; conditions that today are minor inconveniences, like a broken bone or the flu, might have proved fatal to our distant ancestors. Ancient healers worked very hard to develop methods for curing the ailing members of their tribe, but only with limited success.

In the beginning, no doubt, medical lore was shared by all members of small tribes, and any available person might act quickly to treat a wound or find the right plant for a sick person to chew; but as the groups grew larger and people began to specialize in certain activities, a few people would come to be regarded as the chief healers. In most cases, this was one of the responsibilities of the shaman, who would treat the sick with a combination of religious rituals and practical remedies; some decisions about the medical care of important individuals might be made by chieftains; and since they were the ones who were the experts in identifying and gathering useful plants, older women might naturally become the persons consulted about the use of herbal remedies. Eventually, healing might become the informal part-time job of several individuals, each called upon to deal with certain sorts of medical problem.

For some conditions, one approach developed by ancient humans was to engage in crude forms of surgery. Their best-known technique was trepanation, cutting a small hole in a person's skull. This might have been helpful in relieving the painful pressure caused by brain tumors or in treating certain types of injuries to the skull, but many believe that it was more often employed as a treatment for mental problems, such as epilepsy (though it is by no means clear that ancient humans regarded the head as the center of the intellect, an insight that eluded some ancient cultures). Interestingly, one theory is that trepanation was first performed on sheep to treat the condition known as staggers, a neurological disorder caused by tapeworm larvae underneath the scalp that causes sheep to move unsteadily, and when people found the procedure was occasionally successful, they began to treat humans in the same fashion. The holes in the skull were created in various ways: most frequently, the surgeon would use a flint or obsidian scraping tool to first make an incision, then enlarge it until there was a small circular depression that was removed. They would also employ a device called a bow drill, which rapidly rotated a pointed shaft to drill a series of holes in a circle. To modern observers, these processes seem both extremely dangerous and incredibly painful, but studies indicate that up to two-thirds of the patients survived the procedure, and skulls show that some people underwent trepanation several times. And to ease their pain, patients may have been given alcohol, perhaps in conjunction with forms of opium or cannabis.

While skulls with such holes are found all over the world, trepanation may not have been as common as was once believed, because it happens to be a form of surgery that can always be detected because its effects are so obvious. Other types of surgery, though their signs are less obvious, may have been just as frequent, as indicated by some ancient surgical tools that have been discovered, including saws, forceps, scalpels, and needles. The most common operations were probably digging out spear points and arrowheads, removing large tumors, and amputating damaged limbs, using the most suitable cutting tools in each case. In ancient Australia, however, evidence has been discovered of an ancient amputation apparently effected by means of cauterization; literally, the diseased or wounded limb was burned away, probably by digging a hole, placing the limb within it, and starting a fire in the hole. Observations of African tribes by early explorers suggest that their ancestors may have developed the ability to successfully perform Caesarian sections, and there are signs that our ancestors practiced acupuncture, not only ancient Chinese people but the Aleutians of North America as well. There is also occasional evidence of ancient dentistry, such as a molar discovered with a hole drilled into it, apparently by a bow-drill, probably in order to remove a cavity that had caused an abscess. Beeswax, detected in one of these holes, may have been commonly used as a filling.

To deal with other health issues, ancient people were wise enough to basically let the body heal itself. When someone broke a bone in her arm or leg, she would be told to remain motionless, and mud or clay would be placed over the limb to harden into a protective cast. Generally, though, skeletons indicate that the broken bones were positioned clumsily and healed imperfectly, so that the afflicted person never regained full use of the damaged arm or leg. Other cuts and wounds were covered with animal fat and pieces of animal skin to serve as a bandage.

Prehistoric people also discovered, and made use of, various herbal remedies, consuming certain plants for certain conditions. Some of these may date back to the Neanderthals; their graves typically include six flowers, all from plants with known medicinal uses, suggesting that the flowers may have been placed there to relieve the suffering of the deceased person in the afterlife. These plants, also used by some later humans, were the grape hyacinth, which has diuretic effects; the hollyhock and ragwort, both used as pain relievers; yarrow, administered to ease constipation; St. Barnaby's thistle, given to people suffering from fevers; and the woody horsetail, which functioned as a stimulant. Other plants that were employed as medicines include orchid bulbs, chewed on to relieve stomach aches; cornflowers, applied to treat eye problems; eucalyptus leaves, which relieved congestion; chamomile, consumed to ease stress; and feverfew, used to reduce the pains of arthritis. In addition, a fungus that grew on birch trees was used as a laxative, and cumin seeds were eaten to relieve constipation and indigestion. In early South America, ancient people discovered that they could relieve their pain by chewing coca plants, now the source for the drug cocaine. Indeed, it seems that our ancient ancestors in various parts of the world found and ingested many sorts of psychoactive plants that remain popular in various forms, such as hemp or cannabis, the opium poppy, tobacco, and betel leaves (still chewed as a stimulant throughout Asia). Some experts have even speculated that agriculture may have originated not to produce food, but to provide a steady source of such medicinal drugs.

Still, while we can celebrate our ancestors for discovering and using some good remedies, they also came up with many useless or counterproductive remedies. If someone complained of heart pains, for example, they might be advised to eat leaves that were shaped like the human heart, and if a person's skin looked reddish due to an illness, their friends might assume that it was due to an excessive amount of blood in their body and begin draining blood from the affected area, a practice that endured well into recent centuries. There were also many conditions that they were completely unable to ameliorate, particularly infectious diseases, which became especially problematic when humans began to live in settled communities close to large numbers of animals. Examinations of ancient skeletons have shown that ancient people regularly contracted diseases like cholera, influenza, measles, malaria, smallpox, and typhoid fever; many older people suffered from arthritis and rheumatism; and there are signs of diseases caused by poor nutrition, such as rickets and scurvy. In such cases, all

HERBS FOR HEALING

Accompanying the rise of modern medicine, there has been a renewed interest in the herbal remedies discovered by ancient healers; numerous books promote their benefits, and health-food stores sell herbal remedies in tablet form. Interestingly, in some cases, scientific studies indicate that an herbal remedy may actually be effective. The herb chamomile, for example, was long administered to relieve stress, and recent research has confirmed that the herb is a good treatment for gastrointestinal problems like diarrhea, indigestion, and colic in infants. Paradoxically, however, the research to date has not yet demonstrated that it actually functions to reduce anxiety as was once believed.

A HOLE IN THE HEAD?

Of all the healing methods developed by prehistoric healers, trepanation—drilling small holes in people's skulls—undoubtedly seems the most bizarre and counterproductive to modern observers. However, demonstrating that few ancient beliefs are ever completely abandoned, a handful of modern eccentrics, like Bart Huges and Joey Mellen, have advocated trepanation as a way to improve the speed and quality of people's thoughts by relieving pressure on the brain; Huges and Mellen even performed the procedure on themselves in the late 1960s. Needless to say, medical research has proved that there are absolutely no benefits to the procedure.

people could do was to depend upon the rituals of the shaman, who might burn incense, dance around the patients, and chant invectives in hopes of removing the demons from their bodies. If the suffering people thought that such actions would be effective, their belief alone might have had a beneficial effect, suggesting that the ancient shamans did inadvertently devise one form of treatment that is known to work in some cases: the placebo effect. But only the beginning of civilization would bring the first efforts to develop a systematic and scientific approach to the maintenance of human health.

Further Reading

Arnott, Robert. 1997. *Surgical Practice in the Prehistoric Aegean*. Munich, Germany: Gustav Fischer Verlag.

Arnott, Robert, Stanley Finger, and C.U.M. Smith, editors. 2003. *Trepanation: History, Discovery, Theory*. Lisse, The Netherlands: Swets & Zeitlinger.

Aufderheide, Arthur C., and Conrado Rodriguez-Martin. 1998. *The Cambridge Encyclopedia of Human Paleopathology*. Cambridge and New York: Cambridge University Press.

Johns, Timothy. 1996. *The Origins of Human Diet and Medicine: Chemical Ecology*. Tucson: University of Arizona Press.

Kelly, Kate. 2009. *The History of Medicine, Volume 1: Early Civilizations: Prehistoric Times to 500 C.E.* New York: Facts on File.

Prioreschi, Plinio. 1996. *The History of Medicine, Volume 1: Primitive and Ancient Medicine*. Second edition. Omaha, NE: Horatius Press.

Documents

From Parry, Thomas Wilson. 1918. *Surgery of the Stone Age: A Ballad of Neolithic Times*. London: J. Bale.

The British doctor Thomas Wilson Parry had a keen interest in trepanation, the process of boring holes in the human skull, which was common during prehistoric times. He theorized that ancient surgeons may have done this as a cure for epilepsy, creating a hole so that the presumed demon in a person's head could escape, and he wrote this playful poem to describe such a procedure.

"This patient must be *now* trephined,
Let all the others go;
To-morrow when the sun is up
My magic I'll then show."

Two men the epileptic bore
And laid him on a trunk,
And when the wretch was coming round
He showed some signs of funk.

No questions put they to the man;
The doctor cleared his throat,
Then, bringing flints from out his hut,
Took off his hairy coat.

A crowd had gathered all around,
To watch the bloody deed;

Their curiosity was stirred
To see his devil freed.

With sharp flint flake the surgeon made
A cruciform incision;
The blood did spurt, the wound it hurt,
The crowd laughed in derision.

The two assistants pressed the flaps
To stop the blood from running;
The Medicine-Man did scheme and plan,
He was so full of cunning.

He scraped the pericranium,
Until the skull was bare;
Then scratched the bone with a sharp stone,
It did not matter where.

He scraped that bone and scratched and
    scraped—
The scratches made a groove,
The groove a basin-like ellipse.
The patient did not move.

The fact was this, when he came round
So rotten did he feel,
He fainted when he found himself
The centre of such zeal.

The hollow soon became a hole,
'Twas all but through the bone,
His diploë,* you well might see,
But still he made no moan.

The inner table only now
Protected his soft brain,
One final scrape and he did make
That hole a window-pane.

The devil stirred within his skull
And with a fearful yell,
Escaped from out its prison-house
To seek its own in hell.

*The soft tissue between the two layers of bone
in the skull

From London, Jack. 1907. *Before Adam.* New York:
Macmillan.

*In this passage, novelist Jack London vividly
describes how a prehistoric man would have treated
an arrow wound.*

My next dream, in the order of succession, begins
always with the flight of Lop-Ear and myself through
the forest. . . . Lop-Ear and I, in a cautious panic, are
fleeing through the trees. In my right leg is a burning
pain; and from the flesh, protruding head and shaft
from either side, is an arrow of the Fire-Man. Not only
did the pull and strain of it pain me severely, but it
bothered my movements and made it impossible for
me to keep up with Lop-Ear.

At last I gave up, crouching in the secure fork of
a tree. Lop-Ear went right on. I called to him—most
plaintively, I remember; and he stopped and looked
back. Then he returned to me, climbing into the fork
and examining the arrow. He tried to pull it out, but
one way the flesh resisted the barbed lead, and the
other way it resisted the feathered shaft. Also, it hurt
grievously, and I stopped him.

For some time we crouched there, Lop-Ear nervous and anxious to be gone, perpetually and appre-
hensively peering this way and that, and myself
whimpering softly and sobbing. Lop-Ear was plainly
in a funk, and yet his conduct in remaining by me, in
spite of his fear, I take as a foreshadowing of the altruism and comradeship that have helped make man the
mightiest of the animals.

Once again Lop-Ear tried to drag the arrow
through the flesh, and I angrily stopped him. Then he
bent down and began gnawing the shaft of the arrow
with his teeth. As he did so he held the arrow firmly
in both hands so that it would not play about in the
wound, and at the same time I held on to him. I often
meditate upon this scene—the two of us, half-grown
cubs, in the childhood of the race, and the one mastering his fear, beating down his selfish impulse of flight,
in order to stand by and succor the other. And there
rises up before me all that was there foreshadowed,

and I see visions of Damon and Pythias, of life-saving crews and Red Cross nurses, of martyrs and leaders of forlorn hopes, of Father Damien, and of the Christ himself, and of all the men of earth, mighty of stature, whose strength may trace back to the elemental loins of Lop-Ear and Big-Tooth and other dim denizens of the Younger World.

When Lop-Ear had chewed off the head of the arrow, the shaft was withdrawn easily enough. I started to go on, but this time it was he that stopped me. My leg was bleeding profusely. Some of the smaller veins had doubtless been ruptured. Running out to the end of a branch, Lop-Ear gathered a handful of green leaves. These he stuffed into the wound. They accomplished the purpose, for the bleeding soon stopped. Then we went on together, back to the safety of the caves.

Hunters

As best we can determine, the primates who would evolve into modern humans were originally herbivores, exclusively eating plants; however, at some point two to three million years ago, our ancestors developed a taste for meat, a shift in their diets that may have played a crucial role in the development of human intelligence. After all, once people have identified which forms of plant life are edible and nutritious, and that knowledge can be passed on to the next generation, finding and gathering such plants is not an intellectually demanding task. Yet someone attempting to locate, track down, and kill a fast-moving animal faces a series of difficult puzzles to solve, so effective hunters must be smart as well as strong. Further, successful hunters would be most likely to have more children who would also be successful hunters, gradually making the species more intelligent through the process of natural selection. Eating meat changed humans in other ways, requiring large teeth that could effectively chew raw meat and a digestive system that could handle fats, though people eventually learned to master fire and cook their meat to make it easier to consume.

People tend to speak of prehistoric hunters as men, because in the remote tribes who seemingly have retained the habits of their distant ancestors, anthropologists generally observed a division of labor based on gender; all men are trained to become hunters and warriors, while all women are trained to become gatherers and food preparers. In ancient times, however, some anthropologists have suggested that such dividing lines were not observed, and even some contemporary evidence indicates that both men and women may have engaged in both hunting and gathering. In almost all cultures, the men who hunt also help women gather plants, and in the Ju'/hoansi culture of modern Namibia, women accompany and assist the male hunters. In addition, it is certainly interesting that in Greek mythology, the deity associated with hunting was a woman, Artemis, described as an expert hunter and archer; clearly, the ancient Greeks did not think it unusual to envision a woman performing these roles. Other ancient cultures, including Egypt and the Inuit people of modern Canada, also worshipped hunting goddesses.

The earliest hunters may have been able to subdue a few animals with their bare hands if they were wounded or elderly, but hunting could not become a reliable source of food until humans were able to use tools. Undoubtedly, as depicted in the film *2001: A Space Odyssey* (1968), the first tools they employed were found objects, like bones and tree branches, that could be wielded as clubs to bludgeon animals; later, humans would carve suitable pieces of wood specifically for that purpose. Yet animals could easily avoid being clubbed by running away, so humans needed some way to wound a fleeing animal. The first solution to the problem was probably a spear. Using a special stone, a man would chip away at another stone until it had a sharp point; then, the pointed stone would be tied, using ropes made from plants, to the end of a long stick, so that a hunter could forcefully fling the stick at an animal and penetrate its skin with the pointed stone. An improved version of the spear, the atlatl, was especially shaped to be thrown effectively.

Since spears had only a limited range, most cultures developed a better weapon, the bow and arrow: a thin strip of animal muscle with some elasticity was attached to a long piece of wood (the bow) and used to propel a stick (the arrow) with a thin pointed stone attached to it (the arrowhead). Ancient cultures also created many other sorts of devices that could kill mobile animals, such as slings to propel small stones

This image of a prehistoric hunter, from about 4000–3000 BCE, wielding a bow and arrow, was found in the Tassili n' Ajjer mountain range of present-day Algeria. (DeAgostini/Getty Images)

(the precursors to today's slingshots) and blowguns that aimed poisoned darts. Australia's ancient aborigines created a uniquely curved throwing weapon, the boomerang, that would fly back to the hunter if it missed its mark.

. Despite such improvements in technology, the task of the hunter remained arduous and difficult. Typically starting early in the morning, hunters would carry their weapons on long treks, moving as quietly as possible so that the animals would not notice their presence. When a desired animal was spotted, the hunters would try to creep close enough so that their weapons could be effectively deployed; more often than not, the animal would be alerted by their approach and rapidly flee, though hunters might be able to run after it and subdue it with a well-aimed spear or arrow. Boys would accompany their fathers on hunts in order to learn the craft, but experienced hunters would direct

the hunt and actually attempt to kill the animals. After long days of walking and running over vast amounts of territory, though, even the best of hunters might return to their tribes empty-handed, forcing them to eat only the plants gathered by the women while hoping for better luck on the next day.

Hunting undoubtedly played a role in the development of many human crafts. To improve their chances, it is believed that prehistoric hunters sometimes painted pictures in caves showing animals being killed, as portents of eventual success, so they may have been humanity's earliest artists. When hunters brought back large animals, they must have entertained their tribes by sitting around the fire and describing how they managed to kill their prey, helping to develop the art of storytelling. One of the first instances of domesticated animals may have been dogs who were trained to help hunters track down their prey. And while animals were killed primarily to provide food, hunters and their female companions gradually devised many other uses for the carcasses that were brought home: animal furs could be cut and sewn together to serve as human clothing, and bones could be carved to become flutes or small sculptures. Elephants were often hunted almost exclusively for their valued ivory tusks, which could be employed for a variety of purposes. The bodies of dead animals even inspired an ancient form of prophecy, called *extispicium*, based on careful examination of their entrails.

When humans abandoned a completely nomadic life to periodically settle in certain areas, they devised another way to capture animals—the trap. One simple system involved digging a large hole and covering it with a thin layer of leaves; when an animal stepped into the area, it would fall into the hole, where it could be easily killed. Humans also learned to craft nets that could be concealed on the ground under leaves; the nets would then surround and elevate the surprising animals, rendering them helpless. In desert cultures, special sorts of walls called desert kites were used to force animals into enclosures or drive them off a cliff. Later cultures devised more elaborate sorts of traps that would lure animals into cages.

After many generations of progress, early humans became very accomplished hunters, as evidenced by the bones found at various archaeological sites.

PREHISTORIC HUNTING TODAY

While modern hunters usually employ modern weapons, there are small numbers of people who deliberately limit themselves to the techniques of ancient hunters. There has been a surprising amount of interest, for example, in reviving the use of an early spear, the atlatl, for hunting, and in 2006, the state of Pennsylvania officially sanctioned this weapon for hunting deer. Of course, it seems very unlikely that such primitive weapons will ever supplant rifles and revolvers, but there may long remain a few hunters who enjoy the challenge of following in the footsteps of their distant ancestors.

A MAMMOTH COMEBACK?

The prehistoric hunters of Europe became so efficient at killing woolly mammoths that, by all accounts, they drove these large animals to extinction—something that modern people deeply regret. However, as if to atone for this ancient human sin, growing numbers of contemporary scientists are intent upon bringing this creature back to life by means of cloning. While some are skeptical that this can be accomplished, their determined efforts to locate more mammoth remains, facilitated by the global warming that is bringing more of them to the surface, are increasing the chances of finding suitable amounts of the fresh blood and tissue that might make such cloning possible.

Excavations of the Zhoukoudian caves in China, for example, indicate that prehistoric hunters were successfully killing a number of large animals, including rhinoceroses, antelopes, boars, leopards, and cave bears. In ancient Africa, humans hunted elephants, hippopotamuses, buffaloes, giraffes, and gazelles. The evidence also suggests that one species, the woolly mammoth, was driven into extinction largely by effective human hunting.

Eventually, however, humans began to rely on agriculture as a more reliable source of food, and hunting became less important, for two reasons. A steady supply of plant food meant that hunted animals, while still valued, were no longer essential, and as humans settled down to plant and raise crops, they discovered that animals, instead of being hunted, could be usefully domesticated for various purposes. Some provided food products, such as eggs from chickens and milk from cows, though these animals could also be slaughtered and eaten; others, like pigs, were raised exclusively as meat. Hunting wild animals, then, merely offered some occasional variety in a human diet otherwise consisting of harvested plants and food from domesticated animals. Eventually, in developed societies with many other sources of food, hunting almost exclusively became a sport, as hunters pursued and killed animals for the thrill of the experience, not the reward of a tasty meal. Still, to this day, there remain individuals in rural areas who continue to rely upon hunted animals as a major portion of their diet, just like their ancient ancestors.

Further Reading

Frison, George C. 1991. *Prehistoric Hunters of the High Plains*. Second edition. San Diego: Academic Press.

Frison, George C. 2004. *Survival by Hunting: Prehistoric Human Predators and Animal Prey*. Berkeley and Los Angeles: University of California Press.

Lee, Richard B., and Richard Daly, editors. 1999. *The Cambridge Encyclopedia of Hunters and Gatherers*. Cambridge: Cambridge University Press.

Smith, Christopher. 1992. *Late Stone Age Hunters of the British Isles*. London and New York: Routledge.

Speth, John D. 2010. *The Paleoanthropology and Archaeology of Big-Game Hunting: Protein, Fat, or Politics?* New York: Springer.

West, Dixie Lee. 1997. *Hunting Strategies in Central Europe during the Last Glacial Maximum*. Oxford: British Archaeological Reports.

Documents

From Renarde, Georges François. 1929. *Life and Work in Prehistoric Times*. Translated by R. T. Clark. 1929. New York: Alfred A. Knopf.

In this passage, the French historian paints a vivid picture of how struggling early humans gradually developed the ability to hunt animals.

At first man found himself in a real state of inferiority as compared with the big animals on which he hoped to feed. He had not the strength of the bull or the buffalo, the swiftness of the stag or the horse, the wings of the pigeon or the heron. Beside the elephant, the rhinoceros and the mammoth he was but a pygmy. But he possessed what will secure for him the dominion of the world, intelligence, and he gained the day over his adversaries however redoubtable and however agile by sheer force of patience and ingenuity.

In the beginning he could count on nothing but his own strength. . . . He could follow an animal by scent; the examination of a clod of turf told him that his prey had passed that way. He used sight as much as the sense of smell. Broken branches, the movement of the grass, revealed things to him. His ear could catch almost imperceptible sounds. He was also a fine runner, climber, and jumper. He was able to run down the game he had started.

He soon learned to add stratagem to the power which agility of body gave him. Stratagem was necessary in the case of winged game which, when he approached, could soar into the air. . . . He invented all sorts of limes, traps, and snares especially for prey which he did not dare attack openly. A pit covered with grass delivered into his power the elephant or the tiger which fell into it and disemboweled itself on the sharp stakes. Traps of this kind are frequently painted on the walls of prehistoric caverns.

For the hunting of large animals bands were formed . . . by shouting and waving of torches [the humans] had driven their prey in panic between them and driven them over the precipice. The animals killed were for the most part young, either because young animals are easier to surprise or because they are more tender to eat.

From London, Jack. 1907. *Before Adam*. New York: Macmillan.

From the perspective of a less advanced human, the writer Jack London created characters in the fictional Before Adam, *which describes early humans' encounters with ancient people who have mastered the art of hunting and are now using their skills to kill other humans.*

It was not until the night of our first day on the south bank of the river that we discovered the Fire People. What must have been a band of wandering hunters went into camp not far from the tree in which Lop-Ear and I had elected to roost for the night. The voices of the Fire People at first alarmed us, but later, when darkness had come, we were attracted by the fire. We crept cautiously and silently from tree to tree till we got a good view of the scene.

In an open space among the trees, near to the river, the fire was burning. About it were half a dozen Fire-Men. Lop-Ear clutched me suddenly, and I could feel him tremble. I looked more closely, and saw the wizened little old hunter who had shot Broken-Tooth out of the tree years before. When he got up and walked about, throwing fresh wood upon the fire, I saw that he limped with his crippled leg. Whatever it was, it was a permanent injury. He seemed more dried up and wizened than ever, and the hair on his face was quite gray.

The other hunters were young men. I noted, lying near them on the ground, their bows and arrows, and I knew the weapons for what they were. The Fire-Men wore animal skins around their waists and across their shoulders. Their arms and legs, however, were bare, and they wore no footgear. . . .

The hunters of the Fire People began to appear more frequently as the time went by. They came in twos and threes, creeping silently through the forest, with their flying arrows able to annihilate distance and bring down prey from the top of the loftiest tree without themselves climbing into it. The bow and arrow was like an enormous extension of their leaping and striking muscles, so that, virtually, they could leap and kill at a hundred feet and more. This made them far more terrible than Saber-Tooth himself. And then they were very wise. They had speech that enabled them more effectively to reason, and in addition they understood cooperation.

We Folk came to be very circumspect when we were in the forest. We were more alert and vigilant and timid. No longer were the trees a protection to be relied upon. No longer could we perch on a branch and laugh down at our carnivorous enemies on the ground. The Fire People were carnivorous, with claws and fangs a hundred feet long, the most terrible of all the hunting animals that ranged the primeval world.

Metalworkers

The ability to work with metals has long functioned as a way to designate the basic stages of human development: the time when people did not use metals and instead depended on stone is called the Stone Age; the era when they mastered an alloy of copper and tin called bronze is called the Bronze Age; and the later period when they learned how to make objects out of a stronger metal, iron, is called the Iron Age. Throughout these eras, humans were also discovering and making use of other metals like gold, silver, tin, and lead. Of course, one reason why these materials loom so large in our understanding of human prehistory is that artifacts made of stone, bronze, and iron have endured to the present time, while ancient items made of flimsier stuff, like wood or fabric, were almost invariably destroyed. But no one can doubt that metal weapons and utensils were significant factors in the gradual development of human civilization.

Human metallurgy began about 8,000 years ago, when humans would occasionally find nuggets of pure gold and copper and hammer these attractive stones into decorative beads; when they discovered that heating metals made them easier to shape, they began using metal both for practical objects—pins and fishhooks—and items of jewelry—pendants and rings. When only small quantities of these metals were needed, they could be obtained by a process of panning: gravel from a river would be mixed with water in a dish and stirred so that lighter materials would spill over the edges, leaving the heavier metal at the bottom of the dish—a technique still used today to find gold. Later, searching for larger amounts of desirable metals, people would go upstream, looking for distinctive colors in the rocks: red signaled iron ore, while copper ore might look green or blue. At first, obtaining useful ores was undoubtedly an informal process, involving individuals digging out rocks, but later mining was done more systematically, using specific tools. First, rocks would be heated by building a fire next to a wall of rock, causing cracks; then, men would place wooden wedges in strategic positions and wield hammers made of stone to break off pieces of rock. These would then be crushed on flat stones using hammers, and bits of ore would be picked up

and collected. Seeking more metal, humans also began to dig trenches and tunnels to reach ores; one might imagine that this work would be done exclusively by strong adult men, but some narrow mine passages discovered in modern-day Israel could only have been accessed by children.

To work effectively with ores, humans had to figure out how to heat them to high temperatures, and their answer was to build furnaces out of clay, place ores inside of them, and heat them with charcoal fires. To use copper, for example, they first obtained reasonably pure metal by a process of smelting that required a temperature of almost 1500 degrees Fahrenheit; making the metal completely molten demanded a more efficient furnace that could attain a temperature of almost 2000 degrees Fahrenheit. Once this was accomplished, people could pour the molten copper into molds to create various objects; the first of these may have been little more than indentations carefully made in sand, but later molds that were bowls of clay produced better results. To deal with the high heat and fumes involved in their work, metalworkers learned to don gloves and place filters over their mouths. Eventually, copper was poured into two-part molds that entirely surrounded the metal to produce more intricately shaped three-dimensional objects. Rarer metals like tin and silver could be handled with similar procedures, although another rare metal, gold, was malleable enough that it could be hammered into shape with little or no heating. Although most researchers have focused their attention on the activities of European metalworkers, people in other parts of the world were learning to use metals as well; prehistoric North Americans, for example, made many objects out of copper mined near Lake Superior, though they worked only with cold metal.

While copper could make useful objects, this common metal was not hard enough for many purposes; the solution devised by ancient humans was to create alloys, mixing two metals together to produce substances with desired qualities. They first discovered and made use of some natural alloys like electrum, a combination of silver and gold, and ancient Europeans sought out a particular sort of copper ore containing some antimony or arsenic that yielded a harder form of copper; however, working with this alloy may have

This copper portrait of a warrior, from the Mississippian culture of North America, is a late example of skilled metalworking that did not involve heating the metal. (UIG via Getty Images)

exposed prehistoric metalworkers to toxic quantities of arsenic, leading them to seek a safer alternative. After some experimenting, they discovered that adding a small amount of tin to copper produced an ideal alloy, bronze, which they formed into ingots to be used immediately or transported elsewhere. To facilitate the production of several similar objects, the metalworkers began to carve and employ molds made of stone, which could be used again and again. Especially elaborate bronze objects were made using the new method of lost-wax casting: the desired shape is sculpted out of wax, clay is placed around the wax, and when the clay is heated the wax melts away, precisely forming the desired mold. Different sorts of bronze objects are found throughout Europe, including weapons, armor, utensils, and jewelry, but the people of ancient Ireland stood out because they made large numbers of bronze horns, reflecting their keen interest in music.

Gradually, the skills of making bronze and forging complex metal objects spread throughout ancient Europe and Asia; by 3000 BCE, copper and bronze utensils are found in many regions, including ancient China. The metalworkers there developed another system of mass production by forming slabs of clay with six indentations shaped like arrowheads, pouring in molten bronze, and placing another mold over it so the bronze could cool to form six arrowheads. Decorative bronze objects and bronze spearpoints have also been unearthed in prehistoric Thailand. Exactly how this wide diffusion of metalworking knowledge occurred remains uncertain. Some groups, coveting the sorts of metal weapons and utensils that they could only import from other regions, may have managed to develop the needed techniques independently, engaging in an early form of reverse engineering. In other cases, metalworkers may have sought greater income by traveling to other regions where their skills would be highly valued. Some even speculate that there may have been emerged a population of itinerant metalworkers, who moved from town to town spreading their new technology.

As metals became more and more a part of human society, they improved lives in many ways, providing cooks with superior utensils and warriors with more effective weapons. Yet they also created social divisions and contributed to the establishment of hierarchies. Powerful people could accumulate precious metals like gold and silver and make their families permanently wealthy; many metalworkers earned large incomes by producing ornaments and jewelry for high-ranking individuals who could thus advertise their elevated status. As the rarest metal known to the ancients, and an unusually attractive one as well, gold in particular became a symbol of wealth and achievement, which remains true to this day. As one result of the increasingly importance of metals, people often assume that metalworkers must have been considered part of the elite class themselves, though others have questioned this view. Still, evidence that metalworkers were valued members of their society comes from ancient religions, which often included smith gods like the Celtic Gofannon, the Norse Wayland, and the Greek Hephaestus.

THE NEW BRONZE AGE

Although ancient metalworkers devised a variety of techniques, the process of creating intricate sculptures using lost-wax casting has remained popular to this day, as many contemporary artists create bronze objects in roughly the same manner as their prehistoric counterparts. However, they understandably take advantage of some modern technology to produce a superior product: instead of making the mold out of clay, for example, they typically use plaster or fiberglass to better reproduce each detail of the wax sculpture, and instead of chiseling away any excess metal from the final sculpture by hand, they will wield electric grinders.

MALEVOLENT METAL

Before they forged the alloy of copper and tin we call bronze, prehistoric metalworkers had discovered and used another form of bronze, which occurs naturally, arsenical bronze—an alloy of copper and arsenic. Later, this alloy was deliberately manufactured. Its properties are similar to those of standard bronze, but it fell out of use, probably because metalworkers deduced that the arsenic they were working with was toxic. Before this discovery, many metalworkers exposed to arsenic may have suffered from nerve damage that made them walk unsteadily; by one theory, the Greek god of metalworking, Hephaestus, was portrayed as lame due to memories of other smiths who had trouble walking.

Throughout the Bronze Age, one can also observe tentative efforts to make use of iron, a much sturdier metal, although dauntingly high temperatures are required to work effectively with this metal. When they eventually learned how to make iron objects, it marked the beginning of the Iron Age and the end of human prehistory, as iron objects are often characteristic of the earliest human civilizations. Over the years, people have discovered and employed innumerable other metals using increasingly sophisticated technologies, but they must still admire their ancient precursors who struggled against considerable odds to employ their limited resources to master the use of these challenging materials.

Further Reading

Barber, Martyn. 2003. *Bronze and the Bronze Age: Metalwork and Society in Britain c. 2500–800 BC*. Stroud, England: Tempus.

Hanks, Bryan K., and Katheryn M. Linduff, editors. 2009. *Social Complexity in Prehistoric Eurasia: Monuments, Metals, and Mobility*. Cambridge and New York: Cambridge University Press.

La Niece, Susan, Duncan Hook, and Paul Craddock, editors. 2007. *Metals and Mines: Studies in Archaeometallurgy*. London: Archetype Publications in Association with the British Museum.

Mei, Jianjun. 2000. *Copper and Bronze Metallurgy in Late Prehistoric Xinjiang: Its Cultural Context and Relationship with Neighbouring Regions*. Oxford: Archaeopress.

Morteani, Guilio, and Jeremy P. Northover, editors. 1995. *Prehistoric Gold in Europe: Mines, Metallurgy, and Manufacture*. Dordrecht, The Netherlands, and Boston: Kluwer Academic.

Yener, K. Aslihan. 2000. *The Domestication of Metals: The Rise of Complex Metal Industries in Anatolia*. Leiden, The Netherlands, and Boston: Brill.

Document

From Lord Dunsany. 1909. "The Sword and the Idol." In *A Dreamer's Tales*. 1910. London: George Allen and Sons.

In this story, the famed fantasy writer envisions how humans might have discovered the art of metalworking by means of an accidental discovery in the ashes of a huge fire.

Loz might have known that after such a mighty conflagration nothing could remain of his small furry beast, but there was hunger in him and little reason as he searched among the ashes. What he found there amazed him beyond measure; there was no meat, there was not even his row of reddish-brown stones, but something longer than a man's leg and narrower than his hand, was lying there like a great flattened snake. When Loz looked at its thin edges and saw that it ran to a point, he picked up stones to chip it and make it sharp. It was the instinct of Loz to sharpen things. When he found that it could not be chipped his wonderment increased. It was many hours before he discovered that he could sharpen the edges by rubbing them with a stone; but at last the point was sharp, and all one side of it except near the end, where Loz held it in his hand. And Loz lifted it and brandished it, and the Stone Age was over. That afternoon in the little encampment, just as the tribe moved on, the Stone Age passed away, which, for perhaps thirty or forty thousand years, had slowly lifted Man from among the beasts and left him with his supremacy beyond all hope of reconquest.

It was not for many days that any other man tried to make for himself an iron sword by cooking the same kind of small furry beast that Loz had tried to cook. It was not for many years that any thought to lay the meat along stones as Loz had done; and when they did, being no longer on the plains of Thold, they used flints or chalk. It was not for many generations that another piece of iron ore was melted and the secret slowly guessed. Nevertheless one of Earth's many veils was torn aside by Loz to give us ultimately the steel sword and the plough, machinery and factories; let us not blame Loz if we think that he did wrong, for he did all in ignorance. The tribe moved on until it came to water, and there it settled down under a hill, and they built their huts there. Very soon they had to fight with another tribe, a tribe that was stronger than they; but the sword of Loz was terrible and his tribe slew their foes. You might make one blow at Loz, but then would come one thrust from that iron sword, and there was no way of surviving it. No one could fight with Loz. And he became ruler of the tribe in the place of Iz, who hitherto had ruled it with his sharp axe, as his father had before him.

Potters

The art of pottery represents one of the major achievements of prehistoric humans, and the innumerable chards of pottery found at archaeological sites testify to the time and energy that they poured into producing these items; indeed, oftentimes archaeologists will spend most of their time digging out and sorting prehistoric shards of pottery. We can speculate that ancient people first observed that clay in the ground, after being moist, would gradually harden, suggesting that if they took moist clay and shaped it into objects, they would harden as well. Since these would break

easily, they later figured out that subjecting the clay to intense heat would make the clay objects harder and more durable. For some cultures, this would be accomplished solely by leaving the completed objects out in the hot sun to dry, then placing them in a bonfire. Other ancient peoples, however, recognized the value of applying more intense heat than the sun or an open fire could produce, so they began to construct small enclosures in which pieces of clay could be placed and subjected to very high temperatures; these were the ancestors of the modern kiln. Since humans at this time were still nomadic, however, it is believed that these crude kilns were hastily built to be used only once before being abandoned.

Despite the usefulness of pottery, there is intriguing evidence that humans first dabbled in ceramics in order to construct works of art. At a site in the present-day Czech Republic, archaeologists found fragments of fire-hardened animal and human figurines that were made about 26,000 years ago, long before the first pots. Eventually, however, they recognized that this technology could be employed to make useful containers of various sizes, though this breakthrough occurred at different times in different societies. Thus, some fragments of genuine pottery have been located that date to around 13,000 years ago, while other cultures did not begin making pots until 6000 BCE.

Since ancient women were the ones who weaved the baskets and bags that had been previously used to carry materials, it was only logical that they also became the first people to make containers out of clay. The potters might begin with adding some particulate material to the clay, such as sand, crushed shells, or plant fibers, which would help to keep the pots from cracking. Then, they might employ the simple technique of molding the clay into a bowl-like shape by hand, a technique sometimes termed pinching and shaping, but this could lead to irregular results. Another method with the same drawback, paddling, involved holding clay next to a stone and battering it with a wooden paddle. It was better, ancient potters learned, to first form the moist clay into long coils; then, using a clay bowl as a base, they would begin to craft the pot by building circular walls with the coils. The women's experience in weaving baskets may have influenced this process, as the completed pots often resemble women baskets. The ancient potters also figured out that coiling worked better if the potters slowly rotated the embryonic pots as they worked, and some cultures experimented with various sorts of platters or bowls as bases to accomplish the coiling more quickly. After the women of many ancient societies mastered the technique of making coil pots, some of them never advanced beyond it, as coil pots were still being made in the twentieth century in some remote Native American and African communities.

A significant improvement in making pottery occurred in ancient Mesopotamia, where the concept of the wheel first emerged, and while wheeled vehicles were undoubtedly the first result of this discovery, the idea was soon applied to making pottery as well. The earliest potter's wheel was a rotating platform, called a tournette, that the potter could spin while she was employing the coiling method. When the ancients figured out the principle of a flywheel, however, the potter could apply her feet to a lower wheel and make the platform holding the pot rotate rapidly and steadily. This allowed potters to develop the technique of "throwing" pots by placing a mass of wet clay on the platform, rotating it, and using their hands to shape the material into a smooth bowl shape as it spun around.

It is around this time and a crucial change in the business of pottery occurred. Previously, making pots had been the responsibility of women, who occasionally did this work while addressing numerous other chores as well. However, as people settled into agrarian communities, there emerged a greater need for large numbers of pots, so that pottery had to become the full-time occupation of certain craftspersons, who would make pots to be purchased by others. These potters, the evidence indicates, were overwhelmingly male. This probably resulted from the general presumption in ancient societies that men should be the ones working outside the home, while the women stayed at home. However, as both the pots and the kilns were becoming larger, this work was now more arduous and dangerous, another reason why it may now have been perceived as a task best suited for men. As another significant development in the history of pottery around this time, it seems that the pots of ancient Mesopotamia were increasingly made by teams of

A culture that thrived in Europe around 4000 BCE is best known for producing pots, like this one, which resembled modern-day beakers. For that reason, they are sometimes described as the "Beaker Culture" or "Beaker Folk." (Heritage Images/Corbis)

men, not individual artisans, as archaeologists have found large numbers of pots with virtually identical designs, suggesting a form of mass production.

Whether the potters were women or men, they were rarely content to leave their pots undecorated, even though such embellishments were not necessary—only the very earliest pots are entirely unadorned. The first technique involved making marks in the sides of the wet pot, using various implements. For example, ancient potters cut notches with sharp objects like awls made of bones; pressed bones, fingers, or fingernails into the pot; scraped pots with a clamshell; brushed the sides of the pot with pieces of cord; or used a sort of comb to produce parallel markings. In a few cases, the potters made holes near the tops of the pots so that they could be hung on ropes. In addition to indentations, potters could also make protruding markings by pulling the wet clay out

PRIZED POTTERY

The prehistoric potters undoubtedly imagined that their pots would only last for several years, anticipating that they would eventually break; yet people generally used them carefully, and large numbers of them have remained intact until the present time, especially in the arid climate of the American Southwest. Today, some ancient pots found in this region are highly valued by collectors who admire their artistry. On eBay, for example, even shards of ancient pottery are available for a few dollars, and well preserved, and colorfully decorated pots are regularly being sold for hundreds or even thousands of dollars.

TWENTIETH-CENTURY COOKING, THE OLD-FASHIONED WAY

Since antiquity, metal pots have generally supplanted ceramic pots for most forms of cooking, but during the twentieth century, this ancient technology reemerged in the form of slow cookers, first marketed nationally by the Rival Company using their copyrighted term "Crock Pot." Invented by Irving Naxon in 1938, the device consists of a porcelain or ceramic pot that is heated to a low temperature by electricity; in these pots, soups and stews can be gradually cooked for several hours. Slow cookers are especially useful for making tough meats more tender, the same reason why prehistoric cooks often engaged in their own form of slow cooking over a small fire.

or applying additional clay to the surface; the same method was used by later potters to make handles for their pots. Potters could also make the surface more shiny and smooth by the process of burnishing, rubbing pebbles on the sides of pots. Oftentimes, in the absence of other evidence, the distinctive style of the decorations on shards of pottery can be used to identify the ancient culture that produced them.

Many ancient potters also enjoyed painting their products. In the ancient Near East, potters used hematite, an iron ore, to make a red paint, while in prehistoric North America, they would boil the Rocky Mountain bee plant to produce a black paint that they applied with a brush made of plant fibers. Although the paint was normally used to make geometric patterns, the potters of ancient China used white, red, and black paints to paint representational art on their pots, showing men hunting, women gathering plants, and fish swimming in the water; these images are greatly valued by archaeologists because of the information they provide about the everyday lives of their creators. In some cases, though, the decorations seem to have symbolic meanings that archaeologists have been unable to deduce. Some have speculated, though, that such pots were designed to convey religious messages from the ruling classes to their subjects, as their mysterious patterns conveyed the inscrutable knowledge only possessed by the elite and thus justified their absolute power.

Overall, the many variations in the shapes and appearance of prehistoric pots testify to our ancestors' boundless ingenuity and creativity. As one small example, when the prehistoric people of the American southeast developed agriculture, they began to boil seeds, but found that their pots broke when filled with boiling water. Accordingly, they painstakingly learned to make thicker, harder pots that could withstand exposure to heated water. Such changes provide archaeologists with valuable data about people who left no written records; one might even regard pots, with their illuminating designs and images, as humanity's first form of writing, tangible symbols that vividly convey the desires and dreams of their ancient creators.

Further Reading

Barnett, William K., and John W. Hoopes, editors. 1995. *The Emergence of Pottery: Technology and Innovation in Ancient Societies.* Washington, DC: Smithsonian Institution Press.

Freestone, Ian, and David Gaimster, editors. 1997. *Pottery in the Making: Ceramic Traditions.* Washington, DC: Smithsonian Institution Press.

Gibson, Alex M., editor. 2003. *Prehistoric Pottery: People, Pattern and Purpose.* Oxford: Archaeopress.

Gibson, Alex M., and Ann Woods. 1990. *Prehistory Pottery for the Archaeologist.* Leicester, England: Leicester University Press.

Jordan, Peter, and Marek Zvelebil, editors. 2009. *Ceramics before Farming: The Dispersal of Pottery among Prehistoric Eurasian Hunter-Gatherers.* Walnut Creek, CA: Left Coast Press.

Woodward, Ann, and J. D. Hills, editors. 2002. *Prehistoric Britain: The Ceramic Basis*. Oxford: Oxbow Books.

Document

From Bandelier, Adolph Francis Alphonse. 1890. *The Delight-Makers: A Novel of Prehistoric Pueblo Indians.* New York: Dodd, Mead, and Co.

In this passage, written by an archaeologist who had studied the Pueblo Indians, a potential suitor meets with a young woman who has become a skillful potter and admires one of her decorated pots.

"Have you any green paint?" the girl asked.

"No, but I know a place where it is found. Do you want any?"

"I would like to have some."

"For what do you use the green stone?"

"Next year I want to paint and burn bowls and pots." Mitsha had no thought of the inferences that he would draw from her simple explanation. He interpreted her words as very encouraging for him, not only because the girl understood the art of making pottery, but he drew the conclusion that she was thinking of furnishing a household of her own.

Hannay improved the opportunity to still further praise her child. She said,—

"Mitsha does not only know how to paint; she can also shape the uashtanyi, the atash, and the asa." With this she rose, went to the wall, and began to rummage about in some recess. Okoya had meanwhile taken one of the girl's hands in his playing with her dainty fingers which she suffered him to do.

"See here," the woman cried and turned around. He dropped the girl's hand and Hannay handed something to him.

"Mitsha made this." Then she sat down again.

The object which Okoya had received from her was a little bowl of clay, round, and decorated on its upper rim with four truncated and graded pyramids that rose like prongs at nearly equal intervals. The vessel was neatly finished, smooth, white, and painted with black symbolic designs. There was nothing artistic in it according to our ideas, but it was original and quaint. Okoya gazed at the bowl with genuine admiration, placed it on the floor, and took it up again, holding it so that the light of the fire struck the inside also. He

shook his head in astonishment and pleasure. Mitsha moved closer to him. With innocent pride she saw his beaming looks, and heard the admiring exclamations with which he pointed at the various figures painted on the white surface. Then she began to explain to him.

"Lightning," said she, indicating with her finger a sinuous black line that issued from one side of the arches resting on a heavy black dash.

"Cloud," he added, referring to the arches.

"Rain," concluded the maiden, pointing at several black streaks which descended from the figure of the clouds. Both broke out in a hearty laugh. His merriment arose from sincere admiration, hers from equally sincere joy at his approbation of her work. The mother laughed also; it amused her to see how much Okoya praised her daughter's skill. She was overjoyed at seeing the two become more familiar.

Okoya returned to his former position, placing the vessel on the floor with tender care; and Mitsha resumed her sitting posture, only she sat much nearer the boy than before. He still examined the bowl with wonder.

"Who taught you to make such nice things?" he asked at last.

"An old woman from Mokatsh. Look," and she took up the vessel again, pointing to its outside, where near the base she had painted two horned serpents encircling the foot of the bowl. . . .

Shamans

Prehistoric people lived in a world of strange phenomena, many of them harmful to their interests, and they were driven to devise explanations for mysterious problems like droughts and diseases. It seemed most logical to posit that there existed beings like themselves with magical powers—gods, spirits, or demons—who were assisting or harming humanity depending upon whether they were pleased or displeased. Through a lengthy process of experimentation, forever inaccessible to detailed scrutiny, they tried doing various things to placate these invisible beings; the actions that seemed ineffective were forgotten and never repeated, while those that seemed to work were remembered and tried again and again.

Eventually, tribes throughout the world built up vast bodies of lore concerning the spiritual inhabitants of their universe and the proper ways to correct the problems that they caused; and learning and applying this knowledge became the task of one special member of each tribe. Different terms have been employed for these figures, such as medicine men, witch doctors, priests, or priestesses, but they are now generally described as shamans.

Exactly how certain people were chosen for this role remains uncertain, but one theory is that, even as children, certain individuals seemed different from others. They may have been subject to fits or inclined to bouts of daydreaming; they may have reported strange dreams or visions; they may have consistently preferred to go off by themselves instead of socializing; or they may have found it difficult to master the basic skills being taught to other children. Various conditions that we would diagnose quite differently today, such as epilepsy, schizophrenia, and Asperger's syndrome, may have once served to identify potential shamans, since people displaying these symptoms would appear to be attuned to the spirit world, not the real world, and hence would be especially well suited for the task of interpreting the will of the gods and manipulating invisible forces. In some cases, children might even announce that they have received a vision that they are destined to become shamans. However they were chosen, the future shamans would then work under the existing shamans, learning all of the necessary lore and rituals, so that they would be prepared to someday assume that role. Apparently, both men and women could be chosen for this position, but the scant evidence of cave paintings, burial remains, and the practices of contemporary tribes suggest that the shamans were usually men.

Being a shaman almost certainly required distinctive styles of clothing; one cave painting in ancient France, called the Sorcerer, is thought by some to depict an ancient shaman dressed as an animal. A body in an ancient German grave similarly indicates that the shaman wore a coyote fur, deer antlers, and a headdress with goose feathers, and a necklace of animal teeth. Shamans may have also tattooed their bodies in distinctive ways; for example, some people believe that the prehistoric Iceman, whose remains

This cave painting in France's Trois Freres cave depicts a man dressed like an animal, wearing fur and horns; the figure is called the Sorcerer because it is believed that he must have been a shaman, perhaps one who performed ceremonies within the cave. (Print Collector/Getty Images)

were discovered in a European glacier, was actually a shaman, who had climbed the mountain to perform a religious ceremony, because his body had several tattoos. Elsewhere in the world, different sorts of clothing distinguished the shaman, and in the jungles of South America, while most people wore loincloths, the shaman walked around naked to identify his special position.

European explorers described Native American shamans as "medicine men," and African shamans as "witch doctors," because their work mainly seemed to involve curing people's illnesses, and that was indeed one of their primary responsibilities. To be sure, cuts and wounds were probably handled by other people, since these had no mystic origins, and minor problems like headaches and stomach aches could be addressed by the herbal remedies known to the women of the tribe. But when someone had a major disease with no obvious cause, the shaman would be called upon to attempt to heal the person. They may have chanted spells and burned incense in an effort to drive away the demon believed to be afflicting the victim, or performed some form of sympathetic magic. One intriguing discovery in present-day Alaska was a burial site of a woman accompanied by a small wooden statue of a woman; such statues are commonplace in themselves, but this particular statue had three holes drilled in its head, chest, and hip. Examination of the woman's body revealed signs that she had suffered from cancer of the jaw and an irregular hip that must have made it painful to walk. It seems likely, then, that the shaman first carved a small statue to represent the sick woman, and then bore holes in the places that were troubling her in an effort to magically remove the diseased parts of her body.

Among other responsibilities, the shamans were also in charge of all of the rituals that marked important stages in life: births, circumcisions, initiations into adulthood, marriages, and deaths. If their homeland was afflicted by a drought, shamans would be expected to perform ceremonies asking the gods to bring rain; if warriors were about to go into battle, shamans might sacrifice an animal to ensure that the gods would grant them a victory. And if tribes were uncertain about where to migrate, or what action to take, they would ask the shaman to enter a trance in order to receive a vision that would indicate which decision they should make.

The trances of shamans have been a topic of debates regarding precisely how they are achieved, though anthropological observations of contemporary cultures provide some clues. As already indicated, some individuals who became shamans may have been naturally inclined to have visions; certain forms of mental training may have been helpful in entering a trance state; and extended fasting could have brought about vivid hallucinations. Psychoactive drugs have been used as well; there is a documented tradition of Native Americans consuming mushrooms that contain psilocybin for their psychedelic effects, and in ancient South America, people prepared a brew of plant leaves, called ayahuasca, to have spiritual visions. Yet

A PREHISTORIC GODDESS

Much of the recent interest in prehistoric shamans involves the belief that many of them were women, providing a new sort of positive role model for young girls. One result was an obscure but cherished video game, first marketed in 1998, called Populous: The Beginning. In this game, the main character is a female shaman living in ancient times. Her task, as the commander of a small tribe, is to use her magical powers and leadership ability to attract and train followers and gradually build a civilization. As her reward for a successful outcome, the shaman becomes a goddess.

SHAMAN OR CON MAN?

While many prehistoric shamans were sincere believers in the efficacy of their craft, it is suspected that some of them were conscious charlatans, offering people potions and performing rituals that they knew full well would have no real effect. Today, similarly, there are some individuals who have engaged in extensive research in order to accurately reconstruct the religions of their ancestors, meriting the title of shaman, while others who call themselves shamans appear to be mostly interested in making money by attracting followers. This is so frequently the case that a popular term has emerged to describe such opportunists: "plastic shamans."

the shamans of prehistoric Africa generally avoided drugs, believing that they made it more difficult for them to control their trances to achieve the desired purpose. Overall, there seems little doubt that these trances are genuine phenomena, though there remains the suspicion that on some occasions, shamans who were struggling to attain the proper mental state may have pretended to go into a trance to placate the concerned tribal members.

There is also a controversial theory, developed by researcher Jean Clottes and archaeologist David Lewis-Williams, that the European cave paintings can be interpreted as representations of the three typical phases of a shamanic trance: stark geometric figures, iconic religious objects, and exotic animals and people. If recording such visions was indeed the primary purpose for ancient cave art, it would suggest that shamans were most valued for their spiritual revelations, not their efficacy in ameliorating practical problems, which was undoubtedly limited in any event. It also means that the shamans, who either produced or supervised this artwork, necessarily must have spent a great deal of time away from their tribes, crouching in deep caves. Yet their theory has not been universally embraced, as much about this striking art still seems mysterious to modern observers.

Complicating all scientific efforts to understand prehistoric shamanism are the energetic efforts of contemporary men and women to follow the teachings of what they perceive to be its ancient wisdom, often on the basis of very little evidence. Some feminists have been particularly attracted to this reconstructed religion because it appeared to involve the worship of a mother goddess, frequently depicted in small statues, and provided wise women with central roles. These people may be exaggerating the stature and significance of prehistoric shamans, whose actual role in the lives of daily people may have been more like that of modern ministers, who preside over ceremonies every week and on special occasions, and are consulted when special problems arise, but otherwise have little interaction with individuals engaged in their daily business. In handling the religious affairs of the tribe, in other words, shamans may have simply been performing one of its important tasks, while other people deal with different, but equally important business.

Further Reading

Aldhouse-Green, Miranda J., and Stephen Aldhouse-Green. 2005. *The Quest for the Shaman: Shape-Shifters, Sorcerers, and Spirit-Healers of Ancient Europe*. London: Thames & Hudson.

Clottes, Jean, and J. David Lewis-Williams. 1998. *The Shamans of Prehistory: Trance and Magic in the Painted Caves*. New York: Harry N. Abrams.

Gusso, Fulvio, and Peter Webster. 2013. *The Dream on the Rock: Visions of Prehistory*. New York: State University of New York Press.

Hayden, Brian. 2003. *Shamans, Sorcerers, and Saints: A Prehistory of Religion*. Washington, DC: Smithsonian Books.

Pearson, James L. 2003. *Shamanism and the Ancient Mind: A Cognitive Approach to Archaeology*. Walnut Creek, CA: AltaMira Press.

Romain, William F. 2009. *Shamans of the Lost World: A Cognitive Approach to the Prehistoric Religion of the Ohio Hopewell*. Lanham, MD: AltaMira Press.

Documents

From Berthet, Elie Bertrand. 1876. *The Pre-Historic World*. Translated by Mary J. Stafford. 1879. Philadelphia: Porter & Coates.

This passage describes a priestess in an ancient tribe, explaining how she maintains her position through a combination of "mysterious ceremonies" and practical wisdom.

Holly-Branch was the priestess of the tribe, though religion then was a mere medley of strange, superstitious, puerile, monstrous, and often cruel rites. The only survivor of her family in consequence of a battle in which her husband and two sons had perished, the old woman, thanks to certain traditional knowledge, had performed the functions of doctor, midwife, and sorceress. She did not exactly plume herself on possessing supernatural power, but used mysterious ceremonies and words adapted to impress untutored imaginations. Besides, she lacked neither experience nor intelligence, and could give good counsel in time of need. Thus she enjoyed much influence among the Wolves, and Gnarled Oak, whom she was nursing for intermittent fever, willingly listened to her advice.

Hurricane therefore had an interest in taking Holly-Branch into his confidence, and, to his great satisfaction, the priestess seemed impressed by the tale. She remained silent a moment, with her eyes fixed on vacancy, as if reflecting or seeing some vision. At last she raised the hand which held the talismanic crescent, and said solemnly, "I see a red light in the sky; it is blood. I hear the ravens croaking in the tops of the pine trees; they scent corpses. Something mutters sullenly in the woods like a fierce wind; it is the distant roar of the conflagration. Young man, your affront shall be avenged. Come with me to Gnarled Oak." This proposal harmonized with the young hunter's secret wishes, so he quickly threw the dead fox over his shoulder and followed Holly-Branch, who had turned toward the village. . . .

Gnarled Oak was in the act of drinking when Holly-Branch entered, followed by Hurricane, who remained in the shade. At the sight of the priestess the chief raised himself on his elbow, his eyes flashing with fury. "Is that you, old martlet?" he cried hoarsely; "you promised to cure me, and you go away when I am suffering. Cure me quickly, or I'll kill you and throw your carcass to the wild dogs." Holly-Branch seemed to be no more moved by these threats than a physician is moved by the powerless rage of a sick child. "Patience, chief," she replied. "This is the sixth day of the moon, that cures everything, and under its influence, holding in my hand the sacred crescent, I have gathered wonderful herbs. I'm going to make you a drink; you will soon be able to dash through the forest at the head of your hunters." And she quietly began to heat the water in an earthen vessel. Gnarled Oak was still shivering on his couch, but he answered in a gentler tone,

"You've cheated me a long time with fine promises, and the sickness always returns. Cure me, and I'll give you plenty of skins, stags' horns, and venison."

[Later,] addressing himself to Holly-Branch, [Gnarled Oak said,] "make haste and cure me, that I may go and seize Sea-Eagle's spear and axe."

"Listen, chief," replied the priestess, serving smoking hot the beverage she had just prepared, and into which she had plunged by turns the two horns of the mystic crescent; " you must drink this. Perhaps you won't be entirely cured of your fever, for you are so fierce, so impatient, that my remedies cannot act thoroughly upon you; but after to-morrow it will not return for a week. During this time you will be able to avenge your insult."

"A week !" cried Gnarled Oak. "I don't ask so much to crush Sea-Eagle and his tribe. Since you promise, old woman, that I shall be able to wield my bow and spear to-morrow, I will not wait much longer. Hurricane," he added, "take the horn near the door and sound it to summon all my 'young men.' I'll give them my orders, that they may prepare for battle." As the hunter was about to execute this command, Holly-Branch interposed: "What are you doing, chief? If you reveal your plans in advance, Sea-Eagle cannot fail to be warned and on his guard. Isn't it better to attack him unexpectedly? The danger will be less and

the advantage greater." We have spoken of the power the sorceress exercised over the mind of the chief, and this time also her counsels were heard. Gnarled Oak recalled Hurricane.

From Lang, Andrew. 1886. "The Romance of the First Radical." *In the Wrong Paradise and Other Stories*. 1886. London: K. Paul, Trench, and Co.

In this story, the famed Scottish writer and collector of folk and fairy tales describes an ancient man who rebelled against the teachings of his tribe's medicine men.

We must also remember that, among the tribes, there was no fixed or monarchical government. The little democratic groups were much influenced by the medicine-men or wizards, who combined the functions of the modern clergy and of the medical profession. The old men, too, had some power; the braves, or warriors, constituted a turbulent oligarchy; the noisy outcries of the old women corresponded to the utterances of an independent press. But the real ruler was a body of strange and despotic customs, the nature of which will become apparent as we follow the fortunes of the First Radical. . . .

The very earliest years of Why-Why, unlike those of Mr. John Stuart Mill, whom in many respects he resembled, were not distinguished by proofs of extraordinary intelligence. He rather promptly, however, showed signs of a sceptical character. Like other sharp children, Why-Why was always asking metaphysical conundrums. Who made men? Who made the sun? Why has the cave-bear such a hoarse voice? Why don't lobsters grow on trees?—he would incessantly demand. In answer to these and similar questions, the mother of Why-Why would tell him stories out of the simple mythology of the tribe. There was quite a store of traditional replies to inquisitive children, replies sanctioned by antiquity and by the authority of the medicine-men, and in this lore Why-Why's mother was deeply versed.

Thus, for example, Why-Why would ask his mother who made men. She would reply that long ago Pund-jel, the first man, made two images of human beings in clay, and stuck on curly bark for hair. He then danced a corroboree round them, and sang a song. They rose up, and appeared as full-grown men. To this statement, hallowed by immemorial belief, Why-Why only answered by asking who made Pund-jel. His mother said that Pund-jel came out of a plot of reeds and rushes. Why-Why was silent, but thought in his heart that the whole theory was "bosh-bosh," to use the early reduplicative language of these remote times. Nor could he conceal his doubts about the Deluge and the frog who once drowned all the world. . . .

Many stories like this were told in the cave, but they found no credit with Why-Why. When he was but ten years old, his inquiring spirit showed itself in the following remarkable manner. He had always been informed that a serpent was the mother of his race, and that he must treat serpents with the greatest reverence. To kill one was sacrilege. In spite of this, he stole out, unobserved, and crushed a viper which had stung his little brother. He noticed that no harm ensued, and this encouraged him to commit a still more daring act. None but the old men and the warriors were allowed to eat oysters. It was universally held that if a woman or a child touched an oyster, the earth would open and swallow the culprit. Not daunted by this prevalent belief, Why-Why one day devoured no less than four dozen oysters, opening the shells with a flint spear-head, which he had secreted in his waistband. The earth did not open and swallow him as he had swallowed the oysters, and from that moment he became suspicions of all the ideas and customs imposed by the old men and wizards. . . . He was no bigot. He kept his word and paid his debts, for no one was ever very "advanced" all at once. It was only when the ceremonious or superstitious ideas of his age and race appeared to him senseless and mischievous that he rebelled, or at least hinted his doubts and misgivings. This course of conduct made him feared and hated both by the medicine-men or clerical wizards and by the old women of the tribe. They naturally tried to take their revenge upon him in the usual way. . . .

When he was dead, the tribe knew what they had lost in Why-Why. They bore his body, with that of Verva, to the cave; there they laid the lovers—Why-Why crowned with a crown of seashells and with a piece of a rare magical substance (iron) at his side. Then the tribesmen withdrew from that now holy ground, and built them houses, and foreswore the follies of the medicine-men, as Why-Why had prophesied. Many thousands of years later the cave was opened when the railway to Genoa was constructed, and the bones of Why-Why, with the crown, and the fragment of iron, were found where they had been laid by his repentant kinsmen. He had bravely asserted the rights of the individual conscience against the dictates of society; he had lived, and loved, and died, not in vain.

Textile Workers

In the earliest stages of their development, human beings wore no clothing at all, but there soon emerged both practical and aesthetic reasons for covering parts of their bodies. Certainly, there were advantages to wearing garments around one's genitals: women could control the flow of blood during menstruation, and men could protect their sensitive testicles against painful blows. And, as people migrated from Africa into regions with colder climates, clothing became necessary to keep their bodies warm. Yet even in prehistoric times, humans clearly found it pleasurable to decorate themselves, whether by tattooing, body painting, or wearing costumes, and distinctive clothing could also help to identify people as members of a particular tribe or persons with a special status, like shamans or chieftains. Thus, at some time between 200,000 and 50,000 BCE, people began a long process of developing useful, comfortable, and attractive items of clothing, and the materials they employed were soon applied to other purposes, such as containers or floor mats.

Since no actual garments from this period have survived, we cannot be sure precisely how clothing originated, but the first materials employed were probably animal furs. While skinning dead animals to get to their meat, ancient humans undoubtedly recognized that their thick furs could be productively employed to cover their own bodies. In the beginning, they may have simply draped large furs around their bodies, but they eventually learned to make garments by taking pieces of fur, punching holes in them with an awl, and tying them together with muscles from the animals. In a site from around 30,000 BCE, researchers discovered a needle made of bone that was clearly designed to stitch furs together with muscles, the first form of sewing. As for the design of their garments, a few remaining bits of clothing suggest that most early humans wore simply designed tunics, a square blanket of material with small holes to accommodate the arms and the head, with a loincloth underneath. To cover people's legs and arms, cylindrical pieces could be attached or sewn on.

Although furs provided warmth during frigid weather, they could be confining and uncomfortable as clothing, and they were often infested with lice. For that reason, prehistoric humans later learned to take animal skins, scape off their fur with tools made of bone or stone, and subject them to a variety of tanning methods; the hides might be dried in the sun, exposed to heavy smoke, covered with salt, or even chewed to make the material more flexible. If harder leather was desired, it could be boiled to make it stiff. These early forms of leather were made from the hides of many animals, ranging from badgers, dogs, and cats to cattle, sheep, and deer. Leather was especially well suited to the production of shoes, which in the beginning were probably only platforms with straps resembling modern sandals, and leather was also employed to make bags and shields and body armor for early warriors. On some occasions, the Neanderthals apparently employed urine to bleach the hides, and ochre to dye them yellow or red, possibly for special items of clothing worn by figures of authority.

At first, all members of the tribe were probably responsible for making their own clothes, a pattern still observed in some remote tribes; gradually, however, making clothes became a specialty of the women, a task addressed after they had finished their daily gathering. They would sit in groups, sewing pieces of leather together while they conversed, assisting each other as needed. Their female children would join them, doing basic chores and gradually learning more complex skills by observing and imitating their mothers.

Leather was never an ideal material for clothing, and around 6000 BCE, women began to seek better alternatives. They first turned to the plants around them, learning how to weave pieces of tree bark, hemp, and grasses to make various garments, including tunics,

capes, and shoes, and these materials were also used to produce baskets, containers, nets, and floor mats. But the best choice for making clothing was the flax plant, which provided fibers of linen that could be woven together to produce attractive and flexible cloth. To obtain the fibers through a process called retting, the women would take dried stalks of flax and immerse them in water or urine so that everything except the fibers would rot; to isolate the fibers, the resulting material was pounded with a bat and combed using a board with thorns.

A few animals also provided new fabrics for clothing. As woolly sheep became commonplace, women began making wool, although getting useful fibers from the sheep involved some labor. First, the sheep's wool had to be thoroughly washed and combed; then, the fibers would be spun on a weighted spike, called a spindle, to produce a fine thread. In ancient China, women figured out how to obtain fibers from the larvae of the silkworm to produce the fabric known as silk, long valued in other parts of the world that did not know how to produce this luxurious material. In prehistoric America, molted snakeskins were gathered and stitched together to make small items of clothing.

To weave fibers effectively, ancient women needed to invent the loom. If only a narrow strip of clothing was required, to make a belt or sash, they would use what is called a band loom, with threads stretched from a band on the woman's waist to a nearby tree branch or stick. But to make larger pieces of cloth, they would use an upright loom, a wooden frame with a crossbar and small weights to hold the threads; other pieces of equipment, such as handle bars and bobbins, were required to sew on such looms, but none of these have survived. We know that these upright looms were first used about 9,000 years ago because archaeologists will often find the two postholes that typically held the loom in position or triangular weights with small holes for the threads. Pairs of postholes close together suggest that, in some cases, women worked together on adjacent looms to create large pieces of cloth up to 10-feet long.

When people had settled into agrarian communities that allowed for the use of such looms, women may have had more time for sewing, since they no longer needed to gather food, and their textiles displayed

None of the prehistoric textile workers' looms, made out of wood, has survived, but we know that they existed because the small stone weights that they employed, like this one, are regularly found at archaeological sites. (UIG via Getty Images)

FURS AND THEIR FOES

Animal furs were the first materials used for human clothing, and they long remained popular garments because of their attractive appearance and the warmth they provided; a desire for profitable animal furs was one driving force behind the early development of the United States interior, and as late as the 1960s, a mink coat was regarded as the most desirable thing that a woman could own. However, defying this long tradition, most people today reject fur garments because of the unnecessary animal deaths that they cause, and a modern celebrity seen wearing a fur coat is likely to face a hostile reaction.

LOVING THE LOOM

One of the most significant inventions of prehistoric times was the loom, which enabled women to transform flax, wool, and silk into thin pieces of cloth. When electric looms were perfected in the nineteenth century, however, the process of making cloth in the developed world largely became the business of large factories. Still, some contemporary hobbyists have remained devoted to the ancient art of making fabric with manual looms, and several companies are in the business of selling these looms. There are also websites that instruct interested readers in how to construct and use their own homemade looms.

increasing variety in their styles and features. Several different patterns in the fabrics have been observed; some pieces of cloth had borders sewn on; one cloth from ancient Europe was decorated with stamped designs; and some textiles were elaborately embroidered. Women also worked hard to dye their fabrics different colors, even though this required a lengthy process of boiling. In addition to the ochre used by the Neanderthals, later textile workers fermented woad leaves to produce a blue color, made bright red dye out of beetles' blood, and found that saffron flowers could provide a yellow. While all women continued to make clothes for their families, some of them started to specialize in this skill and were asked to make special garments for their communities, effectively becoming the first professional seamstresses.

Early archaeologists tended to pay little attention to the amazing complexity and intricacy of ancient textiles, in part because so few examples of this art could be found at their sites; perhaps it was only natural for them to focus more attention on human progress in making tools and weapons. However, modern feminists have subjected ancient weaving to intense scrutiny, properly valuing a form of technology that was almost certainly developed and mastered entirely by women, and a form of technology that was, in its own way, just as important to the rise of civilization as the implements devised by men. People needed warm clothing just as much as spears and arrows to survive in harsh environments, and garments were also a key element in establishing the hierarchal social orders that characterized early settlements. And, as improved techniques enable scientists to garner more information about prehistoric clothing from fragile evidence, we may gain an even greater appreciation for the work of prehistoric textile workers.

Further Reading

Barber, E.J.W. 1991. *Prehistoric Textiles: The Development of Cloth in the Neolithic and Bronze Ages with Special Reference to the Aegean*. Princeton, NJ: Princeton University Press.

Barber, E.J.W. 1994. *Women's Work: The First 20,000 Years: Women, Cloth, and Society in Early Times*. New York: Norton.

Gleba, Margarita. 2008. *Textile Production in Pre-Roman Italy*. Oxford: Oxbow Books.

Gleba, Margartia, and Ulla Mannering, editors. 2012. *Textiles and Textile Production in Europe from Prehistory to 400 AD*. Oxford: Oxbow Books.

Jørgenson, Lise Bender. 1992. *North European Textiles until AD 1000*. Translated by Peter Crabb. 1992. Aarhus, Denmark: University of Aarhus Press.

Teague, Lynn S. 1998. *Textiles in Southwestern Prehistory*. Albuquerque: University of New Mexico Press.

Document

From Waterloo, Stanley. 1897. *The Story of Ab: A Tale of the Time of the Cave Man*. Chicago: Way & Williams.

In this passage, the author describes a garment worn by a prehistoric woman and the techniques she employed to make such garments.

The garment of wolverine skins, sewed neatly together with thread of sinews, was all the young mother wore. Thus hanging from the shoulder and fully encircling her, it reached from the waist to about half way down between the hips and the knees. It was as delightful a gown as ever was contrived by ambitious *modiste* or . . . designer in these modern times. It fitted with a free and easy looseness and its colors were such as blended smoothly and kindly with the complexion of its wearer. The fur of the wolverine was a mixed black and white, but neither black nor white is the word to use. The black was not black; it was only a swart sort of color, and the white was not white; it was but a dingy, lighter contrast to the darker surface beside it. Yet the combination was rather good. There was enough of difference to catch the eye and not enough of glaringness to offend it. The mother of Ab would be counted by a wise observer as the possessor of good taste. Still, dress is a small matter. There is something to say about the cave mother aside from the mere description of her gown. . . .

It was good for the boy that he was so under the maternal dominion, and that, as he lingered about the cave, he aided in the making of threads of sinew or intestine, or looked on interestedly as his mother, using the bone needle, which he often sharpened for her with his flint scraper, sewed together the skins which made the garments of the family. The needle was one without an eye, a mere awl, which made holes through which the thread was pushed. . . .

Toolmakers

For most of the twentieth century, the ability to make and use tools was considered a defining attribute of humanity, and even though we have now found that a few other animals, like chimpanzees, also employ primitive tools, this skill remains the major reason that *homo sapiens* were able to take control of their world, even though they lacked the size, strength, and speed of other species. Tools enabled humans to kill large animals, catch fish, and harvest a wide variety of plants; they also provided the clothing and shelter that humans needed to survive in inhospitable environments. Later, they allowed people to make the transition to settled lives of farming and craft humanity's first works of art. Since sturdy tools of stone and metal have tended to last through the ages, they have remained available to provide modern archaeologists with valuable information about how they were devised and employed.

It was an ancestor of present-day humans, *homo habilis*, who began making tools over a million years ago, although these are not always easy to recognize, since the first tools were little more than slightly altered stones. The early toolmakers learned to strike a stone with another stone, breaking off flakes and gradually shaping them to serve special purposes, which archaeologists can only speculate about. Pointed stones with sharp edges are usually described as hand axes, probably used to cut meat or dig up edible roots; stones with a long straight edge are thought to be scrapers, which removed fur from animal skins and bark from trees; elongated stones with a point are considered knives, which were perhaps wielded to kill small animals at close quarters; a round stone with several faces, termed a polyhedral stone, could have broken animal bones and might have been thrown at running animals to injure them; stones with an extended small point are called borers, which could cut holes in pieces of fur so they could be sewn together to form items of clothing; and stones with more than one of these features were presumably multipurpose tools.

Interestingly, some scientists have speculated that the human mastery of fire was an inadvertent by-product of early toolmaking, as toolmakers noticed that striking certain stones together would produce sparks and figured out that by placing combustible plants nearby, they could use those sparks to start a fire. In addition to the many stone tools found by modern archaeologists, we can assume that from the start, toolmakers were also crafting tools out of wood and animal bones, but these less durable objects only become part of the fossil record in later periods. Thus, for example, archaeologists are confident that humans in prehistoric China were making knives and spear points out of bamboo, but definitive evidence is elusive.

Of course, we cannot be sure who was making these tools, but in the beginning, all men undoubtedly made their own tools, absorbing the necessary skills as they matured. However, as certain individuals became more skillful in the craft, others would begin asking those persons to craft tools for them, and these men would gradually become the tribe's official toolmakers. In some cases, this perhaps became the job of an older man, who would stay behind at the camp to make tools while younger cohorts hunted and fished. Since women were using some of these tools to scrape furs to make leather and crush foods for eating, some of them may have been involved in making tools as well, but only the strongest women could have become adept at repeatedly striking hard stones to produce suitable tools.

Human toolmaking apparently remained largely the same for many thousands of years, but around 500,000 years ago, there are definite signs of improvement. For one thing, humans had learned to seek out certain types of stones that were most likely to break and form hard edges. Five types of stones were particularly popular: flint, which consisted of quartz and various impurities; quartzite, a purer form of quartz; basalt, a gray igneous rock; obsidian, a hard black glass also of volcanic origins; and chalcedony, a combination of the minerals quartz and moganite. An abundance of flakes at certain sites suggests that these were being used as quarries, repeatedly visited by toolmakers in search of certain desirable stones. The techniques of shaping stones also improved, as typical tools became thinner and had sharper edges. One helpful innovation was the idea of making the tools out of the flakes removed from the stones, not the stones themselves; the toolmaker would painstakingly carve the stone into precisely the right shape, and then, with one well-aimed blow, he would break off a large flake with a sharp edge that had precisely the right form to serve as an effective knife or scraper. One common tool made in this manner, called a burin, was mainly employed to engrave markings on stone and wooden objects, though some have argued that it was also used to cut and scrape.

Humans took another step forward when they began to construct and use spears, which were originally long wooden poles with small pointed stones attached to one end with bands of muscle or leather. These indicate that humans were learning to combine different parts made of different materials in order to construct more complicated tools. Toolmakers also developed an early form of mass production, termed the blade core technique, that could create several tools at once: a large piece of flint would be carefully split into two pieces; the toolmaker would then knock off several long flakes from the side, producing up to a dozen useful blades. A final breakthrough in the technology of stone toolmaking came around 15,000 years ago, when humans developed a new method known as grinding. They first would painstakingly tap stones to gradually remove bits of their surface, roughly attaining the desired shape; they would then rub another stone against the stone to smooth it into its final form; and finally, they would polish the stone with wet sand.

NEANDERTHAL TECHNOLOGY

In experimental archaeology, contemporary researchers attempt to understand their ancestors by duplicating the ways that they made objects. One early priority of the field was to figure out how prehistoric humans made their stone tools—which often turned out to be more difficult than they had anticipated. One scientist, Metin Eden, wanted to replicate the so-called "Levallois flakes"—the sharp stone tools of the Neanderthals—and reports that despite his long experience in such work, it took him "about 18 months to master Levallois technology," which he described as "much more difficult to make than any of the modern *Homo sapiens* technologies."

STONE SURGERY

For over a million years, humans made most of their tools out of stone, but eventually abandoned them in favor of metal tools, which were generally more durable and effective. Yet for some purposes, stone may still be the best material. In medicine, for example, some surgeons use scalpels made of obsidian instead of steel, arguing that the obsidian blade is actually sharper and that its cuts heal more quickly. However, perhaps because they must be used very carefully to avoid shattering, the Federal Drug Administration has not officially approved such scalpels for human use.

Tools were also becoming more and more specialized. In later eras, different styles of cutting tools are found close together, suggesting that people were now working with their own tool kits, selecting certain blades for certain tasks. To obtain sharper points, toolmakers turned to bones to craft pointed needles to sew together clothing and harpoons to impale fish in the water; crude wooden forks and stone spatulas were devised to assist ancient cooks; and spearpoints and arrowheads were carefully crafted to fit upon wooden shafts, now shaped to fit into slots and be firmly attached using plant-derived adhesives. When humans began turning to agriculture to sustain themselves, about 10,000 years ago, this required the development of a whole new array of tools, including plows for planting seeds, harnesses to control the animals that pulled the plows, and sickles to harvest the crops. Crafting

profession-specific tools now generally became the responsibility of members of that profession, as hunters were best qualified to craft tools for hunting and fishers were best qualified to craft tools for fishing.

Tools were changing in other ways as well. Some toolmakers began to display the same artistic flair that produced the famous cave paintings by engraving animal images and geometric patterns on their knives, harpoons, and spearpoints; this is also a sign that, as humans settled down into fixed abodes, they were coming to cherish tools as personal possessions, not merely as means to certain ends. When humans finally learned how to make objects out of metal, they began to have access to a wide variety of long-lasting tools with razor-sharp edges, though these would have to be forged by experienced metalworkers heeding the instructions of the warriors, farmers, and food preparers who would actually use them. In a parallel fashion, as genuine civilizations emerged, toolmaking would become the task of professionals who specialized in shaping certain materials—such as masons who handled stone, and carpenters who worked with wood.

Since tools are found wherever people lived, and since many of them obviously required many hours of work, it is easy to assume that prehistoric humans were obsessed with tools, and considering their importance in helping humans to progress, one can reasonably describe toolmaking as the central profession of ancient times. Yet our ancestors also devoted much of their time to activities that did not leave a mark in the fossil records, and their significance should be acknowledged as well—even as archaeologists continue to focus their attention on the evidence provided by tools.

Further Reading

Edmonds, M. R. 1995. *Stone Tools and Society: Working Stone in Neolithic and Bronze Age Britain*. London: Batsford.

Goren-Inbar, Naama, and Gonen Sharon, editors. 2006. *Axe Age: Acheulian Tool-Making from Quarry to Discard*. London and Oakville, CT: Equinox.

Nowell, April, and Iain Davidson, editors. 2010. *Stone Tools and the Evolution of Human Cognition*. Boulder: University of Colorado Press.

Odell, George H., editor. 1996. *Stone Tools: Theoretical Insights into Human Prehistory*. New York: Plenum Press.

Shea, John J. 2013. *Stone Tools in the Paleolithic and Neolithic Near East: A Guide*. Cambridge: Cambridge University Press.

Wilson, Thomas. 2007. *Arrowpoints, Spearheads, and Knives of Prehistoric Times*. New York: Skyhorse Publishing.

Document

From Dopp, Katherine Elizabeth. 1905. *The Tree-Dwellers*. New York: Rand McNally & Co.

This passage from a book for children describes how a young boy of the Stone Age, named Bodo, created two early tools, a stone hammer and knife.

Bodo often cracked nuts with his teeth.
But sometimes he found nuts that he could not crack.
He had never seen or heard of a hammer, so he threw a hard nut against a rock.
The nut did not crack.
So he kept on trying different ways.
At last he struck the nut with a stone.
Its hard shell broke.
How glad Bodo was!
He ate the kernel and then cracked some more nuts with the stone.
This stone was his first hammer.
Sometimes he used a rough stone.
Its rough edges hurt his hand, so he hunted for a smooth stone.
At other times he wrapped one end of a rough stone in grass.
The grass protected his hand.
This was the first handle to his hammer.
Bodo liked to use this hammer.
He liked to use smooth hammer-stones. . . .

Some animals had larger and sharper teeth.
The Tree-dwellers found such teeth in the sand.
They found sharp claws there, too.
They often found sharp bones and horns.
They used such things for cutting for many long years, but at last they made a knife.
It happened when Bodo was cracking a bone.
In some way he broke his hammer.

He picked up the pieces and looked at them.
They were sharp enough to cut with, but the edges hurt his hand.
So he found a smooth pebble and chipped flakes from one end.
Before long he had a sharp point.
He never hafted it; but he left one end smooth, so that it would not hurt his hand.
It was such a weapon as this that was found in the gravel.
You can see that it is something like a spear-head.
Bodo used it when he hunted small animals.
He used it to skin them and to hack off strips of flesh.
Many things had been used as knives before, but this was the first knife that we know man made.

Warriors

In the film *2001: A Space Odyssey* (1968), after a pre-human primate is inspired to use a bone as a weapon, he first wields it to kill a boar and eat its meat, but his very next action is to kill a member of a rival tribe and seize control of their waterhole. Similarly, Jack London's novel *Before Adam* (1907) depicts prehistoric hunters who have begun to stalk their less advanced cousins, slaughtering every one they encounter. In reality, we have no idea whether our ancestors were actually so quick to turn their weapons against each other, and the available evidence seems to indicate that conflicts between people were relatively uncommon during much of humanity's prehistory; the scattered nomadic groups probably had little contact with each other, and if two tribes did begin to hunt in the same area, one of them could probably easily leave to hunt elsewhere.

When people began to settle down in communities and practice agriculture, however, battles between armed men started to become more frequent, as evidenced by the increasing numbers of wounds in ancient skeletons. The usual explanation is that with growing populations, resources were becoming scarcer, inspiring efforts to violently dislodge groups from bountiful areas or seize their assets. There are some early settlements in the Middle East, for example, that were clearly attacked and destroyed by raiders coveting their wealth. Living permanently in certain regions may also have led to the first stirrings of nationalism, as people in one place developed their own customs and values and disliked others with different practices and beliefs, leading in some cases to fierce battles. While fighting for one's tribe had once been the task of any available man, using whatever weapons he happened to possess, the settlements began to train and equip certain men to be warriors, who can be distinguished by the weapons with special decorations that were buried with them.

The general assumption made by archaeologists is that all of the prehistoric warriors were men, but a few tantalizing bits of evidence have been seized upon to challenge this view. After all, the ancient Greeks did report that there had once been a race of warrior women, called the Amazons, and one modern researcher, Lyn Webster Wilde, believes that they may have actually existed, based on the discovery of graves around the Black Sea that have women buried with weapons and armor, suggesting that they had fought in battles; similar graves have also been unearthed in ancient China. It is possible, however, that these were merely women who possessed wealth and power in their societies, as symbolized by the military equipment; perhaps, like some later female rulers, they led warriors into battle but did not actually fight themselves. In any event, one can safely say that, if such prehistoric women warriors did exist, they were relatively rare. However, burial remains suggest that women, and even children, were quite often the victims of war, as they are often found decapitated or with arrowheads in their bodies, indicating that someone had deliberately sought to kill them.

When humans first began fighting with each other, they employed the weapons they had developed to kill animals: a cave painting in Spain showing rows of archers aiming at each other, and the aforementioned arrowheads in skeletons, suggest that the bow and arrow may have been the first weapon used in this fashion, but people were also killed by spears and objects propelled by slings. Around 5,000 years ago, however, warriors began to develop weapons that were especially designed to kill other people. These new weapons included the battle-axe, a large blade attached to a wooden stick; the mace, a club with a

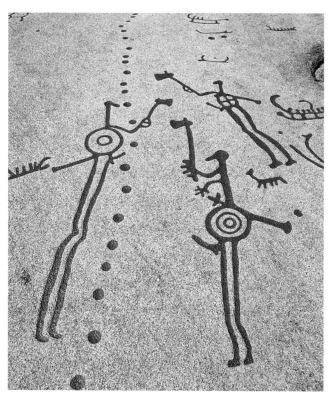

These stylized images from prehistoric Scandinavia show warriors holding circular shields confronting each other while brandishing large axes. The rock carvings were discovered in a pre-Viking settlement, called Vitlycke, in Tanum, Sweden. (UIG via Getty Images)

heavy stone head; and various sorts of knives, daggers, and swords, among the first objects humans ever forged from copper and bronze, since metal blades were sharper and stronger than stone. Such weapons could not have been used against animals fleeing from hunters, but would have been lethally effective for warriors engaged in close combat. Prehistoric warriors also recognized that they could improve their chances of victory with greater mobility, and the major reason that the horse was first domesticated in central Asia may have been a desire to ride them into battle. In ancient India, soldiers made use of another large animal, the elephant, as an excellent mobile platform for throwing their spears and shooting their arrows.

When there emerged men who fought against other men on a regular basis, another logical development was forms of armor to protect them in battle. And, around the time that the new weapons were appearing, signs of such equipment can also be found, made either of thick leather or bronze, though the ancient warriors of North American Arctic regions uniquely devised body armor made of whale bones. Circular or oval shields were held by warriors to fend off attacks, and these could also be used to strike opponents; helmets protected the warriors' heads; and breastplates and tunics prevented grievous wounds to their bodies. Beyond such utilitarian innovations, ancient European warriors also displayed an increasing concern for their appearance: some early cave paintings indicate that warriors were decorating themselves with feathers; the hilts of metal swords were often adorned with gold, enamel, and coral; and figures of animals like birds were attached to helmets, perhaps in an effort to make the warriors look taller and more intimidating. In central Asia, scepters shaped like horses' heads may have merely been emblems of authority, but they could also have served as weapons.

At first, the men employing these weapons and armor were probably part-time warriors, who worked at other occupations but were occasionally called upon to defend their settlements or accompany their chieftain in an attack on their habitual enemies. In prehistoric Europe, however, there eventually emerged a true class of professional warriors. Unattached to any particular community, these soldiers of fortune wandered through the countryside, attacking others whenever it was propitious and making their living off of the goods that they could seize. We know that such bands were both ubiquitous and effective, since so many European communities developed elaborate systems for warding off their armed attacks. One finds evidence of towns protected by barriers made of mounds of dirt, wood, or stone; other settlements were surrounded by deep ditches that could only be crossed by removable causeways; stone towers proved an effective refuge for members of small communities; and a few desperate people lived on artificial islands, called *crannogs*, that they had constructed in the middle of lakes to make them inaccessible to raiders.

Since evidence of ancient European warriors had been studied so carefully, and since Europeans later went on the brutally colonize other regions of the world, the attitude arose in some quarters that the prehistoric Europeans must have been particularly bloodthirsty, in contrast to the more peaceful people elsewhere whom

HELPFUL HELMETS

One of the priorities of the prehistoric warrior was protecting his vulnerable head with a helmet made of thick leather or bronze. While helmets remained commonplace during ancient times, they were at one time abandoned by soldiers seeking improved visibility and mobility. But new forms of hazardous artillery again made helmets a necessity for twentieth-century soldiers, and during both world wars, soldiers in combat wore bowl-shaped helmets made of steel. Today, however, helmets employ a newly created substance, the synthetic fiber Kevlar, which is both lightweight and durable. Kevlar is also used for ballistic vests, a modern form of body armor.

THE MIGHTY SWORD

The first warriors would attack and kill their opponents by wielding weapons with sharp points, like spears, arrows, and swords. With the advent of rifles and other modern weaponry, one might imagine that this approach to combat would become obsolete, but blades have in fact remained important components of recent warfare. In the seventeenth century, French soldiers began using bayonets, swords that were attached to rifles to make them serve as stabbing weapons as well, and Swiss soldiers were famously equipped with multipurpose Swiss Army knives, which are still being manufactured today. The United States also equips its modern soldiers with a variety of knives.

they eventually conquered. But recent research indicates, in fact, that people all over the world frequently engaged in their own ancient wars. Examining the prehistoric Americas, for example, scholars Richard J. Chacon and Rubén G. Mendoza (2007) have concluded that "Warfare was ubiquitous; every major culture area of native North America reviewed herein has produced archaeological, ethnohistorical, osteological, or ethnographic evidence of armed conflict and ritual violence." Armed conflicts were also commonplace in prehistoric Africa, India, and China; indeed, it is difficult to find any culture in the world that did not develop weapons and some traditions of military activity.

To be sure, there are many reasons to condemn warfare and those who engage in it, but it may have played an important role in the rise of civilization. It is often theorized that nations must have been the result of armed conflicts between small communities that eventually produced one victorious chieftain who came to rule over all of them. As in modern times, the desire to more effectively wage war, and defend oneself in war, inspired new technologies in toolmaking, metalworking, and architecture that were later beneficial in other arenas of life. Violence also helped to create hierarchal societies, as victorious warriors and their cohorts became the dominant figures, and these men were the centerpieces of most early works of literature. No one can properly describe human prehistory and history, then, without paying considerable attention to its innumerable warriors.

Further Reading

Chacon, Richard J., and Rubén G. Mendoza, editors. 2007. *North American Indigenous Warfare and Ritual Violence.* Tucson: University of Arizona Press.

Ferrill, Arthur. 1997. *The Origins of War: From the Stone Age to Alexander the Great.* Revised edition. Boulder, CO: Westview Press.

Guilaine, Jean, and Jean Zammit. 2001. *The Origins of War: Violence in Prehistory.* Translated by Melanie Hersey. 2005. Malden, MA: Blackwell.

Keeley, Lawrence H. 1996. *War before Civilization: The Myth of the Peaceful Savage.* Oxford and New York: Oxford University Press.

Pearson, Mike Parker, and I.J.N. Thorpe, editors. 2005. *Warfare, Violence and Slavery in Prehistory: Proceedings of a Prehistoric Society Conference at Sheffield University.* Oxford: Archaeopress.

Wilde, Lyn Webster. 2000. *On the Trail of the Women Warriors: The Amazons in Myth and History.* New York: Thomas Dunne Books.

Document

From Waterloo, Stanley. 1897. *The Story of Ab: A Tale of the Time of the Cave Man.* Chicago: Way & Williams.

In this passage from the novel, two ancient tribes have a long and bloody battle over control of a prized homeland.

Boarface had gone away angry and muttering, and he was not a man to be thought of lightly. His rage over the memory of Ab's trophy did not decrease with the return to his own region. Why should this cave man of the West have sole possession of that valley, which was warm and green throughout the winter and where the wild beasts could not enter? Why had he, this Ab, been allowed to go away with all the tiger's skin? Brooding enlarged into resolve and Boarface gathered together his relations and adherents. "Let us go and take the Fire Valley of Ab," he said to them, and, gradually, though objections were made to the undertaking of an enterprise so fraught with danger, the listeners were persuaded. . . .

The invaders came clambering up the creek's course, openly and with menacing and defiant shouts, for any concealment was now out of the question. They had but few bows and could, under the conditions, send no arrow flight which would be of avail, but they had thews and sinews and spears and axes. As they came with such rush as men might make up a tumbling waterway with slipping pebbles beneath the feet and forced themselves one by one between the heaped stone piles and fairly in front of the barrier there was a discharge of arrows and more than one man, impaled by a stone-headed shaft, fell, to dabble feebly in the water, and did not rise again. But there came a time in the fight when the bow must be abandoned. . . . So the struggle lasted for a long half hour, and when it ended there were dead and dying men upon the barrier, while the waters of the creek were reddened by the blood of the slain assailants. The assault now ebbed a little. Neither Ab nor Hilltop had been injured in the struggle. As the invaders pressed close Ab had noted the whish of an arrow now and then and the hurt to one pressing him closely, and old Hilltop had heard the wild cries of a woman who hovered in his rear and hurled stones in the faces of those who strove to reach him. And now there came a lull. [Soon thereafter] the main body rushed desperately upon the barrier again. What had been good fighting before was better now. Lives were lost, and soon all arrows were spent and all spears thrown, and then came but the dull clashing of stone axes. Ab raged up and down, and, ever in the front, faced the oncoming foe and slew as could slay the strong and utterly desperate. More than once his life was but a toy of chance as men sprang toward him, two or three together, but ever at such moment there sang an arrow by his head and one of his assailants, pierced in throat or body, fell back blindly, hampering his companions, whose heads Ab's great ax was seeking fiercely. And, all the time, nearer the northern end of the barrier, old Hilltop fought serenely and dreadfully. There were many dead men in the pools of the creek between the barrier and the entrance to the valley. And about Ab ever sang the arrows from the rocky shelf. . . . [Later in the battle] Ab rushed in upon his enemy and rained such blows as only a giant could

have parried. Boarface fought desperately, but it was only man to man, and he was not the equal of the maddened one before him. His ax flew from his hand as his wrist was broken by Ab's descending weapon, and the next moment he fell limply and hardly moved, for a second blow had sunk the stone weapon so deeply in his head that the haft was hidden in his long hair. It was all over in a moment now. As Ab turned with a shout of triumph there was a swift end to the little battle. . . .

Ancient Egypt and the Near East, 3200–500 BCE

Introduction

By common consensus, the region around the Tigris and Euphrates rivers in present-day Iraq spawned the first true civilizations, where people lived in cities and worked in specific professions in exchange for money. There, independent city-states were gradually supplanted by the Sumerian empire, the first of several empires that rose and fell in the area, including the Akkadians, Assyrians, Babylonians, and Hittites. These cultures had a powerful influence on other embryonic civilizations in the area and made lasting contributions in fields ranging from architecture and astronomy to literature and law. While there were other, smaller nations in the region that were sometimes independent and sometimes absorbed into nearby empires, the best known of these is the land of Israel, since it became the birthplace of two major religions, Judaism and Christianity; for that reason, its history and culture, recorded in the Bible and elsewhere, have been the subject of intense scrutiny.

Yet the civilization of Egypt dominates the history of the ancient Near East, as it endured as a major power for almost 3,000 years and has continued to fascinate the world long after its heyday. Sustained by efficient agriculture and trade along the Nile River and into the Mediterranean Sea, the people of Egypt, ranging from high officials to lowly peasants, worked hard to forge a unique civilization marked by numerous achievements: impressive monuments, like the Pyramids of Giza; styles of art and dress that were widely admired and imitated; important progress in warfare, science, commerce, and social engineering; and a polytheistic religion with gods that were borrowed by other ancient faiths. Other Egyptian innovations were only appreciated in later times, like its pioneering female pharaohs and the monotheism briefly promoted by the pharaoh Akhenaten (died 1336 BCE). Remarkably, Egypt accomplished all that it did without a currency, as salaries and taxes were paid solely in goods, usually barley or other foods. Distant scholars came to Egypt to study its scrolls and learn its wisdom; consumers craved its distinctive goods; later conquerors ranging from Alexander the Great to Napoleon Bonaparte lingered there to study its structures and artifacts. And as Egypt offered much to the world, it also absorbed technologies and traditions from other cultures, so the saga of ancient Egypt can function as a summary of the saga of civilization in the entire ancient world.

Architects

One of the characteristics of an emerging civilization is the construction of large buildings—usually, to function as palaces, temples, or royal tombs—and unlike smaller structures, these need to be carefully planned beforehand. In ancient Mesopotamia, we do not know the names of the early architects, perhaps because the rulers who commissioned their works wished to receive sole credit for the complete structures, but there are surviving copies of their plans on clay tablets, showing the design and listing the number and types of bricks that would be required. There is also a statue of a king who ruled the southern Mesopotamian state of Lagash, Gudea (died 2124 BCE), who holds a plan for a temple in his lap. In addition to these crude blueprints, scholars believe these anonymous architects also built small models of the planned structures in order to identify any potential issues in their construction; no such models have been found, but the discovery of some miniature bricks in one temple suggests that they existed.

As they strived to achieve large buildings, the Mesopotamian architects learned how to build arches, which could support the roofs of large structures without numerous pillars, and they eventually perfected the characteristic design of their later temples: the ziggurat. These were constructed as a series of platforms on top of each other, each one smaller than the one beneath, to produce a building that resembled the Step Pyramid of ancient Egypt. However, since these were made of mud bricks, and not stone, almost all of the ziggurats eventually collapsed, forcing researchers to deduce their features from ruins and illustrations.

We are more familiar with the architects of ancient Egypt, for these men were prominent public officials who were widely respected for their work. Their official title, *medjeh nesu* or "royal carpenter," indicates that the first men who held this position constructed wooden buildings, though all major projects were eventually made of stone. We often have little biographical information about these royal architects, other than their names and accomplishments, but certain generalizations about them can be made. First, it is often emphasized that architects tended to be of humble birth and worked their way up through the Egyptian bureaucracy by displaying their unusual aptitude. This shows how important their work was considered; instead of entrusting their grand buildings to a relative or friend, pharaohs preferred to seek out the most capable person available. Second, once they attained their high rank, architects spent a great deal of time with their pharaohs, perhaps even becoming their friends as they regularly discussed the progress of their buildings. The pharaoh Amenhotep III (ca. 1388–1349 BCE) clearly became very fond of his architect, who was also named Amenhotep (ca. fourteenth century BCE), since he granted him the unusual privilege of an impressive tomb. And the female pharaoh Hatshepsut (1508–1458 BCE) was so often in the company of her architect, Senenmut (ca. fourteenth century BCE), that it inspired rumors, recorded in graffiti, that they were lovers.

The work of the royal architect began when he met with the pharaoh to make decisions about the nature, size, and location of the proposed structure. The architect himself probably chose the types of stone to be used and estimated the number of workers that would be needed, but scribes in his employ surely handled the details of procuring the materials and recruiting laborers. The architect needed a special form of assistance from astronomers, since it was believed that buildings should be precisely aligned to face in certain directions. We assume that, as in Mesopotamia, the Egyptian architects prepared plans and constructed models before proceeding to construction, but the evidence is scanty: a few sketches on papyrus of courtyards and tombs, and an unimpressive miniature building that may have been created for other purposes. At the chosen site for the project, the architect would also have to conduct certain religious rituals to ensure that the gods would sanction its successful completion.

Once building had commenced, the architects generally had little to do, but they may have been called upon to address problems that arose during construction. This apparently occurred in the case of one of Egypt's earliest pyramids, the notorious Bent Pyramid erected during the reign of the pharaoh Snefru (ca. 2700 BCE). Originally, its sides were designed to rise at a sharp angle of 60 degrees, but because it was unwisely located on a base of soft clay, the builders soon realized that it was becoming unstable. One theory is that alarmed workers began hearing cracking noises within the pyramid, inspiring them to alert the architect of the possibility of a collapse. The improvised solution was to reduce the angle of its sides, first to 55 degrees and then to 45 degrees, so that fewer stones were needed to complete the pyramid and the weight of the projected structure was reduced, placing less pressure on the base. Also, instead of laying the stones at a slight angle, the stones at higher levels were placed horizontally to the ground, which helped to improve the pyramid's stability. The resulting structure looks very odd, but the architect's strategies were effective, since the Bent Pyramid is still standing today, though Snefru probably chose another of his pyramids as his burial site.

The most famous architect of ancient Egypt was Imhotep, who worked for the pharaoh Djoser (both ca. 2600 BCE) and designed the nation's first major pyramid, the Step Pyramid, which still stands to this day;

The unusual shape of ancient Egypt's Bent Pyramid, at Dahshur, may have resulted from its architect's hasty decision, upon realizing that his half-built structure was becoming unstable, to suddenly reduce the angle of its sides to lower its overall weight. It was built around 2575 BCE. (Jorge Lascar)

Djoser so appreciated his work that he allowed Imhotep's name to be placed on one of his statues. This architect also may have lived long enough to serve the next two pharaohs, Sekhemkhet and Huni (both ca. 2600 BCE), and construct pyramids and other structures for them as well. Some have speculated that Imhotep's role may have been more like that of a senior administrator than an architect, and that he delegated the process of planning his structures to subordinates; yet the man was so respected for his wisdom, both in architecture and medicine, that he was worshipped as a god after his death, indicating that his talents must have been genuine. A lesser-known successor of Imhotep, Hemiunu (ca. 2570 BCE) was responsible for the largest pyramid, the Great Pyramid of Khufu (died 2566 BCE), though he may have been assisted by his father Nefermaat (ca. 2600 BCE).

Two other renowned architects lived over a thousand years later. The greatest accomplishment of Hatshepsut's architect, Senenmut, was her magnificent funeral temple, a three-part structure supported by rows of columns in the manner of the Greek Parthenon; yet his close relationship with the pharaoh evidently made him quite unpopular, and after his death, some of his monuments and his sarcophagus were smashed, so he long remained obscure. Amenhotep, who rose from a lowly position as a scribe for the Egyptian army, designed many structures that have not endured through the ages, but two enormous statues of Amenhotep III that were in front of one temple, now called the Colossi of Memnon, are still in place today. But Amenhotep was admired much more than Senenmut since, like Imhotep, he was later regarded as a god.

We mostly think of ancient Egyptian architects because of their pyramids and temples, but they were responsible for many other sorts of structures as well. Before the pyramids, Egyptian pharaohs and high officials were buried in mound-shaped buildings called *mastabas*, and much later, more elaborate versions

A MODERN PYRAMID BUILDER

The most renowned buildings designed by the Egyptian architects were the pyramids; however, while the Egyptians and other ancient civilizations like the Mayans were enamored of such structures, pyramids gradually fell out of favor. However, at least one contemporary architect has had the opportunity to design a pyramid—Veldon Simpson, an experienced hotel architect who was asked to design a Las Vegas hotel in the shape of a pyramid. The completed building, the Luxor, is almost as tall as the Great Pyramid of Giza, but it is made entirely out of modern materials; instead of limestone, for example, it is covered with panels of black glass.

STONE HOMES

Many of the stone buildings designed by ancient architects have proven to be remarkably long-lasting, and while more modern materials remain standard for larger structures, there has been a recent revival of interest in using stones to construct houses. Along with its durability, stone seems a desirable choice because it is natural, readily available, and friendly to the environment. Thus, a number of websites now advise homeowners on how to build their homes out of stone, and in 2012, architect Luca Zanaroli garnered some attention in architectural circles for designing an attractive all-stone house in his native Italy.

of these again came into fashion. The royal architects surely designed the large palaces where the pharaohs lived, and when there arose concerns about defending Egypt against foreign enemies to the north and south, they had to plan the fortresses that were constructed on the Nile Delta and in Upper Egypt. And, when no major projects demanded their attention, architects may have been assigned additional administrative duties, like other members of the Egyptian bureaucracy.

Overall, being an architect was probably one of ancient Egypt's most desirable professions, since their work had such enormous cultural and religious significance to all citizens; indeed, architects are the only people other than pharaohs themselves who are known to have attained the status of gods. All of the brightest

scribes must have competed for the privilege of garnering this position, and a few of them like Imhotep, who are still renowned today, effectively managed to achieve the immortality that all of the Egyptians craved.

Further Reading

Arnold, Dieter. 2003. *The Encyclopedia of Ancient Egyptian Architecture.* Edited by Nigel Strudwick and Helen Strudwick. Translated by Sabine H. Gardiner and Helen Strudwick. Princeton, NJ: Princeton University Press.

Curatola, Giovanni, editor. 2007. *The Art and Architecture of Mesopotamia.* New York and London: Abbeville Press.

Leick, Gwendolyn. 2011. *A Dictionary of Ancient Near East Architecture.* London and New York: Routledge.

Magli, Giulio. 2013. *Architecture, Astronomy and Sacred Landscape in Ancient Egypt.* Cambridge and New York: Cambridge University Press.

Rossi, Corinne. 2004. *Architecture and Mathematics in Ancient Egypt.* Cambridge and New York: Cambridge University Press.

Smith, W. Stevenson. 1998. *The Art and Architecture of Ancient Egypt.* Revised by William Kelly Simpson. New Haven, CT: Yale University Press.

Document

From Rawlinson, George. 1882. *History of Ancient Egypt, Volume 1.* Boston: S. E. Cassino.

In this passage, Rawlinson, a nineteenth-century Egyptologist, describes the high status of architects in ancient Egypt and names some noted architects.

A third learned profession was that of the architect, which in some respects took precedence over any other. The chief court architect was a functionary of the highest importance, ranking among the very most exalted officials. Considering the character of the duties entrusted to him, this was only natural, since the kings generally set more store upon their buildings than upon any other matter. . . . The royal architects, the *Murket*, as they were called, recruited their ranks not unfrequently from the class of princes; and the inscriptions engraved upon the walls of their tombs inform us that, almost without exception, they married either the daughters or the granddaughters of the reigning sovereigns, who did not refuse the Murket this honour. Semnofer, for instance, an architect under the third or fourth dynasty, was married to a lady named Amon-Zephes, the granddaughter of a Pharaoh; Khufuhotep, belonging to about the same period, had for wife a person of the same exalted position; Mer-ab, architect under Khufu, or Cheops, was an actual son of that monarch; Pirson, who lived a little later, married Khenshut, of the blood royal; and Ti, though of low birth himself, married Nofer-hotep, a princess. This last-named architect united in his own person a host of offices and dignities: he was the king's secretary in all his palaces, the secretary who published the king's decrees, the president of the royal Board of Works, and a priest of several divinities. His magnificent tomb is still to be seen at Saccarah in the neighborhood of the Pyramids, a little to the north of the Serapeum, and attracts the general attention of travellers.

Though a position of such eminence as this could belong only to one man at a time, it is evident that the lustre attaching to the head of their profession would be more or less reflected upon its members. Schools of architects had to be formed in order to secure a succession of competent persons, and the chief architect of the king was only the most successful out of many aspirants, who were educationally and socially upon a par. Actual builders, of course, constituted a lower class . . . exposed by their trade both to disease and accident. But architects ran no such risks; and the profession must be regarded as having enjoyed in Egypt a rank and a consideration rarely accorded to it elsewhere. According to [the Greek historian] Diodorus, the Egyptians themselves said that their architects were more worthy of admiration than their kings.

Boat Builders

Most of the world's first civilizations developed around great rivers: the Nile River in Egypt, the Tigris and Euphrates rivers in Mesopotamia, the Indus River in India, and the Yellow River in China. To carry on daily business, their citizens needed boats to transport them up and down these rivers; later, when the empires of the Near East extended their reach to the Mediterranean Sea, ships that could travel on open waters also became essential. However, we know relatively

little about the boats employed by the ancient people of Mesopotamia, except for information gleaned from carvings and illustrations. To carry large goods, they apparently constructed, long flat-bottomed boats with elevated bows and sterns, so the crafts were shaped like the letter U; records indicate that they had to import wood, which was scarce in the region, in order to build these boats. To keep the boats moving, the sailors either relied upon long oars or deployed square sails made of cloth. Smaller boats, made of reeds and covered with animal skins, carried cargoes of grain between cities.

Other ancient civilizations of the Near East had traditions of boat building as well. The Hebrew Bible celebrates the achievement of the legendary Noah, who constructed and sailed an ark capable of carrying pairs of all the world's animals, though later residents of Israel apparently limited their efforts to small fishing boats. A very mysterious ancient race, the Sea People, at one time dominated the eastern Mediterranean Sea and even conquered Egypt. Later, the Phoenicians built an impressive civilization largely due to their seaworthy ships that carried on trade throughout the Mediterranean world. Their cargo ships were usually about 90-feet long and 20-feet wide, propelled by rows of muscular oarsmen and colorful sails.

We are best informed, however, about the boats of ancient Egypt, in large part because it became the custom to include a small model boat in all royal tombs, which the Egyptians believed could be magically enlarged in the afterlife to provide transportation for the deceased; archaeologists have even unearthed a few full-sized boats near larger tombs. One particularly impressive find, in the city of Abydos, was a buried fleet of fourteen ships constructed for the early pharaohs. In addition, the Egyptians provided many written and pictorial depictions of the different sorts of boats that they built and used. The very first boats, limited to the Nile River, were made of papyrus; essentially, they were simple rafts made out of reeds that were tied together, with curved ends rising on both sides. Poor people continued to construct these simple craft for fishing and traveling; however, the officials of ancient Egypt recognized that their regular travel up and down the river required sturdier boats made of wood. This posed a challenge to the early boat

This carved image, found inside one of the early Egyptian tombs known as *mastabas*, shows small papyrus boats being propelled by men wielding long oars. (Jose Fuste Raga/Corbis)

builders because the available wood in Egypt did not provide long planks; true, the men building boats for the pharaohs could rely on expensive cedar imported from Lebanon, but other boat builders necessarily devised methods for joining small pieces of wood to form large planks. These were then combined to form boats using dowels, an adhesive, and strong ropes to bind the planks to each other.

The overall shape of Egyptian boats, to modern observers, seems overly wide, but they were seaworthy despite their lack of streamlining; like the ancient Mesopotamians, the Egyptian propelled their boats with oars and sails. Boats with different designs were constructed for different purposes. To transport groups of animals or the massive stone used for construction projects, there were large, flat barges, which were usually towed by other boats. For other cargo, smaller ships were employed. The boats that carried passengers were about 30- or 40-feet long, and they

were equipped with leather awnings or cabins on their decks, so nobles and officials could rest in the shade while they traveled down the Nile; some even had their own small kitchens, where animals could be butchered and cooked. By the time of the New Kingdom, certain ships were especially built for naval battles, with lots of room to transport soldiers and raised sides to protect against attacks at sea.

Special boats with long, curved ends, imitating the shape of papyrus boats, were constructed for religious purposes, such as carrying statues of gods to be observed during religious festivals or transporting the bodies of dead pharaohs to their tombs. As noted, these funeral boats were sometimes buried alongside of them; archaeologists now call them "solar boats" since the eventual destination of the deceased pharaoh was assumed to be the sun god Re. One example of such a boat, constructed for the pharaoh Cheops or Khufu (ca. 2580 BCE), was unearthed in 1954. This

BUILDING AN ANCIENT EGYPTIAN SHIP

Since their techniques seem crude and dangerous to modern shipbuilders, many wonder how the ancient Egyptians created reliable craft to sail on rivers and seas. Recently, Egyptologist Cheryl Ward participated in an effort to reconstruct the ship used by the pharaoh Hatshepsut (1508–1458 BCE) to travel south to distant Punt (Ethiopia). As reported in a 2010 episode of the documentary series *Nova*, "Building Pharaoh's Ship," their boat did sail successfully on the Red Sea in late December 2008, though builders sometimes had to improvise on the basis of incomplete information; so, believing that their boat required caulking to prevent leaks, they devised a mixture of linen and beeswax, two substances known to the Egyptians.

SAILING DOWN THE NILE

While the peasants of ancient Egypt built their boats out of papyrus, this once-abundant plant is no longer available for their modern counterparts. However, a version of their simple wooden sailboats, the felucca, is still commonplace on the Nile River. Tourists seeking an authentic Egyptian experience enjoy taking a leisurely cruise down the Nile in feluccas, though the boats they are riding in are not exactly like their earlier counterparts; they often incorporate modern materials as well as wood, and they are sometimes equipped with an outboard motor as a backup method of propulsion if the wind is not strong enough.

impressive vessel was over 140-feet long and about 20-feet wide, and while some initially suspected that it was not built for actual use, evidence of soaked wood indicates that it did sail on the Nile. Tomb paintings suggest that these funeral boats were often painted gold and elaborately decorated.

All boats were generally built by carpenters who specialized in this work, supervised by an important government official called the chief of the royal ships. Later, however, wealthy individuals could pay to have ships crafted for their own private use. The ships were constructed in large shipyards, including a renowned site in the city of Memphis and another on the coast of Syria. Given the importance of boats

in ancient Egypt, their builders must have been well trained and generously compensated, and the opportunity to serve as a boat builder was undoubtedly, in many cases, passed on from fathers to sons. The boat builders earned their pay by working very efficiently to complete their assignments; there is one report, for example, of a large ship, over 30 meters in length, that was constructed in a total of seventeen days. Unlike modern boat builders, the Egyptians began by putting together the outer planks of the boat, and then inserted the interior reinforcements. For the curved boats, some planks had to be individually carved with an adze so that they would fit together like the pieces of a puzzle. One tomb illustration shows two carpenters kneeling underneath a boat, elevated by ropes, wielding tools to work on its hull; another displays a raised boat with workers seated inside. Strangely, one of the regular tasks of boat builders was to rebuild the boats they had already built, since evidence suggests that some boats designed for sea travel were first constructed at interior shipyards, then disassembled, carried to the shore of the Mediterranean Sea or Red Sea, and put back together again. One site where this task was carried out, in the present-day city of Mersa Gawasis on the Red Sea, has yielded large numbers of boat fragments and evidence that numerous workers were in residence.

Over the centuries, the boat builders gradually improved their designs, although they never employed modern keels or rudders, which complicated the task of steering the vessels. However, while the first boats required three paddles for steering, they later created a single paddle that could control the motion of the boat with reasonable effectiveness. Their boats grew bigger, with deeper hulls, and for faster travel, they provided boats with larger and more complex sails; the oars were inserted through holes of rope to better keep them in position. As one possible indication of the increasing quality of the boat builders' work, archaeologists rarely find ancient Egyptian shipwrecks, suggesting that their crafts were generally seaworthy (though the Egyptians were also cautious sailors, traveling only during the day and always staying close to shore).

Still, the Egyptians were eventually conquered by the Sea People, who evidently possessed superior boats, and during the final millennium of the pharaohs' rule, the Mediterranean Sea was largely dominated by other cultures, such as the Phoenicians and the Greeks, who greatly advanced the art of shipbuilding. The Egyptians probably imitated some of their innovations in building later boats, but they never became a great naval power. Still, their boats long provided them with reliable transportation on the Nile River, Mediterranean Sea, and Red Sea, and they were central to the development and maintenance of Egyptian culture.

Further Reading

Fabre, David. 2004. *Seafaring in Ancient Egypt*. London: Periplus.

Gilbert, Gregory Philip. 2008. *Ancient Egyptian Sea Power and the Origin of Maritime Forces*. Canberra: Sea Power Centre Australia.

Partridge, Robert B. 1996. *Transport in Ancient Egypt*. London: Rubicon.

Tallet, Pierre, and El-Sayed Mahfouz, editors. 2012. *The Red Sea in Pharaonic Times: Recent Discoveries along the Red Sea Coast: Proceedings of the Colloquium Held in Cairo/Ayn Soukhna 11th-12th January 2009*. Cairo: French Institute of Oriental Archaeology.

Vinson, Steve. 1994. *Egyptian Boats and Ships*. Princes Risborough, England: Shire Publications.

Ward, Cheryl A. 2000. *Sacred and Secular: Ancient Egyptians Ships and Boats*. Philadelphia: The University Museum, University of Pennsylvania.

Documents

From Herodotus. C. 425 BCE. *The History of Herodotus*. Translated by G.C. Macaulay. 1890. London and New York: Macmillan and Co.

Here, the Greek historian describes the cargo boats of the ancient Egyptians.

Their boats with which they carry cargoes are made of the thorny acacia, of which the form is very like that of the Kyrenian lotos, and that which exudes from it is gum. From this tree they cut pieces of wood about two cubits in length and arrange them like bricks, fastening the boat together by running a great number of long bolts through the two-cubit pieces; and when they have thus fastened the boat together, they lay cross-pieces over the top, using no ribs for the sides; and within they caulk the seams with papyrus. They make one steering-oar for it, which is passed through the bottom of the boat; and they have a mast of acacia and sails of papyrus. These boats cannot sail up the river unless there be a very fresh wind blowing, but are towed from the shore: down-stream however they travel as follows:—they have a door-shaped crate made of tamarisk wood and reed mats sewn together, and also a stone of about two talents weight bored with a hole; and of these the boatman lets the crate float on in front of the boat, fastened with a rope, and the stone drag behind by another rope. The crate then, as the force of the stream presses upon it, goes on swiftly and draws on the *baris* (for so these boats are called), while the stone dragging after it behind and sunk deep in the water keeps its course straight. These boats they have in great numbers and some of them carry many thousands of talents' burden.

From Erman, Adolf. 1894. *Life in Ancient Egypt*. Translated by Helen Mary Tirard. 1894. London and New York: Macmillan and Company.

The author explains how the ancient Egyptian carpenters had to overcome some special challenges when they constructed boats.

We shall only indicate here a few of the peculiarities of Egyptian workmanship, peculiarities principally due to the poor character of their materials. If we confine ourselves to the consideration of native wood, we find a complete lack of planks of any great length; the curious art was therefore devised of putting together small planks to form one large one. In boat-making, where fine workmanship was not required, the little boards were fastened the one over the other like the tiles of a roof; this process, which is unmistakably represented in a picture of the Middle Empire, was still in common practice in Egypt in the time of Herodotos, though, like other old Egyptian customs, it is now confined to the Upper Nile. . . .

The following was the method by which they gave the planks of a boat the right curve: when the boat was ready in the rough, the boat-builder of the Old Empire drove a post with a fork at the top into the middle of the bottom. Strong ropes were then fastened to the stern and the bow of the boat, and drawn over the fork; the workmen next stuck poles through these ropes and then twisted them round till the boards of the boat had been curved into the necessary shape. The men had of course to exert all their strength, so that the rope should not untwist, and all their work be in vain.

Carpenters

Along with stone, wood was the material that prehistoric humans most depended upon to make their tools, utensils, and structures, and this remained the case in early civilizations, even as people also mastered the art of metalworking. Yet studying the work of ancient carpenters is sometimes difficult because their products have usually not survived. Yet from a few preserved examples, illustrations, texts, and evidence like postholes, we can get a good sense of their habits and activities.

For example, tablets from the Mesopotamian city of Mari, on the Euphrates River, describe the building of furniture for nobles; carpenters typically connected pieces of wood with ropes, animal muscles, or glue and added leather covering to the chairs. In Assyria, chairs with backs, legs, and arms were built out of seventeen types of wood and sometimes adorned with ivory, copper, silver, or gold. Tables for eating meals were made out of wood with added pieces of metal, and beds were wooden frames that supported mattresses filled with wool. For storage, carpenters crafted wooden chests and crates, and some bowls and plates were also made out of wood. Also, while homes were usually made out of mud bricks, there were occasional wooden houses, and all homes had wooden doors, stairs, and roofs. The larger projects of the Mesopotamian carpenters included bridges, wagons, and boats.

Trained carpenters were from the beginning found in Mesopotamian cities; a tablet from ancient Ur, for example, describes a large workshop which included carpenters and seven other types of craftsmen. The skills of carpentry were typically passed on from father to son, though some carpenters also took on apprentices, and carpenters sometimes worked as part of guilds organized by the government or the temples. We have little information about the tools they employed, but they surely possessed a wide variety of cutting tools, probably made out of bronze.

Carpentry was an important profession throughout the ancient world, since wooden objects were essential to daily life; we know this was the case in ancient Israel, for instance, due to numerous references to carpenters and carpenters' tools in the Old Testament. Yet carpenters sometimes found it difficult to obtain enough suitable wood from the sparse local forests in many regions of the ancient Near East, so nations needed to import timber from places where it was abundant, like Lebanon, renowned for its lush forests of tall trees. This was an especially difficult problem for Egypt, since its native trees only provided wood of a low quality in small pieces; hence, to get larger and better planks of wood, they relied upon Lebanon, Assyria, and distant Punt (present-day Ethiopia). Much of this wood was used to make boats, but since these vessels were so numerous and important to the Egyptian economy, the carpenters who specialized in their construction can be considered a special class of workers.

Egyptian carpenters found many ways to apply their skills, as they built wooden doors, tables, chairs, boxes, statues, and coffins. Since their labors were often immortalized on tomb illustrations, we know a great deal about their methods. Each project required several tools, first made of copper and later of bronze. To cut pieces of wood, carpenters tied them on a wooden pillar and used a handsaw that, unlike modern saws, had to be pulled, not pushed. Axes and adzes roughly shaped the wood; bow drills made holes; and carving was done with chisels hit with a wood hammer. For final polishing, the carpenters applied a piece of sandstone (which was also employed to sharpen tools with blunted blades). If the carpenter had used cheap Egyptian wood, he might have stained it so that it would look like a more expensive imported wood.

The Egyptians did have nails, but for most of their history they were used solely to attach wood to metal; thus, carpenters had to devise a variety of ingenious ways to join pieces of wood together, especially since long planks were often unavailable. For pieces of furniture and coffins, they would typically tie the joints tightly with strips of leather, linen strings, or bands of copper, and at times they could use a type of vegetable glue. They perfected the mortise and tenon joint, cutting a rectangular hole in one piece of wood—the mortise—and inserting a projection of the same shape on another piece of wood—the tenon—and they sometimes employed dowels and hinges as well. Since the chairs and couches they constructed for the tomb of the pharaoh Tutankhamun (ca. 1341–1323 BCE) survived intact for thousands of years until they were unearthed in 1923, their techniques must be regarded as effective.

We are, in fact, most familiar with the pieces of furniture made by Egyptian carpenters because these wooden objects were invariably included in royal tombs, since it was believed that the deceased would need places to sit, rest, and eat in the afterlife. Even when the wood itself has disintegrated, the design of some furniture can be deduced because it was covered with thin sheets of gold that endured through the centuries. Everyday Egyptians undoubtedly got by with a few stools, chairs, tables, and beds with plain designs, and some of these can be found in the tombs of individuals of low rank; however, carpenters crafted more elaborate items for their leaders. The chairs and beds of pharaohs had legs that were carved to resemble animals' feet; their couches might feature carved images of hippopotamuses' or lions' heads; and in addition to gold, their furniture was decorated with ivory and jewels. But we observe pieces of furniture with some more practical features as well. The Egyptians invented a type of folding stool that generals could take with them on their campaigns, and small chests for jewelry had sliding drawers.

In addition to furniture, carpenters were needed to make many other sorts of objects. Soldiers needed well-crafted bows, arrows, and javelins, and an essential emblem of the pharaoh's authority, the scepter, was also made of wood. Temples had tall shrines to elevate statues of the gods to be worshipped, and the roofs of palaces were often supported by wooden columns elaborately carved to look like plants or lotuses. Egyptian children played with wooden balls and toys carved in the shape of people or animals, and to provide security for homeowners, carpenters learned to make wooden locks with pins to secure doors. During the New Kingdom, there arose a demand for a new sort of vehicle, the chariot, for use in battle. These required their carpenters to carefully assemble over fifty pieces of wood, including a wheel with six spokes.

In completing all of their projects, Egyptian carpenters never worked alone; tomb illustrations

THE PHARAOH'S FURNITURE

In the late eighteenth century, Napoleon's military campaigns in Egypt sparked European interest in ancient Egypt, and one of their effects was the development of Egyptian revival furniture, which imitated the designs of Egypt's carpenters. Similar pieces became fashionable after Howard Carter's discovery of Tutankhamun's tomb in 1923, especially since he uncovered many items of elaborately decorated furniture, and these have remained popular in some circles. Today, for example, people with expensive tastes can purchase precise replicas of Tutankhamun's furniture, constructed using the same sorts of wood and coverings of ivory and gold.

SITTING LIKE AN EGYPTIAN

Ancient Egyptian carpenters constructed the world's first folding stools, employing a simple but ingenious design. Two pairs of boards of equal length were connected by a central pivot, so they could be horizontally aligned or extended to form an X shape. The bottoms of each X were attached to two boards, which provided firm support on a flat surface, while the tops were attached to two slanted boards that could be covered with a piece of leather for comfortable sitting. Folding chairs of precisely this sort are still being used, though today they are normally made out of aluminum instead of wood.

invariably show several carpenters inside a single workshop, and while they are sometimes working separately, some tasks needed two or more carpenters working together. There are scenes, for example, of four men constructing a large frame for the door to a tomb, and two men assembling a bed. Occasionally, one of the workers looks smaller than the others, perhaps to represent the son of a carpenter or an apprentice who is learning his craft, the typical way that people entered professions in the ancient world. We know that some of these workshops were maintained by the pharaoh's staff or the temples, which paid the carpenters to work exclusively on their projects, but those which produced furniture for ordinary Egyptians probably supported themselves by selling their goods directly to customers.

Intriguingly, depictions of carpenters working on religious items sometimes include names, a rare honor suggesting that carpenters may have been held in higher esteem than other craftsmen who are invariably anonymous. The job may also have been considered desirable because, in contrast to working with molten metal or enormous stone blocks, carpentry was generally a safe profession, though there is one illustration depicting a minor health problem: a carpenter is using a narrow stick to remove some object from a colleague's eye, probably a splinter. Finally, those who built furniture and small objects could bring a personal style to their work, providing a unique sense of satisfaction when observing the finished product. Scraps of evidence even suggest that, at times, even the pharaohs and nobles expressed gratitude for the striking work of the men who built their beautiful furniture and brought comfort and elegance to their daily lives.

Further Reading

Barnett, Richard S. 2002. *All Kinds of Scented Wood: Wood and Woodworking in the Bible*. Fairfax, VA: Xulon Press.

Harvey, Julia. 2001. *Wooden Statues of the Old Kingdom: A Typological Study*. Leiden, The Netherlands: Brill.

Killen, Geoffrey. 1994. *Ancient Egyptian Furniture, Volume 2: Boxes, Chests and Footstools*. Warminster, England: Aris & Phillips.

Killen, Geoffrey. 1994. *Egyptian Woodworking and Furniture*. Princes Risborough, England: Shire Publications.

Kubba, Shamil A. A. 2006. *Mesopotamian Furniture: From the Mesolithic to the Neo-Assyrian Period (ca. 10,000 B.C.-600 B.C.)* Oxford: John and Erica Hedges.

Whelan, Paul. 2007. *Mere Scraps of Rough Wood?: 17th-18th Dynasty Stick Shabtis in the Petrie Museum and Other Collections*. London: Golden House Publications.

Document

From Erman, Adolf. 1894. *Life in Ancient Egypt*. Translated by Helen Mary Tirard. 1894. London and New York: Macmillan and Company.

Here, the prominent German Egyptologist Adolf Erman describes the typical tools used by ancient Egyptian carpenters.

The tools used by the carpenters and joiners were of a comparatively simple nature; evidently it is not due to the tools that the work was often carried to such perfection. The metal part of all tools was of bronze, and in the case of chisels and saws was let into the handle, whilst with axes and bill-hooks it sufficed to bind the metal part to the handle with leather straps. For rough-hewing the Egyptians used an axe, the blade of which was about the size of a hand, and was bent forwards in a semicircular form. Subsequent work was carried on with a tool that, from its constant employment, might almost be called the universal tool of Egypt. This is the adze of our carpenters, a sort of small bill-hook, the wooden part of which was in the form of a pointed angle with unequal shanks; the bronze blade was bound to the short shank and the longer served as a handle. To work in the details more perfectly a small chisel was used with a wooden mallet to strike it. A large spatulate instrument served as a plane, with the broad blade of which the workman smoothed off the small inequalities of the wood; lastly, a fine polish was attained by continual rubbing with a smooth stone. The saw, like our hand-saws, had but one handle, and it was most tedious work to cut the trunk of a thick sycamore into planks with this awkward instrument. As a rule, the wood that had to be sawn was placed perpendicularly and fastened to a post that was stuck into the ground, the part of the wood that was already sawn was tied up, so that its gaping asunder might not interfere with the work. In very early times a stick on which a weight was hung was stuck obliquely through these fastenings; this was evidently intended to keep them at the right tension, and to prevent them from slipping down. For boring, a drill was employed of the shape customary in Egypt even now; the female screw in which it moved was a hollow nut from the dom palm.

By a happy chance originals of nearly all these tools, which I have enumerated from tomb-pictures, have been preserved to us. A basket was found, probably in one of the Theban temples, containing the tools employed by King Thothmes III, "when he stretched the rope over 'Amon glorious in the horizon'," *i.e.* when he accomplished the foundation ceremonies for the temple of this name. We see that they are tools specially prepared for this ceremony, for they are not suitable for hard work; they give us however a variety of model specimens, from which we can form a very good idea of the simpler tools used by the Egyptian workman.

Embalmers

Surely, one of the reasons why people have remained fascinated by ancient Egypt is the fact that, because of its singular practice of mummification, we can actually look at the bodies of some of the pharaohs and officials who shaped its history, even employing modern forensic techniques to reconstruct their appearance when they were alive. In a sense, the process did provide these deceased Egyptians with a form of immortality, although they were actually anticipating a very different sort of life after death, an endless, peaceful sojourn with their gods. This required, the Egyptians believed, permanent preservation of their bodies, and their embalmers painstakingly developed effective techniques to achieve these ends.

The entire process of mummification typically took about seventy days. Embalmers took care of their business in workshops, where they kept all of the necessary equipment; these were located far away from cities, since the dead bodies exuded repugnant odors despite efforts to conceal them with incense and perfumes. As independent craftsmen, they negotiated a price for their services before the body was delivered and they began their work. To maintain the mystery of these preparations for the afterlife, embalmers never revealed their techniques, privately passing them to the apprentices who learned by working at their sides. Still, the modern researchers who have intensively studied mummies have deduced their usual procedures, building upon the writings of the Greek historian Herodotus, who reported on the embalming done in the Egypt of his day; however, though Herodotus is regarded as generally reliable, some of his observations have been questioned. He claimed, for example, that the embalmers removed the internal organs of poorer individuals by dissolving them with a cedar oil enema, but modern examinations show that their organs were actually taken out in the standard surgical manner.

When they handled pharaohs and other high officials, the embalmers were always supervised by a priest, who ensured that the deceased's body was treated properly and performed religious ceremonies to protect the body from demons; but the priest played no direct role in any procedure. Immediately after the person's death, embalmers would first use a knife to carefully slice the body's left side, and the internal organs—the lungs, stomach, intestines, kidneys, and liver—were removed and placed in small containers called canopic jars to be buried alongside the body; later, these were instead dried, covered with linen, and replaced inside the body. For this part of the procedure, embalmers placed the body on a slanted platform so the bodily fluids would flow into a basin, as shown in one tomb painting. In some cases, male genitals would also be sliced off to be separately preserved. However, no special attention was paid to the brain; instead, they would simply use a narrow hook to pierce a hole in a nostril, allow some brain matter to drain out, pull out any remnants, and discard them. The embalmers were careful to leave the heart inside the body, however, because it was thought that the god Anubis would measure people's virtue by weighing their hearts. After the organs were taken out, all body hair below the neck was shaved off; the bodies were thoroughly washed with palm wine and rinsed off with fresh water from the Nile River; and the mineral natron, a form of salt, was applied to the skin to absorb moisture so the body would be completely dried out, a process that required about forty days.

In the next stage, oils were applied to the skin, while the empty spaces inside the body were stuffed with sawdust, sand, and linen, along with aromatic spices; this was done with deliberation, to provide the body with an ideal shape. Beeswax was applied to keep the person's hair stylishly coiffured. Next, the body was wrapped with hundreds of yards of linen strips that had been immersed in a mixture of resin and other substances, like beeswax, camphor oil, and myrrh, which the embalmers had discovered inhibited decay. The embalmers began with the head, proceeded to the fingers and toes, covered the legs and arms, and finally placed linen around the entire body, producing the familiar appearance of a human figure covered by horizontal white bandages. So that the deceased person would not appear before the gods without a face, the embalmers might paint a face on the facial strips or apply plaster to recreate the person's appearance; by the time of the famous pharaoh Tutankhamun (ca. 1341–1323 BCE), mummies were provided with special masks, made of pure gold for pharaohs.

The embalmers also placed small good-luck charms, termed amulets, inside the strips, along with jewels and small pieces of gold; the body's legs and arms were bound together; and a scroll filled with magic spells was positioned in the hands for additional protection in the afterlife. After more strips of linen were applied and the body was covered with a cloth, it was ready to be sealed in its case and placed in its tomb, a procedure accompanied by elaborate rituals, though these may have been conducted outside the workshops in special tents erected near the tombs.

Most attention, understandably, has been paid to the mummies of pharaohs, but members of the pharaoh's family, priests, and other high officials were granted the privilege of mummification as well. Later, ordinary citizens could also have their bodies mummified, although they necessarily paid lower prices and thus received a lower quality of care. According to Herodotus, the embalmers around 500 BCE offered three levels of service for three different prices, though his descriptions, as noted, have been disputed. But researchers can detect evidence of inferior work in some later mummies. The linen used for their bodies was cheap and coarse; despite the religious significance of a preserved heart, it was often removed along with the other organs of these lesser individuals because it simplified the process of evisceration; and as another cost-cutting device, the brain was often left in place.

Even animals were mummified for various reasons. Some animals like cats, bulls, and crocodiles were considered divine or sacred and hence deemed worthy of such special treatment; some have speculated that mummified animals in royal tombs were placed there as offerings to the gods or as a source of food for the deceased person; and other preserved animals may have simply been the beloved pets of the deceased. For example, one man's mummy was found with a mummified dog resting near his feet, clearly there to provide him with a familiar companion in the afterlife. Mummified falcons were valued as a way to honor the god Horus, but these animals, which are difficult to breed in captivity, were not always available. In such cases, some embalmers defrauded their customers by mummifying a different bird like a hawk and shaping it to resemble a falcon. Some bold

ANCIENT AND MODERN EMBALMING

The modern process of embalming shares some similarities with the work of the ancient Egyptians: internal organs may be removed, and chemicals are used to keep the body from decaying. However, the purpose of the procedure has changed: the Egyptians sought to preserve the body for as long as possible as a key requirement for a successful afterlife, and while mummies might be decorated, there was no particular concern about the appearance of the body underneath the wrappings. Today, embalming is done to keep the body looking lifelike for a few days, so it can be displayed in an open casket, but long-term preservation is not a goal.

REVIVING THE DEAD

It is a tribute to the craftsmanship of the ancient Egyptian embalmers that their mummies are consistently so well preserved as to inspire suspicions that these bandaged bodies might be brought back to life by magical means. Even though an entire subgenre of Hollywood horror films has been based on this theme, such resurrections would be impossible, in large part because the embalmers removed the brains and internal organs of the bodies they prepared for burial. However, specialists in the field of cryonics are now freezing dead bodies intact, a new preservation technique that might actually enable future scientists to bring some corpses back to life.

embalmers even created animal mummies made out of mud and passed them off as the real thing.

In addition to shady practices, an additional problem was that some embalmers were not as skillful as others, and while examining the innumerable mummies that ancient Egypt left for posterity, Egyptologists often find signs of sloppy work. The head of one queen was stuffed with too much material, giving her mummy a cracked and swollen face that surely would have appalled this once-attractive woman. Embalmers forgot to remove a narrow tool used to remove another woman's brain, leaving it to be found inside her skull by modern researchers. In one case, embalmers who perhaps had not begun their work at the proper time sped up the process of drying by subjecting the body to high temperatures, resulting in poor preservation.

The advantage that these craftsmen enjoyed, of course, was that such signs of their ineptitude usually did not appear until the bodies were sealed away in coffins, so relatives could never complain.

As more and more citizens sought to have their bodies mummified, embalming eventually must have been a common profession in ancient Egypt, and although the work had its unpleasant aspects, it provided gainful employment for many men who, like contemporary morticians, found the process of preparing bodies for burial both interesting and fulfilling. And, while it was never their intent, they might have been proud to learn that their generally capable craftsmanship produced many products that have endured for thousands of years to be studied by scientists and displayed in museums.

Further Reading

Brier, Bob. 1994. *Egyptian Mummies: Unraveling the Secrets of an Ancient Art.* New York: W. Morrow.

Dunand, Françoise, and Roger Lichtenberg. 1998. *Mummies and Death in Egypt.* Translated by David Lorton. 2006. Ithaca, NY: Cornell University Press.

Germer, Renate. 1997. *Mummies: Life after Death in Ancient Egypt.* Translated by Fiona Elliott. 1997. Munich, Germany, and New York: Prestel.

Ikram, Salima, editor. 2005. *Divine Creatures: Animal Mummies in Ancient Egypt.* Cairo and New York: American University in Cairo Press.

Ikram, Salima, and Aidan Dodson. 1998. *The Mummy in Ancient Egypt: Equipping the Dead for Eternity.* London: Thames and Hudson.

Taylor, John H. 2001. *Death and the Afterlife in Ancient Egypt.* Chicago: University of Chicago Press.

Document

From Herodotus. C. 425 BCE. *The History of Herodotus.* Translated by G.C. Macaulay. 1890. London and New York: Macmillan and Co.

In this passage, the Greek historian describes Egyptian embalming as it was practiced in the fifth century BCE.

Whenever any household has lost a man who is of any regard amongst them, the whole number of women of that house forthwith plaster over their heads or even their faces with mud. Then leaving the corpse within the house they go themselves to and fro about the city and beat themselves, with their garments bound up by a girdle and their breasts exposed, and with them go all the women who are related to the dead man, and on the other side the men beat themselves, they too having their garments bound up by a girdle; and when they have done this, they then convey the body to the embalming.

In this occupation certain persons employ themselves regularly and inherit this as a craft. These, whenever a corpse is conveyed to them, show to those who brought it wooden models of corpses made like reality by painting, and the best of the ways of embalming they say is that of him whose name I think it impiety to mention when speaking of a matter of such a kind; the second which they show is less good than this and also less expensive; and the third is the least expensive of all. Having told them about this, they inquire of them in which way they desire the corpse of their friend to be prepared. Then they after they have agreed for a certain price depart out of the way, and the others being left behind in the buildings embalm according to the best of these ways thus:—First with a crooked iron tool they draw out the brain through the nostrils, extracting it partly thus and partly by pouring in drugs; and after this with a sharp stone of Ethiopia they make a cut along the side and take out the whole contents of the belly, and when they have cleared out the cavity and cleansed it with palm-wine they cleanse it again with spices pounded up: then they fill the belly with pure myrrh pounded up and with cassia and other spices except frankincense, and sew it together again. Having so done they keep it for embalming covered up in natron for seventy days, but for a longer time than this it is not permitted to embalm it; and when the seventy days are past, they wash the corpse and roll its whole body up in fine linen cut into bands, smearing these beneath with gum, which the Egyptians use generally instead of glue. Then the kinsfolk receive it from them and have a wooden figure made in the shape of a man, and when they have had this made they enclose the corpse, and having shut it up within, they store it then in a sepulchral chamber, setting it to stand upright against the wall.

Thus they deal with the corpses which are prepared in the most costly way; but for those who desire the middle way and wish to avoid great cost they prepare the corpse as follows:—having filled their syringes with the oil which is got from cedar-wood, with this they forthwith fill the belly of the corpse, and this they do without having either cut it open or taken out the bowels, but they inject the oil by the breech, and having stopped the drench from returning back they keep it then the appointed number of days for embalming, and on the last of the days they let the cedar oil come out from the belly, which they before put in; and it has such power that it brings out with it the bowels and interior organs of the body dissolved; and the natron dissolves the flesh, so that there is left of the corpse only the skin and the bones. When they have done this they give back the corpse at once in that condition without working upon it any more.

The third kind of embalming, by which are prepared the bodies of those who have less means, is as follows:—they cleanse out the belly with a purge and then keep the body for embalming during the seventy days, and at once after that they give it back to the bringers to carry away.

The wives of men of rank when they die are not given at once to be embalmed, nor such women as are very beautiful or of greater regard than others, but on the third or fourth day after their death (and not before) they are delivered to the embalmers. They do so about this matter in order that the embalmers may not abuse their women, for they say that one of them was taken once doing so to the corpse of a woman lately dead, and his fellow-craftsman gave information.

Farmers

In ancient Mesopotamia, as in other regions of the world, effective farming was essential in order to provide a growing population with a sufficient amount of food. Two basic systems were employed. In the north, the center of the Assyrian empire, there was enough rainfall to allow for what was called "dry farming" without extensive irrigation. However, in the southern regions of Babylonia and Sumeria, irrigation was needed to provide expanses of land with water from the Tigris and Euphrates rivers and control the water from annual flooding. Large canals up to up to 40-feet

wide fed small canals, about 3-feet wide, that brought the water to the crops; banks and levees prevented flooding and the erosion of canal walls. Constructing and maintaining these canals was necessarily the task of the government, which placed limitations on the freedom of farmers: some had to work on land owned by the king or the temples as tenant farmers, while those lucky enough to own land paid substantial fees or taxes.

Farming was also labor intensive: the plowing, which started in autumn, typically involved three men and four oxen pulling a simple plow with a metal tip; seeding was done by four men with another sort of plow equipped with a funnel that deposited the seeds; and harvesting in the spring required many workers wielding sickles with teeth made of flint. Other chores included applying fertilizer to the crops and fending off hordes of locusts, which the Assyrians liked to catch and eat. Along with family members, farmers regularly had to hire seasonal laborers or, if they could afford them, slaves. The major crop was barley, stored in large cylindrical silos, though the Mesopotamian farmers also grew vegetables like leeks, lettuce, cucumbers, onions, and turnips, usually in smaller gardens. In addition to their oxen, farmers kept sheep, goats, and cows to provide meat, cheese, and yogurt as well as leather and wool.

Through the ancient Near East, farming tended to be much the same, with certain regional variations. Thus, in hilly nations like Israel, the farmers had to construct terraces to provide flat areas suitable for agriculture. Also, since thieves and scavenging animals were a recurring problem, the Israelites constructed watch towers, where men would sit and watch over the fields. Biblical references suggest that grains, grapes, and olives were their most popular crops.

In Israel and ancient Greece, small family forms were the norm, but a quite different system arose in Egypt where, as in southern Mesopotamia, farming demanded extensive irrigation. As the government took control of the construction and maintenance of irrigation canals and dams, all of the land came to be owned by either the pharaoh or the temples. The Egyptian peasants effectively became tenant farmers, paying the government a percentage of the crops they raised (in the form of taxes) in exchange for the privilege of farming on its land. They were also required to spend some of their time digging canals and building dams. Their major crops were two varieties of wheat (spelt and emmet) and barley, to make bread and beer, along with flax and cotton for clothing.

Since tomb illustrations frequently depicted farmers at work (to ensure that food production would continue for the deceased in the afterlife), we have a fairly detailed picture of how Egyptian agriculture worked. In the fall, after the annual flooding was over, farmers would first place their seeds in the ground, sometimes by themselves with a hoe, and sometimes using a plow with a wooden blade dragged by a pair of cows which were guided by a naked boy. Herds of pigs and sheep then ran over the soil to flatten the land and force the seeds deep into the ground. One advantage the Egyptian farmer enjoyed was that his soil already contained some nitrogen, phosphorous, and potassium, so there was no need to use any fertilizers.

When it was time to harvest the crops during the dry season, a scribe would first survey the land and estimate how much grain would be obtained from the field, a way to ensure that unscrupulous farmers did not withhold some of their crops to avoid giving the government its fair share. Then, all available workers formed into teams and, chanting songs to the accompaniment of a flute, they sliced the stalks with sickles made of wood, later replaced by copper and bronze sickles, and gathered them into sheaves; since they worked all day in the hot sun, the workers were permitted to take a few breaks, leaning on their sickles and drinking water from jugs. The sheaves were then placed in nets or baskets and transported by donkeys to a threshing floor. There, cows and donkeys stomped on the sheaves to separate the husks from the grain, a process completed by men and women using scoops and sieves. The grain was finally stored in tubs and measured by the scribe; most of the grain was taken

In this ancient Egyptian fresco, a man is guiding two oxen pulling a plow, while a woman walks behind him, spreading seeds on the ground. (Cascoly Software)

LINGERING LOCUSTS

Ancient Egyptian farmers always had to worry about ravenous locusts, which might at any time descend upon and consume their crops; the problem was immortalized as one of the ten plagues that God afflicted Egypt with in order to persuade the pharaoh to free the Hebrew slaves. Even today, locusts remain a threat to Egyptian agriculture; in early 2013, swarms of locusts again attacked the farms of the Nile Delta, ironically just before the Jewish holiday of Passover, which commemorates the liberation of the Hebrews brought about by locusts and the other plagues.

WATERING CROPS THE EGYPTIAN WAY

One of the Egyptian farmers' most striking innovations was the simple device called the *shaduf*: a bucket hanging from a long stick on a pivot was lowered into the Nile River, a balancing weight on the other end brought it out filled with water, and the stick was swung around so the water could be poured on the garden. The process could be repeated as many times as necessary to provide plants with enough water. To this day, Egyptian farmers continue to employ *shadufs* to irrigation their crops, and schoolchildren learning about Egypt are sometimes assigned to construct their own small *shadufs* as a class project.

away to be placed in the state granaries, but the farmers were given a portion for their personal use.

When the crop was flax, male and female workers pulled the fibers from the ground before they were ripe, inverted them to remove the dirt, took out roots and seeds, placed the fiber in bundles, and left them on the ground to dry out. After a week of drying, the fibers were soaked in water for two weeks, beaten on stones, and combed with a metal tool.

The vegetables grown by the Egyptians came from gardens near the Nile River, which did not require water from irrigation channels. Temples and palaces had large gardens with rows of trees surrounded by high walls, while individual farmers maintained family gardens near their homes. These farmers would diligently bring water from the rivers in pots and pour it into a gridwork of small trenches in their gardens. Later,

however, they came to rely upon an ingenious device called the *shaduf*: a bucket hanging from a long stick on a pivot was lowered into the river, and a balancing weight then elevated the bucket filled with water so it could be swung around and emptied into the garden. Among the vegetables grown in these gardens were cucumbers, lettuce, chickpeas, onions, garlic, radishes, and lentils. Farmers also raised fruits like figs, dates, watermelons, and pomegranates; olives, which were made into oil for cooking and lighting; grapes to be fermented into wine; castor oil plants to provide oil; and colorful flowers to serve as decorations.

Both in their fields and in their gardens, Egyptian farmers had to deal with a wide variety of problems. The cows pulling the plows might trip over a rock and hurt themselves or damage the plow. The growing crops might be eaten by any number of ravenous animals, ranging from locusts, mice, and quails to cows and hippopotamuses. There was little to do be done about the smaller pests, but the birds could be scared with slings or captured in nets and traps, and large animals could be driven away with shouts and sticks. If a farmer was for some reason unable to provide the proportion of grain that the scribe required, the official would arrange for him to be brutally beaten, as depicted in several tomb illustrations. Even worse, as the farmers stepped in mud or waded through canals, they might be afflicted by parasitic worms that would bore into their bodies and cause severe bleeding; they might also be bitten by poisonous snakes or scorpions, which could lead to a quick and painful death.

Some commentators, however, may tend to overstate the amount of hard work and suffering that was part of the Egyptian farmers' lives, for they also experienced some pleasure. At the end of a long day, they derived great pleasure from sitting in their garden in the shade of a tree, drinking beer, and gossiping with friends about local officials and their foibles. Their constant labors gave them the strength and stamina to deal with the demands of their profession, and the pain of an occasional beating could be quickly forgotten. Most important, the effective work of the Egyptian farmers provided them and their fellow citizens with a hearty, healthy, and variegated diet, one of the best in the ancient world. Indeed, while their pyramids and treasures draw more attention, their system of agriculture may represent ancient Egypt's most impressive achievement.

Further Reading

Bowman, Alan K., and Eugene Rogan, editors. 1999. *Agriculture in Egypt from Pharaonic to Modern Times*. Oxford: Oxford University Press.

Cappers, Rene, editor. 2007. *Fields of Change: Progress in African Archaeobotany*. Eelde, The Netherlands: Groningen University Library.

Davis, Ellen K. 2009. *Scripture, Culture, and Agriculture: An Agrarian Reading of the Bible*. Cambridge: Cambridge University Press.

Fairbairn, Andrew S., and Ehud Weiss, editors 2009. *From Foragers to Farmers: Papers in Honour of Gordon C. Hillman*. Oxford and Oakville, CT: Oxbow Books.

Maeir, Aren M., Shimon Dar, and Ze'ev Safrai, editors. 2003. *The Rural Landscape of Ancient Israel*. Oxford: Archaeopress.

Smith, Wendy. 2003. *Archaeobotanical Investigations of Agriculture at Late Antique Kom el-Nana*. London: Egypt Exploration Society.

Documents

From Anonymous. C. 1200 BCE. *The Tale of Two Brothers: A Fairy Tale of Ancient Egypt*. Translated by Charles E. Moldenke. 1898. Watchung, NJ: Elsinore Press.

The opening passage of this ancient Egyptian fairy tale provides a picture of the daily lives of farmers living around 1200 BCE.

Once upon a time there were two brothers of the same mother and father. Anubis was the name of the elder and Batau that of the younger. Now Anubis was married and had a house while his younger brother was his servant. He attended to the clothes, and followed the cattle on the pasture, and did the ploughing and the threshing; in fact he did everything connected with the farm. He was, indeed, an excellent workman and none could be found like him in the whole country. He was, besides, a good brother.

Now for a long time this younger brother was tending the cattle according to his daily wont, returning home every evening, having on his back the herbs of the field that he had gathered while on the pasture, and setting them down before his older brother who passed the time with his wife in eating and drinking. Then he

lay down to sleep in the stable with his cattle as usual. *The next day* he would bake loaves of bread on the fire and place them before his older brother and take some loaves to the field. Here he tended his cattle, pasturing them and walking behind them. But they would tell him where there were good herbs growing, and he would listen to all they told him and drive them where they could find the good herbs they loved so much. His cattle, consequently, thrived under his hands and their young multiplied greatly.

Now when the time of ploughing arrived the older brother said to him: "Come, let us take our yoke of oxen and get ready for ploughing: for the soil is beginning to appear (after the inundation) and is now in excellent condition for ploughing. Do yon, therefore, go to the field with seed. To-morrow we will begin to plough." Thus he said, *and* his younger brother made all the arrangements with which his older brother had charged him.

On the following day they went out on the field with their yoke of oxen and began to plough. They were quite cheerful at their work and not idle for a moment. *Now after a few days* they were again at work in the field *when* the older brother came to the younger and said: "Run and fetch us some seed from the town!" Then he went and found the wife of his older brother sitting in the house and arranging her hair *and* said to her: "Come, give me some seed, that I may take it to the field; for my older brother has sent me saying: 'Run, und don't be long about it'!" *But she* answered him: "Oh, go yourself! open the bin and take as much as you need I am afraid, lest my tresses fall to the ground." *So* the young man went to the stable and took a big basket, which he filled with as much seed as he needed and put on his shoulder full of barley and spelt. . . .

From Erman, Adolf. 1894. *Life in Ancient Egypt*. Translated by Helen Mary Tirard. 1894. London and New York: Macmillan and Company.

As explained in this passage by German Egyptologist Adolf Erman, the ancient Egyptian farmers had to take several steps in order to successfully plant seeds in the harsh Egyptian soil.

The first duty of the farmer is now to plough the land; this work is the more difficult because the plough with which he has to turn over the heavy soil is very clumsy. The Egyptian plough has changed but little: from the earliest period it has consisted of a long wooden ploughshare, into which two slightly-bent handles are inserted, while the long pole, which is tied on obliquely to the hinder part of the ploughshare, bears a transverse bar in front, which is fastened to the horns of the oxen. Such is the stereotyped form of plough, which for centuries has scarcely altered at all; for though under the Middle Empire another rope was added to bind the pole and ploughshare together, and again under the New Empire the handles were put on more perpendicularly and provided with places for the hands, yet these alterations were quite unimportant. Two men are needed for ploughing—one, the plough-man proper, presses down the handles of the plough, the other, the ox-driver, is indefatigable in goading on the animals with his stick. The work goes on with the inevitable Egyptian cries; the driver encourages the ploughman with his "Press the plough down, press it down with thy hand !" he calls to the oxen to "pull hard," or he orders them, when they have to turn at the end of the field, to be "round." There are generally two ploughs, the one behind the other, probably in order that the second might turn up the earth between the furrows made by the other.

If the Egyptians merely wanted to loosen the upper coating of mud, they employed (at any rate under the New Empire) a lighter plough that was drawn by men. Here we see four boys harnessed to the bar, while an old man is pressing down the handles. This plough also differs somewhat from the usual form; the ploughshare consists of two parts bound together, it has also a long piece added on behind and turned upwards obliquely, by which the ploughman guides the plough.

After ploughing however the great clods of the heavy Egyptian soil had to be broken up again before the ground was ready for the seed. At the present day a "cat's claw"—a roller covered with spikes—is drawn over the fields for this purpose; in old times a wooden hoe was used,—the latter seems indeed to have been the national agricultural implement. We could have scarcely formed a correct idea of it from the figure [. . .] which it takes in the hieroglyphs and on the reliefs; happily however we have some examples of real hoes in our museums. The labourer grasped the handle of

this hoe at the lower end and broke up the clods of earth with the blade; by moving the rope he could make it wider or narrower as he pleased. In the pictures of the Old Empire, the men hoeing are always represented following the plough; later, they appear to have gone in front as well; under the New Empire we meet with them also alone in the fields, as if for some crops the farmers dispensed with the plough and were content with hoeing the soil. In the above-named periods wooden hammers were also employed to break up the clods of earth.

After the land had been properly prepared, the sowing of the seed followed. We see the "scribe of the corn" gravely standing before the heap of seed, watching the men sowing, and noting down how often each filled his little bag with seed. When the seed had been scattered, the work of sowing was not complete—it had next to be pressed into the tough mud. For this purpose sheep were driven over the freshly-sown fields. In all the pictures of this subject one or two shepherds with their flocks are to be seen following the sower. Labourers swinging their whips drive the sheep forward; others no less energetically chase them back. The frightened animals crowd together; a spirited ram appears to be about to offer resistance—he lowers his head in a threatening attitude; most of the creatures, however, run about the field in a frightened way, and *plough* it (to use the expression of the inscriptions) *with their feet.*

This trampling in of the seed is only represented in the pictures of the Old Empire; the custom probably continued later, but became less common. When Herodotus travelled in Egypt, he noticed that pigs were employed in the Delta for this purpose; in Pliny's time this practice was spoken of as a long-forgotten custom of doubtful credibility.

Food Preparers

One characteristic of a successful civilization is a well-fed population: cities and cultures develop only in areas where food is available, and any stable government must strive to ensure that their citizens always have enough to eat. Yet people also crave variety and flavor in their diets, so that the residents of ancient cities naturally tended to develop more and more elaborate ways of cooking and preparing their food.

While other grains such as wheat, rye, and millet were occasionally used, the staple of the Mesopotamian diet was barley, baked to make bread and brewed to produce beer. Fish oil, sesame oil, and lard were sometimes added to the bread, as well as extra ingredients like cheese, fruits, fruit juices, honey, and milk. One recipe for special cakes served to nobles, for example, required barley flour, cheese, butter, raisins, and dates. The Mesopotamians also consumed a wide variety of vegetables, including onions, cabbages, beets, cucumbers, and radishes; meat from pigs, cattle, geese, and ducks; and fish and turtles from the rivers. Several of these foods were typically boiled in water and used in various sorts of soups and broths, seasoned with herbs and spices like salt, mustard, mint, cumin, thyme, and marjoram. Some vegetables, and fruits like apples, plums, pears, melons, and grapes, were also eaten without cooking them, though all foods were assiduously washed, reflecting the Mesopotamians' strong concern for hygiene. Their favorite beverages included beer, wine, and milk.

The food was cooked in various ways. Some items might simply be placed upon a bed of hot coals, or on a grill over the coals, resembling a barbeque. The Mesopotamians also had clay ovens and a variety of cooking pots; some pottery molds with animal designs or shaped like fishes, found at one site, were probably used for special royal treats. Cooking at home was usually done by women, and while brewing beer was originally the responsibility of the priestesses of Nintaki, the Mesopotamian goddess of beer, ordinary women later performed this task as well. However, the cooks in the king's palace were always men. The usual pattern in Mesopotamia was to prepare and eat two meals a day.

Food preparation in other regions of the ancient Near East had many similarities to Mesopotamian practices. In Israel, for example, bread made of barley or wheat was the central part of the diet, baked over an open hearth in the center of one's house or courtyard. The fruits and vegetables the Israelites grew and consumed included olives, onions, and figs, and goats provided milk and cheese. On special occasions, they would eat meat from cattle, lambs, goats, and geese,

either cooked on a fire or boiled with vegetables to form a stew. To make one common dish, the cook formed pancakes out of dough, stuffed them with meat or fruit, and baked them on hot coals; according to the Old Testament, such cakes were what Gideon offered the angel who visited him. The most famous meal in the Bible, though, was the feast of Passover, first eaten by the Hebrews in Egypt following God's explicit instructions.

We have a great deal of information about ancient Egyptian eating habits because tombs would typically include both items of food for the deceased and wall illustrations of people preparing dishes. As in Mesopotamia, bread and beer made from barley were usually

This ancient Egyptian statuette from Giza shows a woman immersing loaves of bread and dates in a pot, so that the mixture can ferment to produce beer. This figure now resides at the Egyptian Museum in Cairo. (Alfredo Dagli Orti/The Art Archive/Corbis)

part of every meal. Women enjoyed making bread in their own homes, beginning with grains of barley, which one or two men would crush using a large mortar and pestle; then, the women took over the process, first by grinding the flour using two stones to make it very fine. Then they would mix the flour with milk, yeast, and additional ingredients, knead the resulting dough, and form the dough into loaves shaped like cones, pancakes, or spheres. They would then bake the loaves in a stove or fry them in a pan over a fireplace surrounded by bricks, either in the courtyard or the kitchen. Later, during the New Kingdom, some Egyptians baked the bread in clay ovens shaped like cones. If they wanted beer, women would break up loaves, soak them in water with dates, and leave the mixture for a few days to ferment; it would then be poured through a sieve or cloth to obtain the beer. While wives and daughters were invariably responsible for cooking in the home, nobles and rich men hired men to serve as their cooks.

Although grain for bread and beer was usually obtained from large farms, many Egyptians turned to their own gardens for other types of produce; some people kept hives of bees to supply them with honey. Onions were usually eaten at every meal; fruits and vegetables consumed less regularly included pomegranates, radishes, romaine lettuce, leeks, cucumbers, grapes, and melons; and garlic was frequently used to provide flavor. Making wine required the combined efforts of several family members: grapes were placed in a large, elevated box under a wooden framework, and several men holding on the framework with their hands or ropes crushed the grapes with their feet. The juice ran through pipes into vats and was then poured into large jars that were sealed so the juice would ferment.

In addition to bread and vegetables, the wealthier Egyptians would regularly cook and eat meat from cattle, goats, pigs, geese, and pigeons, usually obtained through hunting, as shown by numerous tomb illustrations showing animals being slaughtered for food. The dead animal was typically placed on a spit and roasted over a fire, though pieces of meat might also be placed in pots with vegetables and herbs like coriander or mint to make stews. Fish from the Nile River were cooked in similar ways, though they were often salted so they could be eaten later. For poor peasants,

ANCIENT EGYPTIAN BEER

Beer, a staple of the Egyptian diet, was made through a simple process of placing pieces of baked bread and dates in water, waiting a few days until the mixture had fermented, and pouring it through a cloth or sieve to remove large particles. Though the resulting alcoholic beverage, thick and sweet, bears little resemblance to the beer preferred by modern drinkers in Western countries, a form of Egyptian beer, called boza or bouza, is still made and marketed in Turkey and Eastern Europe. Modern brewers have learned, however, that by adding some leftover bouza to the original mixture, the time needed for fermentation is reduced to one day.

RESISTIBLE RECIPES

The ancient Egyptians produced no known cookbooks, so efforts to recreate their recipes, based on written descriptions and remnants of food found in tombs, are necessarily conjectural. There are, however, tablets from ancient Mesopotamia that contain recipes for modern chefs to follow. Julie Powell, best known for her efforts to cook all of Julia Child's recipes (as chronicled in the 2009 film *Julie and Julia*), also tried her hand at some Mesopotamian recipes, as described in her 2004 article "The Trouble with Blood" in *Archaeology* (November/December, vol. 57, no. 6.). Its title refers to one unpalatable habit of Sumerian cooks that she queasily imitated: boiling food in animal blood.

however, meat and fish might only be available on special occasions, and they depended on cooked beans and lentils as their main source of protein. When the food had been prepared, all Egyptians would eat with their hands, periodically pouring water over their hands, while they squatted in front of a table.

Cooking and eating were not without hazards for the ancient Egyptians. First, their fireplaces produced a thick smoke that was inhaled not only by the women doing the cooking but also by the other residents of the home. Thick coatings of soot have been found both on pieces of roofs and in mummies' lungs. Flies often infected food, causing dysentery and other intestinal disorders; the process of grinding flour regularly added bits of sand and stone to Egyptian bread; and the growing unpopularity of pork in the Egyptian diet may have resulted from an awareness of the disease trichinosis, usually caused by eating undercooked pork. The bodies of some poor people show signs of malnutrition, while rich people confronted the opposite problem of being overweight, as indicated by several statues and illustrations. Large banquets, a favorite social event for the Egyptians, might also lead to overeating or extreme drunkenness; in one indiscreet illustration a woman is seen regurgitating her food while other guests seem to be walking unsteadily, and another illustration shows men carrying a drunken friend who cannot walk at all.

Still, the Egyptians could be considered luckier than most ancient people because they generally enjoyed more than enough food; famines were constantly feared, but the Egyptian government learned to maintain supplies of grain to keep their people fed whenever they occurred. Indeed, while their diets were not as varied as those of the wealthy, even the poorest people in ancient Egypt could count on an abundance of food as one of their daily pleasures, to be cooked and eaten twice a day in the morning and evening. Even common laborers during the reign of Seti I (died 1279 BCE), according to one stela, or stone pillar, received as their daily wages four pounds of bread, two packages of vegetables, and some meat, enough to feed a man and his family; texts also suggest that the Egyptians greatly enjoyed both preparing and eating their food. And while they left us no cookbooks, a number of modern researchers have drawn upon the available evidence to reproduce some of their recipes, so that people today can again experience the pleasure of ancient Egyptian cooking.

Further Reading

Berriedale-Johnson, Michelle. 1999. *Food Fit for Pharaohs: An Ancient Egyptian Cookbook*. London: British Museum Press.

Bottéro, Jean. 2004. *The Oldest Cuisine in the World: Cooking in Mesopotamia*. Translated by Teresa Lavender Fagan. 2004. Chicago: University of Chicago Press.

Curtis, Robert I. 2001. *Ancient Food Technology*. Leiden, The Netherlands, and Boston: Brill.

Kaufman, Cathy K. 2006. *Cooking in the Ancient Civilizations*. Westport, CT: Greenwood Press.

MacDonald, Nathan. 2008. *What Did the Ancient Israelites Eat?: Diet in Biblical Times*. Grand Rapids, MI: Eerdmans Publishing Co.

Mehdawy, Magda, and Amr Hussein. 2010. *The Pharaoh's Kitchen: Recipes from Ancient Egypt's Enduring Food Traditions*. Cairo and New York: American University in Cairo Press.

Documents

From Exodus 12: 1–20.

In this passage from the version of Exodus *found in the* Torah, *God (who is here called "HaShem," which means "The Name" in the Hebrew language), instructs the Hebrews in Egypt about the meal they must cook and eat that will protect them from the coming plague that otherwise will kill their first-born sons, and the meal they must eat in the future to commemorate this occasion. These rules for celebrating the feast of unleavened bread provide the basis for the Jewish holiday of Passover, or* Pesach, *and for the traditions observed at the Seder dinner.*

1. And HaShem spoke unto Moses and Aaron in the land of Egypt, saying:
2. 'This month shall be unto you the beginning of months; it shall be the first month of the year to you.
3. Speak ye unto all the congregation of Israel, saying: In the tenth day of this month they shall take to them every man a lamb, according to their fathers' houses, a lamb for a household;
4. and if the household be too little for a lamb, then shall he and his neighbour next unto his house take one according to the number of the souls; according to every man's eating ye shall make your count for the lamb.
5. Your lamb shall be without blemish, a male of the first year; ye shall take it from the sheep, or from the goats;
6. and ye shall keep it unto the fourteenth day of the same month; and the whole assembly of the congregation of Israel shall kill it at dusk.
7. And they shall take of the blood, and put it on the two side-posts and on the lintel, upon the houses wherein they shall eat it.
8. And they shall eat the flesh in that night, roast with fire, and unleavened bread; with bitter herbs they shall eat it.

9. Eat not of it raw, nor sodden at all with water, but roast with fire; its head with its legs and with the inwards thereof.

10. And ye shall let nothing of it remain until the morning; but that which remaineth of it until the morning ye shall burn with fire.

11. And thus shall ye eat it: with your loins girded, your shoes on your feet, and your staff in your hand; and ye shall eat it in haste—it is HaShem's passover.

12. For I will go through the land of Egypt in that night, and will smite all the first-born in the land of Egypt, both man and beast; and against all the gods of Egypt I will execute judgments: I am HaShem.

13. And the blood shall be to you for a token upon the houses where ye are; and when I see the blood, I will pass over you, and there shall no plague be upon you to destroy you, when I smite the land of Egypt.

14. And this day shall be unto you for a memorial, and ye shall keep it a feast to HaShem; throughout your generations ye shall keep it a feast by an ordinance for ever.

15. Seven days shall ye eat unleavened bread; howbeit the first day ye shall put away leaven out of your houses; for whosoever eateth leavened bread from the first day until the seventh day, that soul shall be cut off from Israel.

16. And in the first day there shall be to you a holy convocation, and in the seventh day a holy convocation; no manner of work shall be done in them, save that which every man must eat, that only may be done by you.

17. And ye shall observe the feast of unleavened bread; for in this selfsame day have I brought your hosts out of the land of Egypt; therefore shall ye observe this day throughout your generations by an ordinance for ever.

18. In the first month, on the fourteenth day of the month at even, ye shall eat unleavened bread, until the one and twentieth day of the month at even.

19. Seven days shall there be no leaven found in your houses; for whosoever eateth that which is leavened, that soul shall be cut off from the congregation of Israel, whether he be a sojourner, or one that is born in the land.

20. Ye shall eat nothing leavened; in all your habitations shall ye eat unleavened bread.'

From Erman, Adolf. 1894. *Life in Ancient Egypt*. Translated by Helen Mary Tirard. 1894. London and New York: Macmillan.

Here, the renowned nineteenth- and twentieth-century German Egyptologist Adolf Erman describes the ancient Egyptian process of cooking meat and baking bread.

We know very little unfortunately of how the dishes were prepared. The favourite national dish, the goose, was generally roasted over live embers; the spit is very primitive—a stick stuck through the beak and neck of the bird. They roasted fish in the same way, sticking the spit through the tail. The roast did not, of course, look very appetising after this manner of cooking, and it had to be well brushed by a wisp of straw before being eaten. A low slab of limestone served as a hearth; even the shepherds, living in the swamps with their cattle, took this apparatus about with them. In the kitchen of Ymery, superintendent of the domain of King Shepseskaf, the hearth is replaced by a metal brasier with pretty open-work sides. In the same kitchen we see how the meat is cut up on low tables and cooked; the smaller pots have been placed on a brasier, the large ones stand on two supports over the open fire. It is only when we come to the time of the New Empire that we find, in representations of the kitchen of Ramses III, a great metal kettle with feet standing on the fire; the kitchen boy is stirring the contents with an immense two-pronged fork. The floor of the whole of the back part of the kitchen is composed of mud and little stones, and is raised about a foot in order to form the fireplace, above which, under the ceiling, extends a bar on which is hung the stock of meat.

Bread-making held a high place in the housekeeping at all periods, bread in different forms being the staple article of food with the people. We know therefore a good deal about it. We may take it for granted that the Egyptians, at any rate in the older periods, had no mills; we never find one represented in their tombs. On the contrary, in the time of the Middle as well as of the New Empire we find representations of great mortars in which one or two men are "pounding the corn" with heavy pestles, just in the same way as is done now in many parts of Africa. They obtained finer flour however by rubbing the corn between two stones. The lower larger stone was fixed and sloped towards the front, so that the prepared flour ran into a little hollow in the front of the stone. Under the Old Empire the stone was placed on the ground and the woman who was working it had to kneel before it; under the Middle Empire a table hollowed out in front took the place of the lower stone, the woman could then stand, and her work was thus rendered much lighter.

The second thing to be done in the making of bread was the kneading of the dough, which could be done in different ways. Shepherds, in the fields at night, baking their cakes in the ashes, contented themselves with "beating the dough" in an earthen bowl and lightly baking their round flat cakes over the coals of the hearth or in the hot ashes only. Little sticks served as forks for these hungry people to take them out of the glowing embers, but before they could eat them they had first to brush off the ashes with a wisp. It was otherwise of course in a gentleman's house. Here the dough was placed in a basket and kneaded carefully with the hands; the water was pressed out into a pot placed underneath the basket. The dough was then fashioned by the hand into various shapes similar to those we now use for pastry, and these were baked on the conical stove. I purposely say *on* the stove, for the Egyptians seem to have been satisfied with sticking the cakes on the outside of the stove. A picture of the time of the New Empire gives us a tolerable idea of one of these stoves; it is a blunted cone of Nile mud, open at the top and perhaps three feet high. The fire is burning in the inside, the flames burst out at the top, and the cakes arc stuck on the outside. The same picture shows us also the court-bakery of Ramses III. The dough here is not kneaded by hand—this would be too wearisome a method when dealing with the great quantities required for the royal household—it is trodden with the feet. Two servants are engaged in this hard work; they tread the dough in a great tub holding on by long sticks to enable them to jump with more strength. Others bring the prepared dough in jars to the table where the baker is working. As court baker he is not content with the usual shapes used for bread, but makes his cakes in all manner of forms. Some are of a spiral shape like the "snails" of our confectioners; others are coloured dark brown or red, perhaps in imitation of pieces of roast meat. There is also a cake in the shape of a cow lying down. The different cakes are then prepared in various ways—the "snails" and the cow are fried by the royal cook in a great frying pan; the little cakes are baked on the stove.

Miners

The first civilizations developed along great rivers, which offered fresh water and a convenient means of transportation, but they also required another resource—metals for their tools, utensils, weapons, and armor. Small quantities of metals like gold and tin could be obtained from rivers and streams by panning—gradually draining water from shallow containers to expose nuggets of the desired metal—but larger amounts of needed metals demanded the construction of mines in areas where ores were available. If there were no nearby deposits to exploit, as was the case in ancient Mesopotamia, nations had to depend upon trade with other regions for their metals.

The first place in the Near East to profit from exporting metals was Anatolia (present-day Turkey), where copper ores were abundant. Here, after long relying upon ores found on the surface, miners began to dig tunnels into the ground around 3000 BCE, relying upon large wooden shovels. Initially focused on finding copper, the Anatolian miners also began extracting arsenic, after it was discovered that the two metals could be combined to form a stronger alloy, arsenical bronze. They also began to mine other desirable metals, like zinc and lead, but the Anatolians could not provide quantities of tin, the metal needed to make true bronze, so they and others in the area had to import this metal from mines in Afghanistan, Tajikistan, and Uzbekistan.

Mounds of slag discovered around the Anatolian mines indicate that copper ores were not only dug out at these sites, but they were also smelted there in kilns, using firewood from nearby forests, and the relatively pure copper that resulted was poured into molds to form ingots that could be readily transported and sold.

There is little available information about the men who worked at these mines, but we can assume that this unpleasant and sometimes dangerous work was mostly handled by slaves or coerced laborers, while the processing of the ores was supervised by skilled craftsmen. Since Anatolian copper was sought by people throughout the ancient Near East, control of these mines was highly coveted, and though the Hittites flourished while they possessed the copper mines, they were eventually seized by the Assyrian empire, a loss that contributed to the eventual collapse of the Hittite empire.

The mining activities of ancient Egypt are better documented. Although they would have preferred to have mines near the Nile River, they could not find the metals they desired there, so the Egyptians turned to the deserts of Sinai in the East, and Nubia in the south, where there were rich deposits of copper, gold, and silver as well as precious stones like turquoise. Unlike the Anatolians, who worked in their mines throughout the year, the Egyptians did not wish to constantly endure the heat and harsh conditions of their desert mines, so these were mined only when there was a need for some material, and only during times of the year when the weather was more tolerable. Mining, in other words, was carried out by specific expeditions, usually ordered by the pharaoh and supervised by a general, though individual temples would sometimes mount their own, smaller expeditions if they required a certain metal.

We have detailed information about these mining operations because their commanders began by making elaborate plans, which were then carved in stone near an entrance to the mines. After estimating how many people would be needed, he would first gather his personnel. Some soldiers would come along to protect the valuable metals from thieves as they were extracted from the mines and transported back to the Nile River. Convicted criminals, prisoners of war, and other slaves would be responsible for most of the hard work, though entire families of peasants might have been recruited to assist in certain activities, and experienced artisans and metalworkers would handle the processing of the ore. The commander would also need to bring sufficient food and supplies to sustain the miners during the months they would be working.

Once everyone reached the site of the mine, the first priority was to dig a well, so there would be enough water; the people would also need to build some mud-brick huts to live in, effectively establishing a temporary village near the mine. To earn the support of the gods, they would set up shrines to honor Hathor, the goddess of miners, or Amun-Ra, the sun god, since gold was considered his flesh. Then the actual mining could begin. If the metal being mined was gold, the supervisors would locate the veins of quartz that contained the gold and begin digging narrow underground galleries, following the veins. The miners would then enter the passages, carrying their tools—usually, stone axes and chisels—along with oil lamps, to help them see in the darkness, and pots of water to drink. Conditions inside the mines were so stuffy that the men may have taken off their clothing to work. The miners would first break off chunks of ore, leaving them on the ground to be picked up by small boys, who could better navigate through the narrow galleries. After the rocks were carried outside, they would be heated over a fire to make them more brittle. Next, male and female workers would smash the stones into pebbles with stone hammers; then they would place them in mills to reduce them to dust. Finally, the dust was laid out on a table with grooves and rinsed with water, so that the sand would be washed away while the gold fell into the grooves. In mining areas where water was scarce, however, the dust would have to be transported to the Nile River to be washed in this fashion. While most Egyptian gold was obtained in this fashion, some gold was also garnered through a unique system of panning: river sand would be placed in a fleece bag, water would be poured into the bag, and after it was shaken and drained, bits of gold would stick to the fleece.

The Egyptians also mined copper, in much the same manner as the Anatolians, though they used open fires to heat the metal instead of kilns; still, the relatively meager supplies in the Sinai Desert required them to import much of their copper. This was also where they obtained semiprecious stones like turquoise and emeralds; the miners would find a promising site and cut out underground galleries, with the roofs supported by special pillars. They then allowed water to flow into the galleries to wash out the turquoise and emeralds.

NEW GOLD FROM OLD MINES

Egypt was envied throughout the ancient world because it possessed so much gold, extracted from mines in the Sinai Desert and Nubia. One might imagine that, over the course of 3,000 years, the Egyptians would have mined all of the available gold in their region. Yet a modern company, Pharaoh Gold Mines, began looking for Egyptian gold in 1995, and after it was taken over by another company, Centamin, in 1999, its efforts paid off when Centamin opened the first modern Egyptian gold mine in 2009. To date, this mine has produced over 500,000 ounces of gold.

MINORS AS MINERS

The ancient Egyptians often employed young boys in the mines, in part because they could easily fit through their narrow passages, and they thought nothing of subjecting children to the harsh conditions there. Much later, in nineteenth-century Europe and America, the burgeoning demand for coal forced many children to work as miners, until outcries over their appalling working conditions led to bans on such child labor. To this day, however, there are places in South America, Africa, and Asia where children are still working in mines, despite vigorous efforts to outlaw such employment throughout the world.

To a limited extent, the Egyptians also mined tin, lead, and iron, which could be found in Upper Egypt and Nubia.

Mining was undoubtedly arduous and unappealing labor, but it was not without its enjoyable moments; several mines are filled with playful graffiti—pictures of animals and tools—showing that the miners had time for leisurely diversions from their work. Also, the seasonal nature of Egyptian mining meant that people only had to endure the rigors of mining for a limited time before they could return to their homelands. Much later, after Alexander the Great had established a dynasty of pharaohs of Greek descent, the situation was very different, if we are to trust the reports of the Greek historian Diodorus, who visited the Egyptian mines in the first century BCE. While the process of mining remained largely the same, it was now done constantly, regardless of the weather, and it was solely carried out by convicts and slaves, kept in chains and cruelly forced to labor by the foreign soldiers who guarded them until the poor workers collapsed and died. Yet some believe that Diodorus was exaggerating the misery of the Egyptian miners, perhaps due to his awareness that the Greeks themselves had also treated the slaves in their silver mines very harshly. Still, whether their working conditions were benign or torturous, the miners of ancient Egypt hopefully recognized that they were making an important contribution to the artwork and prosperity of their country, which for many today is virtually defined by the gleaming gold and copper artifacts now displayed in museums throughout the world.

Further Reading
Dercksen, Jan Gerrit. 1996. *The Old Assyrian Copper Trade in Anatolia.* Leiden, The Netherlands, and Istanbul, Turkey: The Netherlands Historical-Archaeological Institute.

Esmael, Feisal A., and Majlis al-A'lá lil-Āthār, editors. 1996. *Proceedings of the First International Conference on Ancient Egyptian Mining and Metallurgy and Conservation of Metallic Artifacts.* Cairo: Ministry of Culture, Supreme Council on Antiquities.

Klemm, Rosemarie, and Dietrich Klemm. 2013. *Gold and Gold Mining in Ancient Egypt and Nubia: Geoarchaeology of the Ancient Gold Mining Sites in the Egyptian and Sudanese Eastern Deserts.* Translated by Paul Larsen. Berlin and New York: Springer.

Moorey, P. R. S. 1994. *Ancient Mesopotamian Materials and Technology: The Archaeological Evidence.* Oxford and New York: Oxford University Press.

Nicholson, Paul T., and Ian Shaw, editors. 2000. *Ancient Egyptian Materials and Technology.* Cambridge: Cambridge University Press.

Yener, K. Ashilan. 2000. *The Domestication of Metals: The Rise of Complex Metal Industries in Anatolia.* Leiden, The Netherlands, and Boston: Brill.

Document

From Diodorus. C. 60 BCE. *Diodorus of Sicily.* 12 volumes. Translated by C. H. Oldfather. 1935. Cambridge, MA: Harvard University Press.

In this passage, the Greek historian Diodorus describes conditions in Egyptian mines around 70 BCE, which were presumably similar to the conditions in earlier eras, though some believe that he exaggerated the harshness and cruelty of the miners' treatment.

At the extremity of Egypt and in the contiguous territory of both Arabia and Ethiopia there lies a region which contains many large gold mines, where the gold is secured in great quantities with much suffering and at great expense. For the earth is naturally black and contains seams and veins of a marble which is unusually white and in brilliancy surpasses everything else which shines brightly by its nature, and here the overseers of the labour in the mines recover the gold with the aid of a multitude of workers. For the kings of Egypt gather together and condemn to the mining of the gold such as have been found guilty of some crime and captives of war, as well as those who have been accused unjustly and thrown into prison because of their anger, and not only such persons but occasionally all their relatives as well, by this means not only inflicting punishment upon those found guilty but also securing at the same time great revenues from their labours. And those who have been condemned in this way—and they are a great multitude and are all bound in chains—work at their task unceasingly both by day and throughout the entire night, enjoying no respite and being carefully cut off from any means of escape; since guards of foreign soldiers who speak a language different from theirs stand watch over them, so that not a man, either by conversation or by some contact of a friendly nature, is able to corrupt one of his keepers. The gold-bearing earth which is hardest they first burn with a hot fire, and when they have crumbled it in this way they continue the working of it by hand; and the soft rock which can yield to moderate effort is crushed with a sledge by myriads of unfortunate wretches. And the entire operations are in charge of a skilled worker who distinguishes the stone and points it out to the labourers; and of those who are assigned to this unfortunate task the physically strongest break the quartz-rock with iron hammers, applying no skill to the task, but only force, and cutting tunnels through the stone, not in a straight line but wherever the seam of gleaming rock may lead. Now these men, working in darkness as they do because of the bending and winding of the passages, carry lamps bound on their foreheads; and since much of the time they change the position of their bodies to follow the particular character of the stone they throw the blocks, as they cut them out, on the ground; and at this task they labour without ceasing beneath the sternness and blows of an overseer.

The boys there who have not yet come to maturity, entering through the tunnels into the galleries formed by the removal of the rock, laboriously gather up the rock as it is cast down piece by piece and carry it out into the open to the place outside the entrance. Then those who are above thirty years of age take this quarried stone from them and with iron pestles pound a specified amount of it in stone mortars, until they have worked it down to the size of a vetch. Thereupon the women and older men receive from them the rock of this size and cast it into mills of which a number stand there in a row, taking their places in groups of two or three at the spoke or handle of each mill they grind it until they have worked down the amount given them to the consistency of the finest flour. And since no opportunity is afforded any of them to care for his body and they have no garment to cover their shame, no man can look upon the unfortunate wretches without feeling pity for them because of the exceeding hardships they suffer. For no leniency or respite of any kind is given to any man who is sick, or maimed, or aged, or in the case of a woman for her weakness, but all without exception are compelled by blows to persevere in their labours, until through ill-treatment they die in the midst of their tortures. Consequently the poor unfortunates believe, because their punishment is so excessively severe, that the future will always be more terrible than the present and therefore look forward to death as more to be desired than life. . . .

Officials

The rise of large, centralized governments in Mesopotamia and Egypt inevitably created a need for new sorts of leadership positions: kings and emperors could no longer manage their innumerable responsibilities alone, so tasks had to be delegated to subordinates; and vast areas could only be managed by dividing them into separate administrative units under the control of local officials with a degree of autonomy.

Further, the important work of governance could not be entrusted solely to friends or relatives who may lack the required knowledge and skills; only well-trained, qualified individuals would suffice. Thus, there arose a unique human invention, the bureaucracy, consisting of a hierarchy of appointed officials.

The first Mesopotamian bureaucracies arose in their large temples, and there remained some overlap between religious and secular administration, as priests in the city-states often handled governmental duties as well. They were initially supervised by the local kings, but as city-states were absorbed into larger empires, the officials came under the control of governors appointed by the emperor. Their responsibilities included maintaining employee records, collecting taxes, overseeing construction projects, and resolving legal disputes. One official had the surprising title of "barber": such a worker had initially garnered some power because, by cutting hair in a certain way, he could determine whether a man was regarded as a free man or a slave; later, he took on other roles, including smashing tablets that recorded outdated laws. Another official, the "herald," represented the ancient equivalent of a press secretary: by speaking in public, he provided citizens with information about government policies, and he also, for some reason, supervised the sales of homes. As international relations became more important to these developing states, kings appointed ambassadors who were sent to foreign countries, temporarily or permanently, and authorized them to negotiate on behalf of their governments.

It was the ancient Egyptians, however, who gradually mastered the art of establishing and maintaining a complex bureaucracy. The pharaoh was the supreme authority over all aspects of government, but much of its day-to-day business was handled by his chief subordinate, the *vizier*, who was usually a scribe who had risen through the ranks. During a typical day, the vizier would receive reports from his subordinates, hold personal meetings with the pharaoh and the treasurer, and listen to petitioners with problems to be resolved. In addition to supervising other officials, viziers were personally responsible for some important tasks like repairing dikes, measuring the water levels of the Nile River, and conducting the census; his seal was also required upon all legal documents. In some eras, there were two separate viziers governing Upper Egypt and Lower Egypt.

Since viziers had great power and worked closely with the pharaohs, a vizier could sometimes become the pharaoh himself if his pharaoh died without a clear heir; in one well-known case, the vizier to the pharaoh Tutankhamun (ca. 1341–1323 BCE), Ay (died ca. 1319 BCE), briefly served as pharaoh after Tutankhamun died at a young age with no children. Scholars even believe that one vizier who became a pharaoh, Amenemhet I (died 1962 BCE), obtained that position by leading a coup to overthrow his predecessor, Mentuhotep III (died 1998 BCE), and there are recurring suspicions that Ay killed Tutankhamun in order to seize the throne.

We can obtain a vivid picture of a vizier's life from the tomb of Rekhmire (died ca. 1410 BCE), who served as the vizier to Thutmose III (died 1425 BCE) and his son Amenhotep II (died 1401 BCE). The wall illustrations show Rekhmire performing various duties: passing judgment on some men who had not paid their taxes; receiving gifts from foreign visitors, including jewels, vases, chariots, and animals like elephants and panthers; and examining some craftsmen at work, such as carpenters, sculptors, and potters. There are also images of his wife and three sons, and a lengthy inscription listing his numerous responsibilities. The magnificence of his tomb indicates that he was a talented and respected official; however, since he was never buried in the tomb he prepared, some believe that he later fell out of favor and was removed from office before his death.

Underneath the vizier were a variety of other officials. The priests of the temples were theoretically his subordinates, though they did enjoy some special privileges, like freedom from taxes. Of the other lesser officials, all former scribes, the most important one was the treasurer, who supervised taxation and met with the vizier every day. There were also the overseer of the granaries, who managed Egypt's agricultural products; the overseer of cattle, who kept track of the pharaoh's herds; the steward, who was responsible for managing the pharaoh's properties; and the chamberlain, who was in charge of the palace. There were many other officials with different titles, who each maintained their own personal staffs. Some officials

This scene from the tomb of the pharaoh Tutankhamun shows his vizier Ay presiding over the important "opening of the mouth" ceremony at Tutankhamun's funeral in 1323 BCE, allowing the pharaoh to continue eating and drinking after his death. (Corel)

had several different titles, sometimes suggesting that they performed both priestly and governmental duties; though some suspect that these multiple titles were largely honorific, some officials probably did supervise multiple departments, having demonstrated their administrative abilities. For example, the favorite of the pharaoh Hatshepsut (1508–1458 BCE), Senenmut (ca. fourteenth century BCE), is primarily known as her royal architect, but his other titles indicate that he also performed religious duties as a priest, managed her estates, controlled the storehouses, and was even responsible for tutoring her children.

In addition to the central government, there were local officials who, in the early days of ancient Egypt, effectively became independent authorities, maintaining their own armies and contributing to the collapse of the Old Kingdom. Pharaohs in the Middle Kingdom and thereafter, however, divided Egypt into forty-two districts, called *nomes*, and appointed the officials who governed them, the *nomarchs*, keeping them under their firm control. Their principal responsibilities included maintaining the irrigation canals that were essential to Egyptian agriculture and collecting taxes to be sent to the central government.

In some cases, the Egyptian government functioned as a true meritocracy, as there are many recorded cases of men from humble backgrounds who rose to positions of great authority. However, over time, most positions tended to become hereditary: officials would have their sons trained as scribes, then hire them as their assistants, and train them to perform all of their duties. When the officials died or retired, their sons naturally assumed their jobs, and were soon preparing their own sons to be their successors. In the later eras

SUSPECTED SUCCESSORS

Because Tutankhamun's vizier Ay succeeded him as pharaoh and later married his wife, some scholars speculated that he murdered the young pharaoh to usurp his position. Yet Ay long served both Tutankhamun's father Akenhaten (died 1336 BCE) and Tutankhamun himself as an apparently loyal and effective official, casting doubt on the notion that he would suddenly turn traitor. Perhaps, though, subordinates who replace a dead leader may always be subject to such rumors. For example, ever since President John F. Kennedy was assassinated in 1963, many have asserted that his successor, Lyndon Johnson, must have been involved in his death, although no evidence has emerged to support the theory.

OFFICIAL LOVERS

The female Pharaoh Hatshepsut was frequently observed in the company of her most trusted official, Senenmut, and this led some of her citizens to gossip that he was actually her lover. Throughout history, other female rulers who depended upon male subordinates have faced similar suspicions. A few people have attempted to argue, for example, that England's Queen Elizabeth I had passionate affairs with courtiers Robert Devereux and Walter Raleigh, and that Russia's Catherine the Great enjoyed a long romance with statesman Grigory Potemkin. However, while most historians believe that Catherine and Potemkin were actually intimate, the theories about Elizabeth I are not generally accepted.

of Egyptian history, even the viziers were increasingly the sons of previous viziers; Rekhmire, for example, was the grandson and nephew of two of his predecessors. As another typical consequence of an entrenched bureaucracy, evidence suggests that the numbers of officials kept growing, as more and more things were discovered to keep them busy.

Many members of this expanding corps of officials undoubtedly did their work efficiently and honestly, but some of them must have been corrupt, as suggested by one popular story. A farmer, Khun-Anup, is traveling to sell his grain and passes by the home of an official named Nemtynakht, who decides to seize

his possessions. He forces Khun-Anup to take his donkeys close to a barley field, and when one donkey eats some barley, he uses this "crime" as a pretext to beat the farmer and take all his goods. Khun-Anup then approaches Nemtynakht's supervisor and complains so eloquently that he is eventually awarded all of the official's property. In reality, it seems very unlikely that a humble peasant would actually prevail in such a dispute, but this story must have struck a chord with ancient Egyptians because they were keenly aware of officials like Nemtynakht who were abusing their authority to enrich themselves.

Even without ill-gotten gains, Egyptian officials enjoyed good lives, as they received high salaries, never had to engage in hard physical labor, and were well prepared for the afterlife; examinations of mummies indicate that, overall, they lived much happier and healthier lives than the peasants whose lives they oversaw. Their tomb inscriptions also convey that they felt a genuine sense of satisfaction from the ways that their actions benefited Egyptian society and fully expected the gods to reward them for their exemplary service. And certainly, even if they sometimes made mistakes or failed to meet high moral standards, ancient Egypt could never have prospered and grown as it did without the hard work and dedication of its innumerable officials.

Further Reading

Garcia, Juan Carlos Moreno, editor. 2013. *Ancient Egyptian Administration*. Leiden, The Netherlands: Brill.

Grajetski, Wolfram. 2009. *Court Officials of the Egyptian Middle Kingdom*. London: Duckworth.

Postgate, J.N. 1992. *Early Mesopotamia: Society and Economy at the Dawn of History*. London and New York: Routledge.

Watanabe, Kazuko, editor. 1999. *Priests and Officials in the Ancient Near East: Papers of the Second Colloquium on the Ancient Near East—Its City and Its Life*. Heidelberg, Germany: Universitätsverlag C. Winter.

Wenke, Robert J. 2009. *The Ancient Egyptian State: The Origins of Egyptian Culture (c. 8000–2000 BC)*. Cambridge and New York: Cambridge University Press.

Wilcke, Claus. 2007. *Early Ancient Near Eastern Law: A History of Its Beginnings: The Early Dynastic and Sargonic Periods*. Revised edition. Winona Lake, IN: Eisenbrauns.

Document

From Breasted, James Henry, editor and translator. 1906. *Ancient Records of Egypt: Historical Documents from the Earliest Times to the Persian Conquest.* Volume II. Chicago: University of Chicago Press.

An inscription in the tomb of Rekhmire, who served as vizier to the pharaoh Thutmose III, provides a valuable overview of the responsibilities of the position. However, since the text is not complete, and at times difficult to understand, the description below, by its translator James Henry Breasted, conveys its contents more clearly.

This, the most important inscription known on the organization of the state under the Eighteenth Dynasty, is unfortunately incomplete. Two duplicates found by Newberry fill out many of the lacunae, but the last fifth of the text is very fragmentary. This is especially unfortunate, as the latter part of the inscription is by far the most intelligible and deals with functions easily understood.

The inscription is an outline of the duties of the vizier, of the greatest interest. After prescribing the external arrangements for the vizier's daily sitting in his "hall," as his office is termed, the document proceeds to the daily conference of the vizier with the king, and, immediately subsequent to this, the daily reports of the chief treasurer and the vizier to each other, and of the chief officials to the vizier. These daily duties are now followed by a long list of exceedingly varied functions to be discharged by the vizier, making in all at least thirty. There seems to be no logical order in the enumeration, and the varied character of the list will be evident from a reading of the marginal heads, which may serve in lieu of a table of content here. It will be seen that the vizier is grand steward of all Egypt, and that all the activities of the state are under his control. He has general oversight of the treasury, and the chief treasurer reports to him; he is chief justice, or head of the judiciary; he is chief of police, both for the residence city and the kingdom; he is minister of war, both for army and navy; he is secretary of the interior and of agriculture, while all general executive functions of state, with many that may not be classified, are incumbent upon him. There is, indeed, no prime function of the state which does not operate through his office. He is a veritable Joseph, and it must be this office which the Hebrew writer has in mind in the story of Joseph. The only person other than the king to whom he owes any respect is the chief treasurer, to whom he seems to offer a daily statement that all is well with the royal possessions. Such power is, of course, possible only in a highly centralized state, and Egypt is shown by this inscription to be in the Empire simply a vast estate of the Pharaoh, of which the vizier is chief steward.

Painters

Even before the dawn of civilization, people wanted a variety of colors in their everyday lives, and hence they searched for natural substances that could be turned into different shades of paint, first applying them to the walls of caves and later to everyday objects like pots and furniture. The citizens of early civilizations similarly loved to fill their world with painted designs and images. Unfortunately, unlike their stone statues and metal ornaments, their paint often faded with time, so that we often associate ancient times with stark, unadorned structures and artifacts when in fact these were originally brightly colored with paint.

The people of ancient Assyria were fond of painting their walls with realistic images of people and animals; sometimes, they painted directly on the bricks, while at other times they would cover the walls with plaster before painting them. Some lucky individuals have observed and described these paintings when they were first excavated, but they usually disappear within a week after they are exposed to the air, so we have few very examples of these illustrations, though efforts have been made to reconstruct what they looked like. The Assyrians made their paints from available minerals; for example, tin oxide provided white paint, blue came from copper oxide or lapis lazuli, iron produced a dark brown, and copper yielded green paint. In addition to walls, Assyrian statues were also painted, and bricks were sometimes provided with colorful geometric designs.

The wall paintings that fill Egyptian tombs are better known, because many of them have survived for millennia and are still being admired by tourists today. From the beginning, the images were governed by strict artistic conventions that were maintained for centuries, in part because depictions of people and places often had religious significance. Since the pharaoh was considered a living god, for example, he had to be depicted as a young, muscular man with broad shoulders and a slender waist; one simply could not show a god as old and frail. The pharaoh could only be shown in stiff, dignified poses, and he and his wife were sometimes drawn disproportionately larger than other people in the scene to convey their special importance. As a sign of respect, the people around the pharaoh would be painted standing in neat rows, with all of their feet pointing in one direction. Since the people and places in tomb paintings purportedly had the power to come to life and serve the pharaoh in the afterlife, they had to be shown completely, even if it would result in an odd-looking illustration. For example, paintings of pools incongruously show the fish on top of the water because, in a realistically painted pool, the fish would be invisible under the water; yet it was important to depict the fish in the painting so that when the pool materialized in the afterlife, the deceased could enjoy a pool that contained fish. It was also standard to show human figures with their bodies facing the viewer but their heads turned in profile, allowing the people to see in all directions and thus guard against dangers. Colors were employed to signify a figure's status: gods and goddesses were often given gold, green, or blue skin; men had reddish-brown skin; and women had lighter olive complexions.

Only in depicting lowly figures like craftsmen and animals did painters enjoy a certain amount of freedom, so that these paintings tend to be more lively and variegated. Some excellent examples of such artwork are observed in the tomb of an official of the Eighteenth Dynasty named Menna (ca. 1400 BCE). One panel shows Menna and his family hunting; another depicts farmers harvesting their crops; and there is an energetic scene of birds in flight, a perched bird being approached by a cat, and a large rodent climbing a reed of papyrus. One imagines that these sorts of projects, that did not require adherence to rigid patterns, were especially enjoyable for their artists.

To produce their images, the Egyptian painters used sticks of fibrous wood that were struck repeatedly at one end or chewed to produce bristles; a different brush was used for each shade of paint. Their wall paintings sometimes involved the work of stonemasons, who carved raised figures to be painted, but the composition of some stone walls made such sculpting impossible; in those cases, the walls were left flat and covered with a plaster made from gypsum, chalk, or clay. However, the painters waited for the plaster to dry before applying paint, so that one cannot describe their works as frescoes, though some commentators have employed this term. Images might first be sketched on pieces of stone or wooden boards, as shown by a few surviving examples of such preliminary artwork, and papyrus might have been used as well. A gridwork, applied to both the preliminary drawing and the wall, allowed artists to accurately transfer their designs. The process involved two teams of painters: some would first draw black outlines of figures on the walls, while others would later fill the outlined areas with paint. A few tomb paintings seem to indicate that novices might have been entrusted with some of the painting, but their work was always reviewed and sometimes corrected by experienced artists.

The Egyptian painters probably mixed their paints on the spot, combining powdered minerals with substances like beeswax, gum arabic, and egg whites on their palettes. Carbon was used for black paint; gypsum provided white; a mineral called azurite was initially used to make blue, though painters later employed calcium copper silicate; malachite produced green; yellow ocher yielded yellow; and iron oxide made red and brown. Some colors required two minerals: gray came from mixing gypsum and charcoal, and pink was produced by mixing gypsum and red ocher. To paint within tombs, the painters required light from oil lamps or torches, but they were careful to remove unsightly smoke marks from the ceilings before departing.

During the reign of the pharaoh Akenhaten (died 1336 BCE), an entirely new style of artwork was introduced, often described as Amarna art after the name of Akenhaten's capital, and while its effects are primarily noted in the period's sculptures and reliefs, it can be observed in paintings as well. These illustrations display a new willingness to depict figures realistically, as shown by images of Akenhaten's pot belly and a charming scene of his two daughters sitting and

GUIDELINES FOR PAINTING

Paintings on the walls of pharaohs' tombs could never be improvised on the spot; instead, careful plans were prepared, a gridwork was placed over the sketches, and the designs were transferred by placing a similar gridwork on the walls. This has remained a recommended technique for important projects; it is believed, for example, that the Renaissance artist Michelangelo painted the Sistine Chapel by applying his planned images to the ceiling using a gridwork. And to this day, neophyte portrait artists are advised to begin with a smaller drawing within a gridwork before shifting to their canvasses.

A FAMOUS SHADE OF BLUE

Egyptian painters produced the world's first synthetic pigment, Egyptian blue, using a complex method described by the Roman author Vitruvius: "Sand and the flowers of natron are brayed together so finely that the product is like meal, and copper is grated by means of coarse files over the mixture, like sawdust, to form a conglomerate. Then it is made into balls [and] put in an earthern jar, and the jars in an oven. As soon as the copper and the sand grow hot. . . . [T]hey are reduced to a blue colour." This powder, which yields a distinctive and long-lasting pigment, is still sold to painters today.

relaxing. The most famous piece of art from this era, the famous bust of Nefertiti (ca. 1370–1330 BCE), is generally heralded as a magnificent piece of sculpture, but much of its beauty stems from the way that the woman's face, eyebrows, eyes, and lips were delicately painted. However, because this novel approach to portraiture was linked to the heretical religion that Akenhaten promoted, it was abandoned after his death, and artists returned to their traditional styles. Egyptian art did not really change again until late in its history, when the conquest of Alexander the Great brought Greek artists and artworks to the region, which had some influence on the Egyptian painters.

While the Egyptian painters are best known for their tomb illustrations, they were called upon to decorate a wide variety of objects, including statues, pots, chairs, columns, and the floors of palaces, which might be painted blue to resemble a pond while the ceiling was painted like the nighttime sky. Royal

coffins were elaborately painted; the exteriors were painted to resemble the walls of houses, while the interiors were filled with images of the food and possessions that the deceased would need in the afterlife. Many examples of Egyptian pottery are attractively decorated with Egypt's distinctive blue paint, and the tomb of Tutankhamun (ca. 1341–1323 BCE) includes a wooden chest painted with scenes of the pharaoh riding his chariot into battle. The discoverer of that tomb, Howard Carter, even anticipated that the chest would "probably rank as one of the greatest artistic treasures of the tomb."

The circumstances of their employment are not entirely clear, but it is assumed that most painters worked for pharaohs and other nobles, focusing most of their energies on palaces and tombs; however, temples and wealthy individuals were occasionally allowed to borrow their services for their own projects. Painting was doubtless one of many skills passed through families from generation to generation, or taught to talented outsiders. There are no indications that any painters ever attained the prestige of architects or sculptors, but some painters were undoubtedly known and appreciated by their royal masters, and most of them probably enjoyed their work.

Further Reading

Albenda, Pauline. 2005. *Ornamental Wall Painting in the Art of the Assyrian Empire*. Leiden, The Netherlands, and Boston: Brill.

Davies, W. V., editor. 2001. *Colour and Painting in Ancient Egypt*. London: British Museum Press.

Robins, Gay. 1997. *The Art of Ancient Egypt*. Cambridge, MA: Harvard University Press.

Robins, Gay. 1994. *Proportion and Style in Ancient Egyptian Art*. Austin: University of Texas Press.

Tiradritti, Francesco. 2002. *Ancient Egypt: Art, Architecture, and History*. Translated by Phil Goddard. 2002. London: British Museum.

Tiradritti, Francesco. 2007. *Egyptian Wall Painting*. Translated by Marguerite Shore. 2007. New York: Abbeville Press Publishers.

Documents

From Rawlinson, George. 1882. *History of Ancient Egypt*. Volume 1. Boston: S. E. Cassino.

This Egyptologist is generally not impressed with the artistry of Egyptian painters, although he does acknowledge their useful work and praises their command of their tools.

Egyptian painting was far inferior to Egyptian sculpture; and it may be questioned whether the Egyptian painter ought to be regarded as an artist in the true sense of the word. It was his principal business to add brilliancy to walls and ceilings, either by coloring them in patterns, or by painting in a conventional way the reliefs and hieroglyphics with which they had been adorned by the sculptor. Still, occasionally, he seems to have been called upon to produce pictures in the modern sense, as, for instance, portraits, and figures of men or animals. Of the portraits we have no specimens; but it is not likely that they had much merit. Outlines of men and animals occur in unfinished tombs, boldly and clearly drawn, as a guide to the chisel of the sculptor. We have also some representations of painters at work upon animal forms, from which it would appear that they must have possessed great steadiness of hand and power over the pencil. The painter seems to have held his pot of color in his left hand, while with his right, which he did not support in any way, he painted the animal. A similar absence of support is observable when painters are employed in coloring statues. When the artist was engaged in any complicated work, instead of a single paint-pot, he made use of a palette. This was ordinarily a rectangular piece of wood, porcelain, or alabaster, containing a number of round depressions or "wells," for holding the various colors. Palettes are found with as many as eleven or twelve of these cavities, which indicate the employment of at least eleven or twelve different tints. The cakes of paint, which filled the cavities, were moistened at the time of use, with a mixture of water and gum arable. The painter used slabs and mullers for grinding his colors.

From Erman, Adolf. 1894. *Life in Ancient Egypt*. Translated by Helen Mary Tirard. 1894. London and New York: Macmillan and Company.

In this passage, Erman, a nineteenth-century Egyptologist, describes the first Egyptian paintings that endeavored to portray soldiers in battle realistically.

Ramses II gave the artists who had to perpetuate his deeds a yet harder task to perform. They had not only to show in half-symbolic manner the king and his foes, but faithfully and historically to portray for posterity special events in real battles. We cannot be surprised that the execution of these pictures is far behind the conception. Many details are however quite worthy of our admiration—for instance, there is a dying horse which is excellently drawn; a representation of camp-life that is full of humour, but there is no attempt at unity of composition. Again and again we may see soldiers marching and soldiers formed in square, enemies who have been shot and enemies drowning, chariots attacking and chariots at rest, yet no uniform picture. The fine contrast also between the Pharaoh storming forward, and the king of the Cheta hesitating in the midst of his troops, which occurs in the most extensive of these pictures, does not impress us much in the midst of all this confusion of detail

It was, nevertheless, a great step in advance for Egyptian art when these battle pictures, and the smaller representations of like nature and style, were admitted into the official cycle of pictures. . . .

Pharaohs

Many great empires had traditions of strong, hereditary rulers who displayed impressive wealth and elaborate regalia; but none have garnered as much attention as the pharaohs of ancient Egypt, who stood out for several reasons. Other kings and emperors claimed to govern with the approval of the gods, but pharaohs were uniquely regarded as living gods themselves, imbuing them with a special aura of authority over both governmental and religious matters. The men (and occasional women) that we call pharaohs (though the Egyptians long used another title, *nisu*) controlled Egypt almost continuously for 3,000 years, from the very beginning of civilization to the dawn of the Christian era, and their habit of entombing themselves in enormous structures, or buried treasure troves of golden artifacts, served to keep their memories alive, along with monuments they erected that boasted of their accomplishments.

Pharaohs usually obtained their position through inheritance, though there were many cases of usurpers who seized power when there was no clear heir; these men would typically marry a member of the deposed royal family so they could bolster their legitimacy by connecting themselves to royalty. Even a pharaoh with an undisputed claim to the throne often chose a sister as one of his wives, knowing such a union would unfailingly produce children of pure royal blood. When a new pharaoh was only a child, a member of his family would govern as a regent until he became an adult; this was the way that a few women, like Hatshepsut (1508–1458 BCE), were able to become pharaohs themselves.

The opulent goods found in royal tombs suggest that pharaohs enjoyed lives of luxury, but their lofty positions also required a great deal of daily labor. First, before they appeared in public, pharaohs would first have to don a wig, a pleated kilt, a belt displaying their personal symbol or cartouche, and a heavy necklace; for ceremonial occasions, they would also wear the double crown, signifying their rule of Upper and Lower Egypt, and an artificial beard. The Greek historian Diodorus, who claimed to have researched the records kept by Egyptian priests, reported that rigid regulations governed all of a pharaoh's activities; in the morning, after bathing and dressing, there was a fixed time to review his correspondence, followed by a meeting with a priest to hear prayers and homilies. Then he followed a daily schedule of holding audiences with officials and foreign dignitaries and reaching decisions on issues brought to his attention, though he had some free time to do as he please. The tomb paintings of the pharaoh Akhenaten (died 1336 BCE), who allowed himself to be portrayed with unusual realism, show him relaxing with his wife and playing with his children.

While Egyptian pharaohs are usually depicted at work—riding in battle or presiding over ceremonies—this carved image of the pharaoh Akhenaten, dating from 1345 BCE, unusually shows an Egyptian pharaoh relaxing, enjoying some private time with his wife Nefertiti and children. (Ruggero Vanni/Corbis)

While there were regularly ceremonies to perform and matters that required the pharaoh's personal attention, the Egyptian bureaucracy could generally handle the daily business of governing, so pharaohs could focus much of their energy on projects of their choice. Many of the early pharaohs like Khufu (died 2566 BCE), also known as Cheops, were great builders, overseeing the construction of massive pyramids and temples; some pharaohs like Thutmose III (died 1425 BCE) functioned primarily as generals, leading military campaigns to expand the boundaries of their empire; and a few pharaohs like Akhenaten were primarily preoccupied with religious duties. But almost all of them devoted a great deal of attention to preparing their tombs, both to glorify themselves and to ensure that they would have sufficient goods and services in the afterlife.

Pharaohs are commonly regarded as absolute rulers, but this was not always the case; toward the end of the Old Kingdom, local princes with their own armies gradually gained more and more power, eventually ushering in a period of political uncertainty. Later, during the New Kingdom, the high priests of Amun became a threat to the pharaoh's authority; some even believe that Akhenaten's controversial efforts to promote a new, monotheistic religion of worshiping the sun was partly inspired by his desire to reduce the priests' power. More broadly, Akhenaten's experience demonstrates that pharaohs were also limited by Egypt's strong traditions—for despite his vigorous efforts to promote his new beliefs, they were abandoned immediately after his death, and the nation's former religion was reestablished.

A man named Narmer (ca. thirty-first century BCE) is generally regarded as the first pharaoh, since he is credited with uniting Lower Egypt and Upper Egypt and becoming the first to rule over the entire country; yet little is known about Narmer or his immediate successors in the first three dynasties of pharaohs. The first major pharaoh, Snefru (ca. 2700 BCE), set a pattern for his successors in two ways: he was the first of the warrior pharaohs, using troops to gain territory in Syria and Nubia; and while previous pharaohs had built pyramids, Snefru was the first great pyramid builder, responsible for three pyramids that gradually perfected their design. Yet Snefru also garnered

a reputation as a wise and kindly ruler, as exemplified by a charming anecdote in the story "Khufu and the Magicians": he was purportedly boating in a lake in the company of his magician when one of the female rowers dropped her necklace into the water; sympathizing with her plight, Snefru promptly instructed his magician to drain the water from the lake so the necklace could be retrieved. Snefru's son Khufu also built a noteworthy pyramid, the first and tallest of the three great pyramids of Giza. The other two were built by Khufu's son Khafre (ca. 2570 BCE) and his grandson Menkaure (died ca. 2700 BCE).

There was nothing remarkable about the reigns of most of the pharaohs who are known to have ruled Egypt, but a few have commanded a great deal of attention from modern scholars. Djedefre (ca. 2575 BCE), Khufu's son and immediate successor, is usually overlooked because his brief reign produced only a pyramid that long ago collapsed, but a recent theory suggests that he, not his brother Khafre, actually built the Sphinx at Gaza, since its face resembles Djedefre more than Khafre. A pharaoh who ruled about a thousand years later, Hatshepsut, stands out because she not only served as the regent for her stepson and eventual successor Thutmose III, but she was also one of the few women who ruled in her own name as an Egyptian pharaoh, apparently with great success, since her two decades in power were distinguished by economic prosperity, numerous building projects, and a legendary expedition to the distant land of Punt (modern-day Ethiopia) to obtain valuable goods for her country. Tutankhamun (ca. 1341–1323 BCE), the son and successor of Akhenaten, accomplished little when he ruled Egypt for ten years before dying at the young age of nineteen, but his tomb uniquely was never looted, and its discovery in 1923 by Howard Carter brought to light innumerable treasures and mementos of his life, making him especially fascinating. In particular, there has been much speculation that the young pharaoh was murdered, perhaps by the elderly vizier Ay (died ca. 1319 BCE), who succeeded him as pharaoh and married his sister and wife against her will, since she wrote a very unusual letter to a foreign king asking him to provide her with a husband. Ramses II (ca. 1303–1213 BCE), generally regarded as the greatest pharaoh, ruled for seven decades, fathered

A MODERN PHARAOH

Ancient Egyptians, who regarded their pharaohs as living gods, apparently were not bothered by the absolute rule and luxurious lives of the men (and occasional women) who controlled their lives. Contemporary Egyptians, however, have a different attitude: their last monarch, King Farouk, was overthrown in 1952 due to widespread resentment of his excessive spending and corrupt government, and more recently, the first elected president of Egypt (in June 2012), Mohamed Morsi, quickly became unpopular because citizens thought he was exercising too much power, inspiring a military coup that removed him from office in July 2013. As the ultimate insult, Morsi was regularly denounced and caricatured as a modern-day "pharaoh."

KING TUT IS A HIT

Although his reign was brief and undistinguished, Tutankhamun became ancient Egypt's most renowned pharaoh after his intact tomb, filled with treasures, was discovered by Howard Carter in 1923. He has since become a celebrated figure in popular culture: in the 1960s, the *Batman* television series featured a villain named King Tut, a crazed Egyptologist who imagined himself to be the pharaoh's reincarnation, and in 1978, after comedian Steve Martin performed his song about Tutankhamun, "King Tut," on *Saturday Night Live*, the single became a Top Twenty hit. The video of Martin's memorable performance can still be seen on YouTube.

over a hundred children with various wives and concubines, led many military expeditions to distant realms, and built innumerable monuments and temples, including a renowned cliff-side temple at Abu Simbel, featuring four enormous statues of a sitting Ramses, that was carefully removed and reconstructed in the twentieth century when it was about to be flooded by the Aswan Dam. Finally, late in its history, several pharaohs of Greek descent ruled Egypt, most of them men named Ptolemy, but the dynasty ended with another female pharaoh, Cleopatra (69–30 BCE), who famously romanced the Roman leaders Julius Caesar and Marc Antony in an effort to maintain her nation's independence.

Even as the focus of recent scholarship has shifted to the lives of everyday Egyptian citizens, and not their rulers, the pharaohs remain objects of fascination to researchers, who continue striving to obtain more information about both the famous and obscure figures who governed the nation of Egypt for over 3,000 years. Their treasures draw millions of visitors to museum; their greatest monuments, like the Great Pyramids and the temple of Abu Simbel, attract steady streams of tourists; and for most people today, they still symbolize the wealth, grandeur, and mystery of ancient Egypt.

Further Reading

Baker, Darrell. 2008. *The Encyclopedia of the Egyptian Pharaohs: Volume 1: Predynastic through Twentieth Dynasty (3300–1069 BC)*. Oakville, CT: Bannerstone Press.

Clayton, Peter A. 1994. *Chronicle of the Pharaohs: The Reign-by-Reign Record of the Rulers and Dynasties of Ancient Egypt*. New York: Thames and Hudson.

Dodson, Aidan, and Dyan Hilton. 2004. *The Complete Royal Families of Ancient Egypt*. London and New York: Thames and Hudson.

Tyldesley, Joyce A. 2000. *The Private Lives of the Pharaohs*. New York: TV Books.

Vernus, Pascal, and Jean Yoyette. 2003. *The Book of the Pharaohs*. Translated by David Lorton. Ithaca, NY: Cornell University Press.

Ziegler, Christiane, editor. 2002. *The Pharaohs*. New York: Rizzoli.

Documents

From Breasted, James Henry, editor and translator. 1906. *Ancient Records of Egypt: Historical Documents from the Earliest Times to the Persian Conquest*. Volume IV. Chicago: University of Chicago Press.

In this selection from the Prayer of Ramses III (died 1155 BCE), the pharaoh describes a number of his activities undertaken on behalf of the gods, hoping to win their favor.

Hail to you, gods and goddesses, lords of heaven, earth, and the Nether World, great of foot in the barque of millions of years, by the side of your father, Re. . . I am your son whom your hands created, whom ye crowned as ruler. . . of every land. Ye wrought for me good things upon earth, that I might assume my office in peace.

Was not my heart constant in seeking out mighty benefactions, for your temples? I equipped them with great decrees, recorded in every hall of writings; with their people, their lands, their herds; with their galleys and ships upon the Nile. I restored their temples which formerly were in ruin. I founded for you divine offerings, as an increase of that which was before you. I wrought for you in the gold-houses, in gold, silver, lapis lazuli, and malachite. I made plans for your storehouses. I completed them with numerous possessions. I filled your granaries with barley and spelt, in heaps. I built for you houses and temples, carved with your name forever. I provided their serf-laborers, I filled them with numerous people. . . . I presented to you oblations before you, supplied with every good thing. I made for you storehouses for the "Feast of the Appearance"; I filled them with plentiful food. I made for you table-vessels of gold, silver, and copper by the hundred-thousand. I hewed your barges upon the Nile, bearing a "Great House," overlaid with gold. . . .

I did mighty deeds and benefactions, a numerous multitude, for the gods and goddesses of South and North. I wrought upon their images in the gold-houses, I built that which had fallen to ruin in their temples. I made houses and temples in their courts; I planted for them groves; I dug for them lakes; I founded for them divine offerings of barley and wheat, wine, incense, fruit, cattle, and fowl. I built the "Shadows of Re" for their districts, abiding, with divine offerings for every day. I made great decrees for the administration of their temples, recorded in the hall of writings forever. Behold, the list is before you, O gods and goddesses, that ye may know of the benefactions which I did for your ka's. . . .

From Haggard, H. Rider, and Andrew Lang. 1890. *The World's Desire*. London: Longmans, Green.

In this passage from the famed authors' novel, the disguised Odysseus enjoys a feast with the pharaoh and his wife, conveying the luxurious and ceremonial daily lives of the Egyptian monarchs. Haggard (1856—1925) was a popular adventure writer, and Lang (1844–1912) was a translator of Homer, and prominent folklorist and collector of fairy tales. Their story begins where Homer's Odyssey *ends.*

Trumpets blared as the Wanderer waited, drums rolled, and through the wide thrown curtains swept the lovely Meriamun and the divine Pharaoh Meneptah, with many lords and ladies of the Court, all crowned with roses and with lotus blooms.

The Queen was decked in Royal attire, her shining limbs were veiled in broidered silk; about her shoulders was a purple robe, and round her neck and arms were rings of well-wrought gold. She was stately and splendid to see, with pale brows and beautiful disdainful eyes where dreams seemed to sleep beneath the shadow of her eyelashes. On she swept in all her state and pride of beauty, and behind her came the Pharaoh. He was a tall man, but ill-made and heavy-browed, and to the Wanderer it seemed that he was heavy-hearted too, and that care and terror of evil to come were always in his mind.

Meriamun looked up swiftly.

"Greeting, Stranger," she said. "Thou comest in warlike guise to grace our feast."

"Methought, Royal Lady," he made answer, "that anon when I would have laid it by, this bow of mine sang to me of present war. Therefore I am come armed—even to thy feast."

"Has thy bow such foresight, Eperitus?" said the Queen. "I have heard but once of such a weapon, and that in a minstrel's tale. He came to our Court with his lyre from the Northern Sea, and he sang of the Bow of Odysseus."

"Minstrel or not, thou does well to come armed, Wanderer," said the Pharaoh; "for if thy bow sings, my own heart mutters much to me of war to be."

"Follow me, Wanderer, however it fall out," said the Queen.

So he followed her and the Pharaoh till they came to a splendid hall, carven round with images of fighting and feasting. Here, on the painted walls, Rameses Miamun drove the thousands of the Khita before his single valour; here men hunted wild-fowl through the marshes with a great cat for their hound. Never had the Wanderer beheld such a hall since he supped with the Sea King of the fairy isle. On the daïs, raised above the rest, sat the Pharaoh, and by him sat Meriamun the Queen, and by the Queen sat the Wanderer in the golden armour of Paris, and he leaned the black bow against his ivory chair.

Priests and Priestesses

The civilizations of the ancient Near East did not have any concept of the separation of church and state; rather, governments were closely connected to official religions, and they subsidized priests and priestesses who sometimes had secular responsibilities, while state officials might perform some religious duties. However, while rulers and bureaucrats were almost invariably male, religious doctrines sometimes stipulated that there should be priestesses as well as priests, and these positions provided a rare opportunity for women to achieve significant wealth and power.

In the Sumerian empire, for example, priests would serve goddesses, but priestesses served the gods. Each temple would have both a high priest and a high priestess who controlled staffs of other priests and priestesses as well as a variety of other workers, including guards, weavers, butlers, barbers, scribes, slaves, and treasurers. One special group of employees, the diviners, interpreted omens and made prophecies by slicing open and examining the livers or intestines of sacrificed animals. The chief task of the priests and priestesses was to tend to the temple's statues of the gods, who were treated like living beings. Each day, two lavish meals were placed before the statues for the gods to eat (although, since the statues never consumed their meals, they were later eaten by workers and their families); the statues also were regularly cleaned and covered with fresh clothes. Each statue also had a boat, used to transport the gods to visit other gods or another of their residences, and during religious festivals, the statues would be carried by temple workers through the streets of the city. The priests and priestesses also controlled vast estates engaged in agriculture, animal husbandry, carpentry, weaving, and other crafts, and while these activities brought them great wealth, they also performed charitable services, like lending barley to hungry families or providing homes for orphans.

The situation in ancient Israel, well documented in the Bible and other research, was rather different. Here, there was a tradition of exclusively male priests who inherited their positions by being members of the Levite tribe, the descendants of Moses's brother Aaron, described as the first priest. While priests tended to the holy sanctuaries or temples and supervised animal sacrifices, they were also called upon to promulgate religious doctrines and resolve personal disputes; some early priests became political leaders as well, like Samuel, who wore multiple hats as a priest, judge, prophet, and general, though later priests limited themselves to matters of religion. The priests of Israel were distinguished by their elaborate garments, including an ephod (or skirt), breastplate, robe, girdle, tunic, and crown. A priest could not have any

In this engraving, a nineteenth-century artist depicts the elaborate garments that a Jewish high priest of Ancient Israel would wear during a religious ceremony. (Steven Wynn Photography/iStockphoto.com)

visible physical defects, and he had to abide by certain rules: he was not allowed to have any contact with a dead body, for example, and if he married, his wife had to be a virgin.

The priests of Egypt were more like their counterparts in other Near East civilizations because, unlike the priests of Israel, they also commanded vast resources and exercised great authority over their society. And while a majority of the Egyptian priests were male, some female goddesses like Hathor were originally served by priestesses. By the time of the New Kingdom, however, it appears that priests were entirely male, although women still played some key roles: a noble woman would serve as the "God's Wife of Amun," and women would serve as the musicians who provided accompaniments to rituals. People became priests or priestesses in various ways: some inherited their positions from their fathers; some were appointed by the pharaoh; some were selected by a committee of priests; and a few were able to purchase their positions. Before they began their service, they received extensive training in the rituals and mysteries of the cult of their gods; they were also prepared to perform administrative duties, as they would be in charge of the temples, large expanses of land, and innumerable religious and secular workers. Finally, male priests were circumcised, and all of their body hair was shaven off, so they would be ritually clean as they served their gods.

Officially, the main responsibility of priests and priestesses was to tend to the needs of their god, represented by a statue, though much of the daily work was delegated to four teams of lay priests, who each served for three months of the year, feeding, clothing, decorating, and cleaning their gods. When they were not working in the temples, these lay priests usually held other jobs. We know a great deal about the rituals of caring for the god because they were frequently depicted on the walls of the temple. Each day, the chief priest would remove a seal on the god's chamber and, when the sun rose, remove the god's statue from a sacred box and take off the clothes and the makeup it had worn the day before. After burning incense and placing balls of natron (used by the Egyptians as a sort of breath mint) in front of the god, it would be given new clothes, fresh makeup, and some jewelry.

The god was then presented with a breakfast of meat, fruits, vegetables, bread, cakes, wine, and beer; later, after its lunch and dinner, the god would be returned to its box for the evening. The unused food might first be placed at an altar honoring deceased pharaohs (to ensure their support for the current monarch), then it would be given to the priests. On religious holidays, the god would be placed on a wooden shrine, adorned with numerous jewels, and carried through the streets or given a boat ride down the Nile River.

As another daily task, priests were expected to meet with citizens at the entrances to the temples and deal with the issues they brought to their attention; they might also deliver individuals' questions to the gods and, after considering omens, provide them with an answer. In moments of leisure, they could study the temple's religious scrolls or watch the stars at night. An infrequent but important duty involved the ceremonies associated with the burial of a pharaoh or high official. The priests would first accompany the mummy on its procession to the tomb; there, a priest sacrificed an animal and touched the organs of the mummy with special instruments to ensure that the deceased would regain important abilities like seeing, hearing, and speaking. After the inner tomb was sealed, priests were often paid to continue providing daily food for the deceased in an outer chamber.

We are reminded, though, that priests were often preoccupied with secular matters by a series of letters written by Hekanakhte, an obscure priest who served under the vizier Ipu during the First Intermediate Period (roughly 2181–2055 BCE), to his son Mersu. Hekanakhte often had to travel to the temple's distant properties to handle their business, leaving his son in charge of the temple, but he sent Mersu long letters with instructions to send his father food, to plant certain fields with certain crops at certain times of the year, to allow particular men to rent acres of farmland, and to deal with family problems involving Hekanakhte's elderly mother, his younger sons, and his mistress. In modern terms, one might describe Hekanakhte as an irksome micromanager—as evidence of his dislike for these letters, Mersu left one of them unopened—but perhaps such attention to detail in juggling multiple responsibilities was an essential trait of an effective priest.

FEEDING THE DECEASED

One major duty of priests in ancient Mesopotamia and Egypt was providing their temple gods, who took the form of statues, with daily meals; Egyptian priests sometimes delivered food to the tombs of deceased nobles as well. The notion that gods and people in the afterlife would require sustenance from living followers may seem strange to some modern observers, but other cultures have developed and maintained similar beliefs. In contemporary China, for example, some individuals still pay tribute to their ancestors by placing their pictures in household shrines and periodically placing food in front of them.

LIKE FATHER, LIKE SON

As was the case with many ancient professions, Egyptian priests often sought to pass their positions on to their sons, training them from a young age to assume their responsibilities when they retired. Today, this sort of automatic succession is rare in most religions, since priests and religious leaders must receive a formal education and be officially approved by superiors before assuming positions. However, charismatic evangelists sometimes groom their sons as their replacements; thus, Oral Roberts was succeeded by his son Richard Roberts as president of Oral Roberts University (though he later resigned), and Billy Graham's crusades now are usually led by his son Franklin Graham.

Priests held varying degrees of authority, depending upon their position in the hierarchy. The priest with the most influence was the high priest of Amun, always appointed by the pharaoh himself; this priest and his associates often played an important role in the selection of a new pharaoh, and at times he appeared to be almost as powerful as the pharaoh. Other high priests would gather to meet with the pharaoh every year, offering their input on matters of state, and sometimes accompanied him when he traveled. Below them, each temple had its own head priest and a staff of lesser priests with particular duties, some of whom, as noted, only worked on a part-time basis.

Whether a priest was a friend of the pharaoh, or a minor official in a small temple, there seems little doubt that the priesthood was one of ancient Egypt's most desirable professions, providing its members with a comfortable income, pleasant surroundings, and great prestige in the community. And certainly, most of them earned what they received, since Egypt could not have maintained its efficient government and unified culture without their many contributions.

Further Reading

Arnold, Dieter, Lanny Bell, Ragnhild Bjerre Finnestad, Gerhard Haeny, and Byron E. Shafer. 1997. *Temples of Ancient Egypt*. Edited by Byron E. Shafer. Ithaca, NY: Cornell University Press.

Blackman, Aylward M. 1998. *Gods, Priests, and Men: Studies in the Religion of Pharaonic Egypt*. London and New York: Kegan Paul International.

Fried, Lisbeth S. 2004. *The Priest and the Great King: Temple-Palace Relations in the Persian Empire*. Winona Lake, IN: Eisenbrauns.

Rooke, Deborah W. 2012. *Zadok's Heirs: The Role and Development of the High Priesthood in Ancient Israel*. Oxford: Oxford University Press.

Taggar-Cohen, Ada. 2006. *Hittite Priesthood*. Heidelberg, Germany: Winter.

Teeter, Emily. 2011. *Religion and Ritual in Ancient Egypt*. Cambridge and New York: Cambridge University Press.

Documents

From Herodotus. C. 425 BCE. *The History of Herodotus*. Translated by G.C. Macaulay. 1890. London and New York: Macmillan and Co.

In this passage, the Greek historian describes the appearance and habits of the Egyptian priests that he encountered.

The priests shave themselves all over their body every other day, so that no lice or any other foul thing may come to be upon them when they minister to the gods; and the priests wear garments of linen only and sandals of papyrus, and any other garment they may not take nor other sandals; these wash themselves in cold water twice in the day and twice again in the night; and other religious services they perform (one may almost say) of infinite number. They enjoy also good things not a few, for they do not consume or spend anything of their own substance, but there is sacred bread baked for them and they have each great quantity of flesh of oxen and geese coming in to them each day, and also wine of grapes is given to them; but it is not permitted to them to taste of fish: beans moreover the Egyptians do not at all sow in their land, and those which grow they neither eat raw nor boil for food; nay the priests do not endure even to look upon them, thinking this to be an unclean kind of pulse: and there is not one priest only for each of the gods but many, and of them one is chief-priest, and whenever a priest dies his son is appointed to his place.

From Weigall, Arthur Edward Pearse Brome. 1911. *The Treasury of Ancient Egypt: Miscellaneous Chapters on Ancient Egyptian History and Archaeology.* London: W. Blackwood and Sons.

In this passage, an Egyptologist explains that Egyptian priests, unlike their modern counterparts, enjoyed all of the pleasures of life.

At first sight, in reflecting on the mysteries and religious ceremonies of the nation, we are apt to endow the priests and other participators with a degree of austerity wholly unjustified by facts. We picture the priest chanting his formulae in the dim light of the temple, the atmosphere about him heavy with incense; and we imagine him as an anchorite who has put away the things of this world. But in reality there seems to have been not even such a thing as a celibate amongst the priests. Each man had his wife and his family, his house, and his comforts of food and fine linen. He indulged in the usual pastimes and was present at the merriest of feasts. The famous wise men and magicians, such as Uba-ana of the Westcar Papyrus, had their wives, their parks, their pleasure-pavilions, and their hosts of servants. Great dignitaries of the Amun Church, such as Amen-hotepsase, the Second Prophet of Amen in the time of Thutmoses IV, are represented as feasting with their friends, or driving through Thebes in richly-decorated chariots drawn by prancing horses, and attended by an array of servants. A monastic life, or the life of an anchorite, was held by the Egyptians in scorn; and indeed the state of mind which produces the monk and the hermit was almost entirely unknown to the nation in dynastic times.

Prophets

Since the beginning of civilization, people have shown a keen interest in learning what will happen in the future, and many individuals have stepped forward to claim the power of prophecy. While some of these prophets garnered little attention, as they eked out a meager living by addressing the concerns of ordinary citizens, others—especially in ancient Israel—were widely respected not only as prophets but as authorities on morality and religious doctrines.

The prophets of Mesopotamia, generally referred to as "diviners," worked for the kings, local governments, or the army. Their most common technique was hepatoscopy, examination of the liver of a sacrificed animal, though they also employed extispicy (looking at a sacrificed animal's intestines), libanomancy (watching the movement of smoke from burning incense), and lecanomancy (looking for patterns when oil is poured into a bowl of water). Some diviners sought signs by watching birds in flight, and the Mesopotamians pioneered in the practice of astrology, though it was only in the later Persian empire that the modern techniques of astrology were developed, as the Persian astrologers charted a twelve-sign zodiac and tracked the movements of planets within each sign to make their predictions.

For the ancient Egyptians, one favorite method of predicting the future was the interpretation of dreams. One scroll advised potential interpreters about over 200 events in dreams that heralded future developments; seeing a large cat or diving into a river indicated good fortune, for example, while looking into a mirror or a deep well foretold bad outcomes (respectively, a second wife or loss of one's property). Citizens seeking very specific prophecies about their own lives could visit their local temples and submit a question to its god, and a priest would soon provide an answer. Overall, however, despite numerous modern efforts to discern prophecies in the designs of their pyramids and other structures, the confident and usually prosperous Egyptians appear to have been less concerned about predicting the future than their contemporaries.

The most renowned prophets of ancient times were those in the land of Israel, though their actions and status in society changed over the centuries. The first prophets apparently worked together in guilds, teaching their craft to apprentices. Sometimes accompanied by music, they would shout or chant their poetic prophecies as if in a trance, reinforcing the belief that they were being possessed by a spirit, though skeptics have endeavored to explain this unusual behavior in various ways, including undiagnosed epilepsy, self-delusion, or outright fraud. These early prophets were not always devoted to promoting the worship of the Hebrew god, as they sometimes attributed their powers to other gods, ghosts, or demons. For this reason, early books of the Bible contain warnings against these sorts of false prophets. In the twentieth chapter of Leviticus, the author speaks scornfully of people who "have familiar spirits," or are "wizards," and states that these purported mystics or magicians should be "put to death" by stoning. And the thirteenth chapter of Deuteronomy warns against "a prophet, or dreamer of dreams," who attempts to employ an apparently successful prediction as a way to lure the Israelites to worship other gods; such men should also be stoned to death. It seems that the changing fortunes of ancient Israel may have made many people anxious about the future, creating an opportunity for unscrupulous individuals to profit by claiming to have prophetic abilities.

Yet there soon arose another sort of prophet, people who were accepted as authentic spokespersons for God, and these individuals achieved broad influence over their societies. Surprisingly, despite the generally patriarchal structure of Israelite society, some of these prophets were women, most prominently the biblical judge Deborah, who recruited a military leader, Barak, and joined him in leading her people to a major victory. Their ability to attain popular support and political power suggests that these prophets, unlike their less-reputable precursors, were closely connected to or aligned with established governments. One of them, Samuel, may have originally been a priest, though he effectively ruled his society before yielding power to a king that he personally chose and anointed.

The story of one prophet, Jonah, suggests that in some cases, people felt compelled to enter this profession. Receiving instructions from God to preach

in the heathen city of Nineveh, Jonah instead traveled far away from Nineveh in a ship; only after being swallowed by a large fish and surviving the ordeal did he finally agree to follow God's commands and go to Nineveh. Today, many regard the story of Jonah as fanciful, but its true point may be that prophecy is an avocation forced upon people, not chosen by them.

The later prophets of Israel played a much different role than earlier prophets like Deborah or Samuel. These men were characteristically outsiders, critics of the established leaders, and while they predicted the future, their proclamations were framed as exhortations to the people to change their ways. A typical theme was that God was punishing the Israelites, and would continue to do so, because they were no longer obeying His commandments; however, if they returned to the proper path, God would again bless them with good fortune. Though their teachings were often in conflict with those of the authorities, they employed a new weapon in their efforts to promulgate their views: writing. Once they began to write down their predictions as well as proclaiming them, devoted followers could copy and circulate their words, expanding the prophet's audience beyond the people in his immediate vicinity. Eventually, their pronouncements were accepted as divinely inspired and incorporated into the Old Testament of the Bible (although passages in some books, attributed to a prophet, are usually thought to be the work of another hand).

One of the greatest of these prophets was Isaiah, who lived in the eighth century BCE. Along with condemnations of the leaders and people of his times, he linked his vision of their eventual redemption to the anticipated appearance of a savior, born to the house of David—a prediction fulfilled, in the eyes of Christians, by the later birth of Jesus. Another noteworthy prophet, Jeremiah, seems to have been an irascible and passionate man who was often in trouble with the government because of his dark pronouncements of God's imminent wrath, tempered only by the promise of Israel's eventual reformation and rebirth. The other two men now regarded as major prophets were Ezekiel and Daniel; Ezekiel is best remembered for his extravagantly visual prophecies, including a vision of a chariot in the sky, while Daniel was noted for

POETIC PROPHECIES

Most scholars agree that the Old Testament prophets were speaking primarily to their contemporaries, and their predictions involved the immediate future of the ancient Near East. Still, many modern commentators have discerned predictions of twentieth- and twenty-first-century events in the pages of the Bible. One of the strangest theories, developed by pastor J. R. Church, is that the author of the Psalms foretold events in the last two centuries: the first Psalm predicts events in 1901, the second Psalm events in 1902, and so on, concluding with the 150th Psalm and the end of the world in 2050. However, his creative interpretations of the Psalms have attracted little support.

THE INTERPRETATION OF DREAMS

Most ancient systems of prophecy, such as examining the intestines of dead animals or the movements of birds in flight, are no longer practiced today. However, people remain keenly interested in the interpretation of dreams, the prophetic skill displayed by Daniel that so impressed the Babylonian monarch Nebuchadnezzar. Today, however, they are not regarded as divine messages about the future, but rather as symbols of unconscious desires—the theory of psychologist Sigmund Freud—or distorted reflections of everyday experiences. Still, despite the proliferation of books purporting to explain the significance of people's dreams, some researchers have suggested that, in fact, dreams have no real meaning at all.

being protected by God when placed inside a lion's den. The Old Testament concludes with the work of twelve minor prophets, including Jonah, and we know of several others whose writings were ultimately not deemed worthy of inclusion.

We have little information about how these prophets were able to survive without holding jobs that provided an income, though it is reasonable to assume that their followers, who included wealthy individuals, were willing to provide them with food and shelter, and some may have received support from local temples that embraced their teachings. Their strength was that, unlike prophets interested in personal gain, they were not in the business of making short-term

predictions that were often proven false, undermining their credibility. Rather, the great prophets of ancient Israel adopted a broader perspective on the task of prophecy, regarding their primary duty as promoting religious piety and moral behavior; their predictions of coming ruin for an Israel that did not follow the dictates of God, or eventual salvation for an Israel that would finally see the light and reform its ways, were doubtless heartfelt, but they were also a way to encourage people to change their attitudes in hopes of avoiding future punishments or garnering future rewards. And because of the fundamental integrity underlying their predictions, they are still being studied today, as many people believe that they still have insights to offer about both time-honored principles of morality and the future of our own contemporary world.

Further Reading

Ciraolo, Leda, and Jonathan Seidel, editors. 2002. *Magic and Divination in the Ancient World.* Leiden, The Netherlands, and Boston: Brill.

Day, John. 2010. *Prophecy and the Prophets in Ancient Israel: Proceedings of the Oxford Old Testament Seminar.* New York and London: T. T. and Clark.

De Jong, Matthijs J. 2007. *Isaiah among the Ancient Near Eastern Prophets: A Comparative Study of the Earliest Stages of the Isaiah Tradition and the Neo-Assyrian Prophecies.* Leiden, The Netherlands, and Boston: Brill.

Grottanelli, Cristiano. 1999. *Kings and Prophets: Monarchic Power, Inspired Leadership, and Sacred Text in Biblical Narrative.* Oxford and New York: Oxford University Press.

Huffmon, Herbert Bardwell, John Kaltner, and Louis Stulman, editors. 2008. *Inspired Speech: Prophecy in the Ancient Near East: Essays in Honor of Herbert B. Huffmon.* New York and London: T. T. and Clark.

Stökl, Jonathan. 2012. *Prophecy in the Ancient Near East: A Philological and Sociological Comparison.* Leiden, The Netherlands, and Boston: Brill.

Document

From *The King James Bible.* 1611. Daniel 2:5–48.

In this passage, the Israelite prophet Daniel succeeds in interpreting the dream of the Babylonian king Nebuchadnezzar, although the Babylonian prophets that the king consulted had failed.

The king answered and said to Daniel, whose name *was* Belteshazzar, art thou able to make known unto me the dream which I have seen, and the interpretation thereof?

Daniel answered in the presence of the king, and said, The secret which the king hath demanded cannot the wise *men*, the astrologers, the magicians, the soothsayers, shew unto the king; but there is a God in heaven that revealeth secrets, and maketh known to the king Nebuchadnezzar what shall be in the latter days. Thy dream, and the visions of thy head upon thy bed, are these; as for thee, O king, thy thoughts came *into thy mind* upon thy bed, what should come to pass hereafter: and he that revealeth secrets maketh known to thee what shall come to pass. But as for me, this secret is not revealed to me for *any* wisdom that I have more than any living, but for *their* sakes that shall make known the interpretation to the king, and that thou mightest know the thoughts of thy heart.

Thou, O king, sawest, and behold a great image. This great image, whose brightness *was* excellent, stood before thee; and the form thereof *was* terrible. This image's head *was* of fine gold, his breast and his arms of silver, his belly and his thighs of brass, his legs of iron, his feet part of iron and part of clay. Thou sawest till that a stone was cut out without hands, which smote the image upon his feet *that were* of iron and clay, and brake them to pieces. Then was the iron, the clay, the brass, the silver, and the gold, broken to pieces together, and became like the chaff of the summer threshing floors; and the wind carried them away, that no place was found for them: and the stone that smote the image became a great mountain, and filled the whole earth.

This *is* the dream; and we will tell the interpretation thereof before the king. Thou, O king, *art* a king of kings: for the God of heaven hath given thee a kingdom, power, and strength, and glory. And wheresoever the children of men dwell, the beasts of the field and the fowls of the heaven hath he given into thine hand, and hath made thee ruler over them all. Thou *art* this head of gold. And after thee shall arise another kingdom inferior to thee, and another third kingdom of brass, which shall bear rule over all the earth. And the fourth kingdom shall be strong as iron: forasmuch as iron breaketh in pieces and subdueth all *things*: and as iron that breaketh all these, shall it break in pieces and bruise. And whereas thou sawest the feet and toes, part of potters' clay, and part of iron, the kingdom shall be divided; but there shall be in it of the strength of the iron, forasmuch as thou sawest the iron mixed with miry clay. And *as* the toes of the feet *were* part of iron, and part of clay, *so* the kingdom shall be partly strong, and partly broken. And whereas thou sawest iron mixed with miry clay, they shall mingle themselves with the seed of men: but they shall not cleave one to another, even as iron is not mixed with clay. And in the days of these kings shall the God of heaven set up a kingdom, which shall never be destroyed: and the kingdom shall not be left to other people, *but* it shall break in pieces and consume all these kingdoms, and it shall stand for ever. Forasmuch as thou sawest that the stone was cut out of the mountain without hands, and that it brake in pieces the iron, the brass, the clay, the silver, and the gold; the great God hath made known to the king what shall come to pass hereafter: and the dream *is* certain, and the interpretation thereof sure.

Then the king Nebuchadnezzar fell upon his face, and worshipped Daniel, and commanded that they should offer an oblation and sweet odours unto him. The king answered unto Daniel, and said, Of a truth *it is*, that your God *is* a God of gods, and a Lord of kings, and a revealer of secrets, seeing thou couldest reveal this secret. Then the king made Daniel a great man, and gave him many great gifts, and made him ruler over the whole province of Babylon, and chief of the governors over all the wise *men* of Babylon.

Scribes

While the art of writing originated in ancient Mesopotamia as a way for businesspersons to keep track of their possessions and transactions, it was soon extended to other purposes as well. The earliest samples of writing, found in the city of Uruk, are imperfectly understood, but they appear to consist primarily of pictographs, such as a small picture of an ox, or head of an ox, to represent an ox. Later, these symbols evolved into stylized hieroglyphs representing words or sounds. Initially, scribes cut reeds to make styluses, which they used to make marks on moist

This wall carving, created about 730 BCE, in an ancient Assyrian palace in present-day Iraq, shows two scribes holding their styluses and boards for writing. (Zev Radovan/Land of the Bible Picture Archive)

tablets of clay, though special forms of writing might be engraved upon slabs of other substances like beeswax, metal, or stone.

The useful skill of writing soon spread to all parts of the Sumerian empire, though different regions developed their own styles; after 3000 BCE, however, the writing throughout the area becomes more uniform, suggesting that institutions had been established to train scribes to write in an officially approved manner. We can be sure that such schools existed a thousand years later, since we find numerous classroom exercises and narratives about educational experiences from that era. A listing of 500 scribes from 2000 BCE that includes their fathers' positions demonstrates that only the sons of wealthy individuals were attending these "tablet-schools," though a document naming one female scribe suggests that, on rare occasions, their

daughters might enroll as well. Discipline in these schools was very strict—one student reported being hit with a cane nine times in one day—but students endured the harsh treatment so that, upon completing their education, they could obtain desirable jobs in various government offices or private estates.

The large numbers of clay tablets located in ancient Mesopotamian sites indicate that this system was workable enough for the daily business of running an empire; to keep the contents of sensitive documents secret when they were transported, the Sumerians even devised envelopes, also made of clay, to cover the tablets. However, the ancient Egyptians came up with a better material for writing—long strips of paper made out of the reed papyrus, which could be rolled up and compactly stored as scrolls. To write on papyrus, the scribes would first grind up pigments on a slate, then mix the powder with liquids to produce black ink (for most texts) and red ink (for headings). One end of a reed would be chewed on to separate its fibers and make a brush. Before they wrote, they would have to burnish the papyrus with a rounded stone so the movement of the brush would not be impeded by small irregularities on the surface. Finally, after dipping their brushes in a pot of water to moisten them, they applied the brushes to palettes with small containers of ink and began their writing; these palettes also had slots where scribes could store up to twelve brushes. To erase mistakes, they might employ a wet rag, or simply lick the ink off with their tongues.

The Egyptian system of writing soon became standard through the Near East, as evidenced by numerous scrolls containing the writings of the ancient Hebrews and Greeks. However, another Egyptian innovation in this field was perhaps even more significant. In Sumeria and elsewhere, scribes had been valued as useful professionals, but there is no evidence that they were granted an exalted social status. For the Egyptians, however, being a scribe represented their society's best and most desirable profession. Only scribes were eligible to become priests or high government officials, and even those that did not obtain such positions enjoyed a number of special privileges. They were often able to work as their own bosses, not subject to intense scrutiny and supervision; they were not required to pay taxes; they received generous salaries that provided them with expensive clothing and an abundance of food; and they were also treated with great respect by other illiterate citizens who were awed by their ability to transform their spoken words into written texts and thus immortalize them. Egyptologist John A. Wilson cleverly described the scribes as Egypt's "white kilt" workers, a pun on today's "white collar" workers, which also refers to their clean white clothing, a sign that they did not have to engage in physical labor.

It is little wonder, then, that many Egyptians wanted their sons to become scribes, which normally involved attending a special school, although royal children were usually trained by private tutors, and some temples taught young scribes with an interest in the priesthood. These schools were expensive, so that most of their students came from wealthy families, but poorer families in some cases could manage the cost of educating children who displayed an aptitude for learning; scribes themselves, of course, made sure that their own sons were enrolled. In these schools, beginning students would practice on small pieces of broken stone, since papyrus was too valuable to waste; typically, the instructor would dictate a text, the students would copy it, and the instructor would then critique their work. Students learned to sit on the ground with crossed legs using their kilts, stretched tight by their knees, as a sort of desk to write on; scribes seated in this fashion are often depicted in Egyptian sculptures, additional evidence of the society's high regard for this profession. The students were expected to master two forms of writing, the pictorial hieroglyphs observed on monuments and in tombs and a cursive script used for everyday tasks. Prospective scribes also had to memorize the prayers they must recite prior to writing and vast numbers of the elaborate phrases that characterized administrative prose.

Once they had completed their education, scribes could obtain a variety of different jobs within the labyrinthine Egyptian bureaucracy. Some traveled through the countryside to collect taxes; in temples, scribes carefully copied religious texts and performed other duties; scribes worked for the army, keeping detailed records of their soldiers and supplies; scribes supervised libraries; the most esteemed scribes would be assigned to work in palaces, serving the pharaohs and other members of the royal family; and a few scribes

became the instructors of future scribes. We can obtain a picture of a typical scribe's career by examining the life of Ramose, a scribe who lived sometime during the reign of Ramses II (born ca. 1300 BCE, reigned from 1279 to 1213 BCE), because he left behind on various monuments a detailed record of his activities. He was unusually the son of a common messenger, not a rich man or a scribe, but since his father was in regular contact with high officials, he probably used personal connections to get his son enrolled in a scribal school. He began by working at small temples, one dedicated to the dead pharaoh Thutmose IV (died 1388 BCE), the other established by pharaoh Amenhotep III (died 1353 BCE) to honor his most trusted scribe; one of his duties was to keep track of the cattle that were given to the temples by private estates. He must have been good at his job, for at the age of thirty-five he was promoted to become part of the team constructing the tomb of

EGYPTIAN PAPER

A major innovation of the Egyptian scribes was the use of scrolls made of papyrus for most of their writing, a vast improvement on the clay tablets of ancient Mesopotamia. While paper made of papyrus was long popular in Europe and Asia, it was eventually replaced by parchment, made from animal hides, and later by the paper made from wood pulp that is most common today. However, there are still companies today that manufacture sheets of paper from papyrus grown in Egypt, for customers interested in writing or drawing on the same material that was employed by the Egyptian scribes.

WRITERS FOR HIRE

While most Egyptian scribes worked for the government or the temples, they were also hired by illiterate individuals to write documents for them, like personal letters or complaints sent to officials. Today, while most people can read and write, there are still people who make a good living by writing for other people, such as the ghost writers who write books for celebrities and athletes. Also, technical writers are regularly hired by companies to produced needed materials like user manuals, employee handbooks, brochures, press releases, annual reports, and environmental-impact reports.

Ramses II, working under another scribe named Huy. His major responsibility was maintaining records of the food and supplies provided for the project's numerous workers, but he was paid to perform a number of additional tasks for private individuals: he wrote decorative inscriptions on furniture being prepared for Huy's tomb, and private citizens hired him to transcribe their complaints and send them to government officials. Eventually, he became one of the wealthiest men in the village of workers, marrying and becoming the owner of a large piece of cultivated land, and he started to supervise the preparation of his own tomb. As he aged, a young scribe named Kenhirkhopeshef became his assistant and assumed his position after Ramose died.

Ramose may have been more fortunate than most scribes, but it seems clear that most members of this profession also enjoyed fulfilling and prosperous lives, which is why Egypt's best and brightest young men so often sought this position. And if their society rewarded them generously for their work, the scribes also contributed much to ancient Egypt; indeed, anyone seeking to explain the extraordinary influence and longevity of the Egyptian civilization must consider, as one factor, their high regard for educated people, and their determination to keep all aspects of their government under the constant control of educated people. For ancient Egypt, this most definitely proved a formula for success.

Further Reading

Baines, John. 2007. *Visual and Written Culture in Ancient Egypt*. Oxford and New York: Oxford University Press.

Perdue, Leo G., editor. 2008. *Scribes, Sages, and Seers: The Sage in the Eastern Mediterranean World*. Göttingen, Germany: Vanderhoeck & Ruprecht.

Rollston, Chris A. 2010. *Writing and Literacy in the World of Ancient Israel: Epigraphic Evidence from the Iron Age*. Atlanta: Society of Biblical Literature.

Silverman, David P. 1990. *Language and Writing in Ancient Egypt*. Pittsburgh: Carnegie Museum of Natural History.

Visicato, Giuseppe. 2000. *The Power and the Writing: The Early Scribes of Mesopotamia*. Bethesda, MD: CDL Press.

Wilson, Penelope. 2003. *Sacred Signs: Hieroglyphs in Ancient Egypt*. Oxford and New York: Oxford University Press.

Document

From Myer, Isaac, translator. 1900. *Oldest Books in the World: An Account of the Religion, Wisdom, Philosophy, Ethics, Psychology, Manners, Proverbs, Sayings, Refinement, Etc., of the Ancient Egyptians*. New York: Edwin W. Dayton.

Below are two excerpts from a document generally known as The Maxims of the Scribe Ani, probably written around 1300 BCE. The author, a scribe addressing his son, stresses the importance of written knowledge, praises the wisdom of scribes, and conveys their special status by repeating the point that, unlike other workers, scribes cannot pass their positions on to their sons; rather, the position must be individually earned.

If one comes (to thee) in order to seek thy views (advice), let that be a reason for thee to turn to the divine books.

One comes to seek thy views (advice), let that make thee lean upon the books. . . .

If thou art skillful in the writings, if thou hast penetrated into them, place them in thy heart (*i.e.*, commit them to memory): all thou sayest (then) becomes perfect. If the scribe is employed in any profession whatsoever, he discourses following the writings. There is not a son for the chief of the double-white-house; there is not an heir for the chief of the seal. The great appreciate the scribe; his hand, it is his profession; they do not give it to the children; their misery, it is his good; their greatness, it is his protection.

Thou art versed in letters, thou penetratest (the sense) of the writings; let it remain fixed in thy heart, all thy discourse will become virtuous. The literary man is raised to all employments; it is he who deliberates upon the writings. The chief of the treasury has not a son, the chief of the seal has not an heir. The great (men) appreciate the writer; he fulfills functions which one cannot confide to a child.

Slaves

Slavery, in the ancient Near East and elsewhere, originated at the same time as large national states, and it appeared to be the direct result of newly developed nationalistic feelings. That is, the people who came from different lands, with different languages and customs, were literally regarded as not human, and hence they could properly be treated like pieces of property. Even cultures that developed ideals that seemed clearly in conflict with slavery, like ancient Greece and Israel, continued to sanction such involuntary servitude, unable to perceive what modern people would regard as its fundamental unfairness.

In ancient Mesopotamia, the first slaves were people seized from the mountains surrounding the plains of the Tigris and Euphrates rivers, so that the words for male and female slaves were "mountain-men" and "mountain-women." These unfortunate individuals were owned by the state and employed as soldiers or workers, helping to construct roads, buildings, and canals. When increasing military success brought more and more prisoners of war to serve as slaves, they began doing domestic chores as well. Later, merchants began to purchase foreigners to sell them as slaves, while citizens could be forced into slavery if they were unable to pay their debts; in some cases, families would sell their children into slavery to satisfy their creditors.

While most slaves were still government property, some wealthy individuals could purchase their own slaves to work as maids or servants. Female slaves were often trained to play musical instruments like lyres or harps so they could entertain guests. As a sign of their low status, Mesopotamian slaves sometimes had their hair cut in a distinctive fashion, or they wore shackles; enslaved prisoners of war were brought into town naked; and slaves who ran away might have had marks placed on their foreheads. The legal code of Hammurabi (1772 BCE) specifies that anyone who assists a runaway slave must be put to death, conveying a determination to keep slaves in their place. However, though they were often mistreated, slaves also enjoyed certain rights: they could own property, start a business, borrow money, and get married, and if they married a free person, their children would be free. Most important, prosperous slaves could purchase their own freedom.

Another region where slavery was relatively benign was ancient Israel where, as decreed in the Bible, most slaves had to be freed after six years of

This stone carving from the Assyrian city of Nineveh shows teams of slaves working in a stone quarry, removing and transporting stones, ca. 700 BCE. (Werner Forman/Corbis)

servitude; the Bible also explains how a slave can opt for permanent slavery, suggesting that most slaves were treated kindly. However, the best-known biblical passage involving slavery is its final story about Noah, who got drunk, wandered around naked, and was observed by his son Ham; his other sons Shem and Japheth, by approaching him backward while holding a cloth, then covered his body without seeing him. Subsequently, an angry Noah condemned Ham's son and descendants to be the slaves of the other sons' progeny. In America, this story was seized upon to justify the enslavement of African Americans, the purported descendants of Ham, by the Caucasian and Asian races, purported descendants of Shem and Japheth. Actually, in Israel and everywhere else, there was never any racial element in ancient slavery; a person of any race might be a slave, or might be a free person.

Slavery was also practiced in ancient Egypt, though two popular beliefs about Egyptian slaves have been called into question. First, Egyptologists are now convinced that highly skilled and salaried workers, not slaves, constructed the pyramids; during the era of the Old Kingdom, in fact, slaves were relatively uncommon, though they became more numerous in the Middle Kingdom and thereafter. Second, despite vigorous research, no outside evidence has emerged to confirm the biblical story that the Hebrews were long enslaved in Egypt before they were led to freedom by Moses. It is true that many Egyptian slaves were foreign-born, but as in other ancient kingdoms, they were mostly prisoners of war and their children. Many Egyptians also became slaves when they were convicted of a serious crime or fell too deeply into debt. A few people even chose a life of slavery, in a rich person's home or a temple, anticipating a comfortable life in exchange for their labor.

As was the case in ancient Mesopotamia, most of the Egyptian slaves were owned by the state, often assigned to work in the mines, to build roads, or to assist in the transportation of the large stones used to construct temples; foreign slaves with military experience might become soldiers in the Egyptian army. However, as the numbers of slaves increased, more and more of them became the possessions of individuals. These slaves typically enjoyed easier lives, working in people's homes as maids, servants, cooks, or gardeners, and they sometimes came to be treated like family members; in a few cases, they were allowed to marry into the families they served. For example, the man who served as the barber to Thutmose III (1481–1425 BCE) was given a foreign slave of whom he grew quite fond; the slave was allowed to marry the barber's niece and the barber's will granted him a permanent place in the household. Slaves in the temples or government offices might garner some political power if they displayed a talent for administrative duties, and all slaves enjoyed the right to own land or private property; noting these privileges, a few experts have even argued that Egypt actually had no slaves in the modern sense of the term, preferring to describe them as servants. There was also a general attitude that a person should treat his slaves humanely; in one passage in the Egyptian Book of the Dead, the dead man

IMAGINARY ENSLAVEMENT

Since the Bible states that the Hebrews were enslaved in Egypt, and since it was long believed that slaves had built the pyramids, it doubtless seemed logical to the makers of the film *The Ten Commandments* (1956) to depict the Hebrews as oppressed laborers forced by whip-wielding overseers to construct those immense structures; one scene even shows an elderly woman being whipped as she struggles to perform this arduous task. All of this was absurd: the Egyptians employed able-bodied, skilled laborers to build the pyramids, and while there is much debate about when the Hebrews lived in Egypt, it was certainly over a thousand years after the pyramids were completed.

RUNAWAY SLAVE ACTS

Since the beginning of slavery, unhappy slaves have regularly attempted to run away from their masters and gain their freedom; so, to hold on to their property, slave owners have sought the assistance of their governments to thwart such escapes. It is not surprising, then, that the world's first body of laws, the Code of Hammurabi, includes harsh punishments for anyone who assists a runaway slave. Much later, in the nineteenth century, slave owners in the American South pressured the federal government to force the residents of free states to return runaway slaves, which was one factor contributing to the increased tensions that eventually led to the Civil War.

strives to convey that he is worthy of the gods' company by proclaiming that he did not abuse his slaves.

On the other hand, ignoring any concerns about their afterlife, some owners regularly beat their slaves, inspiring them to attempt to escape. There are records of two workers in the home of Ramses II (ca. 1300–1213 BCE) who ran away and were pursued by one of the pharaoh's archers, though he abandoned the chase after they traveled beyond a distant fortress. Yet a tomb illustration of a bound slave held by a rope indicates that many runaway slaves were successfully recaptured. As another way to keep slaves from escaping, some were tattooed in prominent places; when a man of the Twenty-Seventh Dynasty named Meshullam sought to free one of his female slaves, Tapmut, the official document granting her manumission indicates that she had his name tattooed on her right hand. Also, while it might have been pleasurable to serve as a slave to a pharaoh, such slaves were often killed when the pharaoh died and placed in his tomb to tend to his needs in the afterlife.

Individuals could acquire slaves in various ways. Nobles or officials might give prisoners of war to their employees to serve as their slaves; children would inherit their deceased father's slaves; and if a man's slaves had children, they would become his slaves as well. If a person only needed laborers for a short period of time, he could pay for the temporary use of someone else's slaves, effectively renting them. There were no public slave auctions in the marketplaces of ancient Egypt, but merchants known to handle slaves could be approached, and private arrangements could then be made to purchase slaves.

While records do provide a number of laws governing slavery, and some accounts of individual transactions involving slaves, we have no way of knowing how many slaves there were in the ancient civilizations of the Near East, or how important they were to their economies. A few things, however, seem clear: slavery was generally the fate of captured foreigners of all nationalities; slaves were not routinely mistreated; and slave labor was never essential to industries that mainly relied upon the work of free men and women. Contemporary Americans and Europeans are more interested in ancient slavery than the people who practiced it, in large part because they are still suffering from the ruinous effects of the form of slavery developed by their ancestors, which was far more exploitative and cruel than the institutions maintained by the cultures that flourished thousands of years ago.

Further Reading

Chirichigno, Gregory. 1993. *Debt-Slavery in Israel and the Ancient Near East.* Sheffield, England: Journal for the Study of the Old Testament Press.

Goldenberg, David M. 2003. *The Curse of Ham: Race and Slavery in Early Judaism, Christianity, and Islam.* Princeton, NJ: Princeton University Press.

Kriger, Diane. 2011. *Sex Rewarded, Sex Punished: A Study of the Status "Female Slave" in Early Jewish Law.* Boston: Academic Studies Press.

Redford, Donald B. 2004. *From Slave to Pharaoh: The Black Experience of Ancient Egypt.* Baltimore, MD: John Hopkins University Press.

Snell, Daniel. 2001. *Flight and Freedom in the Ancient Near East.* Leiden, The Netherlands, and Boston: Brill.

Tenney, Jonathan S. 2011. *Life at the Bottom of Babylonian Society: Servile Laborers at Nippur in the 14th and 13th Centuries B.C.* Leiden, The Netherlands, and Boston: Brill.

Documents

From Johns, Claude Hermann Walter, translator. 1904. *Babylonian and Assyrian Laws, Contracts and Letters.* New York: Charles Scribner's Sons.

The Babylonian Code of Hammurabi, originally written around 1772 BCE, includes several provisions regarding slaves, most of which are listed below. They demonstrate that slaves were regarded solely as pieces of property and subject to severe sanctions if they are rebellious or attempt to run away.

15. If a man has induced either a male or a female slave from the house of a patrician, or plebeian, to leave the city, he shall be put to death.

16. If a man has harbored in his house a male or female slave from a patrician's or plebeian's house, and has not caused the fugitive to leave on the demand of the officer over the slaves condemned to public forced labor, that householder shall be put to death.

17. If a man has caught either a male or female runaway slave in the open field and has brought him back to his owner, the owner of the slave shall give him two shekels of silver.

18. If such a slave will not name his owner, his captor shall bring him to the palace, where he shall be examined as to his past and returned to his owner.

19. If the captor has secreted that slave in his house and afterward that slave has been caught in his possession, he shall be put to death.

20. If the slave has fled from the hands of his captor, the latter shall swear to the owner of the slave and he shall be free from blame. . . .

278. If a man has bought a male or female slave and the slave has not fulfilled his month, but the *bennu* disease has fallen upon him, he shall return the slave to the seller and the buyer shall take back the money he paid.

279. If a man has bought a male or female slave and a claim has been raised, the seller shall answer the claim.

280. If a man, in a foreign land, has bought a male, or female, slave of another, and if when he has come home the owner of the male or female slave has recognized his slave, and if the slave be a native of the land, he shall grant him liberty without money.

281. If the slave was a native of another country, the buyer shall declare on oath the amount of money he paid, and the owner of the slave shall repay the merchant what he paid and keep his slave.

282. If a slave has said to his master, "You are not my master," he shall be brought to account as his slave, and his master shall cut off his ear.

From *The King James Bible.* 1611. Exodus 21: 2–11, and Deuteronomy 15: 12–18.

While accepting slavery, the Old Testament of the Bible does require humane treatment of slaves and grants most slaves the option of freedom after six years. However, slaves are also allowed to choose a life of servitude, and the language conveys the expectation that many will make that choice.

If thou buy an Hebrew servant, six years he shall serve: and in the seventh he shall go out free for nothing. If he came in by himself, he shall go out by himself: if he were married, then his wife shall go out with him. If his master have given him a wife, and she have born him sons or daughters; the wife and her children shall be her master's, and he shall go out by himself. And if the servant shall plainly say, I love my master, my wife, and my children; I will not go out free: Then his master shall bring him unto the judges; he shall also bring him to the door, or unto the door post; and his master shall bore his ear through with an awl; and he shall serve him for ever.

And if a man sell his daughter to be a maidservant, she shall not go out as the menservants do. If she please not her master, who hath betrothed her to himself, then shall he let her be redeemed: to sell her unto a strange nation he shall have no power, seeing he hath dealt deceitfully with her. If he take him another wife; her food, her raiment, and her duty of marriage, shall he not diminish. And if he do not

these three unto her, then shall she go out free without money. . . .

And if thy brother, an Hebrew man, or an Hebrew woman, be sold unto thee, and serve thee six years; then in the seventh year thou shalt let him go free from thee. And when thou sendest him out free from thee, thou shalt not let him go away empty: Thou shalt furnish him liberally out of thy flock, and out of thy floor, and out of thy winepress: of that wherewith the LORD thy God hath blessed thee thou shalt give unto him. And thou shalt remember that thou wast a bondman in the land of Egypt, and the LORD thy God redeemed thee: therefore I command thee this thing to day. And it shall be, if he say unto thee, I will not go away from thee; because he loveth thee and thine house, because he is well with thee; Then thou shalt take an awl, and thrust it through his ear unto the door, and he shall be thy servant for ever. And also unto thy maidservant thou shalt do likewise. It shall not seem hard unto thee, when thou sendest him away free from thee; for he hath been worth a double hired servant to thee, in serving thee six years: and the LORD thy God shall bless thee in all that thou doest.

Soldiers

The formation and maintenance of the large empires that defined early civilization required governments to have armies—to keep restive citizens under control and to repel foreign invaders. However, since only limited numbers of men were attracted to the rigor and violence of a military career, some form of conscription often proved essential. In ancient Mesopotamia, forced military service was made palatable by an appealing reward: at the end of their duties, retiring soldiers received their own pieces of land, a practice that endured in later empires.

After their training, Assyrian soldiers were assigned various roles, though the surviving texts are not entirely clear about the division of labor. Illustrations suggest that foot soldiers might fight in battles, serve as messengers, construct roads for battalions on the move, or break down the walls of enemy cities; other soldiers fought while riding on horses. Their weapons included spears, axes, maces, and bows and arrows, and to protect themselves, they carried shields and wore helmets and armor; their horses had some armor as well to cover their vulnerable necks. The Hittites introduced a significant innovation that eventually transformed warfare throughout the ancient Near East: the chariot. While one man held the reins and controlled the horses pulling the vehicle, his passenger was free to concentrate on accurately shooting arrows at the opposing soldiers. As these effective combatants were soon being targeted by enemies, larger chariots were built to hold a third man, who used a shield to block spears and arrows.

Although there are no detailed records of their daily activities, the soldiers' lives could not have been pleasant: there was the constant threat of death in battle, and soldiers separated from their units often died from starvation or exposure to the harsh desert climate. If they were taken prisoner, soldiers were usually stripped naked and forced to march to their enemy's territory; while sometimes kept in line by neck braces or nets, the captured soldiers might also be blinded to prevent them from escaping. If they were lucky, they would be held for ransom and eventually returned to their homes; otherwise, they would be enslaved and forced to perform menial chores for the rest of their lives.

While great empires of the ancient Near East like the Assyrians, Hittites, and Persians maintained large standing armies of professional soldiers, this was not always the case; smaller nations, like Israel, would simply recruit or coerce young men into serving as soldiers whenever the need arose, and they would return to their normal lives after the decisive battles. This also meant that warfare typically involved very little strategy; the opposing armies would meet at a designated location; individual soldiers would advance and attempt to kill as many enemies as possible; and when one side seemed to be prevailing, the other soldiers would flee, conceding victory to their opponents. The stories of Achilles and Hector in Homer's *Iliad*, and of David and Goliath in the Bible, suggest that in some cases armies might have settled their differences by means of individual combat between two chosen warriors.

In the Old Kingdom of ancient Egypt, pharaohs only kept a small battalion of royal guards on duty at all times, but local rulers had their own armies that the pharaohs could employ for major wars. These independent forces, which were not personally loyal to the pharaoh, gradually undermined his authority and may have contributed to the collapse of the Old Kingdom. The pharaohs of the Middle Kingdom, however, directly controlled their own armies. To obtain needed soldiers, scribes would be assigned to recruit a certain quota of soldiers from each village, employing an unknown mixture of coercion and persuasion; some would serve for a certain time and then resume their previous occupations, while others became full-time soldiers. While the principal duty of most soldiers was fighting, Egyptian armies also included large numbers of scribes, who carefully kept track of soldiers and supplies, and a famous story about the pharaoh Ramses II (ca. 1300–1213 BCE), disastrously misled by false information supplied by two enemy spies,

The ancient Hittites revolutionized warfare throughout the Near East by developing chariots; these could rapidly transport two warriors, one who controlled the horse and a comrade who fired arrows at enemies, as shown in this stone carving, ca. ninth century BCE, from Anatolia, present-day Turkey. (Gianni Dagli Orti/Corbis)

indicates that the Egyptian employed their own spies as well.

At first, the equipment used by Egyptian soldiers was not particularly impressive; most soldiers may have only carried a wooden stick and a bow and arrow, though some carried spears, slings, clubs, and axes made of stone or copper. They also wore no armor, depending upon wooden shields with leather covers to block enemy thrusts. This may have been why Egypt was easily conquered by the Hyksos, who brought superior technology to the battlefield. Influenced by these invaders, the Egyptians of the New Kingdom relied upon a number of new strategies and weapons. For the first time, some Egyptian soldiers rode on horseback, and they constructed carefully designed chariots that could move swiftly and skillfully into battle. Their wooden arrows now had copper arrowheads; soldiers carried a variety of metal swords and daggers; copper was gradually supplanted by the stronger alloy bronze; and soldiers sometimes wore helmets and a form of armor, a leather tunic covered with pieces of metal. Other new instruments of war were designed to improve the morale and efficiency of the troops: both larger divisions of 5,000 men and smaller units of 200 men carried standards into battle—iconic wooden or golden statues on long poles that were held up high to guide and rally soldiers—and raucous trumpets were blown to tell soldiers it was time to begin their assaults.

Around this time, the Egyptians also began to engage in naval battles against foreign opponents, although they developed no specific strategies for war in this arena; instead, their ships carried soldiers near enemy vessels, allowing them to board and begin the same sort of hand-to-hand combat that characterized their warfare on land. Also, now concerned about future invasions, the Egyptians began to build fortresses, protected by high walls and ditches, in the northern Nile delta and near the southern border with Nubia. The walls had changing angles of slope to make it difficult for enemy soldiers to use ladders to reach the top. The Egyptians also learned how to attack fortified towns using their own ladders and siege towers on wheels.

Since the New Kingdom pharaohs also engaged in regular campaigns of conquest, their soldiers were mostly seasoned professionals; while conscription

BENEFITS FOR VETERANS

To reward soldiers, ancient Mesopotamian empires gave retired soldiers their own property, a substantial benefit in that era. In the twentieth century, the U.S. government also initiated many programs to assist veterans, such as the G.I. Bill granting soldiers who fought in World War II a free college education. More recently, to encourage men and women to enlist after ending conscription in 1973, the government continued expanding services to veterans, so it became necessary to create a new cabinet office, the Department of Veterans Affairs (VA), to oversee the many agencies assisting veterans. Though the VA was recently shown to be understaffed and poorly managing its responsibilities, new efforts are being made to improve its services.

PROTECTING CAPTURED SOLDIERS

In the ancient Near East, the soldiers of defeated armies could be treated very harshly, as they were often executed or forced into a lifetime of slavery. Today, the nations of the world have taken steps to ensure that prisoners of war are treated more humanely. Specifically, the third Geneva Convention, implemented in 1929, require armies to move their prisoners of war out of combat zones, place them in well-maintained camps, and provide them with adequate food and medical care. They were even guaranteed the right to correspond with their family members shortly after their captivity.

was still commonplace, many men were drawn to the military by the promise of high salaries, rapid promotion, and the privilege of seizing the wealth of defeated opponents. During their training, new soldiers would wear only short kilts as they exercised, wrestled, and practiced with weapons; if someone disobeyed orders, the miscreant would be beaten by the other recruits. They also learned to march to the accompaniment of trumpets and drums, the activity that usually began and ended each campaign. In addition to native soldiers, the Egyptians began to employ mercenary soldiers from the nearby lands of Libya and Nubia, and they became increasingly important components of the Egyptian military.

Commanders in the later Egyptian armies might be granted elaborate tombs, and one of these, the tomb of a warrior named Ahmose who fought under Amosis I (died 1525 BCE) and two later pharaohs, provides some information about his military career. The son of another commander, Abana, he assumed his father's position as the captain of a ship and sailed with Amosis I when he went north to battle the Hyksos. Though he traveled by sea, he fought on the land, evidently very well, since he was promoted to serve on another ship and received both a medal, the "Gold of Valor," and several slaves for his distinguished service. On his tomb walls, he also boasts about repeatedly killing and capturing enemy soldiers before retiring at an advanced age.

Records indicate that Egyptian soldiers were always well fed, and there are many stories about soldiers like Ahmose who garnered great wealth and many honors for their services. Yet there are numerous skeletons of less fortunate soldiers showing stab wounds and missing limbs, and a well-known scribal account seeks to discourage prospective soldiers by describing the exhaustion, disease, and eventual death that they experience. Such documents support the impression that, in comparison to other ancient civilizations, the Egyptians were generally inclined to prefer peaceful lives, though they would fiercely defend their country against invaders and loyally serve pharaohs intent upon foreign conquests. Still, it is other ancient civilizations of the Near East, like the Assyrians and the Hittites, which made the greatest contributions in developing the art of warfare.

Further Reading

Bahrani, Zainab. 2008. *Rituals of War: The Body and Violence in Mesopotamia*. New York: Zone Books.

Darnell, John Coleman, and Colleen Manassa. 2007. *Tutankhamun's Armies: Battle and Conquest During Ancient Egypt's Late Eighteenth Dynasty*. Hoboken, NJ: John Wiley & Sons.

Gabriel, Richard A. 2003. *The Military History of Ancient Israel*. Westport, CT: Praeger.

Hamblin, William J. 2006. *Warfare in the Ancient Near East to 1600 BC: Holy Warriors at the Dawn of History*. London and New York: Routledge.

Morkot, Robert. 2003. *Historical Dictionary of Ancient Egyptian Warfare*. Lanham, MD: Scarecrow Press.

Spalinger, Anthony J. 2008. *War in Ancient Egypt: The New Kingdom*. Malden, MA: Blackwell Publishing.

Documents

From *The King James Bible*. 1611. 1 Samuel 17:1–10, 32, 38–51.

The Old Testament has many accounts of battles fought by the ancient inhabitants of Israel. One of its most famous stories, about the individual combat between David and the Philistine warrior Goliath, includes descriptions of the typical weaponry and armor used in the wars of that era.

Now the Philistines gathered together their armies to battle, and were gathered together at Shochoh, which belongeth to Judah, and pitched between Shochoh and Azekah, in Ephesdammim. And Saul and the men of Israel were gathered together, and pitched by the valley of Elah, and set the battle in array against the Philistines. And the Philistines stood on a mountain on the one side, and Israel stood on a mountain on the other side: and there was a valley between them.

And there went out a champion out of the camp of the Philistines, named Goliath, of Gath, whose height was six cubits and a span. And he had an helmet of brass upon his head, and he was armed with a coat of mail; and the weight of the coat was five thousand shekels of brass. And he had greaves of brass upon his legs, and a target of brass between his shoulders. And the staff of his spear was like a weaver's beam; and his spear's head weighed six hundred shekels of iron: and one bearing a shield went before him. And he stood and cried unto the armies of Israel, and said unto them, Why are ye come out to set your battle in array? Am not I a Philistine, and ye servants to Saul? Choose you a man for you, and let him come down to me. If he be able to fight with me, and to kill me, then will we be your servants: but if I prevail against him, and kill him, then shall ye be our servants, and serve us. And the Philistine said, I defy the armies of Israel this day; give me a man, that we may fight together. . . .

And David said to Saul, Let no man's heart fail because of him; thy servant will go and fight with this Philistine. . . . And Saul armed David with his armour, and he put an helmet of brass upon his head; also he armed him with a coat of mail. And David girded his sword upon his armour, and he assayed to go; for he had not proved it. And David said unto Saul, I cannot go with these; for I have not proved them. And David put them off him. And he took his staff in his hand, and chose him five smooth stones out of the brook, and put them in a shepherd's bag which he had, even in a scrip; and his sling was in his hand: and he drew near to the Philistine.

And the Philistine came on and drew near unto David; and the man that bare the shield went before him. And when the Philistine looked about, and saw David, he disdained him: for he was but a youth, and ruddy, and of a fair countenance. And the Philistine said unto David, Am I a dog, that thou comest to me with staves? And the Philistine cursed David by his gods. And the Philistine said to David, Come to me, and I will give thy flesh unto the fowls of the air, and to the beasts of the field. Then said David to the Philistine, Thou comest to me with a sword, and with a spear, and with a shield: but I come to thee in the name of the LORD of hosts, the God of the armies of Israel, whom thou hast defied. This day will the LORD deliver thee into mine hand; and I will smite thee, and take thine head from thee; and I will give the carcases of the host of the Philistines this day unto the fowls of the air, and to the wild beasts of the earth; that all the earth may know that there is a God in Israel. And all this assembly shall know that the LORD saveth not with sword and spear: for the battle is the LORD'S, and he will give you into our hands. And it came to pass, when the Philistine arose, and came and drew nigh to meet David, that David hasted, and ran toward the army to meet the Philistine. And David put his hand in his bag, and took thence a stone, and slang it, and smote the Philistine in his forehead, that the stone sunk into his forehead; and he fell upon his face to the earth. So David prevailed over the Philistine with a sling and with a stone, and smote the Philistine, and slew him; but there was no sword in the hand of David. Therefore David ran, and stood upon the Philistine, and took his sword, and drew it out of the sheath thereof, and slew him, and cut off his head therewith. And when the Philistines saw their champion was dead, they fled. . . .

From Baikie, James. 1912. *Ancient Egypt.* London: A. and C. Black.

In this passage, the author draws information from an ancient scribal text to describe the hard life of an Egyptian soldier, and provides an overview of a typical Egyptian fighting force.

If the lot of the cavalry soldier is hard, that of the infantry-man is harder. In the barracks he is flogged for every mistake or offence. Then war breaks out, and he has to march with his battalion to Syria. Day after day he has to tramp on foot through the wild hill-country, so different from the flat, fertile homeland that he loves. He has to carry all his heavy equipment and his rations, so that he is laden like a donkey; and often he has to drink dirty water, which makes him ill. Then, when the battle comes, he gets all the danger and the wounds, while the Generals get all the credit. When the war is over, he comes home riding on a donkey, a broken-down man, sick and wounded, his very clothes stolen by the rascals who should have attended on him. Far better, the wise man says, to be a scribe, and to remain comfortably at home. I dare say it was all quite true, just as perhaps it would not be very far from the truth at the present time; but, in spite of it all, Pharaoh had his battles to fight, and he got his soldiers all right when they were needed.

The Egyptian army was not generally a very big one. It was nothing like the great hosts that we hear of nowadays, or read of in some of the old histories. The armies that the Pharaohs led into Syria were not often much bigger than what we should call an army corps nowadays—probably about 20,000 men altogether, rarely more than 25,000. But in that number you could find almost as many different sorts of men as in our own Indian army. There would be first the native Egyptian spearmen and bowmen—the spearmen with leather caps and quilted leather tunics, carrying a shield and spear, and sometimes an axe, or a dagger, or short sword—the bowmen, more lightly equipped, but probably more dangerous enemies, for the Egyptian archers were almost as famous as the old English bowmen, and won many a battle for their King. Then came the chariot brigade, also of native Egyptians, men probably of higher rank than the foot-soldiers. The chariots were very light, and it must have been exceedingly difficult for the bowman to balance himself in the narrow car, as it bumped and clattered over rough ground. The two horses were gaily decorated, and often wore plumes on their heads. The charioteer sometimes twisted the reins round his waist, and could take a hand in the fighting if his companion was hard pressed, guiding his horses by swaying his body to one side or the other.

Round the Pharaoh himself, as he stood in his beautiful chariot, marched the royal bodyguard. It was made up of men whom the Egyptians called "Sherden"—Sardinians, probably, who had come over the sea to serve for hire in the army of the great King. They wore metal helmets, with a round ball on the top and horns at the sides, carried round bossed shields, and were armed with great heavy swords of much the same shape as those which the Norman knights used to carry. Behind the native troops and the bodyguard marched the other mercenaries—regiments of black Soudanese, with wild-beast skins thrown over their ebony shoulders; and light-coloured Libyans from the West, each with a couple of feathers stuck in his leather skull-cap.

Scouts went on ahead to scour the country, and bring to the King reports of the enemy's whereabouts. . . .

Stonemasons

In the terms that we use to describe the period when human civilization emerged—the Bronze Age and the Iron Age—the first metals that people mastered and used extensively are announced as key characteristics of early cultures. Yet the material of the preceding era, the Stone Age, remained important throughout the ancient world. All major public buildings continued to be made of stone, as were most statues; stone tools, utensils, and weapons remained commonplace; and some civilizations began finding new uses for stone, such as paving roads.

In ancient Mesopotamia, building projects involving stone required three types of workers. Unskilled laborers, mostly slaves, carved out rough blocks of stone at quarries and helped to transport them to the construction site; while some stones were placed on boats, they were generally moved on the ground by dragging them on sledges, pulling them with ropes, or placing wooden rollers beneath them, sometimes with the assistance of donkeys or oxen. They also constructed ramps to pull stones up for the upper portions of the walls. Then, before they were put in place,

experienced stonemasons carved the stones into precise shapes, so that they would stay in position without mortar. Finally, so-called "picture-carvers" would sculpt raised images of people and animals on the walls.

Some of the same techniques were used, on a much larger scale, to construct the ancient world's most famous stone buildings, the Great Pyramids of Gaza. Their materials came from the Tula quarries near Giza: large rectangular blocks of limestone were cut on all sides but the bottom using basalt pickaxes or copper tools; then flint or copper wedges freed the block from its base. The stone blocks may have been coated with hot charcoal and doused with cold water to make them easier to remove. Some parts of the pyramids also used blocks of basalt and granite, which were probably cut out using a combination of copper saws and abrasive sand. Evidence suggests that stones were occasionally cut by tools with sharp jewels for points. Canals were dug to transport these blocks close to the site of the pyramids, and they made their final journey to the pyramid by being dragged on sledges. To ensure that the blocks reached the right destination, marks were occasionally placed on the blocks, indicating which pharaoh's tomb they are intended for or where the block is supposed to be positioned.

The next stage in the process was to carve the blocks into their final shapes. To cut exact right angles, the stonemasons employed set squares, not unlike the triangles used by modern draftspersons, and for measurements they had a ruler, one cubit long, divided into seven sections, though some illustrations suggest that long pieces of string with knots were used for measurements as well. After the final carving, the blocks were placed into position, beginning at the center of the planned pyramid and moving outward; set squares with plumb lines attached ensured that the stones were aligned horizontally. Ramps made out of bricks or rubble were used to elevate stones to higher levels, though there is some debate about whether these ramps went straight up, wound their way around the expanding pyramid, or were inside the incomplete pyramid. The stones were then covered on the outside by casing blocks that were made of fine limestone and put in place with a thin coating of mortar made of quartz, gypsum, and

This painting depicts ancient Egyptian stonemasons preparing stones to be used for a wall surrounding a pyramid. (National Geographic Society/Corbis)

lime. The final touch was a capstone of gold or fine limestone, placed on the top of the pyramid.

Constructing these huge pyramids was undoubtedly arduous work for everyone involved, and there was the constant possibility of dangerous injuries, as shown by examination of the bodies of the workers, which are sometimes missing fingers or limbs or show signs of mended bone fractures. Even some workers who did not have such mishaps suffered from compressed vertebrae, a usual consequence of constantly lifting heavy weights. Yet everyone involved, from the manual laborers to the skilled masons, was paid for their work, and they were also motivated by religious fervor, believing that the construction of the pyramids was what their gods desired. As evidence that their morale was good, graffiti indicates that some pyramid workers made up playful names for their groups, like "Friends of Khufu" or "The Drunks of Menkaure."

In addition to their work on pyramids, temples, and other structures, Egyptian stonemasons crafted many other objects. They became quite expert, for example, in the art of making stone pots, vases, vessels, plates, and bowls, made from a wide variety of materials that included limestone, sandstone, granite, and diorite. There are many tomb illustrations showing stonemasons drilling holes in nearly completed vessels, using a special drill. These surfaces of these pots and vases were smoothed using powdered quartz, the same way that large stone blocks were polished. Some special bowls for sauces were made to look like birds, with a curved head and neck as the handle. Also, while the Egyptians came to rely upon copper tools for most purposes, stone tools remained commonplace, especially stone knives, produced by the ancient technique of chipping. These knives, usually made of flint or jasper, were used for circumcision and embalming, since copper knives were considered improper for these important religious rituals.

In tombs, the mummies of pharaohs were placed in sarcophaguses made of stone, and stonemasons

EXTRATERRESTRIAL STONEMASONS?

Despite ongoing research, there remains some uncertainty about how the pyramid builders of ancient Egypt were able to shape their huge stone blocks so precisely and move millions of them into their proper positions. This has inspired modern theories that visiting aliens must have assisted the Egyptians in constructing the pyramids. These speculations, popularized in numerous books and documentaries, ignore the considerable archaeological evidence showing that the Egyptians planned and built the pyramids themselves. It also seems likely that advanced aliens, like twenty-first-century humans, would have long ago abandoned the use of stone in constructing large buildings and thus would lack the expertise to direct such a project.

CUTTING-EDGE TECHNOLOGY

For years, there remained some uncertainty about the techniques employed by the ancient Egyptian stonemasons; in particular, scholars wondered how they were able to cut granite, a very hard rock, with their copper tools. This puzzle was solved by Egyptologist Denys Stocks, who determined through his experiments that the stonemasons probably poured quartz sand on their copper saws, enhancing their ability to cut into the granite. Stocks now serves as a consultant to the Pharaonic Village, a popular tourist attraction in Cairo where visitors can observe trained workers in Egyptian clothing duplicating the feats of ancient Egyptian stonemasons, woodworkers, and metalworkers. (His book, *Experiments in Egyptian Archaeology: Stoneworking Technology in Ancient Egypt*, is listed in Further Reading.)

assisted in the process of carving out the underground chambers that replaced the pyramids as the pharaohs' final resting places. The Egyptians were also fond of stone statues, and much of the work involved was done by ordinary masons; for a large statue of a pharaoh, for example, a rock might be carved into a roughly human shape at a quarry, then transported to a workshop, where other masons would further perfect its form. Only the final stages of detailed portraiture, polishing, and painting the statue would require skilled sculptors and artists. Stonemasons also contributed to

the artwork on the walls of tombs; they would first smooth the walls and spread plaster over them, and after an artist had outlined the figures, they would chip them out to provide a three-dimensional effect before they were painted.

While much of their work was done at construction sites, stonemasons also had workshops where they made smaller objects, but we have little information about them. Illustrations suggest that all sorts of different craftsmen worked together in the same room, but this was probably only a convenient way to show all of the work that had gone into making all of the contents of the tomb. It seems more likely that, as in modern Egypt, artisans had their own special workshops, grouped together in certain sections of the city. Most stonemasons inherited their positions from their fathers, who would train their sons in all of the necessary techniques, but interested young men may have also worked their way into the field as apprentices.

We are also not sure what sort of status the stonemasons enjoyed in their society. On one hand, an official during the reign of Thutmose IV (died 1391 BCE), named Menna, mentioned in his tomb inscription that he had richly rewarded all of the people who worked on his tomb, including the "stone cutters," an indication that their work was appreciated. Yet others might have felt differently; during the reign of Ramses III (died 1155 BCE), for example, some lower-level bureaucrats decided that it was not important to provide the masons and other workers constructing a tomb at Deir el Medina with their promised rations of wheat. After waiting for their rations to arrive, the angry workers staged the first recorded strike in history, insisting that they would not return to work until they had been properly paid. After weeks of negotiation amidst intermittent work stoppages, some senior administrator did address the problem, so that the workers regularly received their wheat during their final two years of service.

The ancient Egyptians used many other materials for their buildings and utensils, including wood, mud, and clay, but these substances wear away over time while stone endures, which may lead contemporary observers to overstate the importance of stone in Egyptian culture. Still, cognizant of the need for structures and artifacts that would last for ages in the afterlife, the Egyptians themselves no doubt appreciated the special virtues of stone, which is why it was invariably employed in their most cherished projects, the pyramids and the temples, and this means that they must also have valued the skilled artisans who worked with stone.

Further Reading

Arnold, Dieter. 1991. *Building in Egypt: Pharaonic Stone Masonry.* Oxford and New York: Oxford University Press.

Dunn, Christopher. 2010. *Lost Technologies of Ancient Egypt: Advanced Engineering in the Temples of the Pharaohs.* Rochester, VT: Bear & Company.

Klemm, Rosemarie, and Dietrich D. Klemm. 2008. *Stones and Quarries in Ancient Egypt.* London: British Museum Press.

Moorey, P.R.S. 1994. *Ancient Mesopotamian Materials and Industries: The Archaeological Evidence.* Oxford and New York: Oxford University Press.

Stocks, Denys A. 2003. *Experiments in Egyptian Archaeology: Stoneworking Technology in Ancient Egypt.* London and New York: Routledge.

Verner, Miroslav. 2001. *The Pyramids: The Mystery, Culture, and Science of Egypt's Great Monuments.* Translated by Steven Rendall. London: Grove Books.

Document

From Baikie, James. 1912. *Ancient Egypt.* London: A. and C. Black.

Here, the author describes a group of stonemasons who have gone on strike because they have not received their wages.

A great noise is heard from one of the narrow riverside streets, and a crowd of men comes rushing up with shouts and oaths. Ahead of them runs a single figure, whose writing-case, stuck in his girdle, marks him out as a scribe. He is almost at his last gasp, for he is stout and not accustomed to running; and he is evidently fleeing for his life, for the men behind him—rough, half-naked, ill-fed creatures of the working class—are chasing him with cries of anger, and a good, deal of stone-throwing. Bruised and bleeding, he darts up to the gate of a handsome house whose garden-wall faces the street. He gasps out a word to the porter, and is quickly passed into the garden. The gate

is slammed and bolted in the faces of his pursuers, who form a ring round it, shouting and shaking their fists.

In a little while the gate is cautiously unbarred, and a fine-looking man, very richly dressed, and followed by half a dozen well-armed negro guards, steps forward, and asks the workmen why they are here, making such a noise, and why they have chased and beaten his secretary. He is Prince Paser, who has charge of the Works Department of the Theban Government, and the workmen are masons employed on a large job in the cemetery of Thebes. They all shout at once in answer to the Prince's question; but by-and-by they push forward a spokesman, and he begins, rather sheepishly at first, but warming up as he goes along, to make their complaint to the great man.

He and his mates, he says, have been working for weeks. They have had no wages; they have not even had the corn and oil which ought to be issued as rations to Government workmen. So they have struck work, and now they have come to their lord the Prince to entreat him either to give command that the rations be issued, or, if his stores are exhausted, to appeal to Pharaoh. "We have been driven here by hunger and thirst; we have no clothes, we have no oil, we have no food. Write to our lord the Pharaoh, that he may give us something for our sustenance." When the spokesman has finished his complaint, the whole crowd volubly assents to what he has said, and sways to and fro in a very threatening manner.

Prince Paser, however, is an old hand at dealing with such complaints. With a smiling face he promises that fifty sacks of corn shall be sent to the cemetery immediately, with oil to correspond. Only the workmen must go back to their work at once, and there must be no more chasing of poor Secretary Amen-nachtu. Otherwise, he can do nothing. The workmen grumble a little. They have been put off with promises before, and have got little good of them. But they have no leader bold enough to start a riot, and they have no weapons, and the spears and bows of the Prince's Nubians look dangerous. Finally they turn, and disappear, grumbling, down the street from which they came; and Prince Paser, with a shrug of his shoulders, goes indoors again. Whether the fifty sacks of corn are ever sent or not, is another matter. Strikes, you see, were not unknown, even so long ago as this.

Storytellers

Oral storytelling surely dates back to prehistoric campfires, where hunters related their latest adventures and shamans elaborated upon their mythological explanations for the creation of the world and puzzling phenomena of nature. As the communities of ancient civilizations emerged, certain individuals came to specialize in this art, regularly performing for rapt and appreciative audiences; for the very best of these people, storytelling undoubtedly became their principal avocation. However, since our distant ancestors left very few written records of their everyday lives, we know very little about the first full-time storytellers. Almost all of our evidence of their existence is based upon observations of contemporary storytellers in largely illiterate cultures, who surely represent a continuation of an older tradition, and written stories from ancient times that clearly began as oral presentations and still show signs, such as verbal asides and references to listeners, indicating that origin. The Babylonian Epic of Gilgamesh, for example, begins by addressing an audience, and Egyptologist Rosalie David has deduced that one of the earliest Egyptian stories, "Khufu and the Magicians," had been long preserved by means of a tradition of oral storytelling before it was committed to papyrus. Some stories in the Bible, such as the Book of Ruth, are also believed by some to have originated as oral narratives.

The men who entertained monarchs and nobles typically presented their stories in the forms of songs or poems recited to a musical accompaniment; we know that such individuals performed for the Mesopotamian kings, and legends of the Greek poet Homer suggest that such minstrels were commonplace throughout the ancient world. However, everyday people enjoyed stories as well, and their needs must have been served by itinerant storytellers who told their tales without any music. Author and Egyptologist Barbara Wertz offered this observation in *Red Land, Black Land: Daily Life in Ancient Egypt* (1978): "Since most Egyptians were illiterate. . . they probably relied on professional storytellers . . . although I must admit I know of no specific evidence to them in Egypt." Still, she vividly imagines a traveling storyteller standing in the center of a village, next to its

jar of water, and delivering a familiar Egyptian tale. Such people were undoubtedly men, since it would have been highly unusual for an Egyptian woman to travel by herself from town to town, and they would probably enter each new village, find a prominent place to speak, and begin telling stories, soliciting donations from the listeners who would gather. A man who especially enjoyed his talents might invite him to have dinner and spend the night at his house, eager to hear more; an intrigued boy might strive to commit the man's story to memory and ask the storyteller for a few tips, hoping to eventually assume the same role.

The storyteller, of course, would bring his own agenda to these private conversations, eager to hear new stories that he could add to his repertoire. Through such contact between storytellers and citizens, an especially good story might spread throughout a wide region or even to a different civilization, as the tale is passed to traders who venture to distant lands. There are reasons to believe, for example, that a story about a man who survived a worldwide flood circulated orally throughout the ancient world and influenced both the Mesopotamian Epic of Gilgamesh and the biblical story of Noah and the flood, since the two accounts have similarities suggesting a common origin. Undoubtedly, itinerant storytellers were also conduits for the latest gossip about high officials, which we are aware of because it occasionally found its way into written records. One scholar, Lisa Schwappach-Shirriff, has found hieroglyphics reporting that one pharaoh's wife was bald, while another pharaoh was reportedly making nocturnal visits to one of his generals, signaling a homosexual relationship. Precisely this sort of scurrilous information might have been conveyed from town to town by storytellers.

While willing to offer provocative observations about leaders while talking with individuals, the Egyptian storytellers encouraged citizens to support the status quo in their stories; the story of "Khufu and the Magicians," for example, emphasizes that the pharaohs governing Egypt at the time were divine, validating their absolute rule. Another story, about a man named Sinuhe, involves the desirability of living in Egypt, as its hero spends most of his life outside of Egypt before finally achieving his fervent wish to return to his homeland. Presumably, storytellers were well aware that their livelihood depended upon the good will of local officials, and hence were reluctant to tell any stories that might seem designed to make people discontented with their situation.

We can garner some sense of the personalities and attitudes of Egyptian storytellers by examining one of their most popular stories. In "The Tale of the Two Brothers," a man named Bata lives with his older brother Anubis, a farmer, and his wife. One day, while Anubis is away, the wife attempts to seduce Bata; when he refuses her advances, she tells Anubis that his brother had tried to rape and beat her. Warned by a cow that Anubis intends to kill him, Bata runs away, and on the side of a stream infested with protective crocodiles sent by a god, he tells Anubis what really happened and, to demonstrate his sincerity, cuts off his penis. The departing Bata then explains to Anubis that he will place his heart in a tree, and if it falls down, Anubis must come to his aid. While a chagrined Anubis kills his wife, Bata proceeds to marry a lovely woman crafted for him by the gods, but she is lured away by the pharaoh, and when she tells him about Bata's heart, he has the tree cut down. Fortunately, Anubis retrieves the heart and places it inside Bata, bringing him back to life. Seeking revenge against his unfaithful wife and the pharaoh, Bata first transforms himself into a bull, which is killed, and then into two trees; a seed from the tree impregnates the wife, who somehow gives birth to Bata. When he succeeds his purported father as the new pharaoh, he has his wife killed and makes Anubis his heir.

This story suggests, first of all, that the storytellers were addressing a predominantly male audience, since its two villains are both deceitful wives (who are eventually killed for their crimes); and since Egyptian women tended to stay at home, the people who gathered around the visiting storyteller would most likely be men. The magical elements may reflect a desire to appeal to children as well as adults, although the Egyptian world view did not exclude the possibility of fantastic occurrences in everyday life. The protagonist Bata wins listeners' sympathy because he is consistently faithful to his brother and clever in devising imaginative ways to achieve his ends, two traits that the Egyptians clearly valued. Finally, the story supports the notion of cosmic justice, as the virtuous are rewarded and the evildoers are punished, sometimes due to the timely intervention of a god.

NEW VERSIONS OF AN OLD STORY

The stories told by ancient Egypt storytellers continue to influence modern authors in various ways. Several writers have adapted classic Egyptian tales for younger readers, and one of twentieth-century Egypt's greatest writers, Naguib Mahfouz (winner of the Nobel Prize for Literature, 1988), launched his career by writing new stories about ancient Egypt, collected in *Voices from the Other World: Ancient Egyptian Tales* (2004). One of these, "The Return of Sinuhe," is a sequel to one of the masterpieces of ancient Egyptian literature, though it adds romantic complications to the original story. The story of Sinuhe was also the basis of a 1954 Hollywood film, *The Egyptian*, starring Victor Mature and Jean Simmons.

KEEPING A TRADITION ALIVE

Storytellers were appreciated in ancient times because there were few forms of entertainment available to ordinary citizens. Today, of course, people have access to many diversions, including books, films, television programs, video games, and the Internet. Nevertheless, individuals throughout the world are struggling to keep the art of storytelling alive. In modern Egypt, for example, a storyteller named Dalia el-Gendi established the el-Warsha troupe in 1987 in order to preserve the stories told by the country's aging storytellers and to train a new generation of storytellers to carry on the tradition.

Over the course of centuries, the art of Egyptian storytelling evolved: the stories became more complicated, suggesting that audiences were growing more sophisticated, and as Egypt began to have greater contact with the other civilizations of the Mediterranean, stories increasingly featured faraway locations and foreign characters. A few later stories are so realistic that some scholars have argued that they are historical accounts of actual events, though this view has been disputed. When the Greek historian Herodotus visited Egypt, he heard many stories that he incorporated into his *Histories*, though some contemporary scholars think that he was far too credulous in believing most of the things that he heard. Still, his experiences show that a tradition of Egyptian storytelling remained vibrant during his lifetime.

For literate individuals, storytelling in the later days of the Egyptian empire was a matter of written texts, and since they are the individuals who recorded its history, they generally failed to document the continuing practice of oral storytelling. Nevertheless, while largely unnoticed and unheralded, such storytelling did remain a part of Egyptian culture long after its civilization declined and fell to foreign conquerors whose followers brought new stories to incorporate into popular storytelling. Even today, contemporary Egyptians are working to preserve stories that have been passed down from generation to generation, and to train people in the ancient art of telling them in an involving manner, much like their ancient ancestors.

Further Reading

Fisher, Loren R. 2010. *Tales from Ancient Egypt: The Birth of Stories*. Eugene, OR: Cascade Books.

Goldman, Shalom. 1995. *The Wiles of Women/The Wiles of Men: Joseph and Potiphar's Wife in Ancient Near Eastern, Jewish, and Islamic Folklore*. Albany: State University of New York Press.

Matthews, Victor Henry, and Don C. Benjamin. 2006. *Old Testament Parallels: Laws and Stories from the Ancient Near East*. Third edition. New York and Maywah, NJ: Paulist Press.

McCall, Henrietta. 1990. *Mesopotamian Myths*. Austin: University of Texas Press.

Schwartz, Howard. 1997. *Reimagining the Bible: The Storytelling of the Rabbis*. Oxford and New York: Oxford University Press.

Simpson, William Kelly, editor. 2003. *The Literature of Ancient Egypt: An Anthology of Stories, Instructions, Stelae, Autobiographies, and Poetry*. Third edition. New Haven, CT: Yale University Press.

Document

From Brooksbank, Frank Henry. 1914. *Legends of Ancient Egypt: Stories of Egyptian Gods and Heroes*. New York: T.Y. Crowell.

This ancient story, retold by a modern writer for young readers, seems to perfectly represent the sort of story that an ancient Egyptian storyteller would relate to his audiences.

A curious story, still believed in by some Arabs of today, is told of this third pyramid. It was haunted by the spirit of a beautiful woman, who lured men to their destruction by her charms. At about the going down of the sun she came forth, and any man she saw and wished to ruin she smiled upon so winningly that he forgot all else for love of her, and wandered about the country trying to find her. Many men have been observed wandering around the pyramid at about the hour of sunset, deprived of their senses, the victims of her charms.

This woman, it was said, was a famous queen, named Nitocris, whose husband was ruler of Egypt. But having incurred the wrath of some of his nobles, he was slain by them. To all appearance Nitocris did not mind this, and she showed no ill will to his murderers. Her feasts were as rich as before, and her amusements as wild and unbridled.

One day she invited all those Egyptians who had had part or lot in her husband's death to a great banquet to be given in a grand apartment underground. When asked why she chose this place for her feast, she replied that the room was to be consecrated, and the banquet was a part of the ceremonies. But in the midst of the meal, when the merriment was at its height, Nitocris secretly ordered her head servant to open certain sluices communicating with the river Nile by underground canals, and the room began rapidly to fill with water. The guests, brought to their senses by this peril, sought to escape, but none could find the door; and, turning to look for Nitocris, they discovered that she was gone. In vain they fought and struggled to get out. Penned securely in this chamber underground, they all were drowned, victims to the Queen's revenge.

Nitocris, knowing that she would be punished for the vengeance she had wreaked, forestalled her subjects. Going to a chamber which had been heated previously by a fierce fire within, she threw herself into the ashes and was consumed.

Ancient Asia, 3000 BCE–500 CE

Introduction

Historians in Europe and North America long focused on the ancient civilizations that seemed to have had the most direct influence on their own culture—the Mesopotamians, Egyptians, Greeks, and Romans. Yet the civilizations that developed in India, China, Japan, and other Asian countries were equally impressive, even if their accomplishments were not as well known in the Western world, and contemporary world histories and textbooks are now properly devoting more attention to the achievements of the ancient workers in southern and western Asia.

While there were earlier cultures that remain poorly understood, ancient India's Vedic culture developed a rich philosophical and literary tradition inspired by the religion of Hinduism, and various smaller empires were eventually unified under the emperor Ashoka (304–232 BCE) in 300 BCE, bringing further advances in mathematics, science, literature, engineering, and philosophy. In large cities and tiny villages, Indians mastered and practiced a wide variety of crafts, often earning little money for their work, though there were also wealthy individuals who enjoyed lives of luxury.

In ancient China, the man generally regarded as China's first emperor, Qin Shi Huang (259–210 BCE), and his successors built upon the achievements of their predecessors to develop a strong government that encouraged scholarship and sponsored grand public projects, though the country's peasants and artisans sometimes suffered under their oppressive rule, leading to rebellions and foreign invasions. Though the cultures that flourished in Southeast Asia were influenced by both China and India, only Chinese culture

had a major impact on the developing civilizations of Korea and Japan, though their greatest moments would come much later.

For many observers, ancient Asia is most noteworthy because it developed a highly spiritual approach to life, creating religions like Buddhism, Jainism, and Taoism that emphasized the illusory nature of the physical world and encouraged individuals to renounce material goods in order to focus on the pursuit of wisdom and virtue. Yet the Indians and Chinese were also skilled in technology, constructing huge canals, irrigation systems, statues, and structures that rivaled anything being built in the Western world. As one sign of their success, the populations of these regions began increasing, as their thriving cultures could support more and more people, so India and China became the world's most populous nations. Virtually all of their citizens were necessarily hard workers, and they have remained hard workers until the present day, often carrying on traditions that have lasted for thousands of years.

Acrobats

One benefit of civilization is that physical activity, once only a chore, now could also become something pleasurable, both to participate in and observe. Throughout ancient Asia, athletic men and women trained themselves to perform in various ways to attract spectators and earn a living. These people were almost invariably poor and little regarded in their societies, and their strenuous labors were rarely celebrated in art and literature, so we are forced to speculate about many aspects of their daily lives; yet scattered bits of evidence demonstrate that acrobatics was the chosen profession of many adventurous people who disdained more reliable but unexciting avocations like farming or carpentry.

The acrobats of ancient India had many opportunities to make money because of their nation's many religious festivals; and while the performance of a play was the usual centerpiece of such occasions, performers of all sorts would hurry to the site of each festival, knowing that large crowds would be gathering there. Acrobats would work in groups that included an orchestra, since the sounds of clarinets, flutes, and drums would help to draw an audience of onlookers. Those who stayed to watch the performance would generally contribute some money, and afterward the proceeds would be divided among the members of the group.

A wall carving found in a Buddhist *stupa* (or mound) at Bharhut depicts one common feat of the Indian acrobats: forming a human pyramid. Fourteen people are involved: seven of them stand on the ground, and on their shoulders are standing four other men. These men are tightly gripping the ankles of two more men on their shoulders, who are in turn supporting a small boy at the very top of the pyramid. The boy's arms are upraised, as if he is responding to appreciative cheers from his audience, and he is brandishing a scarf, an accoutrement associated with acrobats. Perhaps this served as the exciting climax to a typical performance, but the acrobats could amaze and delight their viewers with other daring feats as well. A second image shows a hanging man who is supporting nine other men who are clinging to his feet, while a carving at another site appears to show acrobats climbing up a wall covered with vines; one of the men turns away from viewers and bends over to display his buttocks.

Other Indian acrobats engaged in an early form of tightrope walking, as a rope would be stretched high above the ground and the acrobat would not only walk across the rope, but dance upon it as well. A troupe might include some tumblers, doing somersaults over each other or other obstacles. Another popular act featured a man or woman who balanced precariously at the top of a long pole with a small horizontal bar,

Like their modern counterparts, ancient Indian acrobats dazzled audiences by forming human pyramids; this one, depicted in a Bharhut, India, stupa (a Buddhist shrine), involved fourteen men in four rows. (The Huntington Library)

maintaining their positions by means of shoes with spikes; rapt audiences knew that if these acrobats slipped, they would fall to their death. On the ground, an acrobat could risk his life in a different way by performing an elaborate dance while holding four or five sharp javelins, which could inflict a grievous wound if mishandled. The sword swallower manipulated a dangerous weapon in a different fashion by inserting a sword into his mouth without harming himself; this act of delicate acrobatics, which originated in India, later became commonplace throughout the world.

Like other performers, acrobats were part of the fourth and least respected Indian caste, the *sudras*, and their peripatetic, unsettled lifestyle attracted a special degree of scorn; as Iravati suggested in her 2003 book, *Performing Artistes in Ancient India*, Indian people "despised their way of life but loved their art." One ancient text advises monarchs that when their cities are besieged, they should banish all actors and acrobats, suggesting that such vagabonds did not merit royal protection in times of trouble. However, an intriguing story from the early days of Buddhism, "The Youth Who Married a Female Acrobat," suggests that individuals from higher castes may have occasionally chosen to become acrobats. The son of a royal treasurer, observing acrobats performing for a king, watches a female acrobat and falls in love with her; but her father, also an acrobat in the troupe, insists that he must accompany them on their travels to marry his daughter. The man then resolves to become an acrobat himself, under the tutelage of his father-in-law, and soon he is skillful enough to perform several somersaults while balanced at the top of a pole. But after he performs these feats in front of the Buddha, he is inspired to abandon his career to become one of his followers. It is impossible to know, of course, how many individuals of loftier castes actually abandoned their positions to become acrobats, motivated by love or a strong desire to pursue this art, but the story also presents a general picture of the life of typical acrobats. They were constantly traveling; both men and women worked as acrobats; they were sometimes hired to perform for royal audiences; and their profession was very much a family affair, as the sons and daughters of acrobats would naturally master the art as well and eventually become part of the act.

Acrobats were also part of the social scene in ancient China, as indicated by the famed "terracotta warriors" buried alongside the first Chinese emperor, since their ranks include a few acrobats, evidently there to amuse the troops in between their battles. These figures are bare-chested, indicating that this was typical dress for acrobats, and one of them seems to be holding part of a long pole. It is also known that acrobats were always included in the autumn harvest festivals, and they frequently performed for the early emperors, who played a key role in promoting this art form. As in India, however, these acrobats enjoyed little respect, as they were never allowed to display their skills in theaters. Instead, they would perform in streets or the local marketplace, though wealthy men sometimes hired them to entertain guests in their homes. As one sign of their lowly status, acrobats were sometimes slaves, who had been assigned to specialize in this activity.

Some typical acts of the Chinese acrobats were similar to those in India, such doing somersaults, walking and leaping on tightropes, and balancing on long poles. However, Chinese acrobats on poles would often perform in groups, so that they might, for example, leap from one pole to another. An ancient sculpture shows that they formed human pyramids of three or more people, and they also walked on stilts. One unique aspect of Chinese acrobatics was the regular use of household objects like plates, jars, chairs, and tables; one common act, for example, involved an acrobat balancing several plates while spinning them rapidly, while another involved juggling glass bowls without spilling any of the water inside. Acrobats might entertain audiences by leaping through small hoops with birdlike agility, sometimes adding an element of excitement by igniting the wicker hoops to create rings of fire. The Chinese also pioneered in developing types of performances that combined acrobatics with other arts; some of these finally gave acrobats an opportunity to perform on theatrical stages. The so-called "Jiaodi Opera," which emerged around 200 BCE, took on various forms that might include acrobatics, wrestling, dance, music, and drama, while the "Lion Dance" featured pairs of performers imitating the movements of lions with both dance-like and acrobatic flourishes.

To become an acrobat in ancient China, one had to train for a long time under the supervision of a veteran performer. An acrobat needed to develop a great deal of physical strength in order to support the weight of several other acrobats, but graceful movements of the wrists and legs also had to be mastered, since there were routines that required acrobats to imitate the smooth motions of fish. Acrobats were taught to meditate before each performance to maintain the necessary calm while engaging in life-threatening maneuvers.

Training might begin by teaching apprentices how to stand on their heads or how to juggle several objects with one's hands and feet; then, aspiring acrobats would join with others to learn standard acts like forming a human pyramid. As in India, acrobatics was often a family tradition, and certain regions of China became especially well known for producing skilled acrobats.

Eventually, as was not the case in India, acrobatics became both a widely admired and very respectable profession, practiced by well-paid professionals who solely performed in theaters for eager audiences who paid high prices for their tickets. Today, the best Chinese acrobats regularly tour the world, and while they are now accompanied by orchestras and augmented by colorful lighting and special effects, they are largely performing the same stunts and routines that once entertained a handful of peasants in the streets of ancient China.

ATHLETES AND ARTILLERY

Although Indian acrobats were originally regarded only as entertainers, their culture gradually came to value their skills and routines as helpful forms of exercise. For that reason, selected soldiers in today's Indian army regularly practice acrobatics using a tall wooden pole, and every year, as part of their Victory Day celebrations, they perform for the public. Their typical feats include a soldier balancing on the top of the pole, another breathing fire while hanging from the pole, and teams of soldiers holding their bodies to form geometric designs. Such performances are designed to show that Indian soldiers are strong and well prepared for battle.

DANCING ACROBATS

Today, skilled Chinese acrobats receive salaries from the government, and they mainly perform in theaters throughout the world; however, there are also acrobatic artists who still make their living in the manner of the ancient acrobats of India and China by performing in the streets in order to garner donations from admiring observers. Such individuals can be found today in New York City, where pedestrians are often entertained by energetic break dancers, who show off their amazing acrobatic dance moves on the sidewalks to the accompaniment of raucous music from a boom box next to a basket to collect money.

Further Reading

Deshpande, S. H. 1992. *Physical Education in Ancient India.* New Delhi: Bharatiya Vidya Prakashan.

Fu, Qifeng. 1985. *Chinese Acrobatics through the Ages.* Beijing: Foreign Languages Press.

Fu, Qifeng, and Xining Li. 2003. *A Primer of Chinese Acrobatics.* Beijing: Foreign Languages Press.

Iravati. 2003. *Performing Artistes in Ancient India.* New Delhi: D.K. Printworld.

Thaplyal, Kiran Kumar. 2004. *Village and Village Life in Ancient India.* New Delhi: Aryan Books International.

Wang, Zhengbao. 1982. *The Art of Chinese Acrobatics.* Beijing: Foreign Languages Press.

Document

From Buddhaghosa. C. fifth century CE. *Buddhist Legends.* Volume 3. Translated by George Watson Burlingame. 1921. Cambridge, MA: Harvard University Press.

The story "The Youth Who Married a Female Acrobat" is attributed to a Buddhist monk named Buddhaghosa who lived sometime in the fifth century CE. Its first part, below, describes how a treasurer's son in ancient India marries a female acrobat and then becomes an acrobat himself. The story's conclusion, not presented here, comes when the Buddha watches one of his performances, and the acrobat gives up performing to devote himself to the master.

The story goes that once a year, or once every six months, five hundred tumblers used to visit Rajagaha and give performances for seven days before the king. By these performances they earned much gold and money; in fact there was no end to the gifts tossed at them from time to time. The people stood on beds piled on top of beds, and watched the tumblers perform their feats.

One day a certain female tumbler climbed a pole, turned somersaults thereon, and balancing herself on the tip of the pole, danced and sang as she trod the air. Now on this occasion a certain treasurer's son, accompanied by a companion, stood on top of a pile of beds watching her. The grace and skill with which she managed her hands and feet attracted his attention, and he straightway fell in love with her. He went home and said, "If I can have her, I shall live; but if I cannot have her, I will die right here." So saying, he flung himself down on his bed and refused to take food.

His mother and father asked him, "Son, what ails you?" The son replied, "If I can have that tumbler's daughter, I can live; if I cannot have her, I will die right here." Said his mother and father, "Do not act in this way. We will bring you another maiden, our equal in birth and wealth." But he made the same reply as before and remained lying in bed. His father argued with him at length, but was unable to make him see things in a better light. Finally he sent for his son's friend, gave him a thousand pieces of money, and sent him off, saying to him, "Tell the tumbler to take this money and give his daughter to my son."

"I will not give my daughter for money," replied the tumbler, "but if it be true that he cannot live without my daughter, then let him travel about with us; if he will do this, I will give him my daughter." The mother and father communicated this information to their son. The son immediately said, "Of course I will travel about with them." His mother and father begged him not to do so, but he paid no attention to anything they said, and went and joined the tumbler.

The tumbler gave him his daughter in marriage, and traveled about with him through villages, market-towns, and royal cities, giving exhibitions everywhere. In no long time the female tumbler, after living with her husband, gave birth to a son. As she played with the boy, she would address him as "son of a cart-driver," or "son of a fetcher of wood and drawer of water," or "son of a know-nothing." It appears that the husband used to attend to everything relating to their carts. Wherever they halted, he would fetch grass for the oxen. Wherever they gave an exhibition, he would procure whatever apparatus was required, set it up, and remove it.

It was with reference to duties such as these performed by her husband that this woman employed such terms as these in playing with her son. The husband came to the conclusion that the songs she sang were about himself, and asked her, "Do you refer to me?" "Yes, I refer to you." "In that case I will run away and leave you."

"What difference does it make to me whether you go away or not?" replied the wife. And over and over again she sang the same song. It appears that by reason of the beauty she possessed and the large amount of money she earned, she was utterly indifferent to him.

"Why is it that she is so proud?" thought the husband to himself. Straightway he perceived within himself, "It is because of her skill as a tumbler." So he thought to himself, "Very well! I will learn tumbling-feats myself." Accordingly he went to his father-in-law and learned all the feats that he knew. And he exhibited his art in villages, market-towns, and royal cities, one after another, until finally he came to Rajagaha. And he caused proclamation to be made throughout the city, "Seven days hence Uggasena the treasurer's son will exhibit his art to the residents of the city." The residents of the city caused platform above platform to be erected, and assembled on the seventh day. Uggasena climbed a pole sixty cubits in height and balanced himself on the top of it. . . .

Architects

Throughout the ancient world, rulers and their subjects sought to demonstrate the greatness of their civilizations by erecting large, impressive structures; and while smaller buildings and homes could be successfully constructed by experienced workers, grander projects had to be carefully planned, creating a need for trained architects. In studying ancient India and China, we may not know the names of their greatest architects, or how they lived their lives, but the products of their visionary designs have often survived the ages to attract the attention of modern scholars and tourists.

The earliest civilizations of India are represented today primarily by remnants of small houses. In the Harappan or Indus Valley civilization, homes were generally built out of bricks hardened by fires, but since these had to be small for the hardening process to work, builders were practically limited to structures with only two stories. But the city of Mohenjo Daro did include a large citadel that included a granary, a hall for ceremonial gatherings, and a public bath, evidence that the government was involved in constructing facilities for their citizens. Their cities were also carefully planned gridworks of streets meeting at right angles. The later Vedic culture favored houses made out of bamboo rods tied together with ropes with straw to fill the gaps between them; however, like other ancient peoples, they soon turned to stone for their larger civic projects.

By the time that the *Mahabharata* was written, sometime between the eighth century and fourth century BCE, architecture had become a standard profession. The epic refers to the architect as *sthāpatyah* and *saudhakāra*, and it also describes the Hindu god of architecture, Vishwakarma, who designed the city of Dvārakā, the gods' flying chariots, their weapons, and even a beautiful woman. Both the *Mahabharata* and the *Ramayana* (written around the same time) also refer to a king named Mayasura, a former demon who designed an enormous palace hall. An architect of the Vedic era might be responsible for designing a variety of structures, including palaces, temples, houses, and forts. One carving in the Buddhist mound at Bharhut suggests that architects not only planned buildings but actually participated in the construction process by helping to lay the bricks.

The Vedic civilization also developed a general theory of architecture, called *vastu*, that addressed both the general layout of cities and the design of their buildings. Several texts in Sanskrit explain the principles of this discipline, which incorporates elements of spirituality and astrology. *Vastu* celebrates the square as the basic pattern to follow, inasmuch as it represents order whereas the circle represents disorder. It also stipulates that all streets must run precisely north, south, east, or west, and the drainage system must have the water flow to either the north or east. These texts also address issues like choosing a suitable site and waiting for a propitious time before beginning construction. Interestingly, a recent study indicates that several tenets of *vastu* can be observed in the design of Mohenjo Daro, suggesting that its ideas predated the emergence of Hinduism in India.

By the time of the emperor Ashoka (304–232 BCE), Buddhism was becoming established in India, and this religion brought three types of structures: the *chaitya* (temple), *vihara* (monastery), and *stupa* (a mound for worship and meditation). These were all characterized by elaborate decorations on both the exterior and interior, as well the occasional temples that were carved out of hillside caves; Ashoka himself ordered the construction of many noteworthy structures. Since Alexander the Great had introduced Greek culture to the subcontinent, there also emerged a new school of architecture, *Gandharva*, which incorporated elements of Greek architecture; but architects of the rival *Mathura* school still adhered strictly to the Indian approach.

In its early stages, Chinese architecture differed in some significant ways from Indian architecture. While the homes of peasants were simple structures made of bricks, the favorite material for larger structures was wood, not bricks or stone. In typical Chinese buildings, long wooden pillars in the interior, not the walls, supported roofs made of wooden eaves and covered with ceramic tiles. For both practical and aesthetic reasons, Chinese architects came to prefer buildings that were about six times wider than their height; these could be well supported with pillars, and they enabled architects to convey an ethereal aura by making the roofs look like they were floating in the air. The roofs were curved to reflect a Buddhist belief that this would deflect evil spirits, and to add to their gracefulness, buildings were always symmetrical in their appearance.

Another feature of Chinese architecture was an overriding concern for privacy, both in private and public buildings, which strongly influenced the design of buildings. Walls were everywhere—around the city, around districts within the city, and around individual buildings; royal palaces might even be surrounded by a series of walls, defining spaces successively limited to fewer and fewer visitors. Oftentimes, because of the walls, people were only able to see the roofs of buildings, which is why these were frequently covered with colorful decorations. The Chinese even extended this philosophy to the defense of their country by beginning to construct the famed Great Wall of China to keep out foreign enemies.

One distinctive innovation in Chinese architecture came with the introduction of Buddhism, as believers began to construct *stupas* based on Indian designs. These quickly evolved, however, into the pagoda, a temple that unusually was often made out of bricks, not wood. Eventually pagodas became tall, multistoried buildings that often towered over the other buildings in their vicinity.

Unlike the Indians, the Chinese did not write much about architecture, as its principles were mostly

The Great Stupa in Sanchi, India, one of many large Buddhist shrine structures commissioned by the emperor Ashoka in the third century BCE, is still standing today and impressive to tourists. (Nitya Jacob)

passed by experienced architects to their apprentices. An exception is a text called the *Kaogongji*, a set of writings by anonymous authors that was first compiled sometime around 600 BCE. While this discusses a wide variety of crafts, it includes some guidelines for building cities that reflect the culture's concerns for symmetry and numerology. According to the *Kaogongji*, a city should be shaped like a square, with each side about 4-1/2-kilometers long; on each side, there should be three gates (since three symbolizes the union of earth and heaven). Within, the city should have a gridwork of nine streets running from north to south and nine streets running from east to west; each street must be broad enough to accommodate nine horse-drawn carts (since nine symbolizes heaven). The ruler's palace is at the center of the city, surrounded by a marketplace, offices, and temples.

As a general rule, we do not know the names of the ancient Chinese architects or anything about their lives; however, the career of a somewhat later figure, Yuwen Kai (555–612 CE) provides some clues about the earlier men who were part of this profession. Yuwen Kai was an aristocrat, the son of a noted warrior, who displayed an aptitude for architecture and soon became prominent in the field. He was asked by the emperor Sui Wendi (541–604 CE) to oversee the general design and construction of major buildings for a new capital city, Daxing. The choice was somewhat surprising because Yuwen Kai was a member of a minority, the Xianbei, who were ethnically Mongolian. Clearly, one had to be a member of the higher classes to garner the opportunity to become an architect, but once this status was achieved, these men obtained prestigious assignments on the basis of their merit, not their connections. Still, in contrast to the peasants of ancient China, even the least talented architects undoubtedly enjoyed a respectable income and a comfortable lifestyle.

In general, the other civilizations of Southeast Asia developed styles of architecture that blended Indian and Chinese models, while the Korean and Japanese cultures were exclusively influenced by Chinese traditions. Their architects naturally had to adjust to local conditions: since stone was abundant in ancient Burma and Cambodia, many of their buildings were made of stone, whereas in Japan, where suitable stone was rare, wooden structures became the norm. Yet preferences for an elegant and harmonious design, and for elaborate and colorful decoration, were almost universal throughout ancient Asia. Unfortunately, many of the buildings created by their skilled architects still await discovery within dense jungles or buried beneath debris, while others have been destroyed or badly damaged; however, archaeologists and preservationists are hard at work seeking to find or restore outstanding examples of their craftsmanship.

OLD IDEAS FOR NEW BUILDINGS

Ancient Indian architecture was based upon the principles of *vastu*, which drew upon Hinduism and astrology to develop procedures and designs for the layouts of cities and buildings. While such an approach to architecture might not seem suitable for modern times, there have been periodic efforts to encourage contemporary architects to adapt the doctrines of *vastu* to their work. A recent book, Khushdeep Bansal's *MahaVastu Handbook: Methods and Practical Working Procedures of Vastu Shastra for Professionals* (2012), provides a detailed illustrated guide for architects interested in employing ancient ideas in their cutting-edge projects.

ARCHITECTURE FOR THE DEAD

Among the grandest achievements of the ancient Chinese architects were the imperial palaces, where emperors lived in isolated splendor; regrettably, though, they were invariably destroyed by invaders or new rulers, so we have only a few drawings and descriptions of these structures. But we may garner a better idea of their features from the discovery, in 2012, of the ruins of a palace built near the tomb of China's first emperor Qin Shi Huang (259–210 BCE). Along with the buried army of soldiers that were placed there to protect him, it seems that the emperor also wanted to have an elegant residence for his afterlife.

Further Reading

Behrendt, Kurt A. 2004. *The Buddhist Architecture of Gandhāra*. Leiden, The Netherlands, and Boston: Brill.

Cai, Yanxin. 2011. *Chinese Architecture*. Updated edition. Cambridge and New York: Cambridge University Press.

Harle, James C. 2004. *The Art and Architecture of the Indian Subcontinent*. Second edition. New Haven, CT: Yale University Press.

Lou, Qingxi. 2002. *The Architectural Art of Ancient China*. Beijing: China Intercontinental Press.

Mahajan, Malati. 2004. *A Gate to Ancient Indian Architecture*. New Delhi: Sharada Publishing House.

Wang, Qijun. 2011. *Chinese Architecture: Discovering China*. New York: Better Link Press.

Document

From Manning, Charlotte Speir. 1856. *Life in Ancient India*. London: Smith, Elder.

In this edited passage, the author lists and describes the four major forms of Buddhist architecture in India.

We have already had occasion to observe that Buddhism was an attempt to make general, doctrines hitherto restricted to learned and privileged classes. But the public cannot accept abstractions, and the more vague and negative the doctrine, the more absolute its demand for visible types and images; and consequently in every country the foot-prints of Buddhism are gigantic monuments, pillars, towers, caves, and temples. This architecture is divided into four classes:—

1. Funeral Mounds and Relic-shrines.
2. Pillars and Towers to commemorate events.
3. Convents or Viharas,
4. Chaitya, Caves, or Temples.

Of these by far the most conspicuous class is that first-named, and monuments of this description, have so constantly accompanied Buddhism that an inclination has arisen to treat all traces of analogous mounds or monuments as indications of Buddhism. But this assumes too much; for although we know that Buddhists made memorial mounds and monuments, we are far from knowing that all memorial mounds and monuments were made by Buddhists. . . .

The second form of Buddhist architecture consists of Towers and Pillars set up to commemorate an event or do honour to a building. . . . These pillars are supposed to have stood, like the Jachin and Boaz of King Solomon, in front of some holy edifice, and one such pillar yet remains watching like a sentinel at the entrance of the Viswakarma, Karli, and other celebrated Cave-Temples of western India.

Of towers erected with the same intent, the Tower of Babel was probably the earliest instance; but, although not uncommon at very early periods in western Asia, Buddhists appear first to have introduced them into India. Few of these erections now remain; but happily the custom survived when Buddhism became extinct, and two beautiful Towers of Victory may be seen in Central India, the one erected in the eighth and the other in the eleventh century.

Viharas, or convents, constitute our next division; and these may be regarded as more radically Buddhist than any other form of Buddhist architecture. . . . Religious Brahmans had long been accustomed to dwell in hermitages apart from the bustle of life, and the Brahmavarti, of the Code of Manu, was a district celebrated for such asramas. But the genius of Buddhism required dwellings on a larger scale, and, as we have already remarked, it soon began to seek relief in the magnificence of architecture for the deadness of its worship.

The structural Viharas have all perished in India, but the Caves, which were fashioned in imitation of those wooden prototypes, yet remain to exhibit the stages by which their ultimate perfection was attained. . . . [T]he simplest form [was] a mere verandah added to a natural cavern. In such cases, the preaching-hall was a wooden building erected, when required, for periodical readings of the sacred books. By degrees the Verandahs became more decorated, and the sleeping-cells were arranged around a central hall; and at last we find twenty beautified pillars supporting this hall, and its walls adorned by paintings,—copies of which adorn the Indian Court at Sydenham.

At Anuradhapura, in Ceylon, may be seen the remains of a grand Vihara, erected BC 161 by King Dushtagamini, called the *Loha prasada*, or, *Loha maha paya*, from *loha*, iron, its roof having been of metal. It had nine stories, each containing one hundred apartments; the whole was supported upon pillars of stone, and Baldaeus honours it by marking Anuradhapura on his map as "the place of the thousand pillars." . . . The upper stories of this nine-storied building were of timber, and required frequent renewal, and sometimes the nine stories were reduced to five stories; but the thousand pillars lived through all vicissitudes, and were still in wonderful preservation when seen by Captain Chapman in 1820.

The Chaitya Caves are very imposing. . . . "They consist of an external porch, or music-gallery, an internal gallery over the entrance, and a centre aisle. . . twice the length of its breadth, roofed by a plain waggon-vault; to this is added a semi-dome terminating the nave, under the centre of which always stands a Dagoba or Chaitya." A narrow aisle surrounds the interior, separated from the centre aisle by a range of massive columns, and this smaller aisle or passage is usually flat-roofed. A very interesting part of the arrangement was the manner in which the Cave was lighted: across the front there is a screen, in which there are three doors,—the largest, in the centre, opening to the nave, the others to the side aisles; over the screen the whole front is a great window, usually in the horseshoe form, as seen in the exterior of the Viswakarma; the whole light thus falls upon the Chaitya or Dagoba, and the effect from the dark colonnade is described as most remarkable. . . .

Calligraphers

Virtually every early civilization created some type of writing, to provide governments and individuals with needed records of their possessions and activities; yet the ancient Chinese were unique in developing a way to record their thoughts which was both efficacious and aesthetically appealing. Today, although calligraphy was abandoned long ago for the practical business of daily writing, it has endured and grown as a cherished form of art.

The origins of writing in China are unclear: some have theorized that they learned about writing from the nomads of Central Asia, who had picked up the art from other cultures, but most believe that the Chinese independently came up with the idea. According to

Chinese folklore, a scribe who worked for the legendary Yellow Emperor invented writing after looking at the footprints of birds and deducing that similar marks might be used as symbols. Like Egyptian hieroglyphics, the Chinese characters were originally small pictures that gradually became more and more stylized; for example, a pair of trees with its roots showing came to represent a forest. However, unlike Western cultures, the Chinese never transitioned to a phonetic alphabet.

The earliest Chinese writers are best described as scribes, not calligraphers, because they were not concerned with the beauty of their work, and they did not use ink and brushes to make their marks. Instead, they began by carving characters on bronze vessels and the so-called oracle bones: questions about the future would be carved on the bones, and when they cracked after being heated, a sage would deduce an answer from the pattern of the cracks and inscribe the answer on the bone as well. Later, the Chinese started to write their questions on bones using a brush and ink, and they then adapted the same method to write on other surfaces, such as strips of bamboo, sheets of silk, and tablets of wood; the Chinese then became the first culture to make and use paper out of wood pulp for most of their writing.

Initially, scribes tended to write in a variety of different manners, but after the unification of China under the Qin Dynasty, prime minister Li Si (ca. 280–208 BCE) imposed a uniform style, called the seal script, which became the first of the five basic styles that were accepted as standard in the centuries to come; the others were the clerical, standard, cursive, and semi-cursive scripts. By this time, while writing for practical purposes continued, calligraphy had come to be regarded as an art, usually practiced by aristocrats and officials as a leisure activity. Eventually, calligraphy was enshrined as one of the several essential skills that all literate Chinese people were expected to learn; others included mathematics, archery, dancing, playing the *qin* (a stringed instrument), and riding a chariot. Ambitious young people probably regarded calligraphy as the most important of these arts to master, since the exam they had to pass to become a government official required the use of calligraphy.

For a long time, calligraphy was done exclusively by the wealthy and privileged, since only they had access to the necessary training, the extensive time required for mastery of the art, and the income needed to purchase its expensive supplies. The four required items for calligraphy were termed the "four treasures of the study." First, calligraphers needed solid paint which came in the form of sticks, made out of a combination of soot and gum and placed in molds to harden into sticks. Next, calligraphers used a flat stone to grind the paint sticks and mix the paint with water to produce the paint; some of these stones were decorated with carvings. Third, their brushes were constructed by tying together with silk thread the hairs of animals like rabbits or sheep and gluing them to a small bamboo tube that fit easily in one's hand. Finally, calligraphers were supposed to employ a special sort of high-quality paper, traditionally made by combining wood, fishnets, and rags. Occasionally, calligraphers were also equipped with special holders made of jade where brushes could be placed during pauses so that they would not roll and leave random marks on the paper. Some of these holders were cherished works of art themselves, carefully shaped to look like animals.

Apprentices would learn calligraphy by mastering its seven basic strokes, called the "seven mysteries": a dot, horizontal and vertical lines, a sharp curve, and three types of downward strokes. Through practice, they would master the exact manner in which their arms had to be positioned and their brushes held in a vertical position between the thumb and three fingers; yet the brush also had to be held loosely, so that it was almost ready to fall from one's hand. By varying the pressure they applied, calligraphers could control the width of their strokes, while moving the brush in different directions altered the amount of ink that reached the page. It was common for neophyte calligraphers to first copy the styles of distinguished calligraphers of the past before they gradually developed their own personal styles.

Because the goal of calligraphy was to express the personality and emotions of an individual artist, it had to be created in a certain way. Before beginning work, the calligraphers would meditate, so that they could calmly focus on the work they would be executing. They were expected to estimate and make precisely the amount of paint that they would need to complete their task, so the resulting piece would be produced entirely by one batch of paint, and the process of making it would not be interrupted by the need to make additional paint. Before making an image, calligraphers were advised to first visualize the image in their heads so it would come out exactly as planned. Calligraphers also had to finish each work in one session, so that it would not reflect the different emotions of different times. Needless to say, the calligraphers would ideally be isolated from other people in order to better concentrate on conveying their individual messages.

Calligraphy was never an art that was limited to men; in fact, one of the first major theorists in the field was a woman named Wei Shuo (272–349 CE). The wife of a government official, Wei Shuo was part of a family of noted calligraphers, which included her uncle and cousin. Her pioneering study of calligraphy, *Bi Zhen Tu*, likened the piece of paper to a battlefield, the brush to a weapon, and the paint to its ammunition. A postscript to her text was written by her most famous student, Wang Xizhi (303–361 CE), who is sometimes regarded as the greatest calligrapher who ever practiced the art. He was known, in fact, as the "Sage of Calligraphy" because of his magnificent work, which is now preserved solely in the form of copies made by later artists. Born into a politically prominent family, he quickly shifted from the approach of Wei Shuo to develop his own innovative style while holding a number of government positions. Wang Xizhi enjoyed raising geese, and according to one charming anecdote, he first figured out how to properly move his wrist while writing characters by watching how geese moved their necks. Another legend holds that he enjoyed doing calligraphy sitting next to a pond, and he once dipped his brush in the water so frequently that the water looked black. Wang Xizhi's work was greatly appreciated by the emperor Taizong (598–649 CE), who employed his characters in a textbook for young calligraphers. One of his seven children, Wang Xianzhi (344–386 CE), also became a celebrated calligrapher.

During the early centuries of the Christian era, Chinese calligraphy sparked the practice of the same

This portrait is said to represent Wang Xizhi (303–361 CE), renowned as the greatest Chinese calligrapher, though this image was painted long after his death and may not be an accurate depiction. (Peng Zhen Ge/Redlink/Corbis)

art in the developing culture of Korea; later, it spread to Japan as well. Although the Korean and Japanese calligraphers eventually developed their own styles, employing the somewhat different characters of their national languages, their calligraphy remained closely modeled on the Chinese approach. In each tradition, calligraphers and their works were increasingly valued, so that a skilled calligrapher might earn a high income by means of commissions and sales of their artwork. Yet considerations of potential profit could never be allowed to affect the essentially meditative and deeply personal nature of the art, which has been maintained to this day by means of textbooks and teachers still instructing pupils in techniques that were first developed many centuries ago.

A LONG-LOST LETTER

Although the ancient Chinese calligrapher Wang Xizhi was highly esteemed, none of his works have survived, and his talents can be appreciated today only by examining copies of his writing made by later calligraphers. Yet even these copies are extremely rare. Still, scholars keep searching through old manuscripts hoping to find another example of Wang Xizhi's calligraphy, and in 2013, the Tokyo National Museum made headlines across the world by announcing the discovery of a new copy of his artistry, a piece of paper 10-inches long and 4-inches wide that reproduces part of a letter he had written to a relative.

CALLIGRAPHY AS THERAPY

The process of calligraphy was traditionally preceded by meditation and carried out in a careful, thoughtful manner, with each brushstroke anticipated by mental images. Despite the intense concentration involved, calligraphers found the process relaxing, and this has been confirmed by recent research. A study done at the University of Hong Kong in the 1980s showed that while doing their artwork, calligraphers typically experienced a lower heart rate and lower blood pressure; they also tended to take deeper breaths. This suggested that in some cases, calligraphy might be prescribed by physicians as a way to reduce stress.

Further Reading

Allen, Susan M., Lin Zuzao, Cheng Xiaolan, and Jan Bos, editors. 2010. *The History and Cultural Heritage of Chinese Calligraphy, Printing and Library Work.* Berlin: Walter de Gruyter.

Chen, Tingyou. 2011. *Chinese Calligraphy.* Updated edition. Cambridge: Cambridge University Press.

Li, Xiangping, editor. 2007. *China's Calligraphy Art through the Ages.* Text by Gao Changshan. Beijing: China Intercontinental Press.

Tseng, Yuho. 1993. *A History of Chinese Calligraphy.* Hong Kong: Chinese University Press.

Uyehara, Cecil H. 1991. *Japanese Calligraphy: A Bibliographical Study.* Lanham, MD: University Press of America.

Wang, Youfen, editor and translator. 2008. *Chinese Calligraphy.* New Haven, CT: Yale University Press.

Document

From Lay, George Tradescant. 1841. *The Chinese As They Are: Their Moral, Social, and Literary Character: A New Analysis of the Language: With Succinct Views of Their Principal Arts and Sciences.* London: W. Ball.

In this passage, the author, who had been a British missionary to China, as well as a naturalist who collected plant specimens in Asia, discusses the admiration given to skilled calligraphers in China, and provides some specific information about their techniques.

The Chinese are greatly enamoured with their symbols, as they are of a highly-wrought composition, and therefore not only use them for conveying moral and engaging sentiments, but also for display and embellishment. A capability of executing them with ease and beauty ranks next after the art of composing; and hence a gentleman is expected not only to be a fine scholar, but also a fine penman. The hair pencil, with which they write, is without a rival in delicacy of workmanship and fitness for the specific purpose to which it is applied. It is held in a direction nearly perpendicular to the paper, as remarked in another chapter, and rests upon the nail of the ring-finger; and as the wrist is the fulcrum on which the hand turns, the greatest latitude is given to its movements. . . . Variety in shape and a symmetry of proportion are studied at the same time; straight lines and sharp comers are either avoided, or so treated that their untoward effect is destroyed. Many of the fundamental principles of drawing, as understood by us, are fully recognized by the Chinese in their canons of calligraphy. . . .

The model specimens of Chinese calligraphy have the ground black and the characters white; and they are executed with so much exactness that the eye of the connoisseur cannot detect a fault in them. Some of these I purchased of a dealer in old books for a small sum, which two or three of my Chinese friends were pleased to think a very great bargain. But notwithstanding the rigour and comprehensiveness with which rules are applied in the formation of the characters, a scope is so far allowed for taste, that each virtuoso's handwriting may be known by some of its peculiarities. My teacher seemed to feel a satisfaction in the thought that his friends would say, when they saw any of his best performances, "This is Kwang's writing; we know it by such and such peculiarity in the style." There are several different kinds of hand, which are devoted to their respective purposes. The seal character, composed of widely-parted lines and turnings, is employed for the object indicated by its name. It is only understood by a few; so that when a tradesman wishes to have his name cut upon a seal in this character, he applies himself to some professional man, or learned neighbour. The perfect character is the one that is susceptible of all the graces of which we have been speaking, and is always used where elegance is studied. The running-hand is used by men of business, and consists of abbreviated forms, sweeps, and zigzags, to favour speed in writing. The hands of those who write this with facility are said to fly; it is then something between a scrawl and a flourish, such as foreigners are not very apt to understand or admire. A mixture of the perfect character and the running-hand is often used, both for the freedom of its appearance and the ease of writing. The long and tasteful pair of scrolls which decorate the niche and altar-piece of a Chinese parlour are oftentimes written with this combination of the free and the finished. Many persons are employed in this work, though not always exclusively, as they are sometimes painters or booksellers by trade and profession. The ink is ground upon a large stone, and the result poured into a small pan. In this the artist dips his large brush, and, holding it at a commanding elevation, alternately manages the straight line and the sweep with a sleight so imposing, that a crowd of natives cluster round him to stare in silent wonder and admiration. In the rapid evolutions of the pencil, the loose hairs, instead of combining to shape a single broad stroke, often trace a number of broken lines, and leave the paper in some places untouched; but no pains are taken to mend this defect, because, in the way of freedom, blemishes are esteemed as graces.

Emperors

A man who has absolute authority over vast territories is traditionally called not a king but an emperor, and that is the term usually applied to the men (along with a few female empresses) who ruled over the subcontinent of India, ancient China, and ancient Japan. While some attained this position simply by being the son of a former emperor, others seized the throne, often after assassinating the previous ruler. So, while emperors enjoyed great wealth and many privileges, they also had to work hard to govern wisely and stay vigilant at all times, to avoid providing a potential usurper with an opportunity to act. Only a few chose the path of voluntary retirement, preferring to serve until their natural or unnatural deaths.

We possess little reliable information about the first Indian emperor, Chandragupta (340–298 BCE); as a young man, he reportedly met with Alexander the Great while he was in India, leading some to suspect that the Greek leader inspired his own aspirations to become an emperor. The general belief, however, is that his rise to power was engineered by his crafty advisor Chankakya (370–283 BCE), the purported author of a treatise on governance entitled *Arthashastra* (although textual analysis indicates that it was actually the work of several authors over a period of centuries). Since the deformed Chankakya could not aspire to high office himself, he first assisted Chankakya in an unsuccessful rebellion against the ruling government; then, observing a boy eating a large piece of flatbread by first nibbling at its edges, he set out to first gain control of outlying areas before they would conquer the capital. Once in power, Chandragupta solidified his position with several arranged marriages, apparently governed effectively, strengthened his army, and employed a network of spies to prevent his assassination. He also established the pattern of a visibly lavish lifestyle, appearing in public wearing fine robes while being carried on a golden litter adorned with pearls. Eventually, however, he tired of ruling and abdicated in favor of his son in order to devote himself to the religion of Jainism.

The greatest of all Indian emperors was his grandson Ashoka (304–232 BCE), who demonstrates that emperors can be both astoundingly cruel and astoundingly benevolent. He gained the throne after a lengthy struggle, murdering many of his brothers in the process, and subsequently expanded his empire with a brutal

This evocative portrait of the first Chinese emperor, Qin Shi Huang (259–210 BCE), conveys both his reputed wisdom and his reputed cruelty. (Getty Images)

conquest of the region now known as Odissa, killing over 100,000 people. Yet he publically expressed remorse for its actions and resolved to henceforth lead a government devoted to benign treatment of its citizens and promotion of the Buddhist religion, doctrines conveyed by means of edicts engraved in stone and read aloud in villages. To achieve these goals, Ashoka established a complex administrative system and standardized taxes and punishments throughout his realm.

Ashoka's successors were unfortunately unable to match his successes, presiding over a long period of decline, but a renaissance occurred with the rise of the Gupta Dynasty in the third century CE. Its greatest emperor, Chandragupta II (ca. 350–415 CE), provided his people with unprecedented peace and prosperity and vigorously supported the arts and sciences, inspiring many great achievements in literature, the visual arts, and technology. His court was the home of nine great poets, called the "Nine Gems," who included the

noted playwright Kalidasa (ca. fifth century CE); he also announced his devotion to music by having himself shown on coins as holding a vīnā (a bow-harp). The emperor is best remembered, though, for his romantic adventures before winning the throne: first, his older brother Ramagupta (ca. 345–375 CE) initially took over after his father's death and insisted upon marrying Chandragupta's fiancée Dhruvasvamini (ca. 350–415 CE); then, Ramagupta agreed to turn over his wife to a foreign ruler who coveted her. Enraged, Chandragupta disguised himself as Dhruvasvamini, killed the man as he greeted his purported prize, and then killed his brother and married Dhruvasvamini himself.

Because they continued to reign over their nation until the early twentieth century, people are generally more aware of the Chinese emperors than their Indian counterparts. The first of these, Qin Shi Huang (259–210 BCE), unified China under his rule and maintained his power with unprecedented brutality, executing hundreds of scholars, burning thousands of books, and building roadways and a magnificent palace with conscripted laborers who were tortured or murdered if they disobeyed orders. Yet he also established an enduring tradition of hiring and promoting government workers on the basis of merit, not family connections. He eventually devoting his energies to the pursuit of immortality and may have died prematurely of mercury poisoning, having ingested the element in the belief that it would prolong his life. But he had already arranged for the construction of a magnificent tomb, filled with thousands of statues of warriors, which were only recently unearthed.

Subsequent Chinese emperors, whether they achieved the throne through inheritance, intrigue, or violence, all lived their lives following certain patterns. Most of the time, they were expected to stay within their palace, protected from contact with ordinary citizens by a series of walls. There, constantly surrounded by servants, the emperor performed ceremonies and met with senior officials. He had special robes to wear for every occasion, and for a long time he was the only person in China permitted to wear the color yellow. Although his daily schedule was highly structured in ways he could not always alter, the emperor still had time to relax with family members and friends during elaborate banquets, and he could enjoy performances by skilled singers, dancers, and acrobats.

To justify the rule of their emperors, the Chinese developed the idea of the "Mandate of Heaven." A man became emperor, they argued, because he was divinely chosen as the nation's best possible ruler, and he would remain the heavenly favorite as long as he ruled judiciously and effectively. However, if troubles arose that seemed beyond his ability to handle, it was a sign that he had lost the Mandate of Heaven, and someone else could justly seize power. This doctrine sometimes enabled ambitious commoners to become emperors, as they could cite their successful ascension as proof that the heavens endorsed their rule. For example, China's second great emperor, Liu Bang (256–195 BCE), founder of the Han Dynasty, was a commoner who retained some sympathy for lowly peasants and improved their lives by lowering taxes and limiting use of the death sentence. Even the rare woman to attained the position of emperor, almost invariably as the widow of a dead emperor with an infant heir, might cite such a Mandate of Heaven to rule in her own name; only empress Wu Zetian (625–705 CE) officially made this claim, but other empresses who were nominally regents for young emperors, like empress Deng Sui (18–121 CE), were implicitly supported by the Mandate if they remained in charge, even when the heir became an adult, by ruling their country effectively.

Since their authority was nearly absolute, Chinese emperors could focus their energies on whatever matters concerned them, though they could never forget their central goal of benefiting their subjects and thus justifying their rule. The Han emperor Wen (202–157 BCE) prioritized governmental reforms: he reduced extravagant expenditures, and since efforts to hire qualified people were haphazardly based on their reputations, he instituted the system of exams for civil servants, ensuring that only the most capable individuals would obtain positions. In contrast, his grandson, Emperor Wu (141–87 BCE), is primarily noted for military campaigns that greatly expanded the territory under the emperor's control, and he supported major projects like the construction of a canal that linked his capital city of Ch'ang-an to the Yellow River. He also set up a school to teach Confucianism to government workers. However, his ambitious projects soon left his government without sufficient funds, requiring high taxes that inspired peasant revolts and assassination attempts; as he aged, Wu also grew obsessed with magicians, further upsetting those under his rule. Even though he publically apologized for his poor decisions, he probably escaped a violent death only by succumbing to a fatal illness.

Ancient Japan had its emperors too, but all of the names recorded in their annals prior to 600 CE are usually regarded as purely legendary figures, perhaps created in order to provide actual emperors with an impressive history that would justify their absolute rule. Of course, the early histories of India and Japan feature similarly dubious precursors to the emperors that we know actually existed. But one does not have to believe in imaginary ancestors to appreciate the achievements of the ancient Asian emperors, who despite their occasional incompetence or brutality played a crucial role in the development of their civilizations.

HEIR TO THE THRONE

When China officially became a republic in 1912, its long tradition of being ruled by emperors finally came to an end, though the last Chinese emperor, Puyi, was briefly restored to power five years later. By the laws of succession, his living nephew, Jin Yuzhang, now has the strongest claim to the throne, but he has repeatedly insisted that he has no interest in becoming an emperor, preferring to live in obscurity as a minor government official. Since he is now in his seventies, his daughter Jin Xin may soon become, theoretically, an empress in waiting, though she seems far more likely to continue working as a computer scientist.

A GOD NO MORE

When the Americans occupied Japan after their victory in World War II, many expected that they would remove Japanese emperor Hirohito from power to establish a republic. However, General Douglas MacArthur, perhaps impressed by the role of the British monarchy, decided that an emperor could helpfully function as a unifying force and allowed Hirohito to remain on the throne, though solely as a titular ruler. He did insist, however, that Hirohito make a public declaration that he was, in fact, not divine, and he later demonstrated his affinity with the Japanese people with an unprecedented decision to allow his son Akihito, who later became emperor, to marry a commoner.

Further Reading

Allen, Charles. 2012. *Ashoka: The Search for India's Lost Emperor*. New York: The Overlook Press.

Harrison, Thomas, editor. 2009. *The Great Empires of the Ancient World*. Los Angeles: J. Paul Getty Museum.

Martin, Peter. 1997. *The Chrysanthemum Throne: A History of the Emperors of Japan*. Honolulu: University of Hawaii Press.

Paludan, Ann. 1998. *Chronicle of the Chinese Emperors: The Reign-by-Reign Record of the Rulers of Imperial China*. London: Thames & Hudson.

Shi Fang. 2008. *Lives of Chinese Emperors*. Edited by Lan Peijin. Translated by Zhang Yuan. Beijing: Foreign Languages Press.

Wood, Frances. 2007. *The First Emperor of China*. London: Profile.

Documents

From Kautilya. C. fourth century BCE. *Chanakya's Arthasastra, or, The Science of Politics*. Translated by Rudrapatna Shamasastry. 1908. Mysore, India: G.T.A. Press.

The Arthashastra, *an ancient Indian book of political and military advice for kings, is attributed to a man named Kautilya, believed to be Chanakya, an advisor to the first Mauyra emperor Ashoka. In these two passages, the author presents a dialogue offering various views of the sorts of people that kings should appoint as ministers, and he provides some advice about how the king should conduct himself.*

"The king," says Bháradvája, "shall employ his classmates as his ministers; for they can be trusted by him inasmuch as he has personal knowledge of their honesty and capacity."

"No," says Visáláksha, "for, as they have been his playmates as well, they would despise him. But he shall employ as ministers those whose secrets, possessed of in common, are well known to him. Possessed of habits and defects in common. with the king, they would never hurt him lest he would betray their secrets."

"Common is this fear," says Parásara, "for under the fear of betrayal of his own secrets, the king may also follow them in their good and bad acts. Under the control of as many persons as are made aware by the king of his own secrets, might he place himself in all humility by that disclosure. Hence he shall employ as

ministers those who have proved faithful to him under difficulties fatal to life and are of tried devotion."

"No," says Pisuna, "for this is devotion, but not intelligence (buddhigunah). He shall appoint as ministers those who, when employed as financial matters, show as much as, or more than, the fixed revenue, and are thus of tried ability."

"No," says Kaunapadanta, "for such persons are devoid of other ministerial qualifications; he shall, therefore, employ as ministers those whose fathers and grandfathers had been ministers before; such persons, in virtue of their knowledge of past events and of an established relationship with the king, will, though offended, never desert him; for such faithfulness is seen even among dumb animals; cows, for example, stand aside from strange cows and ever keep company with accustomed herds."

"No," says Vátavyádhi, "for such persons, having acquired complete dominion over the king, begin to play themselves as the king. Hence he shall employ as ministers such new persons as are proficient in the science of polity. It is such new persons who will regard the king as the real sceptre-bearer (dandadhara) and dare not offend him."

"No," says the son of Báhudantí (a woman); "for a man possessed of only theoretical knowledge and having no experience of practical politics is likely to commit serious blunders when engaged in actual works. Hence he shall employ as ministers such as are born of high family and possessed of wisdom, purity of purpose, bravery and loyal feelings inasmuch as ministerial appointments shall purely depend on qualifications."

"This," says Kautilya, "is satisfactory in all respects; for a man's ability is inferred from his capacity shown in work. . . ."

*****

If a king is energetic, his subjects will be equally energetic. If he is reckless, they will not only be reckless likewise, but also eat into his works. Besides, a reckless king will easily fall into the hands of his enemies. Hence the king shall ever be wakeful. . . .

When in the court, he shall never cause his petitioners to wait at the door, for when a king makes himself inaccessible to his people and entrusts his work to his immediate officers, he may be sure to engender confusion in business, and to cause thereby public disaffection, and himself a prey to his enemies.

He shall, therefore, personally attend to the business of gods, of heretics, of Brahmans learned in the Vedas, of cattle, of sacred places, of minors, the aged, the afflicted, and the helpless, and of women;—all this in order (of enumeration) or according to the urgency or pressure of those works.

All urgent calls he shall hear at once, but never put off; for when postponed, they will prove too hard or impossible to accomplish.

Having seated himself in the room where the sacred fire has been kept, he shall attend to the business of physicians and ascetics practising austerities; and that in company with his high priest and teacher and after preliminary salutation (to the petitioners).

Accompanied by persons proficient in the three sciences (*trividya*) but not alone lest the petitioners be offended, he shall look to the business of those who are practising austerities, as well as of those who are experts in witchcraft and Yoga.

Of a king, the religious vow is his readiness to action; satisfactory discharge of duties is his performance of sacrifice; equal attention to all is the offer of fees and ablution towards consecration.

In the happiness of his subjects lies his happiness; in their welfare his welfare; whatever pleases himself he shall not consider as good, but whatever pleases his subjects he shall consider as good.

From Confucius. C. 500 BCE. *The Sayings of Confucius.* Translated by Leonard Arthur Lyall. 1909. London: Longmans, Green.

Below are several maxims of the Chinese philosopher Confucius (551–479 BCE) regarding the art of being a good ruler.

Tzu-kung asked, What is kingcraft?

The Master said, Food enough, troops enough, and the trust of the people.

Tzu-kung said, If it had to be done, which could best be spared of the three?

Troops, said the Master.

And if we had to, which could better be spared of the other two?

Food, said the Master. From of old all men die, but without trust a people cannot stand. . . .

Ching, Duke of Ch'i, asked Confucius, What is kingcraft?

Confucius answered. For the lord to be lord and the liege, liege, the father to be father and the son, son. . . .

Tzu-chang asked, What is kingcraft?

The Master said, To be tireless of thought and faithful in doing. . . .

Chi K'ang, speaking of kingcraft to Confucius, said, To help those that follow the Way, should we kill the men that will not?

Confucius answered, Sir, what need has a ruler to kill? If ye wished for goodness, Sir, the people would be good. The gentleman's mind is the wind, and grass are the minds of small men: as the wind blows, so must the grass bend. . . .

The Duke of She asked, What is kingcraft?

The Master answered, For those near us to be happy and those far off to come.

When he was governor of Chü-fu, Tzu-hsia asked how to rule.

The Master said, Be not eager for haste; look not for small gains. Nothing done in haste is thorough, and looking for small gains big things are left undone.

Farmers

In ancient Asia, as in the rest of the world, agriculture spurred the births of civilizations and sustained their people as they gradually developed cities, governments, and new technologies. Adapting to the special conditions of their own terrains, farmers employed various strategies to produce bountiful harvests of crops for themselves, their governments, and their fellow citizens.

Farming in India dates back thousands of years, though it was first practiced intensively in the poorly documented Harappan, or Indus Valley, civilization. The Indian farmers had the advantage of generally owning their own land, and rulers only imposed a small tax on their output, never more than one-sixth of the total crop. They grew a wide variety of crops, including grains like oats, barley, and wheat; rice; and vegetables and fruits like peas, lentils, jujubes, and dates. They also became the world's first people to cultivate cotton to make cloth. Due to periodic flooding, the soil of the Indus Valley was rich and well suited for agriculture, as it was loosely packed and filled with nutrients; further, the two periods of heavy rain brought by monsoon winds enabled farmers to grow two crops each year. However, it did become necessary to construct elaborate systems of irrigation canals to distribute the river's water, and dams made of bricks were built to keep the river's floods under control. Further, both Indian astrology and astronomy developed in large part to enable farmers to anticipate the arrival of the seemingly unpredictable monsoons and better plan their sowing and harvesting.

Indian farmers crafted and used a number of tools, including wooden plows, sickles, hoes, and axes; in order to measure their acreage, they used bamboo sticks of a fixed length. To fertilize their land, they might apply readily available cow dung; a mixture of sheep and goat manure, barley, and sesame seeds; or a liquid fertilizer called *kunapa* brewed by combining and boiling manure, bones, and pieces of dead animals and fish. They also learned how to select the best seeds, dry them for an extended period of time, and store them beyond the reach of ravenous pests. The Indian farmers were poor by modern standards, forced to live in flimsy straw or wooden huts with their family members and relatives, but they usually grew enough food to meet their daily needs.

The Chinese attributed the invention of their agriculture to a legendary figure, Shen Nong Shi, an emperor who purportedly determined which plants were best to eat and created tools like the plow to enable farmers to grow and harvest them. Yet archaeological evidence indicates that the Chinese were already farming long before any emperors ruled. As in India, Chinese farmers were usually allowed to own their own small pieces of land; still, they regularly had to serve their governments by devoting some of their time to digging canals or building walls, and they always had to pay a portion of their harvests as taxes.

Depending upon where they lived, the Chinese farmers took two different approaches to their work. Conditions in northern China encouraged farmers to specialize in grains, like millet, barley, and wheat, though they also grew fruits and vegetables like lychees

and snow peas. Another common crop was hemp, grown to make textiles, paper, and medicine. Recognizing the importance of agriculture, the Chinese emperor would annually begin the planting season by going to the countryside and pushing a plow to make the first furrow. The techniques of these farmers generally resembled those of farmers in ancient Europe and the Near East: simple plows, first made of wood and later of copper or iron, were dragged across the ground by a pair of oxen led by one farmer to break up the ground, while another walked behind depositing the seeds. If their land was hilly, the farmers would make terraces to provide flat expanses for rows of plants. After the labor-intensive process of harvesting their crops, the Chinese would celebrate with a mid-autumn harvest festival that is still observed today.

In southern China, where the weather was warmer, the staple crop was rice, which required a more complex type of farming. First, the farmers had to find or prepare a large shallow pond, called a paddy, for their rice, which grows best in a few inches of water. The seedlings of rice were then individually placed in the ground. Since these farmers kept few animals to produce manure, they employed their own feces as a fertilizer. After a few months of constantly checking to see that the water level is optimal, the farmers would drain all the water away and, three days later, harvest the dried stocks of rice. Unlike farming in the north, growing rice required organized efforts to construct and maintain large irrigation systems, but the benefits were substantial, since a typical harvest of rice produces far more edible food than a harvest of millet or wheat. This is why, over time, southern China came to have a larger population than the north.

Regardless of where they lived or what crops they grew, the lives of Chinese farmers were far from pleasant: they surely labored from dawn to dusk every day, with only their conical straw hats to protect them from the hot sun, and they might also be called away from their fields on any day to devote their energies to public works projects. Since their harvests were not always bountiful, they frequently struggled to feed themselves and their families. To maximize their yields, farmers learned to plant their seeds in orderly rows, and they practiced crop rotation to avoid depleting the

A brick from an ancient Chinese tomb (from the Han dynasty, ca. 200 BCE–200 CE) shows a farmer guiding a plow, which is being pulled by an enormous ox. (UIG via Getty Images)

soil of nutrients. They also developed the ingenious technique of intercropping, planting a second, different plant in a field where another plant was already growing; this not only made more efficient use of their land, but it also tended to reduce the erosion of the soil and damage caused by insects.

Despite the ingenuity that the Chinese farmers displayed, they generally were not valued or respected members of their society, as indicated by a story told by the philosopher Han Fei-Tzu (ca. 280–233 BCE): a farmer, he said, was pushing his plow when he saw a rapidly running rabbit collide with a nearby tree and kill itself; believing that he had discovered a better way to obtain his food, the farmer stopped plowing and sat down in front of the tree, waiting for another rabbit to run into the tree. The philosopher concocted the tale to make a point about the necessity for change, but it certainly conveys a low estimation of the average intelligence of farmers.

The agriculture practiced by the other cultures in Southeast Asia was strongly influenced by the techniques and habits of Chinese farmers. It is believed, for example, that Chinese rice cultivation first spread to Korea and then to Japan, where farmers began to grow rice in the Chinese manner by setting up paddies, with water added and removed by means of increasingly complex systems of ditches and canals. In some places, however, Japanese farmers discovered that they could grow rice in dry fields, in the same way that they grew grains like buckwheat, sometimes using terraces on hillsides. They also practiced slash-and-burn agriculture and, since much of the terrain of Japan was mountainous and unsuitable for farming, they necessarily had to devote their energies to cutting down forest trees to provide more acreage for their crops. In addition to rice and buckwheat, Japanese farmers also raised a number of fruits and vegetables, including the large radish known as daikon. They generally relied on iron tools, which were initially imported before Japanese metalworkers learned to make their own iron tools, and they stored their grains in elevated granaries that protected them from damaging pests and water.

Farmers throughout Asia ultimately proved, in a sense, to be the victims of their own success. Because they were so efficient in raising ample amounts of food, they brought about large increases in the population, particularly in India and China; but with growing numbers of mouths to feed, occasionally adverse weather conditions were increasingly likely to lead to famines. When the Greek explorer Megasthenes visited India in the third century BCE, he reported that famines were unknown in the country; later, however, famines became depressingly common both in India and China. These then inspired new efforts, which continue to this day, to find new ways to raise increasing amounts of crops on limited amounts of land.

MECHANICAL FARMERS

In ancient Asia, all of the work needed to grow and harvest rice had to be done by hand, requiring many laborers working for long hours. Today, however, agricultural workers are gradually being replaced by machines. Instead of a plow, a mechanical rototiller can break up the soil for planting; instead of human hands planting seedlings, a tractor with a conveyer belt moves seeds to be picked up by hooks and placed in the ground; instead of farmers cutting plants with a sickle, a harvester cuts and gathers the rice; and instead of people removing the husks, a vibrating conveyer belt shakes the husks off.

PREDICTING THE WEATHER

One major problem confronting ancient Indian farmers was trying to predict when the monsoons would arrive and how much rain would fall; no matter how carefully they watched the skies, the annual monsoons would often defy all expectations. To this day, farmers face the same challenge; in fact, impressed by the way that the American *Farmer's Almanac* drew upon farmers' lore to provide generally correct weather predictions, one Indian farmer wrote to request similar weather forecasts for India! More promisingly, a team of Indian, American, and British scientists are now working with supercomputers to construct computer models that might provide more accurate short- and long-range monsoon predictions.

Further Reading

Gopal, Lallanji, and V. C. Srivastava, editors. 2008. *History of Agriculture in India (Up to c.1200 AD)*. New Delhi: Concept Publishing Company.

Hill, Christopher V. 2008. *South Asia: An Environmental History*. Santa Barbara, CA: ABC-CLIO.

Iinuma, Jiro. 1995. *Japanese Farming: Past and Present*. Tokyo: Nobunkyo.

Lu, Tracey Lie Dan. 1999. *The Transition from Foraging to Farming and the Origin of Agriculture in China*. Oxford: Archaeopress.

Ludden, David. 1999. *An Agrarian History of South Asia*. Volume 4, Part 4. Cambridge: Cambridge University Press.

McIntosh, Jane. 2008. *The Ancient Indus Valley: New Perspectives*. Santa Barbara, CA: ABC-CLIO.

Documents

From Megasthenes. C. 300 BCE. *Ancient India as Described by Megasthenês and Arrian*. Translated by John Watson McCrindle. 1877. Calcutta, India: Thacker, Spink, & Co.

Megasthenes was a Greek explorer who stayed in India around 300 BCE and wrote a book, Indica, *about what he had observed. Here, he describes Indian agriculture and the great respect granted to farmers in that country.*

India has many huge mountains which abound in fruit-trees of every kind, and many vast plains of great fertility—more or less beautiful, but all alike intersected by a multitude of rivers. The greater part of the soil, moreover, is under irrigation, and consequently bears two crops in the course of the year. It teems at the same time with animals of all sorts,—beasts of the field and fowls of the air,—of all different degrees of strength and size. It is prolific, besides, in elephants, which are of monstrous bulk, as its soil supplies food in unsparing profusion, making these animals far to exceed in strength those that are bred in Libya. It results also that, since they are caught in great numbers by the Indians and trained for war they are of great moment in turning the scale of victory. . . .

In addition to cereals, there grows throughout India much millet, which is kept well watered by the profusion of river-streams, and much pulse of different sorts, and rice also, and what is called *bosporum*, as well as many other plants useful for food, of which most grow spontaneously. The soil yields, moreover, not a few other edible products fit for the subsistence of animals, about which it would be tedious to write. It is accordingly affirmed that famine has never visited India, and that there has never been a general scarcity in the supply of nourishing food. For, since there is a double rainfall in the course of each year,—one in the winter season, when the sowing of wheat takes place as in other countries, and the second at the time of the summer solstice, which is the proper season for sowing rice and *bosporum* as well as sesamum and millet—the inhabitants of India almost always gather in two harvests annually; and even should one of the sowings prove more or less abortive they are always sure of the other crop. The fruits, moreover, of spontaneous growth, and the esculent roots which grow in marshy places and are of varied sweetness, afford abundant sustenance for man. The fact is, almost all the plains in the country have a moisture which is alike genial, whether it is derived from the rivers, or from the rains of the summer season, which are wont to fall every year at a stated period with surprising regularity; while the great heat which prevails ripens the roots which grow in the marshes, and especially those of the tall reeds.

But, further, there are usages observed by the Indians which contribute to prevent the occurrence of famine among them; for whereas among other nations it is usual, in the contests of war, to ravage the soil, and thus to reduce it to an uncultivated waste, among the Indians on the contrary, by whom husbandmen are regarded as a class that is sacred and inviolable, the tillers of the soil, even when battle is raging in their neighbourhood, are undisturbed by any sense of danger, for the combatants on either side in waging the conflict make carnage of each other, but allow those engaged in husbandry to remain quite unmolested. Besides, they neither ravage an enemy's land with fire, nor cut down its trees.

From the Duke of Zhou. C. 1100 BCE. *The Shi King: The Old "Poetry Classic" of the Chinese.* Translated by William Jennings. 1891. London: George Routledge and Sons.

The following poem, "Life in Pin in the Olden Time," describes the lives of farmers and their families in the district of Pin, though it is attributed to the aristocratic Duke of Zhou (ca. 1100 BCE). It describes the various activities that filled their annual schedules, including plowing, hunting, preparing silk, and harvesting grain, and the role of their overlords in their lives. The poem was included in the ancient anthology generally known as the Shi Jing.

In the seventh month wanes the heat,
In the ninth are garments doled.
Through the eleventh beat winter winds,
Through the twelfth 'tis chill and cold.
How without the clothes and wraps
Could one see the twelvemonth close?

Through the first, at sock and share
(For the ploughing we prepare).
Through the second—lilting toes!
And with wives and children now
Picnic we upon South Lea.
Comes the Steward, pleased is he.

In the seventh month wanes the heat,
In the ninth the clothes we dole,
In the sunny days of Spring
Comes the warbling oriole;
Maids their dainty baskets seize.
And along the narrow paths
Seek the supple mulberry-trees.
Spring days lengthen—all begin
The white wormwood to get in.
One maid's heart feels a smart:
Time is hastening—she must soon
With the Master's son depart.

In the seventh month wanes the heat,
In the eighth thrive rush and reed.
When the silkworm-month arrives,
Then the mulberry leaves we need;
Then with axe and bill we go
Laying vagrant branches low;
Virgin trees we strip, not strike.
In the seventh month pipes the shrike.
In the eighth, from spinning-wheel
Dark and yellow threads we reel,
While our brightest red is spun
To adorn the Master's son.

In the fourth month seeds the grass;
In the fifth cicadas call;
In the eighth is harvest-tide;
In the tenth the leaves will fall.
Through the eleventh we hunt the brock;
Fox and wild-cat, too, we take;
The young Master's furs they make.
In the twelfth the Meet takes place,
Where brave deeds once more be shown;
To our lot the young boars fall,
To the Master's the full-grown.

In the fifth month hoppers grind;
In the sixth their wings they find;
In the seventh out in the fields,
In the eighth in eaves o'erhead,
In the ninth about the door,
In the tenth beneath the bed,—
So do crickets entrance gain.
Holes be filled, smoked out the rats,
Windows stopped, doors plastered o'er.
Ah! wife and children mine.
So things tell the year's decline!
Go indoors, and there remain.

In the sixth month eat we plum and grape;
In the seventh we boil the pulse and rape;
In the eighth, date-trees are stripped;
In the tenth, the rice is clipped,
And Spring-drinks are brewed from it
For old age's benefit.
In the seventh we melons eat;
In the eighth we cut the bottle-gourd;
In the ninth the seed from hemp is stored,
And lettuce cut, and fuel of worthless wood,
And the farm-labourers supplied with food.

In the ninth month we beat down the space
In the garden for the stacking-place;
In the tenth we bring therein the grain,—
Millets, early sown and late,
Rice, and hemp, and pulse, and wheat.
Ah, my tillers of the soil.
When our crops are all got in
Home you go to other toil,
To the homestead industries,—
Thatching while you have the light.

Twisting ropes when falls the night!
—Yet they scarce the housetop gain
When they must begin again
Sowing every sort of grain!

In the twelfth month boring ice,
How the thuds and cracks resound!
In the first we store it up
In the houses underground.
In the next, at early morn.
To the shrine a lamb, with leeks, is borne.

In the ninth month frost is keen.
In the tenth we sweep the stackyards clean.
Then the pair of spirit-flasks are filled,
"Let the sheep and lambs," we cry, "be killed,
Now up to the Master's hall we'll go.
And the horncup there upraise,
Wishing him long life, and endless days!"

Hydraulic Engineers

All humans require ample supplies of water for drinking, bathing, cleaning, and farming, and many ancient people initially addressed this need by living next to lakes and rivers so they could easily wash their bodies and clothing and obtain water to nourish themselves and their crops. But this will not work for large numbers of people or large expanses of cultivated land; instead, some system must be created to transport water from where it is abundant to where it is wanted. And, as early humans gradually developed ways to achieve this goal, the profession of hydraulic engineering first emerged.

In ancient India, unknown individuals figured out several ways to control their water supply, usually with the goal of bringing water to fields of growing crops. The most common system was to dig small channels in rows, allowing water to flow from the rivers to the cultivated land, but dykes and dams were also constructed on the Ganges River and elsewhere to better control the diverted water. In some places, where it was necessary to elevate the river water to get it into the channels, the Indians built wheels with attached buckets that were turned by cows. To move water greater distances, wide canals were created, effectively functioning as artificial rivers with their own channels. In areas where rivers were not nearby, the Indians dug wells to get water for their crops; indeed, one passage in the *Rigveda* indicates that wells were the primary source of water for crops, taken from the ground by wheels. Also, to capture rain water and store water during dry periods, the Indians built large tanks and reservoirs.

At times, private individuals would undertake the construction and maintenance of irrigation systems to meet their needs, but more often the governments of ancient India would take responsibility for such projects, and it is evident that they regarded them as very important. In the *Mahabharata*, it is recommended that a king place guards at the dams, since any sabotage could cause devastating floods and disrupt the steady flow of water to crops. Other texts advise that anyone who damages a tank or irrigation system should be beheaded or drowned. Naturally, local governments imposed large fees or taxes on farmers for providing their fields with reliable sources of water—not entirely without justification, since they had to pay many workers to dig irrigation canals and build dykes. Officials also had to intervene when there were disputes over water: the farmers of one village, for example, might divert the water from a canal toward their lands and away from the lands of a neighboring village, provoking vehement protests from farmers suddenly without a supply of water.

There were also concerns about supplying people with enough water, and while the ancient Indians did not provide homes with running water, there were always municipal wells where citizens could fill their pots, and cisterns that stored water for their needs. And even the cities of the early Harappan civilization had effective drainage systems, allowing people to get rid of their waste water. Houses had latrines and bathrooms, with pipes leading to drains that poured water into channels made of bricks in the streets. The pipes carrying sewage first passed through a pit that captured solids so they would not clog the drains. The governments were also responsible for these services; indeed, the emperor Ashoka (302–232 BCE) boasted in one of his proclamations that he had dug many wells and built many places where both humans and animals could obtain water.

Because hydraulic engineering is rarely depicted in illustrations or discussed in texts, and because its devices and features have rarely been preserved, there remains some controversy about just how advanced the ancient Indians were in this area. Certain writings, for example, suggest that the ancient Indians, around 400 BCE, were employing a basic sort of water wheel, the noria, to obtain power from running water, but the references are ambiguous. If they did create such wheels out of wood, they may have passed the idea onto China, where there is a similarly unreliable report that a government official, sometime around 100 CE, invented a water wheel that provided power to the bellows used to heat the charcoal fires until they were hot enough to melt iron. Some also believe that the Chinese of that era used a water wheel to bring water to the capital city of Lo-Pang.

The ancient Chinese also practiced irrigation, sometimes using their own distinctive technologies: instead of using a wheel pulled by cows to raise water into channels, for example, they might employ a bucket attached to a lever with a counterweight, or a wooden machine with pedals pushed by peasants. They also built roofs over their wells so that pulleys could raise water to the surface. The Chinese faced a special challenge when they pioneered in the cultivation of rice, since that bountiful crop would grow best if it was constantly in shallow water. This required the construction of many irrigation channels to flood the fields and keep the water at the right level. In some cases, several families of farmers might work together to build needed irrigation channels or dykes, but the government often had to do the work; indeed, at times, soldiers would be diverted from their military duties so that they could dig irrigation channels and protect them from saboteurs.

Another problem was that the rivers of China were prone to flooding, and dykes constructed to prevent such disasters were not always effective. In the third century BCE, an official named Li Bing (ca. third century BCE), to deal with the periodic flooding of the Minjuang River, turned to hydraulic engineering by planning and implementing the massive Dujiangyan irrigation system; he earned such renown for its success that he was even deified. Later, in 69 CE, similar problems with the Yangtze River were confronted by

Wang Ching (ca. 25–90 CE), another of the few hydraulic engineers that we know by name. He was born to an aristocratic family that had long ago moved to Korea to escape from political intrigues, and even as a child he demonstrated unusual abilities in mathematics and science. As he developed a reputation as a hydraulic engineer, the government sought his advice for work on the Yangtze, and his ideas were so impressive that officials gave him the resources required to oversee the project. After a careful survey of the region's topography, he supervised the construction of tunnels through hills, gates across the river to maintain a regular flow, and dredging operations to remove impediments to the free movement of its water. His work was so effective that he was given a government position and later promoted to serve as a provincial governor, where he introduced a system of irrigation and promoted the use of plows pulled by oxen to improve the region's agriculture. A man with many interests, Wang Ching also wrote a book about how to read and make use of omens in everyday life, but the text has not survived.

The ancient Chinese also pioneered in building canals for purposes other than agriculture. In 487 BCE, the government dug a huge canal to connect the Yangtze and the Huai rivers, primarily so that troops could be moved more quickly from region to region; this was later lengthened to eventually become China's Grand Canal. Later, in 129 BCE, the government spent three years building a canal from the Yellow River to the capital city of Ch'ang-an, which it was hoped would both provide farmers with a better supply and allow grain to be transported more efficiently to its citizens.

With the exception of Li Bing and Wang Ching, we are not generally familiar with the specific individuals who planned and supervised the Chinese government's many efforts to control the movement of water. However, we can assume that they were educated men who obtained positions in the government and when they demonstrated an aptitude for such work, they were placed in charge of these very important projects. Since these were enormous undertakings, and since unpredictable weather could undermine even the best-planned schemes for controlling the movement of water, these hydraulic engineers were undoubtedly subjected to a great deal of stress, even though the potential rewards of successful work include an

NO LONGER A GRAND CANAL

The greatest achievement of Chinese hydraulic engineering was the Grand Canal, completed in various stages and eventually stretching over 1,100 miles to connect northern and southern China. As one measure of its impressive dimensions, Skylab astronaut Edward Pogue originally reported in 1973 that he had seen the Great Wall of China from space, but it was later realized that he had actually seen the Grand Canal instead. Unfortunately, due to poor maintenance and pollution, boats can no longer travel along its entire length, but ongoing efforts to clean up and repair the canal may eventually restore the waterway to its original glory.

INCREMENTAL IRRIGATION

Irrigation in ancient India and China primarily involved digging channels to bring water to crops; yet this so-called surface irrigation was often unable to deliver water to every plant in an efficient manner. Among other problems, the water in these channels might sink into the ground or evaporate before it reached the crops, and the channels could also become blocked by debris. For that reason, modern hydraulic engineers have developed a different system, drip irrigation, which employs pipes and tiny drippers that can provide each individual plant with regular drops of water.

emperor's praise and a promotion to higher office. And 2,000 years of advances in technology have still not solved all of the problems they faced, since the well-trained and well-educated hydraulic engineers of today's society are still frustrated at times by the same sorts of challenges faced by their ancient colleagues.

Further Reading

Boongaard, Peter. 2007. *Southeast Asia: An Environmental History.* Santa Barbara, CA: ABC-CLIO.

Mays, Larry W., editor. 2010. *Ancient Water Technologies.* Dordrecht, Germany: Springer.

Mithen, Steven. 2012. *Thirst: Water and Power in the Ancient World.* Cambridge, MA: Harvard University Press.

Ortloff, Charles R. 2009. *Water Engineering in the Ancient World: Archaeological and Climate Perspectives on*

Societies of Ancient South America, the Middle East, and South-East Asia. Oxford and New York: Oxford University Press.

Reynolds, Terry S. 1983. *Stronger Than a Hundred Men: A History of the Vertical Water Wheel.* Baltimore, MD: John Hopkins University Press.

Scarborough, Vernon L. 2003. *Flow of Power: Ancient Water Systems and Landscapes.* Santa Fe, NM: SAR Press.

Documents

From Anonymous. 1840. *The Ancient and Modern History of China.* London: Edward Gover.

In the course of describing Chinese agriculture, the unknown author praises their systems of irrigation.

Rice, the great article of food (for bread is unknown) is everywhere grown, except in sandy and dry soils; and in the northern provinces two crops of this precious grain are produced annually, which requires but little attention or labour: water, however, is absolutely necessary to its growth; and Chinese skill and ingenuity have exerted all their powers, inventing hydraulic and other engines, for the purpose of raising this element from the various rivers and lakes which abound throughout nearly the whole of China. To alleviate the evils and calamities which naturally arise out of a dearth or scarcity, a year's produce is always preserved in the public granaries; but even this does not serve to prevent the most horrible scenes of starvation.

To show the high value set upon this grain, and how much it is prized, from the sovereign to the peasant, a high festival is held at the beginning of each seed-time when the emperor fasts and prays for three days, and going forth with great magnificence and pomp, takes a plough in his hands, and opening a furrow with it, casts into the ground the first seed of the season: this is done by all the governors, vice-roys, and lieutenants throughout the empire, on the same day, which is regarded as a universal holiday.

From Parker, Edward Harper. 1908. *Ancient China Simplified.* London: Chapman & Hall.

In this passage, the author discusses some of the achievements of ancient Chinese hydraulic engineers, including Li Bing.

It is difficult to guess how much truth there is in the ancient traditions that the watercourses of the empire were improved through gigantic engineering works undertaken by the ancient Emperors of China. There is one gorge, well known to travellers, above Ich'ang, on the River Yangtze, on the way to Ch'ung-k'ing, where the precipitous rocks on each side have the appearance and hardness of iron, and for a mile or more—perhaps several miles—stand perpendicularly like walls on both sides of the rapid Yangtze River: the most curious feature about them is that from below the water-level, right up to the top, or as far as the eye can reach, the stone looks as though it had been chipped away with powerful cheese-scoops: it seems almost impossible that any operation of nature can have fashioned rocks in this way; on the other hand, what tools of sufficient hardness, driven by what great force, could hollow out a passage of such length, at such a depth, and such a height? It is certain that after Ts'in conquered the hitherto almost unknown kingdoms of Pa and Shuh a Chinese engineer named Li Bing worked wonders in the canalization of the so-called Ch'eng-tu plain, or the rich level region lying around the capital city of Sz Ch'wan province, which was so long as Shuh endured also the metropolis of Shuh. The consular officers of his Britannic Majesty have made a special study of these sluices, which are still in full working order, and they seem almost unchanged in principle from the period when Li Bing lived. . . . Li Ping's engineering feats also included the region around Ya-thou and Kia-ting, as marked on the modern maps.

The founder of the Hia dynasty (2205 BC) is supposed to have liberated the stagnant waters of the Yellow River and sent them to the sea; as this is precisely what all succeeding dynasties have tried to do, and have been obliged to try, and what in our own times the late Li Hung-chang was ordered to do just before his death, there seems no good reason for suspecting the accuracy of the tradition; the more especially as we see that the founder of the Chou dynasty sent his chief political adviser and his two most distinguished relatives to settle along this troublesome river's lower course, as rulers of Ts'i, Yen, and Lu; the other considerable vassals were all ranged along the middle course.

The original Chinese founder of the barbarian colony of Wu belonged, as already explained, to the same clan or family as the founder of the Chou dynasty, and in one respect even took ancestral or spiritual precedence of him, because the emigrant had voluntarily retired into obscurity with his brother in order to make way for a third and more brilliant younger brother, whose grandson it was that afterward, in 1122 B.C., conquered China, and turned the Chou principality, hitherto vassal to the Shang dynasty, into the Chou dynasty, to which the surviving Shang princes then became vassals in the Sung state and elsewhere. Even though the founder of Wu may have adopted barbarian ways, such as tattooing, hair-cutting, and the like, he must have possessed considerable administrative power, for he made a canal (running past his capital) for a distance of thirty English miles along the new "British" railway from Wu-sih to Chang-shuh, as marked on present maps; his idea was to facilitate boat-travelling, and to assist cultivators with water supplies for irrigation.

In the year 485 BC the King of Wu, who was then in the hey-day of his success, and by way of becoming Protector of China, erected a wall and fortifications round the well-known modern city of Yangchow; he next proceeded for the first time in history to establish water communication between the Yangtze River and the River Hwai; this canal was then continued farther north, so as to give communication with the southern and central parts of modern Shan Tung province.

His object was to facilitate the conveyance of stores for his armies, then engaged in bringing pressure upon Ts'i and Lu. . . .

Jewelers

Even in prehistoric times, both women and men liked to make and wear decorative jewelry out of the materials available to them, including stones, wood, seashells, and animal teeth; however, as humans began to form civilizations, a preference developed for jewelry made from shining metals and jewels, even though these were often rare and available only to the wealthiest members of society. Since crafting such items required special skills, professional jewelers emerged in all ancient societies, who generally made and sold their products directly to eager customers.

The people of the Indus Valley civilization regularly wore jewelry, as evidenced by scattered statues and images on pottery showing scantily clad figures wearing necklaces, earrings, and bracelets; archaeologists have also unearthed some ornaments made of gold, silver, copper, bronze, and electrum (a natural alloy of gold and silver), and beads of semiprecious stones like lapis lazuli, cornelian, and jadeite. One elaborate item, a bracelet consisting of six strings of spherical gold beads alternating with small slabs of gold, demonstrates that talented craftspeople must have been hard at work in this society, presumably making and selling their wares in the workshops and stalls of marketplaces in Harappa and Mohenjo-daro.

Jewelry was even more popular in India's later Vedic culture (ca. 1700–500 BCE): their literary epics describe men, women, gods, and goddesses wearing jewelry, and Indians of both genders would don items of jewelry both to enhance their appearance and to display their personal wealth. Indian jewelers created distinctive new pieces for their customers: the *jhala*, a group of gold flowers to be worn on one's back; the *balapasya*, long strings of pearls to wrap around a woman's hair; and the *nupur*, an ankle bracelet with small metal bells. A crown adorned with jewels, the *mukut*, was the everyday dress of monarchs and a special adornment for brides and grooms during their elaborate wedding ceremonies. Indian women also liked to wear long golden chains, sometimes including precious stones, around their waists, as well as jeweled pendants for their foreheads, while men might wear jeweled turbans or earrings made of ivory. Such items were accessible for large numbers of people because the subcontinent of India provided ample supplies of many sorts of jewels, and other jewels could be readily obtained from nearby Sri Lanka, Burma, and Thailand. Thus, Indian jewelers could employ diamonds, beryls, rubies, emeralds, topazes, amethysts, sapphires, pearls, and other jewels in their attractive designs.

Interestingly, some of the people who designed and crafted these objects were women, as shown by a record of the marriage of a hardware salesman and a jeweler. Perhaps then, this was a skill that jewelers often passed on to their daughters as well as their sons, following the standard pattern of professions becoming family traditions. Certainly, examining items from across the centuries, one can discover very little evidence of innovation, or an individual's artistic flair, in Indian jewelry; for the most part, it seems, Indian jewelers were content to rely upon well-established patterns and designs. We can assume that, as in most ancient societies, these jewelers labored in their own workshops that also served as stores, or they brought jewelry to the marketplace to be sold from a stall to passing customers. However, a play from the second century BCE, *The Toy-Cart* by Śūdraka (ca. second century BCE), suggests that wealthy women may have brought jewelers to their homes, where they could make especially commissioned items for these privileged customers.

Though they were not as enthusiastic about jewelry as the Indians, ancient Chinese men and women often wore items of jewelry, though necklaces and bracelets were relatively uncommon; ornaments for the head and hair, such as earrings headdresses, and hairpins, were more popular, as the Chinese generally preferred to display their wealth or status by means of fine clothing instead of jewelry. Typically men would usually wear only one earring of modest dimensions, while women wore two earrings that were often very large and elaborate. Their preferred metal for jewelry was silver, though gold and bronze were also employed. Another favorite material was jade, though this very expensive jewel, more valuable than gold in China, was beyond the incomes of average people, who might instead purchase jewelry made of a similar but cheaper stone, serpentine. Pearls were another option for wealthy women, while attractive seashells might have holes punched in them to serve as less costly pendants. At times, for women who liked the appearance of seashell jewelry but preferred more expensive items, a piece of jade might be carved in the shape of a seashell.

The Chinese especially valued jewelry that featured images associated with good fortune, requiring special artistry on the part of the jeweler, who might have to design tiny dragons, scrolls, turtles, birds, flowers, and phoenixes on their jewelry. One favorite item for women during the Shang Dynasty, for example, was a hairpin shaped like a bird, made of ivory or bone. Men might wear belt hooks, made of bronze with gold and silver highlights that featured images of dragons. To provide wearers with additional luck, blue kingfisher feathers were sometimes attached to pieces

of jewelry, and for persons of noble birth, it was considered proper to bury their jewelry with them instead of passing it on to relatives.

The techniques employed by Chinese jewelers were generally similar to those in other parts of the ancient world. In some cases, metal for jewelry would first be hammered to achieve the proper form, perhaps after some heating to make it softer; in other cases, the metal would be liquefied in a small oven so it could be poured into a mold to harden into a special shape. Working with jade was more difficult, since this hard stone could not be carved and instead had to be painstakingly ground to produce a certain shape; to aid them in this process, Chinese jewelers uniquely developed a compound milling machine that rapidly rotated pieces of jade to more quickly smooth them into complex forms. Then, to carve patterns on jade, jewelers used a metal knife, a sharp piece of quartz,

A RUSH TO GOLD

For a long period of time, Indians had a special fondness for jewelry made of gold, while the Chinese generally preferred silver or jade. Their tastes are changing, however, as China's growing affluence has created a greater demand for gold jewelry; though such items were once sold only in major cities, Chinese jewelers are now expanding into smaller cities as well, and by some estimates, China is now on the verge of overtaking India as the world's largest consumer of the glittering metal. Further, it is believed that about two-thirds of China's gold is used to make jewelry.

JEWELS FROM FARMS

Unlike jewels and metals that are dug out of the ground, pearls for jewelry can only be obtained from oysters at the bottom of the ocean, often found only at great depths. In some parts of Asia, traditions developed of trained pearl divers, usually naked women, who would dive into the ocean and hold their breath while they gathered one or two oysters. This was hazardous work, as divers might die due to cyclones or from the "bends," caused by rising too quickly from deep waters. Today, jewelers obtain all of their pearls from pearl farms, where oysters are carefully bred and prodded to produce pearls in accessible underwater fields.

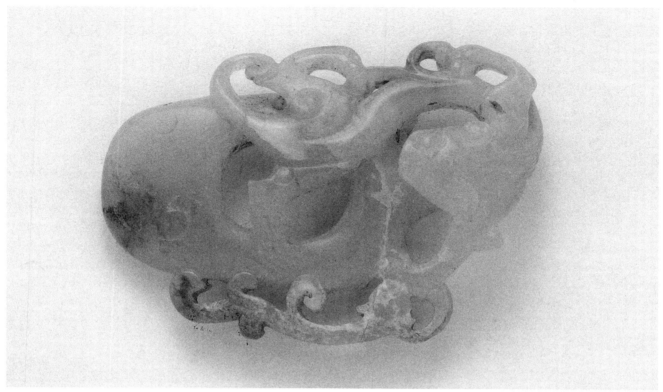

This pendant from Ancient China, carved from yellow jade, which is thought to be from sometime around 206 BCE to perhaps the year 8 CE during the Han dynasty, is decorated with dragons, traditionally valued as images providing good luck. (Heritage Images/Getty Images)

or a spinning stone wheel, propelled either by a foot pedal or running water.

Throughout ancient Asia, one can find impressive traditions of making attractive jewelry. The Scythian nomads of central Asia, for example, were famous for making golden bracelets, necklaces, earrings, and diadems in the shape of animals; in Korea and Japan, a favorite item was the *magatama*, a small bead made of jade or glass; and Burmese jewelers specialized in crafting unique conical headdresses modeled on the shape of the Buddhist *stupa*. However, special attention is merited by the region now known as Indonesia, which has long been renowned by its unusually variegated and beautiful jewelry. An interest in such personal adornment predates any contact with other cultures, since archaeologists have unearthed many pieces in graves from the second millennium BCE. For necklaces and amulets, Indonesian jewelers fashioned beads of gold, silver, glass, and the mineral carnelian; they also crafted rings, necklaces, and hairpins that

were usually made of copper, though some silver and gold may have been used as well. The Indonesian jewelers were fond of a special alloy, *surawa*, which was two-thirds copper and one-third gold. Initially, gold jewelry was relatively rare because the metal had to be imported from India or China, but after gold was discovered in Sumatra, native mines could provide more of their valued material. Later, silver jewelry became a specialty as well, especially the carefully designed silver beads made on the island of Bali.

While their products were cherished, the jewelers of ancient Asia were rarely respected by their societies; they were considered artisans, not artists, and *The Toy-Cart* suggests that rich and powerful people might have treated them like servants, summoning jewelers to their homes to perform chores. Still, they might have been consoled by the thought that they were also among the most influential members of their societies—for since their works were small, easy to transport, and often worn by prominent dignitaries, a culture's distinctive techniques and styles of jewelry could readily be observed and imitated in many distant lands. Further, while few people today are interested in replicating ancient methods for making buildings or weapons, many contemporary craftspeople are dedicated to making jewelry in the same way as their distant ancestors, so that ancient jewelers have had an impact over vast expanses of time as well as space.

Further Reading

Beringen, John, and Others. 2006. *The Art of Silver Jewellery: From the Minorities of China, the Golden Triangle, Mongolia and Tibet*. Milan, Italy: Skira.

Carpenter, Bruce W. 2011. *Ethnic Jewellery from Indonesia: Continuity and Evolution*. Singapore: Editions Didier Millet.

Carpenter, Bruce W., and Anne Richter. 2011. *Gold Jewellery of the Indonesian Archipelago*. Singapore: Editions Didier Millet.

Krishnan, Usha R. Bala, and Meera Sushil Kumar. 2001. *Indian Jewellery: Dance of the Peacock*. Mumbai: India Book House.

Richter, Anne. 2000. *The Jewelry of Southeast Asia*. New York: Harry N. Abrams.

Untracht, Oppi. 1997. *Traditional Jewelry of India*. New York: Harry N. Abrams.

Document

From Śūdraka. C. second century BCE. *The Toy-Cart*. Translated by Arthur Symons. 1919. Dublin: Maunsel.

An ancient play in Sanskrit, also referred to as The Little Clay Cart, *involves a noble but impoverished young man named Charadutta, with a son named Rohasena, who is in love with a wealthy courtesan named Vasantasena. In the first of two passages below, Charadutta describes Vasantasena's luxurious house, where jewelers are crafting new pieces for her; in the second passage, Vasantasena feels sorry for Charadutta's son and gives him all of her jewelry, placing it in his toy cart, and incidentally providing a picture of the typical items worn by wealthy Indian women.*

Charadutta: To be poor is like dying slowly. But what has all this to do with Vasantasena?

Maitreya: A very great deal. Do you know that at the house of Vasantasena the por-

ter dozes in a big chair, as stately as a Brahmin deep in the Vedas; and the very crows, crammed with rice and curds, disdain the rice thrown to the gods?

Charadutta: And if so?

Maitreya: (More and more rapidly.) The kitchen smells like the heaven of Indra, and the gateway, they tell me, to the inner court is like the bow of Indra in the sky. There are jewellers setting pearls and sapphires and rubies and topazes and other jewels; they cut lapis lazuli, polish coral, squeeze out sandal juice, and dry saffron; and there are men and women laughing and singing, and chewing musk and betel, drinking wine; and quails fight, and partridges cry, and cranes stalk about the court, and peacocks dance on the grass and wave their jewelled tails like fans, and in the midst of them, like the mistress of Indra's garden, is Vasantasena!. . . .

*****

Vasantasena: O, my child, you do not know what pitiful things you are saying. (Half-laughing and half-crying [she] takes off her jewels one by one and holds them up to the child and then drops them into the toy-cart.) Here is a little gold chain for you, and I will take this long chain off my neck.

Rambha [her mother]: Vasantasena!

Vasantasena: Do you see this bracelet? A King of the West gave that to me.

Rambha: Vasantasena! the king's bracelet!

Vasantasena: But I don't care for it: I give it to you. And here is another, that was given me by somebody I loved very much; but I don't care for it any longer. You shall have that too.

Rambha: Vasantasena! the bracelet of Rama! Are you beside yourself!

Vasantasena: Silence, mother! And here is a diamond that came from deep under the earth in

Africa, and this pearl was brought up by a diver from a bottomless sea. You shall have them both.

Rambha: All our treasures! O, Vasantasena!

Vasantasena: They are all yours, because you are a child, and Charadutta's, and because you are unhappy. Now I am really your mother.

Rohasena: Why are you crying? I won't take them, because you are crying.

Vasantasena: Now, I am not crying any more. Look, now your cart is more beautiful than any gold cart; it is more beautiful than any cart in the world. Go and play now, child. . . .

Merchants

As in other parts of the world, commerce was an integral part of life in ancient Asia, ranging from humble merchants selling their wares in tiny urban stalls to wealthy entrepreneurs who imported and exported vast quantities of valued goods. These individuals were often respected citizens in their societies, serving on village councils and sought after for charitable donations, yet they were never considered members of the highest social classes.

In ancient India, small businesspersons, members of the third-ranking *vaiśya* caste (below *brahmins* and *ksatriyas*), were typically found in one section of every city, where their small shops were packed together on the streets. These establishments had no doors and were fully open to the street, though their owners would close them with shutters in the evening. Every day, the merchant would sit in the center of the space waiting for customers, perhaps wearing little more than a loincloth because the interior of these buildings was often very hot; when the business day was over, he would retreat to a chamber either behind the shop or on its second floor, where he lived with his wife and family. Customers paid for their goods with coins or shells, though they might also barter their own possessions to get the desired product, and a long process of haggling might occur before the price was agreed upon.

Though there were innumerable sorts of stores, the most common products for sale were milk, oils, perfumes, spices, and alcoholic beverages, and each type of facility had its own distinctive character. The milkman kept his milk in containers of various sizes, and when customers brought vessels to be filled with milk, he would employ a long ladle to pour the milk into measuring cups to dispense precisely the desired amount of milk. Sellers of oil made their own merchandise on the spot by crushing vegetables in a press at the back of their stall. Perfumers displayed a bewildering variety of fragrant incense sticks, oils, perfumes, powders, and pastes, which they prepared themselves, using ingredients purchased from traveling caravans. Sellers of spices, who obtained most of their goods in the same way, had shelves filled with jars of different spices that extended to the ceiling, while others were piled on the floor; some bags of spices were also hanging from poles. Taverns, where customers uniquely lingered to consume the beverages they purchased, were attractively decorated and filled with comfortable chairs; there were also counters where perfumes and flowers were sold, perhaps so that imbibing husbands could purchase gifts to placate their neglected wives.

The sellers of these and other products usually depended upon their scales to determine the weight, and hence the price, of what they were selling. These consisted of a pan that hung on chains from a moving arm; by placing rings on the other side of the arm, one could measure the weight of an object on the pan, though merchants also placed small stone weights on the pan to show customers that the measurement was accurate. Still, some dishonest businesspersons might attempt to adjust their scales to give false readings, requiring the local government to periodically send inspectors to every store to check the scales' accuracy and place a stamp on those that passed muster; a merchant with a faulty scale might be fined or sent to jail. Sellers of certain products also belonged to guilds that would exercise some control over their prices and policies, and those who violated the guilds' laws might be fined or even expelled from the organization. The guilds performed many other functions, such as lending money, resolving disputes among members, and minting coins; their leaders were salaried employees and often had great influence over their communities.

In addition to these established merchants, Indian cities were also filled with independent peddlers, who walked down the streets or stood by bathing areas announcing what products they had to sell. If a merchant was not attracting enough customers to his place of business, he might hire a peddler to take his goods throughout the city. At the other end of the social scale were the wealthy merchants who purchased large amounts to be exported to other countries by means of caravans over land or merchant ships that crossed the ocean. There were many risks involved in such undertakings, but the rewards were great, since people in other lands would pay high prices for Indian goods such as ivory, spices, wood, exotic animals, and jewels. Some Indian merchants specialized in obtaining goods from China, like silk, ceramics, and paper, and reselling them at higher prices in faraway western regions.

Ancient Chinese businesspersons fell into two classes: those who made their own goods, the artisans, were the third of the four classes, while those who merely sold the products made by others, the merchants, were the fourth and least esteemed class because they did not produce anything themselves, depending instead upon the labor of others. Small shopkeepers of both types worked out of small buildings or stalls in special sections of large cities that were surrounded by walls and closed in the evenings. Merchants selling the same products were placed in the same area, supervised by a senior member of the profession. In rows and rows of stalls, vendors sold many different products, including live animals, meat (both raw and cooked), rolls of silk, dried fish, fruit, grains, pottery, weapons, wooden and brass utensils, and slaves; there were also roving peddlers pushing carts or carrying their merchandise. One author in the first century CE claimed that due to the closely packed stalls and many traveling vendors, there was literally no room for a man to turn around.

Adding to the crowdedness were the government officials who constantly patrolled the marketplaces, making sure that the rules were being followed. Indeed, the vendors of ancient China were regulated far more closely than their counterparts in ancient India: basic

THE LURE OF LOW TAXES

The Chinese philosopher Mencius (ca. 372–289 BCE) advised rulers to keep their taxes low to attract more merchants to their cities. He could not persuade any governors to adopt this policy, but his ideas are now being applied by some U.S. state governments. The governor of Texas, Rick Perry, has often visited other states with high taxes, such as Maryland, Illinois, and California, to persuade their businesses to relocate to Texas and reduce their tax bills. Some surveys indicate that his efforts are proving successful; in 2013, for example, Raytheon announced that it was moving the headquarters of its Space and Airborne Systems from California to Texas.

SPICES FOR SALE

For centuries, the most popular products that Indian merchants exported to other countries were their spices; indeed, the main reason that Christopher Columbus sailed eastward was his desire to discover a new trade route to bring Indian spices to Europe. Today, India remains the world's largest exporter of spices, and the demand continues to grow; between 2012 and 2013, Indian spice exports increased by 22 per cent, as cooks all over the world sought spices like coriander, curry powder, chili, fennel, garlic, cumin, mustard, and tamarind. Yet not all Indian spices are sent abroad, as India is also the world's largest consumer of spices.

prices were set by the government, carts for selling goods could only be a precise size, rolls of linen and silk had to be of a certain length and width, fruits and grains could only be sold during the proper seasons, and merchants were not allowed to mix together high- and low-quality food items to deceive customers. If someone was caught violating any of these myriad rules, they would be immediately arrested, and they might be forbidden to open their stalls in the future. Officials in charge of the marketplace collected taxes as well, though they could also be benefactors, making loans to businesspersons who needed money.

Merchants could become wealthy by obtaining a supply of some valuable material, such as salt or silk, that could be profitably exported to other parts of China or to foreign countries. The major problem they faced was transporting these goods, since traveling by land was difficult. The government provided some assistance by building canals, so merchants could place their goods in ships, and spurred by the example of merchant ships from India, Chinese merchants also began to move their goods across the ocean to places in Southeast Asia. Eventually, however, they overcame the challenges of overland travel to transport the most profitable Chinese export, silk, to the west across the continent of Asia, establishing the so-called "Silk Road" (though this system made use of many different routes, not a single road, and conveyed products other than silk, like jewelry and ceramics).

Even if they made a lot of money from such business, however, merchants still commanded little respect in ancient China: there were laws, for example, forbidding them to wear silk or travel in wheeled vehicles. To improve their status, some merchants would purchase property, so they could be considered farmers and hence productive members of society; others paid high prices to give their sons a good education and qualify them for prestigious government positions. They could, however, be consoled by the fact that their wealth did enable them to live in large homes, consume the finest foods, and purchase expensive furniture, while the scholars who were theoretically high above them on the social ladder could rarely afford such privileges.

Further Reading

Chakravarti, Ranabir, editor. 2001. *Trade in Early India.* New Delhi and New York: Oxford University Press.

Guy, John. 1998. *Woven Cargoes: Indian Trade Textiles in the East.* London: Thames and Hudson.

Jayapalan, N. 2008. *Economic History of India: Ancient to Present Day.* Second edition. New Delhi: Atlantic Publishers.

Neelis, Jason. 2010. *Early Buddhist Transmission and Trade Networks: Mobility and Exchange within and beyond the Northwestern Borderlands of South Asia.* Leiden, The Netherlands, and Boston: Brill.

Schinz, Alfred. 1996. *The Magic Square: Cities in Ancient China.* Stuttgart and London: Edition Axel Menges.

Wicks, Robert Sigfrid. 1992. *Money, Markets, and Trade in Early Southeast Asia: The Development of Indigenous Monetary Systems to AD 1400.* Ithaca, NY: Southeast Asia Program, Cornell University Press.

Document

From Mencius. C. 300 BCE. *The Chinese Classics: With a Translation, Critical and Exegetical Notes, Prolegomena, and Copious Indexes: Volume 2: The Works of Mencius.* Translated by James Legge. 1895. Oxford: Clarendon Press.

Unlike other Chinese philosophers, Mencius displayed a keen interest in merchants and their activities, advising rulers to treat them well and employing anecdotes about the marketplace to make certain points. In these passages, the philosopher advises rulers to treat merchants well, imposing few taxes and fees; he attributes the origin of taxes to the actions of one aggressive merchant; he explains the need for unequal treatment of unequal items by describing why this is necessary in the marketplace; and he upbraids a ruler who plans to eliminate his unfair taxes gradually instead of immediately.

"Now if your Majesty will institute a government whose action shall be benevolent, this will cause all the officers in the kingdom to wish to stand in your Majesty's court, and all the farmers to wish to plough in your Majesty's fields, and all the merchants, both travelling and stationary, to wish to store their goods in your Majesty's market-places, and all travelling strangers to wish to make their tours on your Majesty's roads, and all throughout the kingdom who feel aggrieved by their rulers to wish to come and complain to your Majesty. And when they are so bent, who will be able to keep them back?". . . .

"If, in the market-place of his capital, he levy a ground-rent on the shops but do not tax the goods, or enforce the proper regulations without levying a ground-rent;—then all the traders of the kingdom will be pleased, and wish to store their goods in his market-place.

"If, at his frontier-passes, there be an inspection of persons, but no taxes charged on goods or other articles, then all the travellers of the kingdom will be pleased, and wish to make their tours on his roads.

"If he require that the husbandmen give their mutual aid to cultivate the public field, and exact no other taxes from them;—then all the husbandmen of the kingdom will be pleased, and wish to plough in his fields.

"If from the occupiers of the shops in his market-place he do not exact the fine of the individual idler, or of the hamlet's quota of cloth, then all the people of the kingdom will be pleased, and wish to come and be his people."

*****

"Of old time, the market-dealers exchanged the articles which they had for others which they had not, and simply had certain officers to keep order among them. It happened that there was a mean fellow, who made it a point to look out for a conspicuous mound, and get up upon it. Thence he looked right and left, to catch in his net the whole gain of the market. The people all thought his conduct mean, and therefore they proceeded to lay a tax upon his wares. The taxing of traders took its rise from this mean fellow."

*****

Ch'an Hsiang said, "If Hsü's doctrines were followed, then there would not be two prices in the market, nor any deceit in the kingdom. If a boy of five cubits were sent to the market, no one would impose on him; linen and silk of the same length would be of the same price. So it would be with bundles of hemp and silk, being of the same weight; with the different kinds of grain, being the same in quantity; and with shoes which were of the same size."

Mencius replied, "It is the nature of things to be of unequal quality. Some are twice, some five times, some ten times, some a hundred times, some a thousand times, some ten thousand times as valuable as others. If you reduce them all to the same standard, that must throw the kingdom into confusion. If large shoes and small shoes were of the same price, who would make them? For people to follow the doctrines of Hsü, would be for them to lead one another on to practise deceit. How can they avail for the government of a State?"

*****

Tâi Ying-chih said to Mencius, "I am not able at present and immediately to do with the levying of a tithe only, and abolishing the duties charged at

the passes and in the markets. With your leave I will lighten, however, both the tax and the duties, until next year, and will then make an end of them. What do you think of such a course?"

Mencius said, "Here is a man, who every day appropriates some of his neighbour's strayed fowls. Someone says to him, 'Such is not the way of a good man'; and he replies, 'With your leave I will diminish my appropriations, and will take only one fowl a month, until next year, when I will make an end of the practice'."

"If you know that the thing is unrighteous, then use all dispatch in putting an end to it:—why wait till next year?"

Musicians

It can be frustrating to study the music of ancient people, since they usually lacked systems of notation to record their compositions, so all that remains today are the words of their songs and remnants of their musical instruments. Still, by examining written records and observing the still-vibrant traditions of music-making in contemporary societies, one can garner some information about the lives and activities of ancient Asia's musicians.

Ancient Indians loved music, though only members of certain families called *Śailalakas* performed music in public settings. Both men and women would learn to play a variety of instruments, including percussion instruments like drums, tambourines, and cymbals; wind instruments like conches, flutes, and trumpets; and stringed instruments like lutes, lyres, and harps. A special sort of bow-harp, called the *vīnā*, was especially popular, found in many homes and classrooms, but the term was later used for another instrument more like a lute. Illustrations suggest that families would often play such instruments for their private enjoyment, strumming lutes with their fingers or a pick and tapping their feet as they struck tambourines. Wealthy women played the *vīnā* for friends and guests, while shepherds would play flutes to entertain themselves during long hours of watching over their animals.

As for India's professional musicians, they could support themselves in a variety of ways; some performed in the streets to receive donations, while others were hired to perform at weddings, accompany dancers, provide musical accompaniments for plays and religious ceremonies in temples, play music for the women of the royal harem, or entertain the king and other nobles at court. When the king rode through the street on his elephant during public festivals, a full orchestra with huge gongs would accompany him. Drummers might receive special assignments: when the emperor Ashoka (304–232 BCE) wished his people to hear his doctrines, his proclamations were preceded by the beating of a drum; people traditionally boarded ships while drums were playing; and whenever a criminal was captured and beaten, the sound of drumbeats would alert citizens about his punishment. Prostitutes would also work occasionally as professional musicians, playing music at private parties.

For most Westerners, of course, Indian music is defined by the *sitar*, played by skilled artists in theaters full of appreciative listeners and accompanied by the beating of a *tabla*; yet these forms of the lute and drum only became common a few centuries ago, and the sort of respect and admiration their masters garner was not granted to their distant precursors, who were generally regarded as lowly employees. For that reason, we do not know the names of any of ancient India's great musicians, and no works attributed to specific composers have survived. Music itself was greatly valued, especially the music devoted to the Hindu religion, but the musicians who performed it were not.

The situation was somewhat different in ancient China, where music and its performers received more scholarly attention and admiration. The philosopher Confucius (551–479 BCE) believed that in order to govern properly, a man must understand music, which both reflects and imposes the harmony of the universe as a whole; thus, all prospective aristocrats were urged to learn and play music as one of many activities associated with a good education and moral life. If some of these people became especially good at playing their instruments, they would perform for friends and colleagues as a sign of their virtue and merits; practicing what he preached, Confucius himself played the lute and sang, at least according to legend. For these reasons, while the people hired as accompanists might be held in little esteem, a master performer might find that

his services were in high demand. Thus, there were effectively two sorts of musicians in ancient China: hard-working peasants and aristocratic virtuosos.

Persons in the former category could find employment in many arenas. Music was required for many religious rituals, so some musicians worked directly under priests at ancestral shrines, playing music while hymns were sung and ceremonies were performed. Emperors and other high officials had their own groups of musicians to travel with them, entertain guests at banquets, and provide an accompaniment for dancers and other performers. For grand occasions, they would play as part of large orchestras with dozens of musicians; for more intimate gatherings, they would work in smaller ensembles. Some emperors employed individuals who were similar to medieval Europe's court jesters, amusing nobles by playing instruments and singing satirical songs. The Han dynasty's Office of Music employed many musicians and singers as part of their effort to record and preserve both the poetry and music of everyday China, though many of these later lost their jobs as part of an effort to reduce government expenses. Some wealthy families had their own five-person bands to provide them with music whenever it was wanted. Musicians were also hired at play at China's many festivals, and they could even try to support themselves by playing in the streets and asking for donations, either by themselves or along with other musicians or performers like acrobats or jugglers. Sometimes, groups of musicians would travel from town to town to perform, riding on the backs of camels. While most of these people were free citizens, some slaves were also trained to work as musicians.

As for the courtly musicians, some of these were only occasional performers, perhaps asked to play at family dinners or for important visitors. It was the habit of many noble women, for example, to play a lute called the *pipa* in the royal court to entertain their peers. Yet they also enjoyed the music of professional musicians who were so highly esteemed that they were granted the status of court officials. Many of these men were blind, which added to their aura of authority, and they would individually play their instruments while small audiences of aristocrats listened with respectful silence.

Like their counterparts in India, Chinese musicians had many different instruments to play, some of ancient origins. For example, archaeologists have uncovered flutes made out of clay as well as bronze bells and early examples of China's distinctive stone chimes, the *zhong*. As more types of instruments were devised and employed, the Chinese, who were devoted to all aspects of music theory, classified them into eight groups according to the materials used to make them: animal skins, stones, metal, silk, wood, gourds, bamboo, and clay. Uniquely, the Chinese used silk for their stringed instruments, which included a harp (the *konghu*) and the *pipa*. Other common instruments included zithers with twenty-five strings, bamboo mouth organs, wooden clappers, and a bronze drum called the *konggu*, though most drums were crafted from animal skins and struck with bamboo sticks. Another percussion instrument, the *fangziang*, was similar to the *zhong* except that its chimes were

The zither, or *qin*, was a common instrument in Ancient China. From the first century CE, this well-preserved terracotta painted statue from Northern China depicts a bearded man sitting and playing his *qin*. (DeAgostini/Getty Images)

MUSICAL EDUCATION

The ancient Chinese believed that every educated person should learn to play a musical instrument, and many of their greatest thinkers, like Confucius, were known to have that skill. For the same reason, U.S. public schools have often provided students with lessons on how to play instruments like the drums, trumpet, and clarinet; and though such programs have sometimes been eliminated due to budgetary problems, the Chinese belief in the value of such training has been validated by modern studies demonstrating that a musical education does improve children's reading and mathematical skills.

A NEW MASTER OF AN OLD INSTRUMENT

One of the most popular instruments of ancient China was the *pipa*, a four-stringed lute shaped like a pear. While one might imagine that contemporary Chinese musicians would prefer the guitar, there are still artists who prefer this traditional instrument. One of the most prominent of them is Zhou Yi, a woman who has toured the world giving solo concerts, playing both old and modern songs on her *pipa*. Now a resident of New York City, she has also worked with some Western musicians, including Damon Albarn, a member of the British groups Blur and Gorillaz as well as a solo performer.

made of iron instead of stone. Some Chinese instruments were based on models from other cultures, like cymbals from India and gongs from Southeast Asia.

Other cultures of ancient Asia also developed their own distinctive instruments. Indonesia's unique *gamelan* orchestras featured large metal gongs and other pieces of metal struck with hammers, while the ancient Burmese played a sort of xylophone made out of drums, each tuned to one note. The Koreans devised a special drum shaped like an hourglass called the *changgo*; one surface was hit with the musician's hand while the other was hit with a stick. The Japanese were fond of bronze bells and a zither with thirteen silk strings known as the *koto*. As these examples suggest, percussion instruments were often central to the music of Southeast Asia, though the musicians of all its civilizations also played wind and string instruments.

In the final analysis, what may be most striking about the music of ancient Asia is something that was usually of little importance to its musicians: namely, the musical theories that inspired and shaped its traditions. Indian musicians, for example, developed no notion of chords or an eight-note octave, and they valued improvisation and spontaneity in all performances. The Chinese related music to their general theories of nature, so that Confucius celebrated music as a way to express the six basic emotions of happiness, sadness, love, anger, satisfaction, and piety, while others associated the twelve notes of the octave with the twelve months of the year. Despite its vastly disparate theoretical underpinnings, however, the music composed in ancient Asia and represented by its modern descendants can still be appreciated and enjoyed by listeners throughout the world, even as it was appreciated and enjoyed in the nations where it originated.

Further Reading

Falkenhausen, Lothar von. 1993. *Suspended Music: Chime-Bells in the Culture of Bronze Age China*. Berkeley and Los Angeles: University of California Press.

Jie, Jin. 2011. *Chinese Music*. Updated edition. Translated by Wang Li and Li Rong. Cambridge and New York: Cambridge University Press.

McIntosh, Solveig. 2005. *Hidden Faces of Ancient Indian Song*. Aldershot, England, and Burlington, VT: Ashgate.

Mei, Xiao, Bell Yung, and Anita Wong, editors. 2001. *The Musical Arts of Ancient China*. Hong Kong: University Museum and Art Gallery, the University of Hong Kong.

Rowell, Lewis Eugene. 1992. *Music and Musical Thought in Early India*. Chicago: University of Chicago Press.

So, Jenny F. 2000. *Music in the Age of Confucius*. Washington, DC: Freer Gallery of Art and Arthur M. Sackler Gallery.

Documents

From Śūdraka. C. second century BCE. *The Toy-Cart*. Translated by Arthur Symons. 1919. Dublin: Maunsel.

This ancient Sanskrit play conveys how music was a part of the everyday life of both the rich and the poor. As the play opens, an impoverished aristocrat named Charadutta sits in a room filled with musical instruments and tells a friend how much he enjoyed listening to a man sing and play the lute; later, when he visits the wealthy courtesan Vasantansena, she summons musicians so that she can dance for him.

[A room in Charadutta's house, poorly furnished, with a few books and musical instruments, a drum, a tabor, a lute, and pipe, lying about. At the back is a door opening into an outer court or garden, with a wall visible at the back, beyond which is the street. The outer door is not seen. There is a curtained door at the side of the room, leading into the inner part of the house.]

Charadutta: Rebhila sang exquisitely! And as for his lute, it is a sea-pearl; it was more comfortable to my heart than a friend consoling a friend for the absence of the beloved; it had a voice like the very voice of love.

Maitreya: Well, well, for my part I am very thankful to be out of it.
[He sits down, as if tired.]

Charadutta: Rebhila surpassed himself.

Maitreya: Now, there are two things that I can never help laughing at: A woman reading Sanskrit and a man singing a song. The woman snuffles like a young cow when the rope is first passed through her nostrils, and the man wheezes like an old pandit [scholar] who has been saying his beads till the flowers of his chaplet are as dry as his throat; and the one seems to me as ridiculous as the other.

Charadutta: Is it possible that you did not admire Rebhila's marvellous skill? His voice was at once so sweet and so passionate, so flowing and yet so precise, so full of the ecstasy of delight, that I half fancied I was listening to a woman whom I could not see. And now, though the music is over, I can still hear the voice and the lute, the hurrying, rising, sinking, the pause and return of the wandering melody.

*****

Charadutta: A duty calls me; I must go back.
Vasantansena: You are my guest. I have only music and dancing to welcome you; but do you not love music? Nay, be seated. [They sit down.]
Charadutta: More than anything in the world.
Vasantansena: I love music so much that my body follows it wherever it goes. When I dance, it is to say more clearly, and in my own voice, what music says. We will have music, and I will dance for you. Call in the musicians.
[Maid goes into the inner part of the house and returns presently with musicians.]
Charadutta: I have often dreamed of a dance which should be more articulate, more human, than music: dance that dance to me, Vasantasena, for I have never seen it. . . .

From Parker, Edward Harper. 1908. *Ancient China Simplified*. London: Chapman & Hall.

In this passage, the author discusses the importance of music and musicians in ancient China.

Take, for instance, the subject of music, which always played in Chinese ceremonial a prominent part not easy for us now to understand. One of the chief sights of the modern Confucian residence is the music-room, containing specimens of all the ancient musical instruments, which, on occasion, are still played upon in chorus. . . . As we have said before, the ancient emperors, at their banquets given to vassals and others, always had musical accompaniment. . . . Confucius' view a century later was that music best reflected a nation's manners, and that in good old times authority was manifested quite as much in rites and ceremonies as in laws and pronouncements. . . . Before ridiculing the idea that music could in any way serve as a substitute for preaching or commanding, we must reflect upon the awe-inspiring contribution of music to our own religious services, not to mention the "speaking" effect of our Western nocturnes, symphonies, and operatic music generally.

In 562 BC, when a statesman of Tsin (whose fame in this connection endures to our own days) succeeded in establishing a permanent understanding with the Tartars, based upon joint trading rights and reasonable mutual concessions, the principle of interesting the Tartars in cultivation, industry, and so on; as a reward for his distinguished services, he was presented with certain music, which meant that he had the political right to have certain musical airs performed in his presence. This concession ceases to seem ridiculous or even strange to us if we reflect what an honour it would have been to, say, the Duke of Wellington, or to Nelson, had the right to play "God Save the King" at dinner been granted to his family band of musicians. . . . But music also had its lighter uses, for we have seen in Chapter VI how in 549 two Tsin generals took their ease in a comfortable cart, playing the banjo, whilst passing through Cheng to attack Ts'u. Music was used at worship as well as at court; in 527 the ruler of Lu, as a mark of respect for one of his deceased ministers, abandoned the playing of music, which otherwise would have been a constituent part of the sacrifice or worship he had in hand at the moment. Even in modern China, music is prohibited during solemn periods of mourning, and officials are often degraded for attending theatrical performances on solemn fasts. In 212 BC, when the First August Emperor was, like Saul or Belshazzar, beginning to grow sad at the contemplation of his lonely and unloved greatness, he was suddenly startled at the fall of a meteoric stone, bearing upon it what looked like a warning inscription. He at once ordered his learned men to compose some music treating of "true men" and immortals, in order to exorcise the evil omen. . . .

Philosophers

In the Western world, philosophy emerged as part of a secular tradition of studying the world that included mathematics and science; in the cultures of ancient India and China, however, philosophy was considered an aspect of religion, and leading thinkers were devout followers, or even founders, of major faiths. Still, philosophers throughout the world shared a concern for exploring the ways that humans should behave, and a dedication to a contemplative lifestyle, priorities that transformed several thinkers of ancient Asia into figures who are still studied and respected today.

The philosophical ideas of ancient India first emerged in the anonymous Vedic hymns, probably written between 1500 and 1200 BCE, collectively termed the *Vedas*; later, one school of Indian philosophy emerged, *Mimamsa*, that stressed their authority in all matters, first espoused by the philosophy Jaimini (ca. fourth century BCE). Later, a series of treatises, the *Upanishads*, addressed philosophical issues more directly between the fifth century and second century BCE. These works, along with others like the *Bhagavad Gita*, became the basis of another philosophical school, the *Vedanta*. A third school, *Samkhya*, embraced a form of dualism, first articulated by the philosopher Ishvarakrishna (ca. third century CE), while Kanada (ca. second-third century CE) founded the school of *Vaisheshika*, which unusually concerned itself with the material world and adopted an early version of atomic theory to explain the universe. Another philosopher, Gautama (ca. second century BCE), advanced the doctrines of a fifth school, *Nyaya*, which emphasized logical thinking, and Pantajali (ca. second century BCE) first presented the basic beliefs of the sixth classic school, *Yoga*, which focused on helping people achieve complete control over their bodies and minds through exercise and meditation.

Scholars can generally deduce approximately when these early philosophers lived by examining their writing, but other biographical information is usually unavailable. However, we can assume that their experiences were similar to those of a later philosopher, Shankara (ca. 700–750 CE), who became the subject of several biographies—though they are filled with fanciful stories, which no one today regards as plausible. He was reportedly born into the Brahmin class, which seems logical, since only someone from that caste would have access to the sort of education needed to become a learned philosopher. Perhaps saddened by the early death of his father, he became a religious ascetic and studied under the pupil of another noted philosopher, Gaudapada (ca. eighth century CE),

before embarking upon a series of travels throughout India in search of additional wisdom. Eventually, he came to focus on teaching his doctrines in various Indian villages, probably supporting himself by means of generous benefactors and students who sought his instruction (four of them are known by name). Other Indian philosophers, no doubt, similarly adopted a lifestyle of voluntary poverty and few possessions, traveling around without worrying about obtaining food and shelter while they focused their energies on developing and writing down their conclusions.

We know a bit more about the ancient Chinese philosophers, particularly since the works of the two most prominent figures, Confucius (551–479 BCE) and Zhuangzi or Chuang-tzu (369–286 BCE), led to the establishment of religions based on their doctrines. Though Confucius was reportedly the son of a provincial governor, he grew up as a poor person because his elderly father died when he was very young and his mother received only a small tract of land as a pension. As an adult, he first held some minor government positions before leaving for unknown reasons to become an itinerant philosopher, welcomed in various courts by nobles who enjoyed his wise company. Finally, he was able to establish a permanent school in Beijing and attracted many students, who supported him with their fees (though Confucius generously allowed them to pay whatever they could afford). Through the texts that he assigned as readings and his own lectures, the philosopher stressed his primary goal, to create good governments by training rulers to be superior men, whose virtue would lead them to invariably make correct decisions and encourage citizens to emulate their exemplary behavior.

While innumerable sayings are attributed to Confucius, it is believed that he wrote nothing himself, though his later disciples gradually systemized the teachings that became the basis of the religion of Confucianism. Of these, the most important interpreter of Confucius' teachings was probably Mencius (ca. 371–289 BCE), whose life was in many respects similar to that of his mentor. He also lost his father at a young age, though his mother raised him well, moving her family so that her son could attend a good school and encouraging him to become a scholar. After serving for a short time in the Chinese government, he left his

Although this silk painting was created during the Song dynasty (960–1279), more than a thousand years after Confucius's death in 479 BCE, it is undoubtedly accurate in depicting the way that the philosopher would instruct a circle of students. (Howard Sochurek/Time & Life Pictures/Getty Images)

position and began traveling in order to promote his version of Confucianism, which emphasized that rulers must treat their subjects humanely. Unfortunately, when none of the sovereigns he approached expressed any interest in implementing recommended policies like lowering taxes and providing financial support for the elderly, he settled in his home province and devoted himself to teaching students, who eventually compiled his sayings and anecdotes about his life into a book called the *Mencius.*

Another follower of Confucius, Mozi or Mo-tzu (ca. 470–391 BCE), broke away from his doctrines to establish a competing school, known as Mohism, which unusually emphasized devotion to a divine will and rejected the elaborate rituals of Confucianism. Like Confucius, he briefly worked for the government but spent most of his life as a traveling philosopher, hoping to find nobles who would embrace his teachings; however, he also wrote a lengthy treatise, also

called *Mozi*, articulating his beliefs with the clear logic that was his most celebrated virtue. Still, Mohism soon faded into obscurity, while the Confucianism that it once challenged remained prominent.

A rival to Confucius who had a more enduring impact was a shadowy figure named Laozi or Lao-tzu (ca. sixth century BCE), who may or may not have actually existed, although the founding text of Daoism, the *Daodejing*, is attributed to him. (Modern scholars, however, believe that it is the work of several unknown authors.) He purportedly worked in a royal court during the Zhou Dynasty and met with Confucius, who praised his wisdom even though Laozi criticized the philosopher for being too ambitious. Yet the most important Daoist thinker was the later philosopher Zhuangzi, whose work, also named *Zhuangzi*, offered a fuller and more eloquent version of its tenets. Like other Chinese philosophers, he worked as a government official in the province of Meng, and we

PHILOSOPHY SET TO MUSIC

George Harrison of the Beatles was well known for his devotion to Indian music, yet he was also fascinated by Eastern philosophy; thus, when Juan Mascaro sent him a copy of his anthology of religious writings, *Lamps of Fire* (1958), Harrison eagerly read its selections from Asian texts, and one of them, a passage written by philosopher Laozi, so impressed the musician that he employed almost identical language in the lyrics to his 1968 song, "The Inner Light." However, he provided no official credit for the ancient author, as the song's music and lyrics were attributed only to Harrison.

A POPULAR PHILOSOPHER

In the early days of the Communist regime in China, the teachings of the philosopher Confucius were regarded as impediments to progress and officially discouraged; more recently, however, the government has embraced Confucius as an icon of traditional Chinese culture, and more and more citizens are studying the philosopher and sending their children to Confucian schools. In 2006, a professor at Beijing Normal University, hosted a successful television program that explained the maxims of Confucius, and her subsequent book on the same subject sold four million copies, about twice as many copies as the 2002 Chinese translation of *Harry Potter and the Sorcerer's Stone* by J. K. Rowling (1965–).

one had to be the son of socially prominent parents, who could provide him with the high-quality education that he would need in order to pursue philosophy. Once they had completed their educations, aspiring philosophers were qualified to become government officials and usually accepted such positions; however, they often grew dissatisfied with the life of a bureaucrat, or failed to curry favor with the right people due to their habit of forthrightly expressing their views. So, they would usually resign from the government and support themselves by entertaining royal patrons and teaching students. If their ideas were unusually innovative or unusually persuasive, they could attract enthusiastic followers from all over China by means of their own writings, or the writings of their disciples, and they might become celebrated as the founders of important schools of philosophy, or even a religion. And if their achievements did not bring them great riches or fame during their own lifetimes, they were presumably not bothered by this, since they would invariably teach their followers that they should never strive for such unimportant rewards and instead devote themselves solely to becoming wiser and better people. Strangely, though, the renown and respect that they now enjoy serves as evidence of the value of their philosophies.

Further Reading

Collinson, Diane, and Robert Wilkinson. 1994. *Thirty-Five Oriental Philosophers*. London and New York: Routledge.

Ivanhoe, Philip J., and Bryan W. Van Norden, editors. 2005. *Readings in Classical Chinese Philosophy*. Second edition. Indianapolis, IN: Hackett Publishing Company.

King, Richard. 1999. *Indian Philosophy: An Introduction to Hindu and Buddhist Thought*. Edinburgh, England: Edinburgh University Press.

Leaman, Oliver, editor. 2001. *Encyclopedia of Asian Philosophy*. London and New York: Routledge.

Mou, Bo, editor. 2009. *History of Chinese Philosophy*. London and New York: Routledge.

Van Norden, Bryan W. 2009. *Introduction to Classical Chinese Philosophy*. Indianapolis, IN: Hackett Publishing Company.

get some idea of his personality and daily life from comments in his writings. He is described as someone unconcerned with his personal appearance, wearing ragged clothes and worn-out shoes that had to be held together with string. When his wife died, he refused to mourn, citing doctrines that would make such displays inappropriate, and he instructed his followers that his own death should not be marked by a lavish funeral. All of this, of course, was perfectly in accord with the teachings of Daoism, which promoted a mystical vision of a universe that could be understood and embraced only by people who renounced the essentially illusory material world.

One could chronicle the lives of several other ancient Chinese philosophers and their characteristic doctrines, but their careers and experiences generally followed the same pattern. To become a philosopher,

Documents

From Mencius. C. 300 BCE. *The Chinese Classics: With a Translation, Critical and Exegetical Notes, Prolegomena, and Copious Indexes: Volume 2: The Works of Mencius.* Translated by James Legge. 1895. Oxford: Clarendon Press.

In three passages from Mencius, the philosopher builds upon a king's fondness for music to make a point about good government, expounds upon the characteristic viewpoint of the philosopher, and explains the ways that a philosopher can teach others.

Mencius. . . said, "Your Majesty, I have heard, told the officer Chwang, that you love music;—was it so?" The king changed colour, and said, "I am unable to love the music of the ancient sovereigns; I only love the music that suits the manners of the present age."

Mencius said, "If your Majesty's love of music were very great, Ch'î would be near to a state of good government! The music of the present day is just like the music of antiquity, as regards effecting that."

The king said, "May I hear from you the proof of that?" Mencius asked, "Which is the more pleasant,—to enjoy music by yourself alone, or to enjoy it with others?" "To enjoy it with others," was the reply. "And which is the more pleasant,—to enjoy music with a few, or to enjoy it with many?" "To enjoy it with many."

Mencius proceeded, "Your servant begs to explain what I have said about music to your Majesty.

"Now, your Majesty is having music here.—The people hear the noise of your bells and drums, and the notes of your fifes and pipes, and they all, with aching heads, knit their brows, and say to one another, 'That's how our king likes his music! But why does he reduce us to this extremity of distress?—Fathers and sons cannot see one another. Elder brothers and younger brothers, wives and children, are separated and scattered abroad'. Now, your Majesty is hunting here.—The people hear the noise of your carriages and horses, and see the beauty of your plumes and streamers, and they all, with aching heads, knit their brows, and say to one another, 'That's how our king likes his hunting! But why does he reduce us to this extremity of distress?—Fathers and sons cannot see one another. Elder brothers and younger brothers, wives and children, are separated and scattered abroad'. Their feeling thus is from no other reason but that you do not allow the people to have pleasure as well as yourself. . . .

"If your Majesty now will make pleasure a thing common to the people and yourself, the royal sway awaits you."

*****

Mencius said, "Confucius ascended the eastern hill, and Lû appeared to him small. He ascended the T'âi mountain, and all beneath the heavens appeared to him small. So he who has contemplated the sea, finds it difficult to think anything of other waters, and he who has wandered in the gate of the sage, finds it difficult to think anything of the words of others.

"There is an art in the contemplation of water.—It is necessary to look at it as foaming in waves. The sun and moon being possessed of brilliancy, their light admitted even through an orifice illuminates.

"Flowing water is a thing which does not proceed till it has filled the hollows in its course. The student who has set his mind on the doctrines of the sage, does not advance to them but by completing one lesson after another."

*****

Mencius said, "There are five ways in which the superior man effects his teaching.

"There are some on whom his influence descends like seasonable rain.

"There are some whose virtue he perfects, and some of whose talents he assists the development.

"There are some whose inquiries he answers.

"There are some who privately cultivate and correct themselves.

"These five ways are the methods in which the superior man effects his teaching."

Kung-sun Ch'âu said, "Lofty are your principles and admirable, but to learn them may well be likened to ascending the heavens,—something which cannot be reached. Why not adapt your teaching so as to cause learners to consider them attainable, and so daily exert themselves!"

Mencius said, "A great artificer does not, for the sake of a stupid workman, alter or do away with the marking-line. I did not, for the sake of a stupid archer, charge his rule for drawing the bow."

From Lao Tzu. C. sixth century BCE. *The Sayings of Lao Tzu*. Translated by Lionel Giles 1904. London: Orient Press.

In these passages, the philosopher speaks of his predecessors and describes how a philosopher can attain wisdom through inaction.

The skillful philosophers of the olden time were subtle, spiritual, profound, and penetrating. They were so deep as to be incomprehensible. Because they are hard to comprehend, I will endeavour to describe them.

Shrinking were they, like one fording a stream in winter. Cautious were they, like one who fears an attack from any quarter. Circumspect were they, like a stranger guest; self-effacing, like ice about to melt; simple, like unpolished wood; vacant, like a valley; opaque, like muddy water. . . .

The Sage occupies himself with inaction, and conveys instruction without words.

Is it not by neglecting self-interest that one will be able to achieve it?

Purge yourself of your profound intelligence, and you can still be free from blemish. Cherish the people and order the kingdom, and you can still do without meddlesome action.

Who is there that can make muddy water clear? But if allowed to remain still, it will gradually become clear of itself. Who is there that can secure a state of absolute repose? But let time go on, and the state of repose will gradually arise.

Be sparing of speech, and things will come right of themselves.

A violent wind does not outlast the morning; a squall of rain does not outlast the day. Such is the course of Nature. And if Nature herself cannot sustain her efforts long, how much less can man!

Attain complete vacuity, and sedulously preserve a state of repose. . . .

Without going out of doors one may know the whole world; without looking out of the window, one may see the Way of Heaven. The further one travels, the less one may know. Thus it is that without moving you shall know; without looking you shall see; without doing you shall achieve.

The pursuit of book-learning brings about daily increase. The practice of Tao brings about daily loss. Repeat this loss again and again, and you arrive at inaction. Practise inaction, and there is nothing which cannot be done.

Poets

All over the world, one finds traditions of writing poetry, at first designed to be spoken or sung for audiences, and later to be read silently. Yet more so than others, the cultures of ancient Asia greatly esteemed the art of poetry and its practitioners: many of its most respected religious and philosophical texts were written in verse, and an ability to write poetry was considered a key characteristic of properly educated people.

The earliest Indian poems, written down and collected as the *Rigveda* around 300 BCE, are believed to date from around 1500 BCE and thereafter; their anonymous authors recited and memorized their poems to be passed orally from generation to generation. As hymns to Hindu gods and goddesses, these poems were probably written by priests to be recited at religious rituals, and while often eloquent, they sometimes seem deliberately mysterious. Other short poems of a similar nature were written later, and sometime between 1000 and 500 BCE, there emerged an early version of the first major achievement of Indian poetry, the *Mahābhārata*; like Homer's *Iliad*, it originated as an account of a great war, though it was later edited and expanded to include more religious material. The text itself credits a single author, whose named can be rendered Vyasa or Vyasadesa (reportedly ca. fifteenth century BCE), but experts agree that this massive work must have emerged from multiple authors of several generations before a definitive version was committed to paper between 200 BCE and 200 CE. Episodes from this epic were performed by professional singers, called *sūta*, whose improvisations and additions may have found their way into the final text. The other masterpiece of early Indian poetry, the *Ramayana*, was probably written around the same time, purportedly by a man named Valmiki (reportedly ca. fifth century BCE); legend has it that he was the son of a fisherman, later adopted by a family of hunters, though it is difficult to see how such a person in that era could have become a poet.

This eighteenth-century painting depicts a scene from the *Ramayana,* one of ancient India's greatest poems, in which a celestial messenger named Narada converses with the poem's reputed author, Valmiki, who probably lived in the fifth century BCE. (The Walters Art Museum)

By the time of the Gupta Empire (roughly 320 to 550 CE), poetry had become one of the eighteen subjects that all members of the Brahmin caste had to learn, and writing poetry that required complicated techniques was a common activity among members of the royal court. To demonstrate his skill, for example, one poet produced a poem with no "s" sounds; another wrote a poem that had one meaning if read left to right, and another meaning if read right to left. There were regular competitions staged in large gardens or halls, launched by a noble or even the king himself, that challenged poets to address a certain theme in a unique way, inspiring contestants to include clever puns, riddles, and rhetorical flourishes. Winners sometimes received a prize in the form of money or a valuable object, but even when they only a garnered a title like "master of knowledge," poets energetically competed to gain a reputation that could be profitable in other ways. Some poets effectively made a living by traveling from royal court to royal court, seeking victories in such competitions; at times, poets were so eager to triumph that they bribed the judges.

One noted Indian poet, Kalidasa (ca. fifth century CE), reportedly came to his vocation in an unusual manner. Although he was a commoner, he was so strikingly handsome that a princess agreed to marry him, though she was distressed because he was not well educated. After praying to the goddess Kali for assistance, Kalidasa abruptly developed the ability to write eloquently and became a famous poet and playwright. While the story is fanciful, Kalidasa's name suggests that he was of foreign birth, though his writings reflect a familiarity with the Brahmin caste. There is also a legend, not generally accepted as true, that he was murdered by a prostitute while visiting a friend in Sri Lanka.

Chinese poetry developed in a different manner; instead of composing epics or telling stories, poets concentrated exclusively on brief, highly emotional lyrics; also, as expressions of the poet's personality, Chinese poems were as a rule unrelated to religious matters. The pattern of Chinese poetry was set by the first major collection of poems, the *Shijing*, compiled sometime during the life of Confucius (551–479 BCE), though many of its poems are thought to be much older. These poems were most likely written to be sung with a musical accompaniment, although a different style of poetry that originated in southern China was chanted, not sung. These poems were typically written by educated nobles and officials as a diversion from their duties and as a way to demonstrate their talents and convey their thoughts; it was never their primary source of income.

Qu Yuan (339–278 BCE), the first Chinese poet we know by name, led a troubled life, which inspired his often sorrowful poetry. Born a noble, he originally worked as a trusted adviser to a provincial ruler before being forced out of office due to political infighting. He then traveled through southern China, observing local rituals and writing poems until he finally committed suicide by jumping into the Miluo River; the Dragon Boat Festival reportedly grew out of efforts to find his body in the river. His most noted poem, "Lisao," builds upon his sorrowful response to his own exile to describe a poet who wanders through faraway lands and Heaven itself in an effort to end his depression.

In the royal courts of the Qin Dynasty, a new form of poetry flourished, called *fu*, focused on rhetorically sophisticated treatments of unimportant subjects that foregrounded the poet's cleverness but rarely seemed substantive. One master of the form was Yang Xiong (53 BCE–18 CE), a scholar who became so famous for his poetry that he was offered a high position in the government. When a new emperor seized the throne and was about to have him arrested, he jumped out of a tall building and suffered grievous injuries; fortunately, the new emperor belatedly realized that this quiet poet represented no threat to his rule and did not further persecute him. Eventually, Yang Xiong abandoned *fu* poetry as inconsequential and instead devoted himself to philosophy.

CHINESE POEMS FROM THE UNITED STATES

The poets of ancient China were greatly esteemed by one twentieth-century American poet, Ezra Pound, who was given the notes of scholar Ernest Fenollosa and transformed what he read into a book of poems entitled *Cathay*. Later critics point out that neither Fenollosa nor Pound understood Chinese, and Pound regularly misread Fenollosa's notes, so Pound's poems are not accurate translations. Yet Pound's defenders argue that he was actually striving to write original American poems based on Chinese models, not translations, often with impressive results. Today, with several good translations of the original poems available, readers can compare them to Pound's efforts and make their own judgments.

POETRY ON BROADWAY

Ancient India's greatest epic poem, the massive *Mahābhārata*, contains over 200,000 lines, and its sprawling story would not immediately seem suitable material for a Broadway play. Yet in 1987, famed director Peter Brook offered Broadway audiences a nine-hour stage adaptation of the lengthy poem, though it was sometimes split into three three-hour plays staged on successive nights. A version of the production was later filmed and aired on television, cut down to a mere six hours. Surprisingly, *another* play based on the *Mahābhārata* also opened in 1987, though this more modest off-Broadway version only lasted two hours and featured two male actors as its entire cast.

During this time, educated persons of high birth were not the only authors of poetry; everyday citizens were also writing and sharing songs that often complained about the problems and injustices they regularly faced. Perhaps as another response to the elegant artificiality of *fu* poetry, the Han Dynasty set up a special government agency, the Office of Music, to collect and record these anonymously written poems; one of them, "The Orphan," describes the hard life of a parentless boy, while "Southeast the Peacock Flies" recounts the sad story of a couple who were driven to suicide by the husband's harsh mother. But literary poets continued producing impressive works as well. Cao Zhi (192–232 CE), the son of a renowned general, emulated both his father and brother by writing poetry that was soon recognized as superior to theirs. Unfortunately, after his brother became emperor, the jealous man strove to make his younger brother's life miserable, inspiring some of his best poems. Another noted poet, Tao Quin (365–427 CE), was long obliged to work as a bureaucrat because his once-wealthy family had lost its money; but eventually, he withdrew from public life to become a rural farmer, resting after a hard day of labor by growing flowers, drinking wine, and writing poems.

Inspired by Chinese models, the ancient Japanese also began writing poems, although these were initially anonymous songs that were not written down until later. Even in early examples of their work, however, Japanese poets brought different priorities to their writing, focusing more on their native myths and legends. They were also devoted to celebrating the geography of Japan in lengthy descriptions of rivers and mountains. However, a true literary tradition of Japanese poetry comparable to the Chinese genre did not emerge until the seventh century CE and thereafter.

Overall, it is difficult to generalize about the poets of ancient Asia, who one could say were different sorts of people who developed different forms of writing for different purposes. Yet all of these poets combined the words of their native languages to create poems of remarkable beauty and profundity, though it appears that, all too often, the only reward for their labors was obscurity and lives of painful sadness. However, like their modern counterparts, the hardships they faced did not prevent them from carrying on with their memorable work.

Further Reading

Barnstone, Tony, and Chou Ping, editors and translators. 1996. *The Art of Writing: Teachings of the Chinese Masters*. Boston: Shambhala.

Chan, Kwan-Hung, translator. 2011. *Bouncing Pearls: Ancient Chinese Poetry*. West Conshohocken, PA: Infinity Publishing.

Hinton, David, editor and translator. 2008. *Classical Chinese Poetry: An Anthology*. New York: Farrar, Straus and Giroux.

Ōoka, Makoto. 1997. *Poetry and Poetics of Ancient Japan*. Translated by Thomas Fitzsimmons. Santa Fe, NM: Katydid Books.

Schellling, Andrew, translator. 2008. *Dropping the Bow: Poems from Ancient India*. Second edition. Buffalo, NY: White Pine Press.

Sharma, T. R. Srinivasta, editor, with C.K. Seshadri and June Gaur. 2000. *Ancient Indian Literature*. Three volumes. New Delhi: Sahitya Akademi.

Document

From Ch'in Chua and Hsu Shu. C. first century CE. *A Hundred and Seventy Chinese Poems*. Translated by Arthur Waley. 1918. London: Constable and Company.

Ch'in Chua (ca. first century BCE-first century CE) was a Chinese poet and governmental official who married another poet, Hsu Shu (ca. first century BCE-first century CE). When he was called to work in Beijing while his sick wife was living with her parents, he had no opportunity to say goodbye to her, and so he wrote and sent her three poems; she replied with a poem of her own. Below are the third of Ch'in Chua's poems to his wife and her response.

Solemn, solemn the coachman gets ready to go:
"Chiang, chiang" the harness bells ring.
At break of dawn I must start on my long journey:
At cock-crow I must gird on my belt.
I turn back and look at the empty room:
For a moment I almost think I see you there.
One parting, but ten thousand regrets:
As I take my seat, my heart is unquiet.
What shall I do to tell you all my thoughts?
How can I let you know of all my love?
Precious hairpins make the head to shine
And bright mirrors can reflect beauty.
Fragrant herbs banish evil smells
And the scholar's harp has a clear note.
The man in the Book of Odes who was given a quince
Wanted to pay it back with diamonds and rubies.
When I think of all the things you have done for me,
How ashamed I am to have done so little for you!
Although I know that it is a poor return,
All I can give you is this description of my feelings.

*****

My poor body is alas unworthy:
I was ill when first you brought me home.
Limp and weary in the house—
Time passed and I got no better.
We could hardly ever see each other:
I could not serve you as I ought.
Then you received the Imperial Mandate:
You were ordered to go far away to the City.
Long, long must be our parting:
I was not destined to tell you my thoughts.
I stood on tiptoe gazing into the distance,
Interminably gazing at the road that had
    taken you.
With thoughts of you my mind is obsessed:
In my dreams I see the light of your face.
Now you are started on your long journey
Each day brings you further from me.
Oh that I had a bird's wings
And high flying could follow you.
Long I sob and long I cry:
The tears fall down and wet my skirt.

Scholars

Young people have always been eager to learn from their elders, though this was long an informal process of watching people perform various tasks and listening while they explained a skill or told an old story about the creation of the world. However, the invention of writing made it possible for a new sort of learner to emerge: scholars, who would primarily obtain an education by reading the writing of others and would often contribute to the education of future scholars by writing their own works. In ancient societies where few people had the opportunity to learn how to read and write, such individuals were greatly respected, and they were often the only individuals who were eligible to serve in high positions. Yet the life of a scholar had its problems as well, described in the writings of some unhappy scholars that have survived to the present day.

In ancient India, all male children of the higher castes—Brahmin, Kshatriya, and Vaishya—would receive a basic education from tutors or a local school, where a teacher holding a rod to discipline miscreants would teach them how to read and write. Then, some would begin their formal education with an initiation ceremony that awarded them the special string representing their caste that they would wear for the rest of their lives, and bonded them to the *guru*, or holy man, who would serve as their instructor for the next twelve years. They then left their families to live in an *ashram*, a remote spiritual center sometimes termed a "forest university." There, students studied a variety of subjects depending upon their caste. These included disciplines like medicine, philosophy, astronomy, and mathematics, and skills like painting, poetry, playing a musical instrument, archery, and boxing. Students also learned how to meditate, and they were trained to be humble, hospitable, self-controlled, and courteous at all times. However, their education generally emphasized the grammar of Sanskrit, the rituals of Hinduism, and the sacred texts, the *Vedas*. Although reading and writing were part of the curriculum, the sacred *Vedas* were not written down for a long period of time, so that students had to laboriously memorize texts preserved solely by oral tradition. The lives of these aspiring scholars were far from easy: they slept on rushes, had to get up at dawn, were required to remain celibate, and were not allowed to seek shelter in the rain. They also had to do a number of daily chores, including gathering wood for fuel, watching the ashram's cows, and going off to beg in the streets and bring all the food he was given back to his guru.

After his education was completed, a young man would participate in another ceremony, receiving the bamboo stick, umbrella, and turban that symbolized his status as an educated man. He might, however, choose to remain at the ashram to engage in further learning, or travel to one of India's few universities, possibly to eventually become a *guru* himself, teaching students and authoring his own texts. The scholar Pānini (ca. fourth century BC), for example, wrote the first treatise on Sanskrit grammar, the *Ashtadhyayi*; virtually nothing else is known about his life, though there is a legend that he was killed by a lion, perhaps while walking through a jungle, preoccupied with his thoughts. Other educated men would be hired by governments to produce necessary documents like official decrees, letters, and judges' rulings. Eventually, a special caste of these workers emerged, called the *Kāyastha* caste, who were considered members of either the Brahmin caste or the Kshatriya caste of warriors and leaders.

Although they were not permitted to formerly attend schools, many women of ancient India did receive an education, since a scholar named Patañjali (ca. second century BCE) refers to female scholars, female teachers, and even a book written by a female scholar. Presumably, the daughters of nobles and wealthy men would sometimes receive private tutoring and gain an opportunity to do their own writing and teach other privileged young women, though they would never be allowed to enter or work at an ashram.

The ancient Chinese considered scholars one of their four basic social classes—the others being peasants, artisans, and merchants—and they were the most highly respected because of their ability to read and write. Generally, education was only available to children of the privileged classes, although a precocious young boy might gain the opportunity to attend school and compete for a government position; at times, an entire village might band together to provide the necessary financial support for a potential young scholar in their community. Wealthy children were often taught by private tutors in their homes; as in India, this was the only way that women could become educated, since they were not allowed to attend schools. However, more so than other ancient cultures, the Chinese were open to the idea of educated women, so that female scholars and poets were far from uncommon.

For boys, their education would take place in district schools far from their homes, where they would typically live and study for nine years between the ages of ten and twenty. The standard curriculum might have different emphases, but it would typically include calligraphy, mathematics, dancing, playing a lute called the *qin*, archery, and riding a chariot. They would also spend a great deal of time learning Confucian rituals and studying Confucian philosophy; indeed, the emperor Wu (141–87 BCE) established a special school for future government officials that focused exclusively on the classics of Confucianism. While the students at that school were usually the sons of nobles and bureaucrats, including the prince himself, the brightest boys from the provinces might also be able to attend, usually by being sponsored by an official in their district. In some cases, noted philosophers would establish their own schools and attract students eager to learn from an especially wise man. Whether the school they attended was nearby or far away, all students were forbidden to have any contact with family members and old friends, and no women were even allowed within a school.

Upon finishing his studies, a Chinese boy would officially become a man, in a ceremony that involved adopting an adult hair style and receiving the hats and robes that symbolized his new status. Though

STRESSFUL TESTS

The ancient Chinese originated the concept of employing a highly competitive exam as a way to choose people to work for the government. In more recent times, another exam, the *gaokao*, is employed in China to select the students who will be allowed to attend universities. This system inspires a great deal of stress in Chinese teenagers, who study for countless hours, preparing for a single exam that may literally determine the course of the rest of their lives. Seeking alternatives for their children, wealthy Chinese parents sometimes decide to send them to U.S. universities, which can be very expensive but are less stringent in their admissions policies.

SCHOLARS TURNED POLITICIANS

Much of the material that Chinese scholars had to learn seemed unrelated to any tasks they would perform as government officials, yet it was believed that a purely academic education would improve their job performance. In the contemporary United States, many scholars with PhD degrees become university professors, and a few of them, after writing books and earning tenure, have entered the government by being elected to the U.S Senate. They include California's S. I. Hayakawa, formerly an English professor at San Francisco State University; Minnesota's Paul Wellstone, formerly a government professor at Carleton College; and Massachusetts's Elizabeth Warren, formerly a professor at Harvard Law School.

he could now become a warrior or enter other professions, a typical ambition was to work for the government. Initially, this process involved writing letters to various officials boasting of one's skills and accomplishments, hoping to be hired on the basis of his claims. However, this system was obviously open to abuse, since nepotism and cronyism could place unqualified men in high positions; to address the problem, the emperor Wen (202–157 BCE) instituted a system of mandatory exams for prospective officials. These exams, which had to be written in elegant calligraphy, stressed detailed knowledge of Confucian texts and doctrines, which was seemingly irrelevant to the duties of a civil servant; however, the Chinese believed that a man who was learned in classical philosophy would be well equipped to master whatever mundane tasks were required in his position. These tests were highly competitive: many men took the exams, but only a few passed and qualified for government employment. It was not unusual, then, for aspiring bureaucrats to spend years preparing to take the test, working intensely on their own or studying under hired tutors.

In one key respect, though, the education of a Chinese scholar did not prepare him for this sort of career; for we know of several men who attained government positions but quickly grew tired of the routine labors and political infighting that they often involved and chose instead to resign and devote their lives to the further study of the philosophy they had first learned as students. They may have been competent bureaucrats, in other words, but a stimulating education in less worldly matters often made him bored bureaucrats, ready to abandon government work for the life of a full-time scholar, even though it provided them with less income and privileges. These are the scholars who became ancient China's first historians, poets, literary critics, philosophers, and political theorists, leaving behind texts that are still studied and appreciated, while their less able colleagues who devoted their lives to the daily business of government left no records of their necessary but forgettable work and made no significant contributions to Chinese culture. But scholars in all societies, one might say, are often appreciated more after their deaths than they were during their lifetimes.

Further Reading

Chatterjee, Mitali. 1999. *Education in Ancient India: From Literary Sources of the Gupta Age*. New Delhi: Dorling Kindersley Printworld.

Chidatman, Swami. 2009. *Ancient Indian Education*. New Delhi: Anmol Publications.

Kinney, Anne Behnke. 2004. *Representations of Childhood and Youth in Early China*. Stanford, CA: Stanford University Press.

Lee, Thomas H. C. 2000. *Education in Traditional China, a History*. Leiden, The Netherlands, and Boston: Brill.

Nylan, Michael. 2011. *Yang Xiong and the Pleasures of Reading and Classical Learning in China*. New Haven, CT: American Oriental Society.

Scharfe, Hartmut. 2002. *Education in Ancient India*. Leiden, The Netherlands, and Boston: Brill.

Documents

From the Self-Help Department, Women's Bible School, Presbyterian Mission. C. 1870. *Legends of Ancient China*. China: Presbyterian Mission.

This modern retelling of an old legend, "Djang Liang and Whang Hsi Gung," describes the unusual way that young boy was able to receive an education as a scholar by demonstrating his deference and punctuality to a philosopher.

Djang Liang, a student, was walking along one day when he came to a bridge and saw an old man sitting there with his shoe on the ground in front of him. With unusual courtesy Djang Liang stooped and put the shoe on the foot of the old man, who was really one of the Sages in disguise. The sage was so pleased with this act of courtesy that he told the boy to come to the bridge very early the next morning and he would tell him what would affect his whole life. The boy went to the bridge very early, but the sage was there ahead of him, and all he received that morning was a lecture on his lazy habits. He was told to go again, and the next morning went at dawn, but still the Sage was ahead of him and he was reprimanded very severely this time and told to come again on the third morning. This time the boy went to the bridge right after his supper, and spent the night there! When the Sage came at dawn he was greatly pleased to find Djang Liang there ahead of him, and gave him instruction of such value that when he grew up he became a great general.

From Parker, Edward Harper. 1908. *Ancient China Simplified*. London: Chapman & Hall.

In this passage, the author offers the general Chinese definition of scholars and provides an anecdote about a scholar who strongly desired to see his name added to the government's official records.

The ancient classification of people was into four groups. The scholar people employed themselves in studying tao and the sciences, from which we plainly see that the doctrine of tao, or "the way," existed long before Lao-tse, in Confucius' time, superadded a mystic cosmogony upon it, and made of it a socialist or radical instead of an imperialist or conservative doctrine. . . .

In 496 BC it is recorded of a scholar at the Emperor's court that, being anxious to see his own name in the "Springs and Autumns," he suggested to the Emperor that for a long time no complimentary mission had been sent to Lu. The result was that he was sent himself, and is thus immortalized: it does not follow from this that the knowledge of Confucius' coming book had penetrated to the Chou court, because "Springs and Autumns" was already the accepted term in Lu for "Annals," long before Confucius adopted the already existing general name for his own particular work. In 496 Confucius had left Lu in disgust, and had gone to Wei—the capital of Wei was then on, or near, the then Yellow River (now the River Wei), between the two towns marked "Hwa" and 'K'ai' on modern maps—where he collected materials for his History; but he did not begin it until the year 481; so probably the ambitious scholar simply hoped to appear in the "Springs and Autumns" of Lu, as they had already been called before Confucius borrowed the name, just as Sz-ma Ts'ien borrowed the name Shi-ki.

Sculptors

Sculpture, in a sense, allows modern people to come face to face with their distant ancestors, staring at life-sized, and sometimes eerily lifelike, replicas of

One of the most famous creations of ancient Indian sculptors is this small statue of a dancing girl from the city of Mohenjo Daro, whose assertive stance and facial expression seem surprisingly modern, for a young woman of approximately 2500 BCE. (National Museum of India, New Delhi, India/Bridgeman Images)

individuals who died long ago and the animals that accompanied them; and less realistic statues of gods, goddesses, and imaginary creatures provide access to their thoughts and beliefs. Looking at these works, we also become curious about the people who carved them and their artistic methods, although limited data may force us to rely upon speculation in reconstructing their daily lives.

The surviving sculptures of India's ancient Harappan civilization are small figurines, made of stone or bronze; the best known of these is a bronze "dancing girl," a naked woman wearing a necklace and bracelet with her hand on her hip. Her pose and facial expression strongly suggest that there was no religious intent behind her creation; rather, this tiny statue was crafted as a household decoration, perhaps even a toy, and sold by its sculptor in the marketplace of Mohenjo Daro. Later, in Vedic India, such items were more often made out of wood or ivory, though many of these items have not endured through the centuries. To create wooden statues, sculptors would work closely with carpenters, who would prepare basic shapes for the sculptors to carefully carve into finished images. The best ivory statues, it was believed, were formed from ivory taken from live elephants instead of dead ones, even though taxes made this product very expensive. Some examples of these popular items, always purchased right after they were finished by eager customers, have been found at archaeological sites in Afghanistan, dating from around 100 BCE, and they demonstrate that their sculptors were skillful artists who employed sophisticated techniques. In addition to standalone statues, sculptors also created decorative pieces used to adorn walls, doorways, and pieces of furniture. Another impressive achievement of the ivory sculptors was the porticos of the Buddhist *stupa* of Sānchī, which were filled with intricate carvings of animals and human figures. As was the case for most ancient professions, one usually became an ivory sculptor because that was their father's avocation, and ivory sculptors were also represented by one of ancient India's influential guilds.

We are more familiar with the work of stone sculptors, primarily because of their contributions to the walls of temples and holy monuments. While these artists were surely hired and supervised by priests, gurus, and monks, one has to suspect that they were also inspired by their own religious fervor as they carved their innumerable images. Indeed, their usual tendency was to crowd as many people and animals into available spaces as possible, each individually characterized, so observers might stare for hours at a wall, constantly noticing interesting new figures or details. Hindu temples also included separate statues of their principal gods or goddesses, made out of stone, clay, or bronze. Such images had to represent the sculptor's very best work, as statues of gods were not only looked at but also clothed, bathed, and decorated with flowers.

Sculptors in stone did not only work in buildings; it also became common to carve large temples and

monuments out of hillsides and natural caves, such as the huge statues of Buddha that were long observed on a cliff in Afghanistan. For such projects, the sculptors might have to work on wooden scaffolds or dangle from ropes as they chiseled the rock into the desired form. Oddly, despite the prominence of these and their other works, Indian sculptors were generally not respected as artists; the ancient Hindu hymns collected as the *Rigveda*, for example, do not even mention them.

Among the earliest known examples of Chinese sculpture are the bronze statues crafted by sculptors of the mysterious culture of Sanzingdui, which flourished during the twelfth and eleventh centuries BCE. One striking example of their work is a life-sized statue of an elongated man with large circular holes in his hand, suggesting that he was designed to hold some sort of pole or decoration made of a less enduring material. Ancient sculptors were working with jade as well, as evidenced by the small jade figurines in the shapes of animals that were uncovered in the tomb of female military leader Fu Hao (ca. twelfth century BCE). Since metal tools were not in use at that time, the pieces of jade must have been broken off by stone hammers and painstakingly shaped using grindstones; later, sculptors would carve jade with bamboo drills that had bronze tips and polish the pieces with rough sand or leather-covered wheels. Scholars have speculated that early jade items were used by shamans to purportedly control mystical forces and carry out their rituals, though small jade objects were eventually fashioned exclusively as household ornaments.

By the time of the first Chinese emperor, Qin Shi Huang (259–210 BCE), there must have been a long tradition of sculptors in China, as he was able to employ many of them to complete various projects. He gathered many bronze weapons, for example, and had them melted down to make twelve large statues. He is now better known, of course, for commissioning the creation of over 7,000 terracotta statues of soldiers to be placed in his enormous tomb. These were made out of clay near the site of the tomb and baked inside large kilns that could reach temperatures up to 2000 degrees Fahrenheit, making the statues extremely hard and explaining why they remained intact for 2,000 years. The statues were also painted so they would appear lifelike, though the once-bright colors have largely vanished. Interestingly, since Qin Shi Huang had ordered that no two statues could be exactly alike, one suspects that, along with many other models, the sculptors working on this army used themselves as models, so that when examining these statues' faces, we may in some cases be looking at the men who carved them. Other tombs from this general era also contain clay and bronze statues, though it is not known whether these came from the deceased person's home or were especially constructed for burial.

When monks brought Buddhism to China, they also introduced the Indian habit of carving images of the Buddha and other men and animals on the stone walls of temples, in caves, and on hillsides. These images, and other freestanding statues, tended to face the viewer, emphasize the face, and represent figures at rest rather than figures in motion. Chinese sculptors produced so many images of the Buddha that when the Sui Dynasty emperor Wen (541–604 CE) set out to have them repaired, it is estimated that over one and half a million pieces were worked on by the artisans he hired. While much of this work reflects a strong Indian influence, Chinese sculptors of all kinds never portrayed naked or nearly naked figures, except for a few pieces that were designed not to be displayed in public, but rather to instruct medical students.

In addition to stone, bronze, jade, and clay, Chinese sculptors also used ivory, although it usually came from rhinoceros horns instead of elephant tusks. Their intricately carved ivory items often adorned the desks of bureaucrats and scholars. For many of China's peasants and other nonprofessional artists, a popular hobby was carving figures out of bamboo, a cheap and readily available material; though they did not always last long, some of these pieces became collectors' items.

We do not know the names of any ancient Chinese sculptors because their work was not considered genuine art, like poetry or calligraphy; no aristocrat would ever have been advised or encouraged to develop this skill. Rather, all sculptors were part of the third-ranked class of artisans, who labored in cramped workshops and sold their small statues and figurines in marketplace stalls. Larger statues requiring more time were commissioned by wealthy men and women, and sculptors would occasionally be paid

to travel in order to work for special projects like palaces, temples, and tombs, living in temporary quarters while they labored. Yet these unknown men must have regarded themselves as artists, feeling a special sense of satisfaction whenever they completed an especially fine statue or added a unique flourish to a wall carving. Sadly, none of them would ever have been so bold as to add their signature to their works, so it remains impossible to attribute statues of special beauty to the individual sculptors who crafted them.

LOST STATUES RETURNING

Among the major achievements of Buddhist sculpture were two enormous statues of the Buddha, 120- and 180-feet tall, which were carved into the cliffs of present-day Afghanistan. Unfortunately, when the country was controlled by the extremist group known as the Taliban, they destroyed those statues with explosives in 2001, regarding them as offensive to their Islamic beliefs. Today, however, with the help of sculptor and art historian Bert Praxenthaler (ca. 1960–), the current government of Afghanistan is working to rebuild the statues by collecting their shattered pieces and combining them with new material.

VERY BIG BUDDHAS

The old tradition of sculpting enormous statues of the Buddha has endured into modern times. Thus, in 1993, the Po Lin Monastery of Hong Kong unveiled a huge bronze statue of the Buddha, which looks out on the city and now attracts tourists who walk through its base and eat dinner at its vegetarian restaurant, even though they must take a long bus ride and climb 240 steps to reach the hillside statue. An even larger bronze statue of a standing Buddha, in China's Jiangxi province, was completed in 2013; to make it even more impressive, it has been covered with gold plating.

Further Reading
Ganapathi, V. 2002. *Indian Sculpture and Iconography: Forms and Measurements*. Middletown, NJ: Grantha Corporation.

Howard, Angela Falco, Li Song, Wu Hung, and Yang Hong. 2006. *Chinese Sculpture*. New Haven, CT: Yale University Press.

Klokke, Marijke J., editor. 2000. *Narrative Sculpture and Literary Traditions in South and Southeast Asia*. Leiden, The Netherlands, and Boston: Brill.

Pal, Pratapaditya. 2002. *Indian Terracotta Sculpture: The Early Period*. Mumbai, India: Marg Publications.

Schroeder, Ulrich von. 2008. *108 Buddhist Statues in Tibet: Evolution of Tibetan Sculpture*. Chicago: Serindia Publications.

Sullivan, Michael. 1999. *The Arts of China*. Fourth edition. Berkeley and Los Angeles: University of California Press.

Document

From Manning, Charlotte Speir. 1856. *Life in Ancient India*. London: Smith, Elder.

In 399 CE, a Chinese Buddhist monk named Fa-Hian (337–ca. 422 CE) visited India and wrote about his journeys. This author partially quotes from, and partially paraphrases, his account. In the selected passages below, he describes the various sorts of statues and monuments that he encountered, demonstrating that the works of sculptors could be found almost everywhere in ancient India.

The religious buildings of this town are described as peculiarly magnificent: one temple was eighty-four years in building, occupying three kings' reigns. Sculptures are particularized, and gold and silver images decorated with precious stones, also gilded windows and doorposts of gold. . . .

[Fa-Hian] sees the gigantic statue of Maitrya, which on certain occasions glistens with light, and he visits the scenes of all the extravagant legends of Buddha's sacrifices, and sees the Pillars set up in commemoration. . . .

A story is told of elephants who did temple-service in an abandoned Vihara, where "the elephants are seen to come taking water in their trunks to water the ground;" this may possibly explain the device on the pillars at Kennary, where elephants sprinkle water upon dagobas. The woods, he says, are filled with monuments, but he could not visit them from their being so much infested by tigers and white elephants; from which we may infer that the present formidable Tarai, or jungle, was even then beginning to encroach upon human habitations. . . .

"In the kingdom of Magadha," says Fa-Hian, "the towns and villages are large; the people rich, fond of discussion, but compassionate and just in action; and the paintings and sculptures such as this age could not produce.". . .

Fa-Hian mentions a pillar on which is inscribed, "The great Asoka gave. . . to the religious of the four quarters: he ransomed it from them for money, and this he did three times." At a town called Nili he saw another pillar surmounted by a lion, with an inscription recording the foundation of the town. . . .

But image-worship was also fully established; and an image of blue jasper, holding in its hand a pearl of inestimable value, was to our traveller "dazzling and majestic beyond expression."

Shamans

The religious leaders and visionaries of ancient Asia are rarely described as "shamans," as there are special words used for these figures in each culture and each religion. But it is a functional umbrella term for the various men and women, such as Hindu priests and Buddhist monks and nuns, who announced and practiced their religion's doctrines, working to establish traditions that endure to the present day.

For a male Brahmin in ancient India, becoming a holy man was enshrined as one of the four stages of life: after being a student (the *Bhahmachari* stage), he was supposed to marry, raise a family, and enjoy the experience of an ordinary life (the *Grihastha* stage); then, after his oldest son was married and thus prepared to head the family, he could retire to a distant ashram, abandon all of his worldly concerns, and devote himself to religious study and meditation while instructing young students (the *Vanaprastha* stage); finally, having achieved the necessary wisdom, he would enter the *Sannyasi* stage and become a wanderer, visiting holy places and meeting with leaders who valued his company and sage advice. To demonstrate their detachment from the world, these men would wear only a loincloth, or even go naked, and their few possessions included sandals, a bowl for begging food, and bundled manuscripts of holy texts. Not all men chose to abandon their friends and family for such an impoverished existence, but those who did were greatly respected and happily supported by all citizens. Some achieved the status of Hindu priests, who presided over sacrifices and other rituals.

For Indian Buddhists, becoming a religious mentor involved different steps. A man would first go to live at a monastery, shave his head, don a yellow robe, and begin an extended period of instruction under an experienced monk; then, after an initiation ceremony, he would become a monk himself, dedicating himself to a life of poverty and virtue. His daily routine would involve begging for food in the morning, eating a single meal around noon, and spending the rest of the day privately teaching students or speaking with any interested citizens in public gatherings. Buddhist women could undergo a similar process to become nuns, though they had to wait a longer time before ordination and follow even stricter rules than their male counterparts. Over the centuries, as the monasteries grew into larger institutions, the practice developed of having the oldest monk serve as the leader, while others were assigned specific tasks like gardening, supervising the building, sewing clothes, and managing supplies of food and water. Some Buddhist monasteries became renowned educational institutions, such as the monastery of Nalanda, and these would attract students of all religions who came from great distances. Other Buddhist monks played a role in the building of the religion's distinctive centers for meditation, the *stupas*, and in carving enormous statues in honor of the Buddha. They especially came to dominate the culture of ancient Tibet, still renowned for its many monasteries in the mountains that would entertain visitors from distant lands in search of wisdom.

The related religion of Jainism maintained its own monasteries, though their monks, nuns, and laypersons were often subject to even harsher expectations; one sect, for example, demanded that males constantly remain completely naked and forbid them to possess anything, even a bowl for begging. They were often required to travel in order to recruit new members of their religion, though they were not allowed to ride on animals or in vehicles; if they faced persecution for their religious beliefs, however, they had the right to disguise themselves and temporarily break the Jain rules to avoid unjust punishment. In other places, however, these missionaries were welcomed because they were believed to possess magical powers.

We know little about the earliest religions of ancient China, probably overseen by independent shamans wielding magical objects and performing forgotten ceremonies, but religious practices were eventually taken over by the imperial government of the emperors, who valued religion as one mechanism for justifying and maintaining their control. The chief preoccupation was the worship of ancestors, whose approval was deemed necessary for any successful enterprise. Accordingly, the government established shrines all over the country to honor the ancestors of emperors of the Han Dynasty, and priests were hired to maintain these shrines and conduct ceremonies to provide the ancestors with food and sacrifice animals on their behalf. These priests, however, were not expected to provide moral guidance to ordinary citizens, and their lives were not subject to complex rules; their major responsibilities were to correctly carry out all of their necessary rituals, properly maintain their shrine, and instruct the acolytes who would someday take their place. There were other priests who would specialize in the proper ceremonies for launching a war, for opening negotiations or gatherings of nobles, and conducting funerals; some practiced forms of divination to obtain answers to important questions from the ancestors. As was the case with many ancient professions, being a priest was often a family tradition, as the secret knowledge of the rituals would be passed from father to son. The emperor also functioned as a sort of priest, since this divinely favored individual was expected to lead several important public rituals every year.

Another sort of religious leader was the sorcerer or sorceress; these generally self-appointed figures claimed that they could enter a trancelike state and be possessed by gods, perform rituals to dispel evil spirits, cure people's ailments, and bring rain in times of drought. They supported themselves by charging clients, ranging from high government officials to ordinary citizens, for their services. Many of these individuals were little more than expedient charlatans, but it is from this tradition, many believe, that the religious of Daoism developed, as mystically inclined men came to form groups, develop doctrines, and estab-

This photograph shows the ruins of Nalanda, the ancient Buddhist monastery that became a renowned center for religious education. Located in present-day Bihar, India, it dates back to at least the fifth century BCE. (Hideyuki Kamon)

lish a priesthood dedicated to this developing faith. Another religion that sprang from ancient China, Confucianism, uniquely emphasized a moral code instead of the worship of divine beings, and it accordingly led to no official hierarchy of priests, although Confucius (551–479 BCE) and his followers also embraced traditional practices like ancestor worship.

After traveling monks brought Buddhism to China, Buddhist monasteries were established throughout the country, attracting monks and nuns who dedicated themselves to a monastic existence. There was resistance, however, to the traditional practice of celibacy, as many Chinese strongly believed that every man should have a son to maintain his family lineage. As in India, many of these monasteries became centers of learning, collecting and preserving many valuable manuscripts, and despite the spiritual priorities of Buddhism, some of its Chinese monasteries surprisingly came to function as banks, pioneering in the use of paper currency. Another surprising development in Chinese Buddhism came around 500 CE, when its Shaolin Monastery established a unique tradition of

fighting monks, skilled at using a staff in man-to-man combat.

Ancient Asia has never suffered from a shortage of religions: Hinduism, Buddhism, Jainism, Confucianism, and Daoism have remained major religions throughout the centuries; Christianity and Islam have attracted innumerable converts and came to dominate entire countries; and two major new religions would later emerge: Shinto in medieval Japan and Sikhism in fifteenth-century India. Most of these faiths were dominated by religious leaders who promoted their beliefs both in their writings and teachings and in the humble way that they led their lives. Yet it should be noted that in ancient India and China, every head of the household also served as a sort of priest, as he would maintain his house's individual shrine to a god or ancestor and lead small ceremonies that also involved the participation of family members. Further, one can argue that these recurring gestures had a greater impact on the daily lives of citizens than the words and actions of the priests and monks who served as the public representatives of their religions,

DISGRUNTLED WITH A GURU

In ancient India, young people hoping to gain wisdom would go to study under a holy man, or *guru*, living a humble life in a remote *ashram* while they absorbed his teachings. The practice has remained commonplace in modern times, and Westerners learned about this unique system of religious education in the 1960s when four very famous musicians—the Beatles—traveled to India to be trained by the Maharishi Mahesh Yogi, noted practitioner of "transcendental meditation." Yet they quickly grew disillusioned with the man and his doctrines, and John Lennon wrote a song attacking him, entitled "Maharishi." Later, though, he changed its name to "Sexy Sadie."

BUDDHISM IN 140 CHARACTERS

One of the traditional duties of Buddhist monks is to teach others about their faith. Today, the world's most famous Buddhist monk is the Dalai Lama (1935–), official leader of the Tibetan Buddhists, and he is fulfilling this ancient responsibility in a very modern way by setting up a Twitter account and periodically conveying his wisdom within the limit of 140 characters. For example, on September 20, 2013, he advised his followers to "Use your human intelligence in the best way you can; transform your emotions in a positive way." His lengthier reflections are posted on his Facebook page.

since they were often valued for their roles in the culture's occasional festivals and grand rituals but otherwise may have had little impact on everyday citizens. Still, by happily giving food to the holy men who begged in their streets, or leaving donations at a local temple, the people of ancient Asia always displayed their respect for the men and women who devoted their lives to their religion.

Further Reading

Chaudhuri, Saroj Kumar. 2008. *Lives of Early Buddhist Monks: The Oldest Extant Biographies of Indian and Central Asian Monks.* New Delhi: Abha Prakashan.

Daswani, Rekha. 2006. *Buddhist Monasteries and Monastic Life in Ancient India: From the Third Century BC to the Seventh Century AD.* New Delhi: Aditya Prakashan.

Liu, Xinru. 1994. *Ancient India and Ancient China: Trade and Religious Exchanges, AD 1–600.* Oxford and New York: Oxford University Press.

Oddie, Geoffrey A., editor. 1996. *Religious Traditions in South Asia: Interaction and Change.* Richmond, Great Britain: Curzon.

Poo, Mu-chou. 1998. *In Search of Personal Welfare: A View of Ancient Chinese Religion.* Albany: State University of New York Press.

Verma, B.R., and S.R. Bakshi, editors. 2005. *Hinduism, Buddhism and Jainism in Ancient India.* New Delhi: Commonwealth.

Document

From Manning, Charlotte Speir. 1856. *Life in Ancient India.* London: Smith, Elder.

This passage describes the role of Hindu priests in the ceremonial preparation and drinking of an intoxicating beverage called soma-juice.

Some of the Vedic hymns would lead one to suppose that to *kindle* fire on the altar was the duty to which man first awoke; but other passages speak of fire as "constantly kindled" in the house of a pious worshipper, and it is therefore probable that he only gave "fresh vital air" to the flames at sunrise, and then made his offering of ghee or butter to whichever God he desired to invoke; but when the soma-juice was presented, a public ceremonial called a Soma-yága appears to have been held. On these occasions an additional fire was kindled, by means of a species of churn made of acacia, called *arani* wood: one piece of the wood was drilled into the other, and the upright piece pulled by a loose string, after the fashion by which Hindus make butter. In one address to Indra he is entreated to come "when they bind the churning-staff (with a cord), like reins to restrain (a horse)." A large shed was constructed, called the *Yajna-sálá.* Seven priests attended, each having a distinct title and office; the Rishi, or Raja, at whose expense the festival was given, acting as *Hotri,* or invoker. At a daily morning sacrifice only two persons are mentioned as officiating,—the Purohita, who superintended, and the Hotri, who invoked the Gods. The Sama-Veda gives hymns from the Rig-Veda, arranged in a ritual, to be used on these occasions, and the priests are exhorted to sing the birth of the Gods and the praise of the Gods in alternate lays, with a sound as regular as that of the dripping of the soma-juice. Very little allusion is made to animal sacrifices, but they were probably not unknown, for the priests are to make as much noise as "dogs driven away hungry from a sacrifice." The soma-juice was at any rate the more important portion of the offering; the plants were gathered on the hills by moonlight, and brought home in carts drawn by rams. "Indra," it is said, "found this treasure from heaven, hidden like the nestlings of a bird in a rock, amidst a pile of vast rocks, enclosed by bushes;" the stalks are bruised with stones, and placed with the juice in a strainer of goats'-hair, and are further squeezed by the priest's ten fingers, ornamented by rings of flattened gold. Lastly, the juice, mixed with barley and clarified butter, ferments, and is then drawn off in a scoop for the Gods, and a ladle for the priests, and then they say to Indra, "Thy inebriety is most intense, nevertheless thy acts are most beneficent."

Warriors

No region of the ancient world, it seems, was ever completely at peace, and this is true of Asia as well. Following a standard pattern, petty warlords battled against each other until the most successful ones controlled more and more territory; eventually, the most powerful of these leaders were called emperors, masters of vast realms served by professional armies. While there were commonalities in the ways that different regions waged war, they also responded to their own special circumstances by developing new technologies and techniques for killing their enemies.

The warriors of ancient India, for example, wielded many weapons that were similar to those of their compatriots elsewhere: maces with wooden handles and heads made of limestone; copper and bronze swords and knives, which sometimes had sharp edges on both sides; and slings, spears, javelins, and bows and arrows for attacking foes from a distance. But the Indian bows were made of bamboo, and their arrowheads were distinctively thin, with extended barbs that made them especially lethal. For that reason, Indian warriors relied on arrows more than any

other weapon. The Indians also took advantage of the many elephants that inhabited their country to effectively transform that large animal into the world's first tank, which could carry several armed soldiers into battle in a helpfully elevated position. Later, platforms were placed on the elephants to carry the warriors, and swords were placed on their trunks. Eventually, it became standard for Indian armies to have four divisions: the chariots, the elephants, soldiers riding horses, and archers on foot. Initially, these warriors did not employ any armor, often going into battle with bare chests, although much later helmets and breast plates became common. (Because of India's high temperatures, though, soldiers could not endure wearing a lot of weighty armor.)

Around 1700 BCE, India was invaded by Aryans from the north who brought further innovations: massive, four-wheeled chariots pulled by four to six horses, which could carry up to six archers into battle on a moving platform several feet above the ground. The Indians adopted their design and, about a thousand years later, created a lethal variation, the scythed chariot, which had sharp blades on its wheel to wound or kill any enemies it passed by. The Aryans also introduced weapons made of iron to the subcontinent. The two great epics of ancient India, the *Ramayana* and the *Mahābhārata*, both probably written sometime between 800 and 400 BCE, describe other unique weapons: the *pasa*, a triangular array of rope with attached weights that could be used to strangle an enemy, and the *sudarshana chakra*, a metal disc with edges that was thrown at opponents like a modern frisbee to inflict slashing wounds. Indian soldiers might also wield crushing hammers on long sticks or clubs made of iron.

Still, while weapons like these were helpful to soldiers engaged in individual combat, the most valuable innovations involved the invention of creative ways for soldiers to work together in battle. In the "eagle" formation, for example, the best fighters would lead, advancing in the shape of an eagle's beak and head, while the fastest-moving soldiers on foot and in chariots would accompany them on each side, forming the "wings," while other soldiers marched behind them, composing the "body." In the "lotus" formation, experienced archers would gather at the center of the "flower" while "petals" of soldiers on foot or on horseback would surround and protect them. The Indians also learned to support their soldiers with wagons filled with supplies and civilian workers like carpenters, surgeons, engineers, and astrologers, who determined when the omens were favorable for battle.

Ancient India contributed to the advancement of warfare in another, very different fashion, by developing and promoting the ideal of ethical warfare. As the task of leading soldiers into battle became associated with one of India's four basic castes, the Ksatriya or warrior caste, its members were taught that warriors should only fight other warriors, avoid harming women, the elderly, and children, and cease fighting when one's opponent is no longer able to fight. They were also told to refrain from attacking their opponent's envoys and to never damage the lands and property of the people they fought. As one sign of the way that warriors were respected for their high values, it is significant that in the portion of the *Mahābhārata* known as the *Bhagavad Gita*, the god Krishna takes the form of a chariot driver in order to instruct Prince Arjuna about moral and religious values.

The governments of ancient China first relied upon peasants drafted to serve in their armies for two years armed only with crude spears, maces, and bows and arrows; but like the ancient Indians, they learned about the effectiveness of chariots and bronze weapons from invading soldiers from central Asia. The Chinese chariots, pulled by two or four horses, carried an archer, a driver, and a soldier holding a lengthy spear (almost 18-feet long), While most soldiers remained poorly equipped recruits, there also emerged a group of elite warriors who employed better weapons, including the crossbow, a bow that propelled arrows more powerfully because it was attached to a horizontal stick, and the dagger-axe, a long-handled weapon with both a spear point and a dagger-like blade. To protect themselves, Chinese warriors held shields, wore helmets made of bronze, and put on leather shirts covered with bronze plates.

Like the ancient Indians, the Chinese mastered new fighting techniques as well as weapons. Foot soldiers, archers, and soldiers on horseback would fight together in formations, and making use of China's many rivers, they pioneered in naval warfare as well,

constructing huge fortress ships that became bases within enemy territory, equipped with catapults to hurl stones or balls of fire at opponents. Around the fifth century BC, a general named Sun Tzu (544–496 BCE) is credited with writing *The Art of War*, a treatise on effective strategies for waging war that has remained influential to this day in a wide variety of disciplines. Around 200 BCE, the Qin Dynasty established China's first professional army, so that wars would now be fought by seasoned, lifelong veterans of combat instead of poorly prepared peasants. As fighting became a full-time vocation, soldiers also embraced effective new weapons, such as swords made of iron, stronger compound bows, and the stirrup, which gave mounted soldiers much more control over their steeds. Also, weary of constant invasions from the west, China

WANDERING WARRIORS

We have learned a great deal about ancient Chinese warriors from the army of statues buried with the first Chinese emperor, Qin Shi Huang, since these clay soldiers were also equipped with chariots and weapons like swords, spears, and bows and arrows. While most items were left at the site as a tourist attraction, traveling exhibitions have also traveled to museums all over the world. A typical show might include nine soldiers, a statue of a horse, and a wide assortment of other items like armor, bowls, and jade ornaments. The tomb's chariots, though, are represented only by replicas, since the originals are too fragile to transport.

A METALLIC ELEPHANT

The most distinctive feature of Indian warfare was its use of elephants to carry warriors into battle and provide them with an elevated platform from which to attack enemies. Ponderous but powerful, these elephants were the basis for the chess piece the rook (said to have similar qualities) and famously inspired Carthage's general Hannibal to use the animals in his war against the Roman Empire. Their vulnerability to cannons finally ended their role in combat, but they were still used for wartime construction projects. Interestingly, acknowledging the elephant's role as the world's first tank, the Germans of World War II named one of their tanks the "Elefant."

This seventeenth-century painting shows two characters from the *Bhagavad Gita*, part of the epic poem *Mahabharata*, as they prepare for battle: the god Krishna, in front, who serves as instructor and charioteer for the man in the chariot, the warrior prince Arjuna. (Jupiterimages)

took a new approach to defensive warfare by beginning to construct the Great Wall of China, designed to prevent incursions from reaching the interior of the country.

Although we know little about the daily lives of Chinese soldiers during the Qin Dynasty, we have a fascinating picture of what they looked like, thanks to the discovery in 1974 of over thousands of statues of warriors that were buried alongside the first Chinese emperor, Qin Shi Huang (259–210 BCE) in Lintong County, Shaanxi Province, evidently sculpted and placed there to protect him in the afterlife. Remarkably, each statue is a distinct individual. Among the interesting variations observed, some had no armor, some had partial armor, and some wore extra clothing over their armor for additional protection. As their weapons, most carried bows and arrows, though some

held spears. These statues suggest that soldiers were also concerned about their appearance: their clothing was brightly colored (though most of the colors have faded over time), their moustaches and hair were carefully combed, and some of them wore ribbons, that were either purely decorative or announced their rank. A few figures look more like musicians or acrobats than soldiers, perhaps indicating that armies were regularly accompanied by entertainers to keep the soldiers occupied when they were not fighting. (As another form of recreation, there is evidence of a long tradition of archery contests, in which soldiers competed for prizes.)

The warriors of ancient Asia often figure in poems expressing sorrow over losses in battles, but many of them were well paid and well fed despite the hardships they had to endure. They also enjoyed one advantage over their counterparts elsewhere: they rarely had to travel far from home. While the Indians and Chinese fought among themselves, and fought against foreign invaders, they manifested no desire to extend their rule far beyond their native territories, so they never created vast, multinational empires like those of Alexander the Great and the ancient Romans. For this reason, their many accomplishments in both the mechanics and the philosophy of warfare long remained unknown to the Western world, though they are now intensively studied and widely appreciated.

Further Reading

Brekke, Torkel, editor. 2006. *The Ethics of War in Asian Civilizations: A Comparative Perspective.* London and New York: Routledge.

Peers, Chris. 2006. *Soldiers of the Dragon: Chinese Armies 1500 BC–AD 1840.* Oxford: Osprey.

Sandhu, Gurcharn Singh. 2000. *A Military History of Ancient India.* New Delhi: Vision Books.

Sawyer, Ralph D., translator. 1993. *The Seven Military Classics of Ancient China.* Boulder, CO: Westview Press.

Sawyer, Ralph D., and Mei-chün Sawyer. 2011. *Ancient Chinese Warfare.* New York: Basic Books.

Wang, William S.-Y. 2013. *Love and War in Ancient China: Voices from the Shijing.* Hong Kong: City University of Hong Kong Press.

Documents

From *The Bhagavad Gita: The Song of the Master.* C. 400 BCE. Translated by Charles Johnston. 1908. New York: Quarterly Book Department.

This opening passage provides a picture of an Indian army preparing to begin a great battle.

King Duryodhana, beholding the Pandu army drawn up for battle, coming to Drona, his instructor, addressed to him this word:

Behold, O instructor, this mighty host of the sons of Pandu, marshalled by thy wise pupil, Drupada's son;

Heroes are here, mighty archers, equal to Bhima and Arjuna in battle, Yuyudhana and Virata, and Drupada of the great chariot;

Dhrishtaketu and Chekitana, and Kashi's valorous king; Purujit and Kuntibhoja and Shaivya, bull of men:

The victorious Yudhamanyu and Uttamaujas the valorous, Subhadra's son and the sons of Draupadi, with great chariots all.

Hear now, best of the Twice-born, who are our chiefest men, my army's captains; that thou mayest know their names, I tell them to thee;

Thyself and Bhishma, Kama and Kripa, conqueror in battle, Ashvatthama and Vikarna, and Somadatta's son;

And many other heroes who give their lives for me, variously armed, all skilled in war.

Our force which Bhishma leads is inadequate; their force which Bhima commands is strong;

Therefore, do ye all support Bhishma, holding the several places allotted to you, O worthy warriors!

Then enkindling his ardor, the elder Kuru, the martial grandsire, loudly blew his conch-shell, sounding the lion note.

Thereupon sounded conches, drums, great drums, cymbals and trumpets, till the sound grew to a tumult.

Then standing together in their great chariot yoked with white horses, Krishna, slayer of Madhu, and Arjuna, son of Pandu, blew their godlike conches.

He of the flowing hair blew the conch called Fivefold, and the conqueror of wealth blew the God-given; and he of the wolf-maw, terrible in deeds, blew the Reed-note;

King Yudhishthira, the son of Kunti, blew Unending-victory; Nakula and Sahadeva blew the conches Well-sounding and Pearl-flowered;

And the mighty archer, the king of Kashi, and Shikhandin of the great chariot, Dhrishtadyumma, Virata and Satyaka's unvanquished son;

Drupada and the sons of Draupadi, his daughter, O monarch, and Subhadra's son of mighty arms, blew their conches on all hands, on this side and on that;

And the sound pierced the hearts of Dhritarashtra's sons; the din made heaven and earth resound.

Then Pandu's son, he of the monkey-banner,
  looking toward the sons of Dhritarashtra
  set over against him, while the arrows were
  already falling, grasped his bow;
And thus, O monarch, he spoke to him of the
  flowing hair: Draw up my chariot, O unfallen
  one, between the two armies;
That I may view those ranged against us ready to
  fight, with whom I must do battle in this clash
  of war;
That I may see those who are about to fight, gathered here to work the will of Dhritarashtra's
  evil-minded son in battle!

From Ch'u Yuan. C. 300 BCE. *A Hundred and Seventy Chinese Poems.* Translated by Arthur Waley. 1918. London:
Constable and Company.

*This poem was written by Ch'u Yuan, also called
Qu Yuan (343–278 BCE), who is considered the great-
est of the ancient Chinese poets. This description of
soldiers who died in combat is generally referred to as
"Battle," though its literally translated title would be
"Dying Prematurely on Behalf of Country."*

"We grasp our battle-spears: we don our
  breast-plates of hide.
The axles of our chariots touch: our short
  swords meet.
Standards obscure the sun: the foe roll up like
  clouds.
Arrows fall thick: the warriors press forward.
They menace our ranks: they break our line.
The left-hand trace-horse is dead: the one on the
  right is smitten.
The fallen horses block our wheels: they impede
  the yoke-horses!"
[The soldiers] grasp their jade drum-sticks: they
  beat the sounding drums.
Heaven decrees their fall: the dread Powers are
  angry.
The warriors are all dead: they lie on the
  moor-field.
They issued but shall not enter: they went but
  shall not return.
The plains are flat and wide: the way home
  is long.

Their swords lie beside them: their black bows,
  in their hand.
Though their limbs were torn, their hearts could
  not be repressed.
They were more than brave: they were inspired
  with the spirit of "Wu" [military genius].
Steadfast to the end, they could not be daunted.
Their bodies were stricken, but their souls have
  taken Immortality—
Captains among the ghosts, heroes among
  the dead.

Weavers

The history of textiles, to an extent, can be regarded
as humanity's extended efforts to find more comfortable, and more attractive, materials for their
clothing—although, of course, they also found many
other uses for each new fabric they devised. In many
ways, the ancient residents of Asia engaged in this
process in a typical fashion, progressing from animal
hides and leather to fabrics and developing a variety
of looms to weave threads into pieces of cloth. However, they also made their own unique contributions to
the history of weaving: the Indus Valley civilization of
India was the first to make cotton, while the Chinese
invented the fabric known as silk.

It is not known exactly when the ancient Indians
began cultivating cotton to make fabric, but unearthed
scraps of cotton and wooden spindles dating back to
3000 BCE indicate that cotton was made by people of
the Indus Valley civilization, and references to cotton
in the collection of hymns called the *Rigveda*, dating
back to 1500 BCE, show that it was commonplace by
that time. A major difficulty in making use of cotton
fibers, which remained until the invention of the cotton gin in the nineteenth century, was separating the
seeds from the floss. Indian women, after the cotton
was harvested, would first let it dry for three days;
then a wooden cylinder would be rolled over the cotton to remove the seeds. To separate and clean the
fibers, early weavers would beat them, which sometimes caused them to break; later, vibrations from a
bow with a string loosened the fibers more gently.
A spindle was employed to spin the fibers into yarn,

which could then be woven into fabric on a loom. Like weavers in other civilizations, the women of India learned to create various sorts of patterns in their fabric through weaving, and often added embroidery as well; for special fabrics, some gold or silver thread could be added.

The Indians enjoyed clothing and fabrics that were brightly colored, but the process of dying cotton was unusually complicated. First, a special chemical called a mordant had to be applied so that the color would endure; aluminum oxide was often employed for this purpose. To create attractive patterns, the mordant could be stamped onto the fabric with a wooden block, so colors would only appear in certain areas. The Indians derived their dyes from plants, such as saffron, which provided yellow; indigo plants, for blue; and madder plants, for red. Other colors came from mixtures: indigo with tannin produced black, while red and blue dyes could be combined to make purple and yellow and blue dues made green.

Cotton was probably India's most common fabric, often employed for the large pieces of cloth that people wrapped around themselves: saris for women and dhotis for men. But India also produced fabrics made out of wool and flax, and the nation became well known for a fine type of linen called muslin. In addition, the Indians learned how to make their own form of silk, using a native species of silkworms, but this especially elegant and comfortable fabric originated further to the East, in ancient China.

According to a Chinese legend, it was the wife of the Yellow Emperor who first invented silk about 5,000 years ago, as she sought out silkworms that could make the same sort of silk that the Silkworm Goddess had provided her husband; and in fact the earliest archaeological evidence of its use in China dates from around this time. It is also assumed that women originally learned how to make and weave silk, perhaps after gathering the cocoons of silkworms, believing them to be a new sort of fruit, and stumbling upon their special properties. Another fanciful legend attributes this discovery to a woman who inadvertently dropped a cocoon into her tea and noticed the threads starting to unravel. However the skill originated, women generally remained responsible for all stages of silk production throughout Chinese history. Indeed, in the provinces that made silk, virtually every woman would participate at some time in the labor of its creation; it was considered so important that, emulating the emperor's practice of ritually beginning the plowing of seeds for crops, the empress would officially launch the annual process of silk production.

In the beginning, women would gather silkworm cocoons in the wild, but raising silkworms later became a more organized process, now termed sericulture. The young silkworms were kept in special houses and fed their favorite food, mulberry leaves, which the women cut off the trees with axes and gathered in baskets. The houses also protected the silkworms from loud noises or powerful odors, since it was believed that these might have a negative effect on their filaments. A month or so later, when they were ready to start spinning, the silkworms would be placed on straw; and after they had attached themselves to the straw and spun their cocoons, the women would gather the cocoons and soak them in hot water in order to kill the moths before they chewed their way out of the cocoons. The immersion process also helped to separate the filaments, though the cocoons had to be twisted or placed on spinning wheels to achieve complete separation. Then, the women attached pieces of filaments to their waists, kept them taut with wooden bars held by their feet, and wrapped other filaments around them to produce silk threads. Silk of the highest quality would use threads consisting or six or seven filaments, while combining more filaments would yield a coarser fabric. Chinese women also employed a spinning wheel to make their thread.

When it was time to weave the filaments into pieces of cloth, the women turned to their looms, usually relying on a loom driven by a foot petal. They learned to create elaborate patterns in their products, mastered the art of dying the silk various colors, and added embroidery for certain pieces. At first, only the emperor and the nobles were permitted to wear silk clothing, as the common people had to use fabrics made of hemp or ramie; but over time, everyone had access to silk, though it remained more expensive than other materials. The Chinese also found many other uses for silk, including household decorations, lines for catching fish, musical instruments, and paper for

A FAILED EXPERIMENT

Since silk is a highly desirable fabric, nations all over the world have attempted to import silkworms and their favorite food, mulberry trees, to establish their own silk industries. All efforts to do so in the United States, however, have been fruitless. The most disastrous effort was led by Professor Étienne Léopold Trouvelot (1827–1895), who strangely thought that the secret to making U.S. silk was to develop a hardier variety of silk-worms by interbreeding them with gypsy moths. Not only were his experiments unsuccessful, but some of the gypsy moths he brought to Massachusetts acciden-tally escaped into the wild to become one of America's most destructive insect pests.

GUARANTEED TO BE HANDMADE

For centuries, the weavers in the Indian city of Varanasi earned a living by individually sewing beau-tiful saris with embellishments like golden flowers. Yet while they were long able to command high prices for their products, these weavers recently found it difficult to compete both with popular Western clothing and cheaper, machine-made saris imported from China. To protect this ancient industry, the Indian government passed a law in 2006 to ensure that only handmade saris from the city could be sold as "Varanasi saris," and a special mark was created to identify those authentic garments.

writing and painting. Eventually, pieces of silk were so valued in China that they even came to function as a form of currency; in addition, and since other cultures were long unaware of how to make this material, it was long one of China's most profitable exports.

In both India and China, weaving was originally a process that occurred in every home, as the women of the household were expected, as one of their duties, to weave fabrics and make clothing for their families. However, as the export of fabrics like cotton and silk became an important source of income, they were increasingly made in urban workshops, where teams of weavers working at large looms could produce fab-rics more quickly and efficiently. An unfortunate pat-tern was also established that has endured to this day: small factories, controlled by male entrepreneurs, that exploited female workers by forcing them to labor for long hours to receive little pay.

Just as the other cultures of central Asia were heavily influenced by Indian weaving, those of west-ern Asia largely modeled their production of fabrics on Chinese techniques; but they sometimes developed their own distinctive approaches to the art. Ancient Japan, for example, created an early form of tie-dyeing called *shibori*, in which fabrics are manipulated into three-dimensional shapes in order to produce unusual patterns on the dyed cloth; so, diagonally draping a fabric on a pole can yield images that resemble fall-ing rain. In Indonesia, weavers learned to create a fab-ric with intricate designs known as batik: one applies beeswax to the fabric, using a small pouring tool called a canting to position the wax in certain ways, adds a dye, applies beeswax again, adds a second dye, and continues the process until the desired pattern is achieved. Overall, one cannot overpraise the endless ingenuity of the women weavers of ancient Asia, who constantly struggled to find innovative ways to create new and attractive fabrics, and no single survey of their artistry can ever describe all of their contribu-tions to the art of weaving.

Further Reading

Brown, Claudia, editor. 2000. *Weaving China's Past: The Amy S. Clague Collection of Chinese Textiles*. Phoenix, AZ: Phoenix Art Museum.

Cheng, Weiji. 1992. *History of Textile Technology of Ancient China*. Rego Park, New York, and Beijing: Sci-ence Press.

Dusenbery, Mary M. 2004. *Flowers, Dragons, and Pine Trees: Asian Textiles in the Spencer Museum of Art*. New York and Manchester, England: Hudson Hills Press.

Hua, Mei. 2011. *Chinese Clothing*. Cambridge: Cambridge University Press.

Singh, Kiran. 1994. *Textiles in Ancient India: From Indus Valley Civilization to Maurya Period*. Varanasi, India: Vishwavidyalaya Prakashan.

Wilson, Verity. 2005. *Chinese Textiles*. London: Victoria and Albert Publications.

Documents

From Manning, Charlotte Speir. 1856. *Life in Ancient India*. London: Smith, Elder.

In this passage, the author discusses the ancient Indian techniques for making fine fabrics out of cotton.

For the antiquity of weaving we have evidence in the *Rig-Veda*, where we read of the rat gnawing the "weaver's threads"; and again in the Code [of Manu], where the weaver is required to return in the woven fabric a greater weight than he received in the raw cotton; the reason being that he is obliged to keep his threads immersed in rice-water, which necessarily increases their weight. Moist air facilitates weaving, and is indispensable for the finest qualities; it is on this account that Masulipatam and Dhacca maintained their pre-eminence, and could only be rivalled in the dry north-west by the contrivance of underground workshops. The strange appearance of an Indian spinning-wheel, made of richly carved wood and bound round by unsightly threads, was explained by the late Professor Cowper, who discovered that the clumsy-looking threads give a "tension and elasticity" not to be procured in any other way. These wheels are now silenced by the machinery of Manchester, and the time may soon arrive when it will appear incredible that a fabric of ten yards in length and one yard wide should weigh only [3.1 ounces], and pass readily through a small ring. Similar to this must have been the "woven air" of Sanskrit literature, and the robe in which a woman exhibited herself in Buddhist story and was punished for going about unclad. The muslin had been sent to Kosala as a present from the King of Kalinga.

From Parker, Edward Harper. 1908. *Ancient China Simplified*. London: Chapman & Hall.

In passages about clothing and the leisure activities of the ancient Chinese, the author describes the work of female weavers.

Silk was universally known. When the Second Protector (to be) was dallying with his lady-love in Ts'i, the maid of his mistress happened to overhear important conversations from her post in a mulberry tree; the presumption is that she was collecting leaves for the silkworms. Again in 519, a century later, there was a dispute on the Ts'u-Wu frontier (North An Hwei province), about the possession of certain mulberry trees. Cotton (Gossypium) was unknown in China, and the poorer classes wore garments of hempen materials; the cotton tree (Bombyx) was known in the south, but then (as now) the catkins could not be woven into cloth. . . .

As a rule, however, it is to be feared that the wealthy Chinese classes in ancient (as in modern) times found their chief recreation in feasting, literary bouts, and female society. Curiously enough, nothing is said of gambling. Women are depicted at their looms, or engaged upon the silk industry; but it is singular how very little is said of home life, of how the houses were constructed, of how the hours of leisure were passed. In modern China the bulk of the male rural population rises with or before the dawn, and is engaged upon field or garden work until the shades of evening fall in; there is no artificial light adequate for purposes of needlework or private study; even the consolations of tobacco and tea—not to say opium, and now newspapers—were unknown in Confucian days. It is presumed, therefore, that life was even more humdrum than it is now, except that women at least had feet to walk upon.

Ancient Greece, 2000–30 BCE

Introduction

Ancient Greece was both culturally and geographically diverse. Its story begins with the poorly understood civilization of the Myceneans, centered on the island of Crete, which collapsed around 1100 BCE, leading to a long period of decline until the eighth century BCE brought a cultural renaissance, marked by the beginning of the Olympic Games and the first masterpieces of Greek literature, the *Iliad* and *Odyssey* of Homer (ca. 800–701 BCE). This is also when the Greeks began to extensively colonize the lands of the Mediterranean Sea, expanding the Greek world to include settlements on numerous islands, the west coast of present-day Turkey, and the east coast of Italy. The Greeks developed a system of independent city-states, each with its own distinctive government and society, though they were loosely united by cultural events like the Olympic Games and joined forces to defend their country against the Persian Empire. Modern impressions of ancient Greek life mostly focus on the city-state of Athens, renowned for its democracy and pioneering philosophers, though Sparta also commands attention because of its uniquely militaristic culture, and many prominent thinkers emerged from city-states that were far away from Greece itself. Eventually, in the fourth century BCE, the ancient Greeks lost their independence, as their nation was taken over first by the Macedonians and later by the Romans; however, these conquerors also spread Greek culture and ideas throughout Europe and the Middle East.

Despite their many differences, there were some common factors that shaped the lives of all ancient Greeks. These include a rugged, mountainous terrain that made farming difficult and encouraged people to travel primarily by sea; a devotion to their polytheistic religion, illuminated by the classic stories of Greek mythology that energized their literature; and shared interests in athletic achievement, the natural world, and defeating foreign invaders. Looking down upon those individuals who were forced to work for a salary, the Greeks idealized people who supported themselves, whether they were farmers growing crops or craftsmen selling their products. This commitment to independence in the face of constant challenges is reflected in the adventurous spirit that the Greeks displayed in endeavors ranging from their voyages throughout the Mediterranean to their innovative contributions to mathematics, science, philosophy, politics, and literature, which are still studied and admired today.

Actors

In the early days of Greek drama, there were no real actors, only singers in the chorus who were occasionally asked to step forward and speak as one of the characters in the play; and, with masks to wear that clearly identified the characters being portrayed, there was no immediate need for acting ability. However, as the number of characters in the plays increased from one to three, and the focus of attention gradually shifted from the chorus to those characters, performers began altering their voices and movements to match the roles they were playing, ranging from gods and goddesses to soldiers and slaves, and certain individuals began to earn special recognition for their talents in doing so. And, as they also began to earn a significant income for their work, these people became the world's first professional actors. Even though Greek plays regularly featured prominent female characters, women were never permitted to act on the Greek stage, as both male and female parts were taken by male actors.

On stage, actors looked very different than they did in real life. First, their faces were always concealed by masks; since these were made from cork or linen, no actual masks have survived, but artistic representations of theatrical masks suggest that they had large openings for the actors' mouths and eyes, and the masks' faces were shaped to convey strong emotions—sorrow for tragedies and happiness for comedies. (To this day, an iconic image for theater is a pair of masks, one smiling, one frowning.) The masks were equipped with special mouthpieces to make voices resonate, so the actors could be better heard in the outdoor theaters where plays were performed.

Actors also wore a special projection on their masks, called an *onkos*, and shoes with thick soles, which together functioned to make them look especially tall. The men playing women wore additional padding to change the appearance of their bodies, and while many actors merely donned long robes, they were sometimes required to wear elaborate costumes. These were especially outlandish in the comedies; for example, in the plays of Aristophanes (ca. 446–386 BCE), characters might wear baggy pants with huge phalluses, while members of the chorus would be dressed as animals like frogs or birds.

Ancient Greek actors also faced some special challenges. Since the outdoor theaters were designed for large audiences, actors had to gesture extravagantly so that even audience members in distant rows could see what they were doing. Since there were only three

This painting from an ancient Greek wine vessel shows a young actor removing his mask after portraying a much older character, ca. 350 BCE. (UIG via Getty Images)

actors, all actors had to play multiple roles, and hence would have to rush into a structure behind the stage, called the *skene*, to change their masks or costumes while the chorus provided an interlude. Props were occasionally employed on stage—especially weapons like swords or spears—and when the *skene* evolved from a tent into a permanent wooden or stone building, actors were sometimes asked to deliver lines from its roof. Finally, in some plays, actors were placed in the large crane called the *mêchanê* which would elevate them so that, portraying gods, they could be lowered onto the stage; like modern stage effects, the *mêchanê* undoubtedly malfunctioned at times, perhaps injuring an actor.

While the actors portraying individual characters were most prominent on stage, the twelve men who made up the chorus continued to play a role in the drama, since their songs provided important information about story developments and they occasionally interacted with actors. Members of the chorus had to have both good singing voices and a certain amount of dancing ability, since choruses typically danced rhythmically around the stage while singing their songs. In some plays, members of the chorus might also serve as extras, portraying a crowd of observers to the action.

Initially, actors in the annual dramatic competitions were not credited, but even during the era of Aeschylus (ca. 525–456 BCE), the two actors who regularly performed in his plays, Cleander and Mynniscus (both ca. fifth century BCE), were respected throughout Athens for their talents. Later, festivals began to award prizes to both outstanding playwrights and outstanding actors, and to prevent playwrights from gaining an unfair advantage in the competition by recruiting the best actors, it became customary to randomly assign actors to playwrights. By the fourth century BCE, prominent actors were sometimes allowed to alter the scripts of classic playwrights; scholars speculate, for example, that an incongruous speech near the conclusion of Sophocles's play *Antigone* (ca. 441 BCE) was not written by Sophocles (ca. 497–406 BCE) himself, but by a later actor who wanted to expand his speaking role. Eventually, however, the Athenian authorities passed a law to end this practice.

The first man to become famous for his acting skills was probably Polus, who lived in Athens dur-

ing the fourth century BCE. Two anecdotes attest to his abilities: first, he reportedly gave lessons in elocution to Demosthenes (384–322 BCE), who was thus able to overcome his speaking difficulties to become one of ancient Greece's greatest orators. Then, to effectively portray the grief of Electra in a production of Sophocles's tragedy, he brought an urn containing the ashes of his own son on stage. Polus was able to earn vast sums of money for his work; by one report, he once received one Attic talent—about $150,000 in modern U.S. currency—for giving only two performances. The other renowned actors of his era, like Aristodemus and Neoptolemus (both ca. fourth century BCE), also became extremely wealthy; one assumes that most of their income came from acting, along with fees for giving acting lessons or leading acting classes.

Eventually, much like the great actors of nineteenth-century Europe and America, prominent actors primarily made their living by traveling throughout Greece in small companies, performing the classic plays of Aeschylus, Sophocles, and Euripides (480–406 BCE). To protect their own interests, actors in 275 BCE organized a guild, called the Artists of Dionysus, which included both actors and other theatrical workers. In some cases, actors toured with their own choruses and supporting crew; later, it became more common for the actors to travel by themselves, performing alongside a local chorus and crew that was already familiar with the standard repertoire of plays. As actors became more and more popular, they began to receive special privileges as well; for example, to clearly designate one actor as the star performer, the three actors came to be classified as the protagonist, deuteragonist, and tritagonist, and protagonists might make additional demands; for example, according to Aristotle, the actor Herodotus (ca. fourth century BCE) always insisted that he had to come on stage before any other actors. Theater historians have also wondered why, as actors came to dominate the plays, the Greeks never expanded their casts beyond three actors, so each part could be played by a separate actor; one theory is that influential actors fought to maintain the three-actor rule because they did not want to share the spotlight with multiple performers, who would also reduce the time they were on stage. As a sign of how they were valued by their societies,

GREEK THEATER AS THE GREEKS SAW IT

Although the plays of Aeschylus, Sophocles, and Euripides are regularly performed today, actors generally follow the modern conventions of drama: they wear no masks, and both male and female actors play roles. In the 1960s, however, the Tyrone Guthrie Theatre in Minneapolis, Minnesota, staged a version of Aeschylus's *Oresteia* trilogy, entitled *The House of Atreus*, which strived to emulate the Greek style of performance, employing male actors for all parts and having them wear large, elaborate masks. The success of this production, which later toured the country, demonstrated that actors could still effectively employ the Greek style of acting to arouse the emotions of rapt audiences.

ACTING WITH STRINGS ATTACHED

Ancient Greek actors were regularly required to stand within a crane, the *mêchanê*, which lowered them from a great height to the stage below as they portrayed gods descending from the clouds to intervene in the affairs of humans. In Aristophanes's comedy *The Clouds*, the *mêchanê* is used to show the philosopher Socrates floating in space, symbolizing his detachment from real-world concerns. On today's stage, actors appear to fly by wearing a harness attached to invisible strings—the device always employed, for example, by the actors playing Peter Pan, Wendy, John, and Michael in productions of J. M. Barrie's *Peter Pan* and its musical adaptation.

actors were usually exempt from compulsory military service, and some city-states recruited actors to serve as ambassadors, since they were well known and experienced travelers with excellent speaking skills.

Outside of festivals and large theaters, another form of drama later emerged in Greece during the Hellenistic Age, although it is poorly understood and only sketchily documented. While referred to as "mime," these performances featured actors voicing scripted dialogue, as indicated by a few surviving texts by a writer in the third century BCE named Herodas. These short plays, involving everyday people and their sometimes bawdy adventures, were apparently performed by traveling troupes in whatever venues they might

find in cities they visited. Clearly, there was much less prestige, and much less income, to be garnered from these scattered productions, but they did provide Greek actors with another way to make a living if they could not obtain roles in traditional dramas.

Overall, as acting became a highly visible and profitable profession in ancient Greece, there was a corresponding decline in the craft of writing plays, since audiences now came to theaters to see a particular actor, not to enjoy the work of a particular playwright. Thus, there was no need to encourage anyone to write new and original plays, as both actors and audiences were content to keep staging new productions of the classic plays of earlier centuries. Still, given the similar proclivities of modern society, it is hard to criticize the Greeks for becoming more devoted to charismatic celebrities than to talented authors.

Further Reading

Ashby, Clifford. 2000. *Classical Greek Theatre: New Views of an Old Subject.* Iowa City: University of Iowa Press.

Bassi, Karen. 1998. *Acting Like Men: Gender, Drama, and Nostalgia in Ancient Greece.* Ann Arbor: University of Michigan Press.

Easterling, Pat, and Edith Hall, editors. 2002. *Greek and Roman Actors: Aspects of an Ancient Profession.* Cambridge: Cambridge University Press.

Wiles, David. 2000. *Greek Theatre Performance: An Introduction.* Cambridge: Cambridge University Press.

Wiles, David. 1991. *The Masks of Menander: Sign and Meaning in Greek and Roman Performance.* Cambridge: Cambridge University Press.

Wilson, Peter. 2000. *The Athenian Institution of the Khoregia: The Chorus, the City, and the Stage.* Cambridge: Cambridge University Press.

Document

From Aulus Gellius. C. 170 CE. *The Attic Nights of Aulus Gellius.* Translated by John C. Rolfe. 1927. London: William Heinemann.

In this passage, the Roman author Aulus Gellius (ca. 130–180 CE) relates the story of how the Greek actor Polus was able to demonstrate true grief on the stage.

There was in the land of Greece an actor of wide reputation who excelled all others in his clear delivery and graceful action. They say that his name was Polus, and he often acted the tragedies of famous poets with intelligence and dignity. This Polus lost by death a son whom he dearly loved. After he felt that he had indulged his grief sufficiently, he returned to the practice of his profession.

At that time, he was to act in the *Electra* of Sophocles at Athens, and it was his part to carry an urn which was supposed to contain the ashes of Orestes. The plot of the play requires that Electra, who is represented as carrying her brother's remains, should lament and bewail the fate that she believed had overtaken him. Accordingly, Polus, clad in the mourning garb of Electra, took from the tomb the ashes and urn of his son, embraced them as if they were those of Orestes, and filled the whole place, not with the appearance and imitation of sorrow, but with genuine grief and unfeigned lamentation. Therefore, while it seemed that a play was being acted, it was in fact real grief that was enacted.

Architects

If asked, the ancient Greeks would say that the first architect was the legendary Daedalus, the figure from Greek mythology whose accomplishments included the construction of the intricate labyrinth wherein the monstrous minotaur lurked. Although few people today believe that such a man actually existed, he did function as a sort of patron saint for both architects and sculptors, since the dividing lines between the two professions were not always clear; sometimes, sculptors would also design buildings, while architects would provide their projects with sculptures. More commonly, however, these tasks were assigned to separate individuals; thus, we know that architects Ictinus and Callicrates (both ca. fifth century BCE) combined their talents to design the Parthenon, the famous building that was completed in 438 BCE, but sculptor Phidias (ca. 490–430 BCE) was responsible for its central statue of Athena and friezes of raised figures on its walls.

While today's architects only provide the design for buildings, the architects of ancient Greece were more involved in the entire process of construction.

The architect would first be commissioned by a city government to create a certain sort of structure, often in exchange for a large sum of money. After the architect received his instructions, the process presumably began with a sketch of the planned building, like a modern blueprint, done on papyrus; no examples of such sketches survive, but many architects would later carve their plans onto one of the stones of the building, to serve as a permanent guide for the original builders and perhaps for later craftsmen repairing or expanding the structure. (We know of such blueprints in stone because an archaeologist discovered one on the ruins of the Temple of Apollo at Didyma.) Then, the architect would not only decide upon the sort of stone to be used for the building—usually limestone for ordinary structures, marble for special projects—but would also go to the quarry and personally supervise the choice of particular stone materials that seemed best suited for his project, and he would instruct the carvers who shaped the pieces to be transported from the quarry to the building site. During this work, we can assume the architect was accompanied by one or more apprentices, who sought his tutelage to receive the training that would someday enable them to become architects themselves.

When all necessary materials for construction were present, the architect would then be in charge of the workers who actually constructed the building. These included craftsmen, who carved stones into their final, precise shapes so that they would fit together and remain in place without the use of mortar; common laborers, who would set up wooden scaffolding and move stones into position; metalworkers, who crafted the building's supportive fittings and adornments; sculptors, who carved the three-dimensional images on friezes and sometimes carved separate statues for the building's interior; and painters, who gave the bare stone material some decorative color, like the bright red, green, and blue paint that once adorned the Parthenon. Only when the building was completed to the architect's satisfaction would workers be allowed to cease their labors.

Greek architects applied their skills to a variety of structures. As one unusual example, we know the name of one architect from the sixth century BCE, Eupalinos of Megara (ca. sixth century BCE), because

This photograph shows what is universally regarded as the greatest achievement of ancient Greek architecture, the temple called the Parthenon, completed in 438 BCE, and still visited by thousands of tourists every year, who climb the hill of the Acropolis of Athens to see it. (Pedre/iStockphoto.com)

the historian Herodotus (484–425 BCE) praised one of his achievements, an enormous tunnel on the island of Samos, which provided the city with fresh water. Another architect, Phaeax of Agrigentum (ca. fifth century BCE), is oddly most renowned for the sewers he designed for his home city. Sostratus of Cnidus (ca. third century BCE) designed and constructed the world's first lighthouse, at the port of Alexandria in Egypt, which was completed sometime between 280 and 247 BCE, while the architects Satyros and Pythius (both ca. fourth century BCE) were responsible for an enormous tomb, the Mausoleum at Halicarnassus, completed between 353 and 350 BCE. The lighthouse and mausoleum were later designated as two of the Seven Wonders of the Ancient World. Another variety of architecture was practiced by Hippodamus of Miletus (498–408 BCE), generally regarded as the world's first city planner, as he prepared designs for several Greek cities during the fifth century BCE. He was also one of the few architects who wrote about his work, though none of his texts have survived.

However, Greek architecture as a whole is most strongly associated with the grand temples that were regarded, both in their day and in centuries thereaf-ter, as the field's greatest achievements. To sustain the roofs of such structures, the Greeks needed to employ long, cylindrical columns, and their differing features define the three basic styles of Greek architecture, developed by anonymous architects over the centuries. Doric columns were plain and had no base, while Ionic columns had a base and a scroll at their top. Corinthian columns, which appeared later during the Hellenistic period, had elaborate floral decorations at their top. Because these columns tended to appear curved from a distance, Greek architects developed the habit of making columns wider in the middle, which actually made them look straight and contributed to the restrained beauty of their appearance. While the Parthenon is now considered the greatest Greek temple, the ancients actually singled out another example, the Temple of Artemis at Ephesus, as one of their Seven Wonders, though it was long ago destroyed; the temple was financed by Croesus of Lydia (ca. 595–547 BCE), famous for his enormous wealth, and designed by the architect Chersiphron and his son Metagenes (both ca. sixth century BCE). Its construction began in 560 BCE; it was destroyed in 356 BCE, rebuilt, and destroyed again in 268 CE by raiding Goths.

THE AMERICAN PARTHENON

The greatest achievement of ancient Greek architecture, the Parthenon, has suffered extensive damage in the centuries since its completion under the supervision of the sculptor Phidias and architects Callicrates and Ictinos. The Greek government is striving to reconstruct the Parthenon, but acknowledges that it will never be restored to its original appearance. However, to see what it once looked like, one can visit Nashville, Tennessee, where a full-sized replica of the Parthenon was built in 1897 by architects William B. Dinsmoor (1886–1973) and Russell E. Hart (ca. twentieth century); the first building used wood and plaster, so it rapidly deteriorated, but a rebuilt version of concrete stands to this day.

HOW TO CHOOSE AN ARCHITECT

For important civic projects like temples, the leaders of Greek city-states would typically seek out renowned architects to design the buildings and supervise their construction. In the twentieth century, however, governments may hold competitions, inviting any interested architect to submit a design and having experts select the most suitable plan. Thus, an unknown architect may earn the job over better-known rivals. This occurred in 1957, when a design presented by an obscure Danish architect, Jørn Utzon (1918–2008), was surprisingly selected for the Sydney Opera House in Australia. His striking vision, featuring large white shells as the roof, has made the structure a leading tourist attraction.

In addition to such civic projects, most Greeks also owned and lived in their own private homes; these were usually made of bricks of dried mud, with some wooden support and a foundation of stone. None of these structures have survived, but we have deduced some of their floor plans; houses were generally rectangular, with several rooms around a central courtyard with an altar for worship of a god. Some ancient architect must have created this basic design that then became the norm, but all homes tended to be slightly different, indicating that individual owners applied their own rudimentary architectural talents to create homes that suited their particular preferences.

Though some of their designs were widely admired, architects in general were not as highly esteemed as other Greek artists and thinkers, as shown in various ways. While the Muses of Greek mythology presided over the arts, none were associated with architects, suggesting that they were not regarded as genuine artists like poets and dancers. Furthermore, it was common for the ancient Greeks to produce accurate or purported portraits of major figures like Homer (ca. 800–701 BCE), Plato (ca. 428–378 BCE), and Demosthenes (384–322 BCE); however, they produced no portraits of any architects. And while the names of prominent architects have been preserved, there is generally little biographical information available; even in the cases of the men who designed the Parthenon, Ictinus and Callicrates, all we know is the names of a few other buildings they were responsible for. Only a few anecdotes provide us with glimpses in the lives of prominent architects; the Roman architect Vitruvius (ca. 80–10 BCE), for example, relates that the architect Callimachus (ca. 310–240 BCE) was inspired to create the elaborate design of Corinthian columns when he happened to observe a plant that had begun to grow around and through a basket placed on a tomb. And we are aware that an architect from a later era, Aelius Nicon (ca. second century CE), was a kindly and devoted father solely because his son, Galen (ca. 129–200 CE), became a famous physician and wrote about him in one of his books.

Still, even if the Greeks did not value it as much as later generations, architecture was arguably the most influential of all the Greek arts, since scores of later architects have imitated its style in their own buildings; many prominent buildings in Washington, D.C., including the Library of Congress, Supreme Court Building, and Lincoln Memorial, closely resemble ancient Greek temples. For many, structures with stately columns and friezes of human figures epitomize the grandeur and artistry of ancient Greek culture, and although it is damaged, the Parthenon continues to attract thousands of tourists who come to admire its stately beauty. It is ironic, then, that we know so little about the architects who designed this famous building and others of its type.

Further Reading

Barnow, Finn. 2002. *The City of the Landowner: Urban Systems and Urban Architecture in the Antique Greek World and the Roman Empire.* Copenhagen: Royal Danish Academy of Fine Arts, School of Architecture Publishers.

Darling, Janina K. 2004. *Architecture of Greece.* Westport, CT: Greenwood Press.

Jenkins, Ian. 2006. *Greek Architecture and Its Sculpture.* Cambridge, MA: Harvard University Press.

Senseney, John R. 2011. *The Art of Building in the Classical World: Vision, Craftsmanship, and Linear Perspective in Greek and Roman Architecture.* Cambridge and New York: Cambridge University Press.

Tzonis, Alexander, and Phoebe Giannisi. 2004. *Classical Greek Architecture: The Construction of the Modern.* Paris: Flammarion.

Winter, Frederick E. 2006. *Studies in Hellenistic Architecture.* Toronto: University of Toronto Press.

Documents

From Pausanias. C. 170 CE. *Description of Greece.* Translated by W.H.S. Jones. Five volumes. 1918–1935. London: William Heinemann.

In the passage from his Description of Greece, *the Greek geographer Pausanias (ca. 110–180 CE) provides a detailed description of the greatest triumph of Greek architecture, the buildings of the Acropolis in Athens, completed in the fifth century* BCE.

There is but one entry to the Acropolis. It affords no other, being precipitous throughout and having a strong wall. The gateway has a roof of white marble, and down to the present day it is unrivaled for the beauty and size of its stones. Now as to the statues of the horsemen, I cannot tell for certain whether they are the sons of Xenophon or whether they were made merely to beautify the place. On the right of the gateway is a temple of Wingless Victory. From this point the sea is visible, and here it was that, according to legend, Aegeus threw himself down to his death. . . .

On the left of the gateway is a building with pictures. Among those not effaced by time I found Diomedes taking the Athena from Troy, and Odysseus in Lemons taking away the bow of Philoctetes. There in the pictures is Orestes killing Aegisthus, and Pylades killing the sons of Nauplius who had come to bring Aegisthus succor. And there is Polyxena about to be sacrificed near the grave of Achilles. Homer did well in passing by this barbarous act. I think too that he showed poetic insight in making Achilles capture Scyros, differing entirely from those who say that Achilles lived in Scyros with the maidens, as Polygnotus has represented in his picture. He also painted Odysseus coming upon the women washing clothes with Nausicaa at the river, just like the description in Homer. There are other pictures, including a portrait of Alcibiades, and in the picture are emblems of the victory his horses won at Nemea. There is also Perseus journeying to Seriphos, and carrying to Polydectes the head of Medusa, the legend about whom I am unwilling to relate in my description of Attica. Included among the paintings—I omit the boy carrying the water-jars and the wrestler of Timaenetus—is Musaeus. . . .

Right at the very entrance to the Acropolis are a Hermes (called Hermes of the Gateway) and figures of Graces, which tradition says were sculptured by Socrates, the son of Sophroniscus, who the Pythia (the priestess of Apollo at Delphi) testified was the wisest of men, a title she refused to Anacharsis, although he desired it and came to Delphi to win it. . . . Hard by is a bronze statue of Diitrephes shot through by arrows. . . . Near the statue of Diitrephes—I do not wish to write of the less distinguished portraits—are figures of gods; of Health, whom legend calls daughter of Asclepius, and of Athena, also surnamed Health. There is also a smallish stone, just large enough to serve as a seat to a little man. On it legend says Silenus rested when Dionysus came to the land. . . .

From Aristotle. C. 340 BCE. *Politics.* C. Translated by H. Rackham. 1932. London: William Heinemann.

Here, the philosopher Aristotle discusses the life and ideas of Hippodamus of Miletus, the architect who is also regarded as the world's first city planner.

Hippodamus, son of Euryphon, a Milesian (who invented the division of cities into blocks. . . and who also became somewhat eccentric in his general mode of life, owing to a desire for distinction, so that some people thought that he lived too fussily, with a quantity of hair and expensive ornaments, and also a quantity of cheap yet warm clothes, not only in winter, but also in summer, and who wished to be a man of learning in natural science generally), was the first man not engaged in politics who attempted to speak on the subject of the best form of constitution. His system was for a city with a population of 10,000, divided into three classes. He made one class of artisans, one of farmers, and the third the class that fought for the city in wars, and was the armed class. He divided the land into three parts: one sacred, one public, and one private: sacred land to supply the customary offerings to the gods, common land to provide the warrior class with food, and private land to be owned by the farmers. He thought that there are only three divisions of the law, since the matters about which lawsuits take place are three in number: outrage, damage, homicide. He also proposed to establish one supreme court of justice, to which were to be carried up all the cases at law thought to have been decided wrongly, and this court he made to consist of certain selected elders.

Athletes

Among its many lasting contributions to world culture, ancient Greece essentially created the idea of the professional athlete. True, the young men who regularly participated in Greece's greatest competition, the Olympic Games, received no official payment for their victories, famously competing solely for the honor of wearing a crown of laurel leafs. Yet other competitions did provide the winners with valuable awards, as indicated by the epic poem by Homer (ca. 800–701 BCE), *The Iliad*, wherein the games held at the funeral of Patroclus offered the victors oxen, cauldrons, precious metals, women, and other rewards. In other cases, the cities that produced victorious athletes granted them a cash prize, a pension, or free meals. Even discounting such financial gains, noteworthy victors became admired celebrities in their society, the first people in history to garner such recognition solely for feats of physical strength and dexterity. At times, sculptors would be hired to carve statues of victorious athletes; poets like Pindar (ca. 522–443 BCE) would be commissioned to write odes celebrating their achievements; their images might be placed on coins; and a few famous athletes were even worshipped as gods

after their deaths. Even if their achievements were not outstanding enough to warrant such honors, retired athletes could obtain regular employment in the gymnasiums found in every Greek city as figures called *paidotribai*, whose various roles combined the functions of office manager, physical education teacher, personal trainer, and coach.

To the Greeks, being in good physical condition represented an important cultural ideal of almost religious significance; one could say that, in a sense, all Greeks were expected to become athletes by regularly exercising their bodies in the gymnasiums. Their competitions were also religious festivals, with events regularly interspersed with religious ceremonies. Games were considered so important that not even major wars interrupted the famous Olympics, which were always held every four years beginning in 776 BCE while all the city-states of Greece maintained a truce; their occurrence was so regular that it became the basis of the Greek calendar. Yet the sacred nature of the Olympics also brought upon their eventual downfall in 393 CE, as the Christian Roman emperor Theodosius banned all such festivals because they were linked to a pagan religion.

Athletic training began in childhood, as all boys, starting sometime between the ages of eight and twelve, would go to the gymnasiums found in every city to engage in regular exercise and sports. There, they would learn the rituals of preparing for athletic activity: removing all of their clothing, washing themselves in a fountain, covering their bodies with olive oil, and finally sprinkling themselves with fine sand; when they were finished, they would diligently remove the oil and sand with a scraping device called a *strigil* and then wash themselves with a sponge. All of their physical activities were also performed to a musical accompaniment provided by a flute player.

Whenever boys demonstrated special strengths or skills, they would be singled out for additional training and encouraged to become competitive athletes (though only free Greek citizens were allowed to compete). Prior to major events like the Olympics, prospective participants in each city would train for one year before competing in trials to determine which athletes would be sent to the competition. In addition to regular exercise and practice, prospective athletes

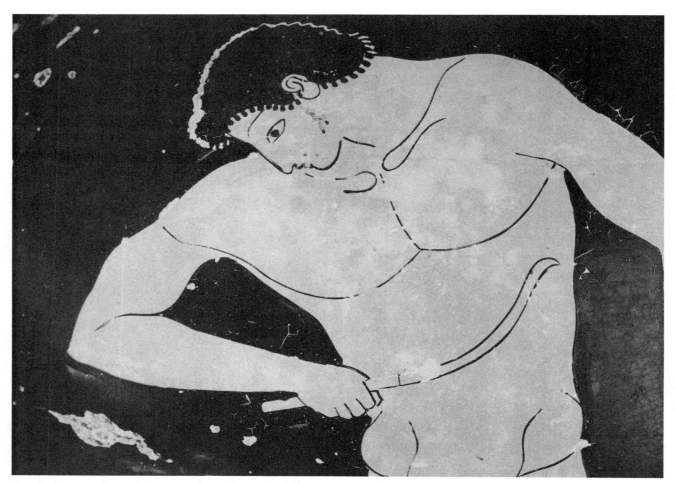

A painting on a large jar, or *amphora*, from the fifth century BCE shows a naked Greek athlete scraping the oil and sand off of his body with a *strigil*. (Erich Lessing/Art Resource, NY)

were usually advised to avoid sexual activity, and some followed special diets that were believed to promote strength and endurance; favored foods included dried figs and pork.

It is not clear why the athletes were always required to compete in the nude; one ancient historian, Pausanias (ca. 110–180 CE), attributed the practice to the example of one athlete, Orsippos of Megara, who won an Olympic race in 720 BCE by continuing to run after his loincloth fell off; others reported that nudity originated with the athletes from Sparta. Certainly, nudity provided a complete freedom of movement that the athletes must have welcomed, as ancient Greece lacked the sorts of form-fitting clothing that enables modern athletes to perform effectively while maintaining their modesty. It is also true that the Greeks

considered the naked human body to be aesthetically appealing, especially when the body in question was a superbly conditioned young man, and hence would have regarded nudity as nothing to be ashamed of. (From the perspective of the Greeks, though, the athletes were not entirely nude, since they would tie together their foreskins with a string so that the tips of their penises were not exposed.)

Men would generally avoid being naked in the presence of women, who were not permitted to observe their exercise and training; some traditional beliefs also hold that they could not attend athletic competitions. However, because competitions were also religious events, priestesses were granted a prominent place in the audience; some authorities state that only married women were forbidden to attend events,

ATHLETES FOR ART'S SAKE

As young men in superb physical condition who were accustomed to being naked in public, ancient Greek athletes were regularly employed as sculptors' models during the era when virtually all sculptures depicted male nudes. Today, also appreciating their superbly developed bodies, photographers often ask both male and female athletes to pose in the nude for their photographs. As one prominent example, the sports publication *ESPN The Magazine* annually produces a "Body Issue" featuring photographs of prominent athletes who are not wearing any clothing, although certain body parts are strategically concealed.

WARS OVER SPORTS

Even when ancient Greece was in the midst of wars, all of its city-states demonstrated their high regard for athletics by observing a truce during the Olympic Games, so that men from all city-states could gather to peacefully compete against each other. Today's nations, clearly, do not value athletics to the same extent, since on three occasions the modern Olympic Games have been cancelled due to wars—in 1916, 1940, and 1944—and some nations have boycotted other Olympic Games for political reasons. In 1980, for example, the United States and many other nations boycotted the Moscow Games to protest the Soviet Union's invasion of Afghanistan.

which could be observed by young maidens; and other authorities claim that women were allowed to watch the foot races but were banned at other events. There is also the well-known story of one athlete's mother who disguised herself as a man to watch her son compete; while she was discovered and forcibly removed, she was not otherwise punished, suggesting that such surreptitious observers may have been more common than is generally believed.

At the Olympics and other festivals, Greek athletes competed in only a limited number of events. There were four types of foot races, each of a different length; however, there was no equivalent to the 26-mile race now known as a marathon, even though the event is based on the purported achievement of an ancient Greek soldier who ran that distance to announce an

important victory. Athletes also competed in forms of boxing, wrestling, and a brutal combination of the two called the *pankration*; and there was a combined event, called the pentathlon, in which athletes sprinted, jumped, hurled a javelin, threw a discus, and wrestled. Finally, there were horse races and chariot races; as an exception to the general policy, the charioteers wore tunics while competing, although the jockeys who rode the horses were naked.

While the Greeks informally played some team sports, only individual competitions were included in formal competitions; there were also no events in which athletes were judged on the basis of their style or grace. Instead, victory was achieved by the runner who first reached the finish line, the discus thrower who threw the discus the farthest, or the wrestler who first forced his opponent to touch the ground three times. The major role of the judges was to make sure that no athletes were breaking the rules; for example, while competitors in the *pankration* could generally do anything they pleased to defeat an opponent, they were not allowed to engage in biting or deliberate eye-gouging. On a few occasions, boxers received hefty fines after it was discovered that they were bribing opponents to lose their matches.

While male athletes received more attention, there were also female athletes in ancient Greece; however, while men competed in multiple events, women were limited to foot races. Their major competition, the Heraea, was held every four years like the Olympics. In contrast to male athletes, the women always wore a tunic, perhaps revealing one of their breasts but nothing more. The mythical figure of Atalanta, who was renowned both for her speed as a runner and her skills with a bow and arrow, suggests that archery was another common pastime of female athletes, but there are no records of formal competitions in this field. Unlike the modern Olympics, male and female competitions were always separate events; however, wealthy women could enter their horses in male competitions like the Olympics and, if their horses won, they would be recognized as the victors in those events.

While the Greeks generally esteemed their athletes, it should not be assumed that these men were universally admired. That noted contrarian, the playwright Euripides (480–406 BCE), fiercely criticized athletes in a surviving passage from his lost satyr play *Autolykos*, ridiculing them as vain, pampered figures who contributed nothing of value to their societies. The life of an ancient Greek athlete may also seem more desirable than it actually was because we now remember only the greatest athletes who were celebrated in statues, poems, and stories; the athletes who never earned to right to participate in major competitions, and athletes who lost every event they entered, surely garnered far less happiness from their efforts and must have sometimes succumbed to poverty, drunkenness, and despair. Still, the sad fates of these unsuccessful athletes did not discourage innumerable Greek youth from seeking victories in future competitions; perhaps, as the contemporary world also demonstrates, the glamorous allure of a successful career in athletics will always attract very many people who will compete to become one of the very few winners.

Further Reading

Crowther, Nigel B. 2007. *Sport in Ancient Times*. Westport, CT: Praeger.

König, Jason. 2010. *Greek Athletics*. Edinburgh: Edinburgh University Press.

Kyle, Donald G. 2007. *Sport and Spectacle in the Ancient World*. Malden, MA: Blackwell.

Miller, Stephen G. 2004. *Ancient Greek Athletics*. New Haven, CT: Yale University Press.

Miller, Stephen G. 2004. *Arete: Greek Sports from Ancient Sources*. Berkeley: University of California Press.

Scanlon, Thomas F. 2002. *Eros and Greek Athletics*. Oxford: Oxford University Press.

Documents

From Lucian. C. 170 CE. *Lucian: Volume IV*. Translated by A. M. Harmon. 1925. London: William Heinemann.

In this passage from a dialogue, Anacharsis, *written by the Roman satirist Lucian (ca. 125–180 CE), a foreign philosopher named Anacharsis visits Athens, where he converses with Solon about Athenian customs, including wrestling.*

[Anacharsis:] And why are your young men doing all this, Solon? Some of them, locked in each other's arms, are tripping one another up, while others are choking and twisting each other and groveling together in the mud, wallowing like pigs. Yet in the beginning, as soon as they had taken their clothes off, they put oil on themselves … very peacefully. I saw it. Since then, I do not know what got into them that they push one another about with lowered heads and butt their foreheads together like rams. And see there! That man picked the other one up by the legs and threw him to the ground, and then fell down upon him and will not let him get up, shoving him all down into the mud. And now, after winding his legs around his middle and putting his forearm underneath his throat, he is choking the poor man, who is slapping him sideways on the shoulder . . . so that he may not be strangled completely.

[Solon:] It is only natural, Anacharsis, that what they are doing should have that appearance to you, since it is unfamiliar and very much different from Scythian customs. In a similar way, you yourselves probably have much in your education and training which would appear strange to us Greeks if one of us should look in upon it as you are doing now. But have no fear. It is not insanity, and it is not out of brutality that they strike one another and tumble each other in the mud, or sprinkle each other with dust. The thing has a certain usefulness, not unattended by enjoyment, and it gives much strength to their bodies. As a matter of fact, if you stop for some time, as I think you will, in Greece, before long you yourself will be one of the muddy or dusty group, so delightful and profitable will the thing seem to you.

From Philostratus. C. 250 CE. *The Story of Greek Athletics as Told by the Greek and Roman Writers of More Than Twelve Centuries: A Collection of the Literary Sources in English Translation*. Translated by Rachel Sargent Robinson. 1927. Champaign, IL: Daniels & Shoaff.

Gymnasticus, *a treatise written in the third century AD, is attributed to Philostratus, but there are three known authors with that name, and it is uncertain which of the three wrote this text, which describes the physical qualities and skills needed by various Olympic athletes. In this passage, the author discusses wrestling and the brutal combination of boxing and wrestling known as pankration.*

Let us proceed to those aspiring to wrestle. The regulation wrestler should be tall rather than in proportion, but built like those in proportion, with neither a long neck, nor yet one set down on the shoulders. The latter type of neck is not ill-adapted but looks rather deformed than athletic, and to anyone who is familiar with the two kinds of statues of Hercules, ever so much more pleasing and godlike are the high-born types and those without short necks. The neck should stand straight as in a handsome horse that is conscious of its own worth, and the throat should extend down to each collar bone. The shoulder blades should be drawn together, and the tips of the shoulders erect, thus lending to the wrestler size, nobility of aspect, force, and superiority in wrestling. A well-marked arm [i.e., with broad veins] is an advantage in wrestling. . . . It is better to have a chest which is prominent and curved outward, for the organs rest in it as though in a firm, well-shaped room. . . . In my opinion, persons with hollow, sunken chests should neither strip nor engage in exercises, for they suffer from stomach trouble, and they have unsound organs, and are short-winded.

Pankratiasts . . . must employ backward falls which are not safe for the wrestler and grips in which victory must be obtained by falling. . . . They must have skill in various methods of strangling; they also wrestle with an opponent's ankle and twist his arm, besides hitting and jumping on him, for all these practices belong to the *pankration*, only biting and gouging prohibited. The Spartans allow even these practices, but the Eleans and the laws of the games exclude them.

Farmers

Although people usually regard ancient Greece as an urbanized culture, almost eighty percent of its citizens lived on farms and devoted most of their energies to raising crops, both to feed themselves and to sell in their city's *agora*, or marketplace. While some parts of Greece had large farms owned by wealthy men who employed hundreds of laborers and slaves to farm their many acres of farmland, most of the city-states developed policies that allowed numerous citizens to own small family farms, consisting of a few acres that were

handled by a single farmer, his family members, and perhaps a few slaves or paid seasonal laborers. Indeed, to a large extent the Greeks envisioned farming as the ideal life, allowing individuals to remain close to nature and achieve the important goal of *autarkeia*, or self-sufficiency. As Xenophon (ca. 430–354 BCE) stated in his *Oikonimikos*, "I am fully persuaded as to the propriety of making agriculture the basis of life. I see it is altogether noblest, best, and pleasantest to do so." Later, Greek poets like Theocritus, who lived sometime in the third century BCE, developed a form of poetry, termed pastoral, explicitly devoted to celebrating the virtues of rustic life.

However, while Theocritus's herdsmen seem to enjoy plenty of leisure time to engage in friendly poetic competitions, the lives of the people who made their living by growing crops and tending livestock could actually be rather arduous, for several reasons. The terrain of Greece was hilly, so that by one estimate, only twenty percent of the land was suitable for farming. Further, the soil tended to be very poor, despite regular use of fertilizers like ash and manure; to keep the soil productive, the Greeks generally left their fields fallow after each harvest, and they developed a system of rotating crops. The climate was also less than ideal, since Greece's hot, dry summers could damage growing plants even though farmers would dig many small channels to bring water to their crops. One strategy that farmers employed, recommended by the poet Hesiod (ca. 700 BCE) in his *Works and Days*, was to plant in the autumn and harvest in the spring, to avoid exposing crops to the summer heat, but heavy rains would sometimes wash away the seeds. As another necessary chore, every stage in the process would have to be accompanied by a sacrifice or religious ritual, to ensure the cooperation of the gods in achieving a bountiful harvest.

The technology of farming in ancient Greece was also rather primitive. To prepare the soil and plant their seeds, farmers had to depend upon a simple type of wooden plow with an iron blade, dragged through the ground by donkeys, mule, or oxen; the farmer or his slave would walk behind the animals with a hoe to crush clumps of earth while dropping and burying seeds into the ground. Sometimes the ground was so hard that the farmer would need to use a pickaxe to further loosen the soil for seeding. When the crops were fully grown, they would have to be harvested by hand, as every available laborer would cut them down with a curved sword or sickle; even the women of the house would participate in gathering the crops, since the work had to be completed quickly.

The Greek farmers were limited in the crops they could raise; grapes, figs, and olives were their most successful products, especially since they could be planted on hillsides. However, since grains were harder to grow in the Greek soil, only a few regions were able to grow barley and wheat, requiring the city-states to rely primarily on imported grain to make their breads. In some regions of Greece, farmers were able to grow some vegetables (onions, lentils, peas, garlic, and cabbages), fruits (cherries, pears, plums, dates, and apples), and herbs (sage, thyme, mint, and oregano). Farmers could also profit by growing flowers, which were sold to be used in the wreaths and garlands observed at every city-state's numerous festivals.

Raising livestock was another common occupation, since animals could productively graze on hillsides that were unsuitable for agriculture. Unlike modern farmers, the Greeks used cattle mainly for various tasks, and goats were the principal suppliers of milk. Sheep were raised to obtain wool for clothing; pigs were regularly slaughtered as sacrifices or meat; and horses were raised by wealthy farmers for soldiers to ride in battle. These animals, not kept in pens, were allowed to roam, but they had to be constantly watched and guided by herdsmen to ensure that they did not start eating the crops. Since honey was the only source of sweetness in the Greek diet, some farmers were also beekeepers.

Images on Greek pottery provide information about some of the specific techniques employed to harvest certain crops. For example, olives grew on tall trees, so that men would have to stand on the ground and use sticks to dislodge the ripe olives from the branches; when olives were too high to be reached by the sticks, boys would have to climb the trees to pick them and throw them to the ground, where they would be gathered by the women. To produce olive oil, the olives were crushed into pulp to remove their pits and placed in baskets; then, an olive press would employ large counterweights to apply great pressure to the baskets and produce the oil. Grapes would be hand-picked to the rhythm provided by a man playing a flute, gathered in large baskets, and dropped into elevated vats so that they could stomped by barefoot men and women into a liquid. A spout at the bottom of the vat would direct the liquid into jars, where it would be left until it fermented into the wine that accompanied most Greek meals. When grain was harvested, it would first have to be threshed, typically by laying the sheaves on a floor where they could be trampled by a team of mules, forced to walk in circles while attached by a rope to a central pillar. The women would then grind the grain by hand using a stone mortar and pestle.

In addition to the basic tasks of growing and harvesting crops, ancient Greek farmers needed to be masters of other arts as well. Without calendars or almanacs to guide them, farmers had to be amateur astronomers, tracking the movements of the Moon and stars in order to determine exactly when crops should be planted and harvested; in some cases, observing the annual migrations of birds provided important signals as well. A farmer would need to build his own plow out of the wood found in forests, a skill described at length in Hesiod's *Works and Days*. While the Greeks did have some veterinarians, or *hippiatrikoi*, who specialized in taking care of animals, their services could be expensive, so that most farmers had to learn how to treat and cure their own sick animals. Finally, to make a profit from their surplus crops, farmers would have to transport them to the city, perhaps by constructing and sailing a small boat, and sell them in small stalls within the *agora*, so they would need to be skillful in bargaining with customers to obtain the best price.

Despite the demands and hardships of farming, it seems clear that most farmers enjoyed their daily lives, as is suggested by a play by Aristophanes (ca. 446–386 BCE), *The Peace*, which takes place at a time when many rural laborers had been forced to move to Athens because of the Peloponnesian War. As peace seems imminent, a character named Trygaeus expresses a longing to get back to his former occupation: "I also burn to go into the country and to turn over the earth I have so long neglected. Friends, do you remember the happy life that Peace afforded us formerly; can you recall the splendid baskets of figs, both fresh and dried, the myrtles, the sweet wine, the

PASTORAL POETS

Today, much of our information about ancient Greek farming comes from Hesiod, a farmer who decided to concentrate on writing instead. In modern times, other noteworthy individuals have been both farmers and writers. For example, the twentieth-century poet Robert Frost, although he was raised in the city of San Francisco and aspired to become a poet, spent nine years primarily supporting himself by working on a farm in New Hampshire, writing poems whenever he could. While he later abandoned farming for teaching until his poetry garnered global renown, he continued to live in the country, and he drew upon his farming experiences to produce some of his best-loved poems.

FAVORITE FLUIDS

In ancient Greece, most agriculture was carried out on small family farms, and the evidence suggests that the two most profitable products for their farmers were olive oil and wine, since shipwrecks frequently contain numerous *amphoras* (ceramic containers) filled with these liquids for delivery to other nations. Today, much about Greek agriculture has changed, but small family farms remain most common, and while wine is no longer a major export, the country remains one of the world's largest producers of olive oil. By one report, Greece is now the third-leading exporter of olive oil, behind Italy and Spain.

violets blooming near the spring, and the olives, for which we have wept so much?" Perhaps modern scholars tend to deemphasize the Greek affection for agriculture because so many of the writers they study were city dwellers, but there are fortunately a few writers who were also farmers, like Hesiod, Xenophon, and Theocritus, to remind us of how central this profession was to the people of ancient Greece.

Further Reading

Burford, Alison. 1993. *Land and Labor in the Greek World*. Baltimore, MD: John Hopkins University Press.

Foxhall, Lin. 2007. *Olive Cultivation in Ancient Greece: Seeking the Ancient Economy*. Oxford: Oxford University Press.

Hanson, Victor David. 1999. *The Other Greeks: The Family Farm and the Agrarian Roots of Western Civilization*. Second edition. Berkeley and Los Angeles: University of California Press.

Hanson, Victor David. 1998. *Warfare and Agriculture in Classical Greece*. Revised edition. Berkeley and Los Angeles: University of California Press.

Isager, Signe, and Jens Erik Skydsgaard. 1992. *Ancient Greek Agriculture: An Introduction*. New York and London: Routledge.

Nelson, Stephanie. 1998. *God and the Land: The Metaphysics of Farming in Hesiod and Vergil: With a Translation of Hesiod's Works and Days by David Grene*. Oxford: Oxford University Press.

Document

From Hesiod. C. 700 BCE. *Hesiod, the Homeric Hymns, and Homerica*. Translated by Hugh G. Evelyn-White. 1914. London: William Heinemann.

In this passage from Works and Days, *the ancient Greek poet Hesiod provides some advice on how and when a farmer should plow his land.*

So soon as the time for ploughing is proclaimed to men, then make haste, you and your slaves alike, in wet and in dry, to plough in the season for ploughing, and bestir yourself early in the morning so that your fields may be full. Plough in the spring; but fallow broken up in the summer will not belie your hopes. Sow fallow land when the soil is still getting light: fallow land is a defender from harm and a soother of children.

Pray to Zeus of the Earth and to pure Demeter to make Demeter's holy grain sound and heavy, when first you begin ploughing, when you hold in your hand the end of the plough-tail and bring down your stick on the backs of the oxen as they draw on the pole-bar by the yoke-straps. Let a slave follow a little behind with a mattock and make trouble for the birds by hiding the seed; for good management is the best for mortal men as bad management is the worst. In this way your corn-ears will bow to the ground with fullness if the Olympian himself gives a good result at the last, and you will sweep the cobwebs from your bins and you will be glad, I ween, as you take of your garnered substance. And so you will have plenty till you come to grey springtime, and will not look wistfully to others, but another shall be in need of your help. But if you plough the good ground at the solstice, you will reap sitting, grasping a thin crop in your hand, binding the sheaves awry, dust-covered, not glad at all; so you will bring all home in a basket and not many will admire you.

Historians

Since the beginning of civilization, people have displayed an interest in remembering important events of the past, but they tended to lack any concern for strict accuracy in recording those events; stories were refashioned to match the attitudes and expectations of their audiences, and mythical gods and magical elements might be freely intermingled with the facts. Thus, most scholars are confident that there is much historical truth in ancient texts like the *Iliad* and *Odyssey* by Homer (ca. 800–701 BCE), but they also recognize that they contain other, less truthful material added to provide audiences with a more entertaining story. The ancient Greeks, largely due to the works of two men named Herodotus (ca. 484–425 BCE) and Thucydides (460–395 BCE), introduced the idea that it was important to report to provide posterity with trustworthy accounts of what had actually happened during important periods of a nation's history. In doing so, historian Torrey James Luce has argued, these pioneering historians were strongly influenced by Homer in two important respects: they strived to emulate his dramatic manner of writing in telling their stories of wars and warriors, often referring to his *Iliad* in their writings, but they recoiled against his willingness to mingle historical truths with fanciful inventions. True, they were not as meticulously accurate as contemporary historians: Herodotus's work contains mythology as well as history, and Thucydides openly admitted that he himself had actually written the speeches attributed in his text to historical figures. Still, unlike previous narratives about the past, their texts can be regarded as genuine histories, largely based on first-hand accounts and careful research.

While these individuals, and other ancient historians whose works and reputations have survived, were widely known and respected, it is difficult to regard being a historian as a profession in the modern sense, since there was no obvious way for such people to earn money directly from the labor of researching and writing a historical text. Most of the Greek historians we know about, it seems, came from wealthy or politically powerful families and hence possessed the wherewithal to pursue their interests without being concerned about compensation. Historians also suffered from the perception, endorsed by the great philosopher Aristotle (384–322 BCE) in his *Poetics*, that their works were less valuable than literature, since literature could present the universal truths of the human condition while history was limited to particular facts about particular people that may or may not illustrate important principles. However, there were undoubtedly some financial rewards to be garnered from becoming a renowned historian. In Athens, for example, after Herodotus read aloud from his *Histories*, completed around the middle of the fifth century BC, the Athenians were reportedly so pleased by his efforts that they awarded him a substantial prize, equivalent to about $60,000 in modern currency. Noted historians also were surely welcome as guests for extended periods of time in the homes of nobles and rich families, and they may have been paid to work as tutors for their children as well.

The first man that we can describe as a historian was probably Hecataeus of Miletus, who lived sometime in the fifth or sixth century BCE. Only fragments of his major works, the *Periegesis* and the *Genealogies*, have survived, but the frequently quoted opening line of the later work proclaims his innovative determination to produce a genuine history: "Hecataeus of Miletus speaks thus. I write what seems to me to be true; for the Greeks have many tales which, as it appears to me, are absurd." It is believed that Hecataeus had a strong influence on Herodotus, the man described by the Roman orator Cicero as the "father of history" and the first historian whose complete text has been preserved, since he was clearly familiar with his writings and refers to him in his *Histories*. Herodotus was born in the Greek colony of Halicarnassus on the coast of Asia Minor (present-day Turkey), which was then ruled by Persia. Since he came from a prominent family, he was free to investigate historical matters by traveling extensively throughout the Mediterranean world, including a visit to Athens where he socialized with the playwright Sophocles (ca. 497–406 BCE).

Based on what he had learned, Herodotus then set out to record the history of the successful Greek wars against the Persians. While his writings, as already indicated, included a great deal of mythology, hearsay, and errors, he was still much more accurate and thorough than any previous chroniclers of past events, and his work was praised for that reason.

The other major historian of classical Greece, Thucydides, was born into wealth, but he did not lead an easy life, as he served in the Athenian military during the Peloponnesian War against Sparta, keeping detailed notes of all his experiences. After serving as

The facial expression on this bust of the Greek historian Thucydides, who lived during the fifth century BCE, is intended to convey both the toughness of a military veteran and the wisdom of a renowned historian. (DeAgostini/Getty Images)

the general who headed an unsuccessful naval expedition, he was exiled from Athens and spent many years traveling before returning to Athens in 404 BCE to begin writing his *History of the Peloponnesian War*, which was still incomplete at the time of his death in 396 BC. Except for the eloquent speeches that he composed for the leaders in his narrative, such as the famed Funeral Oration of Pericles (495–429 BCE), Thucydides was so scrupulously factual in describing the major events of the conflict that modern historian Will Durant has described him as "the father of the scientific method in history."

A third historian, Xenophon (ca. 430–354 BCE), first studied under Socrates (ca. 469–399 BCE) before becoming a general and finally turning to a writing career. Along with other texts on various subjects, he produced a continuation of Thucydides's work, the *Hellenica*, which completed the story of the Peloponnesian War; however, his most highly acclaimed work, the *Anabasis*, related his own story about participating in a Greek expedition against the Persians and the soldiers' subsequent efforts to return to Greece. He was able to support himself as an author because, while fighting for Sparta against the Persians, he had captured a wealthy Persian and received a substantial ransom for his safe return. Another prominent historian who lived during the Hellenistic period, a man named Polybius (ca. 200–118 BCE), was initially a political and military leader in Arcadia, but after the Roman conquerors of Greece deported the country's prominent figures to Italy, he survived by working as a tutor in Rome and eventually began to write history. In his major text, the *Histories*, he described the rise of Rome and its successful effort to dominate Greece; however, only lengthy excerpts from that work and his other writings have been preserved.

Discussions of the ancient Greek historians tend to focus on major figures like Herodotus, Thucydides, Xenophon, and Polybius because the writings of the other Greek historians, for the most part, have been entirely lost or are represented today only by brief quotations and references in other sources. We know, for example, that an historian named Ephorus produced, sometime in the fourth century BC, no less than twenty-nine volumes that endeavored to relate the entire history of the known world, but no

SPURIOUS SPEECHES

In writing his history of the Peloponnesian War, the Greek historian Thucydides freely admitted that he himself composed some speeches attributed to historical figures, including the famed Funeral Oration of Pericles. Later historians have taken similar liberties; for example, the Revolutionary War patriot Patrick Henry is now best remembered for delivering a stirring speech in which he declared, "Give me liberty or give me death." However, this speech did not appear in print until seventeen years after his death, in a biography by William Wirt, and while Wirt claimed that the text was based on the detailed memories of witnesses, most historians believe that Wirt wrote the speech himself.

MAKING AND WRITING HISTORY

Xenophon first served as a general in Greece's Peloponnesian War, and he later wrote part of its history, continuing Thucydides's account in his own *Hellenica*. This combination of history maker and history writer has occasionally been observed in later eras. In the 1940s, Winston Churchill served as Great Britain's prime minister during World War II, and following the Allied victory he wrote a definitive, six-volume history of the war, beginning with *The Gathering Storm* (1948). After the final volume was published in 1953, Churchill was given the Nobel Prize in Literature largely to honor his massive and eloquent history of the war he had helped to win.

copies of these works have ever been discovered. Dozens of other historians are similarly remembered for their contributions, and if the later historian Plutarch (ca. 46–120 CE) is to be believed, there were literally hundreds of ancient Greek historians. However, since their treatises are not available, modern scholars seeking information about ancient Greek history are often obliged to rely on historians who worked well after Greece had been conquered by Rome, such as Plutarch, who wrote in the first century CE; his *Parallel Lives* offered paired biographies of prominent Greeks and Romans, and he also produced a biography of Alexander the Great (356–323 BCE).

Overall, while there is much to appreciate about the work of the ancient historians, modern scholars can find them frustrating as well. Their literary flourishes at times seem to compromise the value of their writing as an historical record, and almost invariably, the Greek historians focused their attention on wars, and on the military and political leaders involved in those wars. While these conflicts were certainly important to the people that they affected, we would also like to know more about conditions in ancient Greece during its long periods of peace, and more about the everyday lives of the men, women, and children who were not part of the nation's social and political elite. Instead, for the history of such matters, interested investigators are obliged to ignore the Greek historians and glean whatever data they can from other forms of Greek literature like poetry, drama, and philosophy.

Further Reading

Foster, Edith, and Donald Lateiner, editors. 2012. *Thucydides and Herodotus*. Oxford: Oxford University Press.

Hunt, Peter. 1998. *Slaves, Warfare, and Ideology in the Greek Historians*. Cambridge: Cambridge University Press.

Luce, Torrey James. 1997. *The Greek Historians*. New York: Routledge.

Luraghi, Nino, editor. 2001. *The Historian's Craft in the Age of Herodotus*. Oxford: Oxford University Press.

Marincola, John. 1997. *Authority and Tradition in Ancient Historiography*. Cambridge: Cambridge University Press.

McGing, Brian. 2010. *Polybius' Histories*. Oxford: Oxford University Press.

Document

From Polybius. C. 130 CE. *Polybius: The Histories*. Volume 1. Translated by W. R. Paton. 1922. Cambridge, MA: Harvard University Press.

In beginning his book, the Greek historian Polybius refers to previous historians in announcing the importance and value of history.

Had the praise of History been passed over by former chroniclers, it would perhaps have been incumbent upon me to urge the choice and special study of records of this sort as the readiest means men can have of correcting their knowledge of the past. But my predecessors have not been sparing in this respect. They have all begun and ended, so to speak, by enlarging on this theme: asserting again and again that the study of History is in the truest sense an education and a training for political life, and that the most instructive, or rather the only, method of learning to bear with dignity the vicissitudes of fortune is to recall the catastrophes of others. It is evident, therefore, that no one need think it his duty to repeat what has been said by many, and said well. Least of all myself, for the surprising nature of the events which I have undertaken to relate is in itself sufficient to challenge and stimulate the attention of everyone, old or young, to the study of my work. Can anyone be so indifferent or idle as not to care to know by what means, and under what kind of polity, almost the whole inhabited world was conquered and brought under the dominion of the single city of Rome, and that, too, within a period of not quite fifty-three years [219–167 BCE]? Or who again can be so completely absorbed in other subjects of contemplation or study, as to think any of them superior in importance to the accurate understanding of an event for which the past affords no precedent?

Household Managers

While the women of ancient Greece were rarely given an education, and were barred from most professions, Greek wives were always responsible for the management of their homes, a task that could require both strenuous physical labor and considerable intelligence. This was particularly true because Greek husbands tended to spend most of their time away from home, so they were rarely available to provide assistance or advice; in contrast, Greek wives were generally expected to spend their entire lives at home, except to visit and speak with female neighbors, attend religious festivals, or participate in important rituals like weddings and funerals. In poor families, the wife might have to do most of the household chores herself, assisted only by her female children and perhaps a single slave; a wealthy woman, in contrast, would effectively function as the administrator of a large staff of slaves and hired servants who would take care of all required tasks.

All respectable women were expected to become wives, but their marriages were usually arranged by their families, so that romantic love was rarely an element in these pairings; rather, men and women might have sexual relationships before marriage, but the man would eventually feel obliged to get married, often not until they reached the age of thirty, for the primary purpose of having sons to carry on his family. These men would typically seek a woman no older than fifteen who came from a suitable family, not a woman that they were attracted to, and the marriage was always arranged by speaking to the prospective bride's male relatives. As illustrated by the Greek myth of Persephone, who was forcibly abducted to become the wife of Hades, the god of the underworld, women never had any choice about who they would marry. As was the case in other ancient societies, then, marriage was more like a business arrangement: the man provided his wife with financial security in exchange for her bearing children and tending to household duties. Husbands and wives might have little daily contact—even in their homes, which were typically divided into men's and women's quarters—and in some cases actively disliked each other; the philosopher Socrates (469–399 BCE), for example, was reputed to spend almost all of his time away from home in part because he could not bear the company of his wife Xanthippe (ca. 420–360 BCE). Still, it is reasonable to assume that husbands and wives regularly conversed, and that wives could exercise some influence over their husbands' decisions. For example, in a speech reportedly written by Demosthenes (384–322 BCE) to argue for the conviction of a woman named Neaera, jurors were advised to find her guilty because an acquittal would anger their wives.

Since children, especially male children, were considered so important, and since the Greeks lacked any techniques for birth control, Greek wives were regularly pregnant while doing their daily tasks, and they would give birth in their homes, assisted solely by a midwife and female friends and relatives. Many women died in childbirth, largely due to poor sanitary practices. If a Greek wife for any reason was unable to bear children, Aristophanes (ca. 466–386 BCE) suggests in his play *The Thesmophoriazusae* that she might pretend to be pregnant and, at the moment of purported birth, smuggle a purchased baby into her home, but one cannot be sure if this farcical playwright was serious in making this claim.

One task of the household manager was the daily preparation of food. There were typically two meals: a small lunch, or *ariston*, and a large dinner, or *deipnon*. Bread, which could either be baked at home or purchased from a baker, was the main dish, usually made from the grain barley, since wheat was difficult to grow in Greece; the bread was accompanied by olive oil (used instead of butter), cheese, onions, and honey. Various sorts of fish and seafood would sometimes be cooked over an outdoor fire in warm weather, while an indoor brazier was employed in the winter; and eels were especially appreciated. Vegetables and nuts might be served raw, or cooked in a broth or soup, while meat was a rare delicacy. Daily meals involved simple recipes and could be prepared quickly, but more elaborate dishes would have to be prepared for the large banquets that the Greeks regularly enjoyed—though the women of the house would never participate, as their role was solely to cook the food and serve it to their husbands and their male guests.

In addition, sewing required a great deal of the household manager's attention, since women were expected to make the clothes worn by all members of their families, and material was also needed for bedding and wall coverings. They would begin by purchasing and cleaning some suitable wool, then extracting the fibers with a special comb; next, the wool would be dyed in a vat. Finally, after spinning the wool by hand, the women would use a loom to sew the wool into large, rectangular pieces of fabric and fashion them into the relatively simple robes and tunics favored by the Greeks and other items. However, some pieces of the women's own clothing, such as jewelry, would have to be purchased during one of the household manager's rare shopping trips outside the home.

Another major responsibility of the household manager was to watch and educate her children, and while slaves undoubtedly provided some assistance, we can assume that the wife herself handled much of this work. Both boys and girls would be under the wife's supervision until the age of seven, when the boys would start receiving instructions in schools or

HOUSEHUSBANDS

Unless they were very wealthy, ancient Greek women were forced into the role of household manager, since they were not allowed to hold other jobs. This situation remained commonplace throughout the world until recent times, when women demanded and obtained the right to enter any profession they preferred. Some women, however, are still choosing to be stay-at-home mothers, tending to their children and domestic duties; growing numbers of men are similarly deciding to become "househusbands," taking care of the home while their wives go to work. These men have founded an organization, the National At-Home Dad Network, to provide support for those who are finding fulfillment in this nontraditional role.

A WOMAN'S WORK

The most famous household manager of ancient Greece, Socrates's wife Xanthippe, is also the most reviled; for while contemporaries only praised her, later writers described her as shrewish and intemperate. Perhaps her reputed anger stemmed from the fact that she was surely one of the busiest women in Athens, since her perpetually absent husband was never around to assist in managing their home or raising their three sons. And to this day, wives regularly complain that their husbands do not do their share of household work, even though the pattern now is for both husbands and wives to have full-time jobs.

from male tutors. Although girls received no formal education, some mothers taught their female children how to read and write, and they would also learn arts such as cooking, sewing, and playing a musical instrument. In addition to their roles as teachers, the household managers were also expected to take care of sick or elderly relatives, and they were in charge of their household budgets; thus, they had to be careful that the family's money was spent carefully, even though men would usually do most of the shopping. The visible sign of the wife's authority in this area was the set of keys that she carried to open the rooms that contained supplies; so, if a husband wanted some extra onions or another bottle of wine, he would have to ask his wife to unlock the door, allowing her to monitor, and perhaps control, his consumption of the family's resources.

Household managers also faced some arduous chores. For one thing, since the ancient Greeks generally lacked indoor plumbing, it was necessary to regularly walk to a local well or fountain in order to fill containers of water and bring them back to the house; a poor woman would often have to do this herself, though her wealthier counterparts would usually have slaves bring water. In homes that were also farms, the women would have to milk the goats and the sheep every day, and at harvest time they would participate in gathering the crops. One can also assume that many other household tasks, such as washing dishes, washing and mending clothes, and cleaning, occupied much of a woman's daily schedule.

Despite such labors, however, and their many daily responsibilities, there can be little doubt that household managers enjoyed some leisure time as well; the plays of Aristophanes, for example, suggest that they would always find some time to gossip with their neighbors and exchange complaints about their husbands. Many of these women must also have found it genuinely rewarding to prepare certain dishes, or interact with their children, and when their husbands were away fighting during times of war, they enjoyed complete control the affairs of their households. Still, many women must have found it frustrating to be limited to the business of managing their homes, as evidenced by the rare women like Sappho (died ca. 570 BCE) and Aspasia (ca. 470–400 BCE) who ventured into all-male fields like literature and education while continuing, one assumes, to tend to their domestic duties. As is true of many other civilizations, then, ancient Greece shamefully underutilized the talents of its female citizens by forcing them to always stay at home.

Further Reading

Ault, Bradley A., and Lisa C. Nevett, editors. 2005. *Ancient Greek Houses and Households: Chronological, Regional, and Social Diversity*. Philadelphia: University of Pennsylvania Press.

Blundell, Sue. 1995. *Women in Ancient Greece*. Cambridge, MA: Harvard University Press.

Brulé, Pierre. 2003. *Women of Ancient Greece*. Edinburgh: Edinburgh University Press.

Lefkowitz, Mary R., and Maureen B. Fant, editors. 2005. *Women's Life in Greece and Rome: A Source Book in Translation*. Third edition. Baltimore, MD: John Hopkins University Press.

MacLachlan, Bonnie, editor. 2012. *Women in Ancient Greece: A Sourcebook*. London and New York: Continuum.

Nevett, Lisa C. 2001. *House and Society in the Ancient Greek World*. Cambridge: Cambridge University Press.

Document

From Xenophon. C. 370 BCE. *Xenophon: Memorabilia and Oeconomicus*. Translated by E. C. Marchant. 1923. London: William Heinemann.

In this passage from Xenophon's Oeconomicus, *Ischomachus tells Socrates how he instructed his wife to manage their home.*

"Now," [said Ischomachus], "after seeing [the perfect ordering and organization of a ship's cargo], I told my wife: 'Considering that sailors aboard a merchant vessel, even though it be a little one, find room for things and keep order, though tossed violently to and fro, and find what they want to get, though terror-stricken, it would be downright carelessness on our part if we, who have large storerooms in our house to keep everything separate and whose house rests on solid ground, fail to find a good and handy place for everything. Would it not be sheer stupidity on our part?'

"How good it is to keep one's stock of utensils in order, and how easy to find a suitable place in a house to put each set in, I have already said. . .

"[So] we immediately set about [sorting and organizing the furniture]. We began by collecting the vessels we use in sacrificing. After that, we put together the women's holiday finery, and the men's holiday and war garb, blankets in the women's quarters, blankets in the men's quarters, women's shoes, men's shoes. Another category consisted of arms, and three others of implements for spinning, for bread making, or for cooking; others, again, of the things required for washing, at the kneading-trough, and for table use. All these we divided into two sets, things in constant use and things reserved for festivities. We also put by themselves the things consumed month by month, and set apart the supplies calculated to last for a year. This plan makes it easier to tell how they will last to the end of the time.

"When we had divided all the portable property. . . we arranged everything in its proper place. After that, we showed the servants who have to use them where to keep the utensils they require daily, for baking, cooking, spinning, and so forth; handed them over to their care and ordered them to see that they were safe and sound. The things that we use only for festivals or entertainments, or on rare occasions, we handed over to the housekeeper, and after showing her their places and counting and making a written list of all the items, we told her to give them out to the right servants, to remember what she gave to each of them, and when receiving them back, to put everything in the place from which she took it. . . .

"When all this was done, Socrates, I told my wife that all these measures were futile, unless she saw to it herself that our arrangement was strictly adhered to in every detail. I explained that in well-ordered cities, the citizens are not satisfied with passing good laws; they go further, and choose guardians of the laws, who act as overseers, commending the law-abiding and punishing law-breakers. So I encouraged my wife to consider herself a guardian of the laws of our household. And just as the commander of a garrison inspects his guards, so must she inspect the household goods whenever she thought it well to do so. . . . She was to make sure that everything was in good condition. Like a queen, she must reward the worthy with praise and honor, so far as in her lay, and not spare criticism and punishment when they were called for."

Mathematicians

Since the dawn of civilization, certain types of mathematics emerged as matters of necessity: numbers and basic arithmetic were essential to commerce, while rudimentary geometry was required when building large structures. Throughout the ancient world, many unknown individuals developed practical mathematical principles and techniques that were passed down from generation to generation in various professions. However, only in ancient Greece did there emerge the key concept that there existed an overarching theoretical structure to mathematics, founded on basic definitions and postulates that could be employed to prove certain theorems to be universally true.

This approach to mathematics is generally credited to the philosopher Thales (ca. 624–546 BCE), often described as the world's first mathematician. Some of the other individuals who contributed to the development of mathematics, however, are unknown; for example, it is almost certain that it was not Pythagoras (ca. 570–495 BCE) himself, but some later mathematician in his school, who first proved the Pythagorean theorem that became associated with his name. However, we do know about some prominent mathematicians who wrote treatises and interacted with major figures in Greek history. Some of these men are also referred to as philosophers, since there were then no clear divi-

The ancient Greek who carved this bust of the Pythagoras probably esteemed him most as a philosopher, not a mathematician, but he is now known primarily for the geometric theorem bearing his name, even though it was one of his followers, not Pythagoras himself, who first proved this theorem. (Jupiterimages)

sions between the fields, and they often worked in fields outside of mathematics; thus, Thales is also highly regarded for his contributions to Greek philosophy and science. It is only today that we tend to identify some of these individuals as mathematicians because that is the area where their work proved most significant.

To be sure, these men did not earn their living by articulating postulates and proving theorems; rather, like mathematicians today, most were employed as educators, typically working as tutors for the children of wealthy individuals or members of the nobility. Others may have had other professions; according to Aristotle (384–322 BCE), for example, after Thales predicted a period of favorable weather that would bring a large harvest of olives, he purchased a large number of olive presses, so he could profitably rent them when they were needed to turn the harvested olives into the olive oil that the ancient Greeks prized. One of the greatest Greek mathematicians, Archimedes (287–212 BCE), was regularly employed by his friend, King Hiero II of Syracuse (270–215 BCE), to solve practical problems; these included the creation of the Archimedes screw, a device that raises water to a higher level, and his ingenious technique for determining that a wreath purportedly made from solid gold actually contained silver as well by immersing it in water and observing how much water was displaced—the discovery he made in a bathtub that supposedly prompted him to run naked through the streets happily shouting "Eureka," or "I have found it." However, scholars and scientists have since decided that although Archimedes was certainly a brilliant early mathematician and engineer, he never wrote of the bath discovery himself, and it was more likely first written about by Vitruvius, a Roman writer, some 200 years later, who either embellished on a story passed along, or who invented it himself. A few noted mathematicians, like Democritus (ca. 460–370 BCE), came from wealthy families and hence were free to pursue their interests without worrying about earning a living. But other mathematicians struggled to support themselves, like Euxodus (480–355 BCE), who grew up very poor; however, recognizing his unusual potential, his friends provided him with funds to travel and learn more about mathematics. Later, he became famous enough to attract paying students and thus earn some needed money.

In pursuing their interests, the Greek mathematicians faced certain obstacles that many may not appreciate. For one thing, since ink and papyrus to write on were considered valuable commodities, one could not waste them to take notes or work out the steps in solving a problem; instead, both students and instructors would use tablets covered with wax, and when they were finished with their work they could smooth out the wax to be written on again. At times, undoubtedly, mathematicians would have to struggle to reconstruct their thought processes in completing a proof because they had no scratch paper to consult. More broadly, they were burdened by a clumsy number system that used letters to represent numbers and offered no straightforward way to perform calculations, though the Greeks did use a form of the abacus, a board with grooves where stones could be placed. They also lacked the useful algebraic notation later developed by Hindu and Arabic mathematicians, so they had to render their equations and problems in words and sentences. This helps to explain why the Greeks were weak in algebra but strong in geometry, where they could readily sketch and reason from figures drawn with rulers and compasses like modern students. Finally, the manuscripts that explained mathematical findings could be difficult to locate, so a mathematician working in a certain area might have to travel to one of the region's few libraries, like the famous facility at Alexandria, to learn what he needed to know, or he might have to consult a well-known mathematician in another city.

One cannot readily summarize all of the many contributions of the ancient Greek mathematicians, but two great achievements—one in practical math, the other in theoretical math—might serve to represent the breadth and significance of their accomplishments. The Greek mathematician Eratosthenes (276–195 BCE) learned that, on one day of the year at noon, the Sun shone directly into a well in the Egyptian city of Syene, indicating that the Sun was directly over the city at that time. He reasoned that the Sun was far enough away from Earth that its rays could be regarded as parallel lines, and on the same day, he went to another city, Alexandria, and found that at the same time a tower cast a shadow of 7.2 degrees. If the two rays hitting the well and the tower were parallel, and if the vertical tower was aligned with a line

ATHLETIC MATHEMATICIANS

Eratosthenes, the Greek geographer and mathematician who first calculated the circumference of the Earth, was also a renowned athlete, described as a champion in five Olympic sports. This unusual combination of talents can also be observed today in the person of Nate Ackerman, who competed for Great Britain as a wrestler at the 2004 Olympic Games before earning a PhD in mathematics from the Massachusetts Institute of Technology in 2006 and becoming a visiting professor of mathematics at Harvard University. And, while not yet a mathematician of Eratosthenes's stature, Ackerman is now publishing original contributions to mathematics in articles for academic journals.

A PRESIDENTIAL PROOF

The most famous achievement of ancient Greek mathematics is the Pythagorean theorem, stating that when one adds the squares of the two sides of a right triangle making up its right angle, the sum equals the square of the third side. We do not know what proof was first devised by Pythagoras or a member of his school, but Euclid's *Elements* presents the oldest known proof, involving the construction of squares adjoining the sides of the triangle. Since that time, over 350 different proofs have been devised; one later proof, employing trapezoids, was developed by a future U.S. president, James Garfield, four years before his election in 1880.

that went to the center of the Earth, that meant that the angle between Earth's center, Alexandria, and Syene was the same as the angle of the shadow, 7.2 degrees, which was about 1/50 of 360 degrees. By obtaining a figure for the distance between the two cities, and multiplying it by 50, Eratosthenes determined that the circumference of the Earth was about 25,000 miles in modern units, a remarkably accurate measurement.

Another famous mathematician, Euclid (ca. 300 BCE), developed an elegant proof that there were an infinite number of prime numbers. He began by assuming that there was a finite number of prime numbers and imagined multiplying all of those numbers together and adding one. That sum, however, could not be divided by any prime numbers in the group, meaning that it was either prime itself or it was divisible by

some prime that was not in the group. In either case, a new prime number had been located, showing by this contradictory result that the original assumption was false, and that there must be an infinite number of prime numbers.

Since the vast majority of the treatises written by ancient Greek mathematicians have been lost, we cannot be sure about exactly how much they actually achieved, and the occasional discovery of a previously unknown text is always exciting to contemporary researchers. One area for investigation involves medieval manuscripts, since scribes sometimes reused older manuscripts made of valuable parchment by scraping off the ink and writing new words on the pages; however, by employing ultraviolet light and computer imaging technology, scientists today can read the erased material. By examining one medieval prayer book in this manner, researchers located several works of Archimedes, three of them previously lost, including one that surprisingly showed the mathematician using the techniques of integral calculus to solve certain problems. Perhaps, then, the accomplishments of Greek mathematics were even more impressive than we know them to be, as may be demonstrated by future rediscoveries of other lost texts.

Still, the ancient Greek mathematicians were also unwilling or unable to pursue certain lines of inquiry, leaving vast areas of mathematics to be developed by later mathematicians. For example, according to one dialogue by Plato (ca. 427–347 BCE), *Theaetetus*, a mathematician named Theodorus discovered that certain numbers, like the square roots of numbers that were not square, were irrational and could not be expressed as fractions, but this notion evidently disquieted the Greeks, and they did no further work in this area. In addition, comfortable with Euclid's postulate that there is precisely one line running through a point that is parallel to another line not containing that point, the Greeks failed to recognize that, by assuming that there is no such line, or that there are more than one such line, one could develop two entirely different, non-Euclidean systems of geometry, as was finally understood in the nineteenth century. Thus, one can credit the Greek mathematicians with laying the foundations of mathematics, but they also bequeathed to their successors many challenges that they did not overcome.

Further Reading

Christianidis, Jean, editor. 2004. *Classics in the History of Greek Mathematics*. Dordrecht, The Netherlands: Kluwer Academic Publishers.

Cuomo, Serafina. 2001. *Ancient Mathematics*. London and New York: Routledge.

Nicastro, Nicholas. 2008. *Circumference: Eratosthenes and the Ancient Quest to Measure the Globe*. New York: St. Martin's Press.

Riedwig, Christoph. 2002. *Pythagoras: His Life, Teaching, and Influence*. Translated by Steven Rendall. 2005. Ithaca, NY: Cornell University Press.

Rudman, Peter S. 2007. *How Mathematics Happened: The First 50,000 Years*. New York: Prometheus Books.

Tuplin, C.J., and T.E. Rihll, editors. 2002. *Science and Mathematics in Ancient Greek Culture*. Oxford: Oxford University Press.

Documents

From Plato. C. 369 BCE. *The Dialogues of Plato*. Volume 4 Translated by Benjamin Jowett. 1892. Oxford: Clarendon Press.

In this excerpt from the dialogue Theaetetus, *the philosopher Plato (427–327 BCE), in the course of making a point about knowledge, explains a way of dividing rational and irrational numbers.*

[Theaetetus:] Theodorus was writing out for us something about roots, such as the roots of three or five, showing that they are incommensurable by the unit: he selected other examples up to seventeen—there he stopped. Now as there are innumerable roots, the notion occurred to us of attempting to include them all under one name or class.

[Socrates:] And did you find such a class?

[Theaetetus:] I think that we did; but I should like to have your opinion.

[Socrates:] Let me hear.

[Theaetetus:] We divided all numbers into two classes: those which are made up of equal factors multiplying into one another, which we compared to square figures and called square or equilateral numbers; that was one class.

[Socrates:] Very good.

[Theaetetus:] The intermediate numbers, such as three and five, and every other number which is made up of unequal factors, either of a greater multiplied by a less, or of a less multiplied by a greater, and when regarded as a figure, is contained in unequal sides; all these we compared to oblong figures, and called them oblong numbers.

[Socrates:] Capital; and what followed?

[Theaetetus:] The lines, or sides, which have for their squares the equilateral plane numbers, were called by us lengths or magnitudes; and the lines which are the roots of (or whose squares are equal to) the oblong numbers, were called powers or roots; the reason of this latter name being, that they are commensurable with the former, i.e., with the so-called lengths or magnitudes not in linear measurement, but in the value of the superficial content of their squares; and the same about solids.

[Socrates:] Excellent, my boys; I think that you fully justify the praises of Theodorus, and that he will not be found guilty of false witness.

From Porphyry. C. 390 CE. *Pythagorean Library: A Complete Collection of the Surviving Works of Works of Pythagoreans*. Translated by Kenneth Sylvan Guthrie. 1920. Alpine, NJ: Platonist Press.

In this passage from The Life of Pythagoras *by Porphyry (ca. 234–305 CE) the later Greek philosopher explains Pythagoras's beliefs about the value of mathematics and the meanings of numbers.*

[Pythagoras] cultivated philosophy, the scope of which is to free the mind implanted within us from the impediments and fetters within which it is confined; without whose freedom none can learn anything sound or true, or perceive the unsoundedness in the operation of sense. Pythagoras thought that mind alone sees and hears, while all the rest are blind and deaf. The purified mind should be applied to the discovery of beneficial things, which can be effected by, certain artificial ways, which by degrees induce it to the contemplation of eternal and incorporeal things, which never vary. This orderliness of perception should begin from consideration of the most minute things. . . .

That is the reason he made so much use of the mathematical disciplines and speculations, which are intermediate between the physical and the incorporeal realm, for the reason that like bodies they have a threefold dimension, and yet share the impassibility of incorporeals; as degrees of preparation to the contemplation of the really existent things; by an artificial reason diverting the eyes of the mind from corporeal things, whose manner and state never remain in the same condition, to a desire for true (spiritual) food. . . .

The Pythagoreans specialized in the study of numbers to explain their teachings symbolically, as do geometricians, inasmuch as the primary forms and principles are hard to understand and express, otherwise, in plain discourse. . . .

Number one denoted to them the reason of Unity, Identity, Equality, the purpose of friendship, sympathy, and conservation of the Universe, which results from persistence in Sameness. For unity in the details harmonizes all the parts of a whole, as by the participation of the First Cause.

Number two, or *Duad*, signifies the two-fold reason of diversity and inequality, of everything that is divisible, or mutable, existing at one time in one way, and at another time in another way. After all these methods were not confined to the Pythagoreans, being used by other philosophers to denote unitive powers, which contain all things in the universe, among which are certain reasons of equality, dissimilitude and diversity. These reasons are what they meant by the terms *Monad* and *Duad*, or by the words uniform, biform, or diversiform.

The same reasons apply to their use of other numbers, which were ranked according to certain powers. Things that had a beginning, middle and end, they denoted by the number Three, saying that anything that has a middle is triform, which was applied to every perfect thing. They said that if anything was perfect it would make use of this principle and be adorned, according to it; and as they had no other name for it, they invented the form *Triad*; and whenever they tried

to bring us to the knowledge of what is perfect they led us to that by the form of this *Triad*. So also with the other numbers, which were ranked according to the same reasons.

All other things were comprehended under a single form and power which they called *Decad*, explaining it by a pun as decad, meaning comprehension. That is why they called Ten a perfect number, the most perfect of all as comprehending all difference of numbers, reasons, species and proportions. For if the nature of the universe be defined according to the reasons and proportions of members, and if that which is produced, increased and perfected, proceed according to the reason of numbers; and since the *Decad* comprehends every reason of numbers, every proportion, and every species, why should Nature herself not be denoted by the most perfect number, Ten? Such was the use of numbers among the Pythagoreans.

Merchants

From one perspective, a majority of ancient Greek citizens could be described as merchants, at least on some occasions. Greek farmers and their families might consume much of the food they raised, but there were usually surpluses of certain crops, and farmers also needed money to purchase the foods and household items that they could not produce themselves. Thus, every year, they would need to bring a portion of their harvests to the city, pay a fee to set up a stall in the ancient Greek marketplace, the *agora*, and sell their goods. A fragment from a lost play by Euboulos, who lived sometime during the fourth century BCE, lists several of the foods that these farmers would typically sell, including figs, grapes, apples, pears, myrtle berries, honeycombs, and chickpeas. In addition, the local fishermen would rush their catches to the agora to be sold on marble slabs, because the Greeks had no way to keep fish cold to avoid rotting. Finally, the artisans of Greek cities—such as carpenters, potters, metalworkers, jewelers, and carpenters—would also have to make a living by selling their wares, either in the workshops where they labored or in their own stalls. In these ways, many Greeks had the regular experiences of trying to attract customers, bargaining with them to obtain the best price for their products, and counting their coins at the end of the day to determine how much they had profited.

However, none of these people would have regarded themselves as merchants, feeling that their principal avocation involving creating goods, not selling goods. Indeed, the Greeks tended to look down on the people who specialized in the marketing of products that were the work of others. These men were called *kapéloi*, and they were generally thought of as disreputable and even dishonest. However, they were also absolutely essential to the functioning of Greek society, since none of the city-states were able to grow all of their own food, or manufacture all of their own goods. Thus, they depended upon merchants who could travel to other lands in cargo ships and bring back necessary items like wheat, silk, spices, wood, and papyrus; the city-states also employed merchants to export certain items, like wine, olive oil and pottery, that they could profitably sell to foreigners. Due to the constant threats of piracy or shipwrecks, being

a merchant of this sort could often involve disastrous losses, but men freely accepted these risks because of the rich rewards that they could earn.

For people who could not regularly travel to the city to obtain what they needed, there was another sort of professional merchant, the peddler, who would travel through rural areas with various items that remote farmers might wish to purchase; while some would carry all their merchandise themselves, most peddlers depended upon donkeys or wagons. In addition to providing necessary items, peddlers could find it profitable to sell jewelry to rural women who could not otherwise obtain such adornments. Sometimes, since farmers did not always have currency on hand, peddlers would engage in barter, obtaining food in exchange for goods, which the peddlers could later sell in the city. There, instead of setting up a stall, these perpetually peripatetic merchants might walk through the streets, calling out what they had to sell to passing pedestrians. A story from Greek mythology reveals that peddling was a longstanding tradition: when

This ancient Greek wine vessel, or *krater*, from the fourth century BCE, shows a fisherman standing in the *agora* (marketplace), slicing up a fish to sell to a waiting customer. (Museo Archeologico, Cefalu, Sicily, Italy/Bridgeman Images)

Achilles's mother tried to keep him out of the Trojan War by dressing him as a woman, the clever Odysseus disguised himself as a peddler and revealed the hero's identity by tricking him into seizing a sword that he had offered for sale.

Another important type of merchant, the banker, emerged only when the city-states were established and began to issue their own local currencies. Thus, for commerce to take place throughout Greece, someone was needed to convert foreign coins into the local currency, creating a need for bankers. These figures also played key roles in financing trading expeditions and offering loans to other businessmen, charging interest rates that varied according to how risky the venture was deemed. Banking represented one of the few opportunities for foreign-born residents or slaves to become wealthy. One well-known example was an Athenian slave who lived during the fourth century BCE, Pasion; he initially worked for a bank and did such excellent work that his owners granted him his freedom. Eventually, he took control of the bank and earned so much money that he was able to provide needed funds to support the government, which eventually gave him an unusual reward by making him a citizen of Athens. Yet bankers, like other merchants, were not universally popular; the philosopher Diogenes (412–323 BCE), for example, initially worked in his father's bank, but he ultimately rejected this profession to both practice and promote a life of virtuous poverty.

Almost universally, the people who worked as merchants were male, although poorer women might assist their husbands in growing crops and crafting objects; wealthy women, however, limited their activities to household duties. Some poor women also worked on their own, performing services as maids, seamstresses, washerwomen, servants, and midwives. There were also the hetaerae, who are often referred to as the prostitutes of ancient Greece, although they might also entertain male customers in other ways by arranging parties, singing, and dancing. In some city-states like Corinth, it was also common for hetaerae to function as madams, owning and operating houses of prostitution and employing other women to perform the services requested by patrons. Needless to say, the women in these professions were generally foreign-born and were not respected by society, but

THE AMERICAN AGORA

Today, in cities outside the developed world, one finds open-air marketplaces recalling the ancient Greek *agora*, where both full-time and occasional merchants set up stalls to sell goods. In the United States, shopping takes place almost entirely within permanent buildings owned and operated by professional businesspersons. However, there are exceptions: at farmers' markets, local farmers bring fresh crops and sell them much like their ancient Greek counterparts; and at swap meets, or flea markets, recurring events in stadiums, drive-in theaters, and warehouses, any interested party can rent a space to sell products. And many come to swap meets, like the *agora*, primarily for the social experience, not the bargains.

INCENTIVES FOR ENTERPRISE

In his essay *Ways and Means*, the Greek historian Xenophon (430–254 BCE) suggested that Athens should offer financial incentives to encourage merchants to do business in their city, such as awards for officials who promptly resolve disputes and front-row seats at theaters for merchants and shipowners. Today, the usual way that U.S. states and cities try to attract business owners involves offering another sort of financial incentive—lower taxes. In particular, some cities have endeavored to revitalize their downtown areas by creating "enterprise zones" where new businesses can take advantage of tax breaks and fewer regulations.

prostitution represented one of the few ways that a woman might become independently wealthy and even famous. Thus, we are familiar with a few hetaerae because they emerged as prominent individuals in their city-states: Phryne of Athens, for example, was the model for the famed statue of Aphrodite by Praxiteles (both lived during the fourth century BCE), and she earned so much money from her trade that she volunteered to finance the reconstruction of the ruined walls of Thebes, though the city elders refused her offer because she insisted upon receiving official recognition for her contributions. Yet attaining such a high position in society also brought risks: both Phryne and another hetaera of that era, Neaira, were brought to trial for their alleged crimes, though these prosecutions were actually inspired by their political enemies.

Although some merchants were based in other areas, most business transactions were conducted in the *agora*, which most cities regulated in various ways. As indicated, all participants needed to pay a fee to set up a stall, and while there were no taxes on sales, imported goods were assessed customs duties, usually no more than two percent of their value. Since some purchases involved the weighing of goods, an official called the *metronomoi* would regularly measure the accuracy of the weights and scales used by merchants, to ensure that customers were not being shortchanged. Another official, the *agoranomoi*, would inspect goods to ensure that they were of reasonably good quality. The stalls in the *agora* were not arranged randomly, as it became the custom for members of certain professions to congregate in the same area, for the convenience of customers. Over time, as the *agora* came to function as a center for all civic activities, these marketplaces were provided with other facilities, such as fountains, courtrooms, statues, monuments, and gathering areas, but buying and selling remained the primary pursuit of the regular visitors.

Despite the vital role that merchants played in Greek society, the general disdain for the profession meant that the Greeks developed, at best, a very crude understanding of the general principles of economics, so that this became one of the few disciplines whose origins cannot be traced back to ancient Greece. Furthermore, since no thinkers were engaged in any effort to understand how the marketplace really worked, our knowledge of many aspects of the ancient Greek economy remains somewhat sketchy, with scattered bits of information gleaned from courtroom speeches, plays, illustrations on pottery, shipwrecks, and histories. Paradoxically, however, because economics is becoming more and more important to today's citizens, much of the recent research into the ancient Greeks has focused on an aspect of their lives that the Greeks themselves rarely examined.

Further Reading

Ameniya, Takeshi. 2007. *Economy and Economics of Ancient Greece*. London and New York: Routledge.

Cohen, Edward E. 1992. *Athenian Economy and Society: A Banking Perspective*. Princeton, NJ: Princeton University Press.

Lyttkens, Carl Hampus. 2013. *Economic Analysis of Institutional Change in Ancient Greece: Politics, Taxation and Rational Behaviour*. London and New York: Routledge.

Reden, Sitta von. 1995. *Exchange in Ancient Greece*. London: Duckworth.

Schaps, David M. 2004. *The Invention of Coinage and the Monetization of Ancient Greece*. Ann Arbor: University of Michigan Press.

Tandy, David W. 1997. *Warriors into Traders: The Power of the Market in Early Greece*. Berkeley and Los Angeles: University of California Press.

Document

From Xenophon. C. 270 BCE. *Scripta Minora*. Translated by E. C. Marchant. 1925. London: G. Heinemann.

In the course of discussing the advantages of Athens as a hub of commercial activity, the historian Xenophon describes, in his Ways and Means, *the activities and virtues of the city's merchants.*

I shall now say something of the unrivalled amenities and advantages of our city as a commercial centre.

In the first place, I presume, she possesses the finest and safest accommodation for shipping, since vessels can anchor here and ride safe at their moorings in spite of bad weather. Moreover, at most other ports merchants are compelled to ship a return cargo, because the local currency has no circulation in other states; but at Athens they have the opportunity of exchanging their cargo and exporting very many classes of goods that are in demand, or, if they do not want to ship a return cargo of goods, it is sound business to export silver; for, wherever they sell it, they are sure to make a profit on the capital invested.

If prizes were offered to the magistrates of the market for just and prompt settlement of disputes, so that sailings were not delayed, the effect would be that a far larger number of merchants would trade with us and with much greater satisfaction. It would also be an excellent plan to reserve front seats in the theatre for merchants and shipowners, and to offer them hospitality occasionally, when the high quality of their ships and merchandise entitles them to be considered benefactors of the state. With the prospect of these honours before them they would look on us as friends and hasten to visit us to win the honour as well as the profit.

The rise in the number of residents and visitors would of course lead to a corresponding expansion of our imports and exports, of sales, rents and customs. . . .

Metalworkers

Few professions in ancient Greece were as arduous and dangerous as metalworking; every aspect of the process of working with metals—mining ores, extracting the desired metals, creating alloys, and forging the metal into useful objects—involved hard labor in hazardous circumstances, often leading to injuries or premature deaths. Yet Greek civilization was dependent upon metal products: soldiers needed metal weapons and armor, all business transactions required metal coins, households employed various sorts of metal bowls and utensils, and wealthy women demanded attractive metal jewelry. Most of the preliminary work of producing such objects, predictably, was assigned to slaves, but the final stage of making the finished products could only be handled by skilled craftsmen.

Before any items could be crafted, the metals first had to be mined and processed from raw ores into pure metal. We know the most about the mining of silver, since Athens maintained a well-documented mine and processing facility in the nearly city of Laurium. After slaves arduously dug out the ore from the narrow corridors of the mine, it would be crushed by other slaves, using mortars and pestles, then ground into even smaller particles with revolving stones; the resulting material would be washed through screens to extract the bits of silver. These would be melted in furnaces and placed in porous cups, or cupels, to separate the silver from lead. The silver could then be transferred to trained silversmiths, who would hammer pieces of silver to create pieces of jewelry, vessels, and utensils.

Another prized metal, gold, was rare, but it required little processing since it could usually be found either in a relatively pure form or combined with silver as the natural alloy electrum; this alloy was one of the first metals used to make coins. After it was mined, gold was typically hammered into thin sheets that could be employed to decorate statues and buildings, though very wealthy Greeks could afford to purchase items of gold jewelry. Gold and silver were also shaped into small coins. In general, however, we do not know a great deal about products made from silver and gold, since only a few have survived; in almost all cases, they were later melted down so that people could reuse these precious metals.

Copper was obtained by smelting the ore malachite in a furnace; the copper was then mixed with molten tin to form the alloy bronze, which was stronger than pure copper. However, some coins of little value were sometimes made of pure copper. Because bronze could be easily melted, it became the preferred raw material for most manufactured objects; typically, the liquid bronze would be poured into stone casts to harden into the desired shape. While great quantities of bronze were used to make armor for soldiers, household items were often made of bronze as well, such as pots and bowls of various sizes and polished hand mirrors. Over the centuries, these bronze products became more elaborate: large pots were provided with handles and small feet to support them, while mirrors might be equipped with stands in the shape of draped women. To make objects like statues and figurines, the metalworker could first sculpt the image in wax, cover the wax with clay, and fire the clay to melt away the wax; the bronze was then poured into the space previously occupied by the wax, and when it was hardened, the clay covering was removed.

Iron was harder to employ because the Greek furnaces could not reach the very high temperatures needed to melt iron; instead, the metal could only be softened. To work with iron, the metal would first have to be placed inside of a blast furnace—a large tower made of bricks and clay that would usually be filled with charcoal and the metal. A bellows would fan the flame to produce the intense heat needed to soften the metal; then, an assistant would hold the hot iron with tongs while a blacksmith hammered it into shape on an anvil. Despite the dangers involved, metalworkers handling iron would often work naked because of the insufferable heat generated by the furnace, and jars of water were kept nearby to quench the men's thirst. Sometimes the furnace's heat would be generated by burning peat moss, which had the additional virtue of adding a bit of carbon to the iron and effectively transforming it into a crude form of steel. The Greeks also figured out that the forged iron objects could be strengthened by immediately placing them in water, a process called quenching, and then slightly reheating them to spread the carbon throughout the iron. Since iron produced in this fashion would be stronger than bronze, it was often used to make swords and spears, which could be crafted by hammers, but armor, which had to be carefully shaped to shield human bodies, could only be made out of the more malleable bronze.

There was no formal system to train all of the people who made these metal objects; instead, interested young men would work as apprentices to experienced metalworkers, and when they had mastered the craft, they could set up their own shops or inherit the facilities of retiring metalworkers. They typically labored in various locales. Some metalworkers maintained large workshops that were invariably located close to the local temple of Hephaestus, the god of artisans, creating a special district of craftsmen in some cities. In other cases, smiths might work in the men's quarters of their own homes, since the Greeks had no zoning laws to prevent such a practice. The metalworkers who specialized in small objects, like jewelers, usually performed their labors inside of their stalls in the *agora*, crafting pieces of jewelry to customers' specifications while they watched. By means of their instructions and feedback, Greek women did influence the design and featuring of Greek jewelry, though this represented their only contribution to the otherwise all-male profession of metalworking.

Although the Greeks valued their metal items, we know relatively little about their creators because metalworkers were not highly regarded by their societies. They suffered from the general stigma attached to all individuals who worked with their hands in exchange for money, and due to the dark fumes and dust generated by their labors, they often looked dirty and disheveled. Even the god who engaged in metalworking, Hephaestus, was described as lame and ugly, and the other gods looked down upon him, though they often asked him to make metal objects for them. In addition, like others who sold their products, metalworkers were regularly suspected of being dishonest, and many of them may have actually cheated their customers, justifying the public disdain. Indeed, there is at least one documented case of such deception:

MODERN METALWORKERS

The metalworkers who crafted weapons and household products for Greek citizens were visible figures in their everyday lives, as evidenced by numerous portrayals of men working with metals on Greek pottery. Much later, Henry Wadsworth Longfellow immortalized a similarly central figure of nineteenth-century American life in his poem "The Village Blacksmith." Today, most individual metalworkers employ a modern tool called the acetylene torch and are called welders; while not as common as the metalworkers of ancient Greece or the blacksmiths of early America, many of these welders also work in small shops and can be approached by customers to perform various tasks, much like their earlier counterparts.

A RIVETING CELEBRITY

To illustrate the importance of metalworking in their daily lives, the ancient Greeks created a god, Hephaestus, who practiced this art at the behest of other gods; he is prominently described in the *Iliad* of Homer (ca. 800–701 BCE) as using flames and bellows to forge metal objects. In modern times, important professions may be represented by fictional celebrities; for example, during World War II, the nation's need for female factory workers was conveyed by means of the iconic Rosie the Riveter, celebrated in songs, posters, and films. (A riveter, of course, is a specialized sort of metalworker who attaches pieces of metal together by driving a bolt through them.)

King Hiero II of Syracuse (270–215 BCE) believed that his goldsmith had used some silver in crafting a crown that was supposed to be made of solid gold, and he asked his friend Archimedes (287–212 BCE) to confirm his suspicions without damaging the crown; the scientist then realized, while sitting in a bathtub, that he could determine the crown's composition by immersing it in water, and when the crown was tested, it did contain silver as well as gold. Surely, there were many honest metalworkers as well, but this anecdote suggests that it might have been temptingly easy to take advantage of patrons who did not happen to know any famous scientists.

As a final reason for their relative obscurity, metalworkers, unlike painters and sculptors, were not thought of as true artists, and they did not sign their works, which is why we do not know the names of any metalworkers. It is also unfortunate that so many of the beautifully crafted products of Greek metalworkers were melted down so their metal could be reused, leaving only scattered evidence of their artistry. Still, in the illustrations on Greek pottery, we can today find preserved, anonymously, the images and habits of some of the individual metalworkers who contributed so much to ancient Greek society.

Further Reading

Blakely, Sandra. 1996. *Myth, Ritual, and Metallurgy in Ancient Greece and Recent Africa*. Cambridge: Cambridge University Press.

Healy, John F. 1978. *Mining and Metallurgy in the Greek and Roman World*. London: Thames on Hudson.

Humphrey, John W., John P. Oleson, and Andrew N. Sherwood, editors. 1998. *Greek and Roman Technology: A Sourcebook: Annotated Translations of Greek and Latin Texts and Documents*. London and New York: Routledge.

Kostoglou, Maria. 2008. *Iron and Steel in Ancient Greece: Artefacts, Technology and Social Change in Aegean Thrace from Classical to Roman Times*. Oxford: John and Erica Hedges.

Stibbe, C. M. 2000. *The Sons of Hephaistos: Aspects of the Archaic Greek Bronze Industry*. Rome : L'Erma di Bretschneider.

Treister, Michael Yu. 1996. *The Role of Metals in Ancient Greek History*. Leiden, The Netherlands, and Boston: Brill.

Document

From Homer. C 750 BCE. *The Iliad of Homer, Rendered into English Prose for the Use of Those Who Cannot Read the Original.* Translated by Samuel Butler. 1898. London and New York: Longmans, Green.

This passage from Homer's Iliad, *describing the home and workshop of the god Vulcan, or Hephaestus, offers a picture of a Greek metalworker engaged in his daily labors. The goddess Thesis is visiting the smith god to ask him to make new armor for her heroic son, Achilles.*

Meanwhile Thetis came to the house of Vulcan, imperishable, star-bespangled, fairest of the abodes in heaven, a house of bronze wrought by the lame god's own hands. She found him busy with his bellows, sweating and hard at work, for he was making twenty tripods that were to stand by the wall of his house, and he set wheels of gold under them all that they might go of their own selves to the assemblies of the gods, and come back again—marvels indeed to see. They were finished all but the ears of cunning workmanship which yet remained to be fixed to them: these he was now fixing, and he was hammering at the rivets. While he was thus at work silver-footed Thetis came to the house. Charis, of graceful head-dress, wife to the far-famed lame god, came towards her as soon as she saw her, and took her hand in her own, saying, "Why have you come to our house, Thetis, honoured and ever welcome—for you do not visit usoften? Come inside and let me set refreshment before you." The goddess led the way as she spoke, and bade Thetis sit on a richly decorated seat inlaid with silver; there was a footstool also under her feet. Then she called Vulcan and said, "Vulcan, come here, Thetis wants you"; and the far-famed lame god answered, "Then it is indeed an august and honoured goddess who has come here; she it was that took care of me when I was suffering from the heavy fall which I had through my cruel mother's anger—for she would have got rid of me because I was lame. It would have gone hardly with me had not Eurynome, daughter of the ever-encircling waters of Oceanus, and Thetis, taken me to their bosom. Nine years did I stay with them, and many beautiful works in bronze, brooches, spiral armlets, cups, and chains, did I make for them in their cave, with the roaring waters of Oceanus foaming as they rushed ever past it; and no one knew, neither of gods nor men, save only Thetis and Eurynome who took care of me. If, then, Thetis has come to my house I must make her due requital for having saved me; entertain her, therefore, with all hospitality, while I put by my bellows and all my tools." On this the mighty monster hobbled off from his anvil, his thin legs plying lustily under him. He set the bellows away from the fire, and gathered his tools into a silver chest. Then he took a sponge and washed his face and hands, his shaggy chest and brawny neck; he donned his shirt, grasped his strong staff, and limped towards the door. . . .

Orators

In a sense, oratory has always been part of the human experience: members of ancient tribes must have argued about where to migrate and when to hunt, and each person would strive to speak as effectively as possible in order to influence the others. Military leaders preparing to lead their soldiers into battle would make speeches to inspire their followers to fight energetically and skillfully. Yet the art of oratory did not become a major concern until the ancient Greeks developed democracy and a legal system. For when rulers gain their position by exercising their military might or inheriting a throne, and thus have absolute authority over all of a nation's affairs, their speaking skills might be useful, but are not necessarily essential; hence, in the *Iliad* and *Odyssey* of Homer (ca. 800–701 BCE), Nestor and Odysseus are praised for their eloquence and ability to persuade others, which enhanced their stature, but the overall commander of the Greek war against Troy, Agamemnon, apparently lacked this talent but governed all of the Greeks nonetheless. However, once citizens begin to have a say in how they are governed, and once the fates of accused criminals are determined by juries instead of leaders, the skill of persuading people to accept one's position becomes crucially important in order to achieve political and legal victories. So it is not surprising that around the fifth century BCE, the Greeks began to manifest an intense interest in the techniques of rhetoric, introducing ideas and approaches that the Romans would further explore and master.

The first renowned Greek orator, Corax of Syracuse, may or may not have existed; he is said to have lived in Sicily during the fifth century BCE, and he rose to prominence when his city Syracuse replaced its tyrant with a democracy, and citizens went to court to regain the properties he had seized. To assist them, he reportedly authored a treatise, *Techne Logon*, or *The Art of Words*, explaining his system for organizing an effective speech. As the art of oratory became established in Sicily, one of its residents, Gorgias of Leontini (483–375 BCE) became so renowned for his rhetorical skills that his city sent him to Athens in 427 BCE as an ambassador, assigned to seek the city-state's support in Leontini's struggle against Syracuse. His speeches impressed the Athenians so much that he was then able to earn a living by teaching rhetoric, amassing a huge fortune before retiring. As historian Will Durant reports, "Traveling from city to city, he expounded his views in a style of oratory so euphuistically ornate, so symmetrically antithetical in idea and phrase, so delicately poised between poetry and prose, that he had no difficulty in attracting students who offered him a hundred minas [about $250,000 in modern dollars] for a course of instruction." Soon there were many similar instructors, called sophists; some were itinerant like Gorgias, while others, like the esteemed orator Isocrates (436–338 BCE), established schools that attracted large numbers of paying students. While Gorgias and other rhetoricians also considered themselves philosophers and wrote treatises on other subjects, they were derided by more sedentary philosophers like Plato (427–347 BCE), who believed that they were more interested in making money than seeking the truth. In one dialogue, *Gorgias*, Plato has Socrates (469–399 BCE) confront the great orator himself and eventually criticize his rhetoric as "not an art at all, but the habit of a bold and ready wit, which knows how to manage mankind: this habit I sum up under the word 'flattery'." Such grumblings, however, had little effect on the popularity of their efforts to teach the art of rhetoric.

One of Gorgias's most significant successors, Antiphon of Athens (480–411 BCE), also adopted an elevated tone in his speeches, but another famed orator who lived in Athens, Lysias (ca. 445–380 BCE), introduced a more natural style of rhetoric. Strangely, however, both men rarely spoke in public; for Antiphon, this was a matter of choice, but Lysias, as the son of a man from Syracuse, had the legal status of a metic, or noncitizen, and thus he was not allowed to speak at Athenian political assemblies or courtrooms. However, these men discovered a new way to profit from their oratorical skills by becoming professional speechwriters, hired by other men to write speeches that they could deliver. Unlike modern speechwriters, who may long remain anonymous, Antiphon and Lysias were quickly identified as the authors of these speeches, and their work was so admired that about fifteen of Antiphon's speeches, and thirty-five of Lysias's speeches, have been preserved.

Pericles, the long-time leader of the city-state of Athens in the fifth century BCE, was renowned for his skills as an orator, although the major speech attributed to him—his "Funeral Oration"—was actually written by the historian Thucydides. (Library of Congress)

However, superior speaking skills soon became associated with another profession—political leaders—as the democracies of Athens and Syracuse were largely controlled during the fourth century BC by a number of eloquent orators. Chief among these was Pericles (ca. 495–429 BCE), the statesman who so dominated Athens in his lifetime that the era is often described as the Age of Pericles. His career demonstrates both the power, and the drawbacks, of effective rhetoric. He first contributed greatly to the development of Athenian democracy by successfully arguing for some major political reforms and advocating the construction of noteworthy projects like the famed Parthenon. However, employing his eloquence, he later persuaded citizens to accept a series of unwise decisions that led directly to Athens's ruinous defeat in the Peloponnesian War. Among the later leaders of Athens who were also significant orators, a man named Demosthenes (384–322 BCE) commands attention because, by some accounts, he was the greatest of the ancient Greek orators, even though he had to struggle to master the art of articulation and was regarded as both physically unattractive and personally disagreeable. He first specialized in being paid to write speeches for litigants before he became active in politics; although he had not been born to wealthy parents, he managed to amass a huge fortune from his legal work. However, some of his contemporaries whispered that his wealth was due in part to large bribes that the Persians had paid him so that Demosthenes would agitate for war against the Macedonians. Yet his main opponent Aeschines (389–314 BCE), also a talented orator, probably enriched himself in a similar fashion by accepting bribes from the Macedonians.

By the time of Pericles, oratory was no longer exclusively limited to men, for the Greek leader entered into a romantic relationship with a foreign-born woman named Aspasia (ca. 470–400 BCE) who was renowned for her skills in this area. Defying the prevailing attitudes, she established her own school to teach rhetoric and philosophy to the young women of Athens; some men also attended her classes. In Plato's dialogue *Menexenus*, the great philosopher Socrates speaks of Aspasia as his instructor in rhetoric, and he even claims that he observed her composing and delivering an early version of the funeral oration later given by Pericles. As a woman, however, Aspasia was never allowed to deliver a speech in public, and citizens appalled by her independent spirit brought her to trial for purported impiety, though she was successfully defended by her lover Pericles.

In recognition of the important roles that oratory had played in Greek history, two figures of the Hellenistic Era—Aristophanes of Byzantium (ca. 257–180 BCE) and Aristarchus of Samothrace (ca. 220–143 BCE)—compiled a list of the ten greatest orators of classical Greece, who were credited with developing and mastering the art of rhetoric. Along with five men who have already been mentioned—Aeschines, Antiphon, Demosthenes, Isocrates, and Lysias—they selected five others—Andocides (440–390 BCE), Dinarchus (ca. 361–291 BCE), Hypereides (390–322

ELECTING THE ELOQUENT

As in ancient Greece, talented orators in recent centuries have been able to become important political figures; in 1896, for example, an obscure congressman named William Jennings Bryan was unexpectedly nominated for the presidency after impressing delegates with a stirring speech at the Democratic National Convention. Many people believe, however, that the growing prominence of television in American life has made oratorical skills more important than ever in achieving political victories. Thus, three recent presidents—John F. Kennedy, Ronald Reagan, and Barack Obama—were elected in large part because of the memorable speaking skills they displayed during televised speeches and debates.

CELEBRITY SPEECHWRITERS

Today, we remember Greek orators like Lysias and Demosthenes largely because we are familiar with speeches that they wrote for other people, which were preserved by ancient admirers. Similarly, some contemporary speechwriters have been acknowledged as the authors of famous political speeches, helping them to move on to careers as independent writers. We know, for example, that Ted Sorensen drafted President John F. Kennedy's 1961 inaugural address, which advised citizens, "Ask not what your country can do for you; ask what you can do for your country," and Peggy Noonan drafted President George H. W. Bush's 1988 acceptance speech, in which he called for a "kinder, gentler nation."

BCE), Isaeus (ca. 300 BCE), and Lycurgus (396–323 BCE)—who now attract less attention though they were renowned and influential in their day. Their lives were later chronicled in a history attributed to Plutarch (ca. 46–120 CE), *Lives of the Ten Orators*. It is striking to note that only three of these men—Isaeus, Isocrates, and Lycurgus—seemed to have lived relatively untroubled lives; of the others, Antiphon and Hypereides were executed, Demosthenes committed suicide to avoid a similar fate, and Aeschines, Andocides, Dinarchus, and Lysias were forced into exile by political opponents. Clearly, although there were rich rewards to be earned from rhetorical skills, they could also create powerful enemies and even put one's life in danger. As some great orators of modern times,

like John F. Kennedy and Martin Luther King Jr., have sadly demonstrated, this is not a problem that was limited to ancient Greece.

Further Reading

Carawan, Edwin, editor. 2007. *Oxford Readings in the Attic Orators*. Oxford: Oxford University Press.

Grethlein, Jonas. 2010. *The Greeks and Their Past: Poetry, Oratory and History in the Fifth Century* BCE. Cambridge: Cambridge University Press.

Roisman, Joseph. 2005. *The Rhetoric of Manhood: Masculinity in the Attic Orators*. Berkeley and Los Angeles: University of California Press.

Wooten, Cecil W., editor. 2001. *The Orator in Action and Theory in Greece and Rome: Essays in Honor of George A. Kennedy*. Leiden, The Netherlands, and Boston: Brill.

Worthington, Ian, editor. 2007. *A Companion to Greek Rhetoric*. Malden, MA: Blackwell Publishing.

Worthington, Ian, editor. 1994. *Persuasion: Greek Rhetoric in Action*. London: Routledge.

Document

From Plato. C. 370 BCE. *The Dialogues of Plato*. Volume 1. Translated by Benjamin Jowett. 1871. Oxford: Clarendon Press.

In this passage from Phaedrus, *the philosopher Plato discusses the art of oratory.*

[Socrates:] Oratory is the art of enchanting the soul, and therefore he who would be an orator has to learn the differences of human souls—they are so many and of such a nature, and from them come the differences between man and man. Having proceeded thus far in his analysis, he will next divide speeches into their different classes: "Such and such persons," he will say, "are affected by this or that kind of speech in this or that way," and he will tell you why. The pupil must have a good theoretical notion of them first, and then he must have experience of them in actual life, and be able to follow them with all his senses about him, or he will never get beyond the precepts of his masters. But when he understands what persons are persuaded by what arguments, and sees the person about whom he was speaking in the abstract actually before him, and knows that it is he, and can say to himself, "This is the man or this is the character who ought to have a certain argument applied to him in order to convince him of a certain opinion"—he who knows all this, and knows also when he should speak and when he should refrain, and when he should use pithy sayings, pathetic appeals, sensational effects, and all the other modes of speech which he has learned—when, I say, he knows the times and seasons of all these things, then, and not till then, he is a perfect master of his art; but if he fail in any of these points, whether in speaking or teaching or writing them, and yet declares that he speaks by rules of art, he who says "I don't believe you" has the better of him.

Philosophers

Ancient Greece was the first civilization that valued the pursuit of knowledge and wisdom as a profession in itself. They termed its practitioners "philosophers," which literally meant "lovers of wisdom," since these men were interested in all forms of knowledge, not only the deep existential, moral, and ethical issues that preoccupy contemporary philosophers. Thus, while the Greek philosophers did found the discipline now known by that name, they also made important, and often pioneering, contributions to fields such as science, mathematics, history, theology, political science, education, and literary criticism. Indeed, almost every field of study at a modern university can trace its origins, at least in part, to an ancient Greek philosopher.

Needless to say, there was no system of formal education or training that certified a man as a philosopher (since this was one of many professions in ancient Greece that were not open to women). One would typically learn from private tutors and then, when he deemed himself to be sufficiently learned, he would become a private tutor himself in order to learn a living. If one earned a reputation as a particularly wise philosopher, there was income to be garnered from nobles and other wealthy individuals who might hire a philosopher to educate their children (as the famed Aristotle [384–322 BCE] was brought to Macedonia by King Phillip [382–336 BCE] to teach his son, Alexander the Great [356–323 BCE]) or might send their children to study under the philosopher for handsome fees. Other philosophers might be employed as

advisers to nobles or political leaders. In some cases, noted philosophers would travel and earn money by teaching in various cities, usually focusing on the skills of rhetoric while addressing other topics as well. As a distinction not observed in modern discussions, these itinerant philosophers were called "sophists," or wise men, and they were sometimes attacked by more sedentary figures like Plato (427–347 BCE) and Aristotle as men solely interested in making lots of money, in contrast to true philosophers who were primarily dedicated to seeking wisdom. Eager to promulgate their thoughts and findings, philosophers regularly wrote treatises which were copied by scribes, distributed to interested parties in other cities, and kept in libraries, but although these writings could boost their reputations and perhaps lead to profitable opportunities, they earned no direct income from this activity. Unfortunately, most of their manuscripts are now lost, known today only because other ancient writers refer to them.

Focused on conveying their knowledge and ideas whenever they wrote, Greek philosophers said little about their daily lives, and we sometimes know very little about the men whose works were respected and influential throughout the ancient world. What biographical information we have usually comes from people writing long after the philosophers had died, so their data cannot always be considered reliable. Consider, for example, Thales, the man regularly cited as the first major philosopher (and first major mathematician as well); we know that he lived in Miletus, a Greek city on the western coast of what is now Turkey, and that he lived roughly from 624 to 546 BCE. He had a son, Cybisthus (ca. sixth century BCE), but it is unclear whether Thales married and had this son or remained unmarried and adopted a nephew. There are reports that he dabbled in business, and he also earned some money by serving as an adviser to the Ionian king Croesus (ca. 595–547 BCE), well known for his great wealth. But Thales is mainly renowned for his major ideas, including the theory that the world is made entirely of water and a number of geometric theorems.

We know more about the later philosophers of ancient Athens, particularly Socrates (469–399 BCE), Plato, and Aristotle, usually regarded as the greatest of

This pencil sketch of the Greek philosopher Socrates (470 BCE–399 BCE) may suggest his difficult personality, but he is considered one of the greatest thinkers of all times, and a key influence on Western philosophy to this day. (So Illustrator/iStockphoto.com)

Greek philosophers. Socrates was unusual in that he refused to earn money by teaching students, preferring the freedom of poverty. Instead, he would spend most of his time in the Athenian marketplace, the *agora*, talking with anyone who chose to share his company. There are three primary sources of information about his life, all regarded as somewhat accurate and somewhat misleading: a play by Aristophanes (446–386 BCE), *The Clouds*, which mocks the philosopher as a bad influence on Athenian youth; the writings of the historian Xenophon (430–354 BCE), suspected of being based largely on second-hand data; and the early dialogues of Plato, which are regarded as mostly genuine if overly reverential accounts of his beliefs (in contrast to the later dialogues, in which Socrates seems to become a mouthpiece for Plato's own ideas). There

is general agreement that he was an ugly, disheveled man, given to walking around barefoot and wearing the same robe again and again, and he may have spent most of his time away from home because his wife, Xanthippe (ca. 420–360 BCE), was said to be a shrewish, disagreeable woman, according to later descriptions of her. While many valued his wisdom, Socrates irritated many Athenian citizens with his attitude of superiority and proclivity for questioning many of society's basic tenets. Eventually, and notoriously, he was put on trial for corrupting youth and failing to honor Greek religion, found guilty, and executed by being forced to drink the poison hemlock.

His most famous pupil, Plato, fared better in life. After associating with and learning from Socrates, he left Athens after Socrates's death to study elsewhere, returning twelve years later to found a school, called the Academy, that became his major source of income. While regularly teaching students, including his most noteworthy successor, Aristotle, he also became a prolific writer (unlike Socrates, who abhorred and condemned writing), and he was widely respected for the ideas expressed in his many dialogues, diligently preserved by later generations. On two occasions, Plato traveled to the city of Syracuse to work as a personal tutor to its new king, Dionysus I (432–367 BCE), but he found the situation so unpleasant that he soon returned to his Academy, which remained a major institution of learning under other philosophers for centuries after his death.

The third major Greek philosopher, Aristotle, followed in Plato's footsteps in some respects: though he was never chosen to head Plato's Academy, he established his own school, the Lyceum, after teaching at a branch of the Academy in the Greek city of Assos in present-day Turkey. As noted, he also worked as a royal tutor until his pupil, Alexander the Great, assumed the Macedonian throne after his father's death. But while Plato had little interest in the physical world, Aristotle made major contributions to fields like astronomy, physics, and zoology while also addressing various subjects like politics, economics, and literary criticism; his *Poetics*, for example, is commonly considered the first work to seriously examine and theorize about literature. There is some controversy, however, about whether the texts

DIDACTIC DIALOGUES

The Greek philosopher Plato effectively invented the form of writing called the dialogue, in which fictional characters carry on conversations to educate readers. Later philosophers expressed themselves in straight-forward expository prose, but Plato's approach was emulated by writers in other fields. The Renaissance astronomer Galileo presented his argument in favor of the heliocentric theory in the form of a dialogue, *A Dialogue Concerning the Two Chief World Systems* (1632); the seventeenth-century writer Izaak Walton wrote a dialogue, *The Compleat Angler* (1653) to explain the art of fishing; and today's U.S. Army instructs new recruits using comic books, wherein fictional soldiers explain skills and policies to other fictional soldiers.

FASCIST PHILOSOPHERS

Plato's apparent espousal of totalitarianism in his *Republic* has drawn a fair share of modern criticism; one historian of science fiction, Sam Lundwall, has even dismissed Plato as "the old Nazi." Yet there is one prominent twentieth-century philosopher, the German Martin Heidegger, who actually was an official Nazi, since he served as a member of Adolf Hitler's National Socialist Party from 1933 to 1945, and while supporters claim that his involvement in Nazism was minimal, he never made any public statements expressing regret or remorse over his official alignment with Hitler's despicable regime.

attributed to Aristotle were written by the philosopher himself or his students (in particular, some aspects of the *Poetics* have led scholars to speculate that the work is actually an assemblage of student notes on Aristotle's lectures). Like Socrates, Aristotle was also charged by Athenian authorities for being "impious," though this was mostly rooted in suspicions that he was overly supportive of the Macedonians who were endeavoring to dominate Greece; however, instead of remaining in Athens to be tried, Aristotle chose to leave the city and spent the rest of his life in the city-state of Calchis.

As the lives of these figures suggest, it could be both profitable, and perilous, to be a philosopher in ancient Greece. On one hand, accomplished philosophers could become wealthy and widely respected figures, but since their methods of thought did not always accord with commonly accepted beliefs, they could also upset authority figures and find themselves in legal trouble. Even before Socrates, for example, another philosopher, Anaxagoras (ca. 510–428 BCE), had been put on trial in Athens because he denied the existence of the Greek gods, forcing him into exile. Still, by choosing to devote themselves to the pursuit of knowledge, the ancient Greek philosophers did benefit in one significant respect: unlike the greatest Greek warriors or the greatest Greek athletes, the greatest Greek philosophers became famous not only during their own lifetimes but for all centuries thereafter, as people from all over the world have continued to study and benefit from their teachings, and attaining such lasting fame was very important to the ancient Greeks. And certainly, in evaluating the contributions that ancient Greece made to world culture, the accomplishments of its philosophers must be ranked as that civilization's greatest achievement.

Further Reading

Blackson, Thomas A. 2011. *Ancient Greek Philosophy: From the Presocratics to the Hellenistic Philosophers*. Oxford: Wiley-Blackwell.

Cohen, S, Marc, Patricia Curd, and C.D.C. Reeve, editors. 2011. *Readings in Ancient Greek Philosophy: From Thales to Aristotle*. Fourth edition. Indianapolis, IN: Hackett Publishing Company.

Long, A.A., editor. 1999. *The Cambridge Companion to Early Greek Philosophy*. Cambridge: Cambridge University Press.

O'Grady, Patricia S., editor. 2005. *Meet the Philosophers of Ancient Greece: Everything You Always Wanted to Know about Ancient Greek Philosophers but Didn't Know Who to Ask*. Aldershot, England, and Burlington, VT: Ashgate Publishing.

Preus, Anthony. 2007. *Historical Dictionary of Ancient Greek Philosophy*. Lanham, MD: Scarecrow Press.

Tankha, Vijay. 2006. *Ancient Greek Philosophy: Thales to Gorgias*. Delhi, India: Dorling Kindersley.

Documents

From Plato. C. 385 BCE. *The Dialogues of Plato*. Volume 1. Translated by Benjamin Jowett. 1871. Oxford: Clarendon Press.

In this passage from the Symposium, *Plato provides a charming glimpse of the daily life of the philosopher Socrates, when he was invited to a banquet given by a renowned playwright of the day, Agathon; accompanied by his student Aristodemus, he is approaching the man's house.*

Socrates dropped behind in a fit of abstraction, and desired Aristodemus, who was waiting, to go on before him. When he reached the house of Agathon he found the doors wide open, and a comical thing happened. A servant coming out met him, and led him at once into the banqueting-hall in which the guests were reclining, for the banquet was about to begin. Welcome, Aristodemus, said Agathon, as soon as he appeared—you are just in time to sup with us; if you come on any other matter put it off, and make one of us, as I was looking for you yesterday and meant to have asked you, if I could have found you. But what have you done with Socrates?

I turned round, but Socrates was nowhere to be seen; and I had to explain that he had been with me a moment before, and that I came by his invitation to the supper.

You were quite right in coming, said Agathon; but where is he himself?

He was behind me just now, as I entered, he said, and I cannot think what has become of him.

Go and look for him, boy, said Agathon, and bring him in; and do you, Aristodemus, meanwhile take the place by Eryximachus.

The servant then assisted him to wash, and he lay down, and presently another servant came in and reported that our friend Socrates had retired into the portico of the neighbouring house. "There he is fixed," said he, "and when I call to him he will not stir."

How strange, said Agathon; then you must call him again, and keep calling him.

Let him alone, said my informant; he has a way of stopping anywhere and losing himself [in thought] without any reason. I believe that he will soon appear; do not therefore disturb him.

Well, if you think so, I will leave him, said Agathon. And then, turning to the servants, he added, "Let us have supper without waiting for him. . . . " Supper was served, but still no Socrates; and during the meal Agathon several times expressed a wish to send for him, but Aristodemus objected; and at last when the feast was about half over—for the fit, as usual, was not of long duration—Socrates entered; Agathon, who was reclining alone at the end of the table, begged that he would take the place next to him; that "I may touch you," he said, "and have the benefit of that wise thought which came into your mind in the portico, and is now in your possession; for I am certain that you would not have come away until you had found what you sought." How I wish, said Socrates, taking his place as he was desired, that wisdom could be infused by touch, out of the fuller the emptier man, as water runs through wool out of a fuller cup into an emptier one; if that were so, how greatly should I value the privilege of reclining at your side! For you would have filled me full with a stream of wisdom plenteous and fair; whereas my own is of a very mean and questionable sort, no better than a dream. But yours is bright and full of promise, and was manifested forth in all the splendour of youth the day before yesterday, in the presence of more than thirty thousand Hellenes.

From Epicurus. C. 280 BCE. *The Library of Original Sources.* Volume 2. Edited by Oliver J. Thatcher; text below translated by C.D. Yonge. 1907. New York and Chicago: University Research Extension.

In this passage from his Letter to Menoeceus, the Greek philosopher Epicurus (341–270 BCE) offers advice to those who are planning to become philosophers.

Let no one delay to study philosophy while he is young, and when he is old let him not become weary of the study; for no man call ever find the time unsuitable or too late to study the health of his soul. And he who asserts either that it is not yet time to philosophize, or that the hour is passed, is like a man who should say that the time is not yet come to be happy, or that it is too late. So that both young and old should study philosophy, the one in order that, when he is old, he may be young in good things through the pleasing recollection of the past, and the other in order that he; may be at the same time both young and old, in consequence of his absence of fear for the future. It is right then for a man to consider the things which produce happiness, since, if happiness is present, we have everything, and when it is absent, we do everything with a view to possess it. Now, what I have constantly recommended to you, these things I would have you do and practice, considering them to be the elements of living well. . . .

Every pleasure is therefore a good on account of its own nature, but it does not follow that every pleasure is worthy of being chosen. . . . To accustom one's self, therefore, to simple and inexpensive habits is a great ingredient in the perfecting of health, and makes a man free from hesitation with respect to the necessary uses of life. And when we, on certain occasions, fall in with more sumptuous fare, it makes us in a better disposition towards it, and renders us fearless with respect to fortune. When, therefore, we say that pleasure is a chief good, we are not speaking of the pleasures of the debauched man, or those which lie in sensual enjoyment, as some think who are ignorant, and who do not entertain our opinions, or else interpret them perversely; but we mean the freedom of the body from pain, and the soul from confusion. For it is not continued drinkings and revels, or the enjoyment of female society, or feasts of fish and other such things, as a costly table supplies, that make life pleasant, but sober contemplation, which examines into the reasons for all choice and avoidance, and which puts to flight the vain opinions from which the greater part of the confusion arises which troubles the soul. Now, the beginning and the greatest good of all these things is prudence, on which account prudence is something more valuable than even philosophy, inasmuch as all the other virtues spring from it, teaching us that it is not possible to live pleasantly unless one also lives prudently, and honorably, and justly; and that one cannot live prudently, and honestly, and justly without living pleasantly; for the virtues are connate with living agreeably, and living agreeably is inseparable from the virtues.

Physicians

For most of human history, the art of healing was closely tied to religion, as shamans treated sick people by combining practical medicine with religious ceremonies designed to remove demons from a sufferer's body or placate the gods believed to be responsible for the ailment. For many centuries, the situation in ancient Greece was much the same, as persons in need of medical care would have to visit religious sanctuaries dedicated to Asclepius, the Greek god of medicine. At night, ailing supplicants would sleep in the temple and hope that the god would provide them with a vision; during the day, however, they may have received more effective assistance, reflecting a new approach to medicine. For in the ruins of these buildings, archaeologists now find both the remains of religious offerings to the gods and some surgical tools, suggesting that the priests of Asclepius could address the problems of sufferers with both religious rituals and practical medical treatments more likely to prove efficacious.

The newer, more scientific sort of medicine may have originated with Asclepius himself, who some believe was a real person who became famed for his medical skills and hence was later deified; if that is the case, then Asclepius might be regarded as the world's first physician, since he must have mastered and relied upon effective healing techniques in order to garner such widespread renown. It is more common, however, to regard another man, Hippocrates of Kos, as the father of medicine. We are confident that this man lived from 460 to 370 BC, and he firmly broke with past beliefs by insisting that all diseases had natural causes that could be successfully treated without appealing for divine intervention. Inspired by his work, other men began to work as physicians outside of the confines of temples, treating their patients in exchange for fees; there were some female physicians as well, though they unsurprisingly specialized exclusively in treating women.

While he rejected religious explanations for various ailments, many of Hippocrates's ideas would be regarded as equally superstitious by modern doctors. His knowledge of human physiology was very limited, since the ancient Greeks abhorred dissection, so his ideas were largely based on observations of the dissected bodies of dead animals. He also embraced the dubious theories of two important precursors, Empedocles of Acragas (ca. 490–430 BCE) and Alcmaeon of Croton (ca. fifth century BCE). These men built upon the naive notion of ancient Greek physics that the world was made up of four elements—earth, air, water, and fire—to argue that there were four corresponding fluids or humors in the human body—black bile, yellow bile, phlegm, and blood—and that physical ailments were due to an imbalance in those humors. This theory inspired a number of useless or counterproductive therapies, like draining blood from patients to reduce fevers believed to be caused by excess blood in the body, or having patients eat foods believed to increase or decrease certain humors linked to certain diseases.

Still, there is much about Hippocrates's techniques to admire, including an emphasis on having sick patients rest and remain immobile and ensuring that the balms and water used in treating patients were always clean. He recommended the use of certain herbs to treat some ailments; for patients with coughs and bronchitis, for example, he would make use of a plant called hyssop, which is now known to actually

This marble statue, completed during Greece's Hellenistic period (323 BCE–31 BCE), depicts the ancient Greek physician Hippocrates, celebrated as the father of medicine. (Library of Congress)

function as an expectorant and cough suppressant and is still employed today as an herbal remedy. He also advised people with skin problems to soak in sulfur baths, which some still esteem for their purported healing effects.

Hippocrates is best known, however, for establishing the code of ethics that to this day has remained central to the practice of medicine, conveyed in forms of the Hippocratic Oath that was long attributed to him (though some recent research suggests that it was actually written after his death). The Oath established, among other important principles, that physicians should always strive to help their patients, should never harm patients, and should respect patient confidentiality. While no contemporary physicians swear to the original Oath, which includes references to the Greek gods Apollo, Asclepius, Hygieia, and Panacea, modern forms of the Oath are now sworn by virtually all new physicians.

Despite this link to past practices, ancient Greek medicine was otherwise very different from the modern discipline. A man did not require any formal training to become a physician, though some people interested in the profession would travel to study at prestigious facilities dedicated to medical research located throughout the Mediterranean world in places like the Italian city of Krotona and the island of Kos. More commonly, prospective physicians would work under established physicians to learn the trade before they began to practice on their own, supporting themselves with the fees that their patients paid to be treated. A man who garnered a reputation for successful healing might become very wealthy indeed; one physician, Democedes of Krotona (ca. sixth century BCE), was hired to cure the king of Persia and was then employed by three Greek city-states, commanding higher and higher salaries at each position.

The treatments prescribed by these physicians were highly variable in their effectiveness. For head ailments, they might drill a small hole in a person's skull, a process known as trepanning, though this was generally not helpful; other surgical procedures might correct problems like a dislocated shoulder, though the process would be extremely painful since the Greeks had no anesthetics. Furthermore, since their hygiene did not meet modern standards, dangerous infections were a common result. For certain conditions, the physician might use herbal remedies: mullein for coughs, smooth sow thistle for stomach aches, and motherwort for heart problems. In some cases, patients could only be directed to rest in bed or abstain from eating in the hopes that this would enable the body to heal itself. Most grievously, physicians had absolutely no way to help patients suffering from infectious diseases. Thus, during the Peloponnesian War, Pericles (ca. 495–429 BCE) unwisely instructed the Athenians to barricade themselves inside their city to resist the Spartans, and the resulting problems in sanitation led to a devastating plague (now thought to be either typhus or smallpox) that killed numerous citizens, including Pericles himself, despite the efforts of numerous physicians.

Greek medicine later began to advance in the Hellenistic period, when the Greek rulers of Egypt briefly allowed human dissections to occur. Allowed to examine human bodies, Herophilos of Chalcedon (355–280 BCE) became the first to determine that the brain controlled the nervous system and recognized for the first time the importance of measuring a person's pulse to determine his or her health. Another physician, Erasistratos of Chilos (304–250 BCE), figured out that the heart functioned as an important pump, forcing fluid through the body. Neither man, though, abandoned the basis theory of humors, and the ban on dissections was soon reimposed, so that new treatments could not be devised on the basis of their discoveries.

In addition to physicians, there were other people who provided the ancient Greeks with specialized forms of medical care. All armies were accompanied by trained surgeons who treated wounded soldiers after each battle. Childbirths were handled by midwives, who worked in the woman's house with the assistance of other females, since no man was allowed to be present when babies were born. At the gymnasiums, the employees known as *paidotribai* would help athletes deal with injuries and pain caused by exercise, becoming the first practitioners of what we would now term sports medicine. It is also possible that certain physicians devoted most of their energies to certain sorts of patients; for example, the tomb of an obscure Athenian physician named Jason depicts him as he examines a naked boy whose stomach is swollen, suggesting that he may have specialized in treating children.

Overall, while many physicians were able to earn a comfortable living from their work, medicine was not a widely respected field, and the reason for this is not difficult to discern: most of the time, physicians were simply unable to assist their patients, since their knowledge was so limited and their treatments were generally ineffective. Today, doctors are universally admired and highly paid precisely because the advances of the last century now allow them to cure most of the ailments they confront, in stark contrast to the physicians of the ancient world.

AN UPDATED OATH

The ancient version of the Hippocratic Oath, purportedly written by Hippocrates himself, is not used in medical schools today, in part because it respectfully references the Greek gods Apollo, Asclepius, Hygieia, and Panaciea. One modern version of the Oath, commonly recited, was written in 1964 by Louis Lasagna, then dean of Tufts University's School of Medicine. In addition to removing the names of Greek gods, Lasagna's oath, unlike the original Oath, interestingly emphasizes the recommended humbleness of the physician, as future doctors must swear to declare their ignorance about certain medical problems and seek the assistance of colleagues in treating patients.

FRAUDULENT PHYSICIANS

While most physicians of ancient Greece strived to apply the best available knowledge to cure their patients, there were also fraudulent physicians who simply tried to take advantage of sick people. In his book *A Day in Old Athens* (1910), William Stearns Davis says, "Vendors of every sort of cure-all abound, as well as creatures who work on the superstitions and pretend to cure by charms and hocus-pocus. In the market there is such a swarm of these charlatans of healing that they bring the whole medical profession into contempt." Today, of course, "charlatans" offering miracle cures are more likely to peddle their wares via Web sites and e-mails.

Further Reading

Gabriel, Richard A. 2012. *Man and Wound in the Ancient World: A History of Military Medicine from Sumer to the Fall of Constantinople.* Washington, DC: Potomac Books.

Jouanna, Jacques. 2012. *Greek Medicine from Hippocrates to Galen: Selected Papers.* Edited by Philip van der Eijk. Translated by Neil Allies. Leiden, Netherlands, and Boston: Brill.

King, Helen. 2001. *Greek and Roman Medicine.* London: Bristol Classical Press.

Longrigg, James. 1998. *Greek Medicine: From the Heroic to the Hellenistic Age: A Source Book.* New York: Routledge.

Longrigg, James. 1993. *Greek Rational Medicine: Philosophy and Medicine from Alcmaeon to the Alexandrians.* New York: Routledge.

Métraux, Guy P.R. 1995. *Sculptors and Physicians in Fifth-Century Greece: A Preliminary Study.* Montreal: McGill-Queen's University Press.

Documents

From Hippocrates. C. 400 BCE. *The Genuine Works of Hippocrates.* Volume 1. Translated by Francis Adams. 1849. London: Sydenham Society.

In The Book of Prognostics, *the Greek physician Hippocrates first explains that physicians, to be credible, and must be knowledgeable about how diseases typically develop and progress; then he proceeds to provide some specifics about what physicians should look for when they first examine their patients.*

It appears to me a most excellent thing for the physician to cultivate Prognosis; for by foreseeing and foretelling, in the presence of the sick, the present, the past, and the future, and explaining the omissions which patients have been guilty of, he will be the more readily believed to be acquainted with the circumstances of the sick; so that men will have confidence to entrust themselves to such a physician. And he will manage the cure best who has foreseen what is to happen from the present state of matters. For it is impossible to make all the sick well; this, indeed, would have been better than to be able to foretell what is going to happen; but since men die, some even before calling the physician, from the violence of the disease, and some die immediately after calling him, having lived, perhaps, only one day or a little longer, and before the physician could bring his art to counteract the disease; it therefore becomes necessary to know the nature of such affections, how far they are above the powers of the constitution; and, moreover, if there be anything divine in the diseases, and to learn a foreknowledge of this also. Thus a man will be the more esteemed to be a good physician, for he will be the better able to treat those aright who can be saved, having long anticipated everything; and by seeing and announcing beforehand those who will live and those who will die, he will thus escape censure.

He should observe thus in acute diseases: first, the countenance of the patient, if it be like those of persons in health, and more so, if like itself, for this is the best of all; whereas the most opposite to it is the worst, such as the following; a sharp nose, hollow eyes, collapsed temples; the ears cold, contracted, and their lobes turned out: the skin about the forehead being rough, distended, and parched; the color of the whole face being green, black, livid, or lead-colored. . . . Also, if the disease be in a more advanced stage either on the third or fourth day, and the countenance be such, the same inquiries as formerly directed are to be made, and the other symptoms are to be noted, those in the whole countenance, those on the body, and those in the eyes; for if they shun the light, or weep involuntarily, or squint, or if the one be less than the other, or if the white of them be red, livid, or has black veins in it; if there be a gum upon the eyes, if they are restless, protruding, or are become very hollow; and if the countenance be squalid and dark, or the color of the whole face be changed—all these are to be reckoned bad and fatal symptoms. The physician should also observe the appearance of the eyes from below the eyelids in sleep; for when a portion of the white appears, owing to the eyelids not being closed together, and when this is not connected with diarrhea or purgation from medicine, or when the patient does not sleep thus from habit, it is to be reckoned an unfavorable and very deadly symptom; but if the eyelid be contracted, livid, or pale, or also the lip, or nose, along with some of the other symptoms, one may know for certain that death is close at hand. It is a mortal symptom, also, when the lips are relaxed, pendent, cold, and blanched.

From Hippocrates. C. 400 BCE. *The Genuine Works of Hippocrates*. Volume 1. Translated by Francis Adams. 1849. London: Sydenham Society.

Below is an English translation of the original "Hippocratic Oath," attributed to the Greek physician Hippocrates.

I swear by Apollo the physician, and Aesculapius, and Health, and All-heal, and all the gods and goddesses, that, according to my ability and judgment, I will keep this Oath and this stipulation—to reckon him who taught me this Art equally dear to me as my parents, to share my substance with him, and relieve his necessities if required; to look upon his offspring in the same footing as my own brothers, and to teach them this art, if they shall wish to learn it, without fee or stipulation; and that by precept, lecture, and every other mode of instruction, I will impart a knowledge of the Art to my own sons, and those of my teachers, and to disciples bound by a stipulation and oath according to the law of medicine, but to none others. I will follow that system of regimen which, according to my ability and judgment, I consider for the benefit of my patients, and abstain from whatever is deleterious and mischievous. I will give no deadly medicine to any one if asked, nor suggest any such counsel; and in like manner I will not give to a woman a pessary to produce abortion. With purity and with holiness I will pass my life and practice my Art. I will not cut persons laboring under the stone, but will leave this to be done by men who are practitioners of this work. Into whatever houses I enter, I will go into them for the benefit of the sick, and will abstain from every voluntary act of mischief and corruption; and, further from the seduction of females or males, of freemen and slaves. Whatever, in connection with my professional practice or not, in connection with it, I see or hear, in the life of men, which ought not to be spoken of abroad, I will not divulge, as reckoning that all such should be kept secret. While I continue to keep this Oath unviolated, may it be granted to me to enjoy life and the practice of the art, respected by all men, in all times! But should I trespass and violate this Oath, may the reverse be my lot!

Playwrights

In ancient Athens, tradition holds that drama was an outgrowth of choral performances. As part of an annual festival to honor the god Dionysus, the Dionysia, audiences would listen to all-male choruses who sang pieces called *dithyrambs*, songs that told classic tales from Greek mythology, and did some dancing as well. Each year, several judges would decide which of the festival's dithyrambs was the best, and its composer was awarded an ivy crown. However, in the year 534 BCE, one legendary composer and performer of dithyrambs, named Thespis (ca. sixth century BCE), created the new style of having one singer step away from the chorus and speak as if he were one of the characters in the story, wearing different masks to alternately portray different people. Since he reportedly did these performances himself, Thespis has long been regarded as the world's first actor, which is why actors today are still sometimes referred to as thespians, but he may also qualify as its first playwright. Unfortunately, little is known about this man's life, and none of his works has survived.

As Thespis's form of drama became popular, the policy developed that playwrights competing in annual festivals would write four plays: a trilogy of related tragedies, and a concluding comedy, the satyr play. Another important innovation was introduced by the first Athenian playwright whose works have been preserved, Aeschylus (ca. 524–455 BCE), who featured two speaking actors in his plays, so two characters could speak to each other in addition to interacting with the chorus. He may have written as many as eighty-two plays, but only seven have survived. Also, while all previous plays had retold classic tales from Greek mythology, Aeschylus wrote the first play based on actual historical events, *The Persians* (472 BCE), drawing upon his own experiences as a soldier in the wars against Persia. As one sign of his significance, one notes that originally, only new plays were performed at festivals; after Aeschylus's death, however, revivals of his plays were officially sanctioned, establishing a precedent for new productions of other older plays as well.

We do not actually know what the Greek playwright Sophocles (ca. 497 BCE–406 BCE) looked like, but a nineteenth-century artist created this sketch showing him as a dignified elderly man. (Georgios Kollidas/ Dreamstime.com)

The second of Athens's great playwrights, Sophocles (ca. 496–405 BCE), introduced a third actor to his plays and abandoned the pattern of connected trilogies of plays; though only 7 of his 123 plays survived, the best known of his works, *Oedipus Rex* (429 BCE), was celebrated by Aristotle (384–322 BCE) as the ideal tragedy and discussed at length in his *Poetics*. The other great author of tragedies, Euripides (480–406 BCE), took great liberties with stories from Greek mythology, producing iconoclastic plays that sometimes resembled comedies more than tragedies. Though contemporary audiences did not always appreciate his works, Euripides was more esteemed by later readers, who unusually preserved about nineteen of his estimated ninety-two plays.

Originally, except for the brief satyr plays, the festivals were devoted exclusively to tragedies, but around 487 BC, comedies were included as well. However, while one day of each festival was devoted to the presentation of the tragic playwrights' four plays, the comic playwrights could only offer one play, and these were performed on a single day. Later, in 440 BC, a separate festival, the Lenaia, was established to exclusively feature comedies. Of the playwrights who specialized in comedy, the major figure was Aristophanes (446–386 BCE), who savagely satirized noted Athenian figures like Euripides and the philosopher Socrates (469–399 BCE); eleven of his forty-two plays have survived. A later playwright named Menander (ca. 342–290 BCE) introduced a gentler style termed the New Comedy, focusing on complications in the lives of everyday people; although he was highly acclaimed in his day, only one of his plays has been completely preserved.

Each year, prospective playwrights would apply to compete at the festival, and the presiding archon would select three tragic playwrights, and three or five comic playwrights; each playwright would then be randomly assigned actors to work with, so that no one could gain an unfair advantage in the competition by recruiting outstanding performers. Initially, the expense of staging the plays, and assembling the chorus, was covered by a wealthy individual, termed the *choregos*, but later the city government would underwrite the productions. Completing a play required a number of different talents, because the playwright would not only have to write dialogue for his actors, but he would also have to create both the music and lyrics for the songs that the chorus would be singing songs. In a modern Broadway musical, these tasks are typically assigned to three individuals who write the script (the libretto), the songs' melodies, and their lyrics; the Greek playwright would do all of these things himself. In addition, each playwright was in charge of the rehearsals for his plays, so that he also functioned as a modern-day director, musical director, and choreographer, instructing the actors on how to move and deliver their lines and teaching the chorus to sing each song and dance in an appropriate manner. (Eventually, however, specialists in music and dancing would assume some of these responsibilities.) Like Thespis, early playwrights would sometimes act in their own productions as well, though later playwrights relied exclusively on experienced actors. As one indication of the complexity of the playwright's work, it is estimated that up to 1,500 people—both performers and behind-the-scenes workers—were involved in the production of the seventeen plays that were performed at each festival; thus, one playwright might have to supervise literally hundreds of temporary employees in the course of preparing his productions.

In some respects, Greek dramas were staged in a manner that is very different from modern practices: all performances were outdoors, with audiences seated on the slopes of a hillside overlooking a flat circular stage with an altar to Dionysus; instead of a full orchestra, the musical accompaniment was provided by a single flute player; as noted, all of the actors wore masks to indicate which characters they were playing; and there were no sets or pieces of furniture on the stage, although the tent where the actors changed their masks and costumes might be painted to resemble the main setting of the play. In addition, no depictions of violence were allowed, so that dramatic events, like Clytemnestra's brutal murder of her husband Agamemnon with an axe in Aeschylus's *Agamemnon* (458 BCE), had to occur offstage, to be later described by a character or the chorus. But playwrights could make use of two special effects. One, a platform on wheels called an *ekkyklêma*, was used to bring large objects into view; the other was a large crane, the *mêchanê*, that could dramatically lower an actor playing a god from a great height down to the stage. The use of this crane inspired the Latin phrase *deux ex machina*, or "god from the machine," and since these gods often appeared to suddenly impose an ending on a story that seemed likely to end differently, the term *deux ex machina* now refers to any arbitrary or artificial device employed to conclude a story.

Clearly, when one considers the time required to write the plays, and to prepare their performances, it seems clear that being a playwright was effectively a full-time job; yet it is not entirely clear how playwrights supported themselves while they devoted themselves to these labors. It is believed that in

PRIZE-WINNING PLAYWRIGHTS

In ancient Athens, the major playwrights would stage their productions at an annual festival, the Dionysia, and one playwright would be awarded a prize for writing the best play. The nearest modern equivalent to this competition occurs in New York City, where every year, a Tony Award for the Best Play presented on Broadway is given to the author of the winning production. Most of the recent playwrights who are likely to be remembered by future generations, such as Edward Albee, Harold Pinter, Neil Simon, Tom Stoppard, and August Wilson, have won this prestigious award.

SOLDIERS' SAGAS

Although almost all Greek tragedies were based on tales from Greek mythology, the playwright Aeschylus uniquely wrote one play, *The Persians*, about the historical efforts of the Persian king Xerxes to conquer Greece; although Aeschylus himself had served as a soldier in the war against the Persians, his play seems to express remarkable sympathy for Greece's defeated foes. In the twentieth century, an American named Oliver Stone fought in the Vietnam War but later wrote and directed a trilogy of films—*Platoon*, *Born on the Fourth of July*, and *Heaven and Earth*—that also took the side of the nation Stone had once battled against.

addition to the honorific crowns, the competitions also provided the winners with monetary rewards, which might have been large enough as to allow individuals to make the activity their principal profession, and the *choregos* who financed each production must have provided playwrights with some financial support as well. Still, some playwrights undoubtedly did other work as well; we know, for example, that Aeschylus originally worked in a vineyard and long served as a soldier, and that Sophocles, who came from a wealthy family, also served as a treasurer and a priest. However, the other great tragedian, Euripides, apparently had no other way to support himself, and since his unconventional plays rarely won in the annual competition, he was eventually obliged to seek out a royal patron, Archelaus (died 399 BCE), the king of Macedonia, who provided him with a place to live in his declining years.

Discussions of ancient drama invariably focus on Athens, since while other city-states had their own theaters and dramatic festivals, none of their plays were preserved. But drama was clearly an important form of entertainment for all of the ancient Greeks, and the playwrights responsible for these productions were esteemed members of their societies. It is a tribute to their talents that many of the surviving Greek plays are still staged today, albeit without the accompanying music and masks that were integral elements in their original productions.

Further Reading

Ley, Graham. 2006. *A Short Introduction to the Ancient Greek Theater*. Revised edition. Chicago: Chicago University Press.

Martini, Clem. 2009. *The Greek Playwright: What the First Dramatists Have to Say to Contemporary Playwrights*. Toronto: Playwrights Canada Press.

McDonald, Marianne, and J. Michael Walton, editors. 2009. *The Cambridge Companion to Greek and Roman Theatre*. Cambridge: Cambridge University Press.

McLeish, Kenneth. 2003. *A Guide to Greek Theatre and Drama*. London: A. & C. Black.

Sommerstein, Alan H. 2002. *Greek Drama and Dramatists*. New York and London: Routledge.

Storey, Ian C., and Arlene Allan. 2005. *A Guide to Ancient Greek Drama*. Malden, MA: Blackwell Publishing.

Document

From Aristotle. C. 355 BCE. *The Poetics of Aristotle*. Translated by S. H. Butcher. 1895. London and New York: Macmillan,

In this passage the philosopher Aristotle (384–322 BCE) advises playwrights on the ideal type of plot for a tragedy.

We must proceed to consider what the poet should aim at, and what he should avoid, in constructing his plots; and by what means the specific effect of Tragedy will be produced.

A perfect tragedy should, as we have seen, be arranged not on the simple but on the complex plan. It should, moreover, imitate actions which excite pity and fear, this being the distinctive mark of tragic imitation. It follows plainly, in the first place, that the change of fortune presented must not be the spectacle of a virtuous man brought from prosperity to adversity: for this moves neither pity nor fear; it merely shocks us. Nor, again, that of a bad man passing from adversity to prosperity: for nothing can be more alien to the spirit of Tragedy; it possesses no single tragic quality; it neither satisfies the moral sense nor calls forth pity or fear. Nor, again, should the downfall of the utter villain be exhibited. A plot of this kind would, doubtless, satisfy the moral sense, but it would inspire neither pity nor fear; for pity is aroused by unmerited misfortune, fear by the misfortune of a man like ourselves. Such an event, therefore, will be neither pitiful nor terrible. There remains, then, the character between these two extremes- that of a man who is not eminently good and just, yet whose misfortune is brought about not by vice or depravity, but by some error or frailty. He must be one who is highly renowned and prosperous—a personage like Oedipus, Thyestes, or other illustrious men of such families. A well-constructed plot should, therefore, be single in its issue, rather than double as some maintain. The change of fortune should be not from bad to good, but, reversely, from good to bad. It should come about as the result not of vice, but of some great error or frailty, in a character either such as we have described, or better rather than worse. The practice of the stage bears out our view. At first the poets recounted any legend that came in their way. Now, the best tragedies are founded on the story of a few houses—on the fortunes of Alcmaeon, Oedipus, Orestes, Meleager, Thyestes, Telephus, and those others who have done or suffered something terrible. A tragedy, then, to be perfect according to the rules of art should be of this construction. Hence they are in error who censure Euripides just because he follows this principle in his plays, many of which end unhappily. It is, as we have said, the right ending. The best proof is that on the stage and in dramatic competition, such plays, if well worked out, are the most tragic in effect; and Euripides, faulty though he may be in the general management of his subject, yet is felt to be the most tragic of the poets.

Poets

In its earliest form—the epic poems written by Homer (ca. 800–701 BCE), probably during the eighth century BCE—Greek poetry was primarily a performance art: poets would chant their poems in front of audiences while providing their own musical accompaniment, strumming on a stringed instrument called the cithara. Their craft also required prodigious feats of memory, as they memorized their lengthy epics instead of writing them down, and these works were preserved for posterity by having younger poets memorize them as well. Nobles and wealthy individuals undoubtedly paid talented poets to present their works at public and private gatherings, so they could support themselves, perhaps handsomely. But biographical information about the earliest Greek poets is very slight; contemporary scholars, for example, are not even sure that a poet named Homer actually existed, theorizing that the epics attributed to him, the *Iliad* and the *Odyssey*,

Even though we are not sure that a Greek poet named Homer from the eighth century BCE really existed, that has not prevented sculptors from attempting to render his likeness, in busts like this one, based on the tradition that he was an old blind man. (Kmiragaya/Dreamstime.com)

actually may have been written by teams of anonymous writers. In addition, later writers like Samuel Butler and Robert Graves have argued, based on textual evidence, that the *Odyssey* must have been written by a woman from Sicily. Still, several cities did claim to be the birthplace of Homer, and some authorities described him as a blind man who had two daughters.

We are more confident that the other great poet of Homer's era, Hesiod (ca. 700 BCE), was a real man, since his *Works and Days* identifies its author as a farmer who worked in Boeotia, in central Greece, and its descriptions of farming reflect knowledge that could only have been garnered from personal experience. Though he abandoned farming for poetry after seeing a vision of the Muses, Hesiod may not have found his new career profitable, as he became embroiled with his brother Perses in a fierce dispute over their father's land. This experience inspired Hesiod's most famous poem, *Works and Days*, in which he addresses Perses and ironically advises him to mend his ways by adopting the habits of a successful farmer; his other great work, *Theogony*, provided a mythological history of the world's creation and its subsequent decline. After he lost the case, Hesiod left Boeotia for the city of Naupactus, where a wealthy man welcomed him as a house guest, but tradition holds that he was later murdered by the man's sons. In addition to Homer and Hesiod, there were other epic poets of their era who related stories from Greek mythology, but with rare exceptions, all that we now know about them is their names and the titles of their poems.

Although the epics of Homer and Hesiod were admired and sometimes imitated by later poets, these men and women generally shifted to shorter and more personal forms of poetry that were usually sung instead of being recited. Since these poets also wrote the music for these poems, we today might describe them as songwriters, not poets, though no records survive of the music that they composed. Their works are referred to as lyric poems because the musical accompaniment was often provided by another stringed instrument, the lyre. Though almost all of these poems survive only in fragmentary forms, they are valued because, unlike the epic poems, they often provide information about the daily lives of their authors. One of the earliest of these poets, Sappho (ca. 630–570

An 1881 painting, Lawrence Alma-Tadema's *Sappho and Alcaeus*, imagines the Greek poet Sappho and her friends listening to another poet, Alcaeus, as he plays an instrument and recites his poetry. (The Walters Art Museum)

BCE), was also the first woman who became renowned for her poetry. She was a wealthy woman who lived on the island of Lesbos, and fragments of her poems often appear to address the privileged young girls whom she was educating in the womanly arts. Because the strong emotions in these poems were thought by some to convey her homosexual passions, Sappho inspired the creation of the term "lesbian" to describe female homosexuals. A male contemporary of Sappho who also lived on Lesbos, Alcaeus (ca. 600 BCE), produced lyric poems with both romantic themes and political commentary.

There is precisely one Greek poet of this sort whose work has survived in a complete form: a man named Pindar (ca. 522–443 BCE), who may be the first person in history who made himself a wealthy man by writing poetry. Born into an aristocratic family in Thebes, he became renowned for the quality of his work at a young age, and he subsequently traveled throughout the Greek world, commissioned by wealthy patrons to write celebratory poems for various occasions, such as festivals, athletic competitions, and military victories.

He first learned to write poetry by studying under a female poet, Corinna (ca. 500 BCE), who was also an early rival, but only a few fragments of her work have been preserved. She also criticized Pindar for failing to include references to Greek mythology in one early poem, perhaps explaining why his extant works—four books of forty-five poems celebrating the winners of athletic competitions—include lengthy passages comparing their subjects to mythological heroes. (Interestingly, there is a report that Corinna later condemned Pindar for including too much mythology in another poem, stating "One should sow with the hand, not with the whole sack.")

Another poet, Anacreon (582–485 BCE), first served as a soldier, but he was by his own admission not a very good one, as he once fled from a battle. He went on to enjoy more success as a poet, since he was long supported by two Greek dictators, Polycrates of Samos (died 522 BCE) and Hipparchus of Athens (died 514 BCE), who considered him a welcome guest. While he wrote on a variety of subjects, he became best known for his drinking songs, so much so that he inspired an eighteenth-century drinking song, usually referenced by its first line, "To Anacreon in Heaven," which provided the melody for Francis Scott Key's "The Star-Spangled Banner." Yet we have very few samples of his work, as is also true of another greatly admired poet, Archilochus (ca. 680–645 BCE), who was regularly compared to Homer; described as the son of a free man and a slave woman, he wandered around the Greek world in search of gold before falling in love with a beautiful woman who inspired many of his poems. However, apparently unable to support himself by writing poetry, he primarily served as a soldier and eventually died in battle.

Ancient Greek poetry can be classified in various ways, but two of its other recognized forms include the elegy, written to commemorate noteworthy dead people, and the dithyramb, which related a story from Greek mythology to be sung by a chorus. The latter form evolved into Greek drama after one composer of dithyrambs, Thespis, had one member of his chorus step forward and speak as an individual character in the story. While later plays had three actors playing various parts and diminished the role of the chorus, all of the dialogue was still written in verse, so that one can regard their authors as both playwrights and poets.

The Hellenistic age brought a number of new developments in Greek poetry. A poet named Theocritus (ca. third century BCE), apparently drawing upon his own experiences of growing up in the Sicilian countryside, created a new form of poetry, pastoral, that celebrated rural herdsmen and their simple, contented lives. Another poet, Callimachus (ca. 305–240 BCE), worked at the famous library of Alexandria and focused on the lives of nobles in his most famous poem, "The Lock of Berenice." A third poet, Apollonius (ca. third century BCE), studied under Callimachus, though the men were later enemies, and he later attempted to revive the epic tradition with his *Argonautica*, a lengthy poem about Jason's legendary quest for the Golden Fleece.

Ancient Greek poetry has sometimes been criticized for its elitist attitude; for based on what we know about the lives of poets, and the surviving samples of their work, it seems clear that, with a few exceptions like Hesiod and Theocritus, Greek poems were written by, for, and about members of Greece's ruling

MUSICAL POETS

The lyric poets of ancient Greece also wrote music for their lyrics, but none of their music has been preserved; today, then, we regard them solely as poets even though, to their audiences, they were more like the singer–songwriters of today. Interestingly, some of the song lyrics of prominent twentieth- and twenty-first-century musicians like Paul McCartney, Bob Dylan, and Joni Mitchell, have appeared in anthologies of poetry, and these artists have also published some original poems. Thus, although their music will always remain familiar, such individuals someday may also be valued primarily as poets.

PASSIONATE POETRY

Although the name of her island inspired the modern term for lesbians, there is actually no compelling evidence that the Greek poet Sappho was in fact homosexual; that belief is based solely upon some of her poems, which express strong feelings for other women. However, Sappho also married a man and had a daughter, suggesting to some that the passions in her poetry were largely platonic. A similar debate has ensued about William Shakespeare, since some of his sonnets convey great affection for a young man; again, though, many commentators cite his marriage to Anne Hathaway as evidence that his attachment to this figure was fraternal more than sexual.

class. While everyday citizens were exposed to poetry at the well-attended dramatic festivals, one suspects that they otherwise rarely heard, or were interested in, the poems of writers like Sappho and Pindar. Yet one cannot deny the enduring influence of their work: the entirety of Roman poetry can be summarized as a collective effort to imitate all forms of Greek poetry, and later poets of the European Renaissance and eighteenth century were similarly inclined to hearken back to Greek and Roman models in writing their own poems. And perhaps it was their very distance from the worries and concerns of ordinary people that enabled the Greek poets to focus on the explorations of human emotions and romantic love that have inspired so many later readers and writers.

Further Reading

Greene, Ellen, editor. 2005. *Women Poets in Ancient Greece and Rome*. Norman: University of Oklahoma Press.

Hunter, Richard, and Ian Rutherford, editors. 2009. *Wandering Poets in Ancient Greek Culture: Travel, Locality and Pan-Hellenism*. Cambridge: Cambridge University Press.

Kivilo, Maarit. 2010. *Early Greek Poets' Lives: The Shaping of the Tradition*. Leiden, The Netherlands, and Boston: Brill.

Lefkowitz, Mary. 2013. *The Lives of the Greek Poets*. Second edition. London: Bloomsbury.

Reisman, Rosemary M. Canfield, editor. 2012. *Greek Poets*. Ipswich, MA: Salem Press.

Schmidt, Michael. 2004. *The First Poets: Lives of the Early Greek Poets*. London: Weidenfeld and Nicolson.

Documents

From Aristotle. C. 355 BCE. *The Poetics of Aristotle*. Translated by S. H. Butcher. 1895. London and New York: Macmillan,

Though Aristotle's Poetics *eventually focuses on drama as "the higher form of art," the philosopher (384–322 BCE) first provides a discussion of the origins and history of poetry.*

Poetry in general seems to have sprung from two causes, each of them lying deep in our nature. First, the instinct of imitation is implanted in man from childhood, one difference between him and other animals being that he is the most imitative of living creatures, and through imitation learns his earliest lessons; and no less universal is the pleasure felt in things imitated. We have evidence of this in the facts of experience. Objects which in themselves we view with pain, we delight to contemplate when reproduced with minute fidelity: such as the forms of the most ignoble animals and of dead bodies. The cause of this again is, that to learn gives the liveliest pleasure, not only to philosophers but to men in general; whose capacity, however, of learning is more limited. Thus the reason why men enjoy seeing a likeness is, that in contemplating it they find themselves learning or inferring, and saying perhaps, "Ah, that is he." For if you happen not to have seen the original, the pleasure will be due not to the imitation as such, but to the execution, the colouring, or some such other cause.

Imitation, then, is one instinct of our nature. Next, there is the instinct for "harmony" and rhythm, metres being manifestly sections of rhythm. Persons, therefore, starting with this natural gift developed by degrees their special aptitudes, till their rude improvisations gave birth to Poetry.

Poetry now diverged in two directions, according to the individual character of the writers. The graver spirits imitated noble actions, and the actions of good men. The more trivial sort imitated the actions of meaner persons, at first composing satires, as the former did hymns to the gods and the praises of famous men. A poem of the satirical kind cannot indeed be put down to any author earlier than Homer; though many such writers probably there were. But from Homer onward, instances can be cited—his own *Margites*, for example, and other similar compositions. The appropriate metre was also here introduced; hence the measure is still called the iambic or lampooning measure, being that in which people lampooned one another. Thus the older poets were distinguished as writers of heroic or of lampooning verse.

As, in the serious style, Homer is pre-eminent among poets, for he alone combined dramatic form with excellence of imitation, so he too first laid down the main lines of Comedy, by dramatising the ludicrous instead of writing personal satire. His *Margites* bears the same relation to Comedy that the *Iliad* and *Odyssey* do to Tragedy. But when Tragedy and Comedy came to light, the two classes of poets still followed their natural bent: the lampooners became writers of Comedy, and the Epic poets were succeeded by Tragedians, since the drama was a larger and higher form of art.

From Anacreon. C. 500 BCE. *Anacreon*. Edited by A. H. Bullen. Translated by Thomas Stanley. 1893. London: Lawrence & Bullen.

In several untitled poems, labeled by translator Thomas Stanley as "On Himself," the Greek poet Anacreon describes his delight in drinking wine as an antidote to life's cares, and his fear of growing old and dying.

IV.

On this verdant lotus laid,
Underneath the myrtle's shade,
Let us drink our sorrows dead,
Whilst Love plays the Ganimed.

Life like to a wheel runs round,
And ere long, we underground
(Ta'en by death asunder) must
Moulder in forgotten dust.
Why then graves should we bedew?
Why the ground with odours strew?
Better whilst alive, prepare
Flowers and unguents for our hair.
Come, my fair one! come away;
All our cares behind us lay.
That these pleasures we may know.
Ere we come to those below.

XXI.

Reach me here that full crown'd cup
And at once I'll drink it up;
For my overcharged breast
Pants for drouth, with care opprest;
Whilst a chaplet of cool roses
My distemper'd brow incloses;
Love I'll drench in wine; for these
Flames alone can his appease.

XXIV.

I am sprung of human seed,
For a life's short race decreed;
Though I know the way I've gone,
That which is to come's unknown.
Busy thoughts do not disturb me;
What have you to do to curb me?
Come, some wine and music give:
Ere we die, 'tis fit we live.

XXV.

When with wine my soul is arm'd,
All my grief and tears are charm'd;
Life in toils why should we waste,
When we're sure to die at last?
Drink we then, nor Bacchus spare:
Wine's the antidote of Care.

XXVI.

When my sense in wine I steep,
All my cares are lull'd asleep:
Rich in thought, I then despise

Croesus, and his royalties;
Whilst with ivy twines I wreathe me
And sing all the world beneath me.
Others run to martial fights,
I to Bacchus's delights;
Fill the cup then, boy, for I
Drunk than dead had rather lie.

XXXVIII.

Old I am, yet can (I think)
Those that younger are out-drink;
When I dance no staff I take,
But a well-fill'd bottle shake:
He that doth in war delight,
Come, and with these arms let's fight;
Fill the cup, let loose a flood
Of the rich grape's luscious blood;
Old I am, and therefore may,
Like Silenus, drink and play.

LII.

When I see the young men play,
Young methinks I am as they;
And my aged thoughts laid by,
To the dance with joy I fly:
Come, a flowery chaplet lend me;
Youth and mirthful thoughts attend me
Age be gone, we'll dance among
Those that young are, and be young:
Bring some wine, boy, fill about;
You shall see the old man's stout;
Who can laugh and tipple too,
And be mad as well as you.

Priests and Priestesses

Religion was very important to the ancient Greeks: each city-state chose one of the Olympian gods as its special protector, constructed many temples to honor their deity, and employed priests and priestesses who were dedicated to their worship. Each of these individuals functioned as an independent agent, since Greek religion lacked any sort of overarching hierarchy or organization; a god's priest at one temple had no more or less authority than that god's priest at another temple, and no one could discipline or defrock a priest or priestess for purported impieties. Also, each temple tended to develop and practice its own rituals, and its interpretation of its god or goddess might be distinctively different as well; thus, priests and priestesses had to learn the practices and beliefs of their own temples, and since they generally served for life, they would never travel or seek employment at other temples.

The principal responsibility of a priest or priestess was to manage the temples, which were regarded as the residences of their gods more than places of worship; oftentimes, they featured a statue representing the god that had to be cared for as if it were an actual person. But priests and priestesses had other duties as well: they would preside over important rituals and social events, such as weddings, funerals, festivals, and athletic competitions; after a birth or death in a house, priests would be summoned to purify the building using fire, sulfur, or the blood of a pig; and priests would administer oaths to public officials. However, since the business of maintaining a temple required little time, and other ritual events occurred only occasionally, being a priest or priestess was rarely a full-time occupation, and the people who served in this capacity often held other jobs as well. We know, for example, that the playwright Sophocles once worked as a priest, but he was also a prominent general and diplomat before turning to drama.

One could become a priest or priestess in various ways. In some cases, cults had hereditary priesthoods, so that a man could pass his position on to one of his sons. In at least one instance in Athens, the chief priestess of Athena was chosen in a lottery of all Athenian women, and in a few cases priests and priestesses would have to win an election. More often, interested people would apply to become a priest at a temple. Suitable candidates would have to come from established families that had long resided in a city; they could never have any physical disabilities or deformities; and there are reports that in some places, wealthy men could effectively buy a position as a priest. Typically, gods were served by male priests, while goddesses were served by female priests, though there were exceptions in some cases; for example, Athena was sometimes served by boy priests, while the famed

sanctuary of Delphi, dedicated to Apollo and noted for its prophecies, was staffed by priestesses. In addition, certain gods and goddesses had special requirements: to serve the goddess Artemis, who was a virgin, potential priestesses also had to be virgins, while Hera, the goddess of marriage, required older, married women as priestesses.

Priests and priestess were compensated in various ways. They usually received a salary; the city-state of Athens, for example, once paid its priestess of Athena about 50 drachma a year, rather modest compensation equivalent to about $1,250 in modern dollars. In addition, supplicants would often bring food and animals to be sacrificed to the god at the temple, and the priests or priestesses would receive a portion of the sacrifices; for example, if an animal was sacrificed, the priests or priestesses might be given its valuable leather hide. Priests and priestesses were also paid fees to preside over certain rituals.

The position of priestess was especially advantageous to women, since this was one of the few professions open to Greek women, and a calling that provided them with special prominence and power. Unlike other women, who were considered the guardians of their husbands or male relatives, priestesses had the authority to act on their own behalf, and they might even own their own homes. They could also travel freely outside of their residences, ignoring the restrictions placed on other women; for example, while most women might be barred from attending the Olympic Games, due to the nudity of the male athletes, the priestesses who performed the event's religious ceremonies were not only allowed, but expected, to observe all of the competitions.

Probably the most important priestesses were the sybils, who delivered prophecies while purportedly possessed by the spirit of the god Apollo; the most famous of these, called the Pythia, served at the temple of Delphi, which was established sometime in the eighth century BCE. Supplicants who wished the oracle to answer their question would first pay a fee and sacrifice a female goat; then, the Pythia purportedly entered a trance, becoming possessed by the god, and in that state she would announce an answer to the question, which was written down and presented to the supplicant by male priests. The prophecies that they

This painting on a vase from the fourth century BCE shows the god Apollo speaking with the priestess who conveyed his prophecies, the Pythia of the ancient Greek temple of Delphi. (DeAgostini/Getty Images)

delivered were notoriously ambiguous, rather compromising their value, as illustrated by one example given by the Greek historian Herodotus (484–425 BCE). When King Croesus of Lydia (ca. 595–547 BCE) asked what would happened if he battled the Persians, he was told that he would "destroy a mighty empire." Anticipating a victory, he attacked and was ruinously defeated, so that the destroyed empire turned out to be his own. Much about the process of delivering these predictions remains mysterious: it was said that the Pythia became entranced by inhaling fumes that issued from the ground, and recent evidence suggests that the temple, built on two fault lines, may indeed have been exposed to narcotic fumes from under-

ground volcanic activity. It has also been suggested that the Pythia was intoxicated by laurel leaves, or that she effectively willed herself into a trance, driven by her sincere religious beliefs. In any event, while her statements during the trance were officially recorded by the male priests, some believe that they may have edited, or even revised, her predictions. In at least one case reported by Herodotus, the Pythia was bribed by a supplicant, King Cleomenes I (died 491 BCE), to provide a favorable answer to his question.

While other temples had speaking oracles that were similar to the Pythia, priests and priestesses might predict the future in other ways as well. At the temple of Dodona in Epirus, priests dedicated to Zeus would

SEX AND THE SINGLE PRIEST OR PRIESTESS

The sexual practices of the priests and priestess of ancient Greece tended to mirror those of the deity they served: thus, since Artemis was a virgin goddess, the priestesses of Artemis had to be virgins as well, while the priestesses of Hera, the wife of Zeus and mother of several children, had to be older married women. Similarly, the priests of today's Catholic Church are required to be celibate, in part, in order to emulate the life of one aspect of their deity, Jesus Christ, who never married while he lived on Earth.

PRIESTS, PRIESTESSES, AND POWER

In order for a Greek woman to be powerful and independent, becoming a priestess was almost the only option, since priestesses were the only Greek women whose wealth and authority was not related to the status of their husbands. In America, during the first half of the twentieth century, members of another oppressed group—African American men—sometimes chose to become ministers for the same reason; it was one of the few ways that people in their position could become influential voices in their communities. And later, ministers like Martin Luther King Jr. and Jesse Jackson emerged as key leaders in the civil rights movement.

carefully examine how the wind moved the leaves of oak trees in order to determine future events. Another common method of divination involved sacrificing an animal to their gods, slicing open its stomach, and inspecting its entrails; while anyone might engage in this process, it was often performed or overseen by a priest. Some priests specialized in interpreting dreams believed to be prophetic, or predicting the future by observing birds in flight.

Another important function—healing—was the province of the priests of the god of medicine, Asclepius, whose most famous sanctuary was at the Greek city of Epidauros, reputed to be the god's birthplace. While ailing people primarily went to their temples to pray for divine assistance, the priests at times would also provide them with practical remedies and treatments, effectively functioning as physicians. In certain places, priests and priestesses might have other

special responsibilities: in the city-state of Sparta, for example, the priestesses of Artemis presided over a brutal ritual of flogging young boys until they bled.

Overall, while priests and priestesses enjoyed a certain amount of prestige in their societies, they were mostly regarded as public servants, whose primary responsibility was to keep their god happy by providing suitable sacrifices and performing certain rituals. However, they were not believed to have any special understanding of the gods they served, and while they might at times be granted prophetic visions, they were not asked or expected to provide the gods' opinions about current events, and hence they had no special influence over the actions of their societies. Still, if nothing else, they rarely had to worry about their own personal safety, since everyone knew that harming a priest or priestess might provoke damaging reprisals from an angry god.

Further Reading

Connelly, Joan Breton. 2007. *Portrait of a Priestess: Women and Ritual in Ancient Greece*. Princeton, NJ: Princeton University Press.

Dignas, Beate, and Kai Trampedach, editors. 2008. *Practitioners of the Divine: Greek Priests and Religious Officials from Homer to Heliodorus*. Washington, DC: Center for Hellenic Studies, Trustees for Harvard University.

Flower, Michael Attyah. 2008. *The Seer in Ancient Greece*. Berkeley and Los Angeles: University of California Press.

Horster, Marietta, and Anja Klöckner, editors. 2012. *Civic Priests: Cult Personnel in Athens from the Hellenistic Period to Late Antiquity*. Berlin and Boston: Walter de Gruyter.

Mikalson, Jon D. 2005. *Ancient Greek Religion*. Malden, MA: Blackwell.

Price, Simon. 1999. *Religions of the Ancient Greeks*. Cambridge: Cambridge University Press.

Document

From Herodotus. C. 425 BCE. *The History of Herodotus*. Translated by G.C. Macaulay. 1890. London and New York: Macmillan and Co.

In this passage, the Greek historian Herodotus (ca. 484–425 BCE) interestingly describes a priestess of the Oracle of Delphi who appears to adjust a dire prophecy in order to address the concerns of her supplicants.

For the Athenians had sent men to Delphi to inquire and were preparing to consult the Oracle; and after these had performed the usual rites in the sacred precincts, when they had entered the sanctuary and were sitting down there, the Pythian prophetess, whose name was Aristonike, uttered to them this oracle:

"Why do ye sit, O ye wretched? Flee thou to the uttermost limits, leaving thy home and the heights of the wheel-round city behind thee! Lo, there remaineth now nor the head nor the body in safety—Neither the feet below nor the hands nor the middle are left thee—All are destroyed together; for fire and the passionate War-god, urging the Syrian car to speed, doth hurl them to ruin. Not thine alone, he shall cause many more great strongholds to perish, Yes, many temples of gods to the ravening fire shall deliver—Temples which stand now surely with sweat of their terror down-streaming, Quaking with dread; and lo! from the topmost roof to the pavement Dark blood trickles, forecasting the dire unavoidable evil. Forth with you, forth from the shrine, and steep your soul in the sorrow!"

Hearing this the men who had been sent by the Athenians to consult the Oracle were very greatly distressed; and as they were despairing by reason of the evil which had been prophesied to them, Timon the son of Androbulos, a man of the Delphians in reputation equal to the first, counselled them to take a suppliant's bough and to approach the second time and consult the Oracle as suppliants. The Athenians did as he advised and said: "Lord, we pray thee utter to us some better oracle about our native land, having respect to these suppliant boughs which we have come to thee bearing; otherwise surely we will not depart away from the sanctuary, but will remain here where we are now, even until we bring our lives to an end." When they spoke these words, the prophetess gave them a second oracle as follows:

"Pallas cannot prevail to appease great Zeus in Olympos, Though she with words very many and wiles close-woven entreat him. But I will tell thee this more, and will clench it with steel adamantine: Then when all else shall be taken, whatever the boundary of Kecrops Holdeth within, and the dark ravines of divinest Kithairon, a bulwark of wood at the last Zeus grants to the Triton-born goddess Sole to remain unwasted, which thee and thy children shall profit. Stay thou not there for the horsemen to come and the footmen unnumbered; stay thou not still for the host from the mainland to come, but retire thee, turning thy back to the foe, for yet thou shalt face him hereafter. Salamis, thou the divine, thou shalt cause sons of women to perish, or when the grain is scattered or when it is gathered together."

This seemed to them to be (as in truth it was) a milder utterance than the former one; therefore they had it written down and departed with it to Athens: and when the messengers after their return made report to the people, many various opinions were expressed by persons inquiring into the meaning of the oracle. . . .

Sailors

From the earliest days of Greek civilization, traveling by sea was important, since their nation was surrounded by bodies of water and the mountainous terrain made it difficult to travel by land. Greek mythology is filled with stories of maritime adventurers, including the heroic Argonauts led by Jason, who voyaged in search of the Golden Fleece, and Odysseus, who made many sea journeys as he sought to return to his homeland of Ithaca. But there were practical reasons for the Greeks to master the art of sailing. Wars were regularly settled by decisive battles at sea; ships brought Greek colonizers in search of new homes to attractive locales on Mediterranean islands, the west coast of present-day Turkey, and the east coast of Italy; and almost all of Greece's exported and imported goods were transported by sea. Thus, even a man who was known to despise sea travel, the Greek poet Hesiod (ca. 700 BCE), included in his didactic poem *Works and Days* some advice on sailing, presumably for the benefit of farmers who would need this skill to sell their crops in distant markets.

Greek ships depended upon two sources of energy: oars, used to propel small vessels, and sails, which harnessed wind power to proper large ships (though these also carried oars to be employed if necessary).

Their crews could range in size from three or four men to several dozen, depending upon the size of the ship. Most of the ships sailing the Greek seas were merchant ships, carrying cargo to various destinations. The man who owned a merchant ship, the *naukleros*, did not always travel on his voyages, but when he was there he was in charge of the expedition. Otherwise, the ship was primarily controlled by its captain, or *kybernetes*, who steered the ship at the helm and also functioned as the ship's navigator, using his knowledge of geography and astronomy to keep the ship on course to its destination. Ordinary sailors, the *nautai*, would man the oars, maneuver the sails, and perform other routine tasks during the voyage; these men could either be slaves or hired employees. Since there were no passenger ships of the modern sort, travelers would also voyage on merchant ships, which were happy to take on passengers as an additional source of income; almost invariably, passengers would travel with a servant who would prepare their food and tend to their other needs.

Life on board such ships was not always pleasant. The sailors and most passengers would spend all their time on the deck, exposed to the elements, though sailors always wore hats to protect against the sun, and canvas tents could provide a modicum of privacy while sleeping. A few ships, however, did have cabins that offered more comfortable lodging for wealthy passengers. Even experienced sailors would experience seasickness, especially when the waters were rough. To supplement the stored food that was brought on sea voyages, some sailors would catch and cook some fish; one ivory plaque, for example, shows a ship with a single sailor holding a fishing rod with a fish on its end. This activity might have also served as a welcome diversion for sailors, since their trips could take a very long time if the winds were not favorable, and voyages were further prolonged because captains, lacking accurate charts or advanced navigational techniques, rarely took the most direct routes to their destinations; instead, they tended to stay very close to the shore and never sailed at night.

In addition, the crews of trading ships were regularly threatened by another group of individuals who made their living by sailing: pirates. One can find very little specific information about these universally reviled renegades, who made their living by boarding ships engaged in trade and seizing their goods, forcing their crews into slavery, or holding prominent individuals for ransom. If vulnerable ships were not available, pirates would sometimes attack coastal towns, destroying buildings and looting their valuables. Since vast wealth could be gained from such activities, it is hardly surprising that this profession attracted many individuals and remained commonplace throughout the Mediterranean world, even though Athens at the peak of its naval power was able to temporarily control this problem.

Even if ships were able to avoid pirates, they might crash into the shore or sink beneath the sea, doomed by their captains' limited navigational skills or fierce storms; the usual result was the deaths of all crew members. As one sign of how frequent such disasters were, the *Odyssey* of Homer (ca. 800–701 BCE) significantly reports that its hero Odysseus was the victim of two shipwrecks, emerging as the sole survivor on both occasions. Hoping to avoid such perils, Greek ships would begin each voyage with a sacrifice to the sea god Poseidon, asking for his protection while at sea, and they would conclude each successful voyage with another offering to the god to express their gratitude. Also, as a more practical measure, ships began to limit their voyages to the summer months, when threatening weather was less common. Still, shipwrecks remained common, and though tragic events in their time, they have proven a boon to modern archaeologists, since many valuable artifacts and works of art have been retrieved from sunken ships. Almost all surviving examples of bronze sculptures, for example, have been retrieved from shipwrecks. One particularly intriguing find was a rusted device, called the "Antikythera mechanism," which was apparently used to predict the movements of stars and planets and may have greatly benefited navigators; however, its function and purpose remain poorly understood.

Some sailors were also warriors, fighting on behalf of their city-states; in particular, Athens was renowned for waging effective naval battles. The Greeks primarily relied upon warships called triremes, which were propelled during battles by three rows of men pulling

This marble carving from the fifth century BCE shows a stylized row of sailors propelling their trireme, a warship, with oars. (iStockphoto.com)

oars. These ships typically had crews of about 200 men: 170 oarsmen, a few navigators, and a small force of hoplites, or soldiers. Their primary strategy was to rapidly approach enemy vessels and strike them with the bronze battering rams on their bows, hoping to sink or damage the ships; if they managed to stay afloat, the hoplites would board the crippled vessel to attack its crew. Sometimes, the trireme would also attempt to smash the oars of the other ship so that it could not get away from the attackers. Later, since triremes were relatively lightweight and often difficult to control in heavy winds, the Greeks developed larger warships with four or five rows of oars, termed quadriremes and quinqueremes, which were more easily kept on course; as an added benefit, these ships were able to carry catapults that could hurl fire bombs at opposing ships.

Needless to say, all Greek sailors were men, but the historian Herodotus (484–425 BCE) interestingly describes a rare female warrior as a participant in naval battles: Artemisia (ca. 480 BCE), the female ruler of the Greek city-state of Halicarnassus, who personally commanded five ships of soldiers to fight for the Persian king Xerxes (died 424 BCE) against Greece.

She intelligently told Xerxes to avoid fighting the Greeks at sea, since they excelled in such battles, but he ignored her advice, with ruinous results for the Persians. There is also an intriguing coin, minted in the second century CE, which shows an Amazon holding an anchor, perhaps referring to legends of other seafaring women.

While two epic poems—Homer's *Odyssey* and the *Argonautica* by Apollonius of Rhodes (ca. third century BCE)—offer glimpses of the lives of sailors at sea, the Greeks generally spoke very little about the profession of sailing and the everyday lives of sailors. We can assume, however, that their lives gradually grew easier as Greek civilization progressed: larger ships meant smoother voyages, trade routes became familiar, and the construction of lighthouses, beginning with the famed Lighthouse of Alexandria in 280 BCE, helped to reduce the numbers of disastrous shipwrecks. The Greeks, in fact, had to worry about the well-being of their sailors, since they depended so heavily on imported goods that arrived by sea; so, these men were reasonably well paid, and they were always able to enjoy themselves, like modern sailors, whenever their ships came to shore. All things

MODERN ODYSSEYS

The most famous sailor of ancient Greece was undoubtedly the heroic Odysseus, who spent twenty years at sea while striving to reach his homeland; but this man may have never existed, and most scholars agree that Homer's accounts of his voyages in the *Odyssey* are largely fanciful. Nevertheless, two twentieth-century researchers did attempt to retrace Odysseus's journeys in their own ships, relying upon a close reading of Homer's text and their own observations of Mediterranean geography, and both of them later wrote books about their investigatory travels: Timothy Severin's *The Ulysses Voyage: Sea Search for the Odyssey* (1987), and Hal Roth's *We Followed Odysseus* (1999).

INVENTING PIRATES

Although it is rarely regarded as one of their greatest achievements, the ancient Greeks effectively invented the profession of piracy, since their numerous trading ships, laden with valuable goods, first inspired many sailors to make their living by attacking vessels and commandeering their crews and possessions. To this day, the practice has remained tempting to experienced sailors in need of funds, as demonstrated by the impoverished nation of Somalia, where residents today regularly take to the sea to seize control of passing ships, confiscate their cargoes, and hold their passengers for ransom.

considered, despite its hardships and hazards, sailing may have been one of ancient Greece's more rewarding professions.

Further Reading

Beresford, James. 2013. *The Ancient Sailing Season*. Leiden, The Netherlands, and Boston: Brill.

Mark, Samuel. 2005. *Homeric Seafaring*. College Station: Texas A&M University Press.

Morrison, J. S., J. F. Coates, and N. B. Rankov. 2000. *The Athenian Trireme: The History and Reconstruction of an Ancient Greek Warship*. Second edition. Cambridge: Cambridge University Press.

Morton, Jamie. 2001. *The Role of the Physical Environment in Ancient Greek Seafaring*. Leiden, The Netherlands, and Boston: Brill.

Spyrou, Stella, and Costas Lymbouris, editors. 1994. *The Ancient Greek Sailing Ship of Kyrenia*. Cyprus: Cyprus Ministry of Education and Culture.

Strauss, Barry S. 2004. *The Battle of Salamis: The Naval Encounter That Saved Greece—And Western Civilization*. New York: Simon & Schuster.

Documents

From Apollonius of Rhodes. C. third century BCE. *The Argonautica*. Translated by R. L. Seaton. 1912. London: William Heinemann.

After Jason announces that it is time to launch the Argo, Apollonius's description of the process provides a picture of Greek sailors at work.

[Jason:] "Now at last let us propitiate Phoebus with sacrifice and straightway prepare a feast. And until my thralls come, the overseers of my steading, whose care it is to choose out oxen from the herd and drive them hither, we will drag down the ship to the sea, and do ye place all the tackling within, and draw lots for the benches for rowing. Meantime let us build upon the beach an altar to Apollo Embasius (1) who by an oracle promised to point out and show me the paths of the sea, if by sacrifice to him I should begin my venture for King Pelias."

He spake, and was the first to turn to the work, and they stood up in obedience to him; and they heaped their garments, one upon the other, on a smooth stone, which the sea did not strike with its waves, but the stormy surge had cleansed it long before. First of all, by the command of Argus, they strongly girded the ship with a rope well twisted within, stretching it tight on each side, in order that the planks might be well compacted by the bolts and might withstand the opposing force of the surge. And they quickly dug a trench as wide as the space the ship covered, and at the prow as far into the sea as it would run when drawn down by their hands. And they ever dug deeper in front of the stem, and in the furrow laid polished rollers; and inclined the ship down upon the first rollers, that so she might glide and be borne on by them. And above, on both sides, reversing the oars, they fastened them round the thole-pins, so as to project a cubit's space. And the heroes themselves stood on both sides at the oars in a row, and pushed forward with chest and hand at once. And then Tiphys leapt on board to urge the youths to push at the right moment; and calling on them he shouted loudly; and they at once, leaning with all their strength, with one push started the ship from her place, and strained with their feet, forcing her onward; and Pelian Argo followed swiftly; and they on each side shouted as they rushed on. And then the rollers groaned under the sturdy keel as they were chafed, and round them rose up a dark smoke owing to the weight, and she glided into the sea; but the heroes stood there and kept dragging her back as she sped onward. And round the thole-pins they fitted the oars, and in the ship they placed the mast and the well-made sails and the stores.

Now when they had carefully paid heed to everything, first they distributed the benches by lot, two men occupying one seat; but the middle bench they chose for Heracles and Ancaeus apart from the other heroes, Ancaeus who dwelt in Tegea. For them alone they left the middle bench just as it was and not by lot; and with one consent they entrusted Tiphys with guarding the helm of the well-stemmed ship.

Next, piling up shingle near the sea, they raised there an altar on the shore to Apollo, under the name of Actius and Embasius, and quickly spread above it logs of dried olive-wood. Meantime the herdsmen of Aeson's son had driven before them from the herd two steers. These the younger comrades dragged near the altars, and the others brought lustral water and barley meal, and Jason prayed, calling on Apollo the god of his fathers. . . .

From Xenophon. C. 340 BCE. *Scripta Minora*. Translated by E. C. Marchant. 1925. London: G. Heinemann.

A text called The Athenian Constitution *has been attributed to Xenophon (ca. 430–354 BCE), though many believe that it is the work of another author. In this passage, while discussing the policies of ancient Athens, the author praises sailors and conveys that sea travel was an important aspect of ancient Greek life.*

First, I want to say this: there the poor and the people generally are right to have more than the highborn and the wealthy, for the reason that it is the people who man the ships and impart strength to the city. The steersmen, the boatswains, the sub-boatswains, the look-out officers and the shipwrights—these are the ones who impart strength to the city far more than the hoplites, the highborn, and the good men. This being the case, it seems right for everyone to have a share in the magistracies, both allotted and elective, for anyone to be able to speak his mind if he wants to. . . .

In another point the Athenian people are thought to act ill-advisedly: they force the allies to sail to Athens for judicial proceedings. But they reason in reply that the Athenian people benefit from this. . . . [For] were the allies not to go away for judicial proceedings, they would honour only those of the Athenians who sail out from the city, namely generals, trierarchs, and ambassadors. As it is now, each one of the allies is compelled to flatter the Athenian populace from the realization that judicial action for anyone who comes to Athens is in the hands of none other than the populace (this indeed is the law at Athens); in the courts he is obliged to entreat whoever comes in and to grasp him by the hand. In this way the allies have become instead the slaves of the Athenian people.

Furthermore, as a result of their possessions abroad and the tenure of magistracies which take them abroad, both they and their associates have imperceptibly learned to row; for of necessity a man who is often at sea takes up an oar, as does his slave, and they learn naval terminology. Both through experience of voyages and through practice they become fine steersmen. Some are trained by service as steersmen on an ordinary vessel, others on a freighter, others—after such experience—on triremes. Many are able to row as soon as they board their ships, since they have been practising beforehand throughout their whole lives.

Sculptors

Whenever people think of ancient Greece, the first thing that comes to mind may well be its statues—usually, marble images of standing young men, completely nude, though there are also statues of nude women and robed figures. Undecorated and often lacking limbs, broken off during the last 2,000 years, such statues virtually define for many the lost dignity and artistry of the ancient world. Yet we know very little about the people who chiseled these statues, except for some biographical information about a few famous sculptors that reveals some general truths about their lives.

The ancient Greek civilizations, it is believed, first carved statues out of wood and later shifted to two favored materials, bronze and marble. However, wooden statues decayed quickly, and bronze statues were often melted down so that their valuable bronze could be reused; for that reason, the statues that survive today are usually made of marble, though other substances, ranging from precious gold and ivory to common limestone, were employed as well. The naked male body, invariably a handsome, muscular young man, emerged at an early stage as the favorite subject of sculpture; when women were depicted, they were shown wearing robes until the fourth century BCE, when female nudes (previously regarded as pornographic) also became acceptable. During the Hellenistic Era, when Greece was controlled by the Macedonians, sculptors changed their styles as they were exposed to, and influenced by, other Mediterranean cultures. More diverse subjects became common, including clothed men, children, and animals, and historian Will Durant observes at this time a shift from sculpture that "idealized its types" to efforts "to realize in stone something of human individuality and feeling." As one aspect of this new focus, a sculptor who lived in the fourth century BCE, Lysistratus, introduced a new technique for achieving verisimilitude in renderings of human faces by placing plaster on the face of the person being depicted and using the cast while carving the statue.

A young man who wished to master the art undoubtedly began by apprenticing under an experienced sculptor; in some cases, there were long family traditions of sculptors who passed on their skills and techniques to their sons. Once on his own, a sculptor would begin getting his own assignments from either governments or wealthy individuals, who would pay a commission to obtain a sculpture, specifically precisely what they required; for example, if a local athlete was victorious in the Olympic Games, civic leaders might hire a sculptor to make a statue of the athlete that would be placed in the *agora* to celebrate his prowess. Most sculptors were based in particular cities, though one later sculptor, Alexandros of Antioch (ca. first century BCE), was

described as itinerant, traveling from city to city in search of work.

The process of making a sculpture would begin with a large piece of marble being chiseled into a roughly human shape, mechanical work that was probably done mostly by assistants and apprentices. Then, the sculptor would pick up his chisel and carefully shape the statue into its final form. As models, sculptors would typically employ the muscular young athletes that they had observed in competitions, an experience that also influenced their artwork. For as experts have noted, Greek sculptures can project a special aura of energy, as if the artist was capturing a figure in motion instead of a static, posing model; in providing this quality, the sculptors were surely drawing upon their memories of regularly seeing such naked men walking, running, and wrestling in athletic contests.

Completing the carved image did not end the work of the sculptor, since statues were typically painted with bright colors to make them seem lifelike, gold leaf was sometimes placed over the marble, and adornments like gems and other pieces of jewelry were sometimes attached as well. In all cases, the centuries have worn away the paint and removed these added touches, creating the impression that the ancient Greeks enjoyed looking at bare marble statues when precisely the opposite was the case.

One of the first sculptors whose name has been preserved is the Athenian Pheidias, who lived approximately from 480 to 430 BCE; his two most famous works, no longer extant, were the statue of Zeus at Olympia, deemed one of the Seven Wonders of the Ancient World, and the Athena Parthenos, an elaborately adorned statue of the goddess Athena that was placed inside of Athens's Parthenon. The statue of Zeus was seen and described by the Greek geographer Strabo (ca. 64 BCE–24 CE): "it was made of ivory, and it was so large that, although the temple was very large, the artist is thought to have missed the proper symmetry, for he showed Zeus seated but almost touching the roof with his head, thus making the impression that if Zeus arose and stood erect he would unroof the temple." He also noted that Pheidias had been assisted by his nephew, the painter Paneanas (ca. 450 BCE), who added color to Zeus's garments. With only such verbal descriptions of his Zeus, we cannot be sure what it looked like, but several reliable copies of Pheidias's statue of Athena have survived that convey its ornate beauty. One might imagine that such an esteemed talent would have no difficulty earning enough money to enjoy a comfortable life, yet Pheidias was accused of stealing some of the valuable gold and ivory that were used for his statue of Athena. Many have speculated that someone else committed the crime, and that Pheidias was charged solely for political reasons; nevertheless, he was convicted, and the sculptor might have spent years in prison if the people of Olympia had not paid to obtain his freedom and his services in sculpting their statue of Zeus.

If Pheidias perfected the classic gravitas of Greek sculpture, his most noteworthy successor, Praxiteles (ca. fourth century BCE), brought a new aura of erotic beauty. Commissioned to create a statue of Aphrodite for the city of Cos, he employed the noted courtesan Phryne (ca. fourth century BCE) as a model and shocked residents by presenting a statue of a completely naked goddess. To placate the outraged citizens of Cos, he quickly provided them with another, clothed Aphrodite, but it was the original nude statue, purchased by another city, Cnidus, that became a major tourist attraction, and its popularity helped to make statues of naked women socially acceptable. Two other statues by Praxiteles, of the love god Eros and a satyr, depicted attractive young men, but only copies of these statues are available today.

As individual sculptors grew more concerned about their reputations, the practice developed of placing an inscription on the bases of statues, which named their creators. It was the discovery of such an inscription that enabled scholars to identify a previously obscure figure, Alexandros of Antioch, as the man who crafted what Durant calls "the most famous statue in the Western world," the Venus de Milo, between 130 and 100 BCE. This sculpture, now displayed at the Louvre Museum in Paris, is admired for its stately beauty despite the unfortunate loss of the goddess's arms; as an especially effective instance of Greek sculpture's dynamic qualities, the robe covering the goddess's body appears about to fall off, adding to the statue's erotic appeal. Another renowned statue from the period, Laocoön and His Sons, depicts the

The most famous Greek statue, the *Venus de Milo*, was long attributed to the famed Greek sculptor Praxiteles, but an inscription on its base revealed that it was actually the work of another, less renowned, sculptor, Alexandros of Antioch. (Radu C. Rosca/Dreamstime. com)

Trojan man and his two sons writhing as they are attacked by sea serpents; unusually, it represented the combined work of three different sculptors, Agesander, Polydorus, and Athenodorus (all ca. 50 BCE).

Statues were considered a very important part of Greek cities, and the men who carved them were considered important figures who have remained esteemed and influential artists. The irony is that virtually no one in later times has had the opportunity to observe an accurate representation of their works, since the painted colors, jewelry, and other decorations that they added to their statues have long been lost, and no one has desired to reconstruct their original

A SURREALIST'S SCULPTURE

The most famous work of a Greek sculptor, the Venus de Milo carved by Alexandros of Antioch, inspires modern interest for two reasons: its undeniable beauty, and the mystery of its missing arms. It is believed that her left arm was outstretched holding an apple, while her right arm was close to her body, helping to hold up her robe, and some contemporary artists have attempted to reconstruct what her arms looked like. However, the most prominent artist to attempt his own version of the Venus de Milo, the surrealist Salvador Dali, did not replace her arms, but whimsically added several furniture drawers to her body, decorated with pompons. The 1936 piece is titled *Venus de Milo with Drawers*.

SCANDALOUS STATUES

Although ancient Greek sculptors were careful to conceal female genitalia in their statues of otherwise naked women, they felt absolutely no inhibitions about displaying the genitals of male subjects. Later civilizations, finding this openness offensive, developed the habit of covering the private parts of Greek statues, and statues that imitated the Greek style, by using bits of shrubbery—often, the large leaf of the fig tree. To be more subtle, employees of Great Britain's prudish Queen Victoria carved a stone fig leaf, which they attached to a copy of Michelangelo's David whenever the queen was present. Fig leaves were also used to cover the genitals of painted nudes.

appearance. Strangely, to modern eyes, rare instances of painted, decorated versions of classic Greek statues seem artless and garish, in contrast to the gravitas and restraint of the bare statues. Thus, one might say, it is the unfinished stage of classic Greek sculpture, not its final form, that became a powerful influence on later sculptors like Michelangelo, who only imagined that in carving his famous David he was emulating ancient Greek precursors, since they would have actually regarded his unadorned statue as incomplete.

Further Reading

Jenkins, Ian. 2006. *Greek Architecture and Its Sculpture*. Cambridge, MA: Harvard University Press.

Métraux, Guy P. R. 1995. *Sculptors and Physicians in Fifth-Century Greece: A Preliminary Study*. Montreal: McGill-Queen's University Press.

Neer, Richard. 2010. *The Emergence of the Classical Style in Greek Sculpture*. Chicago: University of Chicago Press.

Palagia, Olga, and J. J. Pollitt, editors. 1996. *Personal Styles in Greek Sculpture*. Cambridge: Cambridge University Press.

Spivey, Nigel. 2013. *Greek Sculpture*. Cambridge and New York: Cambridge University Press.

Spivey, Nigel. 1996. *Understanding Greek Sculpture: Ancient Meanings, Modern Readings*. New York: Thames and Hudson.

Document

From Strabo. C. 18 CE. *Geography*. 8 volumes. Translated by John Robert Sitlington Sterrett and Horace Leonard Jones. 1917–1932. London: William Heinemann.

In his Geography, *the ancient Greek historian Strabo describes the most famous statue of the sculptor Pheidias.*

At the outset the temple [of Olympia] got fame on account of the oracle of the Olympian Zeus; and yet, after the oracle failed to respond, the glory of the temple persisted none the less, and it received all that increase of fame of which we know, on account both of the festal assembly and of the Olympian Games, in which the prize was a crown and which were regarded as sacred, the greatest games in the world. The temple was adorned by its numerous offerings, which were dedicated there from all parts of Greece. Among these was the Zeus of beaten gold dedicated by Cypselus the tyrant of Corinth. But the greatest of these was the image of Zeus made by Pheidias of Athens, son of Charmides; it was made of ivory, and it was so large that, although the temple was very large, the artist is thought to have missed the proper symmetry, for he showed Zeus seated but almost touching the roof with his head, thus making the impression that if Zeus arose and stood erect he would unroof the temple. Certain writers have recorded the measurements of the image, and Callimachus has set them forth in an iambic poem. Panaenus the painter, who was the nephew and collaborator of Pheidias, helped him greatly in decorating the image, particularly the garments, with colors. And many wonderful paintings, works of Panaenus, are also to be seen round the temple. It is related of Pheidias that, when Panaenus asked him after what model he was going to make the likeness of Zeus, he replied that he was going to make it after the likeness set forth by Homer in these words: "Cronion spoke, and nodded assent with his dark brows, and then the ambrosial locks flowed streaming from the lord's immortal head, and he caused great Olympus to quake."

Slaves

Slavery was both ubiquitous and universally accepted throughout the ancient world; even in the renowned birthplace of democracy, the city-state of Athens, few people ever questioned the logic or morality of some people becoming the property of other people. In the first book of his *Politics*, for example, the philosopher Aristotle (384–322 BCE) does note that some people "affirm that the rule of a master over slaves is contrary to nature, and that the distinction between slave and freeman exists by law only, and not by nature; and being an interference with nature is therefore unjust." However, he immediately refutes this position, arguing that "the lower sort are by nature slaves, and it is better for them as for all inferiors that they should be under the rule of a master."

In ancient Greece, virtually anyone might be unfortunate enough to become a slave, simply by wandering too far from home and being kidnapped or by having one's ship seized by pirates; the militaristic city-state of Sparta even conquered a neighboring country, Messenia, and absorbed its entire population as slaves called *helots*. In some cases, poor families would sell one of their children into slavery; a person with enormous debts might be forced into slavery; and there is the singular tale of one physician in the fourth century BCE, Menecrates of Syracuse, who agreed to treat certain patients only if they would become his slaves after he saved their lives. A person could also be born into slavery as the child of slaves. However, it was an especially common consequence of being on the losing side of a war, since defeated soldiers were regularly forced into slavery by the victors. Once captured, slaves would be forced to stand naked in the marketplace to be inspected by prospective buyers, who might range from wealthy men with hundreds of slaves to a poor man who could only afford to buy one or two. Once enslaved, people would generally remain slaves for the rest of their lives, but slavery in ancient Greece was not necessarily a permanent condition; a few slaves might be freed by their owners, the process termed manumission, or they might earn enough money to purchase their freedom.

There were numerous slaves in ancient Greece, especially in Athens, where they may have outnumbered the free citizens. They could be owned either by individual families or by the government, and in both cases they did most of society's daily work. In households, male slaves were frequently employed as farmers or tutors to the children, while female slaves handled domestic duties like cooking, cleaning, and weaving. When working for the government, slaves might engage in manual labor, helping to construct buildings or repair roads, but they could also be assigned to office work, serving as jury clerks or public notaries. The most arduous and perilous work assigned to slaves was mining, as they were forced to work in ten-hour shifts, digging ores out of narrow underground chambers lit only by a few lamps. By one account, up to 30,000 slaves labored in the famed silver mines of Laurium, constantly afflicted by the poisonous fumes generated by the process of smelting the silver ores, and historian H.D.F. Kitto notes that these "slaves were often worked until they died."

Today, much of our knowledge about the daily lives of Greek slaves is conjectural, since they were rarely discussed or described in written texts. We know that their relationships with families began with an initiation ceremony that brought them under the aegis of the goddess Hestia, protector of family life. In the *Odyssey* of Homer (ca. 800–701 BCE), the warm way that Odysseus's slaves greet him upon his return indicates that in some cases, slaves were treated like members of the family, as is also suggested by the fact that a few slaves were buried alongside their masters. On the other hand, slaves were routinely punished by being beaten, and slaves who attempted to escape, after being recaptured, would be branded using a hot iron both to punish them and to identify them as potential runaways.

We also learn a few things about slaves because they are occasionally mentioned in written laws. They were never permitted to participate in elections, and their testimony could be accepted in court cases only if it was obtained by means of torture. While it was officially against the law to subject slaves to violent abuse, they were not allowed to represent themselves in court, so a tortured slave would have no real way to obtain justice unless the mistreatment was reported by a free citizen. In some cases, however, a slave might escape abuse by seeking asylum within a temple, which would generally require the owner to sell the slave to someone else.

The individual slaves whose names have entered the history books were atypical because of their unusual achievements. In Athens during the fourth century BCE, a slave who worked as a banker, Pasion, became so wealthy that he donated needed funds to the government and was eventually rewarded with his freedom. When he died, he stipulated in his will that another freed slave, Phormio, should assume control of his businesses. A number of ancient sources also insist that there was once an ugly Greek slave named Aesop (ca. 624–564 BCE) who was intelligent enough to earn his freedom and become involved in diplomacy while also writing the famed animal fables widely attributed to him. However, since there is considerable disagreement about when and where this man lived, some modern authorities suspect that Aesop actually never existed.

Slaves also appear occasionally as characters in ancient Greek literature. One noteworthy example is the dialogue *Meno* by Plato (427–347 BCE), wherein Socrates (469–399 BCE) addresses a slave owned by Meno, a Thessalonian political leader, and through a series of questions prods the slave to state the Pythagorean theorem. Socrates's argument is that all humans possess innate knowledge from previous lives, as shown by the fact that even the brain of an uneducated slave actually contains geometric theorems, but a modern reader would conclude, quite differently, that he was really demonstrating that the Greeks' little-esteemed slaves did possess the intelligence to learn mathematics. There is also a scene in the play *The Frogs* by Aristophanes (446–386 BCE) wherein two slaves speak disrespectfully about their

STORYTELLING SLAVES

Telling stories about animals may be appealing to slaves, since such seemingly innocuous tales can convey disguised criticisms of masters who demanded subservience. This may be why the legendary Greek slave Aesop wrote animal fables, or at least why later readers believed that such stories were the work of a slave. In the nineteenth century, a white American, Joel Chandler Harris, socialized with slaves on a Georgia plantation and subsequently wrote a series of animal fables, called the Uncle Remus stories, based on stories they had told him. While these have been criticized as racist, others discern in them elements of an authentic tradition of African American folklore.

ASSERTIVE UNDERLINGS

Although actual Greek slaves surely had to be obedient and deferential at all times, the comedies of Aristophanes sometimes featured sarcastic, assertive slaves as characters. This convention is sometimes followed in modern depictions of servants; thus, the comic strip and television series *Hazel* (1961–1966), and the television series *Benson* (1979–1986), respectively, featured a maid and a butler who seemed far wiser and more domineering than the masters that they ostensibly served. In the case of *Benson*, the character even advanced from being a governor's butler to becoming his state's budget director and, later, its lieutenant governor.

masters, interestingly suggesting an awareness among slave owners that their possessions were not always as happy and respectful as they were obliged to act in the presence of their masters. Resourceful, insolent slaves would also become standard characters in the later comedies of Menander (ca. 342–290 BCE).

Overall, based on the information that we can glean, there can be little doubt that the lives of most slaves involved little more than day after day of monotonous labor, with little prospect of eventual relief through manumission or a peaceful retirement. Still, even if their lives were not pleasant, they generally were not unduly harsh, and there are few indications that rebellious or runaway slaves were commonplace in most of the Greek city-states. The situation was different, however, in Sparta. It is believed that the city-state developed its militaristic culture in large part because of the constant fear that their helots, who vastly outnumbered the Spartans, might revolt, demanding constant vigilance and military might to keep them in line. And, even though the lives of helots seemed in some respects arguably better than those of slaves in other city-states—they lived more like medieval serfs than slaves, bound to pieces of land, and they were considered the property of the government as a whole, not individuals—they did in fact rebel on several occasions, despite being constantly observed and monitored by their nervous overseers. Still, it was not until the second century BCE, when Sparta lost all of its power and influence, that the helots were finally freed from their centuries of oppression.

Despite this singular instance of a massive release from slavery, no such fate awaited the other slaves of ancient Greece, as the owning of slaves remained an integral part of Greek culture and the other cultures that succeeded it. Only on rare occasions were slaves able to escape from their status due to their own extraordinary efforts or a kindly master. Still, even if they were no better or worse than other ancient cultures in embracing slavery, one can at least credit the Greeks with developing the idea of democracy, which would, almost 2,000 years later, inspire prominent individuals in the Western world to advocate, and eventually achieve, an end to this reprehensible institution.

Further Reading

Bradley, Keith, and Paul Cartledge, editors. 2011. *The Cambridge History of Slavery, Volume One: The Ancient Mediterranean World.* Cambridge: Cambridge University Press.

Forsdyke, Sara. 2012. *Slaves Tell Tales: And Other Episodes in the Politics of Popular Culture in Ancient Greece.* Princeton, NJ: Princeton University Press.

Garlan, Yvon. 1988. *Slavery in Ancient Greece.* Ithaca, NY: Cornell University Press.

Hunt, Peter. 2012. *Slavery in Ancient Greece and Rome.* Oxford: Wiley-Blackwell.

Hunt, Peter. 1998. *Slaves, Warfare, and Ideology in the Greek Historians.* Cambridge: Cambridge University Press.

Wrenhaven, Kelly L. 2012. *Reconstructing the Slave: The Image of the Slave in Ancient Greece.* London: Bristol Classical Press.

Document

From Aristophanes. 424 BCE. *A Metrical Version of The Acharians, The Knights, and The Birds.* Translated by John Hookham Frere. 1840. London: Pickering.

In this passage from Aristophanes's The Knights, *a slave complains about another slave, conveying the sorts of petty rivalries and brutal treatment that Greek slaves regularly had to endure.*

[Demosthenes:] [Our master is] A Man in years,
A kind of bean-fed husky testy character,
Choleric and brutal at times, and partly deaf.
It's near about a month now, that he went
And bought a slave out of a tanner's yard
A Paphlagonian born, and brought him home,
As wicked a slanderous wretch as ever lived.
This fellow, the Paphlagonian, has found out
The blind side of our master's understanding,
With fawning and wheedling in this kind of way:
"Would not you please to go to the bath, Sir? surely
It's not worth while to attend the courts to-day."
And, "Would not you please to take a little refreshment?
And there's that nice hot broth—And here's the threepence
You left behind you—And would not you order supper?"

Moreover, when we get things out of compliment
As a present for our master, he contrives
To snatch 'em and serve 'em up before our faces.
I'd made a Spartan cake at Pylos lately,
And mixed and kneaded it well, and watched the baking;
But he stole round before me and served it up:
And he never allows us to come near our master
To speak a word; but stands behind his back
At meal times, with a monstrous leathern fly-flap,
Slapping and whisking it round and rapping us off.

Sometimes the old man falls into moods and fancies,
Searching the prophecies till he gets bewildered;

And then the Paphlagonian plies him up,
Driving him mad with oracles and predictions.
And that's his harvest. Then he slanders us,
And gets us beaten and lashed, and goes his
   rounds
Bullying in this way, to squeeze presents from us;
"You saw what a lashing Hylas got just now;
You'd best make friends with me, if you love
   your lives."
Why then, we give him a trifle, or if we don't,
We pay for it; for the old fellow knocks us down,
And kicks us on the ground, and stamps and rages,
And tramples out the very guts of us. . . .

Soldiers

From the *Iliad* of Homer (ca. 800–701 BCE) to the chronicles of later historians, the ancient Greeks left us many stories about their wars, and the men who fought those wars. Clearly, fighting on behalf of one's country was regarded as a highly important activity; thus, while we esteem Aeschylus (ca. 342–290 BCE) today as a great playwright, his tombstone was solely devoted to honoring his exploits as a soldier. Warfare was also a skill that the Greeks became very good at: the city-states warred against each other almost constantly, though most of their conflicts were brief, and they joined forces to defeat Persian armies that were significantly larger than their own forces.

Only one city-state—Sparta—maintained a standing army, which effectively consisted of all of its adult male citizens. Beginning at the age of seven, Spartan boys were sent to live at a boarding school, called the *agoge*, where they received rigorous military training; as adolescents, they would undergo a rite of passage by being sent to the countryside to live on their own for an extended period of time and to kill at least one of the Spartan slaves, or helots. Then, when they were twenty years old, they would be assigned to live in barracks, ready to fight on any occasion; indeed, trusting its army to effectively spring to its defense if the city were attacked, Sparta uniquely had no walls. After twenty years of active duty, Spartan soldiers became reserves, and they might be asked to perform some military duties even after the age of sixty.

The other city-states of Greece relied entirely upon part-time soldiers, usually farmers and other laborers who were recruited when needed to fight on behalf of their city-states. In fact, it was customary to avoid fighting wars during the time when farmers needed to harvest their crops. In Athens, all men were first trained to fight between the ages of eighteen and twenty; for the next thirty years, they could be called to active duty at any time to battle enemies; and from the age of fifty to sixty, they would be assigned to guard Athenian territory whenever the younger soldiers were deployed elsewhere. Only at the age of sixty, after forty-two years of potential service, were the Athenian men finally freed from all military responsibilities. Generally, city-states only recruited their own citizens to serve as soldiers, but toward the end of the classical period, when Greece was afflicted by civil wars, city-states began to hire foreign mercenaries as well.

Most Greek warriors were known as *hoplites* because of their characteristic shields, the *hoplons*. These circular shields, made of wood and coated with bronze, were held in one hand to protect their owner, while the other hand held a long spear, the *dolu*, that was used to stab enemy soldiers. The heavy shields of the hoplites could also be employed as a weapon to strike one's foes, and soldiers carried a smaller sword, called a *xiphos*, which they relied on if their spears broke or were dropped. For additional protection, soldiers usually wore helmets, breastplates, and greaves, or leg armor, all made of bronze. These items had to be purchased and maintained by individual soldiers, since governments did not provide them; this meant that it was always the wealthiest soldiers who had the best equipment, while poorer men might go into battle with inadequate armor or inferior weapons like clubs or javelins. Soldiers also carried knapsacks with foods like cheese, bread, and onions, though they mostly relied on the food that they could find or seize while traveling. It is estimated that the total weight of the items carried by hoplites was seventy pounds, requiring great physical strength and stamina.

Initially, as described by Homer, Greek soldiers tended to fight as individuals, but later they learned to advance within a formation called the phalanx, enabling teams of men to hold their shields together to

This painting of two opposing soldiers, on a storage jar, or *amphora*, from 500–480 BCE, shows their characteristic equipment and weapons—long spears, circular shields, body armor, and helmets. (J. Paul Getty Museum)

form an impenetrable wall as they marched into battle. Opposing sides would first meet to agree upon a site for the battle, so there were never any surprise attacks; then, the two sides would advance toward each other. A successful outcome usually depended upon the soldiers remaining in their positions as they approached and attacked their foes; if the formation started to break up, soldiers became more vulnerable to enemy spears, and panicked soldiers might begin to flee, even removing some of their heavy armor in order to run more quickly, though this also made it easier to kill them. Most battles were over in less than an hour.

If Greek soldiers did not die in battle, other unpleasant fates awaited them if they survived as the losers of a battle. There were some cases when opposing armies would exchange their prisoners, but it was more common for the victorious side to enslave their defeated enemies, forcing them to return with them to endure lives of drudgery. During the especially bitter Peloponnesian War (from 431 to 404 BCE), enemy soldiers would often be slaughtered even if they peacefully surrendered. Wounded soldiers often died not from their wounds but from infections, since the Greeks did not understand the need to keep wounded areas clean.

While most of the soldiers in Greek armies were hoplites, there were other personnel who performed special duties. These included couriers, who ran quickly across the countryside to deliver news to and from the army's home city-states; surgeons, who tended to wounded soldiers; and diviners, who were regularly asked to determine the will of the gods and decide upon propitious times for military initiatives, often by sacrificing an animal and examining its entrails. Larger armies might also be accompanied by cooks to prepare food and blacksmiths to repair armor and weapons. In the war against the Persians, the Greeks sent three spies to investigate the army of Xerxes (died 424 BCE); as the Greek historian Herodotus (484–425 BCE) recounts, the spies were captured and about to be executed when Xerxes cancelled the order, allowed the spies to observe his army, and set them free, convinced that their honest report of his military might would persuade

A MODERN GREEK ARMY

One of the most familiar images of ancient Greek life is the armored hoplite, wearing his distinctive helmet and holding his spear and circular shield. This figure has remained fascinating to many modern citizens, so much so that in 2001, a group of men established the Hoplite Association in order to construct and wear the armor of the hoplites, carry replicas of their weapons and equipment, and recapture their romanticized lifestyle. In addition to donning the regalia of the hoplite at various events, members of this association have been employed to portray Greek soldiers in films and documentaries.

A NATION OF SOLDIERS

The city-state of Sparta was powerful, in large part, because it effectively transformed its entire male population into a standing army, providing the city with a large, well-trained military force, which eventually enabled the Spartans to defeat Athens and dominate Greece. A modern-day equivalent to Sparta, perhaps, is the nation of North Korea, which despite its relatively small population has made itself a force to be reckoned with in world politics by building and maintaining the world's largest army, with almost ten million men and women, about forty percent of its total population.

the Greeks to surrender. Yet the Greeks remained determined to fight for their freedom and undoubtedly benefited from the information that their spies provided.

While the hoplites, wearing their characteristic helmets and armor and holding their shields, dominate our image of the Greek warrior, other sorts of soldiers began to play larger and larger roles in battles. First and foremost, many Greek soldiers were also sailors, serving on ships called triremes that would first ram, and then attempt to board, enemy vessels. On land, we know from Homer that archers were regularly involved in ancient Greek conflicts, and around the fifth century BCE they again emerged as key players, prized for their ability to strike down enemies from a distance. Another weapon sometimes employed was the sling, a leather bag attached to cords that allowed soldiers to fling small stones at opponents. Also, as

the Greeks came into contact with the armies of other civilizations, they adopted some of their practices, including the use of cavalry—sword-wielding soldiers on horseback—and chariots drawn by horses, which could quickly maneuver fighters in and out of battles. In the fourth century BCE, Greek armies began to employ siege engines, large portable structures that could attack fortified cities by battering down their gates or hurling large stones over their walls. As early forms of biological and chemical warfare, armies would sometimes throw people infected with smallpox or the plague into enemy cities, and the Spartans would blend sulfur and tar together, set the mixture on fire, and employ it to damage buildings and fortifications.

Overall, considering their many important contributions to civilization, one might regret that the ancient Greeks devoted so much of their time and energy to warfare; yet the Greeks themselves might respond that it was precisely their dedication to fighting for their freedom that enabled them to produce the art, literature, and philosophy that we now admire. It is also true that renowned authors like the playwright Aeschylus and historian Xenophon (430–354 BCE) had previously served as soldiers, and drew upon their experiences to produce their greatest works. More broadly, for better or worse, the Greeks' prowess on the battlefield must be regarded as a key aspect of their society that deeply influenced all of their endeavors.

Further Reading

De Souza, Philip. 2003. *The Greek and Persian Wars, 499–386 B.C.* New York: Routledge.

Kagan, Donald, and Gregory Viggiano, editors. 2013. *Men of Bronze: Hoplite Warfare in Ancient Greece.* Princeton, NJ: Princeton University Press.

Lee, John W. I. 2007. *A Greek Army on the March: Soldiers and Survival in Xenophon's Anabasis.* Cambridge: Cambridge University Press.

Lendon, J. F. 2005. *Soldiers and Ghosts: A History of Battle in Classical Antiquity.* New Haven, CT: Yale University Press.

Santosuosso, Antonio. 1997. *Soldiers, Citizens, and the Symbols of War: From Classical Greece to Republican Rome, 500–167 B.C.* Boulder, CO: Westview Press.

Van Rees, Hans. 2004. *Greek Warfare: Myths and Realities.* London: Duckworth.

Documents

From Xenophon. C. 370 BCE. *Xenophon: Hellenica.* Volume I. Translated by Carleton L. Brownson. 1918. London: William Heinemann.

In this passage from Hellenica, *the writer and former general Xenophon describes how the Spartan general Agesilaus (444–360 BCE) prepared his troops for battle.*

When spring was just coming on [in 395 BCE], he gathered his whole army at Ephesus. And desiring to train the army, he offered prizes both to the heavily-armed divisions, for the division which turned out to be in the best physical condition, and to the cavalry divisions, for the one which displayed the best horsemanship. And he also offered prizes to light infantrymen and archers, for all who should prove themselves best in their respective duties. So one might have seen all the gymnasiums full of men exercising, the hippodrome full of riders, and the javelin throwers and bowmen practicing. In fact, he made the entire city where he was staying a sight worth seeing, for the central part of the city was full of all sorts of horses and weapons, offered for sale, and the copper workers, carpenters, smiths, leather cutters, and painters were all engaged in making military weaponry, so that one might have thought that the city was really a workshop of war. And one would have been encouraged at another sight also: Agesilaus in the forefront, and after him the rest of the soldiers, returning garlanded from the gymnasiums and dedicating their garlands to Artemis. For where people reverence the gods, train themselves in deeds of war, and practice obedience to authority, may we not reasonably suppose that such a place abounds in high hopes? And again, believing that to feel contempt for one's enemies infuses a certain courage for the fight, Agesilaus gave orders to his heralds that the barbarians who were captured by the Greek raiding parties should be exposed for sale naked. Thus the soldiers, seeing that these men were white-skinned because they never were without their clothing, and soft and unused to toil because they always rode in carriages, came to the conclusion that the war would be in no way different from having to fight with women.

From Homer. Ca. eighth century BCE. *The Iliad of Homer, Rendered into English Prose for the Use of Those Who Cannot Read the Original.* Translated by Samuel Butler. 1898. London and New York: Longmans, Green.

In this passage from the Iliad, *relating how the hero Achilles prepared for battle, Homer describes the typical armor and weapons of the soldiers in his era.*

In the midst of them all Achilles put on his armour; he gnashed his teeth, his eyes gleamed like fire, for his grief was greater than he could bear. Thus, then, full of fury against the Trojans, did he don the gift of the god, the armour that Vulcan had made him. First he put on the goodly greaves fitted with ancle-clasps, and next he did on the breastplate about his chest. He slung the silver-studded sword of bronze about his shoulders, and then took up the shield so great and strong that shone afar with a splendour as of the moon. As the light seen by sailors from out at sea, when men have lit a fire in their homestead high up among the mountains, but the sailors are carried out to sea by wind and storm far from the haven where they would be- even so did the gleam of Achilles' wondrous shield strike up into the heavens. He lifted the redoubtable helmet, and set it upon his head, from whence it shone like a star, and the golden plumes which Vulcan had set thick about the ridge of the helmet, waved all around it. Then Achilles made trial of himself in his armour to see whether it fitted him, so that his limbs could play freely under it, and it seemed to buoy him up as though it had been wings. He also drew his father's spear out of the spear-stand, a spear so great and heavy and strong that none of the Achaeans save only Achilles had strength to wield it; this was the spear of Pelian ash from the topmost ridges of Mt. Pelion, which Chiron had once given to Peleus, fraught with the death of heroes. Automedon and Alcimus busied themselves with the harnessing of his horses; they made the bands fast about them, and put the bit in their mouths, drawing the reins back towards the chariot. Automedon, whip in hand, sprang up behind the horses, and after him Achilles mounted in full armour, resplendent as the sun-god Hyperion. Then with a loud voice he chided with his father's horses saying, "Xanthus and Balius, famed offspring of Podarge—this time when we have done fighting be sure and bring your driver safely back to the host of the Achaeans, and do not leave him dead on the plain as you did Patroclus."

Tyrants

The tyrants, or dictators, who long governed the city-states of ancient Greece were different than their modern counterparts in several respects. Despite the negative connotations of the term in modern discourse, tyrants were often welcomed as attractive alternatives to hereditary rulers, and since they were usually wealthy men, they were rarely tempted to exploit their positions for personal gain. Indeed, their governance was sometimes regarded as enlightened and benign: Aristotle (384–322 BCE) praised one Athenian dictator, Peisistratus (died ca. 527 BCE), as a "statesman" distinguished by his "temperate" rule, and a tyrant on the island of Rhodes, Cleobulus (ca. sixth century BCE), was celebrated as one of ancient Greece's Seven Sages, respected for his wise rule, poetry, and frequently quoted aphorisms. Still, the city-states generally came to dislike their despotic rulers and drove them out of office, though many again succumbed to tyranny after periods of more democratic governments.

In Greece's early days, societies were usually governed by hereditary kings, as described in the epic poems of Homer (ca. 800–701 BCE), and this remained the usual pattern until the seventh century BCE. This was the time when the term "tyrant" was first coined by the poet Archilochus (ca. 680–645 BCE) to describe Gyges (died ca. 688 BCE), ruler of Lydia (a region of present-day Turkey), who attempted to conquer Greece; there are also many stories about a tyrant in Argos, Pheidon (ca. seventh century BCE), who is credited with establishing Greece's systems of weights and measures and once presiding over the Olympic Games. However, since reports of his accomplishments span a period of 150 years, many historians believed that this man never existed. The earliest tyrant described in trustworthy accounts was Cypselus (died 627 BCE) of the city-state of Corinth, who seized power in 657 BC, slaughtering or exiling the unpopular aristocrats who had previously ruled. The Greek historian Herodotus (484–425 BCE) tells the story that, before his birth, an oracle proclaimed that the baby

Centuries after Periander's death sometime in the seventh century BCE, a Greek sculptor carved a bust of the tyrant; this photograph shows the surviving Roman copy of the original Greek sculpture. (Vanni Archive/ Art Resource, NY)

would someday threaten the city's rulers, inspiring them to send men to kill the newborn boy; however, the would-be assassins could not bring themselves to kill the adorable infant, so Cypselus survived and eventually fulfilled the prophecy. Both he and his son Periander (died 585 BCE) ruled until they died, but Periander's propensity for violence made him increasingly unpopular with his constituents, and the third representative of the dynasty, Periander's nephew, was assassinated after four years in office.

As tyrants became more and more common in the seventh and sixth centuries BCE, the pattern observed in Corinth was generally repeated: the first tyrants enjoyed broad public support and significantly improved their societies, but the sons or relatives who succeeded them proved to be unwise rulers and were eventually overthrown. As is often the case, we are most familiar with political events in Athens, which had established a system of having wealthy aristocrats annually elect an official, the archon, to govern the city-state. But despite reforms instituted by the statesman Solon (ca. 638–558 BCE) that were designed to strengthen this system, his friend Peisistratus used military forces to seize control of Athens, first temporarily and later permanently. As the city's tyrant, he was appreciated for his beneficial construction projects, policies that brought Athens economic prosperity, and his support for the arts, especially poetry and drama. But after his death his son Hippias (died ca. 480 BCE) took over Athens, assisted by his brother Hipparchus, and when Hipparchus was murdered in 514 BCE, the tyrant became a paranoid and brutal ruler and was soon forced into exile. A few years later, memories of Hippias's excesses helped to inspire the democratic reforms of Cleisthenes (ca. 570–500 BCE), which gave Athenian citizens more ability to control their own destinies.

As was true of twentieth-century Latin America, ancient Greek tyrants were frequently generals who exploited their military victories to garner popular support and take control of their city-states. This happened in Syracuse, a Greek city-state in modern-day Italy, where a general named Gelon (died 478 BCE) successfully defeated an invading force from Carthage; when he gave a speech describing the battle, he dramatically offered to resign his position, but his appreciative audience instead proclaimed him their tyrant. However, after the rule of Gelon and his successor, his brother Hieron (died 467 BCE), proved unpleasant, the residents of Syracuse established a democracy. Sixty years later, however, the city-state was taken over by another tyrant, Dionysius the Elder (432–367 BCE), who was reviled by later Greek historians, though his forty-year reign suggests to some that his rule could not have been as awful as their reports indicate. Demonstrating that tyrants had ample time to pursue other interests, Dionysius the Elder fancied himself a poet, and while audiences at the Olympic Games responded negatively to a recital of his poems, one of his plays, *The Ransom of Hector*, did win the prize at an Athenian festival, suggesting that he may have had some genuine talent (or, perhaps, that he had successfully bribed the judges). His victory proved costly, though,

since by one account, the tyrant then killed himself with his excessive drinking while celebrating his triumph. There are also rumors that he was poisoned at the behest of his son, who then took control of Syracuse. Dionysius the Younger (397–343 BCE), however, was much less successful as a ruler, and after being forced out of office, he emulated his father in another way by becoming a poet.

Even though the tyrants originally emerged as a reaction against hereditary monarchs, they also followed the pattern of bequeathing power to their sons; this propensity also led to the only known example of a female tyrant, Artemisia of Halicarnassus (ca. 480 BCE), who gained her position after the death of her father, Lygdamis (ca. 450 BCE). Herodotus describes her role in the Persian wars, as she allied herself with the Persian king Xerxes (died 424 BCE), gave him advice that he unwisely ignored, and personally led her naval forces into battle. It is surprising that we otherwise have little information about this singular woman, who must have been an intelligent and popular ruler; however, the decision of this Greek tyrant to join forces with one of Greece's bitterest enemies must have aroused resentment in some quarters, while other commentators may have preferred to forget that a woman had once been effective in this traditionally male profession. (An analogy might be made to the Egyptian efforts to erase the reign of the female pharaoh Hatshepsut from their historical records.)

Sparta was the only city-state that entirely avoided the era of tyrants by establishing a government that was a unique mixture of monarchy, tyranny, oligarchy, and democracy. There were two hereditary kings, but they shared power with two other groups: a council of thirty elderly men, the *gerontes* or *gerousia*, who were chosen by election but served for life, and a panel of five ephors, elected annually, who could be regarded as temporary tyrants, since they ultimately had the greatest authority. The *gerontes* would also allow important decisions to be made by all citizens, as determined by a voice vote, which gave the people a direct role in their government in addition to their ability to choose their rulers. Though it seems strange to modern observers, this system of government proved to be effective, and it endured until Greece was conquered by the Romans.

DEFENDERS OF TYRANNY

After experiences with forms of both democracy and dictatorship, the philosopher Plato concluded, in his pioneering utopia *The Republic*, that the ideal state would effectively be a tyranny, governed by "philosopher-kings" who would make wise decisions to benefit their citizens. Almost all modern Americans, however, would regard a democracy as the superior form of government. An interesting exception was the late psychologist, B.F. Skinner, who drew upon his background in behavioral psychology to argue in his own utopia, *Walden Two* (1948), that people would be happiest if their lives were rigidly controlled by benevolent overseers.

AUTHORITARIAN AUTHORS

One prominent Greek tyrant, Dionysius the Elder of Syracuse, attracted great ridicule in his day because he also aspired to be a poet; when his poetry was recited at one of the Olympic Games, audience members reportedly hissed to show their displeasure. Some modern tyrants have also sought recognition as writers; during the final years of his reign, for instance, the Iraqi dictator Saddam Hussein published four novels, which were widely criticized. Some have also speculated that the dictator was unprepared for the 2003 invasion because he was focused on completing his novels.

Just as one can value the good tyrants for eliminating the evils of entrenched hereditary rule, the bad tyrants had the beneficial effect of inspiring democratic reforms, in Athens and elsewhere. One Athenian innovation was particularly designed to prevent future tyrannies: every year, if there was a man who seemed likely to become a tyrant, citizens could vote to force him into exile for ten years; the pieces of clay on which they wrote their votes, *ostraka*, inspired the modern verb "ostracize," meaning to shun or exclude. Even Athens, however, was eventually driven back to tyranny, for after its defeat in the Peloponnesian War, Sparta imposed a system of government by a council of thirty rulers, described by historians as "the Thirty Tyrants," though they were later overthrown. It is interesting to note, though, that looking back on the experiences of Athens, the philosopher Plato (427–347 BCE) concluded that the ideal form of government

was not democracy, but a form of tyranny—the "philosopher-kings" that he placed in charge of his imagined utopia in *The Republic* (380 BCE). Clearly he felt that, despite their deficiencies, there were some advantages to having a tyrant as a ruler, and while few modern observers would agree with his opinion, they must also acknowledge that the tyrants of ancient Greece made significant contributions to the success of their civilization.

Further Reading

Cartledge, Paul. 2009. *Ancient Greek Political Thought in Practice*. Cambridge: Cambridge University Press.

Forsdyke, Sara. 2005. *Exile, Ostracism, and Democracy: The Politics of Expulsion in Ancient Greece*. Princeton, NJ: Princeton University Press.

Lewis, Sian. 2008. *Greek Tyranny*. Exeter, England: Bristol Phoenix Press.

McGlew, James F. 1993. *Tyranny and Political Culture in Ancient Greece*. Ithaca, NY: Cornell University Press.

Morgan, Kathryn A., editor. 2003. *Popular Tyranny: Sovereignty and Its Discontents in Ancient Greece*. Austin: University of Texas Press.

Sancisi-Weerdenburg, Heleen. 2000. *Peisistratos and the Tyranny: A Reappraisal of the Evidence*. Amsterdam: J.C. Gieben.

Document

From Aristotle. C. 443 BCE. *Aristotle on the Athenian Constitution*. Translated by Sir Frederic G. Kenyon. 1891. London: G. Bell & Sons.

In this passage from The Athenian Constitution, *the philosopher Aristotle describes and praises the governance of the Athenian tyrant Peisistratus.*

Such was the origin and such the vicissitudes of the tyranny of Peisistratus. His administration was temperate, as has been said before, and more like constitutional government than a tyranny. Not only was he in every respect humane and mild and ready to forgive those who offended, but, in addition, he advanced money to the poorer people to help them in their labours, so that they might make their living by agriculture. . . . At the same time his revenues were increased by the thorough cultivation of the country, since he imposed a tax of one tenth on all the produce. For the same reasons he instituted the local justices, and often made expeditions in person into the country to inspect it and to settle disputes between individuals, that they might not come into the city and neglect their farms. It was in one of these progresses that, as the story goes, Peisistratus had his adventure with the man of Hymettus, who was cultivating the spot afterwards known as "Tax-free Farm." He saw a man digging and working at a very stony piece of ground, and being surprised he sent his attendant to ask what he got out of this plot of land. "Aches and pains," said the man; "and that's what Peisistratus ought to have his tenth of." The man spoke without knowing who his questioner was; but Peisistratus was so pleased with his frank speech and his industry that he granted him exemption from all taxes. And so in matters in general he burdened the people as little as possible with his government, but always cultivated peace and kept them in all quietness. Hence the tyranny of Peisistratus was often spoken of proverbially as "the age of gold"; for when his sons succeeded him the government became much harsher. But most important of all in this respect was his popular and kindly disposition. In all things he was accustomed to observe the laws, without giving himself any exceptional privileges. Once he was summoned on a charge of homicide before the Areopagus, and he appeared in person to make his defence; but the prosecutor was afraid to present himself and abandoned the case. For these reasons he held power long, and whenever he was expelled he regained his position easily.

Ancient Rome, 1000 BCE–500 CE

Introduction

In many respects, the citizens of ancient Rome achieved the first modern civilization. The two forms of government they perfected—the functional democracy of the Roman Republic and the efficiently administered Roman Empire—became models for many future nations. During the centuries when they controlled much of Europe, North Africa, and western Asia, the Romans happily absorbed the best features of every nation they encountered, ranging from Greek literature and philosophy to the fighting techniques of European barbarians, and they developed a culture based on a shared language and shared values, not ethnic backgrounds, so people living anywhere in the Empire could learn Latin, become Roman citizens, travel to Rome, and achieve high positions in society. The Romans were the first to enjoy numerous amenities of life that today's people take for granted, like a trustworthy postal system, running water, glass containers and windows, and educational institutions that produced a generally literate citizenry. And while Romans could work just as hard as their counterparts in other nations, they benefited posterity with their singular interest in improving the experiences of leisure time: they ate gourmet food, drank vintage wines, decorated buildings with colorful artwork, and found innumerable ways to relax and enjoy themselves, whether by lounging in the public baths, watching gladiatorial contests, attending religious festivals, listening to debates in the Roman Senate, or traveling to faraway lands as tourists.

One other aspect of ancient Rome makes it seem especially contemporary: unlike other cultures that were regularly forgotten and rediscovered, Rome has remained a constant presence in every civilization that emerged after its official fall in 476 ce. Its language, Latin, was long the preferred tongue of educated people throughout the territories it once governed, and large numbers of its literary works were preserved by repeated copying to be studied by new generations of students and scholars. The achievements of their soldiers and diplomats, carefully recorded in their stories, became familiar stories that are still part of today's popular culture, depicted in films, television programs, and video games. Tourists from all over the world travel to Italy to examine enduring remnants of its culture, ranging from the massive Colosseum and amazingly preserved ruins of Pompeii to decorous glassworks and pieces of jewelry displayed in museums. Indeed, it is impossible to summarize all of the accomplishments of this society, or the many jobs that the Romans did so well for so long, especially since ongoing research keeps uncovering new achievements to appreciate. And in that context, the well-known flaws and foibles of the Romans, and their occasional crimes and excesses, can readily be forgiven.

Barbers and Hairdressers

The Romans, more so than the citizens of other ancient cultures, were very concerned about the appearance of their hair, and even the poorest people would devote some time every day to cutting and styling their own hair, probably with the assistance of family members. For those who could afford their services, however, there emerged a tradition of professional barbers, or *tonsors*, for men, and hairdressers for women. They did their work in different circumstances: while very rich men might employ personal barbers who lived in their homes, most barbers had their own barber shop, or *tonstrina*, where customers would congregate to get a haircut or shave. Hairdressers, however, typically came to the houses of the women they served, and some were the permanent employees or slaves of one wealthy client. The Romans rarely wrote about their hair and the people who worked on it, but thanks to numerous images of prominent Romans' heads in sculptures, paintings, and coins, we have a good picture of how the hairstyles crafted by barbers and hairdressers changed over the centuries.

While early Roman men allowed their hair to grow long and often had beards, it became the fashion in the last century of the Roman Republic to have short hair and clean-shaven faces; indeed, for a while, a man could not serve in the Roman Senate until he had shaved off his beard. Common citizens cut their own hair with bronze razors, but professional barbers used superior razors made of iron and soothed their customers' faces using a lotion with the key ingredient of spiders' webs. (Shaving was often painful because the Romans applied no soap or shaving cream.) To keep the hair in place, oils were applied, and barbers sometimes heated an iron to provide men with curly hair, though some derided this style as decadent. Later, the emperor Hadrian (76–138 CE) made beards popular again after he decided to grow a beard to conceal a conspicuous blemish; over a century later, when the emperor Constantine (272–337 CE) chose the clean-shaven look, beards again became unfashionable. The faces of male slaves, to announce their lowly status, had to look different from the faces of free citizens; thus, when beards were frowned upon, slaves were expected to grow beards, and when prominent citizens began to wear beards, slaves were instructed to shave their faces.

Roman women long favored the rather simple style of keeping their long hair in a bun at the tops of their heads; only little girls and prostitutes were allowed to let their hair hang down their shoulders. During the first century CE, more elaborate hairstyles became popular, forcing hairdressers to wield their curling irons quite frequently in order to provide their clients with the numerous curls on their heads and foreheads that they requested; in some cases, women

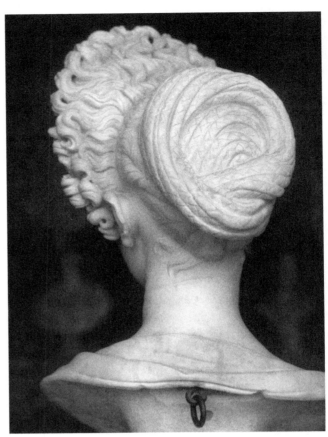

This bust of a wealthy woman in Rome, carved around 90 CE, shows one of the elaborate hair styles that were then becoming popular. (Allan T. Kohl/Art Images for College Teaching)

might have several rows of curls piled on top of their heads. In the second century CE, women began to demand braids in their hair, woven from long strands of hair and wrapped around a crowning bun. Eventually, women's hairstyles grew so complex that several specialists were required to meet the demands of wealthy clients: *cosmetae* were female servants who prepared lotions and perfumes that were applied to the hair; *matrices* washed and brushed the hair and rubbed oil on the scalp; and *ornatrices* prepared braids, styled the hair, and decorated hair with ribbons and jewels. One sculpted image on a monument from Roman Germany shows a seated women surrounded by four female attendants, all working on her hair.

Seeking variety in the appearance of their hair, both men and women sought to change the color of their hair, so that barbers and hairdressers had to develop and employ various forms of hair dye. Soaking walnut shells in olive oil produced a brown dye, lotions made of saffron flowers made hair look blonde, and quicklime provided a reddish color. Blonde hair, once associated with prostitutes, became increasingly fashionable in the later days of the Empire; the mad emperor Commodus (161–192 CE), for example, insisted on having his hair dyed blonde, even though the process of giving him precisely the shade he desired might take several hours. If men and women damaged their hair with these crude dyes, or simply wanted to avoid using dyes, they might also wear wigs, usually prepared by special workers using hair from slave girls; the blonde hair of slaves from northern Europe was considered especially desirable, though black hair from India was also imported. Instead of complete wigs, some hairdressers placed hairpieces shaped like crowns onto their clients' hair or used pieces of artificial hair to provide the hair with additional volume. The very wealthiest of men and women might, for special occasions, sprinkle gold dust into their own hair or into their wigs; the emperor Caligula (12–41 CE) was one prominent Roman who notoriously favored a blond wig with gold dust.

As noted, the lifestyles of the barbers and hairdressers who worked on people's hair were very different. The male barbers were usually free citizens who owned and operated their own shops, employing assistants who might someday inherit the shop or start their own business; some, however, might work exclusively for one wealthy client. Roman barbers typically presided over a very social experience: as was later the custom in the United States, several men might linger for a while in their neighborhood barber shop, chatting with their favorite barber or the other customers about current events. In many cases, a barber shop might become a local center of activity, attracting visitors who simply came to talk or employers who would arrange to interview a prospective employee at that familiar locale. Because the buildings in ancient Rome were usually very small, a barber might have to take a customer out into the street to cut his hair or shave his face in the midst of bystanders, making his work even more public. A typical session would begin by summoning the client waiting on a bench to sit in a chair and be covered by a piece of cloth.

The hair was cut with crude iron scissors; if clients requested it, their hair would be curled or dye; and as a finishing touch, oils and perfumes would be applied. If we are to believe the Roman satirists Martial (ca. 38–103 CE) and Juvenal (ca. 55–127 CE), the work of a talented barber could prove very profitable indeed, as they make barbed comments about humble barbers who have become rich landowners.

In contrast, female hairdressers were often slaves, and they invariably worked inside the home, since women did not want their hair preparation observed by anyone else; an unusually skillful worker, however, might earn her freedom and serve clients as a paid employee. In contrast to male habits, one suspects that any conversations with hairdressers were invariably

SARTORIAL SEAMSTRESSES

Although we have many images of Roman hairstyles in paintings and sculptures, contemporary stylists are still trying to determine some of the secrets behind their elaborate creations. One researcher who calls herself a "hair archaeologist," Janet Stephens, recently made an important discovery: while it was previously believed that Roman women kept their hair in place by using hairpins, Stephens figured out that hairdressers actually sewed their clients' hair together with the use of a needle and thread, and her evidence was convincing enough to earn her a 2008 publication in the *Journal of Roman Archaeology*.

THE UNKINDEST HAIRCUT OF ALL?

Busts and portraits provide innumerable images of the haircuts of Roman men, so that they can still have an influence on contemporary stylists. In the 1990s, one style that became popular, the Caesar haircut, was explicitly modeled on the haircut of the dictator Julius Caesar (100–44 BCE). The man's hair is cut very short, with short bangs extended downward on the forehead. Among the many celebrities who have been observed wearing a Caesar haircut are the actor George Clooney and rap artist Eminem. Naturally enough, actor Russell Crowe also chose a Caesar haircut when he portrayed a Roman gladiator in the film *Gladiator* (2000).

focused on getting the woman's hair precisely right before she was willing to be seen; there are many stories of hairdressers spending hours preparing a woman's hair, only to be met with bitter complaints about one errant curl. The *ornatrix* might also be asked to pull out gray hairs, cut off unneeded hair, add pieces of artificial hair, or apply an early form of hair mousse to keep everything in place. She was often required to perform the additional task of applying makeup to the woman's face and arms.

Considering the amount of attention that the Romans devoted to their hair, one could readily accuse them of vanity, and some of their fellow citizens felt exactly the same way, as they repeatedly chastised men who wore fancy curls or women whose hair towered a foot above their heads. Yet it can also be argued that feeling good about their appearance helps people to feel good about themselves, and the knowledge that their hair was impeccably coiffured in the latest style may have contributed to the immense sense of self-esteem that enabled the Romans to conquer much of the world and make many significant advances. And they bequeathed their extreme concern for hairstyling to later Western cultures, so that today, literally millions of people make a living by preparing hair products and working on people's hair in manners that often seem very similar to the activities of the ancient Romans.

Further Reading

Cleland, Liza, Glenys Davies, and Lloyd Llewellyn-Jones. 2007. *Greek and Roman Dress from A to Z*. London and New York: Routledge.

Edmondson, Jonathan, and Allison Keith, editors. 2008. *Roman Dress and the Fabrics of Roman Culture*. Toronto: University of Toronto Press.

Evans, Maria Willington. 1994. *Hair-Dressing of Roman Ladies as Illustrated on Coins*. Iola, WI: Paaka Enterprises.

Olson, Kelly. 2008. *Dress and the Roman Woman: Self-Presentation and Society*. London and New York: Routledge.

Sebesta, Judith Lynn, and Larissa Bonfante, editors. *The World of Roman Costume*. Madison: University of Wisconsin Press.

Sherrow, Victoria. 2007. *Encyclopedia of Hair: A Cultural History*. Westport, CT: Greenwood Press.

Documents

From Juvenal. C. 100 CE. *The Satires of Juvenal, Persius, Sulpicia, and Lucilius*. Translated by Lewis Evans. 1850. London: Henry G. Bohn.

In this passage from the sixth satire of Juvenal (ca. 55–127 CE), the satirist describes how slave girls elaborately style the hair of a vain, wealthy woman.

The government of her house is no more merciful than the court of a Sicilian tyrant. For if she has made an assignation, and is anxious to be dressed out more becomingly than usual, and is in a hurry, and has been some time already waited for in the gardens, or rather near the chapels of the Isiac procuress; poor Psecas arranges her hair, herself with disheveled locks and naked shoulders and naked breasts.

"Why is this curl too high?" Instantly the cowhide avenges the heinous crime of the misplacing of a hair. What has poor Psecas done? What crime is it of the poor girl's if your own nose has displeased you?

Another, on the left hand, draws out and combs her curls and rolls them into a band. The aged matron assists at the council, who, having served her due period at the needle, now presides over weighing out the tasks of wool. Her opinion will be first taken. Then those who are her inferiors in years and skill will vote in order, as though their mistress's good name or life were at stake. So great is the anxiety of getting beauty! Into so many tiers forms her curls, so many stages high she builds her head; in front you will look upon an Andromache, behind she is a dwarf—you would imagine her another person. Excuse her, pray, if nature has assigned her but a short back, and if, without the aid of high-heeled buskins, she looks shorter than a Pigmy maiden; and must spring lightly up on tip-toe for a kiss. No thought meanwhile about her husband! not a word of her ruinous expenditure! She lives as though she were merely a neighbor of her husband's, and in this respect alone is nearer to him—that she hates her husband's friends and slaves, and makes grievous inroads on his purse.

From Martial. C. 86–103 CE. *The Epigrams of Martial, Translated into English Prose*. Translator unidentified. 1860. London: Henry G. Bohn.

The satirist Martial (ca. 38–103 CE) mentions barbers several times in his Epigrams, *published between 86 and 103 CE. In these four examples, he criticizes a barber who advanced in his social status for lacking other skills; he sarcastically complains about a very slow barber; he chastises a friend for making too many demands on his own barber; and he attacks the butchery of an inept barber.*

[Book VII] LXIV. To Cinnamus

You, Cinnamus, who were a barber well known over all the city, and afterwards, by the kindness of your mistress, made a knight, have taken refuge among the cities of Sicily and the regions of Ætna, fleeing from the stern justice of the forum. By what art will you now, useless log, sustain your years? How is your unhappy and fleeting tranquillity to employ itself? You cannot be a rhetorician, a grammarian, a school-master, a Cynic, or Stoic philosopher, nor can you sell your voice to the people of Sicily, or your applause to theatres of Rome. All that remains for you, Cinnamus, is to become a barber again.

[Book VIII] LXXXIII. On Lupercus

Whilst the barber Eutrapelus is going the round of Lupercus's face, and carefully smoothing his cheeks, another beard springs up.

[Book VIII] LII. To Caedicianus

Caedicianus, I lent my barber (a young man, but skilled in his art even beyond Nero's Thalamus, whose lot it was to clip the beards of the Drusi) to Rufus, at his request, to make his cheeks smooth for once. But, at Rufus's orders, he was so long occupied in going over the same hairs again and again, consulting the mirror that guided his hand, cleaning the skin, and making a tedious second attack on the locks previously shorn, that my barber at last returned to me with his own beard full grown.

[Book XI] LXXXIV. On Antiochus, an Unskilful Barber

Let him who does not wish yet to descend to the waters of Styx, avoid, if he be wise, the barber Antiochus. The knives with which, when the maddened troop of Cybele's priests rage to the sound of Phrygian measures, their white arms are lacerated, are less cruel than the razor of Antiochus. More gently does Alcon cut a strangulated hernia, and hew broken bones with his rude hand. Antiochus should deal with needy Cynics, and the beards of Stoics, and denude the necks of horses of their dusty manes. If he were to shave Prometheus under the Scythian rock, the Titan would again, with bared breast, demand his executioner the vulture. Pentheus would flee to his mother, Orpheus to the priestesses of Bacchus, were they to hear but a sound from the barbarous weapon of Antiochus. All these scars, that you count upon my chin, like those that sit upon the brow of an aged boxer, were not produced by the nails of an enraged wife, but by the steel and cursed hand of Antiochus. Of all animals the goat alone has any sense; he wears his beard, that he may not risk himself under the hands of Antiochus.

Cooks

One thing that the ancient Romans loved was good food, and they devoted a great deal of their time and energy to its preparation. Even the poorest citizens could take advantage of a vibrant economy that imported a wide variety of edible items from throughout the Roman Empire, and the wealthy would seek out exotic foods and devise elaborate recipes to provide guests with memorable banquets that might last for ten hours. And from several sources of information—writings about food, paintings of banquets, and remnants of food in ruined buildings like bones and seeds—we have a good idea of how a typical Roman meal was prepared.

The physical circumstances of cooking at home were not pleasant. Those who could not afford any devices for cooking were obliged to do their cooking outside, over open fires, though some cities provided public ovens that were available to anyone in the community. However, most Romans probably had a kitchen with two appliances. For baking, they had a dome-shaped oven; first, a fire was allowed to burn inside, then it was swept away so the dough could be placed inside of the heated chamber. By the time the Roman Empire was at its height, however, women generally stopped baking their own bread and instead would purchase it from numerous bakeries in the marketplace, which offered inexpensive products. For broiling, frying, or boiling, there was a hearth made of bricks or stone with a bed of charcoal; bronze or ceramic pots were hung on chains above the charcoal, or a pan would be set on top of a gridiron. To stir and handle the food, cooks used utensils made of copper like spoons, dippers, and ladles. Although there was a small vent in the roof or the wall to release the smoke, the kitchens would still become uncomfortably hot and smoky, and considerable labor was involved in constantly squatting by the oven and carrying heavy pots or large *amphoras* filled with wine or water.

Various people were responsible for doing the cooking. Poor women had to cook for their own families, with the assistance of their female children. If a family could only afford a few slaves, one of them would probably be assigned to handle all of the cooking. Wealthy Romans would have several slaves working in their kitchens, each specializing in one area; one woman would bake pastries, for instance, while another man cooked the meat. As interest in foreign cuisine burgeoned, rich people sought slaves from Asia Minor and Egypt who could bring new recipes to their kitchens. Outside the home, some people made

a living by cooking and selling food in the marketplace for Romans who lacked the time to prepare their own foods. They might offer simple fare like freshly baked bread with cooked vegetables, but one could also find homemade stew or cooked sausages taken directly from the pan. Cooks also worked as part of the Roman army, providing soldiers on the march with their standard rations of biscuits, cheese, bacon, and wine and preparing dinners with poultry, beef, fish, vegetables, and fruit for soldiers in camps.

The Roman cooks took special steps to improve the flavor of their cooked food. Honey was the major ingredient to provide sweetness, though foods might also be cooked with fruits; vinegar made foods taste sour. To vary the taste of breads, they would occasionally mix some cheese into the dough, and they regularly used spices like fennel, mint, mustard, or anise. Cooks for wealthy families had access to more expensive spices imported from India like pepper, ginger, cinnamon, cloves, and nutmeg. The Romans were fond of using sauces, and they often purchased one popular fish sauce called *garum*, that was made

This fresco painting, completed sometime in the second century CE, shows two Roman cooks preparing to cook a small animal. (J. Paul Getty Museum)

by boiling the parts of fish that are usually not eaten, like the intestines, fins, and heads, in a mixture of olive oil and herbs and letting it ferment into a paste. They could also prepare their own sauces; after starting with a mixture of cumin and other spices, the cook would crush and add some fruits like dates and raisins, or nuts like almonds and walnuts, and pour in flavorful liquids like *garum*, honey, milk, wine, or vinegar. Finally, if the sauce needed to be thickened, the cook would add wheat starch, dates, or eggs.

The typical pattern of Roman eating was to have a light breakfast and lunch before one major meal at the end of the day. For most Romans, the first two meals might involve little preparation, as one might eat some previously baked or purchased bread along with a few olives or raisins, a small piece of cheese, and some uncooked nuts like walnuts and almonds; in the early days of Rome, though, a customary meal for everyday citizens was a form of porridge made from wheat. Like the ancient Greeks, the Romans spread olive oil on their bread as their substitute for butter, though they might also soak bread in wine or sprinkle some salt on it. The second meal of the day, larger than the first, would often include cold leftovers of meat and vegetables from the last night's dinner. For the major meal of dinner, which usually occurred around sunset, typical dishes might include vegetables like cabbage, onions, asparagus, turnips, radishes, and beets that were either eaten raw or boiled, along with some cooked pork or sausage, the most frequently eaten meat. Birds for cooking like geese, ducks, and peacocks were also sold in the marketplace, along with rabbits, pike, and eels, but beef was only a rare treat, available to everyday Romans only when it was distributed at festivals. Since most Romans could not afford to eat meat every day, the protein in some meals might come only from cooked eggs or cheese. For a dessert, they might bake various pastries and cakes using honey.

Needless to say, wealthier eaters enjoyed more elaborate dinners, typically involving three courses. First, as an appetizer, they might eat eggs, snails, olives, or jellyfish filled with sea urchins. The main course would include cooked vegetables and expensive meats like fish, oysters, lampreys, parrots, or flamingos, flavored with nuts, pork, or dates. Some unusual dishes became well known; for example,

Lucius Aelius (101–138 CE), once designated as a future emperor, devised a pie containing a pig's udder and meat from a boar, peacock, and pheasant, and it was much enjoyed by his patron, the emperor Hadrian (76–138 CE). Finally, the dessert would consist of pastries and fruits like pears, apples, and figs.

We have learned a great deal about Roman cooking because of the survival of a lengthy cookbook, purportedly written by the first-century gourmet Apicius (ca. first century CE), and sometimes simply named the *Apicius*, though it is also known as *De Re Coquinaria* or *The Art of Cooking*. The attribution is understandable, since Apicius was notorious for an obsessive devotion to eating only the finest food that eventually impoverished the once-wealthy man; however, scholars now know that the book was written sometime in the fourth or fifth century CE, long after Apicius died,

PROTEIN FOR ROMAN PALATES

Ostriches were once commonplace in northern Africa and western Asia, and they were regularly imported to Rome, where the birds were a favorite food of wealthy Romans; the *Apicius*, in fact, includes several recipes for cooked ostrich. As the Arabian ostriches were hunted to extinction and African ostriches became rarer, the bird disappeared from the European diet and was long unknown to U.S. cooks. Recently, however, a number of Americans have established ostrich farms, and the ostrich meat they raise can now be purchased at many supermarkets, bringing a touch of ancient Rome to modern U.S. meals.

VENERABLE VEGETABLES

Many of the recipes found in the classic Roman cookbook called the *Apicius* are complex, or they require ingredients that will seem strange or unpalatable to modern cooks. However, the book also provides a simple method for cooking vegetables that virtually anyone today could easily and unhesitatingly replicate. So, if modern people would like to eat some vegetables cooked the Roman way, all they have to do is to place the washed vegetables in a pan, add pepper, cumin, and broth, and cook them slowly until they are soft and ready to eat.

though some believe that he is personally responsible for some of its recipes. Some of these are relatively simple, including instructions for preparing a soufflé by combining milk, honey, and eggs, slowly baking the mixture until it is firm, and sprinkling pepper on it before it is eaten. Others are more complicated, such as a recipe for a sort of fish fricassée: the cook first places pieces of fish and leeks in a pan and boils them in a mixture of wine, beef broth, and olive oil; spices are added and the liquid is again brought to a boil; one finally adds wheat starch to thicken the sauce and sprinkles it with pepper. It is possible that some Roman cooks, like their modern counterparts, learned their recipes by reading other cookbooks like the *Apicius* that are now lost, but it is more likely that such lore was passed down orally from experienced cooks to their apprentices.

As rich citizens of the Roman Empire became more and more concerned about eating fine food, the best cooks could advance from the status of slavery to become valued employees whose services were greatly appreciated; and while most continued to work for a single employer, some were undoubtedly hired to provide their services to other wealthy people who had enjoyed their dishes. However, beyond the issue of their remuneration, Roman cooks probably most appreciated the pleasure of consuming their own food, for such a passion must have motivated them to enter this profession.

Further Reading

Bonifay, Michel, and Jean-Christophe Tréglia, editors. 2007. *LRCW 2: Late Roman Coarse Wares, Cooking Wares and Amphorae in the Mediterranean: Archaeology and Archaeometry.* Oxford: Archaeopress.

Curtis, Robert I. 2001. *Ancient Food Technology.* Leiden, The Netherlands, and Boston: Brill.

Edwards, John. 2009. *The Roman Cookery of Apicius.* New York: Random House.

Faas, Patrick. 1994. *Around the Roman Table: Food and Feasting in Ancient Rome.* Translated by Shaun Whiteside. 2003. New York: Palgrave Macmillan.

Giacosa, Ilaria Gozzini. 1992. *A Taste of Ancient Rome.* Translated by Anna Herklotz. 1992. Chicago: University of Chicago Press.

Renfrew, Jane A. 2006. *Roman Cookery: Recipes and History.* Revised edition. Swinton, England: English Heritage.

Documents

From c. fourth century CE. *Cookery and Dining in Imperial Rome: A Bibliography, Critical Review and Translation of the Ancient Book Known as Apicius de re Coquinaria.* Translated by Joseph Dommers Vehling. 1936. Chicago: W. M. Hill.

A Roman cookbook, called the Apicius, *was apparently written sometime in the fourth century CE. It is traditionally attributed to Marcus Gavius Apicius, a noted gourmet who lived sometime in the first century CE, but modern scholars agree that he could not have been its actual author. Below are five of the recipes found in this book.*

Honey refresher for travelers:

The wayfarer's honey refresher (so called because it gives endurance and strength to pedestrians), with which travelers are refreshed by the wayside, is made in this manner: Flavor honey with ground pepper and skim. In the moment of serving, put honey in a cup, as much as is desired to obtain the right degree of sweetness, and mix with spiced wine, not more than a needed quantity; also, add some wine to the spiced honey to facilitate its flow and the mixing.

Supreme style cooked peas:

Cook the peas with oil and a piece of sow's belly. Put in a sauce pan broth, leek heads, green coriander, and put on the fire to be cooked. Of tid-bits [i.e., finely-chopped meats or seasonings] cut little dice. Similarly cook thrushes or other small [game] birds, or take sliced chicken and diced brain, properly cooked. Further cook, in the available liquor or broth, Lucanian sausage and bacon; cook leeks in water. Crush a pint of toasted pignolia nuts. Also crush pepper, lovage, origany, and ginger, dilute with the broth of pork, tie. Take a square baking dish, suitable for turning over; oil it well. Sprinkle [on the bottom] a layer of crushed nuts, upon which put some peas, fully covering the bottom of the squash dish. On top of this, arrange slices of the bacon, leeks, and sliced Lucanian sausage. Again cover with a layer of peas and alternate all the rest of the available edibles in the manner described until the dish is filled, concluding at last with a layer of peas, utilizing everything. Bake this dish in the oven, or put it into a slow fire [covering it with live coals], so that it may be baked thoroughly. [Next make a sauce of the following]: Put yolks of hard-boiled eggs in the mortar with white pepper, nuts, honey, white wine, and a little broth. Mix, and put it into a sauce pan to be cooked. When [the sauce is] done, turn out the peas into a large [silver dish], and mask them with this sauce, which is called white sauce.

Crane or duck with turnips:

Take out [entrails]. Clean, wash, and dress [the bird], and parboil it in water with salt and dill. Next, prepare turnips, and cook them in water, which is to be squeezed out. Take them out of the pot and wash them again, and put into a sauce pan the duck, with oil, broth, a bunch of leeks, and coriander. The turnips, cut into small pieces: these put on top of the [duck], in order to finish cooking. When half done, to give it color, add reduced must. The sauce is prepared separately: pepper, cumin, coriander, laser root moistened with vinegar and diluted with its own broth [of the fowl]. Bring this to a boiling point, thicken with roux. [In a deep dish, arrange the duck]; on top of the turnips [strain the sauce over it]. Sprinkle with pepper and serve.

Pig's paunch:

Clean the paunch of a suckling pig well with salt and vinegar, and presently wash with water. Then fill it with the following dressing: pieces of pork pounded in the mortar, three brains—the nerves removed—mix with raw eggs, add nuts, whole pepper, and sauce to taste. Crush pepper, lovage, silphium, anise, ginger, a little rue; fill the paunch with it, not too much, though, leaving plenty of room for expansion, so that it does not burst while being cooked. Put it in a pot with boiling water, retire and prick with a needle so that it does not burst. When half done, take it out and hang it into the smoke to take on color. Now boil it over again and finish it leisurely. Next take the broth, some pure wine, and a little oil, open the paunch with a small knife. Sprinkle with the broth and lovage; place the pig near the fire to heat it, turn it around in bran [or bread crumbs], immerse it in brine, and finish [the outer crust to a golden brown].

Spiced hare:

[The well-prepared hare]: Cook in wine, broth, water, with a little mustard [seed], dill, and leeks with the roots. When all is done, season with pepper, satury, round onions, Damascus plums, wine, broth,

reduced wine and a little oil; tie with roux, let boil a little longer, [baste], so that the hare is penetrated by the flavor, and serve it on a platter masked with sauce.

From Juvenal. C. 100 CE. *The Satires of Juvenal, Persius, Sulpicia, and Lucilius*. Translated by Lewis Evans. 1850. London: Henry G. Bohn.

In these passages from his fifth satire, Juvenal (ca. 55–127 CE) provides a picture of two very different sorts of Roman meals: the fine foods that a wealthy man, Virro, reserves for himself, and the humbler fare that he gives to his guests.

See, too, with what grumbling another of these rascals hands you bread that can scarce be broken; the mouldy fragments of impenetrable crust, which would make your jaws ache, and give you no chance of a bite. But delicate bread, as white as snow, made of the finest flour, is reserved for the great man. Mind you keep your hands off! Maintain the respect due to the cutter of the bread!. . . .

See! with how vast a body the lobster which is served to your patron fills the dish, and with what fine asparagus it is garnished all round; with what a tail he seems to look down in scorn on the assembled guests, when he comes in raised on high by the hands of the tall slave. But to you is served a common crab, scantily hedged in with half an egg sliced, a meal fit only for the dead, and in a dish too small to hold it. Virro himself [the host] drowns his fish in oil from Venafrum; but the pale cabbage set before you, poor wretch, will stink of the lamp. . . .

Your patron will have a barbel [a fish] furnished by Corsica, or the rocks of Tauromenium, when all our own waters have been ransacked and failed; while gluttony is raging, and the market is plying its unwearied nets in the neighboring seas, and we do not allow the Tyrrhene fish to reach their full growth. . . . Virro is presented with a lamprey of the largest size from the Sicilian whirlpool. For while Auster keeps himself close, while he seats himself and dries his wet pinions in prison, the nets, grown venturesome, despise the dangers even of the middle of Charybdis, An eel awaits you—first-cousin to the long snake—or a coarse pike from the Tiber, spotted from the winter's ice, a native of the bank-side, fettened on the filth of the rushing sewer, and used to penetrate the drain even of the middle of Suburra. . . .

Before Virro himself is the liver of a huge goose; a fat capon, as big as a goose; and a wild boar, worthy of the spear of the yellow-haired Meleager, smokes. Then will be served up truffles, if it happen to be spring, and the thunder, devoutly, wished for by the epicure, shall augment the supper. . . .

Virro will order to be served to himself and his brother Virros such noble apples, on whose fragrance alone you are allowed to revel; such as the eternal autumn of the Phaeacians produced; or such as you might fancy purloined from the African sisters. You feast upon some shriveled windfall, such as is munched at the ramparts by him that is armed with buckler and helmet: and, in dread of the lash, learns to hurl his javelin from the shaggy goat's back.

Couriers

Wealthy Romans often owned properties in distant locations, and the government faced the increasing challenge of exercising administrative control over provinces that were very far away from the capital city. For obvious reasons, then, there emerged during the time of the Roman Republic some professional couriers who could reliable transport letters from city to city. Surprisingly, although the term *courier* is taken from the Latin word for running, the Roman themselves actually used a different word, *tabellarii*, to describe their couriers. While some of these individuals were slaves, others were free citizens who earned a salary for delivering these documents. We otherwise know little about these early messengers, but after the emperor Augustus (63 bce–14 ce) officially established the Roman Empire, he acknowledged the increasing importance of such long-distance communication by setting up a government agency, the *cursus publicus*, that officials could use to send messages along the fine roads that were being constructed and maintained by the Roman army; and the workings of this institution—in effect, the world's first postal service—are much better documented.

At first, the *cursus publicus* relied upon a series of runners: one man would run to a certain location and hand letters to another runner who would in turn carry them to the next runner; however, one problem with this system is that the man who actually gave the message to its recipient knew nothing about its contents and could not answer any questions about it. So, the process was changed so that a single courier would make the entire journey, using animals like horses or mules attached to wagons. Reasonably enough, only strong young men were recruited for this often arduous travel. Local governments were required to provide the animals, but an edict from an official during the reign of Tiberius (42 bce–37 ce) stipulates that they must be paid for their use. When fresh animals were not immediately available, it was apparently the habit of some couriers to seize a mule or horse from a local farmer, though the practice was officially frowned upon. The primary duty of the courier was to deliver important messages to generals and officials as well as announcements about newly implemented laws, but he might also carry private letters from soldiers to their relatives back home; so, we have a copy of a charming letter, sent in the second century ce, from a young Egyptian man who joined the Roman army, was sent to Naples, and wanted to let his family know that he was alive and well. We are fortunate that its recipients threw the letter away, so it could be preserved for almost 2,000 years in the arid Egyptian sand.

While their work was initially limited to carrying documents, couriers were soon asked to transport people and baggage as well. Their passengers were usually soldiers and bureaucrats, while the freight might include the food for soldiers that came from a tax called the *annona militaris*. Later, couriers were also responsible for both collecting and delivering this food. On rare occasions, even private citizens might ride with couriers; Pliny the Younger (61–112 ce), then serving in a province in Asia Minor, wrote a letter to the emperor Trajan (53–117 ce) apologizing because he had misused his position to authorize his wife to travel back to Rome with a courier so that she could be with her aunt after her uncle's death. After the conversion of the emperor Constantine (272–337 ce) and the establishment of Christianity as the official state religion, church officials could also use the services of the *cursus publicus*, and as the Empire shrank, they became increasingly frequent clients.

To assist the couriers who worked for the *cursus publicus*, the Roman government set up some special facilities along its roads. *Mansiones* were large buildings where couriers could stay overnight, enjoying a bath, dinner, and a good night's sleep in a comfortable bed before embarking the next morning with new animals. Generally, *mansiones* were located from twenty-five to thirty-five miles apart, since that was the average distance of a day's travel for most individuals. The *mansiones* could be used by other official travelers, as long as they could provide the proper document, called a *diploma*, which bore the emperor's signature. To avoid abusive overuse of these facilities, though, only diplomas with a recent signature were considered valid.

In addition to the *mansiones*, the government constructed smaller buildings to further assist couriers. During the day, they could stop at smaller relay stations, called *mutationes*, to change their animals, and if there were places where couriers were being preyed upon by roving bandits, the government set up structures, called *stationes*, where soldiers were posted to guard couriers and other travelers. A copy of a Roman map, made in medieval times, has survived, which shows all available facilities throughout the Roman Empire, also indicating precisely which services are provided at each site; presumably, couriers traveling to distant lands were supplied with such maps to guide them during their journeys.

The pace of the courier's travel varied: if their business was not particularly important, or if they were carrying a lot of baggage, they might travel at the leisurely pace of an ordinary traveler. However, according to an estimate in Lionel Casson's *Travel in the Ancient World* (1994), they generally went a bit faster, averaging about fifty miles in one day, and if they had important news to convey, they could move even more quickly. For example, when there was a rebellion in the army near the Rhine River, a message about it reached the emperor Galba (3 BCE–69 CE) in nine days, indicating that a courier had moved at the impressive rate of 150 miles per day.

The professional couriers of the *cursus publicus* could be either slaves or free men, though they might officially work for other government agencies; however, soldiers were often used as couriers, especially by emperors and provincial governors, who preferred trusted men from their personal guard to deliver confidential information. At times, high-ranking officials might also be asked to deliver messages, especially if they required the sort of quick reply that only someone with some clout could demand.

If one did not have access to the services of the *cursus publicus*, delivering messages across long distances could be troublesome indeed, though the lucky circumstance of a friend about to embark upon a journey might provide an opportunity to send a letter to faraway recipients. However, the delivery of letters within the city of Rome was relatively easy, and professional assistance was not required. Instead, the letter writer would write his letter on a foldable tablet covered with wax, seal the folded tablet with tied

MESSENGERS LIKE GODS

The Romans were the first civilization to develop a reliable system for transporting letters and packages over long distances, which was essential to their maintenance of a vast empire. Today, even when many documents can be sent electronically, there remains a huge demand for similar messenger services, ranging from large organizations like the United States Postal Service, Federal Express, and United Parcel Service to local businesses that deliver items within a single city. One of these innumerable businesses, the Mercury Messenger Service, is even named after the ancient Roman god of couriers.

STAYING IN TOUCH WITH SOLDIERS

Anyone reading the histories of ancient Rome will recognize that fast, efficient messengers played a crucial role in their ability to achieve military victories. But in another ancient nation, Persia, King Cyrus experimented in the sixth century BCE with another method of communication—carrier pigeons. Much later, these birds also emerged as the most effective way for French soldiers to stay in touch during World War I. Indeed, one of the French pigeons, named Cher Ami, was awarded the Croix de Guerre for her heroic service in rescuing almost 200 U.S. soldiers.

thread and a blob of wax marked with a signet ring, write the name of the recipient on the outside, and hand the tablet to any available slave, who probably welcomed the opportunity to get out of the house and enjoy a walk through the streets of Rome. We assume that such letters were frequently written, though most of these ephemeral communications written on wax have not survived; however, at a site from Roman Britain, some unusual tablets were unearthed with messages written in ink, and some passages from these could still be read, including a comment that a needy soldier was being sent some sandals, socks, and underwear. In addition, Pliny the Younger uniquely copied and published all of his correspondence, providing posterity with valuable information about Roman life.

Even in the declining days of the Empire, the soldiers continued to repair the roads, and the couriers still delivered messages, demonstrating how much the Romans valued communication; however, the messages now were more likely being sent from the Vatican to distant churches. Indeed, the fact that Catholic officials, and later lay scholars, contrived to stay in touch with colleagues throughout Europe during the next millennium is a tribute to the precedents set by the Roman couriers, who long enabled their employers to effectively maintain a vast empire. And to this day, images of Mercury, the Roman god of messengers, are often employed to represent those who deliver messages quickly and efficiently.

Further Reading

Adams, Colin, and Ray Laurence, editors. 2001. *Travel and Geography in the Roman Empire*. London and New York: Routledge.

Black, E.W. 1995. *Cursus Publicus: The Infrastructure of Government in Roman Britain*. Oxford: Tempus Repartum.

Casson, Lionel. 1994. *Travel in the Ancient World*. Baltimore, MD: John Hopkins University Press.

Graham, Mark W. 2006. *News and Frontier Consciousness in the Late Roman Empire*. Ann Arbor: University of Michigan Press.

Laurence, Ray. 1999. *The Roads of Roman Italy: Mobility and Cultural Change*. London and New York: Routledge.

Traina, Giusto. 2007. *428 AD: An Ordinary Year at the End of the Roman Empire*. Translated by Allen Cameron. 2009. Princeton, NJ: Princeton University Press.

Document

From Julius Caesar. C. 45 BCE. *Caesar's Commentaries on the Gallic and Civil Wars: With the Supplementary Books Attributed to Hirtius, Including the Alexandrian, African, and Spanish Wars*. Translated by William A. McDevitte and W. S. Bohn. 1869. New York: Harper and Brothers.

The writings of Julius Caesar (100–44 BCE) about his military career contain frequent references to messengers, conveying how important these men were to the success of his campaigns. In this passage from Book V of his Commentarii de Bello Gallico, *usually known in English as* The Gallic Wars, *he describes a time during his battles in Europe when another general, Quintus Tullius Cicero (102–43 BCE—not the famed orator, but his brother) was under attack and unable to contact Caesar because his messengers were being killed; finally, one of his slaves is able to deliver his request for assistance. Caesar, who writes about himself in the third person, then sends messengers to other generals to assemble a force to come to his aid.*

Chapter XLV. In proportion as the attack became daily more formidable and violent, and particularly, because, as a great number of the soldiers were exhausted with wounds, the matter had come to a small number of defenders, more frequent letters and messages were sent to Caesar; a part of which messengers were taken and tortured to death in the sight of our soldiers. There was within our camp a certain Nervian, by name Vertico, born in a distinguished position, who in the beginning of the blockade had deserted to Cicero, and had exhibited his fidelity to him. He persuades his slave, by the hope of freedom, and by great rewards, to convey a letter to Caesar. This he carries out bound about his javelin; and mixing among the Gauls without any suspicion by being a Gaul, ho reaches Caesar. From him they received information of the imminent danger of Cicero and the legion.

Chapter XLVI. Caesar having received the letter about the eleventh hour of the day, immediately sends a messenger to the Bellovaci, to M. Crassus, questor there, whose winter-quarters were twenty-five miles distant from him. He orders the legion to set forward in the middle of the night, and come to him with dispatch. Crassus sets out with the messenger. He sends another to C. Fabius, the lieutenant, ordering him to lead forth his legion into the territories of the Atrebates, to which he knew his march must be made. He writes to Labienus to come with his legion to the frontiers of the Nervii, if he could do so to the advantage of the commonwealth: he does not consider that the remaining portion of the army, because it was somewhat further distant, should be waited for; but assembles about 400 horse from the nearest winter-quarters.

Emperors

Since so many of the Roman emperors were notoriously incompetent, profligate, debauched, or even demented, one might be surprised that the Roman Empire lasted for almost 500 years. Yet the government as a whole was well organized and capable, even when its leader was not, and there was a peculiar but well-established procedure to minimize the disruptive effects of inferior emperors: when an emperor died, his son, adoptive son, or a male relative would usually take his place; if he proved to be a wise and talented ruler, he generally remained in office for the rest of his life; and if he instead demonstrated that he was not well suited for this role, he would be assassinated and replaced, usually by another relative or an ambitious general. Then, if the new emperor was also found lacking, he would suffer the same fate, and the process would continue until a good emperor was placed at the helm. The only problem with this jerry-built system was it sometimes enabled ambitious would-be emperors to eliminate reasonably effective emperors, or emperors who were never given time to display their merits.

Even during the Roman Republic, the country had sometimes been under the authoritarian rule of temporary dictators, but when a man named Octavian (63 BCE–14 CE) finally emerged as the victor of the long power struggle that followed the assassination of Julius Caesar (100–44 BCE), he renamed himself Augustus and effectively established himself as Rome's

This famous statue of the first Roman emperor, Augustus (63 BCE–14 CE), is known as the Augustus of Primaporta, the city where it was found. He is depicted wearing a military uniform, and gesturing imperiously, to convey an aura of absolute authority. (Library of Congress)

first emperor, though he allowed the institutions of the Republic to remain in place. He called himself *Princeps Civitatis*, or "first citizen," and endeavored in some respects to act like an ordinary Roman: the emperors would wear only a laurel wreath, not a crown, and only the purple color of his toga would distinguish him from other Romans. Augustus also insisted that his wife and daughter dress unostentatiously and carry on the standard practice of women weaving and sewing their own family's clothing. Asserting no absolute right to govern Rome, Augustus introduced the fiction that an emperor's powers were given to him by the Senate even as he ruled without any concern for others' opinions. Yet Augustus proved to be an intelligent and benign ruler who benefited his country in many ways. His new standing army helped to expand the

Roman Empire; he oversaw the development of a government of trained civil servants that could efficiently handle the daily tasks of controlling vast territories; and he launched many building projects to improve the capital city.

However, while he lived modestly, to set an example for his constituents, Augustus also made his deceased mentor Julius Caesar a god, setting a precedent that led to the later deification of Augustus and other emperors and perhaps encouraged some of his successors to govern imperiously and behave indulgently, though they often displayed their worst behavior only when far away from Rome. Thus, Augustus's successor Tiberius (42 BCE–37 CE) spent much of his time at an estate on the island of Capri, filled with pornographic books and young slaves of both sexes constantly available to satisfy the sexual desires of Tiberius and his guests. But Tiberius and the next emperor Caligula also greatly expanded the emperor's hillside palace, and the unstable Caligula (12–41 CE) made additional enemies by actually making himself a god during his own lifetime; these and other excesses soon led to his assassination. Then, after the capable emperor Claudius (10 BCE–54 CE) was apparently undone by palace intrigue, the emperor Nero (37–68 CE), after the burning of Rome in 64 CE, made himself very unpopular by constructing a huge new palace, the Golden House, which included a statue, thirty-three-feet high, of a naked Nero. Shrewdly, subsequent emperors demolished the Golden House and built on its site the Colosseum to entertain the citizens of Rome.

After Nero's death led to a succession of three emperors who served only briefly, a general named Vespasian (17–79 CE) became emperor and inaugurated an era when emperors would be chiefly distinguished by their military achievements. He was succeeded by his two sons, Titus (39–81 CE), who served only two years before succumbing to illness, and Domitian (51–96 CE), who was disliked for his brutal and authoritarian governance and eventually assassinated, though Rome did bring much of Britain under its control during his reign. Rome was then ruled by his advisor Nerva (30–98 CE), described by Italian philosopher Niccolò Machiavelli as the first of Rome's "Five Good Emperors" since they were

all skilled administrators who behaved responsibly in their private lives. Three of these men in particular stand out. Trajan (53–117 CE) led campaigns that further expanded the Empire in Europe and western Asia; Hadrian (76–138 CE) then decided that the Empire was large enough and devoted his energies to firmly establishing its control over existing provinces. His most noteworthy effort to achieve that goal was the construction of Hadrian's Wall across central Britain to protect Roman territory from northern barbarians. Finally, while Marcus Aurelius (121–180 CE) was often preoccupied by efforts to suppress rebellions in Europe, he also found time to write a distinguished work of philosophy, generally called his *Meditations*.

Unfortunately, Marcus Aurelius was succeeded by a son, Commodus (161–193 CE), who probably qualifies as the very worst of Rome's emperors. Apparently insane, Commodus wasted vast sums of money on frivolous entertainment and capriciously ordered the deaths of anyone who displeased him. He publically frolicked with both male and female lovers, and wishing to be regarded as a mighty hero, he would personally fight in the Colosseum against some of Rome's greatest gladiators, who were naturally wise enough to let him win every match. As he inattentively allowed corrupt subordinates to loot the Empire's treasury, there was burgeoning discontent with his rule, and declaring himself a god and dressing like Hercules did not improve his reputation. After other unsuccessful efforts, he was finally assassinated at the age of thirty-two. Commodus ushered in a long era of undistinguished emperors who were frequently murdered by ambitious rivals and struggled to maintain the Empire in the face of almost constant rebellions and invasions.

Contemporary commentators frequently judge the Roman emperors on the basis of something they probably would have regarded as unimportant: how they dealt with the growing numbers of Christians in Rome. Some emperors like Hadrian were tolerant toward Christians, while others violently persecuted them as a threat to the Roman religion. The cycles of benign treatment and suppression largely ended after the reign of the emperor Constantine I (272–337 CE), who converted to Christianity. It was

GALACTIC EMPERORS

Since Rome's government ruled by an emperor was long successful in controlling a vast expanse of territories, it might seem logical to employ a similar system to govern an even larger realm, interstellar space. According, two of science fiction's grandest sagas—Isaac Asimov's *Foundation* series and George Lucas's *Star Wars* films—have depicted futuristic empires headed by a single man, which rule over thousands of planets throughout the galaxy. However, recalling Rome's fall as well as its rise, both epics also envision that their empires will eventually collapse and disappear, leading to temporary chaos and the ultimate emergence of a more benign government.

A CRAZED CELEBRITY

Although some of Rome's finest emperors, like Trajan, Hadrian, and Marcus Aurelius, have been virtually invisible in popular culture, the corrupt, demented Caligula has appeared in many modern stories, usually as an iconic representative of Roman decadence. He was the subject of a play by French author and philosopher Albert Camus, *Caligula* (1944), which inspired two film adaptations (1966, 1975), and noted U.S. novelist Gore Vidal scripted his own version of the emperor's strange career, filmed as *Gore Vidal's Caligula* (1979). This notorious emperor has even appeared in such unlikely venues as episodes of the television series *Red Dwarf* and *Xena, Warrior Princess*.

only during the reign of Theodosius I (346–395 CE), however, that Christianity became the official religion of the Roman Empire, ending the sanctioned worship of the old Roman deities. Emperors also began to play a role in church affairs; Constantine, for example, convened the Council of Nicaea in 325 CE to solidity Christian doctrines (as articulated in its Nicene Creed), and Theodosius I oversaw another gathering in the city of Constantinople to resolve disputes within the church.

Constantine and Theodosius also played critical roles in a crucial development, the splitting of the Roman Empire. Constantine had established a residence in the Greek city of Byzantium, renamed Constantinople in his honor, and it effectively became the

Empire's eastern capital. The two parts of the Empire then grew increasingly distant, and Theodosius I became the last man to officially rule all of its territory, as it was officially divided after his death, with one of Theodosius's sons, Honorius (384–423 CE) taking over the Western Empire while another, Arcadius (378–408 CE) ruled the Eastern Empire. However, a series of weak and obscure emperors proved unable to prevent the decline and fall of the Western Empire, though the Eastern Empire, now termed the Byzantine Empire, would endure for another millennium.

Despite their enormous wealth and many privileges, most emperors probably did not really enjoy their positions. The competent and conscientious emperors were constantly bedeviled by the innumerable problems that arose in their vast Empire, while the weak and decadent emperors were tormented by fears that others were plotting against them, suspicions usually confirmed when they found themselves being assassinated at an early age. Still, there were many emperors who apparently lived long and happy lives, blessed by generally untroubled times, effective subordinates, and loyal family members, and even the less fortunate emperors could intermittently feel fulfilled because they were playing a role in sustaining one of history's greatest empires.

Further Reading

Bauman, Richard. 1989. *Lawyers and Politics in the Early Roman Empire: A Study of Relations between the Roman Jurists and the Emperors from Augustus to Hadrian*. München, Germany: C.H. Beck.

Kean, Roger Michael. 2009. *A New History of the Roman Emperors: From Augustus to Romulus Augustulus: 30 BC-AD 476*. North Melbourne, Australia: Alto Books.

Levick, Barbara. 2000. *The Government of the Roman Empire: A Sourcebook*. Second edition. London and New York: Routledge.

Santosuosso, Antonio. 2001. *Storming the Heavens: Soldiers, Emperors, and Civilians in the Roman Empire*. Boulder, CO: Westview Press.

Scarre, Christopher. 1995. *Chronicle of the Roman Emperors: The Reign-by-Reign Record of the Rulers of Imperial Rome*. London and New York: Thames and Hudson.

Southern, Pat. 1998. *Augustus*. London and New York: Routledge.

Documents

From Tacitus. C. 100–110 CE. *Tacitus: The Histories.* Volume 1. Translated by W. Hamilton Frye. 1912. Oxford: Oxford University Press.

In this passage from his Histories, *the Roman historian Tacitus (c. 56–117 CE) describes the reasons why the elderly emperor Galba [3 BCE–69 CE], who succeeded Nero, proved unable to hold onto power.*

The State of the Empire

The troops in the city had long been inured to the allegiance of the Caesars, and it was more by the pressure of intrigue than of their own inclination that they came to desert Nero. They soon realized that the donation promised in Galba's name was not to be paid to them, and that peace would not, like war, offer opportunity for great services and rich rewards. Since they also saw that the new emperor's favour had been forestalled by the army which proclaimed him, they were ripe for revolution and were further instigated by their rascally Praefect Nymphidius Sabinus, who was plotting to be emperor himself. His design was as a matter of fact detected and quashed, but, though the ringleader was removed, many of the troops still felt conscious of their treason and could be heard commenting on Galba's senility and avarice. His austerity—a quality once admired and set high in soldiers' estimation—only annoyed troops whose contempt for the old methods of discipline had been fostered by fourteen years of service under Nero. They had come to love the emperors' vices as much as they once reverenced their virtues in older days. Moreover Galba had let fall a remark, which augured well for Rome, though it spelt danger to himself. "I do not buy my soldiers," he said, "I select them." And indeed, as things then stood, his words sounded incongruous.

Galba's Position

Galba was old and ill. Of his two lieutenants Titus Vinius was the vilest of men and Cornelius Laco the laziest. Hated as he was for Vinius' crimes and despised for Laco's inefficiency, between them Galba soon came to ruin. His march from Spain was slow and stained with bloodshed. He executed Cingonius Varro, the consul-elect, and Petronius Turpilianus, an ex-consul, the former as an accomplice of Nymphidius, the latter as one of Nero's generals. They were both denied any opportunity of a hearing or defence—and might as well have been innocent. On his arrival at Rome the butchery of thousands of unarmed soldiers gave an ill omen to his entry, and alarmed even the men who did the slaughter. The city was filled with strange troops. A legion had been brought from Spain, and the regiment of marines enrolled by Nero still remained. Moreover there were several detachments from Germany, Britain, and Illyricum, which had been selected by Nero, dispatched to the Caspian Pass for the projected war against the Albanians, and subsequently recalled to aid in crushing the revolt of Vindex. These were all fine fuel for a revolution, and, although their favour centred on nobody in particular, there they were at the disposal of any one who had enterprise.

It happened by chance that the news of the death of Clodius Macer and of Fonteius Capito arrived in Rome simultaneously. Macer, who was undoubtedly raising a disturbance in Africa, was put to death by the imperial agent Trebonius Garrutianus, acting under Galba's orders: Capito had made a similar attempt in Germany and was killed by two officers, Cornelius Aquinus and Fabius Valens, without waiting for instructions. While Capito had a foul reputation for extortion and loose living, some people yet believed that he had withheld his hand from treason. His officers, they supposed, had urged him to declare war, and, when they could not persuade him, had gone on to charge him falsely with their own offence, while Galba from weakness of character, or perhaps because he was afraid to inquire too far, approved what had happened for good or for ill, since it was past alteration. At any rate both executions were unpopular. Now that Galba was disliked, everything he did, whether right or wrong, made him more unpopular. His freedmen were all-powerful: money could do anything: the slaves were thirsting for an upheaval, and with so elderly an emperor were naturally expecting to see one soon. The evils of the new court were those of the old, and while equally oppressive were not so easily excused. Even Galba's age seemed comic and despicable to a populace that was used to the young

Nero and compared the emperors, as such people will, in point of looks and personal attraction.

From Marcus Aurelius. C. 170–180 CE. *The Thoughts of the Emperor Marcus Aurelius Antoninus.* Translated by George Long. 1890. Boston: Little, Brown, and Company.

In his Meditations, *also referred to as his* Thoughts, *the emperor Marcus Aurelius (121–180 CE) began by listing what he had learned from various people; his ideas on governance were prominently influenced by a friend or relative named Severus, referred to as his "brother," and by his adoptive father and predecessor, the emperor Antoninus Pius (86–161 CE).*

From my brother Severus. . . I received the idea of a polity in which there is the same law for all, a polity administered with regard to equal rights and equal freedom of speech, and the idea of a kingly government which respects most of all the freedom of the governed; I learned from him also consistency and undeviating steadiness in my regard for philosophy; and a disposition to do good, and to give to others readily, and to cherish good hopes, and to believe that I am loved by my friends. . . .

In my father I observed mildness of temper, and unchangeable resolution in the things which he had determined after due deliberation; and no vainglory in those things which men call honors; and a love of labor and perseverance; and a readiness to listen to those who had anything to propose for the common weal; and undeviating firmness in giving to every man according to his deserts; and a knowledge derived from experience of the occasions for vigorous action and for remission. . . .

I observed too his habit of careful inquiry in all matters of deliberation, and his persistency, and that he never stopped his investigation through being satisfied with appearances which first present themselves; and that his disposition was to keep his friends, and not to be soon tired of them, nor yet to be extravagant in his affection; and to be satisfied on all occasions, and cheerful; and to foresee things a long way off, and to provide for the smallest without display; and to check immediately popular applause and all flattery; and to be ever watchful over the things which were necessary for the administration of the empire, and to

be a good manager of the expenditure, and patiently to endure the blame which he got for such conduct; and he was neither superstitious with respect to the gods, nor did he court men by gifts or by trying to please them, or by flattering the populace; but he showed sobriety in all things and firmness, and never any mean thoughts or action, nor love of novelty. And the things which conduce in any way to the commodity of life, and of which fortune gives an abundant supply, he used without arrogance and without excusing himself; so that when he had them, he enjoyed them without affection, and when he had them not, he did not want them. . . .

He was also easy in conversation, and he made himself agreeable without any offensive affectation. He took a reasonable care of his body's health, not as one who was greatly attached to life, nor out of regard to personal appearance, nor yet in a careless way, but so that through his own attention he very seldom stood in need of the physician's art or of medicine or external applications. He was most ready to give without envy to those who possessed any particular faculty, such as that of eloquence or knowledge of the law or of morals, or of anything else; and he gave them his help, that each might enjoy reputation according to his deserts; and he always acted conformably to the institutions of his country, without showing any affectation of doing so. Further, he was not fond of change nor unsteady, but he loved to stay in the same places, and to employ himself about the same things; and after his paroxysms of headache he came immediately fresh and vigorous to his usual occupations. His secrets were not many, but very few and very rare, and these only about public matters; and he showed prudence and economy in the exhibition of the public spectacles and the construction of public buildings, his donations to the people, and in such things, for he was a man who looked to what ought to be done, not to the reputation which is got by a man's acts. . . .

There was in him nothing harsh, nor implacable, nor violent, nor, as one may say, anything carried to the sweating point; but he examined all things severally, as if he had abundance of time, and without confusion, in an orderly way, vigorously and consistently. And that might be applied to him which is recorded of Socrates, that he was able both to abstain from, and to enjoy, those things which many are too weak to abstain from, and cannot enjoy without excess. But to be strong enough both to bear the one and to be sober in the other is the mark of a man who has a perfect and invincible soul, such as he showed in the illness of Maximus.

Farmers

It is not often celebrated, but farming was the major business of ancient Rome and probably its most common profession. It is difficult, however, to offer generalizations about Roman farmers, since they were different sorts of people who labored in many different situations. In the early days of the Roman Republic, small family farms were the norm, and some of these did remain in operation in the centuries that followed. However, as Rome expanded to control all of Italy, the government typically seized the land of the groups that resisted its rule and either held it as government property or awarded it to favored individuals, such as aristocrats or former soldiers. Eventually, most Roman agriculture came to involve large estates controlled by the emperor, wealthy landowners, or entire communities, where tenant farmers and slaves did most of the work, primarily for the benefit of absentee owners. Land was frequently sold or leased to other individuals or confiscated by the government, even as the people who were actually growing the crops remained the same.

Whether they were working on their own property or property that belonged to others, Roman farmers were always limited to specific fields that were demarcated by hedges, fences, walls, or ditches, and one of their responsibilities was to carefully maintain these boundary lines to avoid any disputes over land. The crops that they grew were determined by local conditions and the marketplace. The three most important crops, by most accounts, were grapes, grains, and olives. Growing grapes was theoretically forbidden outside of Italy, but the law was ignored in the hilly regions of France and Spain; most farmers who grew grapes used them to make wine, an avocation that demands separate attention, though some might be set aside to be sold as food. Grains like wheat, barley,

and millet were always important, though barley and millet were usually only used to feed animals; since grains could be easily preserved and transported long distances, they came to be most commonly grown in distant outposts of the Empire like Egypt, Germany, and Britain. Olives were a popular crop in Italy, Greece, and North Africa. However, the Romans did enjoy variety in their diet, so they also grew some rice, as well as many other types of fruits, vegetables, and nuts, including dates, figs, apples, plums, pears, cherries, peaches, almonds, hazelnuts, and walnuts. Herbs were raised to flavor foods and make medicine; hemp, cotton, and flax were grown for fabrics; and trees were planted to provide timber.

Practicing a form of crop rotation, most Roman farmers would plant on only half of their land at one time, so the nutrients in the other half would be replenished. The process of growing crops began with plowing the land. To plant their seeds, most Roman farmers depended upon a simple type of plow called an ard, usually pulled by one or two oxen; since these animals were costly, an entire village might band together to purchase, and share the services of, a team of oxen. Because the ard only produced a shallow furrow, successful farming usually required cross-plowing, traversing the area twice at right angles, and a field might have to be plowed six times before it was ready for planting. Another problem was that the ard could not deal with hard soils, so these lands were not farmed until the later days of the Empire, when a heavier plow was developed, which could cut into firmer ground. Some small farmers prepared the soil without a plow, instead using hoes and spades, tools that were also helpful in removing weeds and harvesting plants that grew underground. After plowing, the land had to be fertilized with manure, another time-consuming process, since the manure was typically blended into the soil by hand. By one estimate, an entire family would have to labor for six days in order to fertilize one acre.

Then, finally, the land was ready for seeding, but since Roman farmers scattered their seeds by hand and lost many seeds that way, they needed many seeds, often requiring them to save one-fourth of each crop in order to have enough seeds for the next planting. After the seeds were in the ground, the farmers had to

This carving, from the first or second century CE, shows Roman farmers plowing, spreading seeds, and carrying sheaths of harvested crops. (Museo del Sannio Benevento/DeAgostini/Getty Images)

further loosen the soil with hoes and remove weeds with their hands. When it was time to harvest the crops, farmers usually used scythes and sickles to cut them down by hand. One advantage the Roman farmer had was that these tools were usually made of iron, so they were stronger and more effective than the bronze tools of earlier cultures.

While many vegetables, once harvested, were ready to be eaten, grains required special attention. A major innovation of Roman agriculture was the *carpentum*, or harvesting machine, which was designed to harvest grain; this was uniquely pushed, not pulled, by a donkey or an ox. It consisted of a bin mounted on wheels with several long blades attached to its bottom. As the animal pushed the machine forward, the blades cut the ears of grain off of the stalks, and they fell into the bin. Next was the process of threshing, isolating the valued grain from the unwanted chaff. At first, the Roman farmers would simply throw the grain on threshing floors and either strike it with tools called flails or have animals walk over the grain; later, they probably learned to use the Greek device called a *tribulum*, a board with small flints that was dragged over

the grain. An improved version of the tribulum, the Punic cart, employed rollers with tiny razors. Finally, to winnow the grain, it was tossed into the air, so the wind could blow the chaff away while the grain fell to the floor. Roman farmers would also grind their grain into flour; the simplest method involved by placing the grain on a large flat stone and rubbing it with another stone, but they also used machines with rotating stones propelled either by humans or donkeys. Eventually, however, the Romans began to build large watermills, which produced flour far more efficiently, and farmers would bring their grain to these watermills to be processed into flour.

When farmers harvested olives, they had to pick them up very gently, because the tender olives were easily bruised. While farmers might sell some of their olives to be eaten, it was usually most profitable to turn the olives into olive oil, which was not only used in place of butter but also served as soap, fuel for lamps, and a key ingredient in lotions and perfumes. Some authorities advised crushing the olives immediately, while others said it was best to wait a few days. After the olives were washed, the Romans employed

GRAND GARDENS

As many Romans who owned farms grew more and more wealthy, they no longer needed to raise crops to earn income; instead, it became the habit to turn large expanses of land into vast gardens, which featured artificial lakes, rows of hedges and colorful flowers, and pathways for strolling guests. This practice was revived during the European Renaissance, and some of these palatial gardens are still being maintained today. Tourists, for example, can visit such an enormous garden at the French Palace of Versailles and examine the carefully cultivated beauty once enjoyed by wealthy Roman farmers.

WHEN YOU CAN'T KEEP THEM DOWN ON THE FARM

According to one theory, a decline in the numbers of Roman farmers, leading to the dominance of large farms, was sparked by the wars against Carthage: farmers conscripted to fight in the wars moved to cities after experiencing their more stimulating lifestyles. And as rural depopulation made properties cheaper, wealthy people could purchase vast stretches of land. The same process was observed in Europe and United States after World War II, though the problem was anticipated as an effect of World War I in a 1918 song by Joe Young, Sam M. Lewis, and Walter Donaldson: "How You Going to Keep Them Down on the Farm after They've Seen Paree?"

a special mill to crush the olives and remove the pits; the crushed olives were then placed in bags or baskets and pressed, at first by hand and later with special machines with levers that applied even more pressure. The resulting liquid consisted of bitter water with oil that rose to the top, which was collected with a ladle and poured into vessels. A by-product of the process of pressing, a sort of black sludge, was used for various purposes—as a fertilizer, insect repellant, pesticide, or grease. It was also fed to sick sheep as a medicine.

In addition to their crops, Roman farmers also raised several different types of animals. Cattle provided milk and dairy products, sheep produced wool, and the skins of both sheep and goats were made into parchment. The meat from pigs was very popular; birds like ducks and geese offered both eggs and meat; bees were a valuable source of honey, the only source of sweetness in the Roman diet; mules and donkeys pulled plows and vehicles; and dogs assisted in hunting and herding. Tending to the needs of these animals, as well as their crops, undoubtedly kept farmers very busy throughout the year; perhaps this is why the poet Virgil (70–10 BCE), in his poetic treatise on farming, the *Georgics* (ca. 29 BCE), unusually did not emphasize the pleasures of rural life, but rather characterized the life of the farmer as a constant battle against the forces of nature. Still, Roman farmers surely enjoyed many moments of leisure as well, along with a quiet sense of satisfaction from their many productive labors.

Further Reading

Bowman, Alan, and Andrew Wilson, editors. 2013. *The Roman Agricultural Economy: Organisation, Investment, and Production.* Oxford and New York: Oxford University Press.

De Ligt, L., and S.J. Northwood, editors. 2008. *People, Land, and Politics: Demographic Developments and the Transformation of Roman Italy 300 BC-AD 14.* Leiden, The Netherlands, and Boston: Brill.

Erdkamp, Paul. 2005. *The Grain Market in the Roman Empire: A Social, Political and Economic Study.* Cambridge and New York: Cambridge University Press.

Kehoe, Dennis P. 2007. *Law and the Rural Economy in the Roman Empire.* Ann Arbor: University of Michigan Press.

Nelson, Stephanie A. 1998. *God and the Land: The Metaphysics of Farming in Hesiod and Vergil.* Oxford and New York: Oxford University Press.

Rosenstein, Nathan Stewart. 2004. *Rome at War: Farms, Families, and Death in the Middle Republic.* Chapel Hill: University of North Carolina Press.

Documents

From Virgil. C. 29 BCE. *The Georgics of Virgil.* Translated into English Verse by Herbert Gardner Burghclere. 1904. London: John Murray.

In this passage from The Georgics, *the Roman poet Virgil (70 BCE–19 CE) poetically describes the processes of plowing the land, burning the soil to improve its fertility, planting the seeds, setting up a system of irrigation, and removing weeds.*

When springtime comes and brings the warm
    west wind,
When from the hoary-headed mountain streams
The molten ice, and all the clodded fields
Crumble and thaw, then let my plough be set
Deep in the tilth, my straining oxen groan.
And stubborn furrows make the
    ploughshare flame
With a new splendour.

Best that land rewards
Your thrifty farmer's vow which twice the sun
And twice the frost has felt. For him forthwith
Shall be a mighty garnering and his barns
Bursting with grain.

But first our care must be,
Or ever we would drive the iron share
Athwart the glebe in some new plain, to learn
What winds are wont to blow; the character
And variance of the skies; the ancient arts
Thus in a shift of seeds your lands may take
Rest as in idleness, nor cease the while.
As fallows must, their grateful recompense.

And often you will find it well to burn
The garnered fields and set the flimsy straw
A-crackling in the flames. Whether perchance
The land in this wise finds some unknown force,
Some fat enrichment; or that every fault
Thereof is purified by fire and all
The useless humours purged; or that the heat
By its own virtue loosens secret pores
And paths unseen whereby the sap may flow
To the young grasses; or, it may be, binds
Firmer the earth, and knits the gaping veins.
Lest showers should subtly harm, or the
    fierce sun
With a too passionate majesty consume.
Or the bleak north winds sear with piercing cold.

Who with his mattock breaks the sleepy clods
And harrows them with hurdles osier-twined

Shall largely serve the land; nor such a one
Does golden Ceres with indifference eye
From her Olympian heights; he too does well
Who drives the furrow through the glebe
    and then
With a cross-ploughing cleaves the up-turned
    plain.
And tireless disciplines the ground, and rules
Right royally his fields.

Pray, husbandmen,
For summer showers and tranquil winter-time;
The dust of winter days shall fill the land
With joy, and with a joy most great the corn;
Never shall Mysia vaunt her tilth so high
And even Gargarus look with wonderment
Upon his granaries.

And what of him
Who hurls the seed, and soldier-wise pursues
The onslaught, grappling the soil, and scattering
The masses of lean sand? Then to his crop
Summons the flood and leads the attendant rills.
So when the burning fields are all aglow
And the herb meet to die, see! from the brink
Of its steep path he woos the watercourse.
Hither it tumbles hoarsely murmurous
And wakes the way-worn stones and,
    bubbling on,
Quenches the thirsty plain.

Or him again
Who, lest beneath the over-laden ears
The haulms be bowed, crops the rank
    herbage down
In its young leaf, what time the tender growth
First tops the trenches:

Or of him who strives
With bibulous sand to suck the stagnant ooze
Out of the marsh, and finds his special task
When in some changeful moon the rivers rise
In turbulent flood, till far and wide the slime
Covers the land, and all the channelled dikes
Sweat with a faint warm reek?

Yet after all,
Ply as we may our arts, toil as we may.
Both man and beast, till and re-till the ground,
No jot the less do we endure the plague
Of the Strymonian crane or noxious goose.
Or bitter-rooted endive, or the bane
Chill shadows cast around.

So hath he willed,
The great All-father, that we husbandmen
Might tread no easy path, since he it was
Who earliest woke the meadows with our craft.
And made our cares the whetstone of our wits,
Nor suffered drowsy sloth to dull his realm. . . .

Yet straightway trouble falls upon the wheat;
A plague of mildew eats up all the straw,
And wastrel thistles through the fields uprear
Their horrent spikes. The crops begin to die;
Along the ground there creeps a tangled growth
Of caltrops, cleavers, and their kind. Then up,
Lording it o'er the glittering harvest, spring
Harsh darnels and wild barren oats.

And thus,
Unless you chase the weeds with constant hoe,
And scare the birds, and prune the darkening
    shade.
And with your prayers draw showers from
    heaven—alas!
Your lot shall be with vainly covetous eye
To watch your neighbours pile their ricks,
    and then
Go fill your empty belly in the woods
Under the shaken oaks.

From Cicero. 44 BCE. *Cicero's Three Books of Offices,
or Moral Duties; Also His Cato Major, an Essay on Old
Age; Laelius, an Essay on Friendship; Paradoxes; Scipio's
Dream; and Letter to Quintus on the Duties of a Magistrate.*
Translated by Cyrus R. Edmonds. 1850. London: Henry
G. Bohn.

In this passage from Cato Major, an Essay on Old
Age, *the Roman writer Cicero (106–43 BCE) describes
farming as one of the pleasures of old age.*

I come now to the pleasures of husbandmen,
with which I am excessively delighted; which are
not checked by any old age, and appear in my mind
to make the nearest approach to the life of a wise
man. For they have relation to the earth, which never
refuses command, and never returns without interest
that which it hath received; but sometimes with less,
generally with very great interest. And yet for my part
it is not only the product, but the virtue and nature of
the earth itself delights me; which, when in its softened and subdued bosom it has received the scattered seed, first of all confines what is hidden within
it, from which harrowing, which produces that effect,
derives its name (*occatio*); then, when it is warmed by
heat and its own compression, it spreads it out, and
elicits from it the verdant blade, which, supported by
the fibers of the roots, gradually grows up, and, rising on a jointed stalk, is now inclosed in a sheath, as
if it were of tender age, out of which, when it hath
shot up, it then pours forth the fruit of the ear, piled
in due order, and is guarded by a rampart of beards
against the pecking of the smaller birds. Why should
I, in the case of vines, tell of the plantings, the risings,
the stages of growth? That you may know the repose
and amusement of my old age, I assure you that I can
never have enough of that gratification. For I pass over
the peculiar nature of all things which are produced
from the earth: which generates such great trunks and
branches from so small a grain of the fig or from the
grape-stone, or from the minutest seeds of other fruits
and roots: shoots, plants, twigs, quicksets, layers, do
not these produce the effect of delighting any one even
to admiration? The vine, indeed, which by nature is
prone to fall, and is borne down to the ground, unless
it be propped, in order to raise itself up, embraces with
its tendrils, as it were with hands, whatever it meets
with; which, as it creeps with manifold and wandering
course, the skill of the husbandmen, pruning with the
knife, restrains from running into a forest of twigs, and
spreading too far in all directions.

Accordingly, in the beginning of spring, in those
twigs which are left, there rises up as it were at the
joints of the branches that which is called a bud, from
which the nascent grape shows itself; which, increasing in size by the moisture of the earth and the heat
of the sun, is at first very acid to the taste, and then

as it ripens grows sweet, and being clothed with its large leaves does not want moderate warmth, and yet keeps off the excessive heat of the sun; than which what can be in fruit on the one hand more rich, or on the other hand more beautiful in appearance? Of which not enjoy the advantage, as I said before, but also the cultivation and the nature itself delights me: the rows of props, the joining of the heads, the tying up and propagation of vines, and the pruning of some twigs, and the grafting of others, which I have mentioned. Why should I allude to irrigations, why to the diggings of the ground, why to the trenching by which the ground is made much more productive? Why should I speak of the advantage of manuring? I have treated of it in that book which I wrote respecting rural affairs, concerning which the learned Hesiod has not said a single word, though he has written about the cultivation of the land. But Homer, who, as appears to me, lived many ages before, introduces Laertes soothing the regret which he felt for his son, by tilling the land and manuring it. Nor in deed is rural life delightful by reason of corn-fields only and meadows and vineyards and groves, but also for its gardens and orchards; also for the feeding of cattle, the swarms of bees, and the variety of all kinds of flowers. Nor do plantings only give me delight, but also engraftings; than which agriculture has invented nothing more ingenious.

I can enumerate many amusements of rustic life; but even those things which I have mentioned, I perceive to have been rather long. But you will forgive me; for both from my love of rural life I have been carried away, and old age is by nature rather talkative, that I may not appear to vindicate it from all failings.

Gladiators

While there is much to admire about the ancient Romans, commentators have long been puzzled and appalled by their peculiar fondness for gladiatorial contests; huge crowds would gather in arena to watch armed men (and a few women) violently kill each other or be killed by ravenous animals. There has also been intense curiosity about the lives and emotions of people whose profession involved the constant threat of death, accompanied by the cheers of delighted spectators.

It is believed that the origins of the gladiatorial games can be traced back to rites performed at Etruscan funerals called *munera*, especially since the earliest known gladiatorial battle did occur at a Roman funeral in 264 BCE. But these became purely sporting events by the first century BCE, frequently staged by the dictator Julius Caesar (100–44 BCE) in an effort to win the support of the Roman people. Since the usual weapon employed was a sword called the *gladius hispaniesis*, the people wielding them came to be known as gladiators. The burgeoning popularity of contests often resulting in death required the constant recruitment of new gladiators in various ways; criminals (both men and women), prisoners of war, and purchased slaves were the usual candidates, though a man could also volunteer to become a gladiator in exchange for a fee. Needless to say, officials invariably singled out for muscular young men for this sort of work. Depending upon their crimes, criminals could become two types of gladiators: if sentenced *ad gladium*, or to the sword, they would fight other gladiators and, if successful, could enjoy long careers in the arena. However, if they were sentenced *ad bestias*, or to the wild animals, they were destined to be slaughtered by a lion or another large predator.

Once assigned to fighting, gladiators had to undergo training, usually in one of four "schools," or *ludi*, run by the government, which employed a number of guards, doctors, masseurs, and weapon makers, though the most important employee was the *lanista*, the man who trained prospective gladiators to fight. At first, the prospective gladiator, or *tiro*, would practice only with wooden weapons and wooden dummies, but when the men were almost ready for battle, they would switch to actual weapons made of steel and practice fighting against each other. Unsurprisingly, the discipline these men had to endure was brutal: they were forced to live in barracks that resembled prisons and mostly fed meat, which was believed to increase their savagery. If they ever disobeyed orders, they would be mercilessly flogged, and as they were mostly criminals or slaves, they were constantly kept under lock and key. At the beginning of their training, all gladiators would give up their old names and, like

This relief carving from the first century CE shows Roman gladiators killing wild animals, the activity that generally preceded the battles to the death between human combatants. (Print Collector/Getty Images)

many modern actors, they would assume an appealing stage name for their gladiatorial careers.

Gladiators were classified into a variety of groups, depending on the equipment they had for their battles. The *eques* began by riding a horse, but concluded by fighting on the ground, using a lance and sword and protected by several pieces of armor. The *murmillo*, however, was always on foot, had only a sword and shield, and wore only a helmet, loincloth, and minimal armor on their wrists and ankles; a similar gladiator called a *secutor* wore a different helmet. The *thraex* carried a rectangular shield and a curved sword, and the *hoplomachus* had a lance, dagger, and round shield. The *provocator* was well protected by a helmet, breastplate, shield, and armor for his legs and

arms, while a *retiarius* was virtually naked, except for a loincloth and pieces of armor on his arms and shoulders; his special weapons were a trident, a net, and a dagger. Gladiators were usually designated for one of these roles based on their physiques: a man who was heavy and moved slowly might become a heavily armored *provocator*, while a thinner man who moved very quickly would be an ideal *retiarius*, depending on his agility for his survival.

Gladiatorial contests were relatively infrequent—perhaps no more than one or two every year—but they always attracted many spectators and earned a lot of money. Whenever an event was scheduled, the arenas would make arrangements with the *ludi* to obtain a certain number of gladiators for their games. The fees paid would vary tremendously: a neophyte gladiator might be obtained for a little as 1,000 *sesterces* (very roughly, 500–1500 dollars in modern currency), while a famed veteran might command over 100,000 *sesterces*. It was customary for all combatants, even those scheduled to fight each other, to have dinner together the night before. Captured prisoners of war from other countries who were assigned to fight sometimes committed suicide beforehand, while another disobedient gladiator, the renowned Spartacus (ca. 109–71 BCE), escaped from his captivity to lead a lengthy slave rebellion against Rome.

During a typical day at the arena, the festivities would begin with all of the gladiators marching in front of the cheering crowds while a band played music, but they did not immediately begin fighting. Instead, there were preliminary events involving wild animals; a condemned criminal might be mauled to death by a lion, while a variety of other animals—lions, tigers, leopards, panthers, or bears—would fight against each other. Finally, gladiators would come on to the scene to kill the surviving animals. There would then be a break for the spectators to eat lunch, interspersed with some lighter entertainment, such as the distribution of lottery tickets for free prizes, a theatrical sketch, or two ostriches unleashed to be chased and roped by men on horseback. Then, the gladiatorial battles would begin, usually with the fighters loudly insulting each other before they started fighting. If a gladiator was killed during a battle, a man dressed as Charon, who ferries the dead in Roman mythology, would come on the scene to strike the corpse with a hammer to ensure that he was not pretending to be dead. If a fighter was downed without being killed, he could appeal to the crowd for mercy by raising his fist with one finger outstretched, but more often than not, he would be greeted by the audience's famous gesture of down-turned thumbs, and the victorious gladiator would then deliver a fatal wound with his sword. (Interestingly, though, some researchers believe that the downturned thumb was actually the request for mercy, while the thumbs-up gesture demanded death.) An occasional battle between two armed women would be regarded as a welcome change of pace. When the last battle was over, all the winners who were fit enough to walk would come back to be saluted by the crowd.

A life of constant battling may not seem appealing, but successful gladiators could also anticipate some significant rewards. Like modern-day athletes, gladiators who won a series of contests would become celebrities, their names recorded in graffiti as "the glory of the girls" or "what the girls sighed for," and their overseers would begin to pamper these valuable pieces of property instead of brutalizing them. Nobles would eagerly visit these gladiators to watch them train; female visitors might seek romantic liaisons; and some gladiators might marry and have children. Most significantly, after a long career of glorious victories, a gladiator might finally receive, during an event's final ceremony, a wooden sword, symbolizing that he was now allowed to permanently retire from the arena. A free man who received this honor might retire with

LET THE GAME BEGIN

Since Roman gladiators are among the world's most famous battlers, and since fighting games have been a staple of the video game industry, it was virtually inevitable that several games would feature gladiators. The most authentic of these is a 2005 video game called *Colosseum: Road to Freedom*. The main character is a slave living during the reign of the emperor Commodus (161–192 CE), and his goal is to earn enough money to buy his freedom by winning a series of battles in the Colosseum wielding weapons like swords, axes, chains, and hammers. Interestingly, Commodus himself appears as one character in the game.

FEMALE FIGHTERS

As a novelty introduced during some later series of gladiatorial games, two women would be brought into the arena to battle against each other. More recently, pairs of female combatants are becoming more common in a modern-day sport that resembles a gladiatorial battle, boxing. Experimentally featured during the 1904 Olympic Games, women's boxing was forbidden in most countries until the 1980s. But it became an officially sanctioned sport in the next decade, and was included in the 2012 Olympics. One prominent female boxer, now retired, was Laila Ali, daughter of famed heavyweight champion Muhammad Ali.

his considerable earnings to enjoy a comfortable life, while a slave would become a *lanista*, still working hard to prepare new gladiators for combat but secure in the knowledge that he would never again have to risk his own life. We have no reliable statistics to show how often gladiators typically lived long enough for such a fate, but it seems clear that many of them were killed rather quickly; it was rare for one gladiator to win more than ten battles, though some might survive up to thirty contests, and there is a report of one gladiator who actually prevailed in eighty-eight contests.

Despite the popularity of gladiatorial contests, such violent entertainment did not seem to accord with Christianity, so the emperor Constantine (ca. 272–373 CE), after converting to Christianity, attempted to end these events in 325 CE. However, despite official disapproval, battles between gladiators continued for another hundred years or so before they finally ended. In a sense, though, Roman gladiators never stopped fighting, since their exploits have remained alive in the popular imagination, continuing to fascinate scholars and to figure prominently in all depictions of the Roman Empire in both literature and film.

Further Reading

Auguet, Roland. 1994. *Cruelty and Civilization: The Roman Games.* London and New York: Routledge.

Dunkle, Roger. 2008. *Gladiators: Violence and Spectacle in Ancient Rome.* Harlow, England, and New York: Pearson/Longman.

Jacobelli, Luciana. 2003. *Gladiators at Pompeii.* Los Angeles: J. Paul Getty Museum.

Matthews, Rupert. 2004. *The Age of the Gladiators: Savagery and Spectacle in Ancient Rome.* Edison, NJ: Chartwell Books.

Plass, Paul. 1995. *The Game of Death in Ancient Rome: Arena Sport and Political Suicide.* Madison: University of Wisconsin Press.

Wiedemann, Thomas E. J. 1992. *Emperors and Gladiators.* London and New York: Routledge.

Document

From Seneca. C. 40 CE. Letter. *Readings in Ancient History: Illustrative Extracts from the Sources: Volume 2: Rome and the West.* Translated by William Stearns Davis. 1913. Boston: Allyn & Bacon.

In this letter to a friend, written during the reign of Caligula (12–41 CE), the philosopher Seneca (4 BCE–65 CE) describes gladiatorial contests as displays that do not merit the attention of a thoughtful man.

There is nothing so ruinous to good character as to idle away one's time at some spectacle. Vices have a way of creeping in because of the feeling of pleasure that it brings. Why do you think that I say that I personally return from shows greedier, more ambitious and more given to luxury, and I might add, with thoughts of greater cruelty and less humanity, simply because I have been among humans?

The other day, I chanced to drop in at the midday games, expecting sport and wit and some relaxation to rest men's eyes from the sight of human blood. Just the opposite was the case. Any fighting before that was as nothing; all trifles were now put aside—it was plain butchery.

The men had nothing with which to protect themselves, for their whole bodies were open to the thrust, and every thrust told. The common people prefer this to matches on level terms or request performances. Of course they do. The blade is not parried by helmet or shield, and what use is skill or defense? All these merely postpone death.

In the morning men are thrown to bears or lions, at midday to those who were previously watching them. The crowd cries for the killers to be paired with those who will kill them, and reserves the victor for yet another death. This is the only release the gladiators have. The whole business needs fire and steel to urge men on to fight. There was no escape for them. The slayer was kept fighting until he could be slain.

"Kill him! Flog him! Burn him alive!" (the spectators roared) "Why is he such a coward? Why won't he rush on the steel? Why does he fall so meekly? Why won't he die willingly?"

Unhappy as I am, how have I deserved that I must look on such a scene as this? Do not, my Lucilius, attend the games, I pray you. Either you will be corrupted by the multitude, or, if you show disgust, be hated by them. So stay away.

From Martial. C. 86–103 CE. *The Epigrams of Martial, Translated into English Prose.* Translator unidentified. 1860. London: Henry G. Bohn.

In a series of his Epigrams *given the title "On the Public Shows of Domitian," the satirist Martial (ca. 38–103 CE) focuses on gladiatorial contests; his poems include three tributes to a gladiator named Carpophorus who specialized in fighting against animals, and the story of two equally matched combatants who were both declared victors. Also, his other* Epigrams *include a celebration of another skilled gladiator named Hermes.*

["On the Public Shows of Domitian"] XV. On Carpophorus

That which was the utmost glory of thy renown, Meleager, a boar put to flight, what is it? a mere portion of that of Carpophorus. He, in addition, planted his hunting-spear in a fierce rushing bear, the monarch in the realm of the northern pole; he also laid low a lion remarkable for its unheard-of size—a lion, which might have become the hands of Hercules; and he then, with a wound from a distance, stretched lifeless a fleet leopard. And when at length he carried off his prizes, he was still in a condition to engage in new combats.

XXIII. On Carpophorus

The bold right hand of the still youthful Carpophorus now directs with unerring bow the Noric hunting-spears. He carried two steers on his shoulders with ease; to him succumbed the bubalus and the bison. Fleeing from him, the lion fell headlong among the darts of others. Go now, impatient crowd, and complain of the tardy delay to which you are exposed.

XXVII. On Carpophorus

Had the ages of yore, Caesar, given birth to Carpophorus, [barbarian lands would not have boasted of their monsters]. Marathon would not have feared the bull, the woods of Nemea the lion, Arcadia the Maenalian boar. Had Carpophorus armed his hands, one deadly stroke would have sufficed for the hydra; by him would the whole of the Chimera have been stricken down at once. He would have yoked together the fire-breathing bulls without the assistance of the Colchian princess; he could have conquered either monster of Pasiphae. Could the fable of the marine prodigy be revived, he alone would release Hesione and Andromeda. Let all the glories of the praise bestowed on Hercules be counted up; it is more to have subdued twenty animals at one time.

XXIX. On Priscus and Verus

While Verus and Priscus were prolonging the combat, and the valour of each had been for a long time equal, quarter for the combatants was demanded with great clamour. But Caesar obeyed his own law. The law was to fight with a stated reward in view, till by his thumb *one of the pair proclaimed himself vanquished*: but, as was allowed, he frequently gave them dishes and gifts. An end, however, was found for the well-matched contest: equal they fought, equal they resigned. Caesar sent wands to each, to each the meed of victory. Such was the reward that adroit valour received. Under no other prince save thee, Caesar, has this ever happened, that, when two fought with each other, both were victors.

[*Epigrams*, Book V] XXIV: On Hermes, an Eminent Gladiator

Hermes is the pride of his age in martial contests; Hermes is skilled in all kinds of arms; Hermes is a gladiator and a master of gladiators; Hermes is the terror and awe of his whole school; Hermes is he of whom alone Helius is afraid; Hermes is he to whom alone Advolans submits; Hermes is skilled in conquering without a blow; Hermes is his own body of reserve; Hermes makes the fortunes of the letters of seats; Hermes is the object of care and anxiety to the actresses; Hermes walks proudly with the warlike spear; Hermes threatens with Neptune's trident; Hermes is terrible with the helmet shading the face; Hermes is the glory of Mars in every way; Hermes is everything in himself, and thrice a man.

Glassblowers

Thousands of years ago, ancient technicians learned how to make glass; basically, one mixed together sand, ashes, and powdered limestone and heated the mixture, perhaps adding other substances to color the glass. According to one dubious legend, glass was first discovered when some shipwrecked sailors used chunks of natron (sodium carbonate) to hold hot cooking pots over fires in the sand, and the natron and sand merged to form glass. From Mesopotamia, where archaeologists have discovered ancient beads of glass, the art of glassmaking moved to Alexandria in

Egypt, and then to Rome. For centuries, the Romans relied upon three time-tested techniques. To make bottles, molten glass could be placed around a mud mold that was then broken and removed. Heated glass rods could also be fused together, and one could cut and carve large blocks of glass to make various shapes. The Romans later learned to pour molten glass into molds, to grind the piece to its final form, and reheat it to make it shinier. However, all of these methods required considerable skill and a great deal of time, making glass items too costly for most people.

Everything changed in the first century BCE, when glassmakers in a region of present-day Syria under Roman rule made a discovery: liquid glass would adhere to iron. Someone was then inspired to construct a long iron tube and dip one end in molten glass, heated in brick furnaces fueled with wood. By blowing hard through the other end of the pipe, one could produce a glass bubble that could be manipulated to harden into many complex shapes; some glassblowers even learned how to make bottles that were shaped like animals or helmets. Further, one could make glass items in this manner quickly and easily, and by repeatedly blowing glass into prepared molds made of clay, wood, or metal, an artisan could produce large numbers of identical pieces, though the molds would eventually break, requiring the glassblower to make a new mold using a previously produced glass object.

Though almost everyone could now afford to purchase glass bowls and decorations, these were ill-suited for export, since they were so easily broken. The solution was to have each major city develop its own glassmaking industry, and this is precisely what occurred. We know of major glass businesses in Rome, the southern Italian city of Puteoli, the northern Italian city of Aquileia, and the German city of Cologne, and we assume that virtually every Roman province had its own smaller facilities, though remnants of their equipment is rarely found. But in 2005, archaeologists uncovered evidence of a thriving glass industry in one of the most distant outposts of the Roman Empire, present-day London; there, the artisans apparently specialized in reheating broken pieces of glass to make new items. In Rome, bits of broken glass, along with similar fragments of tile, stone, and pottery, were recycled in another way to form the many colorful mosaics that decorated walls and floors.

The Roman glassblowers soon found many ways to improve their products. Applying old knowledge to their new skill, they quickly mastered the art of making glass in many bright colors by adding metals and ores: iron oxide (often already present in the sand) made glass a bluish green, cobalt produced a deeper blue, a mixture of lead and antimony yielded yellow, and manganese could provide a pink or purple color. However, most of their customers came to prefer glass that was perfectly clear and untinted, which became the standard form. Special glass cutters called *diatretarii* engraved decorative flourishes and even human and animal figures on the sides of vessels. Glassworks could also be made more attractive by brushing them with more liquid glass, adding blobs of glass, or applying some paint or golden trim.

Glassblowers also used this newly mastered material to make other objects. Glass beads remained popular; larger pieces of glass were used for necklaces, earrings, and pendants; and small glass pieces were made for board games. Decorative glass plaques were sold to be hung on walls, and some individuals paid to have busts of their heads made of glass. Most significantly, Roman glassblowers in the first century CE made the first glass windows, allowing people to bring sunlight into their homes without any accompanying winds, odors, or noises. At first, the glass was blown into a flat wooden mold to make window glass, but this produced slabs of glass of an uneven width. Later, glassblowers learned to blow an elongated glass bubble, shape it into a cylinder, cut the cylinder, and flatten it into a square or rectangular sheet of uniform thickness. Unfortunately, since glass windows long remained rather expensive, only Rome's wealthy citizens could afford to install them in their homes, though they were commonly found in public baths to provide the facilities with light, but no cooling drafts.

Over the centuries, the Roman glassblowers kept experimenting with their techniques, with often impressive results. One particularly striking piece, dating from the fourth century CE, is a chalice called the Lycurgus Cup because it features an image of Thrace's King Lycurgus. When light shines on the front of the chalice, it looks green, but when light shines through it from

The unusual technique that a Roman glassblower employed to produce the unique appearance of the famed Lycurgus Cup made in the fourth century BCE, and shown here, was not fully understood until the 1990s. The glass changes color from green to red when held up to light coming from behind. (DeAgostini/Getty Images)

raw glass from sand and minerals, as this was done by other professionals called glassmakers, who would then sell chunks of glass to glassblowers to heat and shape. To save money, glassblowers might also purchase pieces of broken glass from street vendors. However, to make their purchased glass hot enough to blow, their constantly burning furnaces needed to reach temperatures as high as 2200 degrees Fahrenheit, and while the iron pipes were typically four- to five-feet long, the furnace and glass were still close enough to make the glassblowers uncomfortably hot as they worked in their small, stuffy workshops. Simply holding an iron pipe and blowing through it all day represented significant physical labor, yet shaping bubbles into precisely the desired shapes also demanded delicate craftsmanship. But the demand for their products kept their businesses profitable, and especially skillful glassblowers might even label their products to attract customers seeking high-quality goods. Thus, for example, a glass cup from around 50 CE has an inscription indicating that it was made in the workshop of a glassblower named Ennion. Furthermore, if they were willing to travel, glassblowers might be able to earn a great deal of money, since cities seeking to launch their own industries would typically hire glassblowers from far away to come and teach the art to their own artisans. It is possible that some glassblowers spent most of their careers as itinerant educators, moving from region to region to show people how to construct and use their equipment.

We may not know much about their daily lives, but we can be sure that there were very many glassblowers in ancient Rome, for no ancient people loved glass as much as the Romans, and despite the inherent fragility, innumerable glass items from the Roman Empire have been preserved to the present day, treasured by collectors or displayed in major museums. The astounding variety and elegance of their works shows that they must have been drawing upon a vast body of glassmaking knowledge and lore, passed orally from generation to generation, since there are surprising few written accounts of this ubiquitous art. So, today's archaeologists and craftspersons must sometimes struggle to reconstruct techniques that were perfected long ago by the ancient Roman glassblowers.

behind, the glass looks red. For decades, scientists were unable to determine how the Greeks achieved this effect, but in 1990, researchers finally determined that the Romans had placed incredibly tiny particles of silver and gold within the glass, and when light hits the particles, their electrons vibrate in ways that produce different colored lights when viewed from different angles. Since the metal particles were sometimes as small as 50 nanometers (1/1000th the size of a grain of salt), the Roman glassblowers had effectively developed an early form of nanotechnology.

The work of the Roman glassblowers was not easy. They were usually spared the labor of manufacturing

ROMAN GLASS FOR MIDDLE-EARTH

While techniques of glassblowing have ostensibly improved over the centuries, there remain individuals who are dedicated to making glass in exactly the same way as the ancient Romans. Two men in Great Britain, Mark Taylor and David Hill, have set up a business, Roman Glassmakers, to make and sell authentically produced items, heating up glass made of Roman materials in Roman furnaces and shaping them in the Roman manner. Since their items are new but look like antiques, the men were recently hired to make glass objects for Peter Jackson's trilogy of films based on J.R.R. Tolkien's *The Hobbit*.

FRAGILE BUT DURABLE

Although glass items are usually regarded as fragile, a large piece of glass can actually endure almost indefinitely as long as it is not dropped or mishandled. And, since Roman glassblowers produced innumerable vessels and objects, it is not surprising that many of them have survived to the present day. The University of Pennsylvania Museum of Archaeology and Anthropology, for example, staged a 1998 exhibition that featured over 200 pieces of Roman glass produced between 100 BCE and 600 CE. Now carefully preserved by skilled curators, these items are likely to last for another 2,000 years.

Further Reading

Fleming, Stuart J. 1997. *Roman Glass: Reflections on Cultural Change*. Philadelphia: University of Pennsylvania Museum of Archaeology and Anthropology.

Newby, Martine, and K. S. Painter, editors. 1991. *Roman Glass: Two Centuries of Art and Invention*. London: Society of Antiquaries of London.

Shepherd, John, and Angela Wardle, editors. 2009. *The Glass Workers of Roman London*. London: Museum of London Archaeology.

Stern, E. Marianne. 2001. *Roman, Byzantine, and Early Medieval Glass: 10 BCE to 700 CE: The Ernesto Wolf Collection*. Ostfildern, Germany: Hatje Cantz.

Stern, E. Marianne. 1995. *Roman Mold-Blown Glass: The First through Sixth Centuries*. Toledo, OH: Toledo Museum of Art.

Whitehouse, David. 1997–2003. *Roman Glass in the Corning Museum of Glass*. Three volumes. Corning, NY: Corning Museum of Glass.

Document

From Middleton, John Henry. 1885. *Ancient Rome in 1885*. Edinburgh: A. & C. Black.

An author who examined the ruins of ancient Rome in 1885 found that glass was extensively used in decorating Roman buildings, and he mentions that the Romans also used pieces of glass to light fires.

[In the "House of Livia," "a Roman house of the time of Augustus":]

The *Triclinium* [dining room], also, has a series of columns on a plinth; the panels are mostly vermilion, and above is a frieze of rudely painted sham marble; and above that; small panels containing glass vessels full of fruit. The fruit seen through the transparent glass is cleverly rendered.

[In the Palace of Severus:]

These baths were all sumptuously decorated in the usual way with marble linings and enrichments of porphyry, alabaster, and brilliant glass mosaics, many of the coloured *tesserae* of which still lie thick among the rubbish.

[In the description of the Temple of Vesta, the requirement that Vestal Virgins keep their sacred fire lit at all times is discussed:]

A survival of this prehistoric custom appears to have existed in the rule which enacted that, if the sacred fire ever did go out, it was to be rekindled by the primitive method of friction, and the negligent Vestal was to be punished by scourging. In later times the much easier method of relighting by a burning glass was permitted.

[In the House of the Vestals:]

Among the many fragments which were found during the excavations are included almost all the fine Oriental marbles, granites, porphyries, and alabasters, which were used during the period of Rome's greatest magnificence, and in many parts the walls appear to have been further decorated with the brilliant jewel-like mosaics made with *tesserae* of coloured glass. . . . A large and handsome marble bath opened out of this upper room; it is now approached by a wooden bridge. It is lined with slabs of *pavonazetto*, *cipollino*, *Africano*, and white marble. In the top of one of the recesses above this bath there are still remains of its lining of brilliant mosaics with *tesserae* of coloured glass.

[In the Colosseum:]

The marble colonnades were plated with gold, the gratings which defended the *Podium* from the beasts were of gold (or gilt) wire; the *zonoe*, or walls which divided the tiers, were studded with mosaics of precious stones (that is of the jewel-like glass *tesserae*); awnings and cushions were of silk, and fountains poured forth jets of perfumed water.

[In the Baths of Caracalla:]

Some of the ground-floor mosaics were of a very elaborate sort of *opus sectile*, with patterns formed not of small square *tesserae*, but of thin slices of porphyry and marble, shaped into patterns, with flowing lines and leaf-shaped ornaments, each piece fitted with great accuracy to the next, a much more expensive and elaborate method of mosaic work than the *opus tesselatum*.

An immense number of *tesserae*, made of glass in very brilliant colours, of almost jewel-like appearance, are strewn about the building. These glass mosaics were used for the walls or vaults, not for pavements.

Historians

It is a sign of the enormous self-confidence felt by the Romans that they were so concerned about recording their own achievements, and those of their distinguished ancestors, for posterity. Many of Rome's finest writers specialized in writing history, and the works that were carefully preserved through the centuries have remained central texts in teaching the Latin language. The Romans first learned this art from the Greek historians, and the first Roman historians actually wrote in the Greek language, since this was long regarded as the language of serious discourse throughout the Mediterranean world. Indeed, since Greece had fallen under Roman rule, and since many Greek writers traveled into other Roman realms, it can be difficult to distinguish later Greek historians from early Roman historians. Polybius (ca. 200–118 BCE), for

example, is generally thought of as a Greek historian, because he was born and grew up in Greece; still, since he later moved to Rome, he has also been classified as a Roman. While many texts from Roman historians have survived, it is often difficult, if not impossible, to establish precisely when they were written, though textual evidence sometimes provides clues.

Using language as a criterion, one would argue that the first Roman historian was Cato the Elder (234–149 BCE), since he was the first to write a history in Latin, called the *Origines*, which related the history of Rome from its founding; however, like many works of Roman history, only fragments of this text have been preserved. Because Cato the Elder was also a distinguished senator and politician, it could also be said that he set a precedent for later leaders who would turn to the writing of history during and after their careers. Unsurprisingly, the most prominent of these individuals often focused on their own experiences; thus, Cato's *Origines* included accounts of his own military campaigns. But a more famous history written by a successful general is a text usually called *The Gallic Wars*, by Julius Caesar (100–44 BCE), though its official title is *Commentarii de Bello Gallico*. It is also known that the emperors Augustus (63 BCE–14 CE) and Claudius (10 BCE–54 CE) wrote autobiographies, but these have not survived. Unlike modern politicians, these men did not write their memoirs to earn money, particularly since they usually came from wealthy families and regularly profited more directly from their public service. Instead, these writings were designed to bolster their reputations and perhaps, from their perspective, to set the record straight about matters that were being distorted by their opponents. In this regard, *The Gallic Wars* can be interpreted as both a description, and a defense, of Caesar's sometimes controversial military exploits.

Not all historians, though, were renowned officials; there are no records, for example, indicating that one renowned Roman historian, Livy (ca. 59 BCE–17 CE), ever held any public office, but there are reports that he was a friend of Augustus who began writing history at his behest, and that he encouraged the youthful Claudius to write his own histories (which like his autobiography are lost). Livy may even qualify as the world's first full-time historian, since he must have devoted every year of his adult life to the task of writing a history of Rome that occupied 142 volumes. We otherwise know little about his life, though he grew up in the city now known as Padua before moving to Rome and becoming famous for his historical writings; in fact, a letter from Pliny the Younger (ca. 61–113 CE) relates that one man from Spain traveled to all the way to Rome only to look at a historian he greatly admired. Unfortunately, because he was so prolific, later copiers often chose to preserve summaries of his books instead of their entire texts, so that most of his massive work, though praised for its prose style, is no longer available for modern readers.

We are more familiar with the lives of the other two men viewed as Rome's greatest historians, Sallust (86–35 BCE) and Tacitus (ca. 56–117 CE), because they also served in the Roman Senate. Sallust, however, was removed from the Senate because he had opposed Cicero (106–43 BCE) and later became a supporter of Julius Caesar (100–44 BCE) before abandoning his political career after he was charged with the crime of extortion. With no grand ambitions to be comprehensive in his history, Sallust focused on thorough examinations of specific events: *Bellum Catilinae*, or *The Conspiracy of Catiline*, relates how the senator Catiline (108–62 BCE) plotted to take over the government in 63 BCE; *Bellum Iugurthinum*, or *The Jugurthine War* describes a Roman war against a North African king named Jugurtha (160–104 BCE); and the *Historiae*, or *The Histories* (ca. 38 BCE) is a history of the Roman Republic from 78 to 67 BCE, providing an insider's perspective on the events that followed the death of the dictator Sulla (138–78 BCE). Only portions of the third text survive, though, and Sallust may have died before completing it.

Before retiring from public life, Tacitus had become renowned as an orator and political leader, and although his background is uncertain, his marriage to the daughter of the general Agricola (40–93 CE) undoubtedly helped him advance to several government positions during the reigns of Domitian (51–96 CE) and Trajan (53–117 CE). In fact, one of his lesser works, *De Vita et Moribus Lulii Agricola*, or *On the Life and Character of Agricola*, was a biography of his noted father-in-law. In the same year, 98 CE, when it appeared, he also published *De Origine et Situ Germanorum*, usually called

This drawing, probably executed by an English artist in the nineteenth century, depicts a bust of the Roman historian Tacitus (ca. 56–117 CE). His best-known works, his *Annals* and his *Histories*, together tell the stories of all Roman emperors from Augustus to Domitian. (Library of Congress)

the *Germania*, which provided an unusually sympathetic portrayal of the German tribes. Tacitus is better known for two larger texts, usually called his *Annals* and his *Histories*, which together tell the stories of all Roman emperors from Augustus (63 BCE–14 CE) to Domitian. One theme that reverberates throughout his work, the damaging effects of authoritarian rule, may help to explain why he abandoned his political career to write history instead.

While many other writers produced histories along conventional lines, a few who departed from the norm also command attention. A young poet named Lucan (39–65 CE), the nephew of the playwright Seneca the Younger (4 BCE–65 CE), was a favorite of Nero (37–68 CE) before the apparently jealous emperor, who also viewed himself as a poet, forbid him to read his poetry

BLOGGING FROM ANCIENT ROME

Although not an historian in the conventional sense of the term, Aulus Gellius (ca. 125–180 CE) provided a valuable service to later historians by writing *Attic Nights*, a massive, twenty-volume compilation of notes and comments on various subjects that provide valuable information about aspects of Roman life neglected by other historians. As indicated by its title, he began writing its materials, in no particular order, during each evening while he was living in Attica, a region of ancient Greece. One can argue that he was history's first blogger, writing daily about whatever happened to be on his mind and publishing the results for any interested person to read.

IMPERIAL AUTHORS

The emperors Augustus and Claudius wrote autobiographies, providing a record of major events during their reigns, though these have not survived, and Marcus Aurelius wrote a series of reflections about his life, usually termed his *Meditations*, which made him one of ancient Rome's most admired authors. In modern America, it is the habit of all former presidents to write their own memoirs, ostensibly fulfilling their obligation to history, though they can also earn millions of dollars from this work (sometimes delegated almost entirely to ghostwriters). One former president, Jimmy Carter, has written several books on various subjects, including a historical novel, *The Hornet's Nest: A Novel of the Revolutionary War* (2003).

in public. He then involved himself in an unsuccessful conspiracy against Nero, leading to his forced suicide. But he was able to complete most of a lengthy history, told entirely in verse, of the struggle between Julius Caesar and Pompey (106–48 BCE); though its official title is the *Bellum Civile*, or *The Civil War*, it is usually called the *Pharsalia* because its account of that famous battle was the poem's most outstanding passage. There were also a few writers who produced willfully disorganized compilations of miscellaneous information and observations, mingling historical anecdotes with comments on other subjects like grammar, literature, and science.

Aulus Gellius (ca. 130–180 CE) began his contribution to history, the *Noctes Atticae* or *Attic Nights*, by writing whatever came to mind every night while he was staying in Greece, eventually producing twenty volumes of material. A later writer, Macrobius (ca. 400 CE), devoted seven volumes to his *Saturnalia*, a dialogue between several Romans attending a banquet, which served as a device for the presentation of numerous explanations and commentaries, including an extended critique of the poet Virgil (70–19 BCE). Surprisingly, later scholars valued these chaotic, rambling texts more than the more focused works of other historians, since both of them were almost completely preserved despite their length. There were also several Roman writers who focused on biographies, beginning with Nepos (ca. 110–24 BCE), who completed sixteen volumes collectively titled *De Viris Illustribus*, or *On Famous Men*; surviving excerpts include a complete book about non-Roman generals and brief biographies of the statesman Cato the Elder and Cicero's friend Atticus (ca. 112–53 BCE). Men wrote autobiographies as well; the most distinguished of these was the *Confessions*, written by the Christian Saint Augustine (354–430 CE), in which the author describes his early, dissolute life and conversion to Christianity with unusual frankness and thoughtfulness.

For the most part, the Roman historians are trusted as reliable sources by their later counterparts, although they sometimes included dubious legends alongside their historical accounts, and some are suspected of allowing their political biases to unduly influence their factual presentations. But many of these historians are more esteemed as prose stylists; indeed, in an era when little prose fiction was written, history was probably the ideal outlet for writers who wished to tell stories about dramatic events and involving characters, and the long history of Rome provided more than enough subject matter of this kind. Their best works, then, offer engaging entertainment as well as valuable information.

Further Reading

Feldherr, Andrew. 2009. *The Cambridge Companion to the Roman Historians.* Cambridge and New York: Cambridge University Press.
Grant, Michael. 1995. *Greek and Roman Historians: Information and Misinformation.* London and New York: Routledge.

Kraus, Christina Shuttleworth, and A.J. Woodman. 1997. *Latin Historians*. Oxford and New York: Oxford University Press.

Mellor, Ronald. 2012. *The Historians of Ancient Rome: An Anthology of the Major Writings*. Third edition. London and New York: Routledge.

Mellor, Ronald. 1999. *The Roman Historians*. London and New York: Routledge.

Potter, David. 1999. *Literary Texts and the Roman Historian*. London and New York: Routledge.

Documents

From Tacitus. C. 100–110 CE. *Tacitus: The Histories*. Volume 1. Translated by W. Hamilton Frye. 1912. Oxford: Oxford University Press.

In the opening passage of his Histories, *the Roman senator and historian Tacitus provides an overview of the era he will cover, dramatically summarizing both its many problems and its instances of noble behavior.*

I propose to begin my narrative with the second consulship of Servius Galba, in which Titus Vinius was his colleague. Many historians have dealt with the 820 years of the earlier period beginning with the foundation of Rome, and the story of the Roman Republic has been told with no less ability than truth. After the Battle of Actium, when the interests of peace were served by the centralization of all authority in the hands of one man, there followed a dearth of literary ability, and at the same time truth suffered more and more, partly from ignorance of politics, which were no longer a citizen's concern, partly from the growing taste for flattery or from hatred of the ruling house. So between malice on one side and servility on the other the interests of posterity were neglected. But historians find that a tone of flattery soon incurs the stigma of servility and earns for them the contempt of their readers, whereas people readily open their ears to the criticisms of envy, since malice makes a show of independence. Of Galba, Otho, and Vitellius, I have known nothing either to my advantage or my hurt. I cannot deny that I originally owed my position to Vespasian, or that I was advanced by Titus and still further promoted by Domitian; but professing, as I do, unbiassed honesty, I must speak of no man either with hatred or affection. I have reserved for my old age, if life is spared to me, the reigns of the sainted Nerva and of the Emperor Trajan, which afford a richer and withal a safer theme: for it is the rare fortune of these days that a man may think what he likes and say what he thinks.

The story I now commence is rich in vicissitudes, grim with warfare, torn by civil strife, a tale of horror even during times of peace. It tells of four emperors slain by the sword, three several civil wars, an even larger number of foreign wars and some that were both at once: successes in the East, disaster in the West, disturbance in Illyricum, disaffection in the provinces of Gaul, the conquest of Britain and its immediate loss, the rising of the Sarmatian and Suebic tribes. It tells how Dacia had the privilege of exchanging blows with Rome, and how a pretender claiming to be Nero almost deluded the Parthians into declaring war. Now too Italy was smitten with new disasters, or disasters it had not witnessed for a long period of years. Towns along the rich coast of Campania were submerged or buried. The city was devastated by fires, ancient temples were destroyed, and the Capitol itself was fired by Roman hands. Sacred rites were grossly profaned, and there were scandals in high places. The sea swarmed with exiles and the island cliffs were red with blood. Worse horrors reigned in the city. To be rich or well-born was a crime: men were prosecuted for holding or for refusing office: merit of any kind meant certain ruin. Nor were the Informers more hated for their crimes than for their prizes: some carried off a priesthood or the consulship as their spoil, others won offices and influence in the imperial household: the hatred and fear they inspired worked universal havoc. Slaves were bribed against their masters, freedmen against their patrons, and, if a man had no enemies, he was ruined by his friends.

However, the period was not so utterly barren as to yield no examples of heroism. There were mothers who followed their sons, and wives their husbands into exile: one saw here a kinsman's courage and there a son-in-law's devotion: slaves obstinately faithful even on the rack: distinguished men bravely facing the utmost straits and matching in their end the famous deaths of older times. Besides these manifold disasters to mankind there were portents in the sky and on the earth, thunderbolts and other premonitions of good and of evil, some doubtful, some obvious. Indeed never has it been proved by such terrible disasters to Rome or by such clear evidence that Providence is concerned not with our peace of mind but rather with vengeance for our sin.

From Sallust. C. 40–35 BCE. *The Catiline and Jugurtha of Sallust, Translated into English.* Translated by Alfred W. Pollard. 1882. London: Macmillan and Company.

In this passage from the beginning of Sallust's Catiline, *the historian explains why it is difficult to write history, and why he abandoned public life to become a historian.*

It is a fine thing to serve the state by action, nor is eloquence without its glory. Men may become illustrious alike in peace and war, and many by their own acts, many by their record of the acts of others, win applause. The glory which attends the doer and the recorder of brave deeds is certainly by no means equal. For my own part, however, I count historical narration as one of the hardest of tasks. In the first place, a full equivalent has to be found in words for the deeds narrated, and in the second the historian's censures of crimes are by many thought to be the utterances of ill-will and envy, while his record of the high virtue and glory of the good, tranquilly accepted so long as it deals with what the reader deems to be easily performable, so soon as it passes beyond this is disbelieved as mere invention.

As regards myself, my inclination originally led me, like many others, while still a youth, into public life. There I found many things against me. Modesty, temperance, and virtue had departed, and hardihood, corruption, and avarice were flourishing in their stead. My mind, a stranger to bad acquirements, contemned these qualities; nevertheless, with the weakness of my age, I was kept amid this sea of vice by perverse ambition. I presented a contrast to the evil characters of my fellows, none the less I was tormented by the same craving for the honours of office, and the same sensitiveness to popularity and unpopularity as the rest. At last, after many miseries and perils, my mind was at peace, and I determined to pass the remainder of my days at a distance from public affairs. It was not, however, my plan to waste this honourable leisure in idleness and sloth, nor yet to spend my life in devotion to such slavish tastes as agriculture or hunting. I returned to the studies I had once begun, from which my unhappy ambition had held me back, and determined to narrate the history of the Roman people in separate essays, wherever it seemed worthy of record. I was the more inclined to this by the fact that my mind was free alike from the hopes and fears of the political partisan.

I am about, therefore, with the utmost truth I can, briefly to relate the history of the conspiracy of Catiline, for I account this affair as in the highest degree memorable for the novelty both of the crime itself and of the danger it involved.

Household Managers

As in other ancient cultures, married Roman women were in charge of their homes, supervising children and slaves and ensuring that all necessary tasks are completed, and this was usually their only official role, since women were not allowed to hold public office or enter most professions. However, they also had many rights and privileges not available to women in other parts of the world. While some Roman wives remained legally controlled by their husbands, that was only one type of Roman marriage, termed *in manu*; but a woman could also remain somewhat independent of her husband with a different sort of marriage, *sine manu*, and while she was still theoretically governed by a man—her father—she practically had the freedom to own her own property and manage her own affairs. Further, both husbands and wives were free to divorce their spouses and remarry, something that became fairly common during the Roman Empire. Still, most women stayed with their husbands and maintained their households, though discreet adultery was not unknown.

A woman would begin managing her home at an early age, since she might get married at early as the age of twelve, and it was unusual for a woman to be unmarried by the time she reached the age of twenty. She did not necessarily have to be a skillful cook, as this was a chore that could be relegated to slaves, but it was considered important that women spin their own wool and personally sew the clothes worn by family members; even the emperor Augustus (63 BCE–14 CE) insisted that his wife Livia (58 BCE–29 CE) and daughter Julia the Elder (39 BCE–14 CE) fulfill these duties. The other major duty of the Roman wife was to keep records of the family budget and household possessions. Since this rarely required a great deal of time, the days of a wealthy woman might primarily be spent checking to make sure that the slaves were properly preparing meals, cleaning clothes, and keeping the house tidy. Many men sought to advance their careers by inviting influential people to banquets at their homes, so their wives would have extra tasks to perform on certain days, supervising the preparation of special foods, arranging for the entertainment, and being the perfect hostess for her guests.

Women were expected to take personal responsibility for the raising of their children, teaching both boys and girls at an early age until they could be entrusted to a tutor or sent to school, and training their daughters in arts ranging from sewing and cooking to playing the harp and singing. Surprisingly, however, many Roman marriages did not produce children, and scholars are not sure why this is the case. Since most Roman marriages were arranged, a few couples may have completely refrained from sex, as the man satisfied himself with female or male prostitutes or slaves, and the growing ease of divorce may also have led to fewer children. A number of Roman women practiced forms of birth control, which are discussed in medical texts; some recommended techniques would have been effective—like placing olive oil or honey into one's vagina or inserting a woolen pessary—but others were fanciful, like strapping a cat's liver onto the woman's leg. Abortions were an option, though these could be painful or life-threatening, and it is not known if they were rare or commonplace. Augustus grew very concerned about the low number of births and enacted several laws to address the problem; these included penalties for unmarried people and childless couples, and a benefit for any woman who had three children: legal freedom from all forms of male guardianship. But his reforms had little effect.

In any event, while the absence of children did not materially affect the lives of poor women, who still faced many daily chores, there were large numbers

A bust of Julia Domna (170–217 CE), the Roman empress who became one of the most powerful and influential wives of ancient Rome. The well-educated second wife of the emperor Septimus Severus (145–211 CE), she was one of her husband's most trusted advisers. (Araldo de Luca/Corbis)

of wealthy wives who had a great deal of free time during the day. Some devoted themselves to traditional pastimes like embroidery or playing a musical instrument, and they could also spend their days shopping, but the satirist Juvenal (ca. 55–127 CE) bitterly attacked women whose leisure activities were less conventional, like seeking out the company of handsome gladiators or lingering at the public baths, hoping to catch a glimpse of some naked men. Like all Roman wives, they were free to visit the forum, watch a play, or listen to the debates in the Senate. Women might study current events, develop opinions, and state them publicly, embarrassing their husbands; try their hand at writing poetry; or participate in male activities like fencing or hunting. Some women became obsessed with their personal appearance; while all women who stepped outside the house were expected to don modest clothing that covered most of their bodies and have their hair carefully styled, some might spend hours having their slaves arrange their hair in intricate patterns, applying several layers of makeup, covering their bodies with perfume, and putting on items of jewelry like earrings, pins, bracelets, and necklaces.

If a woman's husband had some political power, she might also exercise a certain amount of influence over his decisions, becoming an important person in her own right. The examples we are most familiar with the women who were the wives and mothers of Roman emperors, especially those who were part of the family of Augustus. Less renowned, but perhaps

UNOFFICIAL RULERS

The women married to Roman emperors, not content to limit their attention to domestic affairs, often involved themselves in political decisions and sometimes had great influence, like Julia Domna, wife and chief adviser to the emperor Septimius Severus. In modern times, the wives of U.S. presidents have sometimes exercised great authority as well. The most extreme case was Edith Wilson, the second wife of President Woodrow Wilson. After her husband suffered a severe stroke in 1919, she effectively took control of the U.S. government, controlling everyone's access to Wilson and making major decisions in his name.

LIVING LIKE EVERYDAY WOMEN

The emperor Augustus insisted that his wealthy wife sew his own clothes, like other Roman wives, in order to emphasize that his seemingly elevated life was actually in keeping with the habits of typical Roman families. More recent political wives have also presented their lifestyles as modest to serve their husbands' political interests. In 1952, when vice-presidential candidate Richard Nixon was embroiled in a financial scandal, he delivered his "Checkers" speech to emphasize that he had not personally profited from a trust fund set up by supporters. To prove this point, he noted that his wife Pat Nixon did not own a fur coat, only a "respectable Republican cloth coat."

even more influential, was Julia Domna (170–217 CE), the second wife of the emperor Septimus Severus (145–211 CE). The well-educated daughter of a Syrian priest, Julia quickly became one of her husband's most trusted advisers; not even pretending to care about household affairs, she accompanied him on his military campaigns, though that aroused opposition in some quarters. After Severus's death, she arranged for her sons Caracalla (188–217 CE) and Geta (189–211 CE) to serve as co-emperors, but Caracalla decided to kill his brother. This could not have made his mother happy, but Julia continued to serve as Caracalla's adviser, at home and when he was campaigning, until his assassination in 217 CE, which drove her to commit suicide.

While satirists and others would criticize women who departed from social norms, women were also encouraged to behave in certain ways by means of positive examples. Augustus, for example, sought to present his wife Livia as an ideal Roman wife, conveying her sense of modesty by never wearing expensive jewelry or fancy clothing. Another exemplary spouse often spoken of was Lucretia (died 510 BCE), the wife of Collatinus (ca. 500 BCE); as the legend goes, Collatinus was drinking with friends when they decided to have a contest to determine who had the most virtuous wife. When they surprised the women at home, most were discovered wasting their time by gossiping with friends, but Lucretia was dutifully sewing, so Collatinus won the contest. A defeated rival, Sextus (ca. 500 BCE), later entered her bedroom at night and forcibly raped her; she informed Collatinus about what had happened and then committed suicide, feeling that she had betrayed her husband, albeit unwillingly. Reportedly, mothers would tell their daughters the story of Lucretia before they were married to explain how an ideal wife should behave.

As another expression of their appreciation for good wives and mothers, the Romans celebrated them with an annual festival that officially honored Lucina, the goddess of childbirth, but unofficially functioned as the equivalent of the modern Mother's Day. On this day, while women performed rituals at Lucina's temple, they were allowed to let their hair fall freely on the shoulders, and when they returned home, they received presents from their daughters and their husbands. Unlike modern mothers, however, they still had to work on this day, since it was also a holiday for their slaves; hence, it was the woman's responsibility to personally prepare a dinner for all of her slaves.

It is often suggested that Roman women were generally fortunate, since they enjoyed so many rights and freedoms, but many of them were surely frustrated by the many doors that remained closed to them, and it is not surprising that they were sometimes willing to endure public displeasure by acting in unusually independent ways. Still, others may have been perfectly content to stay and home and capably tend to domestic matters like cooking for their families and teaching their children. And by means of their ongoing research, scholars are hoping to learn more and more about their daily lives.

Further Reading

D'Ambra, Eve. 2007. *Roman Women*. Cambridge and New York: Cambridge University Press.

Fraschetti, Augusto, editor. 1994. *Roman Women*. Translated by Linda Lappin. 1999. Chicago: University of Chicago Press.

Gardner, Jane F., and Thomas Wiedemann, editors. 1991. *The Roman Household: A Sourcebook*. London and New York: Routledge.

Joshel, Sandra R., and Sheila Murnaghan, editors. 1998. *Women and Slaves in Greco-Roman Culture: Differential Equations*. London and New York: Routledge.

Lefkowitz, Mary R., and Maureen B. Fant. 2005. *Women's Life in Greece and Rome: A Sourcebook in Translation*. Third edition. Baltimore, MD: John Hopkins University Press.

Rawson, Beryl, editor. 2011. *A Companion to Families in the Greek and Roman Worlds*. Chichester, England, and Malden, MA: Wiley-Blackwell.

Document

From Maine, Henry Sumner. 1873. *The Early History of the Property of Married Women as Collected from Roman and Hindoo Law: A Lecture, Delivered at Birmingham, March 25, 1873*. Manchester: A. Ireland and Company.

In this passage, a scholar summarizes how married Roman women gained the right to retain ownership of their own property.

I have now abridged a very long, and, in some portions, a very intricate history. The Roman law began by giving all the wife's property to the husband, because she was assumed to be, in law, his daughter. It ended in having for its general rule that all the wife's property was under her own control, save when a part of it had been converted by settlement into a fund for contributing to the expenses of the conjugal household. But, no doubt, the exception to the general rule was the ordinary practice. In all respectable households, as now on the Continent, there was a settlement by way of *dos*. Not that we are to suppose there was among the Romans any such form of contract as we are accustomed to under the name of marriage settlement. The mechanism was infinitely simpler. A few words on paper would suffice to bring any part of the wife's property under the well-ascertained rules supplied by the written law for dotal settlements, and nothing more than these words would be needed, unless the persons marrying wished to vary the provisions of the law by express agreement. This simple, but most admirable, contrivance of having, so to speak, model settlements set forth ready made in the law, which may be adopted or not at pleasure, characterises the French Code Napoleon, and it was inherited by the French from the Romans.

Warning you that the account which I have given you of the transitions through which the Roman law of settled property passed, is, from the necessity of the case, fragmentary, and to some extent superficial, I pass to the evidence of early ideas on our subject which is contained in the Hindoo law. . . .

Orators

The ancient Greeks may have first developed oratory, but the Romans embraced this art with such fervor that it became a defining attribute of their civilization. In the days of the Roman Republic, eloquence was a major pathway to political power, and even as its importance diminished during the Roman Empire, oratory remained central to Roman education and public life. Seeking to perfect their rhetoric, the Romans also crafted the doctrines and terminology that still dominate the teaching of effective argumentation and debate throughout the Western world.

The first great orators known to the Romans came from Greece, long regarded as the best place to learn how to speak in public, and young Romans were regularly taught to deliver speeches in Greek. Long after speaking in Latin became the norm, Greek orators could still prosper by coming to Rome and teaching students. One of these was a man named Isaeus (ca. 100 CE); the namesake of a famed Athenian orator, he moved to Rome during the reign of Trajan (53–117 CE) and became famous for his skills, as he is mentioned by the authors Pliny the Younger (ca. 61–112 CE) and Juvenal (ca. 55–127 CE). Pliny himself, however, was trained in oratory by a homegrown talent, Quintilian (35–100 CE); born in Spain, Quintilian was sent by his father to study rhetoric in Rome, and he eventually established his own school, attracting wealthy students like Pliny and possibly the historian and orator Tacitus (ca. 56–117 CE). The emperor Vespasian (17–79 CE) also appointed him as a consul, apparently as a way of providing this talented speaker with financial support, and he was hired to argue on behalf of accused criminals in courts.

We are most familiar with Quintilian, however, because of the activity that occupied his later years, writing a twelve-volume study of oratory called the *Institutio Oratoria*, or *Institutes of Oratory*, published around 95 CE. This massive text drew upon the writings of previous orators, including the renowned Cato the Elder (239–149 BCE) and Cicero (106–43 BCE), though most of their works on oratory have not survived. Since all of Quintilian's work was preserved, it functions as a valuable compilation of the ideas and knowledge of his predecessors, though Quintilian avowedly made his own contributions to the field in its twelfth and final volume. There, he stresses that an effective orator must also have a strong moral character and explains how orators should choose the cases that they argue and negotiate their fees. He offers advice, then, not only on how to make a good speech, but how to make a living by doing so.

The career of an orator began with his training under a teacher of rhetoric, termed a *rhetor*, after he completed his other education. Already fluent in both Greek and Latin, students would carefully study the speeches of famous Greek and Latin orators, and might be asked to speak in both Greek and Latin, though Latin was naturally emphasized. When they began preparing their own speeches and debating issues with other students, their subject matter invariably involved mythology and history; thus, for example, they might be asked to argue that Homer's Achilles was superior to Odysseus, or *vice versa*. It is not clear why students were never asked to practice speaking about the sorts of topics that would actually come up during an orator's lifetime. Perhaps instructors believed that ancient texts offered more challenging and rewarding material than the mundane matters that might be debated in courts or the Senate; perhaps they wished to avoid antagonizing any students, or their parents, by touching upon current controversies that provoked strong opinions. It is difficult to argue that this teaching method was entirely ineffective, since it produced many fine orators, but even some Romans criticized such preparation as frivolous. Officially, women were never trained to be orators, but a woman named Hortensia (ca. first century BCE) became famous in 42 BCE for giving an impassioned speech to Marc Antony (83–30 BCE), Lepidus (ca. 89–12 BCE), and the future Augustus (63 BCE–14 CE), denouncing a proposed tax.

Many men who learned oratory were not concerned about earning money, since they came from wealthy families; they wanted to improve their speaking skills as a way to obtain government positions. In the time of the Roman Republic, masterful orators like Cato the Elder and Cicero could garner vast political power and have a tremendous impact on Roman society; even under the Roman Empire, orators could rise in the administrative hierarchy and become influential, though the emperor and his close advisors made all of the final decisions. Still, it is telling that some later orators retired from politics to focus on writing history, which they may have regarded as a better way to shape the course of events in their lifetimes.

For orators who were concerned about their incomes, one profitable activity was to defend people who were on trial. Officially, one could not be paid for providing this service, but it seems clear that clients found ways to reward the men who spoke on their behalf. One required no knowledge of the law to argue for a person's acquittal, and the rhetorical strategies

A STIRRING SPEECH?

When most people think of Roman orators, they will immediately recall the speech given by Marc Antony at the funeral of Julius Caesar, a highlight of William Shakespeare's play *Julius Caesar*. Yet the words in that speech were Shakespeare's, not Antony's, and the Roman historian Appian (95–165 CE) gives a rather different account of what happened on that day. Antony actually devoted most of his time to reading various decrees from the Senate that praised and honored Caesar; then he seized the dictator's bloodstained robe and brandished it, inspiring the angered crowd to a riot. His own eloquence, then, had little to do with the effectiveness of his presentation.

PREPARATION FOR POWER

In modern America, the nearest equivalent to the sort of rhetorical education found in ancient Rome would be being a member of a high school or college debate team, which provides extensive training in public speaking and oral argument. And like the Roman schools of rhetoric, such debate teams have proven to represent a good way to prepare for a political career. In fact, eight twentieth-century presidents—Theodore Roosevelt, Woodrow Wilson, Franklin Roosevelt, John F. Kennedy, Lyndon Johnson, Richard Nixon, Jimmy Carter, and Bill Clinton—were former debaters. Another former debater may yet become president: the 2016 front-runner, former Secretary of State Hillary Clinton.

that orators employed may strike modern jurists as very irregular. For example, a speech by Cicero has survived in which he is defending a man named Cluentius, who has been accused by his mother Sassia of poisoning his stepfather Oppianicus (all ca. second century BCE). The real issue in the case, however, as Cicero understood, is that Cluentius had previously accused Oppianicus of trying to poison him, and it was universally believed that he had bribed the judges to find Oppianicus guilty. Sassia's charge, in other words, represented an attempt to punish Cluentius for another crime that she could not safely discuss in front of a judge. For that reason, Cicero devoted most of his speech to explaining that, because of Oppianicus's obvious guilt, Cluentius had no reason to bribe his judges, and the actual charge of poisoning Oppianicus was only addressed briefly. Still, the argument proved effective, as Cluentius was acquitted.

An orator might also be compensated for delivering speeches at funerals, which was a tradition that dated back to the early days of the Roman Republic; indeed, by one tradition, the first funeral oration was delivered by the founder of the Republic, Publicola (died 503 BCE), at the funeral of his colleague Brutus (died 509 BCE). Such a speech, termed a *laudatio*, did not necessarily demand great eloquence, as a mere recitation of the deceased's traits and accomplishments was believed sufficient to arouse the emotions of audiences. But some of these speeches were regarded as oratorical masterpieces, such as Tacitus's speech at the funeral of the prominent Roman soldier Lucius Verginius Rufus (15–97 CE), which cemented his reputation as one of Rome's finest orators.

Finally, as already indicated, noteworthy orators could become instructors of rhetoric. In addition to contemporary accounts, we have learned about what these men taught because they sometimes prepared their own textbooks. The oldest of these, the *Rhetorica ad Herennium*, was written by an unknown author around 90 BCE. Although initially forgotten, it was rediscovered in the fourth century CE and employed as a textbook for several centuries thereafter. Rome's most famous teacher of rhetoric was the Christian Saint Augustine (354–430 CE), who initially moved from Carthage to Rome to find better and more attentive students. After he converted to Christianity, one of his many works was a book called *De doctrina christiana*, or *On Christian Doctrine*; its first three books were published in 397 CE, but in 426 CE he added a fourth book that specifically focused on rhetoric, effectively arguing for a new style of Christian oratory that abandoned the artificiality of traditional Latin rhetoric.

In contrast to their achievements in art, architecture, and literature, the Roman mastery of oratory might be deemed less substantive, as we possess no records of most of their speeches. Still, transcripts of some speeches survive, and we also know from their textbooks the sorts of gestures that they used, allowing modern actors to recreate what it would have been like to hear a Roman orator perform. More to the point, their insights continue to influence the style and substance of both oral and written arguments, so that when contemporary students are advised to avoid *ad hominem* arguments (attacking the person, not the argument), or to avoid emotional appeals (*ad misericordiam*), they are learning the same lessons that Roman students were learning almost 2,000 years ago.

Further Reading

Berry, D.H., and Andrew Erskine, editors. 2010. *Form and Function in Roman Oratory*. Cambridge and New York: Cambridge University Press.

Dominik, William J., editor. 1997. *Roman Eloquence: Rhetoric in Society and Literature*. London and New York: Routledge.

Dominik, William, and Jon Hall, editors. 2010. *A Companion to Roman Rhetoric*. Malden, MA: Wiley-Blackwell.

Graf, Fritz. 1991. *Gestures and Conventions: The Gestures of Roman Actors and Orators*. Cambridge: Polity Press.

Pernot, Laurence. 2000. *Rhetoric in Antiquity*. Translated by W.E. Higgins. 2005. Washington, DC: Catholic University of America Press.

Wooten, Cecil W., editor. 2001. *The Orator in Action and Theory in Greece and Rome: Essays in Honor of George A. Kennedy*. Leiden, The Netherlands, and Boston: Brill.

Document

From Aulus Gellius. C. 170 CE. *The Attic Nights of Aulus Gellius*. Volume I. Translated by John C. Rolfe. 1927. Cambridge and London: Loeb Classical Library.

In his Attic Nights, *the Roman writer Aulus Gellius (ca. 125–180 CE) tells the story of one famous speech given by the statesman and orator Cato the Elder (234–149 BCE) and describes its rhetorical strategies.*

The State of Rhodes is famed for the happy situation of the island, its celebrated works of art, its skill in seamanship and its naval victories. Although a friend and ally of the Roman people, that State was on cordial terms with Perses, son of Philip and king of Macedon, with whom the Romans were at war; accordingly, the Rhodians often sent envoys to Rome and tried to reconcile the contending parties. But when

their attempts at peace-making failed, many of the Rhodians harangued the people in their assemblies, agreeing that if peace were not made, the Rhodians should aid the king in his contest with the people of Rome; but as to that question no official action was taken. When, however, Perses was defeated and taken prisoner, the Rhodians were in great fear because of what had been said and done on many occasions in the popular assemblies; and they sent envoys to Rome, to apologize for the hastiness of some of their fellow-citizens and vindicate their loyalty as a community. When the envoys reached Rome and were admitted to the senate, after having humbly pleaded their cause they left the House, and the senators were called upon for their opinions. When some of the members complained of the Rhodians, declaring that they had been disloyal, and recommended that war be declared upon them, then Marcus Cato arose. He endeavoured to defend and save our very good and faithful allies, to whom many of the most distinguished senators were hostile through a desire to plunder and possess their wealth; and he delivered that famous speech entitled *For the Rhodians*, which is included in the fifth book of his *Origins* and is also in circulation as a separate publication. . . .

It is further to be observed that throughout that speech of Cato's recourse is had to every weapon and device of the art rhetorical; but we are not conscious of their use, as we are in mock combats or in battles feigned for the sake of entertainment. For the case was not pleaded, I say, with an excess of refinement, elegance and observance of rule, but just as in a doubtful battle, when the troops are scattered, the contest rages in many parts of the field with uncertain outcome, so in that case at that time, when the notorious arrogance of the Rhodians had aroused the hatred and hostility of many men, Cato used every method of protection and defence without discrimination, at one time commending the Rhodians as of the highest merit, again exculpating them and declaring them blameless, yet again demanding that their property and riches should not be coveted, now asking for their pardon as if they were in the wrong, now pointing out their friendship to the commonwealth, appealing now to clemency, now to the mercy shown by our forefathers, now to the public interest. All this might perhaps have been said in a more orderly and euphonic style, yet I do not believe that it could have been said with greater vigour and vividness.

Popes

In the gospel of Matthew (chapter 16, verse 18), Jesus Christ tells his apostle Peter (died 64 or 67 CE) that "thou art Peter, and upon this rock I will build my church; and the gates of hell shall not prevail against it. And I will give unto thee the keys of the kingdom of heaven." With these words, according to Catholic doctrine, Jesus assigned Peter to lead the church that would be dedicated to his worship, and when he moved to Rome long after Jesus's death, he became the first pope, St. Peter, and began to create and administer the organization later known as the Roman Catholic Church. However, scholars have almost no information about his life in Rome, and while we know the names of the popes that succeeded Peter after he died sometime around 67 CE, their attributes and actions are similarly unknown. In large part, this is a consequence of the fact that the early Christians in Rome were regularly persecuted, so that all of the church's early activities were necessarily very secretive. Believers would meet in private homes or in the Catacombs beneath Rome and spoke about their religion only to trusted friends.

Still, a few scraps of data can roughly suggest how the early popes lived. Popes were apparently elected by local believers, and they could come from diverse backgrounds: Peter came from ancient Israel, Hyginus (died 142 CE) and Eleutherius (died 189 CE) were originally residents of Greece, Victor I (died 199 CE) was born somewhere in Africa, and Alexander I (died 115 CE) was a native Roman. As the heads of a church that many officials were determined to eliminate, they faced the constant threat of execution; it is believed that Peter was one of the many Christians killed during the reign of the emperor Nero (37–68 CE), perhaps by being crucified, and several later popes, including the third pope, St. Anacletus (died ca. 92 CE), are described as martyrs. They corresponded with Christians in other cities, as suggested by the two letters from Peter that became part of the New Testament, one apparently written when he was in Rome, and

a surviving letter from the pope Clement I (died 99 CE) affirming the authority of priests. Tradition states that Peter baptized new Christians in the Catacomb of St. Priscilla, and later popes like Anacletus presided over the ordination of priests. Popes undoubtedly introduced and standardized many Christian rituals; the pope Alexander I (died 115 CE), for example, is said to have launched the tradition of keeping Christian homes pure by anointing them with a mixture of holy water and salt. A letter written to the pope Soter (died 174 CE) praises his church's generosity to the poor, suggesting that charitable work occupied much of the popes' time.

Toward the end of the second century, when Christians were temporarily facing less persecution, one begins to find more reliable information about the lives of popes. Perhaps the first pope who functioned as a prominent figure in Roman society was Victor I (died 199 CE). A mistress of the emperor Commodus (161–192 CE) named Marcia (died 193 CE) was a Christian, and she invited Victor I to the palace and asked for the names of Christians who had been exiled to work in the mines of Sardinia; she then persuaded Commodus to pardon them. Victor was also determined, once and for all, to have all Christians celebrate Easter on a Sunday, and to pressure the churches in Asia to follow this policy, he convened the first gathering, or synod, of bishops from Italy, who affirmed the Roman preference for Sunday. Victor also acted to expel two vocal heretics from the church and wrote extensively on doctrinal matters, although only his letters on the dispute over Easter have survived.

Throughout the third century CE, the persecution of Christians grew worse and worse, climaxing with an edict by the emperor Valerian (ca. 195–260 CE) that ordered the execution of all Christian bishops and priests. The pope at the time, Sixtus II (died 258), was one of those quickly beheaded, and the papacy was then left vacant for over a year, as it was feared that Sixtus II's successor would be immediately executed as well. Eventually, the persecution ceased, Christianity became legal again, and a new pope, St. Dionysius (died 268 CE), was elected. Yet there was to come a final wave of official war on the Christians during the reign of the emperor Diocletian (245–311 CE) before the persecution permanently ended after the emperor

OLD AND NEW NAMES

In the early centuries of the papacy, it was the habit of each pope to assume a different name; it was not until the third century that one pope, Sixtus II (died 258 CE), chose the name of a previous pope. Later, however, it became the custom for popes to always select a predecessor's name, although Pope John Paul I (1912–1978) and his successor, John Paul II (1920–2005), innovatively combined the names of two previous popes. More recently, Pope Francis (1936–), selected in 2013, became the first pope in over a thousand years to choose an entirely new name.

SAINTLY SERVANTS OF GOD

Despite the fact that little is known about many of these men, all but one of the popes who served in Rome until its fall in 476 CE have been declared saints by the Roman Catholic Church, and large numbers of popes in the following millennium received the same honor. From 1600 to 1900, however, no pope has so far been declared a saint. The twentieth century, though, has been distinguished by several noteworthy popes, and three of them—Pius X (1835–1914), John XXIII (1881–1963), and John Paul II—have already been elevated to sainthood.

Constantine (272–337 CE) converted to Christianity. As attitudes toward Christians kept shifting, the properties of the church were repeatedly seized and then returned, so popes had to keep moving around, but Constantine gave the Lateran Palace in Rome to the church, and this became the pope's official home and the church's administrative center. Constantine also exempted the church from taxation, increasing its wealth and influence. Although we know little about the pope who served during most of Constantine's reign, St. Sylvester I (died 335 CE), he did preside over the construction of several church buildings in the vicinity of Lateran Palace, prominently including the Church of St. Peter. All of these structures have remained the property of the church to this day, though not all of them were incorporated into what became the official territory of the church, called Vatican City or the Holy See.

Before Christianity was embraced by the Roman Empire, the authority of the pope had twice been challenged, as two men now termed antipopes asserted that they, not the officially accepted popes, were the true leaders of the church; however, the problems faced by Pope Liberius (died 366 CE) were unusually severe. The emperor Constantius II (317–361 CE) was seeking to impose his own Christian doctrines on the church, and when Liberius proved uncooperative, he was summarily exiled, and the antipope Felix II (died 365 CE) claimed the papal throne, though most Christians in Rome did not recognize him as their true leader. Two years later, Liberius was allowed to return to Rome; Constantius II wished him and Felix II to rule the church together, but Liberius did not sanction the arrangement. There are great controversies, however, about whether Liberius in some way compromised his faith in order to get Constantius II to end his exile, and because of these suspicions of heresy, Liberius, unlike all of his predecessors, was never declared a saint after his death.

As the Roman Empire weakened in the fifth century CE, it became important for the church to maintain and strengthen its own organization, while also carrying on its battles against various heresies. These were the priorities of the most renowned pope who served under the Empire, Pope Leo I (died 461), often called Leo the Great. Even before becoming pope, Leo had earned a wide reputation as a skilled diplomat, and he was even asked by the emperor Valentinian III (419–455 CE) to negotiate a settlement between a feuding general and administrator in the province of Gaul. Later, perhaps in return for this service, Valentinian III issued an edict against the church's most troublesome heretics, the Manicheans. In 452 CE, Leo I persuaded Attila the Hun (died 453 CE) to abandon his conquest of Italy, and when Vandals briefly occupied the city of Rome in 455 CE, he successfully requested that they refrain from destroying its structures or killing its inhabitants. Leo I also asserted his absolute authority over all doctrinal matters, and he acted decisively to resolve disputes and rebuke church officials who diverged from his policies. We have an unusually good understanding of his personality, since copies of ninety-six of his sermons, and 143 of his letters, have survived, and they are greatly admired for their thoughtfulness and eloquence.

Even after the end of the Roman Empire, the pope remained in Rome and continued to control a large network of churches and monasteries in Europe, Asia, and Africa, functioning as a new sort of Roman emperor who left secular matters to local authorities while governing the religious lives of all believers. And, since millions of people all over the world, from the fifth century to today, have continued to look to the pontiff and his church for guidance, one can argue that, in one respect, the Roman Empire never really fell.

Further Reading

Colllins, Roger. 2006. *Keepers of the Keys of Heaven: A History of the Papacy.* New York: Basic Books.

Duffy, Eamon. 2006. *Saints and Sinners: A History of the Popes.* Third edition. New Haven, CT: Yale University Press.

Ferguson, Everett, editor.1993. *Church and State in the Early Church.* New York: Garland.

McBrien, Richard P. 1997. *Lives of the Popes: The Pontiffs from St. Peter to John Pail II.* San Francisco: Harper San Francisco.

Norwich, John Julius. 2011. *Absolute Monarchs: A History of the Papacy.* New York: Random House.

O'Malley, John W. 2010. *A History of the Popes: From Peter to the Present.* Lanham, MD: Rowman & Littlefield.

Document

From Pope Leo I. C. 450 CE. *Select Sermons of Saint Leo the Great on the Incarnation, with His Twenty-Eighth Epistle, Called the "Tome."* Second edition. Translated by William Bright. 1886. London: J. Masters and Company.

One of the major activities of the early popes was the suppression of numerous heretical beliefs about the nature of the Holy Trinity. In this excerpt from his twenty-eighth sermon, delivered on Christmas, Pope Leo I (died 461 CE) describes and argues against a number of these heresies, focusing special attention on the then-popular arguments of Nestorius (386–450 CE) and Eutyches (380–456 CE), both church officials in Constantinople.

Let the Catholic Faith, therefore, dearly beloved, contemn the vagaries of noisy heretics, who, deceived by the vanity of this world's wisdom, have departed from the Gospel of truth, and, being unable to apprehend the Incarnation of the Word, have made to themselves matter for blindness out of the very cause of illumination. . . . For some have ascribed to our Lord mere manhood; others, mere Godhead. Some have said that there was in Him, indeed, true Godhead, but only the semblance of flesh. Others have declared that He took on Him true flesh, but had not the nature of God the Father; and, attributing to His Godhead what belonged to the human essence, have invented for themselves a greater and a lesser God, whereas in true Godhead there can be no gradation, because whatever is less than God is not God. Others, knowing that there is no interval between the Father and the Son, have yet, from inability to understand the unity of Godhead except in the sense of unity of Person, asserted that the Father was the same as the Son, so that to be born and bred up, to suffer and die, to be buried and rise again, belonged to the self-same (Father,) Who sustained throughout the characters both of the Man and of the Word. Some have thought that the Lord Jesus Christ had a body not of our substance, but composed of higher and subtler elements. Some, again, have supposed that in Christ's flesh there was no human soul, but that the functions of a soul were discharged by the Word's Godhead itself. And their folly passed into this form, that they admitted the existence of a soul in our Lord, but said that His soul was without a mind, because Godhead alone was sufficient to the Man for all purposes of reason. At last these same men dared to aver, that a certain part of the Word had been converted into flesh; so that amid the manifold variations of one dogma, not only was the nature of the flesh and soul dissolved, but even the essence of the Word Himself.

There are also many other portentous falsities, with the enumeration of which I must not fatigue the attention of your Charity. But after diverse impieties, which have been mutually connected by the affinity which exists between manifold blasphemies, these following are the errors which I warn your dutiful and devout minds most especially to avoid. One, invented by Nestorius, attempted some time ago to raise its head, but not with impunity. Another, asserted by Eutyches, has lately broken out, and deserves to be condemned with similar abhorrence. For Nestorius dared to call the Blessed Virgin Mary the Mother of a man only, so that no union of the Word and the flesh should be believed to have been effected in her conception and child-bearing, on the ground that the Son of God did not Himself become Son of Man, but, purely of His good pleasure, took a created man as His associate. This statement could nowise be tolerated by Catholic ears, which were so possessed with the true Gospel as to be absolutely assured that there was no hope of salvation for mankind, unless He Himself were the Virgin's Son Who was the Creator of His Mother. But Eutyches, the profane assertor of the more recent impiety, did indeed fess an union of two natures in Christ, but affirmed that union to have had this effect, that of the two there remained but one, while the essence of the other ceased to exist; which annihilation, in fact, could only take place either by destruction or by separation. Now this is so inimical to sound faith, that it cannot be received without ruin to the Christian name. For if the Word's Incarnation consists in a union of the Divine and human natures, but by this very combination what was twofold became single, then Godhead alone was born of the Virgin's womb, and alone, under an illusory semblance, underwent bodily nourishment and growth; and, to pass over all the changes of human life, Godhead alone was crucified, Godhead alone died, Godhead alone was buried; so that, according to those who think thus, there is no reason to hope for a resurrection, and Christ is not "the firstborn from the dead;" for if there had not been one who could be put to death, there was none who had a right to be raised to life.

Far from your hearts, dearly beloved, be the pestilent falsehoods inspired by the devil!

Priests

Ancient Rome had two very different sorts of priests. For centuries, these men were government employees who managed temples and carried out rituals dedicated to the gods and goddesses of Roman mythology. Then, as the Christian church emerged from the shadows of oppression to become the official state religion, a hierarchy of Christian priests, overseen by the pope and devoted to the Christian God, became prominent figures in city life. Due to ongoing controversies over the requirement that Catholic priests must be celibate males, these early priests have been the subject of intensive study by scholars seeking evidence that would validate or challenge the official doctrines.

The Roman religion, largely borrowed from the Greeks, had many deities and few doctrines; its primary concern was to perform ceremonies and carry out sacrifices to please the gods who governed various aspects of nature and society. Just as the heads of households did these tasks so the gods would assist their families, the government's priests would conduct rituals so the gods would assist the officials and people of Rome. Any man from an aristocratic background without physical defects could be chosen to become a priest, usually by a group of current priests who named several candidates and then voted to choose one of them. Priests normally served for life; since the position rarely required constant labor, most of these men held other jobs as well.

The priests were organized into various groups, termed "colleges." The most powerful of these were the *pontifices*, or pontiffs, sixteen men who were officially in charge of all religious affairs; these prestigious positions were often given to experienced senators. Their duties included determining the dates of all religious festivals and holidays, chronicling each year's major events, and maintaining a large library of religious books. Their nominal leader was the emperor himself, who held the title of *pontifex maximus*, though he did not always involve himself in their activities. The most important public ceremonies, however, were headed by another senior official, the *rex sacrocum* or king of the sacred, who was assisted by his wife, the *regina*.

Members of another college of priests, the *augures*, were responsible for determining if the gods favored a planned initiative, like a long journey or a battle; fifteen men typically handled this responsibility. These men had learned how to observe wild birds in flight or the movements of feeding chickens for signs of divine approval or disapproval. One favorable sign, for example, is a raven on the right side of the sky. A rival group of diviners with less authority, the *haruspices*, examined the entrails of sacrificed animals and watched for bolts of lightning or newborn animals

This wall carving, from about 120 CE, shows one of the ancient Roman priests called *haruspices*, striving to predict the future by examining the entrails of a dead animal. (Duruy, Victor. *History of Rome and the Roman People*, 1884)

with unusual features like an extra head; since one did not kill an animal without good cause, these men were trained to interpret entrails with a bronze model of an animal liver, divided into forty parts.

Priests called *flamines* were also appointed to oversee the worship of major gods, like Jupiter and Mars; while these may have been considered very desirable positions, these men also had limitations placed on their behavior. The *flamen* dedicated to Jupiter, for instance, always had to wear a special cap, could never leave the city in the evening, and was not allowed to eat goat meat or beans; further, since his wife, the *flaminica*, assisted him in his work, he could not divorce her, and he had to give up his post if she

died. Other colleges of priests specialized in certain functions. The *fetiales*, for example, would officiate at declarations of war and the signing of treaties; the *Augustales* were responsible for the worship of the late emperor Augustus (63 BCE–14 CE) and other deified emperors; and the *fratres arvales* performed ceremonies to ensure fertile soil for crops. The priests of the god Mars, the *salii*, were noted for their habit of dancing at festivals and wearing military uniforms, while the only priestesses, the Vestal Virgins, served the goddess Vesta.

In addition to various ceremonies in their honor, the gods of ancient Rome also had temples devoted to their worship, and these were managed by other sorts of priests called *sacerdotes*. In addition to tending to the statue of their gods and performing daily rituals, these men were also administrators, in charge of various temple workers like gatekeepers, guides, servants, and clerks. One common activity at temples was the sacrifice of various animals to the gods, including horses, pigs, sheep, and cows; these animals had to be perfectly formed, and if they tried to get away instead of walking peacefully to the altar, it was considered inauspicious, and another animal would be sacrificed instead.

When foreign slaves came to Rome, or soldiers returned after campaigns in distant countries, they often had different religious beliefs and helped to popularize some unofficial cults that developed their own priesthoods. One popular cult was dedicated to the worship of the Egyptian goddess Isis, and her priests were distinguished by the habit of shaving their heads. Our main sources of information about another popular cult, dedicated to the god Mithras, are illustrations on the walls of the caves they used as temples; apparently, there were seven levels of worshippers, each associated with a planet, and the highest individuals, the Fathers of Saturn, undoubtedly presided over ceremonies as the cult's priests. One series of paintings appears to show a naked man, his eyes covered by a blindfold, being initiated into the cult by two helmeted men who place a crown on his head.

Today, however, we are most interested in the once-despised cult that developed into Christianity. Early Christians were often subject to violent persecution, particularly under the emperor Nero (37–68 CE), so they were necessarily secretive, and

NO WOMEN NEED APPLY?

As part of their effort to persuade the Roman Catholic Church to accept female priests, several scholars have engaged in prodigious amounts of research, searching for evidence that women, in fact, did serve as priests in the early church. However, although women did play a prominent role in the rise of Christianity, and probably presided over some rituals at a time when Christians were only informally organized, there remains absolutely no persuasive evidence that women were ever officially ordained as priests. However, this has not prevented some independent Catholics from ordaining a number of women as priests, although the official church rejects the legitimacy of their actions.

A PARALYZED PRIEST

In the Roman religion, no priests were allowed to have any physical deformities, since it was believed that would displease the gods. In the modern Catholic Church, there is no absolute ban on disabled priests, though candidates might be rejected if their disability would interfere with the performance of their duties; a man with a severe speech impediment, for example, could not conduct a mass. However, ordained, priests who develop disabilities can continue to serve; thus, after priest Kevin Bray was in a car accident in 1967 that left him unable to move his body properly, he remained active as a priest, counseling others who face special physical challenges.

their activities are not always well documented. However, it is believed that they would initially gather in private homes to worship and engage in Holy Communion, probably under the supervision of the homeowner or any experienced believer; they also met in the tunnels underneath Rome known as the catacombs. As the church gradually came out of hiding and began to develop a formal organization, its first officials were known as bishops and *presbyters*, or elders; after 200 CE, the heads of churches were referred to as priests. In documents, terms are often used inconsistently, but it appears that bishops were the church's senior officials, priests were below them in the hierarchy, and deacons were the lowest tier.

Considerable evidence suggests that the early priests were often married men who were presumably sexually active, and it was not until 306 CE that celibacy was officially mandated at the Council of Elvira held in southern Spain. There are also disputed indications that some of the priests were women; images in the Catacombs of St. Priscilla, for example, appear to show a woman presiding over Communion and another woman being ordained as a priest. Needless to say, the Roman Catholic Church fiercely disputes these claims, insisting that the married priests were always celibate after their ordination and while women may have informally handled some religious duties, they were never officially designated as priests.

Christians were sporadically persecuted up until the start of the fourth century, when the religion officially became legal; soon, all pagan religions were outlawed, and their once-lofty priests faded from view. The church was now organized into provinces, like the provinces of the Roman Empire, that were each headed by a former priest promoted to serve as a bishop or archbishop. During Rome's declining days, being a Christian priest must have been one of the most desirable jobs available; these men were supported and protected by a wealthy and powerful institution, and in addition to performing their religious duties, they had ample time to engage in scholarly pursuits, most often focused on resolving theological disputes and firmly establishing the doctrines of the church. We do not always know very much about their daily lives, but many of their writings on religion were carefully preserved by medieval scribes who copied decaying texts onto new pieces of parchment. And even after the empire had fallen, these priests were able to carry on with the work of tending to the needs of their parishioners and conferring with distant colleagues, maintaining a tradition that has endured to the present day.

Further Reading

Beard, Mary, and John North, editors. 1990. *Pagan Priests: Religion and Power in the Ancient World.* Ithaca, NY: Cornell University Press.
Beard, Mary, John North, and Simon Price. 1998. *Religions of Rome: Volume 1: A History.* Cambridge and New York: Cambridge University Press.

Beard, Mary, John North, and Simon Price. 1998. *Religions of Rome: Volume 2: A Sourcebook.* Cambridge and New York: Cambridge University Press.

Ermatinger, James William. 2007. *Daily Life of Christians in Ancient Rome.* Westport, CT: Greenwood Press.

Scheid, John. 2003. *An Introduction to Roman Religion.* Bloomington: Indiana University Press.

Torjesen, Mary Jo. 1993. *When Women Were Priests: Women's Leadership in the Early Church and the Scandal of Their Subordination in the Rise of Christianity.* San Francisco: Harper San Francisco.

Document

From Aulus Gellius. C. 170 CE. *The Attic Nights of Aulus Gellius.* Volume I. Translated by John C. Rolfe. 1927. Cambridge and London: Loeb Classical Library.

In this passage from Attic Nights, *the Roman writer Aulus Gellius (ca. 125–180 CE) describes the various rules associated with the priests and priestesses of Jupiter.*

Ceremonies in great number are imposed upon the priest of Jupiter and also many abstentions of which we read in the books written On Public Priests. . . Of these, the following are in general what I remember:

It is unlawful for the priest of Jupiter to ride upon a horse. It is also unlawful for him to see the classes arrayed outside the religious boundaries of the city, that is, the army in battle array. Hence the priest of Jupiter is rarely made consul, since wars were entrusted to the consuls. Also, it is always unlawful for the priest to take an oath, and likewise to wear a ring, unless it be perforated and without a gem. It is against the law for fire to be taken from the *flaminia,* that is, from the home of the *flamen Dialis* [priest of Jupiter], except for a sacred rite. If a person in chains enters his house, he must be freed, the bonds must be drawn up through a skylight in the ceiling to the roof and from there let down into the street.

He has no knot in his head-dress, girdle, or any other part of his clothing. If anyone is being taken to be flogged, and falls at his feet as a suppliant, it is unlawful for the man to be flogged on that day. Only a free man may cut the hair of the priest. It is not customary for the priest to touch, or even name, a she-goat, raw flesh, ivy, and beans.

The priest of Jupiter must not pass under an arbor of vines. The feet of the couch on which he sleeps must be smeared with a thin coating of clay, and he must not sleep away from this bed for three nights in succession, and no other person must sleep in that bed. At the foot of his bed, there should be a box with sacrificial cakes. The cuttings of the nails and hair of the priest must be buried in the earth under a fruitful tree. Every day is a holy day for the priest. He must not be in the open air without his cap; that he may go without it in the house only recently has been decided by the pontiffs. . . and it is said that some other ceremonies have been remitted, and he has been excused from observing them.

The priest of Jupiter must not touch any bread fermented with yeast. He does not remove his inner tunic except under cover, in order that he may not be naked in the open air, as it were under the eye of Jupiter. No other person has a place at the table above the priest of Jupiter, except for the priest who presides over sacrifices. If the priest has lost his wife, he abdicates his office. The marriage of the priest cannot be dissolved except by death. He never enters a place of burial, he never touches a dead body, but he is not forbidden to attend a funeral.

The ceremonies of the priestess of Jupiter are about the same. They say that she observes other separate ones. For example, she wears a dyed robe, that she has a twig from a fruitful tree in her head-dress, that it is forbidden for her to go up more than three rounds of a ladder. Also, when she goes to a chapel, that she neither combs her head nor dresses her hair.

I have added the words of the praetor in his standing edict concerning the priest of Jupiter and the priestess of [the goddess] Vesta: "In the whole of my jurisdiction, I will not compel the priest of Jupiter or a priestess of Vesta to take an oath." The words of Marcus Varro about the priest of Jupiter... : "He alone has a white cap, either because he is the greatest of priests, or because a white victim should be sacrificed to Jupiter."

Prostitutes

It is not the world's oldest profession, but prostitution was commonplace throughout the ancient world, and in Rome, it was widely accepted as an institution; both female and male prostitutes could be found in many places, and there was no social stigma attached to the men who made use of their services. Further, while almost all prostitutes were slaves, they were generally treated reasonably well and, like other Roman slaves, they were regularly able to gain their freedom and pursue other interests.

A woman might become a prostitute, or *meretrix*, in various ways. If parents who did not want daughters left their female infants exposed in the outdoors, then a common practice, the babies might be found and raised to become prostitutes; destitute families could sell their daughters into the profession; and poor free women without a family might venture into prostitution in order to support themselves. But there emerged a special demand for prostitutes from distant lands, and attractive women brought to Rome as slaves were usually destined for that fate. Dark, exotic beauties from eastern provinces were valued, but as the Roman Empire expanded into northern Europe, blonde women became especially popular, though prostitutes might dye their hair or wear wigs to achieve that appearance. Handsome young boys of all nationalities were also candidates to become prostitutes, since it was not considered improper for married men to have occasional sexual relations with youthful males. Strangely, the man who purchased and controlled prostitutes, called a *leno*, might be a slave himself, since it was not the sort of job that appealed to most Roman citizens; rarely, a woman might also be in charge of a group of prostitutes as a *lena*.

In the beginning, prostitutes would work for a *leno*, but women in particular were often able to purchase their freedom and seek customers independently. Regardless of the circumstances of their employment, all prostitutes had to register with an official called the *aedile* and regularly pay a tax, roughly equivalent to what the prostitute would earn from one client every day. There were also a large number of unregistered prostitutes who escaped punishment because they mostly serviced wealthy and influential men. Female prostitutes were expected to dress in a certain way: unlike respectable Roman women, they always wore togas, and they allowed their hair to fall freely on their shoulders instead of styling it into braids or buns. In contrast, male prostitutes were not associated with any particular form of dress, though they might naturally seek to expose as much skin as possible to attract clients.

Prostitutes would find their customers in various places. One might work in a brothel, called a *lupunar* or *fornix*, where entering customers would first approach the cashier, or *villucus*, to obtain suggestions about which woman might best suit their preferences. Then, they would approach the rooms of individual prostitutes; the ruins of Pompeii suggest that the rooms in a typical brothel were very small, with a mattress on top of a narrow bed, and the walls were all covered with pornographic artwork and lewd graffiti. A prostitute would spend her hours sitting on a stool in front of the door of her room, where a tablet hung that displayed her name and her price; whenever she attracted a customer, she would turn the tablet to the other side, which said *occupata*, or "occupied," while she tended to his needs. There was also a special type of brothel, called a *stabula*, which had only one enormous room where all of the sexual liaisons could be observed by other prostitutes and customers. By the third century CE, the city of Rome had a total of forty-five brothels, which were not allowed to open their doors until the middle of the afternoon. These buildings were notorious for the smoke from lamps that accumulated within facilities that were often poorly ventilated, and they were said to be foul-smelling as well, perhaps explaining why they were typically situated solely in one section of a city. Prostitutes might be also employed by taverns and hotels, which would offer them to interested guests; one surviving hotel bill, for example, lists the charges for a room, hay to feed a donkey, several meals, and the services of a young girl.

In addition to these establishments, prostitutes could be located almost anywhere in the streets of Rome; some itinerant prostitutes became known as *lupae*, or she-wolves, because they purportedly would try to attract customers by howling like a wolf. Most prostitutes, however, tended to congregate in certain areas. They frequently loitered outside or within the public baths, where many people might be seen wearing little or no clothing, and the tombs on streets outside of the city were also a favorite location. Some of the prostitutes there might earn extra income by

LEGAL TENDER FOR ILLICIT LIAISONS

According to one theory, the customers of Roman prostitutes in the first century CE were able to pay for their services with a token that was minted by the government as a benefit for male citizens. This peculiar practice has also been adopted by modern entrepreneurs who have produced and marketed silver tokens, which can be used at several legal brothels in the state of Nevada. Unlike the Roman tokens, however, these do not depict sex acts, only scantily clad females. One Web site is now selling these $10 tokens for the price of $40, on the grounds that these singular items are "collectibles."

HOSPITALITY OF ILL REPUTE

There is no real modern equivalent to the ancient Roman baths, since municipal swimming pools are viewed as places for exercise and active play, not bathing and relaxing. But a soothing experience that the Romans could relate to can be enjoyed at a spa or massage parlor, where customers can take a shower, unwind in a sauna or steam room, and get a tranquilizing massage from a trained masseuse. And while large numbers of these facilities are legitimate businesses, limiting themselves to advertised services, some of them, like the Roman baths, have become thinly disguised centers for organized prostitution.

working as paid mourners at funerals. A character in *Curculio*, a play by Plautus (254–184 BCE), complains about the pimps and prostitutes found in the vicinity of Roman temples. Outside of a temple dedicated to Venus, prostitutes might sell cakes that resembled male and female genitalia to be offered to the goddess. It was generally assumed that women who worked in certain professions, such as singers, dancers, mimes, and actresses, would occasionally be willing to work as prostitutes, though it is unclear just how commonly or frequently this occurred.

Prostitutes also attended an annual festival, the Floralia, that honored an ancient fertility goddess named Flora. According to one fanciful legend, Flora was originally a human prostitute who became wealthy, bequeathed funds after her death to establish a festival on her birthday, and was subsequently deemed a goddess. It might only be appropriate, then, that it was reportedly common for prostitutes to dance naked at these festivals to please customers and engage in playful gladiatorial competitions; by some accounts, the Floralia was intended to function as a celebration of prostitution. (Other sources, however, say that the prostitute turned goddess was actually named Acca Larentia, though her festival, the Larentalia, did not attract prostitutes.)

The unhappiest prostitutes were probably those in the employ of the Roman army, who accompanied the soldiers whenever they were on the march. Since there were many men and few women, a typical prostitute might spend her entire day having sex with one soldier after another, and if there ever came a time when her services were not needed, she might be forced to cook meals, clean up the camp, or repair torn clothing. If a prostitute caught the eye of an officer, however, he might purchase the woman, and then she would only have to sleep with one man.

It is difficult to determine just how much a typical prostitute earned, especially since converting Roman currency to modern values is notoriously difficult, but it is believed that most prostitutes received the equivalent of between $1 and $10 from each customer. Aged prostitutes, or those who worked in the streets, probably earned much less, while especially attractive or talented prostitutes, or those who focused on wealthy customers, undoubtedly earned much more. Though prostitutes were usually paid in cash, Roman emperors in the first century CE reportedly instituted the peculiar custom of distributing, as a free gift to their citizens, special tokens known as *spintria* which anyone could use to purchase the services of a prostitute. How these functioned is not exactly clear, but it is assumed that markings on the token indicated particular services and locations, and after the client handed the prostitute a token, she could take it to a bank to be redeemed for cash. There remains much controversy about these tokens, though, since some have suggested that they originated as a way to assist foreign prostitutes, who lacked the language skills to negotiate a price, or that they were employed for purposes other than purchasing sex.

While prostitutes were ubiquitous in Roman society, there are surprisingly few written accounts of the profession, except for the barbed criticisms of satirists; indeed, it may be archaeologists, not authors, who have provided the bulk of our information in this area, especially from the valuable site of Pompeii. Perhaps the Romans recognized that the popularity of prostitution did not reflect well on their culture, and the rise of Christianity in the third century CE surely helped to make the profession less visible, since church fathers did not approve of this activity. Still, to fully understand the ancient Romans, one must examine both their great achievements and their idle pleasures, such as the readily available services of prostitutes.

Further Reading

Faraone, Christopher A., and Laura K. McClure, editors. *Prostitutes and Courtesans in the Ancient World.* Madison: University of Wisconsin Press.

Hallett, Judith P., and Marilyn B. Skinner, editors. 1997. *Roman Sexualities.* Princeton, NJ: Princeton University Press.

Laurence, Ray. 2009. *Roman Passions: A History of Pleasure in Imperial Rome.* London and New York: Continuum.

McGinn, Thomas A.J. 2004. *The Economy of Prostitution in the Roman World: A Study of Social History and the Brothel.* Ann Arbor: University of Michigan Press.

McGinn, Thomas A.J. 1998. *Prostitution, Sexuality, and the Law in Ancient Rome.* Oxford and New York: Oxford University Press.

Williams, Craig A. 2010. *Roman Homosexuality.* Second edition. Oxford and New York: Oxford University Press.

Documents

From Plautus. *The Comedies of Plautus: Literally Translated into English, with Notes.* Volume 2. Translated by Henry Thomas Riley. 1912. London: George Bell and Sons.

In this opening passage from the play Truculentus: The Churl, *written sometime around 200 BCE, the Roman playwright Plautus (ca. 254–184 BCE) has a man speak about the greedy prostitute who has taken all of his money and is now planning to deceive another lover. Although it is set in Athens, the story conveys a common Roman attitude toward prostitutes, that they are both alluring and untrustworthy.*

[Dinarchus:] Thus is it in the houses kept by procurers; before you've given a single thing, she's preparing a hundred to ask for; either a golden trinket's lost, or a mantle has been torn, or a female servant bought; or some silver vessel, or some vessel of brass, or expensive couch, or a Grecian cabinet, or there's always something to be lost and for the lover to be replacing for his mistress. And with one common earnestness do we conceal these losses while we are losing our fortunes, and our credit, and ourselves, lest our parents or our relatives should know something; whom, while we conceal it from them, if we were to make acquainted with it, for them in time to restrain our youthful age, we should be giving what has been received from them before to our descendants in reversion; I'd be for causing, that as there are now more procurers and harlots, there should be fewer and fewer of spendthrift fellows than there are at present; for now-a-days there are almost more procurers and harlots than flies at the time when it is most hot. For, if they are nowhere else, the procurers with their harlots are around the bankers' shops each day as though on siege. That score is the principal one; inasmuch as I know for certain, that now-a-days there are more harlots ready for the money than there are weights for weighing it. And I really don't know what purpose to say it is to serve that these procurers are thus keeping them at the bankers' shops, except as in the place of account-books, where the sums lent on loan may be set down—the sums received I mean, those expended let no one take count of. In fine, in a great nation, amid numberless persons, the state being tranquil and in quiet, the enemy vanquished, it befits all to be in love who have anything to give. Now, this Courtesan [pointing to the house] Phronesium, who dwells here, has totally expelled from my breast her own name. Phronesium, for Phronesis is wisdom. For I confess that I was with her first and foremost; a thing that's very disastrous to a lover's cash. The same woman, after she had found another out, a greater spendthrift, who would give more, a Babylonian Captain, whom the hussy said was troublesome and odious to her, forthwith banished me from the spot. He now is said to be about to arrive from abroad. For that reason has she now cooked up this device; she pretends that she has been brought to bed. That she may push me out of doors, and with the Captain alone live the life of a jovial Greek, she pretends that this Captain is the father of the child; for that reason does this most vile hussy need a palmed-off child. She fancies that she's deceiving me! Does she suppose that she could have concealed it from me, if she had been pregnant? Now I arrived at Athens the day before yesterday from Lemnos, whither I have been on an embassy from this place on the public service. But who's this woman? It's her servant-maid Astaphium. With her too as well I've had some acquaintanceship.

From Terence. C. 160 BCE. *The Comedies of Terence, Literally Translated into English Prose, with Notes.* Translated by Henry Thomas Riley. 1872. New York: Harper & Brothers.

In his comedy Adelphoe, *or* The Brothers, *the Roman playwright Terence (ca. 195–159 BCE) contrasts an indulgent father, Micio, with his stricter brother Demea, as they separately raise Demea's two sons. In this scene, Demea is aghast to learn that Micio will be allowing a prostitute loved by one of his sons, euphemistically described as a "music-girl," to live in his home, even though he and his other son are about to be married.*

[Demea:] [O rare] corrector! of course it is by your art that twenty *minae* have been thrown away for a Music-girl; who, as soon as possible, must be got rid of at any price; and if not for money, why then for nothing.

[Micio:] Not at all, and indeed I have no wish to sell her.

[Demea:] What will you do with her then?

[Micio:] She shall be at my house.

[Demea:] For heaven's sake, a courtesan and a matron in the same house!

[Micio:] Why not?

[Demea:] Do you imagine you are in your senses?

[Micio:] Really I do think [so].

[Demea:] So may the Gods prosper me, I [now] see your folly; I believe you are going

to do so that you may have somebody to practice music with.

[Micio:] Why not?

[Demea:] And the new-made bride to be learning too?

[Micio:] Of course.

[Demea:] Having hold of the rope, you will be dancing with them.

[Micio:] Like enough; and you too along with us, if there's need.

[Demea:] Ah me! are you not ashamed of this?

[Micio:] Demea, do, for once, lay aside this anger of yours, and show yourself as you ought at your son's wedding, cheerful and good-humored. I'll just step over to them, [and] return immediately. . . . [He departs.]

[Demea alone.]

[Demea:] O Jupiter! here's a life! here are manners! here's madness! A wife to be coming without a fortune! A music-wench in the house! A house full of wastefulness! A young man ruined by extravagance! An old man in his dotage!—Should Salvation herself desire it, she certainly could not save this family.

Satirists

Arguably, one sign of a truly enlightened civilization is a willingness to tolerate criticism of its values and its leaders; so it is not surprising that classical Athens welcomed the comedies of the iconoclastic Aristophanes, who farcically attacked major figures of his era like the philosopher Socrates. However, it was the culture of ancient Rome that first developed a form of literature, satire, that was expressly devoted to humorous but pointed commentaries on society, and spawned a long tradition of satirists in verse and prose whose works are still read today.

The founder of the genre was a writer named Quintus Ennius (239–169 BCE), who had an eclectic background: born in southern Italy, he originally spoke a language called Oscan, received his education in Greek, and learned Latin while serving in the Roman army. He came to the attention of the statesman

This image on a mosaic floor, from the third century CE, purportedly shows the pioneering Roman satirist Quintus Ennius, wearing a laurel crown to represent his poetic skills. (DeAgostini/Getty Images)

Cato (234–149 BCE), who brought him to Rome, where he made a living by teaching students and cultivating wealthy patrons. Only scattered passages from his varied works have survived, but his four books of *Saturae* (ca. 200 BCE), or satires, provided gently didactic essays that made use of personal anecdotes, dialogues, and fables. Closer in spirit to satire in its modern sense were the poems of Gaius Lucilius (ca. 180–103 BCE), the first writer to specialize in the form. Like Ennius, he seems to have been largely supported by influential friends, like the generals Scipio Africanus the Younger (185–129 BCE) and Gaius Laelius the Younger (ca. second century BCE), and he garnered such widespread appreciation for his works that he was given a large public funeral, though these were usually reserved for government officials. Also known only by fragments of his works preserved by grammar-ians, Lucilius apparently progressed from parodies of epic poems to barbed critiques of the conduct of both prominent public figures and everyday citizens.

We are more familiar with the achievements of three noteworthy successors to Lucilius, Horace (65–8 BCE), Persius (34–62 CE), and Juvenal (ca. 55–127 CE), because we can still read many of their complete poems. The son of a former slave, the young Horace faced difficulties because he had sided with Brutus (ca. 85–42 BCE) and Cassius (died 42 BCE) following their assassination of Julius Caesar (ca. 100–44 BCE). Though his father's estate was confiscated by the forces of the victorious Octavian, later the emperor Augustus (63 BCE–14 CE), Horace fortunately still had enough money to purchase a minor government position, which enabled him to befriend Gaius Mae-cenas (70–8 BCE), a diplomat working for Augustus who bought him a house and encouraged Augustus to favor the poet. While he wrote other sorts of poems, like his celebrated analysis of poetry, *The Art of Poetry* (ca. 19–18 BCE), Horace's two books of *Satires* (35 and 29–30 BCE) criticized people like unscrupulous businessmen, prostitutes, and pretentious social climb-ers, while celebrating individuals like himself whose achievements came solely from their own efforts, in contrast to pampered aristocrats.

Persius, unusually, was a wealthy man, inspired to write satires by the example of Lucilius. Not concerned about pleasing any patrons, he wrote very carefully, at a leisurely pace, and had only completed six satires at the time of his death. After criticizing contemporary lit-erature as a sign of moral decline, Persius focused his attention on serious analyses of philosophical questions.

Perhaps the most acerbic of the Roman satirists, Juvenal actually got into trouble because one of his early verses complained that meritorious soldiers like him were not gaining high positions in the Roman army solely because they lacked connections to the imperial court; in response, the repressive govern-ment of the emperor Domitian (51–96 CE) seized his property and exiled him to a remote outpost, proba-bly in Egypt. After Domitian was killed, Juvenal was allowed to return to Rome but apparently lived in poverty, supported solely by the sporadic generosity of patrons; the tone of his poetry suggests that he did not find it easy to make friends. His sixteen satires, published in five books sometime during his later life, savagely attacked officials, women, homosexuals, foreigners, and others that he believed had utterly corrupted the once-noble city of Rome. Eventually, his poems brought him enough money to purchase a farm and enjoy a serene retirement, though he continued writing satires in a slightly mellower spirit.

Two other poets should be mentioned in any survey of Roman satire, though they were not considered specialists in the genre. Seneca (4 BCE–65 CE) came from a prominent family and became a powerful political figure during the reign of the emperor Nero (37–68 CE), whom he once tutored; however, he later withdrew from public life and, accused of conspiring to assassinate Nero, was forced to commit suicide. Though he is better known for his philosophical writings and tragedies, Seneca produced one memorable satire, *The Apocolocyntosis* ("The Pumpkinification of Claudius"), which mocked the notion that emperors would become gods after their deaths; no one is sure when it was written, and some suspect that Seneca was not actually its author. Seneca was also the patron of another occasional satirist, Martial (ca. 38–103 CE), who was born in Spain as the son of Roman citizens and moved to Rome to seek his fortune as a poet. He became noted for writing very short poems, or epigrams, which tend to obsequiously flatter the rich and powerful people who were his potential patrons and harshly condemn the flaws of lesser individuals.

While all of these men were poets, there were also some satirists who wrote prose narratives. One of these is the somewhat shadowy figure of Petronius (died 66 CE), evidently a wealthy man who rose to a high position in Nero's court; like Seneca, however, he had to kill himself after being accused of treason against the emperor. We know little about the plot of his major work, the *Satyricon*, since only a few chapters have survived; it reportedly involved the salacious escapades of a boy and his adult male companions. But the longest available episode, called "The Banquet of Trimalchio," is a richly satirical description of a dinner party given by a wealthy but debauched man who may have been a thinly disguised version of Nero. Another prose satirist, Lucian (ca. 120–180 CE), lived in Greece under Roman rule and actually wrote in Greek, though the Romans were familiar with his

ENDANGERED ENTERTAINERS

The lives of Roman satirists were not always pleasant, as they often faced poverty, persecution, or even death because of their writings. A twentieth-century satirist who also suffered for his work was stand-up comedian Lenny Bruce (1933–1966). Though now regarded as a pioneer for his blunt, spontaneous humor, Bruce was regularly arrested for using obscene language and notoriously convicted in 1964, though he remained free while the case was appealed. Yet because of these controversies, Bruce was banned from television and most night clubs, and unable to pursue his profession, he increasingly turned to drugs and died of an overdose in 1966. He received a posthumous pardon in 2003.

VENERATED VANITY

The best-known work of the Roman satirist Juvenal was probably his tenth satire, generally known as "The Vanity of Human Wishes." This work so impressed the eighteenth-century English writer Samuel Johnson that he undertook to write his own updated version of the satire, published in 1749 as *The Vanity of Human Wishes: The Tenth Satire of Juvenal Imitated by Samuel Johnson*. While faithful to Juvenal's general approach, Johnson did alter his conclusion, emphasizing the Christian faith as the best solution to futile desires in place of Juvenal's advice to merely lower one's expectations. Still, many critics believe that Johnson improved upon the original, praising the poem as his masterpiece.

work. He made his living as an itinerant orator, but apparently tired of traveling and settled in Athens to focus on writing. We do not know when his best known work, *The True History*, was completed, but it qualifies as the first story about human space travel, though its playfully absurd account of a ship that sails to the Moon and the Sun is announced from the onset as a complete lie. One of his lost works, called *Lucius, or The Ass*, may have inspired a similar work by the Roman satirist Lucius Apuleius (ca. 124–170 CE), who was born in present-day Algeria and worked as a teacher of rhetoric before he returned to his home in Africa to marry a wealthy widow. Though he also wrote philosophical texts, he is generally remembered for his story *The Golden Ass*, which relates the misadventures of a man who is turned into a donkey; he ultimately becomes a man again after he begins to worship the goddess Isis. Some have argued that Apuleius's text qualifies as the first true novel, though there are many other candidates for that distinction.

From the lives of these and other Roman satirists who garnered less renown, we can discern potential lessons for anyone with similar literary ambitions. By means of eloquent and witty denunciations of people and their foibles, one can attractive both powerful friends, and powerful enemies. It requires keen political instincts to adjust to changing circumstances and achieve a prosperous and happy existence, like Lucilius and Horace; if they lack sufficient skill in this area, though, the lives of satirists might end in tragedy, which was the fate of Petronius and Seneca. The only consoling thought that might have eased their final moments was the knowledge that, because of their works, they would become better known and more esteemed by future generations than their tormentors.

Further Reading

Braund, Susanna Morton. 1992. *Roman Verse Satire.* Oxford and New York: Oxford University Press.

Dominik, William J., and William T. Wehrle, editors. 1999. *Roman Verse Satire: Lucilius to Juvenal: A Selection with an Introduction, Text, Translations, and Notes.* Wauconda, IL: Bolchazy-Carducci Publishers.

Freudenberg, Kirk, editor. 2005. *The Cambridge Companion to Roman Satire.* Cambridge and New York: Cambridge University Press.

Freudenberg, Kirk. 2001. *Satires of Rome: Threatening Poses from Lucilius to Juvenal.* Cambridge and New York: Cambridge University Press.

Hooley, Daniel M. 2007. *Roman Satire.* Malden, MA: Blackwell.

Keane, Catherine. 2006. *Figuring Genre in Roman Satire.* Oxford and New York: Oxford University Press.

Documents

From Juvenal. C. 100 CE. *The Satires of Juvenal, Persius, Sulpicia, and Lucilius.* Translated by Lewis Evans. 1850. London: Henry G. Bohn.

The tenth satire of Juvenal (ca. 55–127 CE), usually called "The Vanity of Human Wishes," discusses the folly of asking the gods for wealth, power, beauty, *and other blessings that will never bring human happiness. In its concluding passage, presented here, he describes the more modest desires that people should focus on, including the memorable phrase "a sound mind in a sound body."*

Is there then nothing for which men shall pray? If you will take advice, you will allow the deities themselves to determine what may be expedient for us, and suitable to our condition. For instead of pleasant things, the gods will give us all that is most fitting. Man is dearer to them than to himself. We, led on by the impulse of our minds, by blind and headstrong passions, pray for wedlock, and issue by our wives; but it is known to them what our children will prove; of what character our wife will be! Still, that you may have somewhat to pray for, and vow to their shrines the entrails and consecrated mincemeat of the white porker, your prayer must be that you may have a sound mind in a sound body. Pray for a bold spirit, free from all dread of death; that reckons the closing scene of life among Nature's kindly boons; that can endure labor, whatever it be that deems the gnawing cares of Hercules, and all his cruel toils, far preferable to the joys of Venus, rich banquets, and the downy couch of Sardanapalus. I show thee what thou canst confer upon thyself! The only path that surely leads to a life of peace lies through virtue. If we have wise foresight, thou, Fortune, hast no divinity. It is we that make thee a deity, and place thy throne in heaven!

From Martial. C. 86–103 CE. *The Epigrams of Martial, Translated into English Prose.* Translator unidentified. 1860. London: Henry G. Bohn.

At the beginning of his first book of Epigrams, *the satirist Martial (ca. 38–103 CE) defends his manner of writing and introduces himself to his readers.*

[Book 1] To the Reader

I trust that, in these little books of mine, I have observed such self-control, that whoever forms a fair judgment from his own mind can make no complaint of them, since they indulge their sportive fancies without violating the respect due even to persons of the humblest station; a respect which was so far disregarded by the authors of antiquity, that they made free use, not only of real, but of great names. For me, let fame be held in less estimation, and let such talent be the last thing commended in me.

Let the ill-natured interpreter, too, keep himself from meddling with the simple meaning of my jests, and not write my epigrams for me. He acts dishonourably who exercises perverse ingenuity on another man's book. For the free plainness of expression, that is, for the language of epigram, I would apologize, if I were introducing the practice; but it is thus that Catullus writes, and Marsus, and Pedo, and Getulicus, and every one whose writing are read through. If any assumes to be so scrupulously nice, however, that it is not allowable to address him, in a single page, in plain language, he may confine himself to this address, or rather to the title of the book. Epigrams are written for those who are accustomed to be spectators at the games of Flora. Let not Cato enter my theatre; or, if he do enter, let him look on. It appears to me that I shall do only what I have a right to do. . . .

The man whom you are reading is the very man that you want,—Martial, known over the whole world for his humorous books of epigrams; to whom, studious reader, you have accorded such honours, while he is alive and has a sense of them, as few poets receive after their death.

Senators

While ancient Rome is best remembered for its Empire, it must be remembered that it was also long governed as a republic, and its legislative body, the Senate, retained a certain amount of power even after the emperors began to rule. Indeed, one of the most enduring images of Roman life is a meeting of the Senate, where men in togas make speeches and confer on matters of state, and; along with the emperors, its most noteworthy members, like the orator Cicero (106–43 BCE), remain the best-known Roman citizens.

In the days of the Republic, a man became a senator after he was elected by a popular assembly to serve as a magistrate, or administrator. Then, he would be a member of the Senate for the rest of his life, while occasionally serving as a magistrate or provincial governor. Magistrates were typically elected in pairs,

so that one man never garnered too much power; the typical qualifications were an aristocratic background and experiencing working either in the military as a tribune or legate or in the courts as a lawyer. The highest officials were traditionally the consuls, while other administrators held the titles of *censor*, *quaestor*, *aedile*, and *praetor*. While in the Senate, members needed an independent source of income, since they received no salary. The size of the Senate gradually increased; originally, there were only 100 members, but there were later increases to 300, 600, and 900 members under Julius Caesar (100–44 BCE), though the first emperor, Augustus (63 BCE–14 CE) reduced its membership to 600. Eventually, by 384 CE, there were 2,000 senators, and another senate of 2,000 members had been established in the Eastern Empire.

Initially, the magistrates played the largest role in governing Rome, but as the Senate's influence grew, it virtually controlled the country in the second and first century BCE. Officially, it was not a legislative body, since senators were only allowed to propose laws, which had to be ratified by an assembly. However, the Senate could issue decrees that, at least temporarily, had the same effect. The Senate was also in charge of the budget, religious matters, and foreign affairs. Senators would compete for prestigious positions in the government, employing a slave known as a *nomenclator* who would constantly accompany them and remind them of the names of each person they encountered, so they would never offend a potential ally. Ambitious politicians would also spend large sums of money on their political campaigns and, at times, gain an advantage through bribery.

In the later days of the Republic, the Senate came to be dominated by members of certain families, so that a man could effectively inherit a place in the Senate if he had the right family connections, and even men from previously unrepresented families tended to be extremely wealthy. The situation eventually divided the Senate into two factions: the *optimates* supported a Senate dominated by the aristocracy, while the *populares* fought for reforms that would better serve the interests of everyday citizens. Such debates became unimportant after the Senate officially empowered the emperor Augustus and lost much of its previous power, as the emperor could now appoint senators, remove them from office, and veto any action that the Senate took.

Nevertheless, the Senate in the Roman Empire still played a significant role in the government. It retained official authority over the provinces and the state budget, and it could now pass new laws, as long as the emperor approved. The Senate remained a prestigious institution, filled with men from prominent families, so an emperor would be ill-advised to entirely ignore its wishes or openly flout its judgments. If there was an issue that an emperor did not want to deal with, he could place it in the hands of the Senate and allow its members to settle the matter. Finally, in some cases, the Senate could function as a court, trying high officials for offenses like alleged extortion.

Although the Senate could legally convene in any place, it normally met in a building called the Curia, which contained rows of benches arranged in a semicircle where senators could sit anywhere they wished, though the seats in front were usually reserved for former magistrates. One scholar has estimated that the building could not have comfortably held more than 300 people, even though there were many more senators than that. However, many of the senators, who served for life, were extremely elderly and rarely if ever attended; others might be working in the provinces; and some could choose not to attend if they had no interest in the affairs at hand. As a result, the number of attending senators on a given day could be as low as fifty. There were several doors that were kept open so that spectators could stand and observe the proceedings, and a large statue of winged Victory, placed there by Augustus, occupied a prominent position.

After a priest called an *augur* studied some feeding chickens and discerned no signs of divine unhappiness, the business of the Senate would begin. Speeches on a given issue were generally limited to a certain time, determined by a water clock; then, when

The *Ara Pacis Augustae*, or Altar of the Augustan Peace, was commissioned by the emperor Augustus in 9 BCE. This detail from its carving shows Roman senators participating in the dedication ceremony for the altar. (Emi Cristea/ Dreamstime.com)

a matter was ready to be voted on, senators indicated their approval or disapproval by moving either to the left or to the right. Sometimes, one crowd would be visibly larger than the other, but there were cases when the bodies on each side had to be counted to determine the Senate's decision. Sessions could last for dawn to dusk, so that service in the Senate could at times be exhausting; however, it was the normal habit to have no meetings during the months of September and October, unless some issue required immediate attention.

It was undoubtedly more rewarding to serve as a senator during the Republic, as illustrated by the life of one famous senator, Cato the Elder (234–149 BCE), so designated because his great-grandson with the same name, Cato the Younger (95–46 BCE), also served as a senator. At an early age, Cato the Elder impressed veteran politicians with his skillful speeches in court and unassuming habits that contrasted sharply with the profligate habits of other aristocrats; accordingly, he was able to obtain several administrative positions, including military tribune, quaestor, aedile, and governor of Sardinia. Later, he served as consul and as censor. In these roles and as a senator, Cato opposed the excessive spending of the general Scipio Africanus the Elder (236–183 BCE), raised taxes on luxury goods, and most famously, successfully argued that Rome must defeat the North African state of Carthage, insisting in speech after speech in the Senate that "*Carthago delenda est*," or "Carthage must be destroyed." Another famous senator, Cicero (106–43 BCE), employed his oratorical and political skills to thwart the efforts of a would-be dictator named Catiline (108–62 BCE); unfortunately, he was less successful in opposing the future emperor Augustus, who ordered his execution.

Their achievements can be contrasted with those of a later senator, Tacitus (ca. 56–117 CE), who served during the first century of the Empire. Like Cato the Elder, he gained a strong reputation as a legal orator and advanced to a number of administrative positions; however, despite his delivery of a highly praised speech at the funeral of the general Verginius Rufus (15–97 CE), he apparently had little effect on the policies of the imperial government. He then began to focus his energies on writing

A LESSON FOR LEGISLATORS

The late U.S. senator Robert Byrd was intensely interested in the Roman Senate, since he thought that their actions in the last days of the Roman Republic could teach his colleagues a valuable lesson. Specifically, in fourteen speeches in 1993, he argued that "when the Roman Senate gave up its control of the purse strings," or the budget, "it gave away its power to check the executive. . . and the Roman Republic fell." On those grounds, he persuaded the Senate that a proposed constitutional amendment to give the president a line-item veto would make the office too powerful. Byrd's speeches were later published as a book.

A ROMAN SENATOR REBORN

Reading about the Roman Senate during the days of Cicero and Cato, historians may have wondered what a senator from the era would have thought about Rome's later history. Nineteenth-century writer Mary Shelley, author of *Frankenstein* (1818), imagined such an individual visiting the modern world in an unfinished story, "Valerius: The Reanimated Roman," probably written in 1819 though not published until 1976. Her hero was a man from a prominent family who served both as senator and consul, at a time when "the Senate appeared an assembly of demigods," though he declines to describe his experiences, focusing on his reactions to Rome's decline into tyranny and the "superstition" of Christianity.

histories that attributed many of Rome's problems to the damaging effects of political dynasties; presumably, he hoped that his writings might have more of an impact than his actions as a senator and administrator. Another senator, Lucianus (ca. third century CE), sought to influence his country in a different way by attempting to overthrow the emperor Decius (ca. 201–251 CE) while he was away from Rome battling the Goths and make himself the new emperor; ironically, he was defeated by another senator then serving as consul, Valerian (ca. 200–264 CE), who did manage to become Rome's emperor, though he lost his position when he was humiliatingly captured by the Persians.

Whether they had great power or little power, Roman senators remained admired members of their society, and if they could avoid making enemies, they might enjoy long and prosperous careers, engaging in deliberations and occasionally working as administrators. And their dignified service has been an inspiration to many later legislators, like those in Great Britain and the United States, who were able to establish and maintain more successful democracies.

Further Reading

Byrd, Robert C. 1995. *The Senate of the Roman Republic: Addresses on the History of Roman Constitutionalism.* Washington, DC: Government Printing Office.

Everitt, Anthony. 2003. *Cicero: The Life and Times of Rome's Greatest Politician.* New York: Random House.

Hildinger, Erik. 2002. *Swords against the Senate: The Rise of the Roman Army and the Fall of the Republic.* Cambridge, MA: Da Capo Press.

Lintott, Andrew. 1999. *The Constitution of the Roman Republic.* Oxford and New York: Oxford University Press.

Mousourakis, George. 2003. *The Historical and Institutional Context of Roman Law.* Burlington, VT: Ashgate/Dartmouth.

Várhelyi, Zsuzsanna. 2010. *The Religion of Senators in the Roman Empire: Power and the Beyond.* Cambridge and New York: Cambridge University Press.

Document

From Aulus Gellius. C. 170 CE. *The Attic Nights of Aulus Gellius.* Volume I. Translated by John C. Rolfe. 1927. Cambridge and London: Loeb Classical Library.

In his Attic Nights, *Aulus Gellius (ca. 125–180 CE) provides this charming anecdote of a son who accompanies his father to the Senate and cleverly lies to his mother about what the senators were discussing, inspiring a change in the Senate's policy regarding senators and their sons.*

It was formerly the custom at Rome for senators to enter the House with their sons under age. In those days, when a matter of considerable importance had been discussed and was postponed to the following day, it was voted that no one should mention the subject of the debate until the matter was decided. The mother of the young Papirius, who had been in the House with his father, asked her son what the Fathers had taken up in the senate. The boy replied that it was a secret and that he could not tell. The woman became all the more eager to hear about it; the secrecy of the matter and the boys' silence piqued her curiosity; she therefore questioned him more pressingly and urgently. Then the boy, because of his mother's insistence, resorted to a witty and amusing falsehood. He said that the senate had discussed the question whether it seemed more expedient, and to the advantage of the State, for one man to have two wives or one woman to have two husbands. On hearing this, she is panic-stricken, rushed excitedly from the house, and carries the news to the other matrons. Next day a crowd of matrons came to the senate, imploring with tears and entreaties that one woman might have two husbands rather than one man two wives. The senators, as they entered the House, were wondering at this strange madness of the women and the meaning of such a demand, when young Papirius, stepping forward to the middle of the House, told in detail what his mother had insisted on hearing, what he himself had said to her, in fact, the whole story exactly as it had happened. The senate paid homage to the boy's cleverness and loyalty, but voted that thereafter boys should not enter the House with their fathers, save only this Papirius; and the boy was henceforth honoured with the surname Praetextatus, because of his discretion in keeping silent and in speaking, while he was still young enough to wear the purple-bordered gown.

Slaves

All early civilizations had slaves, but they were undoubtedly most numerous in ancient Rome, and most significant to the functioning of their economy and society; indeed, by one estimate, almost half of the population of Rome consisted of slaves. This was in large part a consequence of the Romans' success in regularly expanding their empire, since the standard result of each conquest was a new population of slaves, both prisoners of war and other captured citizens. Thus, for example, taking over Greece and Egypt brought many highly educated slaves to Rome, while the addition of Gaul (modern France) provided the Empire with a vast supply of unskilled laborers. Some pirates would attack cities on the coast and kidnap young people to sell as slaves, but the practice ended when the general Pompey (106–48 BCE) suppressed piracy in the first century BCE. All of the children of slaves also became slaves as well, further increasing their population. At first, Roman slaves were treated very harshly, but fears of slave revolts, and their increasingly integration into Roman life, eventually provided most of them with somewhat better lives.

Once they had been brought to Rome, groups of slaves might be purchased by the government, or individual slaves would be brought to one of the large slave bazaars in the city to be sold to private owners at an auction. Signs would list all the slaves available that day, specifying their gender, approximate age, nationality, and particular talents (such as an ability to read and write). Slaves were displayed to potential buyers while almost naked, perhaps wearing only loincloths, and customers were allowed to feel their muscles, examine their teeth, or interrogate them to determine how well they spoke Latin. Then, the ringing of a bell would announce the start of the auction: many slaves could be purchased for the equivalent of a few hundred U.S. dollars or less, but slaves with valuable assets—like a very attractive young boy or an experienced physician—might cost as much as $4,000.

Once in the possession of citizens or the government, slaves would typically perform a wide variety of tasks; indeed, the only job they were forbidden to perform was serving in the military, as the Romans did not wish to train potentially rebellious slaves to fight. The least fortunate slaves were assigned to work in the mines, where the hazardous conditions routinely led to early deaths. Others served at farms, helping to plow the soil, harvest the crops, and stomp grapes to make wine, and slaves labored in factories that produced pots, tools, and weapons. Most of the gladiators and prostitutes were slaves, as were virtually all household servants and the attendants at baths and other public facilities. Within wealthy households, numerous slaves specialized in particular jobs like cooking meat, baking bread, or styling the matron's hair. The advantage these slaves enjoyed is that, in households filled with slaves, they were only required to perform their assigned duties, which could leave them with a great deal of free time; thus, after the slave baker had finished baking the loaves needed for the day's meals, he could relax for the rest of the day. In poorer households, though, with only a few slaves, each one might have to work long hours.

The educated slaves were given more prestigious tasks. They might work as doctors, scribes, or architects, and slaves were entirely in charge of important government agencies like the Archives and the Mint, though there was some minimal supervision. In businesses, slaves were usually the clerks, bookkeepers, and cashiers, and they often managed the banks and estates owned by wealthy men, who freely entrusted them with important responsibilities. In the homes, qualified slaves might help manage the family budget or teach the children, and if a young slave seemed unusually bright, a slave might be assigned to teach him as well.

Although educated slaves who were valued for their skills might enjoy comfortable lives, many slaves had to endure a miserable existence. Those laboring in mines or factories might be physically abused, as their overseers had no incentive to be gentle while making sure that they worked hard; in the homes, however, injured slaves could not be easily replaced, so violent punishments were generally avoided. Still, it was common for owners to have slaves whipped for even minor matters, like failing to deliver a pot of hot water quickly enough, and large homes might have their own little dungeons to imprison misbehaving slaves. And, on a few occasions, angry masters were known to kill their slaves, which was long one of their rights; there are notorious cases of Romans having unsatisfactory slaves eaten by fish or ants. Even if such brutalities did not occur, however, all household slaves, both females and males, were required to submit to the sexual demands of their owners, and if slaves were ever disobedient, unhappy owners could brand them—perhaps burning "thief" on their foreheads—or could sell them to work in a mine. Agricultural slaves might be kept in chains or branded simply to prevent them from escaping.

In the second century BCE, as there were more and more slaves experiencing such indignities, it is hardly surprising that there were major slave revolts.

In 139 BCE, a slave from Syria named Eunus (died 132 BCE) launched a rebellion in Sicily that raged for eight years, and in 73 BCE, an enslaved gladiator, Spartacus (ca. 109–71 BCE), actually threatened Rome with an army of slaves until he was decisively defeated two years later. Gradually, thoughtful Romans realized that the long-term solution to this problem was to provide better treatment for slaves; thus, a series of laws were implemented to improve the treatment of slaves. The emperor Claudius (10 BCE–54 CE) ordered that if slaves became ill and their masters abandoned them, they should be freed, and his successor Nero (37–68 CE) decreed that officials should investigate when slaves complain about their treatment. Later, Domitian (51–96 CE) made it against the law to castrate male slaves, while Hadrian (68–138 CE) forbid the

CINEMATIC SLAVES

The most famous slave rebellion in ancient Rome, led by Spartacus, has inspired a number of films and television series, including Stanley Kubrick's *Spartacus* (1960), starring Kirk Douglas and Laurence Olivier, and the cable series *Spartacus: Blood and Sand* (2010–2013). America's greatest slave revolt, led by Nat Turner in 1831, has attracted less attention, perhaps because much about this slave and his actions is still poorly understood; however, a documentary that aired as part of the series *Independent Lens*, called *Nat Turner: A Troublesome Property* (2004), combined interviews with experts and fictionalized scenes to explore this event and its ramifications.

A TWENTIETH-CENTURY SLAVE

The very successful Broadway musical written by Stephen Sondheim, *A Funny Thing Happened on the Way to the Forum* (1963), is based on the comedies of the Roman playwright Plautus (254–184 BCE), with a particularly close resemblance to *Pseudolus*, since it borrows the lead character of the clever slave Pseudolus. While it follows other conventions of Roman comedy, Sondheim's musical has one very modern twist: from the very start of the play, Pseudolus is portrayed as desperately anxious to become free, and he gains his freedom as the play's happy ending. Plautus's Pseudolus, in contrast, was perfectly content to remain a slave.

selling of slaves to become gladiators or prostitutes, and declared that owners could not kill their slaves without judicial consent. Eventually, under Antoninus Pius (86–161 CE), a master who ordered the death of a slave could be charged with murder.

It also became more common for owners to free their most esteemed slaves through a process of manumission, though there were legal limits on the number of slaves that they could free upon their deaths, a provision no doubt created to protect the interests of heirs. If slaves performing administrative duties for the government were capable, they would usually be granted their freedom by the age of thirty-five, though they retained their positions as salaried employees. Other slaves were allowed to earn some money so they could eventually purchase their own freedom.

Former slaves might be regarded as inferior to other Romans, but they could eventually become full Roman citizens; indeed, a few of them became quite wealthy. Thus, Petronius (died 66 CE), author of the *Satyricon*, made his bumptious billionaire Trimalchio a former slave. An example from real life is a slave named Musicus Scurranus (ca. first century CE) who worked for the government of the province of Gaul under the emperor Tiberius (42 BCE–37 CE); after his death during a visit to Rome, his tombstone reveals that he had been accompanied by an entourage of sixteen of his own slaves, including a doctor and two cooks. Female slaves had fewer opportunities to prosper, but they could rise to prominent positions if they were favored by wealthy and powerful men. The most prominent example is Caenis (died ca. 74 CE), formerly the slave of Claudius's mother Antonia Minor (36 BCE–37 CE), who became the mistress of the emperor Vespasian (17–79 CE) and, after the death of his wife, emerged as his public companion, effectively serving as his second wife.

All things considered, Roman slaves might have considered themselves lucky, in comparison to the slaves of other ancient civilizations, especially since they were unusually likely to gain their freedom. In fact, one scholar estimates that in the early centuries of the Roman Empire, more than eighty percent of the city's population may have consisted of former slaves. Still, many of the Roman slaves suffered greatly, and no one could have really enjoyed having the status of being someone's property. Only in the centuries to come, however, would people begin to understand the fundamental injustice of this institution.

Further Reading

Bradley, Keith. 1994. *Slavery and Society at Rome*. Cambridge and New York: Cambridge University Press.

Fitzgerald, William. 2000. *Slavery and the Roman Literary Imagination*. Cambridge and New York: Cambridge University Press.

George, Michele, editor. 2013. *Roman Slavery and Roman Material Culture*. Toronto: University of Toronto Press.

Joshel, Sandra R. 2010. *Slavery in the Roman World*. Cambridge and New York: Cambridge University Press.

Launaro, Alessandro. 2011. *Peasants and Slaves: The Rural Population of Roman Italy (200 BC to AD 100)*. Cambridge and New York: Cambridge University Press.

Stewart, Roberta. 2012. *Plautus and Roman Slavery*. Malden, MA: Wiley-Blackwell.

Document

From Plautus. *The Comedies of Plautus: Literally Translated into English, with Notes*. Volume 2. Translated by Henry Thomas Riley. 1912. London: George Bell and Sons.

The clever slave was a stock character in Roman comedy, as well as in Greek comedy. In this passage from the play Mostellaria, *or* The Haunted House, *written sometime around 200 BCE, the Roman playwright Plautus (ca. 254–184 BCE) presents the slave Tranio as first fearful of being flogged if his master Theuropides, after his unexpected return, discovers that his son Philolaches has been having an extended party in his house. But he quickly devises a plan to save himself and Philolaches: he will tell the father that the house is haunted, so he cannot enter.*

[Tranio:] (to himself). Supreme Jove, with all his might and resources, is seeking for me and Philolaches, my master's son, to be undone. Our hopes are destroyed; nowhere is there any hold for courage; not even Salvation now could save us if she wished. Such an immense mountain of woe have I just now seen at the harbour: my master has arrived from abroad; Tranio is undone! (To the Audience.)

Is there any person who'd like to make gain of a little money, who could this day endure to take my place in being tortured? Where are those fellows hardened to a flogging, the wearers-out of iron chains, or those, who, for the consideration of three didrachms, would get beneath besieging towers where some are in the way of having their bodies pierced with fifteen spears? I'll give a talent to that man who shall be the first to run to the cross for me; but on condition that twice his feet, twice his arms, are fastened there. When that shall have been done, then ask the money down of me. But am I not a wretched fellow, not at full speed to be running home?

[Philolaches:] Here come the provisions; see, here's Tranio; he's come back from the harbour.

[Tranio:] (running), Philolaches!

[Philolaches:] What's the matter?. . .

[Tranio:] Your father's here.

[Philolaches:] What is it I hear of you?

[Tranio:] We are finished up. Your father's come, I say. . .

[Philolaches:] What am I to do? My father will, just now, be coming and unfortunately finding me amid drunken carousals, and the house full of revellers and women. It's a shocking bad job, to be digging a well at the last moment, just when thirst has gained possession of your throat; just as I, on the arrival of my father, wretch that I am, am now enquiring what I am to do. . . .

[Tranio:] Be of good courage; I'll cleverly find a remedy for this alarm.

[Philolaches:] I'm utterly ruined!

[Tranio:] Do hold your tongue; I'll think of something by means of which to alleviate this for you. Are you satisfied, if on his arrival I shall so manage your father, not only that he shall not enter, but even that he shall run away to a distance from the house? Do you only be off from here in-doors, and remove these things from here with all haste. . . .

[Philolaches and his friend go inside the house.]

[Tranio:] (to himself). It matters not a feather whether a patron or a dependant is the nearest at hand for that man who has got no courage in his breast. For to every man, whether very good or very bad, even at a moment's notice, it is easy to act with craft; but this must be looked to, this is the duty of a prudent man, that what has been planned and done in craftiness, may all come about smoothly and without mishap; so that he may not have to put up with anything by reason of which he might be loth to live; just as I shall manage, that, from the confusion which we shall here create, all shall really go on smoothly and tranquilly, and not produce us any inconvenience in the results. . . .

[Theuropides arrives, and Tranio tells him to stop knocking on the door and move away.]

[Tranio:] Don't you touch the house. Touch you the ground as well. . . .

[Theuropides:] I'faith, prithee, do speak out now.

[Tranio:] Because it is now seven months that not a person has set foot within this house, and since we once for all left it.

[Theuropides:] Tell me, why so?

[Tranio:] Just look around, whether there's any person to overhear our discourse.

[Tranio:] (looking around). All's quite safe.

[Tranio:] Look around once more.

[Theuropides:] (looking around). There's nobody; now then, speak out.

[Tranio:] (in a loud whisper). The house has been guilty of a capital offence.

[Theuropides:] I don't understand you.

[Tranio:] A crime, I tell you, has been committed there a long while ago, one of olden time and ancient date.

[Theuropides:] Of ancient date?

[Tranio:] 'Tis but recently, in fact, that we've discovered this deed.

[Theuropides:] What is this crime, or who committed it? Tell me.

[Tranio:] A host slew his guest, seized with his hand; he, I fancy, who sold you the house.

[Theuropides:] Slew him?

[Tranio:] And robbed this guest of his gold, and buried this guest there in the house, on the spot.

[So, Tranio goes on to explain, the house is now haunted and must be avoided at all costs.]

Soldiers

Arguably, the greatest achievement of ancient Rome was its army, which conquered vast territories in Europe, Africa, and Asia and maintained firm control over its conquests for centuries. Its soldiers were well trained, superbly equipped, and meticulously organized to function effectively as a military force, and a few skillful fighters of lowly origins were able to advance to prominent positions in the Empire, so the profession provided an element of social mobility within an often rigid class structure. Some of the most renowned Roman leaders, in fact, were former soldiers who had achieved and held on to power with the support of their comrades.

In the days of the Roman Republic, the government often managed huge armies, but their soldiers were temporary recruits who fought a few campaigns and returned to civilian life. After the emperor Augustus (63 BCE–14 CE) established Rome's first permanent army, however, being a soldier became a permanent career, since recruits were generally required to serve up to twenty-five years. Despite the length of service and other restrictions on their lives, such as a ban on getting married (repealed in 197 CE), many young men eagerly volunteered for military service because the pay, which could take the form of money, rations, or a combination of the two, was usually quite generous. Soldiers were also required to place some of their wages in a savings account to provide them with a pension. One attractive payment to soldiers, an allotment of the valuable spice salt, was called the *salarium*, which inspired the modern term "salary." In addition, soldiers were entitled to get a portion of the plunder taken during campaigns; generals might give their soldiers a cash bonus after a significant victory; and retiring soldiers might receive a piece of land. Soldiers could also expect to be well fed: even while on the march, soldiers carried with them an ample supply of biscuits, cheese, bacon, and wine, and camps provided soldiers with expensive cooked meats like beef and mutton as well as seafood, poultry, eggs, and fresh fruit and vegetables. Men in the provinces might also seek a career as a soldier because they could become full Roman citizens after they retired.

To become a soldier, a man had to be a free citizen, in good physical condition, and at least five feet eight inches in height. The official age limit was twenty years, but this requirement was not always enforced; tombstones in Roman Britain, for example, suggest that some of the soldiers were only fourteen years old when they joined the army. Prospective soldiers were trained in many ways, learning how to march in parades as well as setting up a camp, riding a

horse, and swimming. They were regularly required to run about eighteen miles in five hours while wearing armor, to build up their strength and stamina, and they had to keep their armor and weapons clean. Needless to say, though, most of their time was spent honing their fighting skills, which is generally how they spent their mornings. They would begin practicing with wooden swords before progressing to actual javelins and short swords called *gladii*, though a covering was placed on their points to prevent major wounds. They were taught how to protect themselves with a shield, either a small round shield called a *parma* or a larger curved shield that later became standard equipment. Early Roman soldiers had to purchase and use their own armor and weapons, but the army later set up workshops in forts to produce massive amounts of armor, helmets, and weapons, though the quality of the workmanship was not always high. Roman soldiers were also trained in battle tactics. Initially, the Romans relied on the formation known as the phalanx, borrowed from Greek soldiers, in which soldiers holding shields marched

This wall carving from Italy's Campania region shows a row of Roman legionnaires, wearing their distinctive helmets and armor. The soldiers were called legionnaires because the Roman army was organized into divisions called legions, with about 5,600 to 6,000 men per legion. (DEA/A. Dagli Orti/DeAgostini/Getty Images)

into battle next to each other in rows, but because this approach proved ineffective in battling against the barbarians of Gaul, the army adopted the approach of first attacking the enemy forces from a distance with javelins, then sending small groups of soldiers into battle who could move around freely and engage opponents at close range.

The Roman army was organized into legions, which usually had about 5,600 to 6,000 men, which is why the soldiers were called legionnaires. While officials called consuls led the entire army, legions were controlled by lesser officials—tribunes, praetors,

FIGHTING WITH OR AGAINST CAESAR

Even since Julius Caesar (100–44 BCE) published his account of *The Gallic Wars*, commentators have been fascinated by the military strategies he employed, and these have naturally become the subject of logistics games. The most recent of these is a game for personal computers called *Hegemony Rome: The Rise of Caesar*, released in 2014. Its graphics enable players to not only reenact Caesar's classic battles but also engage in the other necessary tasks of warfare, like building forts and bridges. Players also have the option of rewriting history by taking command of the Gauls and defeating the Roman armies.

EQUIPMENT FOR ROMAN SOLDIERS

Since the image of the Roman soldier, wearing armor and holding his spear and shield, is so familiar today, innumerable people have endeavored to recreate his equipment, in various ways. One group is dedicated to making these items precisely as the Romans made them, based on the best available evidence. Other companies freely use modern techniques and materials to make weapons and armor that look exactly like their ancient equivalents. Finally, for those who do not wish to spend money on these expensive purchases, there are Web sites that provide advice for making cheap homemade alternatives, such as using aluminum roof flashing (thin material to prevent leaks) to construct lightweight armor.

or legates. Each legion was divided into ten cohorts, which were in turn divided into groups of 100, termed *centuriae*, under the command of a veteran soldier, the centurion. Later, it was deemed more effective to limit the size of a *centuriae* to eighty men. The centurion could be distinguished from the soldiers he commanded because he was usually on horseback and carried a wooden staff to beat soldiers who were not living up to his standards. Each legion also had a small force about 120 men on horseback who only did advance scouting work and carried messages, as well as other professionals who were also not required to fight; these included clerks, doctors, veterinarians, carpenters, masons, trumpeters, weapon makers, and priests who interpreted the will of the gods called *haruspices*.

In addition to its standing army, Rome also recruited auxiliary troops, or *auxilia*, from its provinces; these were valued because they often had fighting skills that the Romans did normally not employ; for example, Crete provided experienced archers, while soldiers from the Balearic Islands off the coast of Spain were experts in using slings. The auxiliary units were generally organized in the same manner as the regular army, though they might be commanded by a local chieftain instead of a Roman, and eventually the dividing lines between the two forces were blurred, as foreigners might join the legion while Romans would become part of the *auxilia*.

While fighting was the Roman soldiers' primary responsibility, they were also kept busy when they were not needed on the battlefield. About three times a month, they would be forced to make their standard eighteen-mile march, to keep in shape, and along with mock combat, they would engage in other forms of exercise; one unusual activity, the *testudo*, involved soldiers jumping up on each other's heads, a useful way to get over an enemy's wall. Soldiers might also be drafted to do nonmilitary tasks, like building or repairing roads, baking bricks for camp buildings, or moving large stones to construct an outdoor amphitheater.

A special section of the Roman army, the Praetorian Guard, was permanently stationed in Rome under the direct control of the emperor. Since its major responsibility was protecting the emperor, the loyalty of the soldiers was very important, so they were mostly recruited from Italy, although other legionnaires might come from anywhere in the Empire. They also earned three times as much as other Roman soldiers, and while they theoretically answered to the emperor, they could also turn against him, which sealed the fate of the Roman emperor Nero (37–68 CE). At the height of their power, in 193 CE, they murdered the emperor they had installed, Pertinax (126–193 CE), and offered the position to the man who paid them the largest sum of money. After the Senate ordered the execution of the winner, Didius Julianus (ca. 137–193 CE), the next emperor, Septimus Severus (145–211 CE), unsurprisingly dissolved the Praetorian Guard and recruited new soldiers to protect him.

Ancient Rome also had a navy, though it was regarded as less important and less prestigious than its army; for that reason, it was considered an auxiliary force, and it primarily attracted only the very poorest Romans and many foreigners. While a captain, called a *trierarch*, was nominally in charge of each ship, military actions were led by a centurion, typically in command of 50 soldiers and about 150 oarsmen (who might also be called upon to fight if an enemy vessel was boarded). Since ships were typically kept anchored in ports during the winter, sailors had time for other pursuits and in some cases contrived to earn enough money to purchase a slave.

As the Roman Empire declined, its army tried to adjust to the challenge of barbarian armies by relying more on archers and soldiers on horseback, but they were ultimately unable to prevent its complete collapse in 476 CE. Still, just as the Roman soldiers had adapted technologies and techniques from foreign soldiers, the opponents of Rome had also learned much from the Roman army, and scholars continue to research its history, seeking new clues as to why it was such an effective fighting force.

Further Reading

Erdkamp, Paul, editor. 2007. *A Companion to the Roman Army*. Malden, MA, and Oxford: Blackwell.

Fuhrmann, Christopher J. 2012. *Policing the Roman Empire: Soldiers, Administration, and Public Order*. Oxford and New York: Oxford University Press.

Goldsworthy, Adrian Keith. 1998. *The Roman Army at War: 100 BC-AD 200*. Oxford and New York: Oxford University Press.

Keppie, Lawrence. 1998. *The Making of the Roman Army: From Republic to Empire*. New edition. Norman: University of Oklahoma Press.

Le Bohec, Yann. 1989. *The Imperial Roman Army*. Translated by R. Bate. 1994. London: B.T. Batsford.

Southern, Pat. 2006. *The Roman Army: A Social and Institutional History*. Oxford and New York: Oxford University Press.

Documents

From Julius Caesar. C. 45 BCE. *Caesar's Commentaries on the Gallic and Civil Wars: With the Supplementary Books Attributed to Hirtius, Including the Alexandrian, African, and Spanish Wars*. Translated by William A. McDevitte and W. S. Bohn. 1869. New York: Harper and Brothers.

In Book I of Commentarii de Bello Gallico, *or* The Gallic Wars, *Julius Caesar (100–44 BCE) describes one of his early battles with the Gauls, providing a vivid picture of the fighting strategies and weapons of Roman soldiers.*

Chapter XXIV. Caesar, when he observes this, draws off his forces to the next hill, and sent the cavalry to sustain the attack of the enemy. He himself meanwhile, drew up on the middle of the hill a triple line of his four veteran legions in such a manner, that he placed above him on the very summit the two legions, which he had lately levied in Hither Gaul, and all the auxiliaries; and he ordered that the whole mountain should be covered with men, and that meanwhile the baggage [the soldiers' equipment] should be brought together into one place, and the position be protected by those who were posted in the upper line. The Helvetii [a Gallic tribe] having followed with all their wagons, collected their baggage into one place: they themselves, after having repulsed our cavalry and formed a phalanx, advanced up to our front line in very close order.

Chap. XXV. Caesar, having removed out of sight first his own horse, then those of all, that he might make the danger of all equal, and do away with the hope of flight, after encouraging his men, joined battle. His soldiers hurling their javelins from the higher ground, easily broke the enemy's phalanx. That being dispersed, they made a charge on them with drawn swords. It was a great hinderance to the Gauls in fighting, that, when several of their bucklers had been by one stroke of the [Roman] javelins pierced through and pinned fast together, as the point of the iron had bent itself, they could neither pluck it out, nor, with their left hand entangled, fight with sufficient case; so that many, after having long tossed their arm about, chose rather to cast away the buckler from their hand, and to fight with their person unprotected. At length, worn out with wounds, they began to give way, and, as there was in the neighborhood a mountain about a mile off, to betake themselves thither. When the mountain had been gained, and our men were advancing up, the Boii and Tulingi [other Gallic tribes], who with about 15,000 men closed the enemy's line of march and served as a guard to their rear, having assailed our men on the exposed flank as they advanced [prepared] to surround them; upon seeing which, the Helvetii who had betaken themselves to the mountain, began to press on again and renew the battle. The Romans having faced about, advanced to the attack in two divisions; the first and second line, to withstand those who had been defeated and driven off the field; the third to receive those who were just arriving.

Chap. XXVI. Thus, was the contest long and vigorously carried on with doubtful success. When they could no longer withstand the attacks of our men, the one division, as they had begun to do, betook themselves to the mountain; the other repaired to their baggage and wagons. For during the whole of this battle, although the fight lasted from the seventh hour [around 12 noon to 1 PM] to eventide, no one could see an enemy with his back turned. The fight was carried on also at the baggage till late in the night, for they had set wagons in the way as a rampart, and from the higher ground kept throwing weapons upon our men, as they came on, and some from between the wagons and the wheels kept darting their lances and javelins from beneath, and wounding our men. After the fight had lasted some time, our men gained possession of their baggage and camp.

From Lucan. C. 65 CE. *The Pharsalia of Lucan, Literally Translated into English Prose.* Translated by Henry Thomas Riley. 1853. London: Henry G. Bohn.

In this passage from the seventh book of his Bellum Civile, *better known as* Pharsalia, *the poet Lucan (39–65 CE) describes the beginning of the battle of Pharsalia and eloquently conveys the experiences of Roman soldiers in battle and the violence of their warfare.*

Darts innumerable are scattered abroad with various intents. Some wish for wounds, some to fix the javelins in the earth, and to keep their hands in purity. Chance hurries everything on, and uncertain Fortune makes those guilty, whom she chooses. But how small a part of the slaughter is perpetrated with javelin and flying weapons! For civil hatred the sword alone suffices, and guides right hands to Roman vitals. The ranks of Pompey, densely disposed in deep bodies, joined their arms, their shields closed together in a line; and, hardly able to find room for moving their right hands and their darts, they stood close, and, wedged together, kept their swords sheathed.

With headlong course the furious troops of Caesar are impelled against the dense masses, and, through arms, through the foe do they seek a passage. Where the twisted coat of mail presents its links, and the breast, beneath a safe covering, lies concealed, even here do they reach the entrails, and amid so many arms it is the vitals which each one pierces. Civil war does the one army suffer, the other wage; on the one hand the sword stands chilled, on Caesar's side every guilty weapon waxes hot. Nor is Fortune long, overthrowing the weight of destinies so vast, in sweeping away the mighty ruins, fate rushing on.

When first the cavalry of Pompey extended his wings over the whole plain, and poured them forth along the extremities of the battle, the light-armed soldiers, scattered along the exterior of the maniples, followed, and sent forth their ruthless bands against the foe. There, each nation is mingling in the combat with weapons its own; Roman blood is sought by all. On the one side arrows, on the other torches and stones are flying, and plummets, melting in the tract of air and liquefied with their heated masses. Then do both Ituraeans, and Medians, and Arabians, a multitude threatening with loosened bow, never aim their arrows, but the air alone is sought which impends over the plain; thence fall various deaths. But with no criminality of guilt do they stain the foreign steel; around the javelins stands collected all the guiltiness. With weapons the heaven is concealed, and a night, wrought by the darts, hovers over the fields.

Then did Caesar, fearing lest his front rank might be shaken by the onset, keep in reserve some cohorts in an oblique position behind the standards and on the sides of his line, whither the enemy, scattered about, was betaking himself, he suddenly sent forth a column, his *own* wings unmoved. Unmindful of the fight, and to be feared by reason of no sense of shame, they openly took to flight; not well *was* civil warfare ever entrusted to barbarian troops. As soon as the charger, his breast pierced with the weapon, trod upon the limbs of the rider hurled upon his head, each horseman fled from the field, and, crowded together, turning bridle, the youths rushed on upon their own ranks. Then did the carnage lose *all* bounds, and it was no battle that ensued, but on the one hand with their throats, on the other with the sword, the war was waged; nor was the one army able to lay low as many as were able to perish on the other side.

Would that, Pharsalia, for thy plains that blood which barbarian breasts pour forth would suffice: that the streams might be changed by no other gore; that this throng might for thee cover whole fields with bones; or if thou dost prefer to be glutted with Roman blood, spare the others, I entreat; let the Galatians and Syrians live, the Cappadocians and the Gauls, and the Iberians from the extremity of the world, the Armenians and the Cilicians; for after the civil wars these will form the Roman people. Once commenced, the panic reaches all, and to the Fates is an impulse given in favour of Caesar.

They had *now* come to the strength of Magnus and the mid ranks. The war, which in its wandering course, had strayed over whole fields, here paused, and the fortune of Caesar delayed. On this spot no youths collected by the aid of kings are waging the war, and no alien hands wield the sword; this spot contains their brothers, this spot their fathers. Here *is* frenzy, here frantic rage; here, Caesar, are thy crimes. My soul, fly from this portion of the warfare, and leave it to the shades of night, and, myself the Poet of woes so great, let no age learn how great is the license in civil warfare. Perish rather these tears, and perish *those* complaints. Whatever, Rome, in this battle thou hast done, upon it I will be silent.

Tutors and Teachers

In the early days of the Roman Republic, education was informal and limited: male children would be taught by their fathers how to read, write, and fight with weapons, and they would go with their fathers to public events to absorb proper patterns of behavior; girls mastered household skills under the tutelage of their mothers but were not otherwise educated. As they approached adulthood, the sons of wealthy men might become the apprentice of a major politician, while poor youths would learn a trade from their father or another artisan. However, Roman education was fundamentally transformed after the conquest of Greece, as educated Greek slaves were brought to Rome to work as tutors; now, boys were expected to learn two languages, Greek and Latin, and their curriculum might include arithmetic and literature. Girls were commonly educated along with the boys from the ages of five to eleven, although only males received additional education, usually focused on the art of rhetoric.

Children would be educated in two ways. If their parents could afford it, they would be privately tutored at home, usually by an educated slave called a *paedagogus*. These figures could readily oversee young boys and girls, but older children might become rebellious, recognizing that their teacher is a piece of property owned by the family that they have the right to control. Thus, in a play by Plautus (254–184 BCE), *Bacchides*, a wealthy young man named Pistoclerus orders his reluctant tutor Lydus to accompany him to a meeting with a young woman. Rich parents could also hire a qualified free man to come to their house and teach their children, perhaps with better results.

Still, recognizing the value of having children socialize with their peers, even wealthy families might also choose to send their children to a school, though they would retain the services of a *paedagogus* to generally supervise the children and escort them to their classes. A school was also the usual option for ordinary citizens, and although Rome had no public schools, families would strive to find enough money to pay for their children's schooling, since illiteracy was considered socially unacceptable. The quality of these private schools, however, varied wildly, since virtually anyone with a modicum of education could declare himself a teacher, find a suitable room, and open up a school. Needless to say, the wealthy would seek out respected and experienced educators who could command large fees for their services, while the poor might have to settle for any teacher they could afford, even if he was only an unsuccessful shopkeeper who had turned to teaching as his only way to make a living.

Because summers in Rome were deemed too hot for serious study, a Roman school would typically begin its year on September 24, meeting each day from dawn until noon, when there was an extended break; in some cases, classes would resume in the afternoon. Children of all ages would be accepted and could continue attending as long as their fees were paid; each school was normally limited to a maximum of thirty students, all in one room. Sitting among them on a high stool was a single teacher, who was expected to provide students at different levels with productive activities while also maintaining discipline; he was permitted, even expected, to wield his cane to harshly beat any students who misbehaved, though some teachers were criticized for being ill-tempered and overly violent. The corporal punishment could range from a simple blow with a cane to a student being stripped naked and fiercely whipped The curriculum was never fixed, but children would generally first be taught to read and write both Latin and Greek, along with some basic arithmetic, and once those skills were mastered, students would be ask to copy and translate classic literary texts by writers like Homer, Horace (65–8 BCE), and Virgil (70–19 BCE).

Depending upon the quality of the teacher, the physical circumstances of the classroom could range from munificent to wretched. A school for wealthy children might have an anteroom, where the *paedagogi* and other slave attendants might relax and converse while classes are in session. Students would sit at desks and write on papyrus, surrounded by walls covered with maps and paintings of famous events. When it was time to read and copy works of literature, the teacher could offer his students a wide variety of scrolls. In a few of the better schools, there would be a second teacher who specialized in teaching arithmetic, called a *calculator*. A poor school, in contrast, would consist of a small room next to a street, with an open door that offered many distractions; some students might even sit outside under an awning. With no desks, the boys and girls would sit next to each other on the floor or on benches and do their writing on wax tablets, smoothing the wax and starting again when the tablet was filled with letters; the only decorations to suggest a classroom might be a few busts of famous writers. For purposes of copying, a few ragged scrolls would have to be shared by several students. At any time, parents might barge in to loudly berate the teacher for failing to properly educate their children. Some have wondered how such establishments could have functioned as effective schools, but the graffiti found everywhere in Roman ruins suggests that most children actually managed to learn to read and write.

After completing school around the age of eleven, a woman usually received no additional education, though some wealthy girls might have tutors to teach them poetry, dancing, and playing the harp, skills that were thought to make them more attractive as potential wives. Wealthy young men would receive a different sort of higher education under the supervision of a teacher called the *grammaticus*, who would primarily instruct them in Greek and Latin literature, though they might also study mathematics by reading Euclid or learn history from classic texts. Students might be expected to memorize long passages from classic writers and receive some preliminary instruction in the art of making effective speeches.

Rhetoric, though, was the typical focus of the third and final phase of a young man's education, involving a teacher called the *rhetor*. The students would first be taught a rigid, six-part structure to follow in all speeches and would study some illustrative examples; then, they would be asked to write and deliver their own speeches. However, their arguments could not involve current events, but rather had to deal with the actions of historical figures. Thus, a young Roman might urge Alexander the Great to venture into the city of Babylon despite an unfavorable oracle; even the deeds of mythological figures like Agamemnon might be addressed. Students might also engage in mock trials involving hypothetical cases, or asked to debate whether living in a city or living in the country was superior. Purportedly, all of these exercises prepared students to speak effectively in courtroom cases

A ROMAN-STYLE EDUCATION

In ancient Rome, all schools had a single classroom, where students of different ages learned independently while supervised by one teacher. This system was also employed in the early United States, where the "one-room schoolhouse" was standard in small communities with few students and only enough resources to hire one teacher. Even today, some tiny villages far away from other towns educate their children this way. In Mist, Oregon, for example, teacher Joanie Jones typically handles twenty-three children from kindergarten to fifth grade in one room, assisted only by an aide. Interestingly, research suggests that students with this background later score higher on standardized tests than peers from conventional schools.

A LINGERING LANGUAGE

The first subject taught in Roman schools was the Latin language, and this remained an integral part of the European and American curriculum until the twentieth century, when a demand for new languages like Russian and Chinese led many schools to drop their Latin classes. Recently, however, high school Latin classes, though still uncommon, are becoming more popular. Some believe that this is inspired by a desire to perform better on the SAT, since the meanings of vocabulary words can often by deduced by students familiar with Latin roots, while other credit the spells of J. K. Rowling's Harry Potter using Latin words for arousing student interest in the language.

or discussions in the Senate, but even many Romans denounced this sort of teaching as impractical and valueless. Nonetheless, rich parents seeking to advance their sons' careers would pay any price to place them in a prestigious school of rhetoric.

Normally, a Roman man's education would conclude with the *rhetor*, but a few interested youth might pursue some additional instruction; for example, it was not uncommon for wealthy young men to travel to Athens in order to study philosophy. For the most part, though, a man with an interest in such matters would seek a job as a tutor or teacher, since one advantage of these professions is that they provided men with ample time for their own reading and writing. Thus,

it is interesting to note that one of early Christianity's greatest theologians, St. Augustine (354–430 CE), originally earned his living as a renowned teacher of rhetoric. For tutors who were slaves, a common reward was freedom, granted by grateful pupils when they became adults and took charge of the household, and some of the later Roman emperors would exempt teachers from having to perform duties for their community. Rome also pioneered in public education by providing financial support for some schools of rhetoric in Athens and Rome, benefiting both students and instructors. Finally, like all teachers, the tutors and teachers of ancient Rome surely felt a special sense of satisfaction whenever one of their former students excelled in some public sphere, or returned to thank them for their efforts.

Further Reading

Bonner, Stanley. 2012. *Education in Ancient Rome: From the Elder Cato to the Younger Pliny.* London and New York: Routledge.

Joyal, Mark, Iain MacDougall, and John Yardley. 2008. *Greek and Roman Education: A Sourcebook.* London and New York: Routledge.

Laes, Christian. 2011. *Children in the Roman Empire: Outsiders Within.* Cambridge and New York: Cambridge University Press.

Lee Too, Yun, editor. 2001. *Education in Greek and Roman Antiquity.* Leiden, The Netherlands, and Boston: Brill.

Morgan, Teresa. 1996. *Literate Education in the Hellenistic and Roman Worlds.* Cambridge and New York: Cambridge University Press.

Rawson, Beryl. 2003. *Children and Childhood in Roman Italy.* Oxford and New York: Oxford University Press.

Documents

From Aulus Gellius. C. 170 CE. *The Attic Nights of Aulus Gellius.* Volume I. Translated by John C. Rolfe. 1927. Cambridge and London: Loeb Classical Library.

As described in his Attic Nights, *the Roman writer Aulus Gellius (ca. 125–180 CE) once discovered that one renowned teacher was not as well informed as he should have been.*

I inquired at Rome of a certain grammarian who had the highest repute as a teacher, not indeed for the sake of trying or testing him, but rather from an eager desire for knowledge, what *obnoxius* meant and what was the origin and the history of the word. And he, looking at me and ridiculing what he considered the insignificance and unfitness of the query, said: "Truly a difficult question is this that you ask, one demanding very many sleepless nights of investigation! Who, pray, is so ignorant of the Latin tongue as not to know that one is called *obnoxius* who can be inconvenienced or injured by another, to whom he is said to be *obnoxius* because the other is conscious of his *noxa*, that is to say, of his guilt? Why not rather," said he, "drop these trifles and put questions worthy of study and discussion?"

Then indeed I was angry, but thinking that I ought to dissemble, since I was dealing with a fool, I said: "If, most learned sir, I need to learn and to know other things that are more abstruse and more important, when the occasion arises I shall inquire and learn them from you; but inasmuch as I have often used the word *obnoxius* without knowing what I was saying, I have learned from you and am now beginning to understand what not I alone, as you seem to think, was ignorant of; for as a matter of fact, Plautus too, though a man of the first rank in his use of the Latin language and in elegance of diction, did not know the meaning of *obnoxius*. For there is a passage of his in the *Stichus* which reads as follows. . . ."

[Aulus Gellius precedes to quote this passage, and three others by the writers Virgil (70–19 BCE), Sallust (86–35 BCE), and Ennius (239–169 BCE) in which the word is also used differently.]

But our grammarian, with open mouth as if in a dream, said: "Just now I have no time to spare. When I have leisure, come to see me and learn what Virgil, Plautus, Sallust and Ennius meant by that word."

So saying that fool made off; but in case anyone should wish to investigate, not only the origin of this word, but also its variety of meaning, in order that he may take into consideration this Plautine use also, I have quoted the following lines from the *Asinaria*. . . .

From Martial. C. 86–103 CE. *The Epigrams of Martial, Translated into English Prose.* Translator unidentified. 1860. London: Henry G. Bohn.

In two of his Epigrams, *which were published between 86 and 103 CE, the satirist Martial (ca. 38–103 CE) speaks to two teachers: one is asked to stop bothering his neighbors by loudly beating and berating his students, while the other is advised to allow his students to be free during the summer.*

[Book IX] LXVIII. To the Master of a Noisy School in His Neighborhood

What right have you to disturb me, abominable schoolmaster, object abhorred alike by boys and girls? Before the crested cocks have broken silence, you begin to roar out your savage scoldings and blows. Not with louder noise does the metal resound on the struck anvil, when the workman is fitting a lawyer on his horse; nor is the noise so great in the large amphitheatre, when the conquering gladiator is applauded by his partisans. We, your neighbours, do not ask you to allow us to sleep for the whole night, for it is but a small matter to be occasionally awakened; but to be kept awake all night is a heavy affliction. Dismiss your scholars, brawler, and take as much for keeping quiet as you receive for making a noise.

[Book X] LXII. To a Schoolmaster

Schoolmaster, be indulgent to your simple scholars; if you would have many a long-haired youth resort to your lectures, and the class seated round your critical table love you. So may no teacher of arithmetic, or of swift writing, be surrounded by a greater ring of pupils. The days are bright, and glow under the flaming constellation of the Lion, and fervid July is ripening the teeming harvest. Let the Scythian scourge with its formidable thongs, such as flogged Marsyas of Ceiaenae, and the terrible cane, the schoolmaster's sceptre, be laid aside, and sleep until the Ides of October. In summer, if boys preserve their health, they do enough.

Vestal Virgins

Although the ancient Romans borrowed and worshipped the Greek gods (under new names), they approached their religion differently, developing a hierarchal system under the control of the government that contrasted sharply with the Greek system of autonomous temples. They also had differing attitudes toward some deities; thus, while Hestia, Greek goddess of the hearth, was not regarded as a major figure, her Roman equivalent, Vesta, received more attention from officials and citizens, reflecting how the Romans cherished the ideal of a happy domestic life. Her chief temple, the Hall of Vesta in Rome, was considered an important institution, and the Vestal Virgins who managed the temples and its rituals were widely respected figures.

The Romans believed that the Vestal Virgins were first established by the legendary Roman king Numa along with other male priesthoods; according to mythology, after Rhea Silvia gave birth to Romulus and Remus, the legendary founders of Rome, she became a Vestal Virgin so she would not produce an heir to threaten her uncle. Such stories help to explain why the Vestal Virgins were considered a venerable institution, and why it was considered a great honor to be chosen to be one. They were also Rome's only female priesthood, creating intense competition for the few available openings.

At first, only families from the upper classes enjoyed the privilege of offering their daughters as candidates for the positions; later, daughters from less wealthy families could also apply, though no potential priestesses could suffer from any physical deformities and their parents had to be alive. The typical applicants, girls from the age of six to ten, were personally chosen by the head priest, or *pontifix maximus*; there were typically eighteen women selected, but at any time only six would officially be considered Vestal Virgins, as the others worked as novices or supervisors. One experienced Vestal Virgin would be appointed to lead the temple and given the title of *virgo Vestalis maxima*. These women usually served for thirty years—ten as novices, ten as Vestal Virgins, and ten as trainers of novices—but most elected to remain at the temple until their deaths, though some chose to get married; despite their advanced age, they were regarded as desirable spouses because their profession was so highly respected.

The Vestal Virgins had a number of responsibilities, such as ensuring that the fire in the temple's hearth was kept burning at all times, since many believed that Rome's survival depended upon its constant flame; they also made a sacred special salt cake, called the

In the late eighteenth century, sculptor Joseph-Charles Marin carved this statue of a Roman Vestal Virgin wearing her traditional headdress, or *infula*; wraparound cloth, or *palla*; and brooch, or *suffibulum*. Vestal Virgins served at the temple of Vesta, and this female priesthood lasted from the seventh century BCE until the emperor Theodosius I closed the Temple of Vesta in 391 CE. (Los Angeles County Museum of Art)

mola salsa, using grain and salt mixed with water, and they were personally responsible for cleaning and mopping the temple every day. Several holy objects within the temple demanded regular attention as well; surprisingly, one of these, the Palladium, was a statue of another goddess, the Greek Athena (called Minerva by the Romans), which was also regarded as a talisman guaranteeing the safety of Rome. The Vestal Virgins were also asked to safeguard the wills of some important figures like Julius Caesar (100–44 BCE) and Marc Antony (83–30 BCE). The Temple of Vesta was destroyed or damaged several times, but it was always rebuilt promptly, testifying to its importance.

For public duties, the Vestal Virgins would cover their hair with six pieces of artificial hair, kept in place by narrow bands, and don three characteristic garments: the *infula*, a headdress that rested upon their shoulders; the *palla*, a large piece of cloth wrapped around their body; and the *suffibulum*, a brooch that kept the palla in place. They had many tasks to perform. Vestal Virgins regularly had to visit a special spring that was sacred to the Roman water goddesses, the Camenae, to obtain the sanctified water that was needed to perform their rites. At the festival of Fordicia, held every April 15th, the Vestal Virgins would ritually burn a cow, take its ashes, and mix them with the blood from the horse that had been sacrificed after winning a race held on the previous October 15th. Then, as part of the festival of Palilia on April 21st, they would toss the mixture onto a bonfire. During the Vestalia, the festival for Vesta held every June 9th, Vestal Virgins and other priests and officials would carry bundles of rushes from twenty-seven shrines and toss them into the Tiber River to honor the goddess. Since the Vestal Virgins participated in many of the other hundred or so festivals that filled the Roman calendar, they were often very busy indeed.

In exchange for their labors the Vestal Virgins also enjoyed some unusual privileges. While nominally under the supervision of the *pontifix maximus*, they were free to act independently, and indeed were long the only Roman women who could manage their own affairs and sign contracts without the aid of male guardians. They lived comfortably in a large house next to Vesta's circular temple with an enormous garden where they could relax, and the government paid all of their expenses. Unlike most Romans, Vestal Virgins were allowed to ride in chariots within the city; they were granted front-row seats at gladiatorial games, even though women were usually relegated to the back rows; and if someone harmed a Vestal Virgin, they could be put to death. Vestal Virgins could testify in court cases without taking an oath, and had the authority to harbor accused criminals within the temple or intercede with officials to have them freed; their most famous exercise of this right came in 81 BCE, when they prevented Julius Caesar from being killed by the dictator Sulla (138–78 BCE). By some reports, they could free slaves by merely touching them. More broadly, anyone with a problem could request assistance from the Vestal Virgins, and the government would usually do what they asked. Whenever a crisis occurred, officials might even seek the advice of the *virgo Vestalis maxima*. After they died, Vestal Virgins received a public funeral and were among the few people who were buried within the city of Rome.

Still, Vestal Virgins were held to high standards and might suffer if they failed to meet them. If they allowed Vesta's sacred flame to go out, for example, they might be flogged to death, or beaten severely if they did not carry out a duty properly. Their most grievous sin, though, was sexual activity: since Vesta, like Hestia, was a virgin goddess, her priestesses were required to remain virgins throughout their years of service. Vestal Virgins accused of losing their virginity faced a grisly punishment—being buried alive in a small room—if they were convicted of the crime, and their lovers would be beaten to death. However, since even a disgraced priestess could not be allowed to die from starvation, they would be buried with a little food, so they would actually die from suffocation. One Vestal Virgin, Aemilia (died 114 BCE), actually suffered this fate when she was accused of committing incest; two of her colleagues who allegedly committed the same crime, Marcia and Licinia (both died 114 BCE), were initially cleared but later put to death as well. The writer Pliny the Elder (23–79 CE) also tells the story of Tuccia, a Vestal Virgin who served at some unknown time, and was charged with unchaste behavior, but demonstrated her innocence by miraculously carrying water in a sieve. Because their chastity was deemed so important, the deranged emperor Elagabalus (203–222 CE) naturally horrified the Romans when he left his wife to marry a Vestal Virgin, Aquilia Severa (ca. third century CE), which he somehow

A SONG FOR VESTAL VIRGINS

As evidence of their continuing prominence in popular culture, ancient Rome's Vestal Virgins are mentioned in one of the seminal rock songs of the 1960s, Procol Harum's "A Whiter Shade of Pale" (1967), written by band members Gary Brooker, Keith Reed, and Matthew Fisher. However, the authors were evidently not well informed about these priestesses' history, since their enigmatic lyrics indicate that the total number of Vestal Virgins was sixteen, when in fact there were eighteen of them. As another error, the lyrics suggest that their duties regularly took them to the shore of the Mediterranean Sea, which was not the case.

WOULD YOU LIKE TO BE A VESTAL VIRGIN?

When the Roman Empire established Christianity as its official religion and suppressed the worship of Roman gods, the ancient Roman religion effectively vanished, its gods and legends relegated to the category of mythology. Yet in 1998, an organization was founded in Maine, called Nova Roma, that was officially dedicated to the restoration of Roman culture and religion, and one of its activities is recruiting and training priests and priestesses to serve the Roman deities. For the goddess Vesta, the organization hopes to attract six women to become Vestal Virgins, and as of 2014 there were five vacancies; any interested woman can apply for the position at the group's Web site.

imagined would serve to harmoniously unite Roman religion and his own eastern cult; instead, the hostile reaction of his subjects forced him to annul the marriage, though he later returned to her side.

In the fourth century, even after the emperor Constantine (272–337 CE) converted to Christianity, the Vestal Virgins remained in operation, until the emperor Theodosius I 347–395 CE) closed the Temple of Vesta in 391 CE. The last known leader of the Vestal Virgins, a woman named Coelia Concordia, gave up her position in 394 CE and, adjusting to changing times, later converted to Christianity. Yet the Vestal Virgins were never forgotten, and recent scholars have studied them intensely, fascinated by the mysterious and powerful women who played such an important role in Roman society.

Further Reading

Lefkowitz, Mary R., and Maureen B. Fant, compilers. 2005. *Women's Life in Greece and Rome: A Source Book in Translation*. Baltimore, MD: John Hopkins University Press.

Sawyer, Deborah F. 1996. *Women and Religion in the First Christian Centuries*. London and New York: Routledge.

Staples, Ariadne. 1998. *From Good Goddess to Vestal Virgins: Sex and Category in Roman Religion*. London and New York: Routledge.

Takács, Sarolta A. 2008. *Vestal Virgins, Sibyls, and Matrons: Women in Roman Religion*. Austin: University of Texas Press.

Thompson, Lindsay J. 2010. *The Role of Vestal Virgins in Roman Civic Religion: A Structuralist Study of the Crimen Incesti*. Lewiston, NY: Edwin Mellen Press.

Wildfang, Robin Lorsch. 2006. *Rome's Vestal Virgins: A Study of Rome's Vestal Priestesses in the Late Republic and Early Empire*. London and New York: Routledge.

Document

From Aulus Gellius. C. 170 CE. *The Attic Nights of Aulus Gellius*. Volume I. Translated by John C. Rolfe. 1927. Cambridge and London: Loeb Classical Library.

In this passage, the Latin writer Aulus Gellius (ca. 125–180 CE) describes the rigorous selection process underwent by the Vestal Virgins.

Those who have written about taking a Vestal Virgin . . . have stated that it is unlawful for a girl to be chosen who is less than six, or more than ten, years old. She must also have both father and mother living. She must be free, too, from any impediment in her speech, must not have impaired hearing, or be marked by any other bodily defect. She must not herself have been freed from paternal control, nor her father before her, even if her father is still living and she is under the control of her grandfather. Neither one nor both of her parents may have been slaves or engaged in mean occupations. But they say that one whose sister has been chosen to that priesthood acquires exemption, as well as one whose father is a priest or an augur . . . The daughter of a man without residence in Italy must not be chosen, and that the daughter of one who has three children must be excused.

Now, as soon as the Vestal Virgin is chosen, escorted to the house of Vesta and delivered to the pontiffs, she immediately passes from the control of her father without the ceremony of emancipation or loss of civil rights, and acquires the right to make a will.

But as to the method and ritual for choosing a Vestal, there are, it is true, no ancient written records, except that the first to be appointed was chosen by [Rome's second king], Numa …

Now, many think that the term "taken" ought to be used only of a Vestal. But, as a matter of fact, the priests of Jupiter also, as well as the augurs, were said to be "taken" . . . The Vestal is called "Amata" when taken by the chief pontiff, because there is a tradition that the first one who was chosen bore that name.

Winemakers

All ancient civilizations had a fondness for alcoholic beverages, but the Romans had a special devotion to wine, which was part of virtually every meal (though it was almost invariably diluted with water, sometimes as much as eight parts water to one part wine). Because of the enormous demand for wine, there were large vineyards throughout the Italian countryside, and as the Roman Empire expanded, winemaking became commonplace in the provinces of Egypt, Spain, and France as well, making wine of Rome's most important products. It is not surprising, then, that many Roman farmers decided to specialize in growing grapes and making wine, and some became unusually skillful in the art, establishing a tradition of fine Italian winemaking that endures to the present day.

The process of making wine began with the grapes, which were most often grown on the hills outside Rome and in the regions of Piedmont and Tuscany. This involved a great deal of demanding labor, described in great detail in the *Georgics* (ca. 29 BCE) of the poet Virgil (70–19 BCE): vines were usually planted in the spring; the soil was broken up and fertilized with manure; poles were positioned for the vines to grow upon; the vines periodically had to be pruned

and grafted; vineyards had to be diligently weeded and hoed in order to remove other plants and prevent any loss of moisture; and the mature grapes had to be harvested. Needless to say, neither wealthy landowners nor the farmers and winemakers who worked on their estates did any of this work, assigning these tasks to children, elderly people, and slaves. Next, so that they could be transformed into wine, the harvested grapes had to be sorted, so that only the most suitable grapes would be used for the wine. Then, as quickly as possible, the chosen grapes would be placed on an elevated platform floor and slaves, usually wearing only a loincloth, would walk over them to crush them into a pulp, and the liquid immediately resulting from this process would drain into special containers. According to the statesman Cato (234–149 BCE), this liquid was valued as a medicine. To obtain more liquid, the winemakers at large estates would have the pulp placed within a wooden press, consisting of a lever that was firmly forced onto the pulp using ropes or a screwing device; however, humbler winemakers often relied upon repeated stomping to obtain all of their liquid.

The resulting liquid, a grape juice called *mustum*, was sometimes consumed immediately; but more often, it was poured into *doria*, or large barrels, that were coated on the inside with beeswax. The *doria* were either placed in a sunken area next to the press room, to keep the liquid cool, or even buried in the ground, with only their tops exposed. The liquid was then allowed to ferment, usually for about two to four weeks. When it was ready to be sold, the wine was poured into large jars called *amphoras* to be sold and transported to other markets; though the tops of the *amphoras* were sealed, winemakers drilled tiny holes in the stoppers so carbon dioxide would escape. This ended the process of making most wines, but some canny winemakers, seeking to maximize their profits, would soak the already crushed pulp in water for one day and crush it yet again, though the very poor wine that came from its liquid, called *lora*, was usually given only to slaves.

Many winemakers were content to make the cheap, ordinary wines that were part of the regular Roman diet; these were often so sour that drinkers had to mix in some honey as well as water. However, winemakers in some regions, such as Latium and Campania, were

This carving on the sarcophagus of an ancient Roman winemaker shows the deceased man selling some of his wine. (DeAgostini/Getty Images)

esteemed for making special wines that could be sold at high prices and cherished for many years. One wine from this region, Setinian, became the favorite of the emperor Augustus (63 BCE–14 CE) and later emperors because it never upset anyone's stomach; with a flavor like figs, this wine was usually drunk cold, after being chilled by added snow. Another popular wine, Caecuban, was unusually made near the city of Fundi from grapes that were grown in a marsh, not on a hillside; this white wine was often mentioned by the poet Horace (65–8 BCE), who evidently preferred it. However, the construction of a canal by the emperor Nero (37–68 CE) later caused the marsh to be drained, eliminating all wine production in that area. The famed city of Pompeii was also a noted center for fine winemaking, so much so that some unscrupulous winemakers tried to profit by falsely labeling their own wines as

Pompeian products; when the vineyards of Pompeii and other nearby cities were destroyed by the eruption of Mount Vesuvius in 79 CE, it caused a severe wine shortage in Rome, though this was alleviated by desperate efforts to plant new vineyards in other areas.

As a sign of how they were esteemed, the vineyards of Italy even entered into Roman mythology, as the high quality of wines from Mount Massicus in Latium was described as the work of a god. The fabular winemaker Falernus, it was said, once eked out a meager living by farming other crops on the mountain, but one day Bacchus, the Roman god of wine, visited him in disguise and was impressed his kindness toward a stranger, as the elderly farmer happily fed his guest. As an immediate reward, Bacchus miraculously made some wine for Falernus to drink, and decided that he and his land should forever be known for fine wine. Accordingly, when Falernus woke up the next morning, he found that his mountain was now covered with rich vines. Though the wine that the region produced, termed Falernian, eventually fell out of favor, its greatest achievement came in 121 BCE, when it produced a wine, called the Vina Opimia because that was the year that the consul Lucius Opimius (ca. 155–100 BCE) took over Rome; Vina Opimia was renowned for its rich sweetness, saved by many connoisseurs for special occasions, and still discussed over a century after it appeared. This region's wine was also immortalized in *The Satyricon* of Petronius (died 66 CE), as the dissolute host Trimalchio serves his guests an expensive wine called "Falernian Opimian."

The special techniques for producing the finest wines were not always well publicized, but some

OLD WINE FOR NEW BOTTLES

Ordinarily, one would not expect a university to enter the business of making wine, but in 2013, the University of Catania in Sicily, Italy, proudly announced precisely such a venture. This is being done, however, not to make a profit, but rather to rediscover the precise techniques that the ancient Romans employed to make their wine. Historian Mario Indelicato, who is in charge of the project, carefully studied Virgil's *Georgics* and the writings of a winemaker from the first century CE named Columella in order to plant the vines in the Roman manner, and he and his colleagues hope to be drinking a brand new batch of ancient Roman wine by 2017.

A DEADLY DRINK?

In 1983, geochemist Jerome Nriagu proposed the controversial theory that the Roman Empire fell, in large part, because numerous citizens were unknowingly victimized by lead poisoning, only recently recognized as a threat. One problem was their habit of sweetening wine by added lead dust or *mustum* boiled in lead vessels, since that provided a better flavor than *mustum* boiled in bronze or copper vessels. However, others have noted that because the Romans invariably watered down their wine, only habitual drunkards could have absorbed enough lead to endanger their health, and most experts agree that other factors were far more important in explaining the Romans' decline.

winemakers experimented by planting thyme in their vineyards, hoping that this would add flavor to the harvested grapes. They also learned that some wines tasted best if they were allowed to age for long periods of time; the wines from the Alban Hills near Rome, for example, were typically aged for about 15 years. The flavor of some wines could be improved if they were heated, and adding some ingredients to the wine would be helpful as well. As noted, honey could be employed to sweeten any wine; one could also boil some *mustum*, making it more sweet, and pour it into the wine; and knowing nothing about the poisonous effects of lead, the Romans occasionally added bits of lead to wine as a sweetening agent. In addition, putting in some chalk dust would reduce the acidity of some wines, and special herbs and spices were added to produce the distinctive flavor of a form of wine called *conditura*. Cato oddly recommended adding a little marble dust and pig's blood to wine, and a little sea water might be poured into wine that was turning into vinegar in order to make it more palatable.

While wine was made throughout the ancient world, only the Romans focused their energies on developing a broad variety of excellent wines with distinctive qualities, and even after the Roman Empire fell, the winemakers throughout Europe that Rome had trained carried on with proven methods and kept developing new ways to improve their wines. Some have even suggested that viniculture, the art of making wine, represents one of the most important ways that the Romans contributed to world culture. Considering all of their other achievements, one might question such claims, but every person today who likes to drink a glass of fine wine with their dinner owns a debt to the ancient Romans who first made it possible to enjoy that simple pleasure.

Further Reading

Fleming, Stuart James. 2001. *Vinum: The Story of Roman Wine*. Glen Mills, PA: Art Flair.
Heskett, Randall, and Joel Butler. 2012. *Divine Vintage: Following the Wine Trail from Genesis to the Modern Age*. New York: Palgrave Macmillan.
Lawrence, Ray. 2009. *Roman Passions: A History of Pleasure in Imperial Rome*. London and New York: Continuum.

Pellechia, Thomas. 2006. *Wine: The 8,000-Year-Old Story of the Wine Trade*. New York: Thunder's Mouth Press.

Standage, Tom. 2005. *A History of the World in Six Glasses*. New York: Walker & Co.

Unwin, P.T.H. 1991. *Wine and the Vine*. London and New York: Routledge.

Document

From Virgil. C. 29 BCE. *The Georgics of Virgil*. Translated into English Verse by Herbert Gardner Burghclere. 1904. London: John Murray.

In three passages from The Georgics, *the Roman poet Virgil (70 BCE–19 CE) announces that he will now be shifting to the topic of wine, lists some of the types of grapes used to make different types of wine, and describes the best type of soil for growing grapes.*

So far of tillage and the sovereign stars.
Now be my song of Bacchus, nor forget
His bosky thickets and the fruit that decks
The tardy olive.

Come, Lenaean! come.
Lord of the winepress. Father of the vine!
For now is nature laden with thy boons.
And by thy bounty all the joyous earth
With grape-clad autumn teems, and
  brimming vats
Foam with the vintage:

Come, Lenaean! come.
Lord of the winepress. Father of the vine!
Strip off thy buskins, bare thy comely feet
And plunge with me into the purple must. . . .

Of grapes we know
White Mareotic, and the Thasian,
(These for stiff soils, and those for lighter apt)
Psithians more meet for raisin wine, Lagenes,

Whose subtle juice anon betrays the feet
And knots the tongue; Rath-ripe and
  Purple-hued.
And thou, O Rhoetic wine! I search for song
To hymn thee duly; nathless seek thou not
To vie with our Falernian cellarage.
Strong Aminoean, who the homage claims
Of Tmolus and imperial Phanae;
And small Argitis wine, which rivals both
For bulk of must and power to last the years.
Nor can I pass thee by, O Rhodian grape!
Dear to the gods and to the second dish;
Nor, Bumast with exuberant clusters, thee!

But numbers lack to mark each name and kind,
Nor boots it of a truth to tell their tale.
Methinks the man, who sought such numbering.
Would list to reckon up the grains of sand.
Whirled by the West winds over Libyan wastes.
Or, when the wilder passion of the East
Falls on our argosies would count the waves
Which the Ionic ocean rolls ashore. . . .

But where the soil is fat
And joyous with sweet wells, or where the plain,
All lush with grasses, teems with plenteousness.
Such land as we are oft-times wont to view
Far down the mountain in some hollow vale.
Where drips the rivulet from steepy rocks
And brings the kindly ooze—a plain, forsooth,
Which breasts the south and cherishes the fern,
That foe to ploughshares—here your grape
  shall wax
Full lustily anon, with bounteous floods
Of wine, here shall your clusters amply grow.
And brew such liquor as from golden bowls
Flows for the gods' delight whene'er we hear
Hard-by the altar the sleek Tuscan blow
His ivory pipe, and on the groaning dish
Men offer up a steamy sacrifice.

The Byzantine Empire and Russia, 300–1500

Introduction

Despite European perceptions to the contrary, the Roman Empire did not really fall in 476; for the former eastern half of the Empire, with its capital at Constantinople in modern-day Turkey, remained a strong and vibrant political entity for another thousand years. Still, the surviving Byzantine Empire, so designated because the original name of Constantinople was Byzantium, did develop a special character that seems quite distinct from that of its predecessor; for while we think of the Romans as extravagant pleasure seekers, devoted to their gladiatorial contests and gourmet foods, the Byzantines lived in a more Spartan manner, dedicated to the doctrines of the Christian church that increasingly dominated their lives. Also, though western Europeans sometimes described the Byzantines as an "Asiatic" civilization, the most powerful influence on its growth and development was actually ancient Greece, as the Empire adopted the Greek language and embraced Greek literature and philosophy within a new Christian context.

Despite having an impressive army, the Byzantine Empire never matched the military might of the Romans, and it was constantly beset by foreign enemies from the north and east, leading to losses of territory and even brief seizures of its capital. One of these was the first Russian state, Kievan Rus, and while it twice threatened Constantinople, its accomplishments as a whole were not significant, though the country would go on to achieve greatness. In response to foreign challenges, the Empire increasingly sought to maintain its position by means of negotiation and trade, not conquest and intimidation. The complex treaties they worked out with rival nations were often viewed with suspicion, so the word "Byzantine" has entered the language to describe anything that is overly complicated or hard to figure out. Merchants from Western Europe and the Arab world were invited to maintain a permanent presence in Constantinople, making the Empire a valuable conduit for trade between those distant regions. Yet the Byzantine Empire itself was not greatly changed by its regular contact with other cultures. In fields ranging from science and technology to literature and the arts, the Byzantines often seemed willfully stagnant, dedicated to preserving ancient traditions more than breaking new ground.

Still, one must admire the Byzantines for their remarkable tenacity as they fought off threat after threat and preserved their distinctive culture for several centuries until they finally succumbed to a Turkish invasion in 1453. From the eunuchs who managed government affairs to the goldsmiths who fashioned magnificent works of art, all the Byzantines worked very hard on behalf of their nation, and while their efforts were frequently overlooked by scholars, recent research is helping us gain a new appreciation for their many accomplishments.

Actors and Dancers

The performers of the Byzantine Empire worked in two radically different arenas. In its early days, they participated in a variety of raucous and sometimes salacious shows that resembled modern circuses more than the tragedies and comedies of the classic Greek and Roman stage. Then, a government increasingly dominated by Christian values banned such entertainments as immoral diversions, limiting them to the streets and other unofficial venues, and a very different sort of theater emerged under the aegis of the church, dedicated to offering dignified dramas based on stories from the Bible or the lives of saints. Dancers and musicians might also earn a living by entertaining guests at banquets or the Byzantine court.

In the fifth century, Constantinople had four outdoor theaters, but none were offering productions of the literate plays of Aeschylus, Sophocles, Euripides, or Seneca, except perhaps for an occasional scene to add a fleeting air of dignity. Instead, companies of performers with diverse talents worked together to offer programs that might be compared to the vaudeville shows of the twentieth-century United States, generally beginning at noon and lasting several hours into the night. As opening acts or interludes, audiences could be briefly entertained by acrobats, magicians, jugglers, or trainers directing animals to perform tricks. Then, actors might perform pantomimes based on Greek or Roman myths, featuring dancing actors wearing large masks, which resembled modern ballets.

Other mimes would amuse audiences with outrageous stunts and slapstick in loosely structured comedies, also derived from myths, involving romance, violent conflict, and mistaken identities; by some reports, performances occasionally included some improvisation, and actors who mangled their lines would be loudly ridiculed by audience members. There was often an emphasis on visual spectacle, with colorful costumes, painted sets, flashes of light, and sound effects. A latter-day version of the crane, or *mêchanê*, from Greek theater could make it seem as if actors were flying above the stage, and singers, drummers, and musicians playing wind instruments provided background music. Simulated sexual activity and even nudity were not uncommon; according to the Byzantine historian Procopius (ca. 500–565), the future empress Theodora (ca. 500–548) first became famous for appearing in a lurid drama based on the Greek myth of Leda and the Swan; as Leda, Theodora appeared on stage completely naked, except for a belt around her waist required by law, while geese representing Zeus purportedly ravished her, though they were actually eating grains dropped upon her by the slaves who worked in theaters as stagehands.

As portrayed by Procopius, who openly despised her, Theodora was also an enthusiastic prostitute with insatiable appetites who devoted most of her time offstage to an endless series of sexual liaisons; but the reality of her life, and that of other actresses, may have been quite different. True, it was widely believed in Byzantine society that all actresses were willing to sometimes work as prostitutes, and since performers were not paid high salaries, many women undoubtedly agreed to provide this service as a way to augment their incomes. However, their sexual activities may have only been occasional and reluctant. Theodora's life also provides a glimpse of the typical careers of these actors. Her father was a bear trainer and her mother was a dancer and actress; they undoubtedly met while performing together and apparently stayed in the business until they retired, also bringing their three daughters into the profession. Theodora, though, tired of the life of an actress and, like others in her position, was able to find other work; though Procopius omits this information, she converted to Christianity while staying in Alexandria and, upon returning to Constantinople, garnered a respectable job spinning wool in a facility close to the imperial palace, which is how she met the future emperor Justinian I (ca. 482–565). Before they could marry, however, Justinian had to persuade his father Justin 1 (450–527) to repeal a law that made it illegal for high-ranking men to marry actresses—another sign that the profession was considered disreputable.

Still, theater long remained an important aspect of the Byzantine social life; even the emperor could be observed attending performances at Constantinople's large Hippodrome, and Justinian's successor, his nephew Justin II (520–578), reportedly preferred pantomimes to studying. Most plays were not as bawdy as Theodora's notorious exhibition, and even the sexually charged dramas would probably be regarded as unobjectionable by modern standards. (One commentator was appalled by actresses who shockingly bared their arms and legs.) Antagonism toward the theater may have been driven by snobbery, as aristocrats resented the attention paid to the lower-class citizens and foreigners who often found employment there, and there were fears that respectable young men and women might be tempted to abandon loftier pursuits to enter the glamorous world of acting. Pantomimes occasionally ventured into sacrilegious territory, such as sarcastic depictions of adult baptism, which surely upset religious leaders, and there is also the theory that church officials opposed the theater because it lured people away from their masses and took money that might otherwise have been given to the church.

For whatever reason, laws were ultimately passed in the sixth and seventh centuries to forbid performances of mime, Constantinople's theaters were largely abandoned, and most of their actors and dancers were forced to carry as attractions in the city's small taverns, or as street performers, living off the donations of passing observers. Later, it became commonplace for troupes of such actors to tour small villages, acting in whatever venues they could find. Dancers, however, could still find legitimate employment, as they were regularly paid to perform at religious festivals, weddings, banquets, and the royal court. There is an illustration from the eleventh century, for example, showing eight women at court dancing with their hands on each other's shoulders. As it happens, the church also regarded dancing as immoral, and in 692, its Council in Trullo even endeavored to ban dancing in public; but dancing nonetheless endured as a widely accepted form of public entertainment. Dancing was also popular in early Russia, as dancers began to develop the distinctive movements that people still associate with traditional Russian dance: men crouching with their arms crossed over their chests as they rapidly extend their legs.

As for Byzantine actors, they might find jobs in the churches, which were beginning to exploit theater as a way to attract people to masses and convey religious messages. In doing so, it is unclear whether the Byzantine church fathers independently developed this tradition or were influenced by similar religious dramas in Western Europe. One surviving example of an early Christian drama from the Byzantine Empire, called *Christus Patiens*, or *Christ Suffering*, was traditionally attributed to St. Gregory of Nazianzus (ca. 325–389), but scholars have determined that it was actually written in the eleventh century. Describing the last days of Jesus Christ, the poetic drama takes the form of a dialogue between Jesus, Mary, Mary Magdalene, and others. Another Christian play, relating

the biblical story of Shadrach, Meshach, and Abednego surviving in the furnace, was frequently performed before Christmas; a fifteenth-century visitor to Constantinople, Bertrandon de la Brocquière (ca. 1400–1459), reports seeing this drama, suggesting that it long remained popular. There is little reliable information about how these plays were performed, but it is likely that the staging was generally sparse, with minimal use of sets, costumes, and props; professional actors probably took the leading parts, while amateur recruits served as extras.

Byzantine writers generally say little about the various sorts of performances that were available to their compatriots, perhaps deeming them unimportant; yet scraps of information from texts and illustrations suggest that theatrical performances were regularly

ACTRESSES-TURNED-EMPRESSES

In the sixth century, the future emperor Justinian I scandalized Byzantine society by marrying an actress, a profession that branded her a probable prostitute as well. Today, actresses are more respected than Justinian's Theodora, but it remains unusual for rich and powerful men to wed actresses, and such events command public attention. Two twentieth-century examples are Argentinian actress Eva Perón, who married her country's future president in 1945, and U.S. film actress Grace Kelly, who married Monaco's ruler, Prince Rainier III, in 1956. And while they did not wield as much power as Theodora, both women had an impact on their nations, in part due to charitable endeavors.

A REALLY BIG SHOW

On a typical day, a performance in a Byzantine theater might feature a juggler, some mimes acting out a famous story, a scene from a famous play, trained animals doing tricks, a brief comedic drama, and some vigorous acrobatics. Centuries later, a similar format was employed for one of U.S. television's longest running programs, *The Ed Sullivan Show* (1948–1971), originally called *Toast of the Town*. Every week, host Ed Sullivan promised his audience a "really big show" and entertained viewers with a diverse set of acts that might range from an operatic solo to the Beatles and Rolling Stones to a ventriloquist trading jokes with his dummy.

enjoyed by members of this purportedly austere culture, as a citizen during a typical week might watch a solemn drama in church, enjoy energetic dancers at a banquet, and take in a pantomime show at a local tavern. And while actors generally garnered little respect in their society, the church did acknowledge a third-century Roman actor who converted to Christianity, Saint Genesius, as the patron saint of actors, indicating that such professionals could also be good Christians, and Theodora's story suggests that it was sometimes possible for former actors to leave their craft and elevate their social status. But like their counterparts in later times, many Byzantine actors undoubtedly relished the experience of performing before audiences and enjoyed long and fulfilling careers on the stage.

Further Reading

Easterling, Pat, and Edith Hall, editors. 2002. *Greek and Roman Actors: Aspects of an Ancient Profession.* Cambridge and New York: Cambridge University Press.

Garland, Lynda, editor. 2006. *Byzantine Women: Varieties of Experience 800–1200.* Aldershot, England, and Burlington, VT: Ashgate.

Gildenhard, Ingo, and Martin Revermann, editors. 2010. *Beyond the Fifth Century: Interactions with Greek Tragedy from the Fourth Century BCE to the Middle Ages.* Berlin and New York: Walter de Gruyter.

Leyerle, Blake. 2001. *Theatrical Shows and Ascetic Lives: John Chrysostom's Attack on Spiritual Marriage.* Berkeley and Los Angeles: University of California Press.

Nahachewsky, Andriy. 2011. *Ukrainian Dance: A Cross-Cultural Approach.* Jefferson, NC: McFarland.

Neiiendam, Klaus. 1992. *The Art of Acting in Antiquity: Iconographical Studies in Classical, Hellenistic, and Byzantine Theatre.* Copenhagen: Museum Tusculanum, University of Copenhagen.

Document

From Procopius. C. 558. *The Secret History of the Court of Justinian: Literally and Completely Translated from the Greek for the First Time.* Translator or translators unidentified. 1896. Athens: Privately Printed for the Athenian Society.

The Byzantine historian Procopius (ca. 500–565), in the ninth chapter of The Secret History *salaciously described the early career of the empress Theodora (ca. 500–548) as an actress and prostitute. Her work on the stage is a matter of record, though scholars have questioned Procopius's claims that she was an enthusiastic, full-time prostitute, believing it more likely that she provided sexual favors only occasionally.*

As for Justinian's wife, I shall now describe her birth, how she was brought up, how she married him, and how in conjunction with him she utterly ruined the Roman Empire. . . .

As soon . . . as she reached the age of puberty, as she was handsome, her mother sent her into the theatrical troupe, and she straightway became a simple harlot, as old-fashioned people called it; for she was neither a musician nor a dancer, but merely prostituted herself to everyone whom she met, giving up every part of her body to debauchery. She associated chiefly with the theatrical "pantomimes," and took part in their performances, playing in comic scenes, for she was exceedingly witty and amusing; so that she soon became well known by her acting. She had no shame whatever, and no one ever saw her put out of countenance, but she lent herself to scandalous purposes without the least hesitation.

She excelled in raising a laugh by being slapped on her puffed-out cheeks, and used to uncover herself so far as to show the spectators everything before and behind which decency forbids to be shown to men. She stimulated her lovers by lascivious jests, and continually invented new postures of coition, by which means she completely won the hearts of all libertines; for she did not wait to be solicited by anyone whom she met, but herself, with joke and gestures, invited everyone whom she fell in with, especially beardless boys.

She never succumbed to these transports; for she often went to a supper at which each one paid his share, with ten or more young men, in the full vigour of their age and practised in debauchery, and would pass the whole night with all of them. When they were all exhausted, she would go to their servants, thirty in number, it may be, and fornicate with each one of them; and yet not even so did she quench her lust. . . .

She frequently became pregnant, but as she employed all known remedies without delay, she promptly procured abortion. Often, even on the stage, she stripped before the eyes of all the people, and stood naked in their midst, wearing only a girdle about her private parts and groin; not because she had any modesty about showing that also to the people, but because no one was allowed to go on the stage without a girdle about those parts. In this attitude she would throw herself down on the floor, and lie on her back. Slaves, whose duty it was, would then pour grains of barley upon her girdle, which trained geese would then pick up with their beaks one by one and eat. She did not blush or rise up, but appeared to glory in this performance; for she was not only without shame, but especially fond of encouraging others to be shameless, and often would strip naked in the midst of the actors, and swing herself backwards and forwards, explaining to those who had already enjoyed her and those who had not, the peculiar excellences of that exercise.

She proceeded to such extremities of abuse as to make her face become what most women's private parts are: wherefore her lovers became known at once by their unnatural tastes, and any respectable man who met her in the public streets turned away, and made haste to avoid her, lest his clothes should be soiled by contact with such an abandoned creature, for she was a bird of ill-omen, especially for those who saw her early in the day. As for her fellow-actresses, she always abused them most savagely, for she was exceedingly jealous.

Afterwards she accompanied Hecebolus, who had received the appointment of Governor of Pentapolis, to that country, to serve his basest passions, but quarrelled with him, and was straightway sent out of the country. In consequence of this she fell into want of common necessaries, with which she hereafter provided herself by prostitution, as she had been accustomed to do. She first went to Alexandria, and afterwards wandered all through the East, until she reached Byzantium, plying her trade in every city on her way—a trade which, I imagine, Heaven will not pardon a man for calling by its right name—as if the powers of evil would not allow any place on earth to be free from the debaucheries of Theodora. Such was the birth, and such the training of this woman, and her name became better known than that of any other prostitute of her time.

Architects

The Byzantines contrived to design and construct their many buildings by relying upon various sorts of experts. In the early centuries of the Empire, there were the *mechanikoi*, or experts in mechanics, whose knowledge of physics and mathematics enabled them to design its grandest churches. As such individuals became harder to find, structures might be erected by an experienced builder, the *protomaistor* or master, who headed a group of workers described as *oikodomoi* or *technitai*. Stonemasons could be in charge of building structures mostly made out of stone, such as public baths and the palatial estates of aristocrats. The army employed engineers who planned and constructed bridges, roads, and defensive structures, recruiting any available laborers in the vicinity, while the farmers and artisans who lived in villages had enough practical knowledge to successfully build small chapels, houses, workshops, and mills.

The first stage in any construction project was the planning, which was rarely as systematic as one might expect. True, when the emperor Justinian I (ca. 482–565) set out to reconstruct the magnificent church long known as the Hagia Sophia, which had twice been destroyed by rioters, he hired two noted *mechanikoi*, Anthemius of Tralles (ca. 474–558) and Isidore of Miletus (ca. sixth century), to prepare a careful design based on painstakingly accurate geometry. However, a practical-minded *protomaistor* or mason might simply decide upon the structure's overall dimensions, ask surveyors to measure and mark the location of the walls, and have his workers start building, confident that he could address and resolve any issues that arose as the building gradually assumed a final shape. Churches in particular tended to follow a standard pattern that allowed masons to bring them to completion without a great deal of premeditation.

The next step was to obtain the right sorts of materials for the envisioned building. Often these were found or made very close to the construction site: local workshops could make tiles for the roof and bricks for the foundation, stones could be dug out of fields, and there were many quarries to provide limestone. There were increasing numbers of ruins where masons might locate stones or columns that could be incorporated into their new structures. Large quantities of rubble were also needed to be poured between outer and inner walls of stone. If builders wanted something special and had a large budget, they could import green marble or white stones from Greece, or some of Egypt's renowned purple porphyry. Some wood had to be available both to provide temporary scaffolding during construction and to permanently keep roofs in place. To ensure that the pieces of wood and stone to be employed would fit tightly together, builders measured them with sticks that were the length of the standard unit, the *pous* (about 12-1/4 inches), while ropes with knots less accurately determined longer distances.

In constructing the outer walls, builders maintained consistent horizontal bands of marble or stone, and a flat roof could be readily kept in place by placing columns underneath it. Supporting the domes that were so characteristic of Byzantine architecture required different techniques. One could simply construct a cylindrical wall under the dome, or large triangular pieces called *pendentives* could support the dome and leave more open space beneath it. Long experience in putting up similar buildings usually ensured that the walls and roofs did not collapse, even if the plans were haphazard by modern standards. In many cases, more time was devoted to perfecting the appearance of the building's interior. Slabs of marble were favored for the floors. The walls were first covered with plaster, then artists were called in to paint frescos or embed tiny panels of marble, stone, or glass to create colorful mosaics. In some cases, mosaics were placed on floors as well.

The structures most strongly associated with the Byzantine Empire, of course, were its many impressive churches, well known both from detailed contemporary accounts and surviving examples that are still holding services today. The most familiar design, the basilica, was developed during the fourth and fifth centuries. Its primary feature was a large hall, of nave, divided into aisles by rows of columns that held up a flat roof. In the front of the hall was an anteroom or *narthex*, where parishioners would enter the church and perhaps socialize before the mass began. At the far end of the hall was a raised platform or *bema*; this included an altar, tables for Holy Communion and offerings from attendees, and a central chair for the bishop. The central aisle was wide enough to accommodate ceremonial processions that would slowly move from the *narthex* to the altar. The walls were covered with mosaics or frescos that depicted characters and events from the Bible.

The Byzantines also built many monasteries, though these are less celebrated and often spartan in their design. These consisted of several buildings devoted to various purposes, though there were no standard models, as different locations had different requirements, and they were probably constructed gradually by monks and supportive believers without any overall plan. One monastery, built in the desert of present-day Israel around the fifth or sixth centuries, has been excavated and extensively studied. It had four

A TRADITION RESTORED

After the Turks conquered Constantinople in 1453, its great churches were converted into mosques and, as Islam became the government's state religion, the construction of new Christian churches was discouraged or forbidden. However, expressing the religious tolerance that is appropriate for a nation that now belongs to the European Community, Turkey has slowly begun to allow Christians to build new churches. Still, as the minority Christians seek to maintain a low profile, these churches are not as large or ornate as the medieval cathedrals; one of them, built in 2006, is merely a converted house, and stained-glass windows are the only sign of its purpose.

DESIGNING A CAREER CHANGE

When hired to design the Hagia Sophia by Justinian I, Anthemius of Tralles was best known as a mathematician and Isidore of Miletus was noted as a physicist; however, despite their lack of experience as architects, their background enable them to design a magnificent structure. Much later, in the seventh century, an Englishman named Christopher Wren made a similar transition: he was first trained in mathematics and science and devoted several years to scientific work until shifting to architecture, becoming his nation's most celebrated architect. Interestingly, Wren's greatest work was also a church: London's St. Paul's Cathedral.

This church in Mistra, Greece, designed by a Byzantine architect and completed around 1290, has a large central dome, a typical feature of Byzantine architecture. (D.B. Della/Dreamstime.com)

main buildings: a small church for worship services; a residence where the monks each lived in small cells, about ten feet by ten feet; a tower, probably devoted to storing grains and other crops; and a reservoir to provide a supply of water. Around these structures were fields, orchards, and gardens surrounded by walls. Larger monasteries might also include a dining hall, library, bathhouse, and hospital. Decorations in early monasteries were minimal, in keeping with the monks' commitment to a renunciation of worldly pleasures, but later monasteries became more elaborate, as more funds became available.

Along with the large churches found in major Byzantine cities, almost every community, even the smallest one, would build its own churches and monasteries, often due to the determined effort of one lowly individual. A common event described in the lives of saints is that the heroic saint begins to build

a monastery all by himself, but other believers soon come to his aid with money and supplies while others start assisting the saint as he works on the building. We know little about these humble structures because they have not endured, but in Cappadocia, part of present-day Turkey, residents adopted the unique approach of carving little churches out of limestone cliffs that only had room for about twelve visitors. Art historian Lyn Rodley, who has studied these curious structures, believes that they were carved by one mason with a few helpers during a period of seven weeks. After they were completed, the limestone walls were coated with plaster and filled with frescos. In their size and style, these cave churches may be analogous to other rural churches of a more conventional nature.

Strangely, although so much effort was put into the construction of churches, the Byzantines were often disinclined to invest in keeping them well maintained, as bishops and wealthy donors preferred to pay for the construction of new churches instead of the repair of old churches. The same situation arose with the increasingly elaborate monasteries that were emerging in response to their growing popularity. Indeed, beginning with the reign of the emperor Romanos I Lekapenos (870–944), laws were implemented to prevent people from constructing new monasteries if there were others available that could be refurbished.

Like so many aspects of Byzantine life, the art of architecture declined as the Empire shrank and its resources dwindled. Thus, when French traveler Bertrandon de la Brocquière (ca. 1400–1459) toured the city of Constantinople in the year 1433, he noted that some of its churches were still beautiful, but there were only three cloisters surrounding the patriarch's church, instead of the many that it once featured, and he complained that holy relics were not being preserved with properly decorous reliquaries. He would have been horrified to learn that two decades later, after the fall of Constantinople in 1453, its remaining churches would be converted into mosques by the conquering Turks. Nonetheless, the fact that they preserved and maintained these Byzantine structures, instead of tearing them down and replacing them, is a tribute to the talents of the architects and builders who created them; and despite these later alterations, the original artistry that went into the structures that survive can still be appreciated today.

Further Reading

Bouras, Charalampos. 2006. *Byzantine and Post-Byzantine Architecture in Greece*. Athens: MELISSA Publishing House.

Buchwald, Hans H. 1999. *Form, Style, and Meaning in Byzantine Church Architecture*. Aldershot, England, and Brookfield, VT: Ashgate Publishing.

Johnson, Mark J., Robert Ousterhout, and Amy Papalexandrou, editors. 2012. *Approaches to Byzantine Architecture and Its Decoration: Studies in Honor of Slobodan Ćurčić*. Surrey, England, and Burlington, VT: Ashgate Publishing.

Kleinbauer, W. Eugene. 1992. *Early Christian and Byzantine Architecture: An Annotated Bibliography and Historiography*. Boston: G. K. Hall.

Piltz, Elizabeth. 2007. *From Constantine the Great to Kandinsky: Studies in Byzantine and Post-Byzantine Art and Architecture*. Oxford: Archaeopress.

Rodley, Lyn. 1994. *Byzantine Art and Architecture: An Introduction*. Cambridge and New York: Cambridge University Press.

Documents

From Bertrandon de la Brocquière. C. 1459. *Le Voyage d'Outre-Mer*. Excerpt translated by Chedomil Mijatovich. 1892. *Constantine: The Last Emperor of the Greeks, or, The Conquest of Constantinople by the Turks (AD 1453), After the Latest Historical Research*. London: Samson Low, Marston, and Company.

One of our last eyewitness accounts of Byzantine architecture comes from a medieval French traveler, Bertrandon de la Brocquière (ca. 1400–1459), who visited Constantinople in 1433 and later wrote about his journey in a book called Le Voyage d'Outre-Mer. *In this edited excerpt, he describes several churches in the Byzantine capital, though his attention was sometimes drawn more to their holy relics than their overall design.*

The city has many handsome churches, but the most remarkable and the principal church is that of St. Sophia, where the Patriarch resides, with others of the rank of Canons. It is of a circular shape, situated near the eastern point, and formed of three different parts: one subterranean, another above the ground, and a third over that. Formerly it was surrounded by cloisters, and had, it is said, three miles in circumference. It is now of smaller extent, and only three cloisters remain, all paved and inlaid with squares of white marble, and ornamented with large columns of various colours. The gates are remarkable for their breadth and height, and are of brass. This church, I was told, possesses one of the robes of our Lord, the end of the lance that pierced His side, the sponge that was offered Him to drink from, and the reed that was put into His hand. I can only say that behind the choir I was shown the gridiron on which St. Laurence was broiled, and a large stone in the shape of a washstand, on which they say Abraham gave the angels food when they were going to destroy Sodom and Gomorrah. . . .

On this side, near the point of the angle, is the beautiful church of St. George, which has, facing Turkey in Asia, a tower at the narrowest part of the straits. . . .

In the pretty church of Pantheocrator, occupied by Greek monks, who are what we should call in France Gray Franciscan Friars, I was shown a stone or table of divers colours, which Nicodemus had caused to be cut for his own tomb, and on which he laid out the body of our Lord, when he took Him down from the cross. During this operation the Virgin was weeping over the body, but her tears, instead of remaining on it, fell on the stone, and they are all now to be seen upon it. At first I took them for drops of wax, and touched them with my hand, and then bent down to look at them horizontally and against the light, when they seemed to me like drops of congealed water. This is a thing that may have been seen by many persons as well as by myself. In the same church are the tombs of Constantine and of St. Helena his mother, each raised about 8 feet high on a column, having their summit terminated in a point, cut into four sides, in the fashion of a diamond. It is said that the Venetians, while in power at Constantinople, took the body of St. Helena from its tomb and carried it to Venice, where, they say, it is still preserved. It is further said that they attempted the same thing in regard to the body of Constantine, but could not succeed; and this is probable enough, for to this day two broken parts of the tomb are to be seen, where they made the attempt. The tombs are of red jasper.

In the church of St. Apostles is shown the broken shaft of the column to which our Saviour was fastened when He was beaten with rods by order of Pilate. This shaft, above the height of a man, is of the same stone as the two others that I have seen at Rome and at Jerusalem; but this one exceeds in height the others put together. There are likewise in the same church many holy relics in wooden coffins, and any one who chooses may see them. One of the saints had his head cut off, and to his skeleton the head of another saint has been placed. The Greeks, however, have not the like devotion that we have for such relics. It is the same with respect to the stone of Nicodemus and the pillar of our Lord, which last is simply enclosed by planks, and placed upright near one of the columns on the right hand of the great entrance at the front of the church.

Among several beautiful churches I will mention only yet one as remarkable, namely, that which is called Blaquerna from being near the imperial palace, which, although small and badly roofed, has paintings, and a pavement inlaid with marble. I doubt not that there may be others worthy of notice, but I was unable to visit them all. The Latin merchants have one situated opposite to the passage to Pera, where mass is daily read after the Roman manner.

From Ramsay, William Mitchell. 1908. *Luke the Physician and Other Studies in the History of Religion.* London: Hodder and Stoughton.

In this passage, an early twentieth-century historian of religion describes the decline of Byzantine architecture in the last centuries of the Empire.

A deterioration in the builder's art is now manifest. The churches were built on good old plans; but the work was carried out rudely and probably in great haste; yet the haste is rather that of carelessness than of urgent need. There are no signs of loving desire to make the work as good and rich as possible. We cannot, indeed, say how far colour may have been employed to supplement the strictly architectural work; but the style is indisputably rather mean in character. The late churches produce the general impression of a degenerating people, a dying civilisation, an epoch of ignorance, and an Empire going to ruin.

Yet, with all their faults, even these late buildings retain for the most part a certain dignity and an effective simplicity. The tradition of the old Byzantine architecture was preserved in this sequestered nook, so long as the Imperial government maintained itself. It was only when the Empire shrank to narrower limits, and Lycaonia was left to the Turks, that the dignity of the Imperial Church was lost, and its places of worship show themselves plainly to be the meeting-places of a servile population.

What was good in the late architecture was traditional, surviving from an older time. What was bad in it was contributed by the age when the work was executed. The decay of true architectural feeling corresponded to decay in the civilisation of the period.

Bishops

The Orthodox Christian church was probably the important institution in Byzantine society, and its bishops were its most influential representatives. Not only were they in charge of the churches and monasteries in the cities they were assigned to, but they also were the men who, in periodic gatherings called synods, resolved the church's frequent theological debates. Most of them were also literate and scholarly men who expressed their views in writings that have survived, providing some information about their lives and personalities.

The priests who supervised individual churches and dealt directly with parishioners were usually not chosen to become bishops, primarily because many of them had wives, and bishops could not be married. Instead, monks were considered the ideal candidates: they were both celibate and well educated, meeting two requirements of the position, and their years of solitary devotion to prayer and contemplation had, it was believed, purified their souls and prepared them to deal with the world's sometimes sordid business. Needless to say, some monks preferred their cloistered lives and rejected invitations to become bishops, while a number of bishops tired of their responsibilities and retired to return to the monastery. Since it was considered important to have bishops who were familiar with the cities where they worked, new bishops were selected by a vote of all local clergy and church officials, subject to the approval of the bishop governing the region known as the metropolitan. Bishops enjoyed lifetime appointments, though they could be removed by superiors or choose to retire at any time.

Once in office, a bishop had many duties to fulfill. He had to live within his diocese and officially earned no salary, though the church's budget provided for his basic needs. He controlled of all of the church's properties and employees within his city, although some institutions, like monasteries and privately funded facilities, often enjoyed a degree of autonomy. The bishop handled his churches' finances and was expected to do so in a wise and honest manner, with a special concern for building and maintaining churches, and helping poor people, widows, orphans, and invalids. In the later centuries of the Empire, when the government had fewer resources, charitable activities became a greater priority, as bishops strived to build hospitals and "soup kitchens" to provide the poor with free food. The bishop had to visit each of his churches on a regular basis to demonstrate his concern, address their issues, and ensure that the facilities were being well managed. Whenever asked a question about the church's doctrines, he was expected to provide a thorough and accurate answer, which required ongoing reading and research to keep up with current developments. Despite the fact that they were supposed to live exemplary lives in all respects, as models for constituents, many did not live up to those high standards; one Egyptian bishop reportedly took 30 pounds of gold from his church treasury to purchase fancy silverware for his own table.

As a matter of law, bishops were not allowed to accept other positions within the government or army, but they did enjoy a certain amount of authority over secular matters. As advisors to the government, they might be asked to recommend good candidates to fill local positions like the judge called a *defensor civitatis* or the manager of the city's stored food, the *sitōnēs*; if provincial governors were incompetent or corrupt, bishops were expected to notify the emperor. Bishops also participated in distributing government funds for the construction of civic projects like baths, bridges, and harbors.

All communities had bishops, but those in larger cities enjoyed most power and prestige and were given different titles. Bishops who served in provincial capitals were called metropolitans; those in prominent cities had the title of archbishop; and those in the Empire's greatest cities, like Alexandria and Constantinople, termed themselves patriarchs. Unlike other bishops, these higher officials were typically appointed by the emperor, and they did not have to be familiar with the city where they worked; thus, a bishop from the Greek city of Argos might become the metropolitan of the city of Nicaea in present-day Turkey. Emperors could also appoint men who had no prior experience of working in the church to become metropolitans. In some cases, these outside candidates were respected intellectuals who seemed well prepared for such responsibilities; thus, the emperor Theophilos (813–842) was praised when he appointed a famed mathematician, Leo the

Philosopher (ca. 790–869), as the metropolitan of the Greek city of Thessaloniki. But other emperors abused their power and chose manifestly unworthy candidates; the most notorious case was the emperor Romanos I (ca. 870–948), who appointed his own son, Theophylact Lekapenos (917–956), to the church's most powerful position, patriarch of Constantinople, at the age of sixteen. Although somewhat attentive to his responsibilities, Theophylact was also something of a playboy who sought to make Byzantine church services more entertaining with touches of drama and devoted most of his time to the many horses that he owned. Once, he left church in the middle of a service to oversee a horse's birth, announcing his true priorities to the world.

Because the metropolitans usually had no ties to the cities where they served, they often grew dissatisfied with locales that seemed remote and uncultured and longed for the sophisticated and stimulating environment of Constantinople; many letters survive in which they complain about the poor food, filth, barrenness, and lack of reading material in their cities. In particular, the letters of the archbishop and distinguished theologian Theophylact of Ochrid (1055–1107) provide a vivid picture of a worldly intellectual who felt out of place among rude Bulgarian barbarians and fervently requested another assignment. Accordingly, many of the archbishops and metropolitans sought to visit Constantinople as often as possible. Such journeys were completely appropriate when special synods were convened to address major controversies; thus, in 754, a total of 754 bishops attended the Council of Hieria, convened by the emperor Constantine V (718–755), that banned religious images in churches, while about 350 came to the later synod, the Second Council of Nicaea in 787, that officially overturned its decision and reauthorized the church's icons. But such portentous gatherings were rare, as most of the synods regularly held in the capital dealt only with minor concerns; nevertheless, they could serve as an excuse for a trip to Constantinople. Metropolitans might also claim that they need to consult with superiors about an important issue, or personally ask the emperor to provide assistance to their diocese. Once in Constantinople, the metropolitans would seek to delay their return for as long as possible. These sojourns became so problematic that a law was passed preventing metropolitans from staying away from their cities for more than six months. As the boundaries of the Empire shrank, however, many bishops justified their permanent residence on Constantinople on the grounds that the cities they were assigned to were now in enemy territory or embroiled in violent conflicts. At the same time, the church extended its influence outside the Empire's boundaries in the early Russian state, Kievan Rus, where the developing Christian church adopted the structure and doctrines of Constantinople; after the Empire's fall, it became a separate organization, the Russian Orthodox Church.

CELEBRITY BISHOPS

In the Byzantine Empire, bishops were sometimes public figures and theologians as well as church leaders. Theophylact of Ochrid, for example, became popular with his Bulgarian parishioners because he fought for their rights, and he wrote respected commentaries on the Bible. In the twentieth-century United States, a Catholic bishop named Fulton J. Sheen played similar roles: after earning a reputation as a noted theologian, Sheen became a celebrity when a television program featuring his sermons, *Life Is Worth Living* (1951–1957), was unexpectedly successful in prime-time television, earning Sheen two Emmy Awards as an Outstanding Television Personality. He died in 1979, but is now on a pathway that could lead to sainthood.

THE AMERICAN ARCHBISHOP

The highest officials in the Greek Orthodox Church are now elected, since there is no emperor to appoint them, but they otherwise are carrying on with the duties that their predecessors handled in the days of the Empire. Today's leader of the church in the United States is Archbishop Demetrios Trakatellis, at the Greek Orthodox Archdiocese of America in New York City, who has served since 1999. In addition to his writings on theology, Archbishop Demetrios has devoted himself to charitable endeavors and has met with the last three U.S. presidents—Bill Clinton, George W. Bush, and Barack Obama. His Web site provides his demanding schedule of regular appearances throughout the United States.

This is a fifteenth-century image of St. John the Merciful, one of the few Byzantine bishops who was later declared a saint. (DeAgostini/Getty Images)

Bishops may have done their most valuable work in the final days of the Byzantine Empire, when both soldiers and officials repeatedly fled from cities that were being conquered by the Arabs or Turks. In these dire circumstances, the bishops bravely remained with their beleaguered citizens and, as the cities' only officials, would meet with the invaders to establish terms for surrender and achieve the most favorable conditions possible for their citizens. They would then serve precariously as the sole advocates for Christianity within an Islamic territory. Despite these commendable labors, and the many charitable endeavors and learned treatises of earlier bishops, the church as a whole oddly failed to value its bishops, regarding the asceticism of lifelong monks as more admirable than the secular dealings of bishops. For that reason, many Byzantine monks were later recognized as saints, but relatively few bishops were elevated to that status. Still, there were bishops like St. John the Merciful

(died 616), patriarch of Alexandria, whose herculean efforts to benefit the poor could not be overlooked, and they suggest that a life of service to society merits just as much appreciation as a life dedicated solely to spiritual pursuits.

Further Reading

Angold, Michael. 1995. *Church and Society in Byzantium under the Comneni, 1081–1261.* Cambridge and New York: Cambridge University Press.

Hussey, J. M. 2010. *The Orthodox Church in the Byzantine Empire.* Foreword and Updated Bibliography by Andrew Louth. Oxford and New York: Oxford University Press.

Louth, Andrew, and Augustine Casiday, editors. 2006. *Byzantine Orthodoxies: Papers from the Thirty-Sixth Spring Symposium of Byzantine Studies, University of Durham, 23–25 March 2002.* Aldershot, England, and Burlington, VT: Ashgate Variorum.

Mullett, Margaret. 1997. *Theophylacht of Ochrid: Reading the Letters of a Byzantine Archbishop.* Aldershot, England, and Brookfield, VT: Ashgate Variorum.

Sterk, Andrea. 2004. *Renouncing the World yet Leading the Church: The Monk-Bishop in Late Antiquity.* Cambridge, MA: Harvard University Press.

Thomas, John Philip. 1987. *Private Religious Foundations in the Byzantine Empire.* Washington, DC: Dumbarton Oaks Research Library and Collection.

Document

From Synesius. C. 403–414. Letters. Excerpts translated by James Carpenter Nicol. 1887. *Synesius of Cyrene: His Life and Writings.* London: E. Johnson.

Synesius (ca. 373–414) was a Greek Orthodox bishop who spent most of his life in the Greek city of Cyrene on the coast of present-day Libya. After being educated in Athens, his city sent him in 398 to serve as their ambassador in Constantinople, though he returned to Cyrene in 403. He was voted to be bishop of the nearby city of Ptolemais in 410, where he served four years before dying. A respected philosopher, he also wrote a number of letters that survive to reveal his personality and experiences, as the four excerpts below reveal. In the first, he implores his ailing brother to come stay at his pleasant home in Cyrene; in the second, he announces his intent to remain with his wife even after becoming a bishop, finally earning the right to do; in the third, as bishop, he announces the excommunication of two heretics; and in the fourth, a letter dictated as he was dying, he laments the recent deaths of his two sons.

Do you wonder at your chills and poor blood, if you will live in that sultry Phycus? It would be far more surprising if your physique held out against such a climate. But if you will only pay me a visit, by God's help there is a chance of your being set up when you are once out of air tainted with marsh vapours, and have left behind you the tepid salt lagoons lying so stagnant you might call them dead. What charm is there in sitting on the sand of the sea-shore, your only haunt, for where else can you turn? But here you may creep under the shade of some tree, and, if it likes you not, pass from tree to tree; nay from grove to grove, leaping across the stream that runs prattling by. How delightful the breeze that stirs the boughs so gently! Here is the changeful song of birds, the bright hues of flowers, the bushes in the meadows. Side by side are the works of man's hand and the free gifts of nature. The air is laden with perfumes, the earth rich with generous juices. And this grotto, fit home for the nymphs—I will spare it my praises, for it needs a Theocritus to sing it as it deserves.

*****

God and the law and the sacred hand of Theophilus gave [my wife] to me; I declare therefore and bear witness to all men that I will not be separated from her, nor associate with her by stealth, like an adulterer. Paul and Dionysius, the elders who are chosen by the people, will tell Theophilus my resolution in this matter. It is a crucial point, and I regard other difficulties as trifling in comparison with it.

*****

The church of Ptolemais, to all the sister churches throughout the world, addresses the following warning. Let no temple be open to Andronicus and his followers, to Thoas and his followers. Let every house of worship, every sacred precinct, be closed to them. The Devil has no part in Paradise; if he enters by stealth he is expelled. Wherefore to all citizens and to magistrates I make this proclamation, that they go not under the same roof, or sit at the same table with these men. And above all to priests that they salute them not in their life-time nor grant them in death the rites of burial. But should anyone despise our church, for that our city is of small account, and shall receive these men whom it has excommunicated, thinking that they need not obey her because she is poor, then, let him know that he is dividing the church which Christ willed should be one; and whatever he be, Levite or presbyter or bishop, he shall be held by us as in the case of Andronicus, and we will refuse him the hand of greeting, nor eat at the same table with him. Finally we shall do anything rather than grant a share in the sacred mysteries to those who choose the part of Andronicus and of Thoas.

*****

I have dictated this letter lying on my couch. May it find you well, my mother, sister, teacher; you who in all these relations have done good to me My physical weakness springs from mental prostration. The recollection of my lost children is wearing me slowly away. Synesius should have lived only so long as he could escape the evils of life . . . . . . Would that I might either cease to live, or else forget the tombs of my children.

Emperors and Empresses

In the beginning, Byzantine emperors were simply the Roman emperors who happened to live in Constantinople and be in charge of Rome's eastern territories; yet after Rome fell, they increasingly took on their own distinctive character. Like most of their subjects, they began to speak Greek instead of Latin, and abandoning the austere style originally imposed by the first Roman emperor Augustus, they donned ornate clothing and expensive jewelry. More significantly, while they still commanded significant armies, their reduced power obliged them to deal with enemies by means of diplomacy, not military action, and they exercised some authority over what was later known as the Greek Orthodox Church. They also granted their wives a larger role, both publicly and privately, in the governance of their empire, occasionally designating them as empresses; on a few occasions, empresses even ruled solely in their own names.

A man could become the emperor in several ways. It became customary for the current emperor to designate his own successor, who then served as a co-ruler until the emperor died and he assumed full control. Sons and other relatives were frequently chosen for the position, but an emperor might select a successful general or capable administrator to take his place. As in the Roman Empire, usurpers could also attempt to assassinate the emperor and seize the throne. Paradoxically, the Byzantines accepted the absolute authority of their emperors but saw nothing wrong with removing and replacing an emperor who seemed an ineffectual ruler. Most emperors came from the aristocracy, but a few ambitious peasants like Justin I (ca. 450–527) and Basil I (ca. 830–856) managed to rise in the ranks of the army and ultimately make themselves emperors.

Once installed in office, the emperor became a larger-than-life figure to his subjects. His face appeared on their coins, and paintings conveyed his kindness and piety by showing him handing gifts to the Christ Child and the Virgin Mary. During his rare public appearances, he wore a golden crown embedded with jewels and a robe of purple silk, with golden threads that made him glitter in the sunlight. When he and his entourage marched through the city while returning from a foreign campaign or going to greet prominent visitors, the road would be repaired and cleaned, covered with perfumed sawdust, and adorned with banners, plants, and wreaths. Bleachers were erected to accommodate spectators who watched the procession, which began with men holding banners and a huge gold cross. If the procession ended at a church, the emperor removed his crown, stepped into the sacred building, and ritually offered ten pounds of gold and other gifts to its clergymen.

Most of the emperor's time, however, was spent inside his huge residence, the Grand Palace, first erected by the Roman emperor Constantine I (272–327) and expanded and fortified by his successors. This enclave included the emperor's residence, homes for his many employees, chapels and churches, the workshops of his artisans, stables for horses, a field for playing polo, and a small harbor for the emperor's yacht. A typical day began with early morning prayers in a church, followed by meetings with various officials, which typically occurred in a large banquet hall where the emperor sat on a throne. When he was ready for lunch, a palace eunuch cleared the palace of visitors by ritually shaking a set of keys. If foreign dignitaries were granted an audience, the emperor would sit on an elevated throne in an enormous hall behind curtains until they were escorted into the room; then, to the accompaniment of singing, organ music, and roars from mechanical animals, the curtains would part to reveal the gloriously attired emperor, and the dazed visitors would bow.

While regular meetings and occasional ceremonial appearances were part of every emperor's schedule, the efficient Byzantine bureaucracy, like its Roman precursor, also allowed emperors time to pursue their own interests, and their preferred activities varied greatly. Some emperors focused on military matters and personally led their soldiers into battle, like Heraclius (575–641) and Manuel I Komnenos (1118–1180). Others, like Justinian I (ca. 482–565), left the fighting to their generals and stayed in Constantinople to involve themselves with the minutiae of governance; indeed, while examining the text of the *Corpus Juris Civilis*, the massive revision of Roman law completed during his reign, one scholar found a pattern of brusque phrasing that he attributed to Justinian's personal copyediting. Several emperors devoted themselves to scholarly pursuits: Constantine VII (905–959) wrote a number of works, including chronicles of recent Byzantine history and a book of advice for future emperors, *De Administrando Imperio*, while Manuel II (1350–1425) produced poetry, a biography of a saint, religious tracts, and a study of rhetoric. Some emperors were preoccupied with religious matters: the devout Leo II (ca. 675–741) developed the belief, termed iconoclasm, that Christian images were sacrilegious and, in 730, decreed that they should be removed from all churches in his realm, meeting fierce opposition. Another emperor, John VI Kantakouzenos (ca. 1292–1383), actually became a monk after retiring in favor of a popular rival and later endeavored to reunify the Eastern Orthodox and Roman Catholic churches. Finally, while none were as extreme as

Roman emperors like Caligula or Commodus, there were dissolute Byzantine emperors renowned mostly for their leisure activities: Michael III (850–867), dubbed "the Drunkard" for his excessive consumption of alcohol, personally participated in Constantinople's popular chariot races, profligately wasted government funds, and was eventually assassinated, while Alexander (866–913) chased women, neglected his responsibilities, and collapsed and died after an overly vigorous game of polo.

About one-third of the emperor's wives were given the official title of empress, which gave them the authority to mint coins, sign government documents, and control their own staffs and budget. Some had considerable influence over government affairs: Theodora (500–548), Justinian I's wife, personally persuaded her husband and other officials to successfully resist a violent rebellion instead of fleeing and supported several laws that benefited women, banning involuntary prostitution and strengthening their rights to own their own properties. Her niece Sophia (ca. 530–601), who married the emperor Justin II (520–578), took charge of the depleted royal budget and by means of shrewd economizing managed to repay all of its debts; and, at times when her unstable husband was too deranged to govern, she would unofficially but forcefully control the entire government.

Scholars have been especially interested in the empresses who governed as sole rulers. The most effective of these was Irene of Athens (752–803). After marrying the future emperor Leo IV (750–780), she first ruled as regent for her young son Constantine VI (771–797) after Leo IV died from a sudden illness; her first major achievement was to officially end the unpopular policy of iconoclasm and permit the display of religious images. As Constantine VI matured, he and his mother quarreled, and she eventually organized a conspiracy against him that led to his violent blinding and subsequent death in 797, allowing Irene to become the Empire's sole ruler. Many have speculated that the ruthless Irene poisoned her husband and personally ordered her son's death, but there is no proof of these allegations. With no male emperor on the throne, Pope Leo (750–816) asserted his power to fill the purported "vacancy" by proclaiming Charlemagne (ca. 742–814) to be the Holy Roman Emperor,

and Irene responded to this challenge to her rule by ingeniously offering to marry Charlemagne and later arranged a marriage between his daughter and her son. Centuries later, the two daughters of Constantine VII (690–1028), Zoe (978–1050) and Theodora (980–1056), briefly served as co-empresses in 1042, but the irresponsible Zoe resented her more capable sister and hastily found a third husband, Constantine IX Monomachos (ca. 1000–1055), who became emperor and reduced her influence. But after his death in 1055, Theodora returned to serve as sole empress and proved a decisive and assertive ruler, despite her advanced age, though she soon succumbed to disease.

We know little about the private thoughts of the Byzantine emperors and empresses regarding their position. Some may have been haunted by the realization that their empire was steadily declining toward an inevitable fall, though they put on a brave face;

A mosaic image of the Byzantine empress Irene, who capably governed the vast empire for five years before being deposed in 802 CE. (Brian Snelson)

TOO-CLOSE COLLEAGUES

The Byzantine emperor Romanos I (ca. 870–948) aroused controversy in 933 when he appointed his son, Theophylact Lekapenos (917–956), to become the patriarch of Constantinople, the church leader who wielded great political power. More recently, U.S. president John F. Kennedy was similarly criticized in 1961 when he appointed his own brother, Robert F. Kennedy, to become the nation's Attorney General. However, concerned about the propriety of a president granting high offices to close relatives, Congress passed a law in 1967, the Postal Revenue and Federal Salary Act, which made it illegal for a president to choose his wife or a family member to hold a government position.

A SHORT-LIVED EMPIRE

Even as the boundaries of the Byzantine Empire shrunk, its rulers continued to refer to themselves as emperors. That title today has become unfashionable, with one noteworthy exception: in 1976, the president of the Central African Republic, Jean-Bédel Bokassa, renamed his country the Central African Empire and proclaimed himself Emperor Bokassa I. Widely criticized for squandering vast sums of his poor country's money on a lavish coronation ceremony, and for his brutal treatment of his citizens, Bokassa I was removed from office in 1979 and later imprisoned for various crimes. His death in 1996, perhaps, marks the final end of the age of emperors.

others might have imagined that their empire would endure forever and someday regain its former glory. But almost all of them undoubtedly did the best they could to meet the many challenges that they faced.

Further Reading

Dagron, Gilbert. 1996. *Emperor and Priest: The Imperial Office in Byzantium*. Translated by Jean Birrell. 2003. Cambridge and New York: Cambridge University Press.

Evans, James Allan. 2005. *The Emperor Justinian and the Byzantine Empire*. Westport, CT: Greenwood Press.

Garland, Lynda. 2002. *Byzantine Empresses: Women and Power in Byzantium, AD 527–1204*. London and New York: Routledge.

Luttwak, Edward N. 2009. *The Grand Strategy of the Byzantine Empire*. Cambridge, MA: Harvard University Press.

Nicol, Donald M. 1996. *The Reluctant Emperor: A Biography of John Cantacuzene, Byzantine Emperor and Monk, c. 1295–1383*. Cambridge and New York: Cambridge University Press.

Walker, Alicia. 2012. *The Emperor and the World: Exotic Elements and the Imaging of Byzantine Imperial Power, Ninth to Thirteenth Century* CE. Cambridge and New York: Cambridge University Press.

Documents

From Procopius. C. 558. *The Secret History of the Court of Justinian: Literally and Completely Translated from the Greek for the First Time*. Translator or translators unidentified. 1896. Athens: Privately Printed for the Athenian Society.

While the Byzantine historian Procopius (ca. 500–565) praises the emperor Justinian I (ca. 482–565) in The Wars of Justinian, *he evidently grew disillusioned with him and his wife, Empress Theodora (ca. 500–548), as he later wrote another text, termed* The Secret History, *that savagely criticized them for their capriciousness and cruelty. In this edited passage from its thirteenth chapter, he provides an overview of the emperor's repugnant qualities.*

Although Justinian's character was such as I have already explained, he was easy of access, and affable to those whom he met. No one was ever denied an audience, and he never was angry even with those who did not behave or speak properly in his presence. But, on the other hand, he never felt ashamed of any of the murders which he committed. However, he never displayed any anger or pettishness against those who offended him, but preserved a mild countenance and an unruffled brow, and with a gentle voice would order tens of thousands of innocent men to be put to death, cities to be taken by storm, and property to be confiscated. One would think, from his manner, that he had the character of a sheep; but if anyone, pitying his victims, were to endeavour, by prayers and supplications, to make him relent, he would straightway become savage, show his teeth, and vent his rage upon his subjects. . . .

[I]n his zeal to bring all men to agree in one form of Christian doctrine, he recklessly murdered all who dissented therefrom, under the pretext of piety, for he did not think that it was murder, if those whom he slew were not of the same belief as himself. Thus, his thoughts were always fixed upon slaughter, and, together with his wife, he neglected no excuse which could bring it about; for both of these beings had for the most part the same passions, but sometimes they played a part which was not natural to them; for each of them was thoroughly wicked, and by their pretended differences of opinion, brought their subjects to ruin. Justinian's character was weaker than water, and anyone could lead him whither he would, provided it was not to commit any act of kindness or incur the loss of money. He especially delighted in flattery, so that his flatterers could easily make him believe that he should soar aloft and tread upon the clouds. . . .

[W]hat he really thought was always the opposite of what he said, and wished to appear to think. . . . As an enemy, he was obstinate and relentless; as a friend, inconstant; for he made away with many of his strongest partisans, but never became the friend of anyone whom he had once disliked. Those whom he appeared to consider his nearest and dearest friends he would in a short time deliver up to ruin to please his wife or anyone else, although he knew well that they died only because of devotion for him; for he was untrustworthy in all things save cruelty and avarice, from which nothing could restrain him. Whenever his wife could not persuade him to do a thing, she used to suggest that great gain was likely to result from it, and this enabled her to lead him into any course of action against his will. He did not blush to make laws and afterwards repeal them, that he might make some infamous profit thereby. Nor did he give judgment according to the laws which he himself had made, but in favour of the side which promised him the biggest and most splendid bribe. . . . While he was Emperor of the Romans neither faith in God nor religion was secure, no law continued in force, no action, no contract was binding. . . . He would often make men repeated promises, and confirm his promise by an oath or by writing, and then purposely forget all about it, and think that such an action did him credit. . . .

As a rule he dispensed with both rest and sleep, and never took his fill of either food or drink, but merely picked up a morsel to taste with the tips of his fingers, and then left his dinner, as if eating had been a bye-work imposed upon him by nature. He would often go without food for two days and nights, especially when fasting was enjoined, on the eve of the feast of Easter, when he would often fast for two days, taking no sustenance beyond a little water and a few wild herbs, and sleeping, as it might be, for one hour only. . . . Had he spent all this time in useful works, the State would have nourished exceedingly; but, as it was, he used his natural powers to work the ruin of the Romans, and succeeded in thoroughly disorganizing the constitution. His constant wakefulness, his privations, and his labour were undergone for no other purpose than to make the sufferings of his subjects every day more grievous; for. . . . he was especially quick in devising crimes, and swift to carry them out, so that even his good qualities seemed to have been so largely bestowed upon him merely for the affliction of his people.

From Bertrandon de la Brocquière. C. 1459. *Le Voyage d'Outre-Mer*. Excerpt translated by Chedomil Mijatovich. 1892. *Constantine: The Last Emperor of the Greeks, or, The Conquest of Constantinople by the Turks (AD 1453), After the Latest Historical Research*. London: Samson Low, Marston, and Company.

The medieval French traveler, Bertrandon de la Brocquière (ca. 1400–1459) visited Constantinople in 1433, and his report includes his observations of its royal family: the emperor John VIII Palaiologus (1392–1448); his third wife, Maria of Trebizond (died 1439); his brother Demetrios (1407–1470), known as the Despot of Morea, or southern Greece; and his mother Helena Dragas (ca. 1372–1450). They are all seen at a church service; he then watches Maria go off to dine and describes her appearance; and he finally observes Demotrios practicing archery on horseback.

I was curious to witness the manner of the Greeks when performing divine service, and went to St. Sophia on a day when the Patriarch officiated. The Emperor [John VIII Palaiologos] was present, accompanied by his consort [Maria], his mother [Helena Dragas], and his brother the Despot of Morea [Demetrius]. A mystery

[play] was represented, the subject of which was the three youths whom Nebuchadnezzar had ordered to be thrown into the fiery furnace. The Empress, daughter to the Emperor of Trebizonde, seemed very handsome; but as I was at a distance, I wished to have a nearer view. And I was also desirous to see how she mounted her horse, for it was thus she had come to the church, attended only by two ladies, three elderly men, ministers of state, and three of that species of men to whose guard the Turks entrust their wives. On coming out of St. Sophia, the Empress went into an adjoining house to dine, which obliged me to wait until she returned to her palace, and consequently to pass the whole day without eating or drinking.

At length she appeared. A bench was brought forth and placed near her horse, which was superb, and had a magnificent saddle. When she had mounted the bench, one of the old men took the long mantle she wore, passed to the opposite side of the horse, and held it in his hand extended as high as he could; during this she put her foot in the stirrup, and bestrode the horse like a man. When she was in her seat, the old man cast the mantle over her shoulders; after which one of those long hats with a point, so common in Greece, was given to her; at one of the ends it was ornamented with three golden plumes, and was very becoming. I was so near that I was ordered to fall back, and consequently had a full view of her. She wore in her ears broad and flat earrings, set with precious stones, especially rubies. She looked young and fair and handsomer than when in church. In one word, I should not have had a fault to find with her, had she not been painted, and assuredly she had no need of it. The two ladies also mounted their horses; they were both handsome, and wore mantles and hats like the Empress. The company returned to the palace of Blaquerne.

In the front of St. Sophia is a large and fine square, surrounded with walls like a palace, where in ancient times games were performed. I saw the brother of the Emperor, the Despot of Morea, exercising himself there with a score of other horsemen. Each had a bow, and they galloped along the inclosure, throwing their hats before them, which, when they had passed, they shot at; and he who pierced his hat with an arrow, or was nearest to it, was esteemed the most expert. This exercise they have adopted from the Turks, and

it was one in which they were endeavouring to make themselves efficient.

Eunuchs

Today, it is impossible to imagine parents arranging to have their son's testicles removed, or a man volunteering to undergo the procedure. Yet these were common occurrences in the medieval world, especially in the Byzantine Empire, primarily because men who had been castrated, called eunuchs, were preferred, or even required, in some desirable professions, for reasons that made perfect sense to people of that era. Because they were not eligible to serve as emperors, and were regarded as unambitious, eunuchs were ideal candidates to work in the palace bureaucracy as loyal servants to the emperor. As men who were assumed to have no sexual desires, they could be allowed to enter women's quarters to perform various tasks. In the church, since celibacy came to be viewed as a worthwhile goal for clergymen (though it was not always required, as in the Roman Catholic Church), the asexual eunuchs seemed well suited to become monks, priests, or bishops. And, since they seemed to combine the traits of men, women, and children, it was believed that they could readily relate to both sexes and hence function as excellent teachers or physicians. Thus, becoming a eunuch could make one eligible for a number of fulfilling careers.

Officially, castration was forbidden in the Byzantine Empire, and the practice was long frowned upon by the church as well, but the procedure was not dangerous or difficult. In the widely distributed writings of the Roman physician Galen, he explains how to cut off or crush testicles, though he expresses a personal aversion to doing so. Scholars assume that castration was rare in Constantinople but fairly common in distant territories where the authorities were less vigilant. It was also customary to import castrated slaves from foreign lands, and visiting diplomats might present the emperor with castrated slaves as gifts, since it was widely known that he constantly needed eunuchs for his staff.

The eunuchs chosen to work in the palace were first trained by veterans to follow all of the protocols of the royal court. Because they seemed effeminate and did not have beards, they could usually be identified, but they also wore a distinctive uniform, a white tunic and red jacket that were both trimmed with gold. Certain eunuchs with a higher status wore a special sort of necklace with a pearl, and some chose to wear earrings. Depending upon their background, they might be assigned any number of daily tasks: many handled jobs that were elsewhere done by women, such as washing and storing clothes, cooking and serving meals, and dealing with household finances. Others cut the emperor's hair or made his bed. Those with more education might teach children, treat ailments, or offer political advice. The most prestigious eunuch, the *parakoimenos*, protected the emperor by locking himself within the emperor's sleeping quarters every night.

As eunuchs became more and more central to palace operations, they assumed greater responsibilities. A eunuch was in charge of preparing for the emperor's ceremonies, and the *castrensis*, or *majordome*, was a eunuch who supervised other members of his staff. A eunuch called the *papias* made sure that the palace buildings were well lighted and maintained, while the *parakoimenos*, once a sort of bodyguard, had assumed the duties of a prime minister. When the empress Irene of Athens (752–803) arranged to have her son marry the daughter of Charlemagne (ca. 742–814), she sent a eunuch to present-day France to teach the future bride how to handle herself at the Byzantine court. And though the emperor Constantine VII (905–959) is believed to have done much of his own writing, scholars suspect that the text *De Ceremoniis*, commonly called *On Imperial Ceremonies*, was actually written by his palace eunuchs, who were probably more familiar with the minutiae of those elaborate rituals.

One of the most powerful eunuchs in Byzantine history, Basil Lekapenos (died 985), was actually the illegitimate son of the emperor Romanos I Lekapenos (870–948). He was castrated as a boy, presumably to prevent him from ever aspiring to achieve the throne; indeed, this was often a strategy employed to thwart the aspirations of the sons of usurpers or deposed emperors. As a eunuch, he was then able to obtain a job in the palace of his father, and he surely proved himself a capable administrator, since he actually attained his highest position as *parakoimenos* under his father's successor, Constantine VII (905–959), and kept that job under the next three emperors. Many sources report that he poisoned the last of these, John I Tzimiskes (925–976), because the emperor was displeased to discover that Basil Lekapenos had made himself rich after years of service. Perhaps this is why the next emperor, Basil II (958–1025), quickly charged him with treason, seized his property, and sent him into exile.

Even though they might have seemed ill-suited for such masculine roles, some palace eunuchs were also promoted to serve as generals in the Byzantine army. One example was Narses (478–573), one of the generals of Justinian I (ca. 482–565). All that we know about his early life is that he came from present-day Armenia, but we can assume that he was one of the many foreigners who were castrated to work in the emperor's palace, and he must have displayed remarkable abilities, as he became Justinian I's chief treasurer. After helping Justinian I quell a local rebellion, he was appoint to command an army to assist the general Belisarius (ca. 500–565) in the effort to reconquer Italy. After returning to Constantinople to again assist Justinian I in the palace, he was sent back to Italy, this time in command of the entire army, and triumphed in several battles. Four centuries later, a eunuch who served in the personal guard of emperor Nikephoros II (912–969), named Peter Phokas (ca. 940–977), so distinguished himself that the emperor put him in charge of the entire eastern army and he performed capably in that role; he continued to fight for Nikephoros II's successors before dying in battle.

Other desirable positions for eunuchs were in the church, which had abandoned its original opposition to castration to regard eunuchs as ideal practitioners of the celibacy regarded as a key aid in focusing all of one's energies on divine matters. The eleventh-century archbishop of Ophid, Theophylact (1055–1107), wrote a tract that celebrated eunuchs as modern-day counterparts to the early ascetics who rejected physical desires in favor of spiritual pursuits. Certainly, castration was no barrier to advancement in the church, since several eunuchs achieved the high position of patriarch of Constantinople and were later declared saints. In addition, two monasteries, at Mount Aphos and

THE *CASTRATI:* ASEXUAL SINGERS

Long after castration had fallen out of favor for any other purpose, some families still chose to castrate their young sons so that they would retain their excellent, high-pitched voices as adults. The practice died out in the nineteenth century, but one Italian *castrato* from that era, Alessandro Moreschi, (1858–1922), lived long enough to have his voice recorded in 1902, after a long career of singing in the Sistine Chapel Choir. So, even if there are no living representatives of these individuals, we can still listen to Moreschi's recordings and hear the sound of an adult *castrati* voice.

PAINLESS CASTRATION TODAY

In the Byzantine Empire, castration was sometimes employed as a way to control men who were perceived as threats; the illegitimate son of an emperor, for example, might be made a eunuch to prevent him from becoming emperor or having children who might claim the throne. In the twentieth- and twenty-first-century United States, castration has been legal in some states as a way to control convicted male sexual offenders, especially those whose victims have been children. Today, however, while surgery under anesthesia remains a voluntary option in some states, most of these sex offenders are controlled by having them ingest chemicals that reduce their sex drive, but that do not actually castrate them.

Constantinople, were set up especially for eunuchs; some suspect that this stemmed from a desire to separate them from other monks who may have resented the special advantage they had in renouncing sexual activity, though others theorize that effeminate eunuchs were regarded as a temptation for heterosexual monks to engage in homosexual activity. Some of the other monasteries employed monks who were eunuchs to work with nuns, since it was assumed that they would never attempt to seduce the women. Eunuchs were also in charge of church choirs; it was customary to employ castrated boys, or *castrati*, as singers because of their excellent, high-pitched voices, and adult eunuchs were seen as ideal mentors for these youth. In addition, since some of them had also been castrated at a young age, they often had attractive voices as well and could join the *castrati* in beautifully singing hymns.

Eunuchs were found in many ancient societies, but the power and visibility of the Byzantine eunuchs made them unusually prominent in their society, and that remained the case until the eleventh century, when the Komnene Dynasty, beginning with the emperor Isaac I Komnenos (1007–1061), promoted a strong image of masculinity that did not accord with the less-than-masculine eunuchs. In addition, as voluntary celibacy became the idealized lifestyle of priests and monks, the church came to see castration as an improper way to achieve that status. In fact, Theophylact may have written his defense of eunuchs to comfort his brother Demetrios (died ca. 1107), a eunuch, in face of growing opposition to such individuals. Still, eunuchs continued to hold positions in the Empire until its fall in 1453, and they retained roles in Western society even into the nineteenth century, when some choirs continued to include *castrati*. Only today has public opinion turned decisively against a practice now regarded as cruel disfigurement, not a pathway to success.

Further Reading

Brubaker, Leslie, and Julia M. H. Smith. 2004. *Gender in the Early Medieval World: East and West, 300–900*. Cambridge and New York: Cambridge University Press.

Hadley, D. M., editor. 1999. *Masculinity in Medieval Europe*. London and New York: Longman.

James, Liz, editor. 1997. *Women, Men and Eunuchs: Gender in Byzantium*. London and New York: Routledge.

Neil, Bronwen, and Lynda Garland, editors. 2013. *Questions of Gender in Byzantine Society*. Farnham, England: Ashgate Publishing.

Ringrose, Kathryn M. 2003. *The Perfect Servant: Eunuchs and the Social Construction of Gender in Byzantium*. Chicago: University of Chicago Press.

Tougher, Shaun. 2008. *The Eunuch in Byzantine History and Society*. London and New York: Routledge.

Document

From Foord, Edward. 1911. *The Byzantine Empire: The Rearguard of European Civilization*. London: Adam and Charles Black.

Historians in the past frequently criticized the purported decadence of the Byzantine court, emphasizing its employment of eunuchs. Here, another historian condemns such complaints and notes the generally effective work of the court's eunuchs.

A common fault among historians, as the writer sees them, is to study and describe Court society under the impression that it is the reflex of that of a nation. Nothing can be farther from the truth. Court life neither reflects that of the people, nor does it influence it except in a very slight degree; it was, and is, and will be apart from it; courtiers live in a little world of their own.

Court society in the Byzantine Empire was, we are frequently assured, corrupt and vicious. That may well be the case; Satan always finds mischief for idle hands, and the average Court is very idle—busy doing nothing. No doubt Byzantine courtiers were as idle, corrupt, and vicious, as the courtiers of every age, not excepting our own, are likely to be. A good deal of abuse is often levelled at the Court ceremonial and the employment of eunuchs. The latter feature is one peculiarly repulsive to the modern European mind, but the eunuchs as a class seem to have been good public servants. As regards the Court ceremonial, there is no reason to think that the Emperors usually insisted upon its observance, except on state occasions; and, after all, the difference between it and that of modern England or Germany is only in degree. I doubt very much whether Constantinopolitan news-writers were more fulsomely adulatory of their Emperors than journalists to-day—speaking of personages who have little of kingship about them save their sounding titles—often are.

Be this as it may, though Byzantine Court society was no worse, and often better, than many of which I have read and heard, I consider it utterly dissociated from that of the people. Nor do I see that the Eastern Empire had a "taint of weakness derived from its Oriental origin"; its peoples as a whole were not by any means weak or degenerate; the elaborate and gorgeous Court, with its degrading ceremonial, was the outcome of the ideas of a Western Roman Emperor of peasant birth!

Farmers

In some respects, the daily lives of Byzantine farmers were very similar to those of their earlier counterparts, as many of the time-tested tools and techniques of agriculture remained in use. However, the broader circumstances of their work were changing, as farms were increasingly tied to villages as well as large estates, and new technologies were emerging that made some of their tasks easier. Two large bureaucracies—the government and the church—also had a growing impact on farmers, both in imposing new restrictions and providing more contact with the world beyond their lands. Indeed, since there are few first-hand accounts of rural life during the Byzantine era, much of our information comes from the documents kept by those institutions.

Most Byzantine farmers lived in small villages with a few hundred residents while doing their farming on a piece of land they owned in the countryside; at the times when their work was most demanding, they might temporarily live in makeshift quarters closer to their fields. Certain areas in the vicinity of the villages, such as pastures, forests, and rivers, were considered community property, and villagers might also pool their resources for public service projects, like the construction of mills and bridges.

Two types of farming occupied the typical peasant's life: first, he needed to raise enough food to feed himself and his family, and a garden near his home usually provided plants for personal consumption, though there were also gardens located in distant fields. Second, he had to raise crops on his fields, which could be bartered to obtain goods or sold in marketplaces to raise money for taxes and other purchases.

The most common garden vegetables were vetches, chickpeas, and lentils, though dozens of others were occasionally preferred, including onions, cabbage, carrots, cucumbers, kohlrabis, radishes, turnips, and leeks. Some herbs were grown both as flavorings and medicines, such as rosemary, dill, mint, mustard, parsley, and fennel, and a few trees would provide fruits and nuts, like apples, pears, pomegranates, peaches, walnuts, almonds, and chestnuts, as well as shade for relaxing farmers. Beyond utilitarian concerns, farmers would often grow a few flowers in their gardens to serve as decorations. In their fields, farmers typically focused on grains, especially wheat, which was preferred for human consumption, while millet and barley were produced primarily to feed animals. Documents from fifteenth-century Macedonia suggest that about half of the Byzantine fields grew wheat, a third were devoted to barley, and the rest produced millet, rye, and oats. Farms might also have vineyards, to grow grapes that were dried to be eaten as raisins or crushed to make wine, and groves of olive trees to generate olive oil, which was central to the Byzantine diet and also used as a fuel for lamps.

To begin the process of farming, it might be necessary to clear the land by burning away most vegetation and cutting down remaining trees with an axe. Plowing was accomplished with the sole ard, a plow made of iron or wood, which was pulled by oxen to produce furrows that were about three-inches deep; seeds were then dropped into the furrows. In gardens, farmers might plant seeds by hand using a spade. Gardens would be fertilized with human waste from cesspools, while fields employed manure from livestock and domesticated birds. Weeds had to be regularly removed with a rake, spade, or hoe called a *makele*. To harvest their grains, farmers employed a small sickle, a *drepanon*, with a blade made of iron. Though this was not as effective as the longer scythe that had become standard in Western Europe, farmers preferred the *drepanon* because it left more stubble to be eaten by their animals. The harvested grain would then be placed in a basin and crushed by a stone roller.

A major innovation in Byzantine farming was the increasingly common use of large mills to grind grain more efficiently. Some of these were built by rivers, so the flowing water could turn a horizontal or vertical wheel connected by gears to a grinding stone, or millstone. In seventh-century Persia, the wind-powered mill, or windmill, was invented and, a few centuries later, the technology had made its way to the Byzantine Empire and Western Europe. These buildings were typically built and owned by villages to be used by all of their farmers.

Raising animals also occupied an increasing amount of the farmer's time, since people were demanding more and more meat in their diet. Pigs were an excellent choice because they reproduced quickly, required little space, could be fed leftovers and waste, and were tame enough to be cared for by children. Other animals provided both meat and other useful products. Goats and sheep produced milk and cheese, and sheep's wool could be sold to make clothing,

though parasites were a recurring problem; one manual advises farmers to heat a mixture of cedar oil, maple roots, and mandrake and rub it into the sheep's wool to kill ticks and lice. Cows were also a source of milk and cheese, though some farmers found them too expensive to keep because they required large quantities of grain. Chickens laid numerous eggs, and goose feathers were used to fill mattresses and pillows. Some farmers were beekeepers, making honey to add sweetness to food, though sugarcane imported from the Arab world began to be grown in the fourteenth century to provide the Byzantines with sugar. A few animals were kept for the services they provided: oxen pulled plows, while dogs assisted in hunting and herding animals. Finally, Europeans had long sought the secret of making silk, and in 554 CE, according to the Byzantine historian Procopius (ca. 500–565), two

PRESIDENTIAL FARMING

Byzantine farmers devoted their fields almost entirely to grains that they sold, while raising food for their families in smaller gardens near their homes. People in many other cultures have used similar home gardens to provide their own food. In the United States during World War II, government posters and films asked citizens to plant "victory gardens" so they could feed themselves and make more food available for the troops. Even Eleanor Roosevelt, the wife of President Franklin D. Roosevelt, planted a victory garden on the grounds of the White House as a good example for her constituents.

HARVESTING THE WIND

Byzantine farmers were the first Europeans to use windmills to grind their grain into flour, a technology they borrowed from the Persians. Over the centuries, windmills have remained in use for that purpose, but they have also been increasingly employed to pump water from wells and reservoirs. More recently, seeking new sources of energy, manufacturers have developed windmills, called wind turbines, which convert the wind's energy into electricity. Today, when one drives through the deserts of southern California and Nevada, they will regularly observe see rows of towers with rotating blades generating needed energy.

Since goats did not eat as much as cows, many Byzantine farmers preferred to keep them as a source of milk. Here, in a mosaic from the fifth or sixth century CE, a Byzantine farmer milks one of his goats. (Neil Harrison/ Dreamstime.com)

monks secretly brought silkworm eggs from China to the Byzantine Empire, so farmers could begin to raise silkworms and the mulberry trees that provided the leaves eaten by silkworms.

Like their counterparts everywhere and throughout time, Byzantine farmers could be victimized by poor weather, droughts, virulent pests, and fluctuating markets, but the greatest challenge they faced was probably paying their taxes. The rates were high, and farmers were required to pay in cash instead of crops or produce. Oftentimes, farmers were forced to sell their property, leading to increasing numbers of large estates owned by wealthy men who had acquired land previously held by small farmers. Substantial pieces of land were also acquired by the church for rural monasteries, where monks made agriculture one of their daily pursuits. These places often resembled small villages, with a central cluster of buildings—residences, chapels, and workshops—surrounded by fields of grain, vineyards, gardens, and orchards. While some of the agricultural work was done by employees of the estate owner or the monks of the monasteries, parts of

the land were also leased to tenant farmers, who were allowed to grow crops as long as they paid landowners a portion of what they raised.

To the north, the early Russians practiced a form of agriculture that long remained rather primitive, but advanced implements like wooden plows began to become common after the seventh century. The greatest difficulty that Russian farmers faced was the poor quality of their soil, which required them to develop more complex systems of crop rotation. Initially, farmers would plant crops on half of their land and leave the other half fallow, but later farmers learned to divide their lands into thirds: one would be planted in the spring and harvested in the fall, one was planted in the fall and harvested in the summer, and the third was left fallow. Most Russian crops were grown on vast estates owned by princes or monasteries, as in the Byzantine Empire, but evidence suggests that some lands were privately owned by small farmers.

Farming has never been an easy life, but the farmers of the Byzantine Empire and early Russia did have one advantage over many of their predecessors: they were almost entirely free men. As the church grew more and more skeptical about the morality of slavery, there were fewer and fewer slaves, and they mostly worked in cities as servants. Farmers might feel effectively tied to lands they farmed but did not own, like serfs, but they could move away to seek a better life in the city. Still, most farmers chose to remain close to the soil, preferring a life of raising crops and animals in the countryside.

Further Reading

Banaji, Jairus. 2002. *Agrarian Change in Late Antiquity: Gold, Labour, and Aristocratic Dominance.* Oxford and New York: Oxford University Press.

Cooper, J. Eric, and Michael J. Decker. 2012. *Life and Society in Byzantine Cappadocia.* Houndmills, Basingstoke, Hampshire, and New York: Palgrave Macmillan.

Dalby, Andrew. 2011. *Geoponika: Farm Work: A Modern Translation of the Roman and Byzantine Farming Handbook.* Based on a collection by Cassianus Bassus. Totnes, Devon: Prospect Books.

Leibner, Uzi. 2009. *Settlement and History in Hellenistic, Roman, and Byzantine Galilee: An Archaeological Survey of the Eastern Galilee.* Tübingen, Germany: Mohr Siebeck.

Littlewood, Antony, Henry Maguire, and Joachim Wolschke-Bulmahn, editors. 2002. *Byzantine Garden Culture.* Washington, DC: Dumbarton Oaks Research Library and Collection.

Oniz, Hakan, and Erdoğan Aslan, editors. 2011. *SOMA 2009: proceedings of the XIII Symposium on Mediterranean Archaeology, Selcuk University of Konya, Turkey, 23–24 April 2009.* Oxford: Archaeopress.

Document

From Anonymous. C. seventh or eighth century. "The Farmer's Law." Translated by W. Ashburner. 1912. *Journal of Hellenic Studies,* 32, 87–95.

A series of anonymously written Byzantine laws from the seventh or eighth century, now referred to as "The Farmer's Law," establishes a number of regulations to punish misbehavior and resolve disputes.

The Farmer who is working his own field must be just and must not encroach on his neighbor's furrows. If a farmer persists in encroaching and docks a neighboring lot—if he did this in plowing time, he loses his plowing; if it was in sowing time that he made his encroachment, he loses his seed and his husbandry and his crop—the farmer who encroached.

If a farmer without his landowner's cognizance enters and plows or sows let him not receive either wages for his plowing or the crop for his sowing—no, not even the seed that has been cast.

If two farmers agree with the other before two or three witnesses to exchange lands and they agree for all time, let their determination and their exchange remain firm and secure and unassailable.

If two farmers, A and B, agree to exchange their lands for the season of sowing and A draws back, then, if the seed was cast, they may not draw back; but if the seed was not cast they may draw back; but if A did not plow while B did, A also shall plow.

If two farmers exchange lands either for a season or for all time and one plot is found deficient as compared with the other, and this was not their agreement, let him who has more give an equivalent in land to him who has less; but if this was their agreement, let them give nothing in addition.

If a farmer who has a claim on a field enters against the sower's will and reaps, then, if he had a just claim, let him take nothing from it; but if his claim was baseless, let him provide twice over the crops that were reaped.

If two territories contend about a boundary or a field, let the judges consider it and they shall decide in favor of the territory which had the longer possession; but if there is an ancient landmark, let the ancient determination remain unassailed.

If a division wronged people in their lots or lands, let them have license to undo the division.

If a farmer on shares reaps without the grantor's consent and robs him of his sheaves, as a thief shall he be deprived of all his crop.

A share holder's portion is nine bundles, the grantor's one: he who divides outside these limits is accursed.

If a man takes land from an indigent farmer and agrees to plow only and to divide, let their agreement prevail; if they also agreed on sowing, let it prevail according to their agreement.

If a farmer takes from some indigent farmer, his vineyard to work on a half share and does not prune it as is fitting and dig it and fence it and dig it over, let him receive nothing from the produce. . . .

If a farmer takes over the farming of a vineyard or piece of land and agrees with the owner and takes earnest-money and starts and then draws back and gives it up, let him give the just value of the field and let the owner have the field.

If a farmer enters and works another farmer's woodland, for three years he shall take its profits for himself and then give the land back again to its owner.

If a farmer who is too poor to work his own vineyard takes flight and goes abroad, let those from whom claims are made by the public treasury gather in the grapes, and the farmer if he returns shall not be entitled to mulct them in the wine.

If a farmer who runs away from his own field pays every year the extraordinary taxes of the public treasury, let those who gather in the grapes and occupy the field be mulcted twofold.

Goldsmiths

While all societies have valued gold, the Byzantine Empire was especially obsessed with obtaining and employing the precious metal in every facet of their society, from coins and jewelry to art and architecture. Indeed, the nation imported so much of the metal to augment its own supplies that Western Europe experienced a significant shortage of gold from the eighth to tenth centuries. The various Byzantines who mined, refined, and worked with gold were kept very busy indeed, responding to the constant demands of their compatriots.

Under the unified Roman Empire, there had been government-controlled gold mines in Cyprus, Egypt, and present-day Turkey, and the Byzantine government continued to oversee these operations, although some of these were leased to private companies. Archaeologists have thoroughly examined one Byzantine gold mine in the ancient Egyptian town of Bir Umm Fawakhir. After the ore was extracted from the ground, it was crushed and heated to a high temperature near the mine, and since gold is often blended with silver, mercury or salt would be added as a way to extract the silver. Before the refined gold was

transported for use, an official would examine it to guarantee that it was pure. Then, the certified ingots would be sent off to various destinations.

Much of Byzantium's gold was employed to make coins, which were manufactured exclusively by the government in several mints in places throughout the Empire, including Constantinople, Antioch in present-day Turkey, Alexandria in Egypt, and Thessaloniki in Greece. Later, when the Empire lost much of its territory, minting occurred solely in Constantinople. All of the mints were closely guarded and located close to the Mediterranean Sea, to reduce the risk of theft as the new coins were moved from the mint to be transported in ships. Inside the mints, skilled workers first heated the gold and let it flow into small circular molds to produce blank disks; then, while the metal was still soft, the disks were placed inside of a press shaped like a plier, with the desired images for the front and back of the coin—usually a man's head and shoulders or a human figure surrounded by text—imprinted on each side. Closing the press provided each coin with the proper markings. The most common gold coin, called a *solidus* or *nomisma*, became the most common currency both within the Empire and in medieval Europe, because it was recognized to have both official and intrinsic value. The Byzantines also minted two smaller gold coins, the *semissis* and *tremisis*.

To be used for other purposes, gold and silver were brought to specialized workshops called *ergasteria*, which typically had no more than twelve employees: an experienced metalworker who owned the shop, his apprentices, and several slaves. These facilities were closely supervised by the government, which was particularly intent upon preventing goldsmiths from melting down coins and making objects out of them. For that reason, *The Book of the Eparch*, a tenth-century compilation of economic rules and regulations, stipulates that gold and silver could only be worked on in the *ergasteria*. Another law stated that each purchase by a goldsmith could involve no more than one pound of gold, probably as a way to discourage people from robbing the *ergasteria*.

To craft items such as plates, the goldsmiths would usually mix their gold with a little silver to produce a form of the alloy known as electrum. To

The Byzantine Empire was intent on using gold in almost every facet of their society, from coins and jewelry to art and architecture. Here, one of the Byzantine gold coins known as a *solidus*, minted in 945 CE, depicts the then-reigning Byzantine emperor Constantine VII (905–959 CE). (Werner Forman/Corbis)

People seeking to economize might settle for a silver plate with a thin coating of gold, produced by dipping the plate in a mixture of gold and mercury and heating it. Since this procedure produced highly toxic fumes, the goldsmiths must have worked outdoors in order to survive the experience.

Many special items made of gold were created exclusively for the use of the emperor and crafted in his own personal *ergasteria*. Unlike the Roman emperors, Byzantine emperors wore golden crowns that naturally had to be magnificently decorated; thus, one crown featured enamel panels depicting Jesus Christ and several saints and numerous jewels dangling from gold chains. The Grand Palace would also be filled with paintings in gold frames, decorative gold vessels, and furniture covered with gold. In addition, the church had the resources to pay for the crafting of large golden objects to be displayed in its grand cathedrals. These might include several large plates, chalices, and candelabras; there are even reports that some churches had entire altars made of gold, though none have survived. Reliquaries, boxes designed to hold holy relics, were often golden; one of these in a church in Constantinople, which purportedly contained a piece of the cross on which Jesus was crucified, was a large golden box, decorated with images of the Roman emperor Constantine and his mother Saint Helena. An official in Venice also commissioned the goldsmiths of Constantinople to make an altarpiece for an Italian cathedral; now called the *Pala d'Oro*, this beautiful golden panel, decorated with jewels, featured depictions of Jesus and his apostles. If a painting of a saint had apparently demonstrated some special power to assist those who prayed to the image, a goldsmith would be asked to cover its face with a thin layer of gold both as a sign of respect and to protect it from damage.

Considerable craftsmanship is also observed in the larger gold pieces worn as jewelry. Among these were two items typically worn at weddings, the marriage crown and the marriage belt. One impressive example of a marriage belt from the Byzantine era consists of a pair of large medallions, each depicting a couple being married by a priest, connected to twenty-one smaller medallions with religious symbols. Marriage crowns might be made of either gold or silver; a tradition in Greek churches stipulates that the groom should wear

make a plate, the metal would first be hammered into the proper shape; then, it would be decorated using three basic techniques. *Repoussé* was a process of delicately hammering the plate from its projected underside to produce raised images on the surface; using the reverse method, called chasing or embossing, the goldsmith would hammer on the surface to produce sunken images; and to engage in incising, cutting tools would be employed to make marks on the plate. For a large platter showing an elaborate scene from history or mythology, a combination of all three techniques might be required. Wealthy customers could afford plates and other utensils made of pure gold; unsurprisingly, a tenth-century visitor to Constantinople's Grand Palace, the emperor's home, reports a dinner that featured golden utensils, plates, bowls, and flasks.

A CURRENT CURRENCY

The Byzantine Empire minted large numbers of gold coins, which were used throughout Europe and the Middle East, so it is not surprising that many of these coins have survived through the ages. Today, on eBay, anyone can buy a Byzantine gold coin for themselves, at prices ranging from $200 to $1,000. In addition, while Web sites selling gold coins as investments mainly feature recent coins like the American Eagle and South African Krugerrand, some of them are also selling Byzantine gold coins. While no one is using them—or any gold coins, for that matter—to make purchases today, Byzantine coins are still a part of the world economy.

HOW TO BECOME A GOLDSMITH

Byzantine goldsmiths learned their trade by working as apprentices under experienced artisans, and within some families, the art of goldsmithing is still passed on in this fashion. It is now more common, though, to take classes and earn a degree to master and enter this field. For example, at Colorado State University, students can earn a Master of Fine Arts (MFA) degree in Metalsmithing and Jewelry, which requires two years of coursework and one year of preparing pieces for a Thesis Exhibition. Logically enough, given the long history of gold mining in the state, the university advertises that its students will have the opportunity to work with gold.

a gold crown, while the bride wears a silver crown. The crowns of wealthy couples may be very ornate, especially commissioned and fashioned by the goldsmith according to their wishes; others might be content with a crown consisting of a plain gold band. It was long expected that couples would purchase their own crowns and, after their wedding, display them in a case on their bedroom walls; but churches also developed the custom of owning their own crowns and lending them to couples who could not afford such purchases. As another alternative to the services of a goldsmith, some brides and grooms wore crowns made of flowers.

In the later days of the Byzantine Empire, due to simple overuse and the loss of territories with gold mines, there was less and less gold available; as a result, to provide as much glittering material as possible, the government allowed its coins and ingots to contain greater quantities of silver, so items made of pure gold became rarer. This may represent, however, the only way in which the work of the Byzantine goldsmiths meaningfully changed over the centuries; otherwise, as in other areas of the Empire's artistry, the men who created gold objects were content to keep following time-honored patterns. This resistance to innovation, and the fact that goldsmiths never sought to identify themselves, can both be regarded as a consequence of the typically religious character of their work; when devout believers are making images of their God and His saints, they are naturally disinclined to do so with any unique touches or celebratory references to their individual creativity. Hence, virtually all of the golden artifacts from this civilization tend to look like the work of a single artist, who might be identified as the Byzantine Empire itself.

Further Reading

Bernstein, Peter. 2002. *The Power of Gold: The History of an Obsession.* New York: Wiley.

Brown, Katharine Reynolds. 1984. *The Gold Breast Chain from the Early Byzantine Period in the Römisch-Germanisches Zentralmuseum.* Mainz, Germany: Römisch-Germanisches Zentralmuseums.

Cormack, Robin. 1985. *Writing in Gold: Byzantine Society and Its Icons.* Oxford and New York: Oxford University Press.

Hahn, Wolfgang, and William E. Metcalf, editors. 1988. *Studies in Early Byzantine Gold Coinage.* New York: American Numismatic Society.

Meyer, Carol, Lisa A. Heidorn, Walter E. Kaegi, and Terry G. Wilfong. 2000. *Bir Umm Fawakhir Survey Project 1993: A Byzantine Gold-Mining Town in Egypt.* Chicago: Oriental Institute of the University of Chicago.

Temple, Richard, editor. 1990. *Early Christian and Byzantine Art: Textiles, Metalwork, Frescoes, Manuscripts, Jewellery, Steatites, Stone Sculptures, Tiles, Pottery, Bronzes, Amulets, Coins and Other Items from the Fourth to the Fourteenth Centuries.* London: Temple Gallery.

Documents

From Procopius. C. 551. *History of the Wars.* Volume 1. Translated by Henry B. Dewing. 1914. London: W. Heinemann.

In 540, the Persian king Khosrau I, also known as Chosroes, invaded Byzantine territories in Mesopotamia and Syria. The Byzantine historian Procopius (ca. 500–565), in this excerpt from his History of the Wars, *describes how he greedily seized a typical golden reliquary, holding a piece of the True Cross, in the Syrian city of Apamea.*

Now there is a piece of wood one cubit in length in Apamea, a portion of the cross on which the Christ in Jerusalem once endured the punishment not unwillingly, as is generally agreed, and which in ancient times had been conveyed there secretly by a man of Syria. And the men of olden times, believing that it would be a great protection both for themselves and for the city, made for it a sort of wooden chest and deposited it there; and they adorned this chest with much gold and with precious stones and they entrusted it to three priests who were to guard it in all security; and they bring it forth every year and the whole population worship it during one day. Now at that time the people of Apamea, upon learning that the army of the Medes was coming against them, began to be in great fear. And when they heard that Chosroes was absolutely untruthful, they came to Thomas, the chief priest of the city, and begged him to show them the wood of the cross, in order that after worshipping it for the last time they might die. And he did as they requested. . . .

Now when Chosroes had seized all the treasures, and Thomas saw that he was already intoxicated with the abundance of the wealth, then bringing out the wood of the cross with the chest, he opened the chest and displaying the wood said: "O most mighty King, these alone are left me out of all the treasures. Now as for this chest (since it is adorned with gold and precious stones), we do not begrudge thy taking it and keeping it with all the rest, but this wood here, it is our salvation and precious to us, this, I beg and entreat thee, give to me." So spoke the priest. And Chosroes yielded and fulfilled the request.

From O. M. Dalton. 1911. *Byzantine Art and Archaeology.* Oxford: Clarendon Press.

O. M. Dalton was a noted art historian who worked at the British Museum, and his book Byzantine Art and Archaeology *was considered one of the best in the early study of Byzantine art. In this passage, he describes the limited techniques of the Byzantine goldsmiths, in comparison to the accomplishments of their Western European counterparts.*

The work of the Byzantine goldsmiths offers less variety than that of their mediaeval contemporaries in the West, who for about eight hundred years were occupied with the solution of similar problems. There are several reasons for this comparative monotony. In the West there was a succession of striking and fundamental changes in architecture, an art which has imposed its forms upon ecclesiastical metal-work; at the same time different processes of enamelling succeeded and displaced each other, each requiring a fresh treatment and necessitating a new disposal of the surface to be wrought and decorated. In the Eastern Empire the architectural changes from the fifth century to the fifteenth were less pronounced; there the reliquary in the form of a church would therefore alter far less throughout this long space of time than in a country like France, where the Romanesque style was succeeded by various phases of Gothic with arches, pinnacles, and window traceries of different forms. The style of enamelling in the East remaining constant down to the fall of Constantinople, gold plaques of small size continued to be decorated by the cloisonne process, which meant that they were in all centuries applied to larger surfaces of metal in the same way. But in the West the general adoption of the champlevé process on copper in the twelfth century reacted upon artistic metal-work: the craftsman could now dispense with small plaques treated as if they were merely larger precious stones, and was able to cover considerable surfaces with colour embodied as it were in the very substance of the work. The development of the beautiful translucent enamel upon sunk relief admitted further variety, and the process of painting in enamel still more. Lastly, the restricted use of sculpture in the East debarred the Byzantine goldsmith from many delicate devices known to his Western neighbours. He cast and chased bronze but little, making no such bold and beautiful mouldings as were produced on the Rhine and Meuse in the twelfth century, and confining himself as far as figures were concerned to embossing thin plates of silver or gold. In this respect the stationary character of his work is marked when compared with the continual developments which were taking place in Italy, Germany, and France. In the use of niello he was also conservative, never advancing beyond a few figures on a small scale, or a conventional design. In the application of precious stones he adhered throughout to the plain raised setting . . . not attempting the device, known even to the Carolingians, of holding a gem as it were suspended in claws, so that the light might pass completely through it. Nor did he often mass stones together, or arrange them in a close row, except by the old method of *orfèvrerie cloisonnée*, which he maintained after it had been abandoned in Western Europe. He never faceted his gems or pastes, but in this respect was no more backward than his neighbours, who also contented themselves with cabochon gems down to the approach of the Renaissance. Filigree he occasionally used to cover vacant spaces between the stones or enamels, having no canopies or traceries to perform this office, thus adhering faithfully to a method of ornamentation which the West abandoned with the rise of the Gothic style. In a word, Byzantine goldsmith's work, though often sumptuous and highly decorative, is perhaps more conservative than any branch of a very conservative art.

Jewelers

Jewelry was very important in the Byzantine Empire, for two reasons. First, like men and women in other cultures, the Byzantines enjoyed wearing jewelry to improve their personal appearance, though it was becoming more popular with women than with men. Second, as the Christian faith increasingly dominated their lives, Byzantine citizens regularly wore small items of religious significance, both to attest to their faith and, it was hoped, to provide holy protection against harm. Large adornments made of gold, like crowns, were handled by professional goldsmiths, but jewelers might employ small quantities of gold to make smaller items, and they also made use of a wide variety of other materials, such as jewels, enamel, ivory, and glass.

Given the wide demand for jewelry and its relatively high prices, jewelers were probably among the most prosperous craftsmen of Constantinople and surrounding cities. They were typically independent entrepreneurs who owned and operated small workshops, which also served as stores. There, they would sell premade items while working on specially commissioned pieces for wealthy customers. A few jewelers might be employed by a rich family to exclusively make items for their use, and the emperor owned large workshops filled with jewelers making items for his court. Byzantine jewelers could also make items especially designed to be exported to other regions, as evidenced by a Byzantine necklace unearthed in Sicily and a Byzantine pendant found in modern-day Tunisia. The major centers for the production of Byzantine jewelry were Constantinople, Athens, Antioch, and Alexandria, though several jewelers could be found in almost every city of the Empire.

Many items were made of gold, usually in combination with gems or pieces of enamel. One unusual practice was to make gold coins the centerpieces of necklaces or rings, perhaps surrounded by tiny jewels. The most common gemstones were pearls, beryls, and garnets, though the wealthy could afford more expensive jewels like emeralds, amethysts, and sapphires. Such jewels were also placed on golden earrings, brooches, and earrings, though these were sometimes made of silver. To cut their gems, jewelers would employ either a wheel or a chisel called a burin; jewels taken from discarded jewelry might be carved again and placed in new settings. Jewelers also had tools to drill small holes in jewels that would hang in gold chains. To decorate gold items with images, jewelers would employ the three basic techniques of goldsmiths—*repoussé*, chasing, and incising—though it was difficult to produce elaborate patterns on very small objects.

Jewelers were asked to produce several different types of gold jewelry. Women liked to wear golden earrings, brooches, and earrings, and both men and women wore large gold crosses around their necks, sometimes with a central red garnet representing the blood of Jesus Christ. Silver and gold rings were made by heating a small cylinder of metal, bending it into a circle, and connecting the ends by soldering on a flat disk or square, decorated with an image or a jewel. Other popular adornments typically made

These earrings, made after the sixth century, like much Byzantine jewelry, are made of gold and prominently feature pearls and other precious stones. (DeAgostini/Getty Images)

alternating panels of gold and enamel, and dangling on attached gold chains were several jewels and seven pendants, one depicting the Virgin Mary.

Byzantine jewelers also began to imitate the works of the Goths and Huns that had earlier invaded southern Europe, who favored golden buckles and pins decorated with small gems. However, after first producing similar items, they made them even more attractive by developing a new technique called *cloisonné*. The jewelers would first heat and attach gold wires to a gold base, creating intricate patterns with the bent wires. Then, they would place tiny bits of glass in various colors into each section created by the wires and bake the object in a kiln, fusing the class into semitransparent enamel. Finally, the jewelers would polish the enamel using sand to produce brightly colored objects. The same technique was later employed to decorate larger objects like medallions, crowns, and reliquaries, boxes used to store holy relics.

Pieces of jewelry would also be made out of metals other than gold. Silver was both attractive and less expensive, and it became the norm for even the wealthiest purchasers of jewelry in the last two centuries of the Byzantine Empire, since by then gold was scarce. People who could not afford precious metals might wear bracelets or necklaces made of bronze, gilded to look like gold. Byzantine jewelers also revived the use of a striking alloy discovered in ancient Greece called *niello*, a mixture of silver, copper, and lead. Because its black color looked impressively masculine, men came to prefer rings made of *niello*.

Ivory and glass were found in jewelry as well. Women liked to place hairpins carved out of ivory in their hair; later, however, the Byzantine Empire experienced a shortage of the substance, which had to be imported from the distant regions where elephants lived, Africa and India, so jewelers might instead use bone or a semiprecious stone like jasper. Colorful glass bracelets were popular and inexpensive, so virtually any woman could afford to buy them; however, since new glass also became hard to obtain, jewelers relied upon bits of used glass, called cullet, which were considerably cheaper. Testifying to the demand for this material, one shipwreck from the eleventh century near the coast of modern-day Turkey mostly contained vast quantities of cullet.

of gold were the amulets called *enkolpia*. A sort of Christian good-luck charm, these amulets, usually displaying images of Jesus, the Virgin Mary, or saints, were believed to protect their wearers from harm if they were worn on a gold chain around their necks. There were usually not enough room to engrave entire names on small pieces of jewelry, but representative Greek letters might be added: the letters *mu* and *rho* (*MR* or *mr*), for example, would represent "Mother" or the Virgin Mary, while *iota* and *chi* (rendered as either *I X* or *ic*) stood for "J.C.," or Jesus Christ. Some *enkolpia* were designed to hold tiny relics—a fragment of the True Cross, a drop of a martyr's blood, or oil from a lamp in a revered church. While items of this nature worn by everyday people might be small, wealthy women could afford more elaborate pieces of religious jewelry. One necklace consisted of thirteen

TREASURES FROM THE TRASH

Today, one reads regular news stories about people who accidentally throw away valuable objects and are forced to search through heaps of trash in hopes of retrieving them. Strangely enough, something similar may have happened in the Byzantine Empire. In 2013, while excavating a seventh-century trash heap in present-day Israel, archaeologists were stunned to discover 400 gold coins and many pieces of gold jewelry, including a handsome gold ring. Since it is impossible to imagine even the wealthiest man choosing to discard such precious items, one must assume that these were thrown in the trash by accident, undoubtedly upsetting the person or persons who owned them.

A BYZANTINE ALLOY

Although they did not invent the alloy, the Byzantines grew fond of jewelry made out of *niello*, a mixture of silver, copper, and lead, and such items also became common in the first Russian state, Kievan Rus. In the twentieth century, the only nation where jewelers regularly employed this alloy was Thailand, though its version of the substance is technically known as "Siam Silver." If U.S. soldiers vacationing in Thailand decided to pick up pieces of jewelry for their wives, they were probably made of *niello*, so that many U.S. families today have, as family heirlooms, jewelry made of one of the Byzantines' favorite alloys.

Most pieces of Byzantine jewelry were purchased by the people who planned to wear them, or their spouses, but jewelers might receive special orders from individuals with different plans. For example, the Byzantine historian Procopius (ca. 500–565) reports that the general Belisarius (ca. 500–565) liked to bring quantities of necklaces and bracelets with him on his campaigns to be given as awards to soldiers who fought especially well. The emperor would also provide certain high-ranking officials with special rings, called *fibulae*, which announced their privileged position within the government or the army. Some people also sought to obtain jewelry for their animals; Byzantine illustrations show bejeweled racing horses and dogs wearing collars with jewels; sometimes, they were also provided with protective amulets.

Jewelry was less important to the people of ancient Russia, although women there, like women everywhere, regularly wore earrings, necklaces, and bracelets, as well as special sort of necklace, called a *grivna*, made of bronze or silver hoops. Men might wear little more than wedding rings and crosses around their necks. Made by local jewelers, these simple items attracted very little attention outside of Russia, in contrast to the more celebrated products of the Byzantine jewelers, which have been carefully preserved and are displayed today in many museums. But their makers, whose names have all been lost to history, were consciously creating works of art, and they probably hoped that each of their items would be passed down from generation to generation and worn for many years. And while the originals are usually kept within glass cases, modern imitations of their achievements are still adorning the bodies of today's stylish women.

Further Reading

Brown, Katharine Reynolds, Dafydd Kidd, and Charles T. Little, editors. 2000. *From Attila to Charlemagne: Arts of the Early Medieval Period in the Metropolitan Museum of Art.* New York: Metropolitan Museum of Art.

Bruhn, Jutta-Annette. 1993. *Coins and Costume in Late Antiquity.* Washington, DC: Dumbarton Oaks Research Library and Collection.

Entwistle, Chris, and Noel Adams, editors. 2010. *"Intelligible Beauty": Recent Research on Byzantine Jewellery.* London: British Museum.

Evans, Helen C., and William D. Wixom, editors. 1997. *The Glory of Byzantium: Art and Culture of the Middle Byzantine Era, A.D. 843–1261.* New York: Metropolitan Museum of Art.

Hackens, Tony, and Rolf Winkes, editors. 1983. *Gold Jewelry: Craft, Style, and Meaning from Mycenae to Constantinopolis: An Exhibition Held at the Museum of Art, Rhode Island School of Design from February 24, 1983–April 3, 1983.* Louvain-la-Neuve, Belgium: Institut Supérieur d'Archéologie et d'Histoire de l'Art, Colle`ge Erasme.

Ross, Marvin C. 2005. *Catalogue of the Byzantine and Early Mediaeval Antiquities in the Dumbarton Oaks Collection: Volume Two: Jewelry, Enamels, and Art of the Migration Period.* Second edition. Washington, DC: Dumbarton Oaks Research Library and Collection.

Document

From O. M. Dalton. 1911. *Byzantine Art and Archaeology.* Oxford: Clarendon Press.

This British Museum scholar offers an overview of the styles of Byzantine jewelry, as contrasted with those of the ancient Greeks, the Romans, and medieval Europeans, and describes some specific items found at Kyrenia, an archaeological site on the northern coast of Cyprus.

It may be noticed by way of preliminary that Byzantine fashions in the matter of personal ornament differed somewhat from those of the West. In Western mediaeval Europe after Frankish times ear-rings are but rarely mentioned in contemporary literature, and examples are never found belonging to any period much earlier than the Renaissance; nor did bracelets, which were common among prehistoric peoples and among the Romans, find much favour before the fifteenth century. In the Eastern Empire this was apparently not the case, though the ear-rings which we possess happen, like European examples, to be of early date. But we know that bracelets continued in use, both through existing examples and through documentary evidence. Thus in A.D. 831 we read that a chief magistrate presented Theophilus with golden bracelets. The custom of sewing pearls, gems, and even enamelled medallions to the garments may also be conveniently noticed here. The richly embroidered imperial robes were covered in this way until they became so stiff that the grace of draped folds became impossible. Many illuminations and mosaics illustrate this magnificence; while an even better idea may be gained from the royal mantle and other vestures made in mediaeval Sicily under strong oriental influence and now preserved in the Schatzkammer at Vienna.

Roman jewellery has survived in greater quantities than that of the Eastern Empire, partly because great tracts of that empire have been less accessible to the excavator than the Roman provinces, partly because Byzantium was Christian from the beginning and interments are less likely to yield objects of archaeological interest.

At the beginning of the First Period, as we should naturally expect, there is no clear line of demarcation between late Roman and Byzantine jewellery. The combination of large stones of intense colour, such as plasma or carnelian, with gold of an ever-diminishing solidity is a characteristic which became general in the fourth century. The old Greek insistence on beauty of form was gone: it was no longer necessary to model well, or to apply to the creations of the goldsmith's craft that fine restraint which preserved the Greeks from the love of empty splendour. What was now required was not work to be picked up and lingered over by the discriminating eye, but something to attract attention from a distance by almost violent contrasts of light and colour. For this purpose fragile gold-work and stones of inferior quality sufficed: with the Greek perfection of detail, the honest solidity of early Roman work was abandoned. Even from the third century the oriental system of massing table-gems or pastes between narrow cloisons had invaded the Roman Empire, and must have obtained early entrance into Constantinople. We may infer this from the survival of the style upon the Limburg reliquary at a time when it had disappeared in Persia and had practically died out in Europe. . . .

The principal other articles of jewellery found with [the Kyrenia] treasure consisted of three necklaces, one of large cylindrical plasma beads alternating with pearls, the other two of gold chains with crosses and pendants hanging from them, several pairs of ear-rings, a girdle (?) composed of a number of gold coins and four large gold medals. The first of these necklaces and the ear-rings are of an early type, and analogous to jewellery ascribed to the Roman period found in Egypt and elsewhere. The two others are interesting from the character of their pendants, which are in the form of little gold amphorae, and of flat open-work plaques, circular and pear-shaped, with confronted birds and conventional patterns. One of the chains has flat rectangular links of quatrefoil design; both are rather flimsy in construction. The greater number of the coins composing the girdle are of Maurice Tiberius, and all the four large medals, which are stated by numismatists to have been cast and not struck from a die, are of the same emperor: the date is therefore presumably the last quarter of the sixth century. The district of Kyrenia had previously yielded other Byzantine jewels (a chain, ear-rings, &c), probably of much the same date as the treasure just described; and to the same period belongs the interesting gold jewellery discovered at Mersina in Cilicia, now in the Hermitage at St. Petersburg, in which the use of openwork and the pear-shaped pendants noticed in the Kyrenia necklaces are again conspicuous. The latter feature suggests an oriental (Persian) influence. Another treasure, found at Narona in Dalmatia, included four gold rings and an ear-ring: the coins discovered with it ranged from Justin I (518–27) to Tiberius Constantine (A.D. 578–82). One of the rings was inscribed in Latin letters with the name *Urvece* (Urbica?), another with a monogram.

Merchants

As its territories and its military might declined, the Byzantine Empire became most important as a center of commerce. While small merchants continued to serve their local customers, others focused their attention on business arrangements with other nations, which increasingly stationed their own representatives within the Byzantine capital to handle their commercial interests. They enjoyed the benefit of using the stable Byzantine currency, commonly accepted throughout the Mediterranean world, as well as a government that carefully regulated businesses to ensure fair practices.

The merchants most overlooked by history were the artisans, who made and sold their own products in workshops that were also their stores; these men and women included bakers, blacksmiths, candle makers, cobblers, jewelers, perfumers, tailors, tanners, and weavers. These artisans usually did not own their establishments, but rather rented them from the large institution that owned the building—the church, the government, or a wealthy aristocrat. In Constantinople, the merchants' shops were typically located underneath the city's porticoes, or covered walkways, in special sections reserved for each type of business; goods were made and sold on the first floor, while merchants and their families lived on the second floor. Merchants in each category typically were organized into guilds, or cartels, which were supervised by the government and designed to prevent unfair competition.

In trades that purchased raw materials from outside sources, all merchants pooled their resources, paid for the materials in one transaction, and divided them proportionately. In selling merchandise, the profit was not allowed to exceed more than four to six percent of what the product was worth, and products were examined by government officials to guarantee their quality. Most interestingly, merchants were no longer allowed to informally train their children and pass on their trade; instead, in order to work, say, as a tailor, a man first had to pass a sort of test administered by the heads of the guild, to ensure that he could capably make and repair items of clothing. To prevent one person from earning too much money, no one could belong to more than one guild; thus, a tailor was not allowed to double his income by also working as a cobbler.

Other cities also had permanent markets, but much of their business was conducted at large market fairs, where merchants from all over the surrounding region would come to temporarily sell their goods in stalls at certain times every year. For example, in the Greek city of Thessalonoki, the Empire's second busiest center for business, there were two established marketplaces, one for high-quality merchandise and another, less reputable "Slav market," and every year during the festival dedicated to St. Demetrios, there was a huge market fair that attracted numerous merchants from Bulgaria, Italy, and other distant nations. Smaller cities had sections for artisans who provided for local needs like leatherworkers, potters, smiths, and weavers. There were also peddlers who walked through the aisles of the market fairs, selling items from pushcarts or backpacks, and we assume that they traveled through the countryside at other times of the year, offering items to remote villagers who rarely visited the city.

In addition to artisans and other small businesspersons, another category of merchant emerged around the seventh century, men who specialized in importing and selling foreign goods. They typically were not ambitious merchants from the marketplace, but rather well-connected aristocrats who could obtain privileges from the emperor and other high-ranking officials. Armed with seals featuring an image of the emperor, attesting to their special powers, these men

These are examples of the lead seals that empowered certain Byzantine merchants from the tenth or eleventh century to monopolize the marketing of various goods from abroad. (Yale University Art Gallery)

could effectively monopolize the trade in certain prized goods such as silk, although other imported goods, like slaves, could also be highly profitable. Foreign items to be resold could be obtained in two ways: these entrepreneurs could make arrangements with ship owners to bring goods to the ports of Constantinople, or foreign businessmen could travel to certain locations outside of the city to sell their goods under the supervision of government officials. The chief hazard faced by these men was the death or removal of their friend in high places, which might end their business in an instant.

In the tenth century, business activities in the Byzantine Empire expanded, as it regained control of Crete in 961 and thus made Mediterranean sea travel less vulnerable to pirates, and as improving economies in northern Asia and the Middle East encouraged more and more of their merchants to seek new opportunities outside their borders. Thus, while the emerging Russian state of Kievan Rus twice attacked Constantinople, it also negotiated treaties to expand trade relations between the two states. In addition to the Russians, merchants from the Arab world and the Italian city of Venice, instead of rendezvousing with agents outside the city, wanted to actually enter Constantinople to do their business. The government sanctioned the practice but kept a careful eye on these foreign businessmen, as they were supervised by officials, required to state

what sorts of goods they sought to import, and allotted a fixed period of time (usually, no more than three months) to complete their arrangements and leave the city. Soon, some representatives of distant economies, like the Venetians and Turks, were allowed to remain permanently within the capital, where they established close ties with local entrepreneurs to regularly sell the goods they brought and purchase items to send back to their homelands.

While the opportunities for profits kept increasing, both from marketing local goods to local customers and from importing and exporting, entrepreneurs also needed more money to take advantage of those opportunities. One could form a partnership with another person to obtain more resources, but this also meant surrendering some control over one's enterprise and splitting the rewards. For many, taking out a loan seemed the better alternative, despite the risks, and for that reason, the business of moneylending became more and more common. While the church officially frowned upon moneylending, the government understood that it was often necessary, and instead of forbidding the practice, it instead established rules to prevent abuses. Thus, for most loans, the moneylenders could charge no more than four or six percent in interest; for riskier understandings, like sending goods on long sea voyages, one might be permitted to charge up to twelve percent. Later, the limits were raised to about

ARTISAN ENTRANCE EXAMS

In ancient Constantinople, people who wished to enter certain professions had to be tested by experienced professionals in their guilds to establish that they were qualified to hold that job. This remains the case today for many professions in the United States: lawyers must pass their state's bar exams to practice law, for example, while teachers in states like California must pass a standardized test to work in a classroom. Even barbers and hair stylists, in order to join trades that demand little formal education, must pass an exam, which in most states combines a written test with a hands-on demonstration of their ability to capably cut people's hair.

A CENTER FOR TRADE

After New York City resolved to construct a World Trade Center in 1959, few people realize that their plans also inspired the creation of the international World Trade Centers Association to encourage other cities to construct similar centers and establish profitable connections between them. Today, there are over 300 World Trade Centers throughout the world. Appropriately, given its historic importance in promoting international trade, the former Byzantine capital, Istanbul, added its own World Trade Center in 1999. However, while this large complex is impressive, it is not as spectacular as New York's destroyed World Trade Center (or its planned replacement, rising to 1,776 feet), since each of Istanbul's buildings only has seventeen stories.

8-1/3 percent for standard loans and 16-2/3 percent for loans for overseas commerce.

Moneylending was regarded as a disreputable business, and merchants of all sorts had long been considered not entirely respectable citizens, compared to lofty members of the aristocracy and the church hierarchy. All of this changed after the crucial year of 1042: first, the son of a merchant, Michael V Kalaphates (1015–1042), actually became emperor after he married the empress Zoe (978–1050), which initially elated the merchant class; then, when he attempted to exile Zoe and become the country's sole ruler, his former supporters turned against him and successfully demanded Zoe's return. As a result, reforms were enacted that effectively made wealthy merchants members of the aristocracy and allowed them to serve in the senate. Briefly, it seemed that merchants might become the dominant members of their society.

Unfortunately, after the Byzantine Empire had some key military setbacks and lost much of its territory, the merchants experienced a reversal of fortune: the emperor Alexios I Komnenos (ca. 1056–1118) took away all of their newly earned privileges, and seeking the assistance of the Venetians, he granted their merchants significant new rights that made it very difficult for native entrepreneurs to compete with their foreign counterparts. Increasingly, it was the Italian businessmen, especially those from Venice and Genoa, who held the upper hand in the business affairs of the Empire, and as its power declined even further, the Turks who were getting closer and closer to its capital also demanded and received a special status for its businessmen. By the time that the Frenchman Bertrandon de la Brocquière (ca. 1400–1459) traveled to Constantinople in 1433 CE, he observed that its business affairs seemed to be dominated by the Venetians and the Turks. Still, artisans continued to make and sell their goods to their local customers until the city and the Empire fell in 1453, carrying on traditions that in some cases have endured to the present day.

Further Reading

Harvey, Alan. 1989. *Economic Expansion in the Byzantine Empire, 900–1200.* Cambridge and New York: Cambridge University Press.

Hendy, Michael F. 1985. *Studies in the Byzantine Monetary Economy C. 300–1450.* Cambridge and New York: Cambridge University Press.

Laiou, Angeliki F., editor in chief. 2008. *The Economic History of Byzantium: From the Seventh through the Fifteenth Century.* Washington, DC: Dumbarton Oaks Research Library and Collection.

Laiou, Angeliki F., and Cécile Morrisson. 2007. *The Byzantine Economy.* Cambridge and New York: Cambridge University Press.

Mango, Marlia Mundell, editor. 2009. *Byzantine Trade, 4th–12th Centuries: The Archaeology of Local, Regional and International Exchange: Papers of the Thirty-Eighth Spring Symposium of Byzantine Studies, St John's College, University of Oxford, March 2004.* Farnham, England, and Burlington, VT: Ashgate Publishing.

Nicol, Donald M. 1988. *Byzantium and Venice: A Study in Diplomatic and Cultural Relations*. Cambridge and New York: Cambridge University Press.

Documents

From Anonymous. C. 12 century. Excerpt from the *Timarion*. Translated by H. F. Tozer. 1881. "Byzantine Satire." *Journal of Hellenic Studies* 52, 233–70.

The Timarion, *a Byzantine satire written by an unknown author sometime around the twelfth century, includes this description of a festival in Macedonia where innumerable merchants set up booths to sell goods from all over the Mediterranean region.*

The Demetria is a festival, like the Panathenaea at Athens and the Panionia among the Milesians, and it is at the same time the most important fair held in Macedonia. Not only do the natives of the country flock together to it in great numbers, but multitudes also come from all lands and of every race—Greeks, wherever they are found, the various tribes of Mysians [i.e. people of Moesia] who dwell on our borders as far as the Ister and Scythia, Campanians and other Italians, Iberians, Lusitanians, and Transalpine Celts [this is the Byzantine way of describing the Bulgarians, Neapolitans, Spaniards, Portuguese, and French]; and, to make a long story short, the shores of the ocean send pilgrims and suppliants to visit the martyr, so widely extended is his fame throughout Europe. For myself, being a Cappadocian from beyond the boundaries of the empire, and having never before been present on the occasion, but having only heard it described, I was anxious to get a bird's eye view of the whole scene, that I might pass over nothing unnoticed. With this object I made my way up to a height close by the scene of the fair, where I sat down and surveyed everything at my leisure. What I saw there was a number of merchants' booths, set up in parallel rows opposite one another; and these rows extended to a great length, and were sufficiently wide apart to leave a broad space in the middle, so as to give free passage for the stream of the people. Looking at the closeness of the booths to one another and the regularity of their position, one might take them for lines drawn lengthwise from two opposite points. At right angles to these, other booths were set up, also forming rows, though of no great

length, so that they resembled the tiny feet that grow outside the bodies of certain reptiles. Curious indeed it was, that while in reality there were two rows, they presented the appearance of a single animal, owing to the booths being so near and so straight; for lines suggested a long body, while the crossrows at the sides looked like the feet that supported it. I declare than when I looked down from the heights above on the ground plan of the fair, I could not help comparing it to a centipede, a very long insect with innumerable small feet under its belly.

And if you are anxious to know what it contained, my inquisitive friend, as I saw it afterwards when I came down from the hills—well, there was every kind of material woven or spun by men or women, all those that come from Boeotia and the Peloponnese, and all that are brought in trading ships from Italy to Greece. Besides this, Phoenicia furnishes numerous articles, and Egypt, and Spain, and the pillars of Hercules, where the finest coverlets are manufactured. These things the merchants bring direct from their respective countries to old Macedonia and Thessalonica; but the Euxine also contributes to the splendour of the fair by sending across its products to Constantinople, whence the cargoes are brought by numerous horses and mules. All this I went through and carefully examined afterwards when I came down; but even while I was still seated on the height above I was struck with wonder at the number and variety of the animals, and the extraordinary confusion of their noises which assailed my ears—horses neighing, oxen lowing, sheep bleating, pigs grunting, and dogs barking, for these also accompany their masters as a defence against wolves and thieves.

From Bertrandon de la Brocquière. C. 1459. *Le Voyage d'Outre-Mer*. Excerpt translated by Chedomil Mijatovich. 1892. *Constantine: The Last Emperor of the Greeks, or, The Conquest of Constantinople by the Turks (AD 1453), After the Latest Historical Research*. London: Samson Low, Marston, and Company.

In his account of a 1433 visit to Constantinople, the French traveler Bertrandon de la Brocquière (ca. 1400–1459) describes his encounters with the city's many merchants.

There are merchants from all nations in this city, but none so powerful as the Venetians, who have a bailiff to regulate all their affairs independently of the Emperor and his ministers. This privilege they have enjoyed for a long time. It is even said that they have twice by their galleys saved the town from the Turks; but for my part I believe that they spared it more for the holy relics' sake it contains than anything else. The Turks also have an officer to superintend their commerce, who, like the Venetian bailiff, is independent of the Emperor. They have even the privilege, that if one of their slaves should run away and take refuge within the city, on their demanding him, the Emperor is bound to give him up. This prince must be under great subjection to the Turk, since he pays him, I am told, a tribute of ten thousand ducats annually. And this sum is only for Constantinople, for beyond that town he possesses nothing but a castle situated three leagues to the north, and in Greece a small city called Salubria.

I was lodged with a Catalonian merchant, who having told one of the officers of the palace that I was attached to my Lord of Burgundy, the Emperor caused me to be asked if it were true that the Duke had taken the Maid of Orleans, which the Greeks would scarcely believe. I told them truly what had happened, at which they were greatly astonished.

The merchants informed me that on Candlemas-day there will be a solemn service performed in the afternoon, similar to what we perform on that day, and they conducted me to the church. . . .

Physicians

In standard views of the history of medicine, the greatest achievements of ancient times were the works of the Greek Hippocrates and his Roman successor Galen, and no significant progress occurred until the emergence of modern scientific medicine during the Renaissance. Yet this capsule history overlooks the key role played by the physicians of the Byzantine Empire, who not only carefully preserved the ideas of Hippocrates and Galen but also garnered insights from Arab physicians and made their own contributions to the techniques of diagnosing and treating ailments. Most significantly, the Byzantines first developed the key institution of the hospital, where trained physicians worked together to assist the seriously ill, assisted by capable associates who can be regarded as the world's first nurses. And this came at a time when many regions, like the emerging nation of Russia, were still relying upon folk remedies and superstitions to handle their medical problems.

In the later days of the Roman Empire, the Egyptian city of Alexandria became the major center for the education of physicians, and this remained the case after Egypt became part of the Byzantine Empire. There, students worked for four years as apprentices alongside experienced physicians, anticipating the later practice of having aspiring physicians serve as residents. But they were also expected to listen to lectures from the world's first professors of medicine, called *iatroasophistes*, and to study the classic texts of Hippocrates and Galen, as well as the medical encyclopedia compiled by a later Roman physician, Oribasius, and the writings of two Byzantine physicians, Aëtius of Amina (ca. 500) and Alexander of Tralles (ca. 525–600). Both of these men emphasized that hygiene was essential in effective medical treatment, and Alexander argued that a change in diet usually promoted healing better than drugs. Interestingly, Alexander also understood what later physicians would call the placebo effect, noting that lucky charms and folk remedies would be helpful if patients believed in their effectiveness. Another important text was *De Re Medica Libri Septum*, or *Medical Compendium in Seven Books*, written by Byzantine physician Paul of Aegina (ca. 625–690); while it provided accurate summaries of current medical knowledge in all fields, it was especially valued for its section on surgery, as it offered detailed guidance on how to perform over a hundred surgical procedures.

Once ready to practice on their own, physicians might work as they had in the past, seeing clients for fees as independent entrepreneurs, or becoming the personal physicians of noble or wealthy men who could pay for their exclusive service. Physicians were also hired to accompany soldiers who went into battle, treating and bandaging wounds and extracting arrowheads. However, many Byzantine physicians were employed at hospitals, or *xenomes*. The first of these were little more than resorts, located next to remote hot springs, where ailing people could relax

In this illustration from a book of the Byzantine Empire, a physician carefully examines a vial of urine while several patients, including an injured man with crutches, await his attention. (Wellcome Library, London)

in the countryside and soak in the heated water. But as these facilities came under the aegis of the Christian church, they began to offer other services and were constructed within cities to be more accessible to patients. The first type of urban hospital, sometimes called a *nosokomeion*, was a modest building that employed a few doctors, priests, and cooks to address both the material and spiritual needs of the sick, but several larger *xenomes* were soon operating in the city of Constantinople.

Some detailed information about one of Constantinople's *xenomes*, part of the Pantokrator monastery, has been preserved because the hospital had been personally established by the Byzantine emperor John II Komnenos (1087–1143) and his wife Irene (1088–1134). Like other facilities, it was administered by priests and monks but staffed by secular workers: ten male doctors; another doctor devoted to teaching future doctors; a female doctor, or *iatraina*;

several assistants, both female and male, which we would today describe as nurses; a specialist in herbal medicine; and cooks who prepared food for patients. Patients who could afford to do so would pay to be treated, but poor people could receive free medical care with the support of the church. Treatment usually began in a clinic open to anyone who walked in, and if the problem was minor, it would be handled there, probably by trained assistants who were not physicians. Patients with more serious conditions were admitted to one of three sections devoted to surgery, other treatments, and the care of women; altogether, fifty beds were available. After admission, physicians would diagnose patients and treat their ailments, assisted by nurses who were also responsible for giving patients their medicine. In the women's section, the *iatraina* usually had to be overseen by two male physicians, though unsupervised midwives would handle childbirths. The neophyte doctors being educated often included the children of the physicians, carrying on the common tradition of inheriting a family profession.

Patients in the *xenomes* would be treated in a variety of ways. To perform surgeries, physicians would employ a broad range of bronze tools, often unearthed at archaeological sites, such as scalpels, forceps, and probes; common procedures including amputating damaged or diseased limbs, repairing hernias, and removing gallstones. After making their incisions, physicians were always careful to cauterize the area with hot metal or chemicals. For other ailments, physicians could prescribe a variety of drugs: the mandrake root provided an anesthetic; the crushed latex of poppies (the source of opium) eased pain; and the roots of violets were applied to an inflamed eye. Illustrations from manuscripts show physicians draining blood from patients, an ineffective procedure that remained popular for centuries, as well as a patient being hung upside down on a ladder as a treatment for a dislocated backbone.

Byzantine physicians were sometimes able to heal their patients, but there remained many conditions that they could not address. In such cases, afflicted people would seek spiritual assistance by visiting the shrines dedicated to saints who were associated with healing. The shrine of Saint Therapon in Constantinople was one of many that attracted a steady stream of ailing visitors. People would typically sleep near the sacred place, engage in intense prayer, and hope that the saint would appear in a dream to offer assistance. Although the church also supported hospitals, the holy men who supervised these sites regularly insisted that their methods were superior to other forms of medicine. They enjoyed telling the story of a physician in seventh-century Cyprus named Theodore, who found himself paralyzed; he was only cured when two saints, Cyrus and John, came to him in a dream and advised him to drink a mixture of wine and pig lungs. Patients who could not travel to shrines might purchase special amulets, or *phylakteria*, that would purportedly cure conditions like stomach aches, insomnia, and uncontrolled bleeding, or simply pray to saints said to be helpful for specific ailments; a person suffering from smallpox, for example, would be advised to pray to Saint Nicaise.

A TRADITION OF CARING

In the Byzantine Empire, the first hospitals were constructed and funded by churches, which viewed such facilities as a natural extension of their religious duty to help the poor and unfortunate. This tradition of Christian support for medical care has continued to the present day in many places around the world, including the former capital of the Byzantine Empire, Constantinople, now called Istanbul. In 1753, an organization of grocers of Greek descent founded a hospital, the Balikli Greek Hospital, to assist others from their background, and it was soon being supervised by the city's Greek Orthodox patriarch. It now includes a Greek Orthodox church, much like the Empire's hospitals, and continues to provide care to patients today.

ASSISTANCE FOR THE AGED

While the Byzantines founded the institution of the hospital, they also introduced the concept of constructing and maintaining special hospitals, termed *gerocomeia*, that exclusively provided care for elderly people. Since it long remained the case that few people survived to an advanced age, the *gerocomeia* did not become commonplace in other cultures, but today, when our vastly improved medicine allows many people to live very long lives, there are innumerable institutions recalling the ancient *gerocomeia*, usually called nursing homes or assisted living facilities, where elderly citizens are closely supervised and provided with specialized care.

In addition to their work with human patients, the Byzantines pioneered in the field of veterinary medicine, with a special concern for treating the horses that were so vital to communication and warfare. A vast text called the *Hippiatrica*, compiled by an unknown author sometime in the fifth or sixth century, offered a wealth of information about the diseases of horses and methods of treatment, as well as advice on proper feeding, grooming, and breeding. As evidence of continuing interest in this subject, subsequent copies of the book featured added material, and the entire text was revised in the tenth century CE under the emperor Constantine VII Porphyrogenitus (905–959). In addition to other books about horses, there is a Byzantine manual on medical care for dogs. These texts suggest that there were many Byzantines who specialized in veterinary medicine, although we know little about their training and the circumstances of their employment.

Overall, the Byzantines probably enjoyed better medical care than any previous civilization, but this is not to say that they enjoyed healthy lives, as they suffered due to poor sanitation and malnutrition. A particularly grievous problem was periodic plagues: one of these, in the sixth century, may have killed half of the population of Constantinople, and many people died in the fourteenth century when the Black Death visited the Empire before attacking Western Europe. In the face of such diseases, both physicians and priests were helpless. Still, it was largely by building upon the work of the Byzantine physicians and their predecessors that later doctors and scientists were able to vastly improve the field of medicine, prevent catastrophes, and extend the human lifespan.

Further Reading

Bourbou, Chryssi. 2010. *Health and Disease in Byzantine Crete (7th-12th centuries AD)*. Farnham, England, and Burlington, VT: Ashgate Publishing

Grmek, Mirko D. 1993. *Western Medical Thought from Antiquity to the Middle Ages*. Translated by Antony Shugaar. 1998. Cambridge, MA: Harvard University Press.

Miller, Timothy S. 1997. *The Birth of the Hospital in the Byzantine Empire*. Baltimore, MD: John Hopkins University Press.

Prioreschi, Plinio. 2001. *A History of Medicine: Volume 4: Byzantine and Islamic Medicine*. Omaha, NE: Horatius Press.

Scarborough, John. 2010. *Pharmacy and Drug Lore in Antiquity: Greece, Rome, Byzantium*. Farnham, England, and Burlington, VT: Ashgate Publishing.

Scarborough, John, editor. 1985. *Symposium on Byzantine Medicine*. Washington, DC: Dumbarton Oaks Research Library and Collection.

Documents

From Paul of Aegina. C. 675–685. *The Medical Works of Paulus Aegineta, the Greek Physician: Translated into English, with a Copious Commentary*. Volume 1. Translated by Francis Adams. 1834. London: J. Welch.

The major work of the Byzantine physician Paul of Aegina (ca. 625–690), De Re Medica Libri Septum, *or* Medical Compendium in Seven Books, *covers a vast number of subjects related to medical treatment. In the two passages below, he describes the importance of exercise in maintaining health and provides some advice about how to exercise properly.*

XVI. On Exercises.

Exercise is a violent motion. The limit to its violence should be a hurried respiration. Exercise renders the organs of the body less liable to sustain injury, and fitter for their functional actions. It makes the absorption of food stronger, and expedites its assimilation; for it improves nutrition by increasing heat. It also clears the pores of the skin, and evacuates superfluities by the increased motion of the lungs. Since, therefore, it contributes to distribution, care ought to be taken, that neither the stomach nor bowels be loaded with crude and indigestible food or liquids; for there is a danger lest they should be carried to all parts of the body before they are properly digested. It is clear then that exercise ought to be taken before eating. The colour of the urine will point out the proper time for exercise. When it is watery, it indicates that the chyme absorbed from the stomach is still undigested. When it is of a dark yellow colour, and bilious, it shows that digestion had been long ago accomplished. When it is moderately pale, it indicates that digestion has just taken place, and this is the proper time for exercise, after having evacuated whatever excrementitious matters are collected in the bladder and bowels.

XVII. On the Kinds of Exercise.

This is the common effect of all kinds of exercise, that they increase the natural heat of animals; but each species has something peculiar to it. Strong, that is to say, violent exercise rouses the tone of the muscles and nerves. Such are digging, and lifting a heavy burden, while one remains in the same spot, or moves a little; or lifting small weights and walking about as much as one can. Of this kind, is the exercise of scaling a rope, and many such. The swift kinds of exercise are such as do not require strength and violence, namely running, fighting with one's shadow, wrestling with the extremities of the hands, the exercise with a leather-bag, and that with the small ball. This last is compounded of strength and velocity; and such exercises as are strong, may become intense by adding velocity to them. Besides, some kinds of exercise bring the loins into action, and some the hands or legs; others the spine or the chest alone, or the lungs. And exercise ought to be carried on until the vessels become distended, and the skin of a florid hue; and, until then, the motions ought to be strong, equable, and unremitting. Upon this you may see warm sweat, mixed with vapour, break out. It will then be time for you to stop, when any of the symptoms which I have mentioned have undergone a change, namely, when the bulk of the body becomes contracted, or when the florid colour of the skin declines. And, should any of the motions remit, it will then be time to stop; or, if there should be any change in the quantity or quality of the perspiration; for, if it should become smaller in quantity, or colder, we must desist, and besmearing the body with oil, endeavour to restore it. It will then be proper to use the Restorative friction as the masters of gymnastics practise.

From Alexander Van Millingen, with Ramsay Traquair, Walter S. George, and A. E. Henderson. 1912. *Byzantine Churches in Constantinople: Their History and Architecture*. London: Macmillan.

In this study of Byzantine churches, the authors describe the founding of the Pantokrator monastery and the structure of its hospital. It should be noted, though, that other scholars disagree with their views on how the hospital was organized and divided.

The church was founded by the Empress Irene, the consort of John II. Comnenus (1118–1143), and daughter of Ladislas, King of Hungary. She came to Constantinople shortly before 1105 as the Princess Pyrisca, a beautiful girl, "a plant covered with blossoms, promising rich fruit," to marry John Comnenus, then heir-apparent to the crown of Alexius Comnenus, and adorned eight years of her husband's reign by the simplicity of her tastes and her great liberality to the poor. The monastic institutions of the city also enjoyed her favour, and not long before her death in 1126 she assumed the veil under the name of Xené. The foundations of the church were, probably, laid soon after her husband's accession to the throne, and to the church she attached a monastery capable of accommodating

seven hundred monks; a *xenodocheion*, a home for aged men; and a hospital.

But the pious and charitable lady had undertaken more than she could perform, and was obliged to turn to the emperor for sympathy and assistance. Accordingly she took him, one day, to see the edifice while in course of erection, and falling suddenly at his feet, implored him with tears to complete her work. The beauty of the building and the devotion of his wife appealed so strongly to John Comnenus that he forthwith vowed to make the church and monastery the finest in the city, and altogether worthy of the Pantokrator to whom they were dedicated; and so well did he keep his promise, that the honour of being the founder of the church has been bestowed on him by the historian Nicetas Choniates. . . .

The hospital had fifty beds for the poor. It was divided into five wards: a ward of ten beds for surgical cases; another, of eight beds, for grave cases; a third, of ten beds, for less serious complaints; the fourth ward had twelve beds for women; the fifth contained ten beds for what seemed light cases. Each ward was in charge of two physicians, three medical assistants, and four servitors. A lady physician, six lady medical assistants, and two female nurses, took charge of the female patients. The sick were visited daily by a house doctor, who inquired whether they were satisfied with their treatment, examined their diet, and saw to the cleanliness of the beds. The ordinary diet consisted of bread, beans, onions, oil, and wine. Throughout their history the monasteries of Constantinople remembered the poor. . . .

Sailors

Like the ancient Greeks, whose territories largely constituted their shrunken empire, the Byzantines depended upon the sea to transport their people and goods; the Romans had built a number of roads, but they were rarely well maintained, making travel by land time consuming and arduous. While sea voyages could be hazardous, they still represented the fastest and most reliable form of transportation available, so merchant ships were able to attract a steady stream of customers.

To get into this business, any interested man—typically an experienced sailor—could purchase a ship, hire a crew, and function as the ship's owner, captain, and its chief negotiator. Several advances in maritime technology made his work easier. While the Greeks and Romans had started the process of shipbuilding with a hull, and then built a shell upon it, the Byzantines gradually learned to begin with an interior framework and nail planks upon it. While a great deal of caulking was required to prevent leaks, this new procedure took less time, reduced the ship's weight, and could be carried out by cheap, unskilled workers, greatly reducing the cost of ships and making them a reasonable investment for small businessmen. To evade pirates, shipbuilders also made their craft smaller and more maneuverable by using another new invention, triangular lateen sails placed at the front and rear of each vessel, and to keep docked ships in place, previous designs were replaced with heavy iron anchors that resembled their modern counterparts. The typical ship, called a *dorkon*, was only sixty-five feet in length, and it could be efficiently handled with a few skilled crewmen, leaving room for additional cargo.

Once employed by a ship owner, sailors could expect to spend much of their time on land, as many remained reluctant to travel by sea during winter, though some experienced sailors might travel short distances during the legendary "halcyon days" of winter when the weather was briefly temperate. The only mariners who left the port every day were the fishermen, who always kept their small crafts close to shore. When not at sea, sailors were still kept busy, as the wooden ships regularly needed to be caulked or repaired, torn nets and sails needed to be patched, and frayed ropes had to be replaced. Then, when the owner was finally ready to set sail, there were large amounts of cargo to be carried on board and secured. By examining shipwrecks, scholars have learned that they typically carried a wide variety of goods: barrels or *amphoras* of olive oil and wine, large bags of grain, and tools made of iron demanded no special treatment, but delicate pottery and glass vessels had to be handled and stored carefully. It was also at this time that potential travelers would request passage on a ship heading for a desired destination, since there were no ships devoted exclusively to carrying passengers. The

travelers included wealthy tourists, government and church officials, couriers, and pilgrims seeking to visit famous Christian shrines.

After the ship had sailed, the sailors had other chores that demanded regular attention. To keep their ships on course, navigators would rely upon books called *periploi*, which gathered together the knowledge and lore of the Mediterranean sailors of the past centuries; later versions of these books were termed *portulans*. Surprisingly, these volumes contained no maps or illustrations, conveying important information solely in written narratives. Sailors seeking a particular port, for example, might be advised to look for a carefully described landmark or avoid a certain region where dangerous shoals lurked beneath the water. They also needed to constantly adjust the sails as the winds shifted direction and watch for approaching pirate ships. Seeking to predict the weather and avoid storms, veteran sailors would carefully observe the movements of the winds and clouds and the flights of seabirds like herons and gulls. Sailors would also periodically toss nets into the sea to catch some fish that could add variety to an otherwise monotonous diet that largely consisted of hard biscuits and bread, dried meat, and diluted wine. But there would also be time to relax on the top deck in warm weather, talking with the passengers, sharing stories, or playing gambling games. If the ship was damaged by rocks or a storm, however, everyone on board was likely to die, since ships had no life preservers or lifeboats and most Byzantines, even sailors, did not know how to swim. Some could survive, though, by hanging on to a floating piece of their destroyed ship. In the face of these fears, it is hardly surprising that sailors superstitiously relied on religious amulets and icons to protect them and regularly prayed to certain saints, like Saint Nicholas of Sion (ca. sixth century) and Saint Phokas of Sinope (died ca. 303), who were renowned for helping sailors in distress.

In addition to merchant ships, sailors might also be employed by the Byzantine navy, which had become crucially important in defending the Empire against foreign foes. A number of smaller, faster ships, referred to as *ousiakoi, pamphyloi, chelandia,* and *galea,* were used to scout enemies, carry troops, send vital messages, and raid coastal communities to obtain supplies. Most sailors, however, would serve on a larger ship, called the *dromon*, an advanced version of the triremes and quinqueremes used by the ancient Greeks and Romans. Primarily propelled by long rows of oarsmen, though also equipped with lateen sails, a typical *dromon* was about 130-feet long and carried up to 200 men; these included experienced sailors, oarsmen, soldiers, and a few carpenters and sail makers. At the front of each *dromon* was a sturdy battering ram that could strike and damage enemy vessels, while a raised platform at the rear was for archers and men using catapults to hurl stones at nearby foes. A special metal siphon would propel the mysterious incendiary chemical, "Greek Fire," to destroy other ships. During the day, messages would be sent to other vessels by means of smoke signals, colored flags, and blasts from a trumpet; at night, flares and lamps would be used. While sailors mainly devoted their energies to keep their ships on course, they might be asked to assist soldiers with other tasks, especially during battles.

Sailors in the Byzantine navy, like their counterparts on merchant ships, spent a great deal of time on land, since virtually all military campaigns were scheduled only in the spring and summer. Whenever a ship was launched into battle, there were special ceremonies to endure, as priests would anoint the vessel with holy water and the imperial flag was hoisted on the central mast. Life on board was undoubtedly less pleasant, as sailors were surrounded by bustling people instead of piles of goods, and the prospect of dying in battle added one more fear to haunt their daily routines.

While it is often seen as a largely landlocked country, the first Russian state, Kievan Rus, regularly employed ships to engage in commerce down its long rivers and into the Black Sea and Mediterranean Sea. The ship employed for lengthy voyages, called a *lodya*, was constructed out of the trunk of a single oak tree; it was usually about sixty-feet long, held about forty men, and was propelled by a large rectangular sail and fourteen oarsmen. We know little about the lives of early Russian sailors, but their ships are renowned for their use in wars against the Byzantine Empire and, later, between factions of its own

This colorful illustration, now displayed in a Spanish museum, depicts Byzantine sailors deploying their navy's most dreaded weapon—the mysterious "Greek Fire" which burned enemy ships. (Heritage Images/Getty Images)

PASSENGERS AS CREWMATES

Byzantine ships were primarily devoted to carrying cargo, but ship owners earned extra income by taking on passengers as well, who often had no other way to travel long distances. Today, there are many ways for people to travel, but the large cargo ships that sail around the world remain a little-known option, since they generally include cabins for interested passengers. While these voyages are relatively slow and expensive, the food and accommodations are usually excellent, and one often gets the opportunity to interact with some to modern-day sailors, who may ask passengers to join them for dinner in order to enjoy some new company.

LIQUIDS FOR LAUNCHING

To ensure a safe and prosperous voyage, the religious Byzantine sailors would regularly ask a priest to bless their ships with holy water before departing. Much later, during the nineteenth century, Europeans developed a different tradition for the auspicious launch of a new vessel, termed a christening. A woman was invited to take a bottle of champagne, announce the ship's name, and smash the bottle into the ship's bow; then, it was launched into the sea for the first time. Occasionally, though, the bottle of champagne would not break, which was considered a very bad omen.

disintegrating empire. In one attack on Constantinople in 941, Grand Prince Igor Rurikovich (died 945) actually commanded a fleet of 10,000 *lodyas*, though these were almost entirely destroyed by "Greek Fire." As peace was established between Kievan Rus and the Byzantine Empire, however, later Russian ships visited solely to import and export various goods.

In the context of early societies, sailing was an unusual profession in one respect: since sailors spent most of their lives traveling and often did not get married and raise families, they did not regularly pass their avocation down to their sons; instead, it was a job typically chosen by restless young men who were rejecting their traditional professions in favor of the perceived excitement and adventure of the open seas. The shared aspirations of sailors both past and present, then, enable us to understand these ancient sailors even if we lack detailed accounts of their daily lives.

Further Reading

Bass, George F., and Frederick H. van Doorninck Jr. 1982. *Yassi Ada: Volume 1: A Seventh-Century Byzantine Shipwreck*. College Station: Texas A&M University Press.

Beresford, James. 2012. *The Ancient Sailing Season*. Leiden, The Netherlands, and Boston: Brill.

Friedman, John Block, and Kristen Mossler Figg, editors. 2000. *Trade, Travel, and Exploration in the Middle Ages: An Encyclopedia*. New York: Garland.

Lewis, Archibald, and Timothy J. Runyan. 1985. *European Naval and Maritime History, 300–1500*. Bloomington: Indiana University Press.

Macrides, Ruth J., editor. 2002. *Travel in the Byzantine World: Papers from the Thirty-Fourth Spring Symposium of Byzantine Studies, Birmingham, April 2000*. Aldershot, England, and Burlington, VT: Ashgate.

Pryor, John H., and Elizabeth Jeffries. 2006. *The Age of the Dromōn: The Byzantine Navy ca. 500–1204*. Leiden, The Netherlands, and Boston: Brill.

Document

From Anonymous. C. seventh century. *The Rhodian Sea Law*. Translated by Walter Ashburner. 1909. Oxford: Clarendon Press.

A Byzantine body of laws related to sea travel, termed today the Rhodian Sea Law, was compiled sometime between 600 and 800. As shown by the regulations listed below, its primary concern was the resolution of financial disputes, but there are also laws forbidding unsafe activities on the deck and the amount of space allotted to certain sorts of passengers.

Chapters 1–7. A master's pay two shares [of the profits]; a steersman's one share and a half; a master's mate's one share and a half; a carpenter's one share and a half; a boatswain's one share and a half; a sailor's one share; a cook's [?] half a share.

8. A merchant may have on board two boys; but he must pay their fare.

9. A passenger's allowance of space is three cubits in length and one in breadth. [A cubit is roughly half a yard.]

10. A passenger is not to fry fish on board; the captain must not allow him.

11. A passenger is not to split wood on board; the captain must not allow him.

12. A passenger on board is to take water by measure.

13. Women on board are to have a space allowance of one cubit; and a boy. . . of half a cubit.

14. If a passenger comes on board and has gold, let him deposit it with the captain. If he does not deposit it and says, "I have lost gold or silver," no effect is to be given to what he says, since he did not deposit it with the captain.

15. The captain and the passengers and the crew, who are on board together, are to take an oath upon the evangels.

16. A ship with all its tackle is to be valued at fifty pieces of gold for every thousand modii [pecks] of capacity, and so is to come into contribution. Where the ship is old, it is to be valued at thirty pieces of gold for every thousand modii. And in the valuation a deduction is to be made of one third, and the ship is to come into contribution accordingly.

Soldiers

The Byzantine army was a direct descendant of the Roman army that had conquered much of Europe, northern Africa, and western Asia, so it is not surprising that its soldiers were generally effective warriors. Yet during its long history the Byzantine Empire also faced an array of new challenges, as its shrinking borders faced powerful new foes—aggressive tribes to the north and west, and the rising forces of Islam to the east. In response, the government reorganized its armies and encouraged its commanders to master effective strategies, as evidenced by several military handbooks that were compiled and widely distributed, including the sixth century *Treatise on Strategy* by an unknown author; the *Strategikon*, or *Handbook on Strategy*, completed during the reign of the emperor Maurice (539–602); and the *Tactica*, or *Tactics*, probably written by the emperor Leo VI (866–912) sometime around 900. Byzantine rulers also focused more and more of their energies on diplomacy, seeking to avoid potentially ruinous military conflicts.

In the seventh century, the Byzantine Empire replaced the old Roman provinces with large districts called *themes*, which also altered the nature of its military forces. Now, each *theme* had a general, or *strategos*, whose soldiers, or *stratiotai*, were local residents conscripted to serve for a short time. Every owner of land either had to join the army or provide a replacement. Anyone becoming a soldier had to be from eighteen to forty years old, to be taller than five feet, six inches, and to be healthy. The only men meeting these requirements who were exempted from service were criminals, monks, and priests. While soldiers received a salary, they had to provide their own weapons, armor, and horse; generally, they remained within their own theme and were only responsible for protecting that territory and maintaining order within its borders.

Since the *stratiotai* were often untrained and poorly equipped, the central government understandably created a different sort of army to protect its own capital and the surrounding lands. There were five regiments, or *tagmata*, each consisting of over 1,500 men organized into thirty divisions, or *banda*. These were professional, full-time soldiers with superb fighting skills who were stationed in Constantinople and assigned to join the emperor on his military campaigns; the best and most loyal soldiers would be part of the palace guard. Qualified foreigners as well as Byzantine citizens were welcome to enlist in these forces; indeed, the emperor's most renowned and trusted protectors, the Varangian Guard, came exclusively from Russia, Scandinavia, and England. However, in the last days of the Empire, these colorful figures, though armed with axes and large swords, were mostly deployed only in ceremonies.

As in the Roman army, most Byzantine soldiers fought on foot, and much of their equipment was not overly different from that of their predecessors, but its quality varied widely. Some men only wore loosely fitting clothing, though iron helmets and arm and leg armor were not uncommon; however, soldiers mostly protected themselves with their shields, which might be round, elliptical, or triangular in shape. These shields were normally made of wood with a cover of leather and some pieces of iron. Their main weapon was a sword with two edges that was about a yard long, but soldiers might also be equipped with spears, javelins, and axes, generally made of iron. To hurl projectiles at their soldiers, some soldiers carried a leather sling, or *sphendone*. In hand-to-hand combat, such time-tested weapons could be lethally effective.

However, the art of warfare had also changed since the Roman days, in several ways. For one thing, archers were becoming increasing important, since such soldiers could kill enemies from a distance without endangering their own lives. A major innovation, imported from Western Europe during the eleventh century, was the crossbow, or *solenarion*. This heavy device could propel several arrows at the same time with tremendous force, though it was difficult to move around. Cavalry units with soldiers on horseback were playing more of a role in combat, since the Byzantines had bred especially strong horses for that purpose. New technologies also made important contributions, as soldiers could better control their mounts with stirrups, and both riders and horses could now be protected with iron armor. With one arm holding a shield, and the other wielding a mace or the long spear called the *kontarion*, these mounted soldiers would ride in a wedge formation to create openings in the enemy lines. Some members of the cavalry also employed bows and arrows as their primary weapons.

Foes learned to fear the Byzantine army, however, primarily because of two massive weapons that they developed and employed with brutal efficiency. First, while types of catapults had previously been built and used in central Asia and the Middle East, the Byzantines crafted a much more effective version of this weapon that, based on modern reconstructions, could have hurled up to 300 pounds of stones a distance of almost a thousand feet. Instead of rocks, though, the *Tactika* of Leo I suggests that containers filled with poisonous snakes or scorpions might be even more effective, and as an early form of chemical warfare, soldiers could also hurl masses of granular quicklime at their enemies, creating a cloud of dust that might blind or suffocate opponents. An even more potent weapon of this kind was the Byzantine's dreaded "Greek Fire," a liquid substance that caused hugely destructive flames. Its exact chemical composition, kept secret by the Byzantine government, has never been determined, but it was so dangerous that the Byzantines generally launched it at adversaries only during naval battles.

While scholars focus on their activities during combat, the Byzantines were also concerned about the most effective ways for soldiers to travel and maintain themselves during long campaigns; in fact, much of the material in their military handbooks addresses these matters. Commanders were advised to send advance scouts to select advantageous routes and locate supplies of water; and to boost morale, generals were told to conceal healthy prisoners while stripping the most pathetic captives and parading them naked in front of the troops, to suggest their enemies' weakness. To carry food and supplies, troops might be accompanied by hundreds of mules, which also had to be fed and cared for. Camps would ideally be located next to a river, both to provide water and to prevent attacks from one side. Soldiers mostly ate cheese, dry meat, and a type of bread made of milled called *boukellaton*, and drank beer or wine mixed with water.

AN EMBEDDED HISTORIAN

The Byzantine historian Procopius (ca. 500–565) based much of the history of the wars of Justinian I on his own observations as he accompanied the general Belisarius on its major campaigns. As the general's legal adviser, he did not do any fighting, but merely watched and recorded the army's activities. Today, U.S. soldiers serving in foreign countries also include a person whose primary role is not to fight, but to write about its actions; however, they are journalists, not historians, and they are referred to as journalists who are "embedded" in the army. Procopius, one could say, was actually an early journalist of this type.

PAINFUL PETROLEUM

The most feared weapon of the Byzantine army was "Greek Fire," a mysterious liquid that could ignite intense fires and devastate enemy forces. Its composition was kept secret and remains unknown, but descriptions suggest that its major ingredient was petroleum. In the twentieth century, the United States developed its own incendiary weapon containing petroleum, called napalm, and was intensely criticized for employing this burning chemical during the Vietnam War, as it frequently killed or burned civilians. In 1980, an international treaty, later signed by the United States, established that using napalm to attack civilians constituted a war crime.

This illustration from a fifteenth-century medieval manuscript depicts the soldiers of Russian leader Oleg of Novgorod (died 912) as they launch their assault on the Byzantine capital of Constantinople. (Werner Forman/ Universal Images Group/Getty Images)

To supplement their diets, soldiers could hunt in the forest or loot local settlements, though this practice was discouraged, and periods of inactivity would be filled with drills and exercises to keep soldiers occupied and in good physical condition. The chaplains who accompanied soldiers conducted services on Sundays and holidays, comforted dying soldiers, and fervently prayed for military victories. When soldiers were injured, physicians strived to treat their wounds and help them recover.

Needless to say, Byzantine soldiers often had hard lives; along with the constant prospect of death in battle, they might also be threatened by famine, disease, or accidents, and soldiers who engaged in misconduct, ranging from attempted desertion to losing weapons, would usually be brutally executed. But soldiers received a good salary as well as supplies, always received at the proper time, as well as special

gifts and honors for distinguished service. When they retired, they were typically given tracts of land, termed *pronoia*, and there were also opportunities for significant advancement. In fact, some Byzantine emperors, including Justin I (ca. 450–527) and Basil I (ca. 830–856), began their lives as impoverished peasants but, by means of successful military careers, were able to first become generals and later emperors.

For over a thousand years, the Byzantine soldiers successfully defended their realm against a host of enemies, but the invading armies of Islam ultimately proved too strong, and the city of Constantinople was conquered and sacked in 1453, bringing an end to the Byzantine Empire. One of the many threats they had fended off came from a nation to the north, Kievan Rus, the first Russian nation, which twice attacked Constantinople in the tenth century with crudely armed but massive armies that were driven away by the "Greek Fire." Much later, Russia would become a significant military power in its own right, one of the many countries that had benefited and learned from contact with the Byzantine military machine, which is still being studied and appreciated by scholars and military historians today.

Further Reading

Bartusis, Mark C. 1992. *The Late Byzantine Army: Arms and Society, 1204–1453*. Philadelphia: University of Pennsylvania Press.

Birkenmeier, John W. 2002. *The Development of the Komnenian Army: 1081–1180*. Leiden, The Netherlands, and Boston: Brill.

Dąbrowa, Edward, editor. 1994. *The Roman and Byzantine Army in the East: Proceedings of a Colloquium Held at the Jagiellonian University, Kraków in September 1992*. Kraków, Poland: Drukarnia Uniwersytetu Jagiellońskiego.

Haldon, John F. 1999. *Warfare, State and Society in the Byzantine World, 565–1204*. London: UCL Press.

Kyriakidis, Savvas. 2011. *Warfare in Late Byzantium, 1204–1453*. Leiden, The Netherlands, and Boston: Brill.

Treadgold, Warren. 1995. *Byzantium and Its Army: 284–1081*. Stanford, CA: Stanford University Press.

Documents

From Procopius. C. 551. *Procopius*. Volume 1. Translated by Henry Bronson Dewing. 1914. London: W. Heinemann.

The Byzantine historian Procopius (ca. 500–565), after accompanying the general Belisarius (ca. 500–565) in the wars of the Emperor Justinian I (ca. 482–565) against the Persians, wrote a chronicle of that war and the emperor's later wars, usually called The Wars of Justinian. *While beginning its first volume, he describes how the soldiers of the early Byzantine army had better equipment and fought more effectively than their predecessors in ancient times.*

It will be evident that no more important or mightier deeds are to be found in history than those which have been enacted in these wars,—provided one wishes to base his judgment on the truth. For in them more remarkable feats have been performed than in any other wars with which we are acquainted; unless, indeed, any reader of this narrative should give the place of honour to antiquity, and consider contemporary achievements unworthy to be counted remarkable. There are those, for example, who call the soldiers of the present day "bowmen," while to those of the most ancient times they wish to attribute such lofty terms as "hand-to-hand fighters," "shield-men," and other names of that sort; and they think that the valour of those times has by no means survived to the present,—an opinion which is at once careless and wholly remote from actual experience of these matters. For the thought has never occurred to them that, as regards the Homeric bowmen who had the misfortune to be ridiculed by this term derived from their art, they were neither carried by horse nor protected by spear or shield. In fact there was no protection at all for their bodies; they entered battle on foot, and were compelled to conceal themselves, either singling out the shield of some comrade, or seeking safety behind a tombstone on a mound, from which position they could neither save themselves in case of rout, nor fall upon a flying foe. Least of all could they participate in a decisive struggle in the open, but they always seemed to be stealing something which belonged to the men who were engaged in the struggle. And apart from this they were so indifferent in their practice of archery that they drew the bowstring only to the breast, so that the missile sent forth was naturally impotent and harmless to those whom it hit. Such, it is evident, was the archery of the past. But the bowmen of the present time go into battle wearing corselets and fitted out with greaves which extend up to the knee. From the right side hang their arrows, from the other the sword. And there are some who have a spear also attached to them and, at the shoulders, a sort of small shield without a grip, such as to cover the region of the face and neck. They are expert horsemen, and are able without difficulty to direct their bows to either side while riding at full speed, and to shoot an opponent whether in pursuit or in flight. They draw the bowstring along by the forehead about opposite the right ear, thereby charging the arrow with such an impetus as to kill whoever stands in the way, shield and corselet alike having no power to check its force. Still there are those who take into consideration none of these things, who reverence and worship the ancient times, and give no credit to modern improvements. But no such consideration will prevent the conclusion that most great and notable deeds have been performed in these wars. And the history of them will begin at some distance back, telling of the fortunes in war of the Romans and the Medes, their reverses and their successes.

From Leo VI. C. 895–908. *Tactica.* Excerpt translated by Charles William Chadwick Oman. 1885. *The Art of War in the Middle Ages, A.D. 378–1515.* Oxford: B. H. Blackwell.

A Byzantine study of warfare, Tactica, or Tactics, is attributed to the emperor Leo VI (866–912), though some believe that others did most of the writing. In this passage, he discusses the proper strategies when fighting against the Germanic tribe known as the Franks.

The Frank believes that a retreat under any circumstances must be dishonourable; hence he will fight whenever you choose to offer him battle. This you must not do till you have secured all possible advantages for yourself, as his cavalry, with their long lances and large shields, charge with a tremendous impetus. You should deal with him by protracting the campaign, and if possible lead him into the hills, where his cavalry are less efficient than in the plain. After a few weeks without a great battle his troops, who are very susceptible to fatigue and weariness, will grow tired of the war, and ride home in great numbers. . . . You will find him utterly careless as to outposts and reconnaisances, so that you can easily cut off outlying parties of his men, and attack his camp at advantage. As his forces have no bonds of discipline, but only those of kindred or oath, they fall into confusion after delivering their charge; you can therefore simulate flight, and then turn them, when you will find them in utter disarray. On the whole, however, it is easier and less costly to wear out a Frankish army by skirmishes and protracted operations rather than to attempt to destroy it at a single blow.

The Islamic World, 600–1500

Introduction

Arguably, no man has ever affected the world as rapidly and as significantly as the prophet Muhammad (570–632). Followers of the religion he founded rapidly spread throughout the Middle East and northern Africa, not only garnering hordes of converts but also assuming control of every region they conquered. Only two centuries after Muhammad's death, a Muslim empire, with its capital first in Damascus and later in Baghdad, stretched from Spain and Morocco in the west to Persia and present-day Pakistan in the east, making it one of the largest empires in history. Yet the achievements of Islam were not only political, for the caliphs who headed its government were keenly interested in supporting scientific research and the arts. They employed scholars who translated and studied classic works from ancient Greece, Rome, and India, and with the knowledge they gained, these Islamic savants were soon making significant advances in mathematics and science, including their effective creation of the field of alchemy, precursor to modern chemistry. The caliphs also supported a cadre of talented poets and other writers who wrote prose texts ranging from histories and commentaries on Islam to fanciful stories and cookbooks.

However, the triumph of the Islamic world was short-lived, for the bureaucrats who worked for the caliphs lacked the Roman flair for effective administration of distant territories, allowing the provinces to become increasingly assertive and to evolve into independent states. The rulers of these smaller states were not as devoted to encouraging intellectual and artistic endeavors, and they also faced new challenges from a resurgent Byzantine Empire, aggressive merchants from the Italian city of Venice, and armies of European crusaders who were determined to seize the holy land of Israel in the name of Christianity. Eventually, the only genuine Islamic power in the region was a new nation that arose in present-day Turkey, the Ottoman Empire, which took over the Byzantine Empire and other regions formerly governed by the caliphs.

Still, the labors of the many citizens of the early Islamic world were not in vain, as the Europeans employed their texts and findings as the basis for their own Renaissance; indeed, it is hard to see how Europe could have become the dominant power in the world without the information and insights they had obtained from Islamic writers. Ironically, the resurgent Europeans made use of what they had learned to colonize the nations once ruled by the caliphs, though the Muslims would later regain some measure of influence over the world by exploiting a valuable resource that had been unknown to their ancestors—the vast reserves of oil that lay beneath the sands.

Alchemists

Scholars and intellectuals of the Islamic world, as in other early cultures, were not limited by disciplinary boundaries: one man might work in fields as disparate as philosophy, engineering, and medicine, and it is only in retrospect that he might be classified as a specialist in one field, on the grounds that his contributions therein proved most significant to later practitioners. So it is that we now label certain Islamic thinkers as pioneers in the study of alchemy, the precursor to modern chemistry. Indeed, the very term "alchemy" is of Arabic origin, a probable combination of its definite article with a Greek term for metalworking (though there are other theories about the original meaning of the Greek root *chemeia*). Modern observers may ridicule the alchemists' obsession with the chimerical dream of converting lead or other substances into gold, yet as they experimented with chemical reactions that apparently altered the very nature of the materials they were working with, the concept seemed far from illogical. Furthermore, this tantalizing possibility often provided them with the financial support they needed to pursue investigations that also yielded important discoveries about substances and their properties.

A medieval manuscript includes this elaborate image of Abu Mūsā Jābir ibn Hayyān, the Islamic alchemist whose purported writings later fascinated European alchemists. (Print Collector/Getty Images)

One man described as a pioneer in the field is Khalid ibn Yazid (died 704), purportedly a brother of the caliph Muawiyah II (661–684) who later pursued alchemy, but many regard this person as the mythical invention of later writers. We are on solider ground to attribute the birth of alchemy to Abu Mūsā Jābir ibn Hayyān (ca. 721–815), who was later called Geber by the Europeans who avidly studied his works. Little is known about his early life, but he was reportedly the son of a pharmacist who was killed while supporting the Abbasids in their ultimately successful civil war against the Umayyad Dynasty. In the course of this struggle, Jābir forged friendships with members of the Barmakid family, who served as viziers under the early Abbasid caliphs, and thus garnered a position in the court of the caliph Harun al-Rashid (763–809), who reportedly befriended the scientist and often discussed alchemy with him. With handsome support from prominent patrons, Jābir spent his days studying the works of earlier scholars, engaging in his own research, and writing prodigiously about alchemy and other subjects. However, most of the hundreds of books attributed to him are now believed to largely consist of material added to his writings by other Arab scholars in the two centuries after his death, and other works linked to his name were probably produced by a fourteenth-century alchemist, termed the Pseudo-Geber, who probably lived and worked in present-day Spain.

We are reasonably certain, however, that Jābir himself is responsible for several important ideas. He popularized the theory that all metals were composed of a mixture of sulfur and mercury (though these were imagined ideal substances, not the known elements with those names), suggesting that valuable metals like gold could be produced by finding and properly combining these elusive materials, and he developed a complex numerical method to describe the characteristics of various substances. He also performed many experiments using the chemical ammonium chloride, which could make metals soluble and, in his view, offer valuable clues as to their true nature. His works describe how to make key compounds like nitric acid, potash (potassium salts), silver nitrate, and the mixture of acids known as *aqua regia* because it could dissolve precious metals. He is said to have invented important pieces of equipment like the retort and to have developed a better understanding of several key chemicals and their properties. His long career came to a close, however, when his allies the Barmakids lost their power in 803, leading to his arrest and confinement.

Another key figure in the early development of alchemy, Muhammad ibn Zakariya al-Razi (ca. 854–925), primarily made his living as a teacher and physician, but he was keenly interested in the transmutation of elements; in fact, some people whispered that this kindly man was willing to treat patients without being paid because he had secretly discovered how to turn other metals into silver and gold—something that he had to publically deny. Yet he also argued that such transformations could be achieved, rejecting the opinion of skeptics like the philosopher aṣ-Ṣabbāḥ al-Kindī (ca. 801–873) that alchemy was impossible. (Al-Kindī himself also dabbled in chemistry, perhaps becoming the first person to distill pure alcohol.) As he labored to transmute metals, al-Razi became an expert in processes like distillation and gilding other metals to make them resemble gold, and he endeavored to systematically classify substances in a logical manner. His practical contributions to chemistry included a method for making sulfuric acid. There are many stories about how he became blind, but one account attributes his condition to exposure to dangerous chemicals during an experiment. His writings are also valued because they describe in vivid detail all of the equipment that would have been in an alchemist's laboratory, including an alembic (*anbiq dhu khatm*), cauldron (*marjal or tanjir*), oven (*al-tannur*), furnace (*kur*), bellows (*minfakh*), crucible (*bawtaqa*), and various pots and containers to hold liquids.

Two other figures are regarded as central to the history of alchemy, though they also did work in other fields. The elusive Muhammed ibn Umail at-Tamîmî (ca. 900–960) was a recluse who may have lived in Spain, Egypt, Iraq, or all of those places during his lifetime. Strangely, he argued that alchemy was primarily valuable as an allegorical system that offered insights into everyday life and the Islamic faith, though he also wrote treatises on the elements mercury and magnesium which included some practical wisdom. Al-Bīrūnī (ca. 973–1052) is best known for his studies of Indian culture, geography, and astrology, but he is also the first man who figured out how to determine a substance's specific gravity.

There were surely many other alchemists within the Islamic world, either working for wealthy patrons or earning a living as teachers, but we are not aware of their names and accomplishments, for several reasons. Some chose not to write, or their works were not preserved, and others' careers may have been prematurely ended because they fell out of favor in the court. Some alchemists were willfully secretive about their experiments, writing about their work only in cryptic terms that few could interpret correctly. Their official explanation is that secrets that could lead to the transmutation of metals should be reserved for those seeking wisdom, instead of those seeking wealth; more practically, however, they may have believed that they were on the verge of a breakthrough and feared that revealing their discoveries would only give an advantage to their rivals. A tenth-century group of unidentified scholars known as the Brethren of Purity, who produced a massive encyclopedia that included some information apparently written by alchemists, were deliberately mysterious about their work for reasons that remain unclear. In at least one case, the government of the caliphs deliberately suppressed knowledge about an important achievement; for after their fleets attempting to conquer Constantinople were devastated by the Byzantine Empire's mysterious "Greek Fire," the Arabs soon developed their own version of the incendiary compound, though like the Byzantines they never revealed the persons who created it or the ingredients they employed. Their efforts to duplicate the Byzantine invention were not entirely successful, though, since the Arab compound was significantly less powerful.

The work of the Islamic alchemists was not always appreciated by their contemporaries: as noted, some did not believe that their labors could ever yield worthwhile results, while others may have felt that the transmutation of materials created by Allah represented an affront to Islam. But few scientists of their era have been studied as intently as the alchemists by later scholars—at two different times. In the late Middle Ages, European alchemists translated and carefully read many of their texts, hoping to find a way to achieve what their predecessors were unable to

ALCHEMY VINDICATED?

The goal of alchemy—to transform another element into gold by chemical means—has long been recognized as impossible. However, twentieth-century scientists discovered that when an atom's nucleus adds or sheds protons, it becomes the atom of another element. Through radioactive decay, for example, the nuclei of uranium atoms emit protons to create lead atoms. In theory, then, one could direct particles into the nuclei of lead atoms, remove the right number of protons, and make them atoms of gold. Even if this could be done, however, it would take centuries to produce even a sliver of gold dust, and the process would cost more than the gold's value.

REPRESSED RESEARCHERS

Alchemists in the medieval Islamic world, employed by caliphs, were constantly in danger of death or imprisonment if they lost important allies in the government or displeased their overseers. In the twentieth century, scientists employed by authoritarian governments faced similar perils. One prominent example was the renowned Russian physicist Andrei Sakharov, whose opposition to the Soviet regime in the 1970s and 1980s resulted in his arrest, internal exile, and periodic confinement in hospitals. Though he was eventually freed and elected to the Soviet parliament, his years of mistreatment may have led to the heart attack that killed him in 1989 at the age of sixty-eight.

achieve. Then, although most people lost interest in their work when alchemy was thoroughly discredited after the Renaissance, twentieth-century historians of science have rediscovered these figures and recognized how important they were in helping chemistry to advance from a collection of murky ideas to a genuine experimental science. They may have never found a way to turn lead into gold, but what they did accomplish was actually much more valuable.

Further Reading

Edson, Gary. 2012. *Mysticism and Alchemy through the Ages: The Quest for Transformation.* Jefferson, NC: McFarland.

Al-Hassan, A. Y., editor. *Science and Technology in Islam: Technology and Applied Sciences.* Paris: UNESCO Books.

Al-Khalili, Jim. 2011. *The House of Wisdom: How Arabic Science Saved Ancient Knowledge and Gave Us the Renaissance.* New York: Penguin Press.

Al-Khalili, Jim. 2012. *Pathfinders: The Golden Age of Arabic Science.* New York: Penguin Press.

Masood, Ehsan. 2009. *Science and Islam: A History.* London: Icon Books.

Von Martels, Z. R. W. M., editor. 1990. *Alchemy Revisited: Proceedings of the International Conference on the History of Alchemy at the University of Groningen, 17–19 April 1989.* Leiden, The Netherlands, and New York: Brill.

Documents

From Abu Mūsā Jābir ibn Hayyān. C. eighth century. *The Works of Geber, the Most Famous Arabian Prince and Philosopher, of the Investigation and Perfection of the Philosophers-Stone.* Translated by Richard Russel. 1686. London: Printed for William Cooper.

In this passage from a seventeenth-century translation of his works, Abu Mūsā Jābir ibn Hayyān describes the properties of gold and presents some purported evidence that it is possible to transmute copper into gold, though he admits that people have not yet discovered how to do so. It is possible that these statements were added to his text by later Arabian alchemists or the fourteen-century European alchemist called the Pseudo-Geber.

We have already given you, in a General Chapter, the Sum of the Intention of Metals; and here we now intend to make a special Declaration of each one. And first of Gold, we say, Gold is a Metallic Body, Citrine, ponderous, mute, fulgid, equally digested in the Bowls of the Earth, and very long washed with Mineral Water; under the Hammer extensible, fusible, and sustaining the Trial of the Cupel, and Cement. According to this Definition, you may conclude, that nothing is true Gold unless it hath all the Causes and Differences of the Definition of Gold. Yet whatsoever Metal is radically Citrine, and brings to Equality, and cleanseth, it makes Gold of every kind of Metals. Therefore, we consider by the Work, of Nature, and discern, that Copper may be changed into Gold by Artifice. For we see in Copper Mines, a certain Water which flows out, and carries with it thin Scales of Copper, which by a continual and long continued Course it washeth and cleanseth. But after such Water ceaseth to flow, we find these thin Scabs with the dry Sand, in three years time to be digested with the Heat of the Sun; and among these Scales of the purest Gold is found. Therefore, we judge those Scales were cleansed by the benefit of the Water, but were equally digested by heat of the Sun, in the Dryness of the Sand, and so brought to Equality. Wherefore, imitating Nature as far as we can, we like wise alter; yet in this we cannot follow Nature.

From Benton, Kate A. 1900. *Geber: A Tale of the Reign of Harun al Raschid, Khalif of Baghdad*. New York: Frederick A. Stokes Company.

U.S. author Kate A. Benton's Geber: A Tale of the Reign of Harun al Raschid, Khalif of Baghdad *is a fictionalized account of the later days of famed Islamic alchemist Abu Mūsā Jābir ibn Hayyān, known to Europeans as Geber. In this passage, the scientist muses about his unsuccessful efforts to transmute other elements into gold, and berates a slave girl who has taken an interest in his work.*

When morning dawned the house of Geber was silent in its deepest slumber. Even the night-porter nodded in the empty *durka'ah*, the outer hall reserved for waiting slaves and attendants. Only Geber himself watched the white crest of Taurus turn to crimson and gold.

"In truth, Nature will ever be the greater alchemist," he thought, with his eyes upon the daily miracle. "She hath converted darkness into light for many ages, while I am still striving vainly for that talisman which shall merely form good servants for mankind out of the more slavish metals. It would seem that I had bought the secret fairly by the weight of years which I have spent in the search. I have watched the leaden midnight transmuted into the gold of dawn until I am maddened by Nature's triumph and my own failure. Yet can I detect no flaw in the theory which I have matured. It is manifest that many forms of matter, as also many metals, have a common basis. Their individual properties—the differentiations—are just as surely due to a formative force which I in thought can easily separate from the common substratum. Why not also in fact? But how! There lie my years of work. Many wonders have I seen, many precious secrets have I wrenched from Nature's jealous hold, but all of these seem worthless and pale to me beside the one I do not, cannot, obtain."

He paced up and down in deepest thought, his head sunk upon his breast, a frown straightening his heavy brows from their wide arch.

"Gold is the one perfect metal," he continued as he walked. "It is therefore reasonable that a baser metal added unto it will not thereby become pure itself, but will alloy the gold to a lesser purity, even as good cannot mix with evil and remain good. Yet hold! I have seen some natures so filled with the perfection of all good that evil itself upon touching them became transmuted into good. If therefore I could find some substance many times more perfect than gold, that substance might perfect the imperfect. Sulphur and pure mercury—"

"The salt hath turned purely white, Master." The female slave, Gulnare, who had accompanied his daughter in the evening, now appeared before him. "I think it hath more nearly the form thou dost require."

"Who taught thee what I require, or told thee to think concerning what thou wast given to do?" demanded Geber harshly.

"I pray thy pardon if I have exceeded my duty," she replied humbly. "For the rest, I could not for so many years be chosen to aid thee in thy great works, oh Wonder of Wisdom, and not gain some small knowledge of thy desires. The crumbs of food which have fallen from thy table, Master, have but made me the stronger to serve thee."

"Ay! Thou hast a woman's guileful tongue, if also a woman's deft fingers. It was because of thy wit and the shape of thy fingers that I chose thee from out the stupidity of the rest—not because I desired to do thee honour. Dost thou understand that, girl?"

"Truly I understand, Master." One might almost have said that she felt the savage irony of his tone, could slaves feel.

Caliphs

Muhammad (570–632) was not only a religious leader, but a military and political leader as well; at the time of his death, he had conquered and ruled most of the Arabian Peninsula, creating an immediate need to select someone to replace the prophet. His followers promptly elected his friend Abu Bakr (573–634) to take command, but they were initially unsure as to what title to give this person, who was replacing their new religion's prophet but was not a prophet himself. While some referred to him as *Amir al-Mu'minin* (commander of believers), or *Imam* (religious leader), the preferred term became *Khalifat Rasul Allah*, meaning deputy to the Messenger of God; later, he would simply be called a *caliph*. The first four men who held this title served as sovereigns of the expanding Islamic empire and were regarded by many Muslims as the official successors to Muhammad. Later Islamic rulers also called themselves caliphs, although they were not granted the special religious status of the original four.

The early caliphs were embroiled with conflicts, both with the other nations they defeated and within their own ranks. The selection of Abu Bakr sparked the argument that eventually led to the division of Islam into two sects: those who supported the choice became the dominant Sunni Muslims, while Shi'ite Muslims believed that the proper successor was Muhammad's son-in-law Ali ibn Abi Talib (ca. 600–661). The immediate challenge facing Abu Bakr, however, was to consolidate Islamic rule over the lands conquered by Muhammad and carry on his efforts to expand its boundaries. While ostensibly in charge of the generals leading those campaigns, Abu Bakr was otherwise gentle and unassertive, as he continued to earn his living by selling cloth in the marketplace and was most noted for his generosity. Under the next caliph, Umar ibn Al-Khattāb (ca. 584–644), the forces of Islam seized Syria and Egypt from the Byzantine Empire and conquered the Sassanid Persian Empire; this firm and dictatorial ruler also solidified the regime's legal system and instituted a census to ensure that taxes were properly collected to support his growing empire. After he was killed in a petty quarrel, Umar was succeeded by Uthman ibn Affan (577–656), who proved arrogant, incapable of governing, and overly inclined to appoint his relatives instead of competent administrators; the eventual assassination of this unpopular ruler was almost inevitable. Reluctantly, the aging Ali finally assumed the caliphate, but his regime was beset by civil wars and he was finally assassinated as well.

This miniature painting from sixteenth-century Turkey depicts the first four Islamic caliphs: Abu Bakr, Umar ibn Al-Khattāb, Uthman ibn Affan, and Ali ibn Abi Talib. They served as sovereigns of the Islamic empire and were regarded by many Muslims as the official successors to Muhammad. (Universal Images Group)

Although Ali's son Hasan ibn Ali (625–670) was briefly supported as the new caliph, he soon accepted Ali's chief opponent, Muawiyah I (602–680), as the nation's undisputed leader, and he became the founder of its first hereditary dynasty, the Umayyads. Under his rule, the caliphate became a primarily secular monarchy. Unlike the earlier caliphs, who had governed in an unassuming manner, Muawiyah resolved to emulate the emperors of the Byzantine Empire with a conspicuously opulent lifestyle, wearing silken robes and expensive jewelry and sitting on a throne with luxurious cushions. However, he also wished to be accessible to all of his subjects; hence, after a morning meal with his subordinates, he went to a nearby mosque and allowed any citizen to approach him with a petition, either granting the request immediately or ordering an official to investigate his complaint. When he returned to his court for lunch, citizens could also ask for his attention and even enjoy some food with their ruler. Muawiyah I was also noted for his civic projects to improve the appearance of his capital city, Damascus, and his extensive private library. However, his decision to make his son Yazid I (647–683) the next caliph was widely unpopular, and Muawiyah's death in 680 began a long era of conflict within the Islamic world that culminated with the ouster of the Umayyad Dynasty in 750 (though members of the family continued to rule as caliphs in present-day Spain).

The caliphs of the subsequent Abbasid Dynasty presided over what is sometimes known as the "Golden Age of Islam." They shifted their capital to Baghdad and, enjoying great wealth from the Islamic world's many conquests, they indulged in the conspicuously extravagant lifestyle that has long formed the popular image of the Middle Eastern sovereign, as they wore the finest silk clothes and jewelry and enjoyed the company of many attractive women in their large harems—although at least one caliph, al-Amīn ibn Harūn (787–813), notoriously preferred the company of young men and eunuchs. Caliphs resided in an enormous palace complex that included a large hall for official business, a bath house and pool, gardens, a cemetery, and the caliph's private quarters. As symbols of their power, the Abbasid caliphs donned the official mantle of the prophet Muhammad, called the *burda*, and were equipped with a sword and a staff called a *qadīb*. Their servants and employees were required to wear black, which was also the color worn by the caliphs on formal occasions. Among other ceremonial duties, the caliph would appear at the ceremonies that launched the annual *hajj* to Mecca and later welcomed the returning pilgrims. At times, the caliph would join the pilgrimage, providing food, beverages,

gifts, and money to those who accompanied him. The Abbasid caliphs were also noted for their support of scholarship and the arts, particularly Harun al-Rashid (763–809), who sponsored the team of brothers called the Banū Mūsā who were responsible for translating many foreign texts and achieving some mathematical and scientific breakthroughs of their own. This led to the creation of an institution, termed the House of Wisdom, that carried on these activities during the reigns of later caliphs. Poets and other writers were also highly valued by the caliphs, who made them regular visitors to the court.

Of course, caliphs were also necessarily preoccupied with matters of state. They were personally responsible for appointing a broad range of important officials: the vizier who functioned as the empire's prime minister and handled the daily business of government; the generals who led armies into battle; the provincial governors; and their two subordinates, the *amil* who deal with the budget and the *wali* who controlled the military. Caliphs often played a personal role in diplomacy, visiting or hosting foreign dignitaries and negotiating the terms of treaties. Some caliphs asserted their authorities over questions of theology; the caliph al-Ma'mūn ibn Harūn (786–833), for example, was a vigorous supporter of the controversial doctrines of Mu'tazilism and instituted a policy called *minha*, which persecuted scholars who did not agree with its tenets.

More than anything else, though, the Abbasid caliphs were obliged to constantly worry about threats to their own sovereignty. Battles were fought with the still-powerful Byzantine Empire, and the death of Harun al-Rashid led to a bitter civil war between his sons al-Amīn ibn Harūn, who initially took the throne, and al-Ma'mūn ibn Harūn, whose armies soon occupied Baghdad and killed the older brother. Another major problem, however, was the growing assertiveness of their own provincial governors, who resisted the directives of the central government and eventually achieved effective independence. The Turkish soldiers who came to dominate their military forces, the Mamluks, also emerged as a dominant power and were often able to choose the next caliph. By the tenth century, the Abbasid caliphs exercised genuine power only over the city of Baghdad and its vicinity, as other

RELIGIOUS RULERS

The early caliphs were leaders of both their governments and the Islamic faith, and later caliphs also played a role in matters of religion. One modern nation in the region they once controlled, Iran, currently has a similar system; for while the country does have an elected government and legislature, the true rulers of the country have been its Islamic ayatollahs—the famed Ayatollah Khomeini who led the revolution that ousted the Shah of Iran in 1979, and his successor, Ayatollah Khamenei, who took office in 1989 after the Ayatollah Khomeini's death.

CALIPHS AND THE COMMON PEOPLE

Despite his exalted position, caliph Muawiyah I strived to be accessible to all of his subjects, who could approach him while he prayed in the mosque or even join him for lunch to discuss their concerns. Some modern rulers are also determined to stay in touch with ordinary citizens, sometimes employing unusual methods. A prominent example is the Norwegian prime minister Jens Stoltenberg, who in 2013 secretly worked for one day as a taxi driver in order to speak with everyday people and learn what they were thinking. His system was not without its perils, however, as one video suggests that the inexperienced driver was almost in an accident.

caliphs ruled Spain, northern Africa, Egypt, and the regions now known as Libya, Syria, and Iran, and in 1060 even Baghdad itself came under the control of the Persian Seljub Empire.

Even under foreign rule, caliphs were allowed to maintain their royal court, were still recognized as authorities in matters of religion, and occasionally garnered some renewed political power as well until the Mongols finally conquered and destroyed the city of Baghdad in 1258. Even then, the caliph's former soldiers, the Mamluks, officially continued the caliphate in Egypt until the fifteenth century, though they also were only respected as religious leaders. Political power in the Islamic world was now, for the most part, in the hands of different sorts of monarchs called sultans, who confined themselves to secular affairs. Still,

the caliphs have continued to have an impact because of the many scholarly and artistic achievements that they inspired, and they remain alive as exotic, opulent rulers in contemporary popular culture.

Further Reading

Bennison, Amira K. 2009. *The Great Caliphs: The Golden Age of the 'Abbasid Empire*. New Haven, CT: Yale University Press.

Hanne, Eric J. 2007. *Putting the Caliph in His Place: Power, Authority, and the Late Abbasid Caliphate*. Madison, NJ: Fairleigh Dickinson University Press.

Kennedy, Hugh. 2004. *The Court of the Caliphs: The Rise and Fall of Islam's Greatest Dynasty*. London: Weidenfeld & Nicolson.

Marsham, Andrew. *Rituals of Islamic Monarchy: Accession and Succession in the First Muslim Empire*. Edinburgh, England: Edinburgh University Press.

Walker, Paul Ernest. 2009. *Orations of the Fatimid Caliphs: Festival Sermons of the Ismaili Imams: An Edition of the Arabic Texts and English Translation of Fatimid Khuṭbas*. London and New York: I. B. Tauris.

Zaman, Muhammad Qasim. 1997. *Religion and Politics under the Early 'Abbāsids: The Emergence of the Proto-Sunnī Elite*. Leiden, The Netherlands, and Boston: Brill.

Documents

From Háshim, Son of Athap. 660. "A Covenant of 'Ali, Fourth Caliph of Baghdad." Translated by Henry Torrens. 1870. *Journal of the Asiatic Society of Bengal*, 39, Part I, 60–64.

To secure his rule over the present-day country of Albania, the caliph Ali ibn Abi Talib entered in a written agreement with the inhabitants, agreeing to allow them to continue practicing Christianity in exchange for their obedience and their payment of taxes. Written at his behest by an otherwise unknown individual who calls himself "Háshim, son of Athap" (ca. seventh century), this surviving document, translated first into Armenian and later into English, does testify to his desire to be tolerant toward Christians, as shown by the excerpt below.

Praise and thanksgiving to the Creator of the universe, and blessings upon the great chief and benign Muhammad and his sacred tribe.

After all this, it is the purport of the translation of the Covenant, which was written by Háshim, the son of Athap, the son of Valas, according to the command of the blessed chief of the Arabians, and of the Lion of God, of the holy of the holies, of 'Ali, the grandson of Abútálib, the exalted, in Cufic character, in the celebrated domicile of Kharanthala, in the magnificent palace, in the month of Çafar, in the fortieth year of Hijrah.

Whereas certain of the Armenian nation, men of distinction, famous for their erudition and honoured for their dignity, namely, Jacob Sayyid 'Abdul-Shúyukh, and the son of Sahan, and Abraham the Priest, Bishop Isaiah, and several others, forty in number, having communicated with me, and being present in the enactment of this Covenant, solicited me to do this, and have rendered every assistance in their power to our agent whom we had sent to our forts and frontiers, (which was the occasion of our conference and the enactment of this Covenant)—Therefore I have made this Covenant with them on my behalf, as well as on behalf of all tribes of Islam, from east to west. To this end they are, in reality, fully under my fostering care and protection, as long as I live, and after my death, so long as the religion of Islám shall prevail, and the doctrine of Christianity shall continue. It shall be the duty of all potentates and of all princes, and of all men to carry out our Covenant by the help of God, so long as the sea shall be capable of wetting wool, tufts and briers, and rain shall descend from heaven, and grass shall grow from the earth, and stars shall give light, and the moon shall rise upon aliens and strangers. . . .

But if any one shall act against all that I have written concerning the Christians, who have proved themselves worthy of my favor and benevolence, such a person acts against the will of God, who inspired me with grace to do this act of goodness to that nation and to save them from troubles and vexations; for I have entered into a Covenant with them, because they requested and solicited it from me and from all my friends. . . . Because the Christians under my authority are my subjects, and I am ruler over them, it is my duty to have a paternal eye over them, and to protect them from all evils and troubles; and thus a good reward shall be given in heaven both to me and to my nation which is scattered in different parts of the world.

And the scale of taxation fixed by me for these nobles should be strictly adhered to. No demand should be made from them beyond what has already been written down and sanctioned. They should not be molested or oppressed. Their country should not be taken from them. They should not be alienated from their country. The priests should not be deprived of their holy calling. The Christians should not be converted from Christianity. The monks and hermits should not be disturbed in their solitudes, nor removed from their monasteries. Their preachers should not be prohibited to preach. Their habitations and their hereditary lands should not be devastated. Their property should not be meddled with when they build Churches. Nobody should remove or to pull down the bells from the steeples of their Churches. This is the law which I have made for them. But, those who shall infringe my Covenant, by disobeying my behests, shall be transgressors of the ordinance of God, and shall suffer severe punishments and eternal penalties.

Let no crowned head or man of authority of the Musalmáns or believers, compel the Christians to profess the religion of Musalmáns. Nor let them hold any controversies with them on matters of religion, but let them treat them with kindness and tenderness; and, under the shadow of their mercy and clemency, protect them from all sorts of oppression and tribulations, wherever they may be found or wherever they may reside. And if the Christian people be in want of money or in need of pecuniary help for the building of Churches and monasteries, for their national and social assemblies, and for their civil and domestic purposes, the Musalmáns ought to assist them and supply them with the necessary means, by granting them a portion of their superabundant and disowned property. . . .

From 'Aḥmad Ibn Yaḥyā al-Balādhurī. C. ninth century. *The Origins of the Islamic State: Being a Translation from the Arabic.* Volume I. Translated by Philip Khūri Hitti. 1916. New York: Columbia University Press.

In this passage from his history of the early Islamic world, Kitab Futuh al-Buldan or The Origins of the Islamic State, 'Aḥmad Ibn Yaḥyā al-Balādhurī (died 892) explains how two caliphs dealt with the Christians and Jews of the Arabian city of Najran, quoting from statements they issued. One caliph expelled them from the city, while a later caliph reduced their taxes.

'Umar expels them. When abu-Bakr as-Siddik became caliph he enforced the terms agreed upon and issued another statement similar to that given by the Prophet. When 'Umar ibn-al-Khattab became caliph, they [the Jews and Christians of Najran] began to practise usury, and became so numerous as to be considered by him a menace to Islam. He therefore expelled them and wrote to them the following statement:

"Greetings! Whomever of the people of Syria and al-' Irâk they happen to come across, let him clear for them tillable land; and whatever land they work, becomes theirs in place of their land in al-Yaman." Thus the people of Najran were dispersed, some settling in Syria and others in an-Najraniyah in the district of al-Kufah, after whom it was so named. The Jews of Najran were included with the Christians in the terms and went with them as their followers.

The Najranites under 'Uthman. When 'Uthman ibn-'Affan became caliph, he wrote to his *âmil* in al-Kufah, al-Walid ibn-'Ukbah ibn-abi-Mu'ait, as follows:

"Greetings! The civil ruler, the bishop and the nobles of Najran have presented to me the written statement of the Prophet and showed me the recommendation of 'Umar. Having made inquiry regarding their case from 'Uthman ibn-Hunaif, I learned that he had investigated their state and found it injurious to the great landlords whom they prevented from possessing their land. I have, therefore, reduced their taxation by 200 robes—for the sake of Allah and in place of their old lands. I recommend them to thee as they are included among the people entitled to our protection."

Another source for 'Umar's statement. I heard it said by one of the learned that 'Umar wrote them the following statement:—"Greetings! Whomsoever of the people of Syria or al-'Irâk they pass by, let him clear for them tillable land." Another I heard say, "waste land."

Cooks

The people of the early Islamic world were fascinated by the art of cooking, and they wrote many treatises on the subject, though only a few have survived. As their empire grew larger and wealthier, even the poorest citizens had access to new sorts of food, which were generally prepared by wives assisted by their daughters and other female relatives. Wealthier families would spend large sums of money to purchase both male and female slaves from distant lands, such as Egypt, India, and sub-Saharan Africa, who had the knowledge and skill to prepare unfamiliar dishes from their native cuisines. The royal court maintained a staff of several cooks under the direction of a kitchen supervisor called the *qayyim* or *wakīl 'ala'l-matbakh*, who decided upon the daily menus and assigned specific tasks to various cooks; the person designated as the head cook, or *tabbākh*, was expected to ensure that each dish was suitably palatable. Talented cooks could also support themselves by working in one of the many restaurants found in a typical city; customers could either sit there and eat the food they prepared or take it home.

Regardless of where they labored, cooks employed a number of characteristic devices and utensils. For those who could not afford to have ovens at home, there were special facilities called bake-houses where they could cook their foods. Ovens were heated by burning wood or coal, and bread was baked using a special sort of oven called a *tannūr*. This was either a hole in the ground or a large clay cylinder without a covering; a fire was started at the bottom and dough was attached to the sides to be baked. The utensil that cooks relied most heavily upon was a large cauldron called a *qidr* (plural *qudūr*), generally made of stone, clay, or lead, although copper *qudūr* coated with tin were occasionally preferred. These came in various sizes—some were large enough to cook meat from four goats—and their bottoms were covered with grease to reduce the heat from the fire and allow for slow cooking. For frying meat or vegetables, cooks could employ either a steel or stone pan called the *miqlā* or an iron or copper slab called a *tabaq*, while meat was roasted by placing it in a *saffūd*, an iron implement with prongs that held the meat. To grind up spices, cooks used a copper mortar called a *hāwan* or *minhāz*.

As noted, almost everyone could obtain a reasonable variety of foods in their local markets to include in their meals. Chickens were most popular, as people often raised a few chickens in their houses to provide meat and eggs, and the birds were relatively inexpensive to buy. Sheep, goats, cows, and camels

This medieval illustration, probably painted in sixteenth-century Persia, depicts several cooks at an oasis preparing a meal. (Werner Forman Archive)

were also eaten, but never pigs, as Islam prohibited the consumption of pork; during difficult times, the poor would eat locusts. Several types of fish caught in the Tigris River were also a staple of the Islamic diet, although many people could only afford to purchase small fish, and crabs and snails were commonly eaten as well. To bake bread, wheat flour was usually abundant; rural women would grind their own flour, while those in the city could take their flour to a mill—indeed, since it was regarded as tedious labor, some marriage contracts stipulated that the future wife would never be asked to grind flour. Flour made from barley or rice was an acceptable substitute. Vegetables readily available to cooks included beans, eggplants, carrots, onions, asparagus, radishes, and lettuce, while fruits like melons, oranges, bananas, grapes, apples, pomegranates, and dates were usually eaten raw. Dairy products like milk, butter, and cheese were primarily used as ingredients in various dishes. To add flavor to their dishes, all cooks could readily use honey, sugar, salt, and mint, which came from nearby areas, and many stretched their budgets to purchase more costly spices imported from India and China, such as cumin, cinnamon, ginger, and pepper. For cooking, one could purchase animal fat, butter, or olive oil.

Everyday cooks favored a number of standard dishes that even the rich would occasionally enjoy. To make one of these, called *harīsa*, cooks would begin in the afternoon by boiling and shredding pieces of fat and adding wheat flour; in the evening, after hours of simmering, pieces of chicken and some cinnamon would be placed in the mixture; around midnight, it would be stirred until it hardened into a paste and left to simmer until the next morning; and right before it was eaten, more spices and flavorings would be added. Another popular treat, the *'asid al-tamr*, was made by boiling dates, pounding them until softened, cooking them again with oil and walnuts, and placing the cooked material between two pieces of sweet bread. A simple recipe was followed to produce *kabāb*: thin pieces of salted meat were fried without grease and turned over again and again until they were thoroughly cooked; other spices might be applied as well.

Meals favored by the wealthy, unsurprisingly, usually required greater quantities of meat. Preparing *bazmāward* began with a cooked roast that was covered with rose water, walnut, lemon, and vinegar. The roast was then stuffed with bread, cooked an additional hour, sliced, and served with mint. To make *madīra*, the cook would cut some meat, like chicken, into pieces, add salt, and boil them in a pan, tossing in leeks, onions, and spices like coriander and cinnamon right before the meat was completely cooked. The meat was temporarily removed and a mixture of milk, mint, and lemon was boiled in the same pan; the meat was then allowed to simmer in the liquid before it was served. The primary ingredient in a sort of stew called *sikbāj* was pieces of meat that were boiled with cinnamon, salt, and coriander; then, eggplant, onions, carrots, and leeks were added to be partially cooked before vinegar and date juice were poured in and the mixture was brought to a boil. After an hour, raisins, almonds, figs, and saffron were dropped in for additional flavor.

FOREIGN FOOD PREPARERS

Seeking novel dishes for their meals, caliphs liked to employ cooks from faraway places like India and Egypt. Today, the executive chef who is officially in charge of preparing food for the president of the United States also comes from a foreign country. Cris Comerford was born in the Philippines, immigrated to the United States at the age of twenty-three, and after years of working as a chef was hired as the first woman, and first member of a minority group, to prepare food for the United States' leader, his family, and guests. And, while she draws her recipes from the cuisines of many countries, she occasionally includes Filipino favorites in her menus.

OLD OVEN, FRESH BREAD

Common people in the medieval Islamic world baked bread in a cylindrical clay oven called a *tannūr*, placing loaves on its sides to be baked by a fire on the bottom. In 2012, as part of his research for a novel about ancient Israel, author Tim Frank built his own *tannūr* and tried baking some bread, discovering some complexities in this apparently simple method of cooking. His first loaves came out poorly because the dough did not have the right consistency, and he sometimes dropped loaves into the fire while trying to remove them. But the process was not time consuming, as loaves were completely baked in only ten minutes.

The cooks who worked for wealthy patrons, however, could not limit themselves to a few well-known dishes, since they were typically expected to offer their master and his guests a large number of different and exotic foods. When a noted singer named Mukhāriq (died 845) entertained a friend, for example, he provided an ample menu of cooked mutton, fish, vegetables, fruits, bread, and several drinks and desserts. Caliphs might be even more extravagant; by one report, the caliph al-Ma'mūn ibn Harūn (786–833) once provided a lunch with over 300 dishes. However, needing to reduce royal expenses, a later caliph, Abu Mansur Muhammad al-Qahir bi'llah (899–950) limited each of his meals to no more than twelve main dishes, although he permitted himself up to thirty different desserts. Unusual and expensive delicacies were also prized; the prince Ibrahim ibn al-Mahdi (779–839), for

example, once served his guests an extremely costly dish consisting mainly of fishes' tongues. Encouraged to be creative and granted access to the finest ingredients, the cooks of the royal court surely enjoyed their work, though there was also a certain amount of stress associated with their job; there are many reports of cooks being berated by their masters for failing to prepare food that met their high expectations.

Obsessed with food and especially fond of sweets, some caliphs were regarded as gluttons and not infrequently became obese; one caliph, Abu Ja'far Abdallah ibn Muhammad al-Mansur (714–775), died after succumbing to a stomach ailment purportedly caused by overeating. Yet wealthy aristocrats and educated men were also very concerned about healthy eating, as shown by several treatises about the helpful and harmful effects of various foods. Some caliphs employed physicians who were expert in such matters to advise them about what they should eat; the caliph Harun al-Rashid (ca. 763–809) granted his physician, Jabril ibn Bukhtishu (ca. eighth century), the power to remove an unhealthy dish from his table even if this made the caliph unhappy. When the physician failed to appear at one meal, Harun refused to start eating until Jabril arrived to approve of the menu. More so than their predecessors, then, many of the Islamic cooks had to be concerned about making their meals nutritious as well as delicious.

Further Reading

Lewicka, Paulina. 2011. *Food and Foodways of Medieval Cairenes: Aspects of Life in an Islamic Metropolis of the Eastern Mediterranean*. Leiden, The Netherlands, and Boston: Brill.

Jan van Gelder, Geert. 2000. *God's Banquet: Food in Classical Arabic Literature*. New York: Columbia University Press.

Salloum, Habeeb, Muna Salloum, and Leila Salloum Elias. 2013. *Scheherazade's Feasts: Foods of the Medieval Arab World*. Philadelphia: University of Pennsylvania Press.

Waines, David, editor. 2010. *Food Culture and Health in Pre-Modern Muslim Societies*. Leiden, The Netherlands, and Boston: Brill.

al-Warrāq, Ibn Sayyār. C. tenth century. *Annals of the Caliphs' Kitchens: Ibn Sayyār al-Warrāq's Tenth-Century*

Baghdadi Cookbook. Translated by Nawal Nasrallah. 2007. Leiden, The Netherlands, and Boston: Brill.

Zaouali, Lilia. 2007. *Medieval Cuisine of the Islamic World: A Concise History with 174 Recipes.* Berkeley and Los Angeles: University of California Press.

Document

From al-Muhassan ibn Ali. C. 991. *The Table-Talk of a Mesopotamian Judge.* Translated by David Samuel Margoliouth. 1922. London: The Royal Asiatic Society.

As one of the many anecdotes told by Al-Muhassan ibn Ali (ca. 940–944) in his eccentric compilation, The Table-Talk of a Mesopotamian Judge, *he describes a wealthy man who is very attentive toward his food, as his cook unhappily discovers.*

I heard Abū 'Abdallāh Ibn Abī Mūsā Hāshimi say: I was in the presence of Nāsir al-daulah in Baghdad when he asked for something to eat in a hurry, so as to lose no time; they brought him a roast fowl, a loaf of bread, sugar, salt, vinegar, and a little in the way of vegetables. He began to eat while I entertained him, when the chamberlain entered to announce some people who, being respected by him, had to be received. He ordered the fowl to be removed, wiped his hands, and let the visitors enter, with whom he talked. Presently they departed and he ordered the dish to be brought back. It was brought in, and after gazing for a time at the fowl, he angrily asked: Where is *that* fowl?—They said: Here it is.—He vowed by his father that it was not and told them to bring the cook. When the cook was fetched, he asked him whether it was the same fowl?—He was silent. Tell me the truth, he then insisted. The cook admitted that it was not. What then have you done with the other?—When it was removed, he said, we did not know that you would want it back; so one of the small lads took it and ate it. When you asked for it, we took this one, tore off a piece and pulled it about as you had done with the other, hoping that you would not notice, and brought it in.—Ass, said the prince, of that fowl I had torn off the right leg and eaten the left side of the breast, whereas of this one the right part of the breast is eaten, and the left leg torn off. Do not you do this sort of thing again.

Farmers

When many people think of the medieval Islamic world, they envision men on camels riding through a barren desert where engaging in any form of agriculture would be absolutely impossible. In fact, large areas of the Middle East and northern Africa under Islamic rule were suitable for farming, and innumerable people fed themselves and made their living by planting and harvesting various crops. The increasing aridity of the land, however, did make wise management of the soil and intensive irrigation more and more essential, and farmers responded to these challenges with some ingenious innovations.

Throughout the Middle East, farmers for a long time continued to rely upon time-honored tools and techniques commonplace in other regions. The land was prepared for planting with a wooden or iron plow, pulled by a donkey, though horses, camels, and buffaloes were brought in to do this work more efficiently. Seeds were scattered by hand, and crops were harvested by wielding an adze made of wood. The manure of farm animals was collected to be applied as fertilizer, although the Persians later learned to raise pigeons for the express purpose of using their guano to fertilize the land. To deal with certain problems, some farmers still relied upon ancient folklore; for example, it was said that one could remove the weeds called tares from wheat fields by having a youthful virgin hold a rooster and walk through the fields. Farmers generally owned their own land, which was passed within families from generation to generation, though they might also make arrangements to grow crops on someone else's land in exchange for a portion of the harvest. Villages considered lands set aside for grazing and water supplies as community property, and members of long-established families might exercise a loose sort of executive authority over their neighbors.

As for the crops that they raised, wheat was by far the most popular, though other grains like barley were also grown, and fields where water was abundant might be devoted to rice. The lives of farmers who grew wheat were greatly improved by the invention of the windmill, which used the power of the wind to grind their wheat. Farmers also grew vegetables like celery, artichokes, cucumbers, beans, and pumpkins, and orchards were maintained to grow fruits and nuts like pomegranates, apricots, blackberries, figs, carobs, and almonds. Even exotic fruits from tropical climates, like bananas and mangos, could be grown by means of sufficient irrigation. Spices and herbs were also raised, like mint, oregano, saffron, mint, and marjoram. On the fringes of the desert, one of the few plants that could survive in the dry conditions was the date palm; these hardy trees might take several years to reach maturity, but their sweet dates were long a favorite delicacy throughout the Islamic world. Surviving texts on the subject of horticulture advise farmers to move the male flowers back and forth above the female pistils in order to make the palms produce more dates.

During the first millennium of Islamic rule, some new crops gradually became popular as well. Sugar cane, imported from India, finally provided an alternative to honey as a sweetening ingredient, although many farmers continued to keep beehives as a source of honey. Silkworms were also introduced to feed on mulberry leaves and provide the silk that was constantly in demand throughout Europe and Asia. Other plants were raised for purposes other than food: cotton yielded an excellent material for warm-weather clothing; indigo was processed to make an attractive blue dye; henna was the main ingredient in women's makeup; and the opium from poppies was used for medicinal purposes and as a recreational drug.

Gardens filled with flowers were also common throughout the Islamic world, though these were not only pleasant places to take a stroll, but also another source of income for farmers. Fresh flowers could be sold as decorations, but they also provided aromatic substances that were highly prized. Roses yielded rose water, often applied to foods to enhance their appeal; jasmines and violets were key ingredients in perfumes; flowering plants of the *commiphora* family were the source of the sweet-smelling resin myrrh; and another flowering plant, boswellia, was used to make incense such as frankincense.

Farmers also kept some animals: cows could pull plows and provide dairy products, while chickens offered meat and eggs. Tending to animals, however, was generally the main business of the nomadic pastoralists who lived in areas where agriculture could not be practiced and sustained themselves by foraging and herding animals. Farmers and pastoralists usually coexisted peacefully, and to some extent depended on each other for food products, but there were cases where the pastoralists essentially preyed upon settled people by raiding their possessions or forcing them to pay tribute.

While rich soil, seeds, and fertilizer were essential to all of the crops grown by Islamic farmers, their overriding concern always had to be water, which was generally a scarce commodity, and much of their energies were focused on finding sources of water and transporting water to their crops. The ancient Mesopotamian governments had long ago implemented extensive systems of irrigation in the Fertile Crescent formed by the Tigris and Euphrates rivers, just as the ancient Egyptian government had set up similar networks around the Nile River, and the Islamic bureaucracies that now controlled these regions continued to maintain these channels and canals with the assistance of local farmers. The Mesopotamian canals, elevated on dams so the water would easily drain toward crops, had to be regularly examined because even the slightest opening would make the water flow out of the canals to form useless, stagnant pools. Dams were constructed to retain water or channel it toward crops, and new canals were generally made of stone or brick; in some cases, pipes made of lead or tile transported the water. A Middle Eastern innovation that predated Islam was the *ghanat*, an underground channel that took water from the ground and drove it in streams toward reservoirs. These were painstakingly excavated and maintained by hand by farmers who first dug a large vertical hole, began digging horizontally, and removed dirt by means of a box lifted to the surface by a winch over the hole.

Other farmers watered their crops in a variety of ways. In the hilly regions of Syria, farmers could construct terraces that allowed the soil to retain water from rain, although there were also irrigation channels that brought water from the Orontes River. Around desert oases, waterskins made of leather were filled from wells and carried by camels to fields where farmers poured the water into small channels. Where there were rivers, large wooden waterwheels, or *noria*, were kept rotating by the current and propelled water into riverside gardens. Another device that was used

The *shaduf,* a device that raises water from rivers to irrigate crops, was invented in ancient Egypt and was regularly employed by the farmers of the Byzantine Empire and Islamic world. It was still being used in twentieth-century Egypt, as this photograph from 1910 attests. (Library of Congress)

WARS OVER WATER

The main priority of most farmers in the medieval Islamic world was obtaining sufficient water for their crops, and this has long remained a significant problem for farmers in the region. There have been many controversies, for example, over the efforts of the Turkish government, beginning in the 1960s, to construct dams on the Tigris and Euphrates rivers, which reduce the amount of water that reaches Iraq. In response to protests, Turkey agreed in 2008 to periodically open the dams to allow more water to flow downstream, but despite opposition from their neighbors, they are proceeding to build another dam, the Ilisu Dam, that may exacerbate the situation.

A FAVORITE FRUIT

The date palm has long been a popular crop in the Islamic world, as dates are a common treat and are used in many recipes; even today, the top ten date-producing countries were once part of the Islamic empire. However, even as Islamic farmers imported and raised plants from other regions, distant nations have also begun to raise their own date palms. Thus, China is currently the eleventh largest producer of dates, and significant numbers of date palms are also grown in the U.S. states of Arizona, California, and Florida.

to bring water from rivers to crops is the Archimedes screw, essentially a large screw inside a cylindrical container; when it is lowered into a body of water and the screw is turned, the water is raised for easy transport. Egyptian farmers continued to employ the *shaduf,* which elevated river water in a bucket by means of a counterweight.

Despite their continuing efforts to irrigate their crops, many farmers of the medieval Islamic world were essentially fighting a losing battle against a changing climate, which brought drier conditions and made agriculture more and more difficult. In Persia, the incompetence of the government played a role as well: in the tenth century, the last caliphs of the Abbasid Dynasty had ceased maintaining the essential irrigation system of the ancient Mesopotamians, and one of their greatest achievements—the grand Nahrawan Canal that brought water from the Tigris River—was deliberately destroyed in a failed effort to defeat a rebel army and was never rebuilt. Lacking water for their crops, farmers were sometimes obliged to abandon agriculture and become pastoralists, reversing the normal pattern of development. But others were able to carry on with farming, like their ancient ancestors, continuing a tradition of living off the land, which has endured to the present day.

Further Reading

Lambton, Ann K. S. 1988. *Continuity and Change in Medieval Persia: Aspects of Administrative, Economic, and*

Social History, 11th-14th Century. Albany, NY: Bibliotheca Persica.

Magness, Jodi. 2003. *The Archaeology of the Early Islamic Settlement in Palestine*. Winona Lake, IN: Eisenbrauns.

Petruccioli, Attilio. 1997. *Gardens in the Time of the Great Muslim Empires: Theory and Design*. Leiden, The Netherlands, and Boston: Brill.

Van Ruymbeke, Christine. 2007. *Science and Poetry in Medieval Persia: The Botany of Nizami's Khamsa*. New York: Columbia University Press.

Viollet, Pierre-Louis. 2000. *Water Engineering in Ancient Civilizations: 5,000 Years of History*. Translated by Forrest M. Holly Jr. 2007. Madrid: International Association of Hydraulic Engineering and Research.

Watson, Andrew M. 2010. *Agricultural Innovation in the Early Islamic World: The Diffusion of Crops and Farming Techniques, 700–1100*. Cambridge and New York: Cambridge University Press.

Documents

From 'Aḥmad Ibn Yaḥyā al-Balādhurī. C. ninth century. *The Origins of the Islamic State: Being a Translation from the Arabic*. Volume I. Translated by Philip Khūri Hitti. 1916. New York: Columbia University Press.

In his historical text, Kitab Futuh al-Buldan, *translated as* The Origins of the Islamic State, *'Aḥmad Ibn Yaḥyā al-Balādhurī (died 892) at one point discusses various views on what agricultural products are subject to taxes, providing a good picture of the major crops raised in medieval Islamic society.*

It was stated by Yahya ibn-Adam that he heard Sufyan ibn-Sa'id (whose view is the following) say:— "There is no *sadakah* except on four of the products of the soil, i. e., wheat, barley, dates and raisins, provided the product measures five *wasks*." But abu-Hanifah's view is that whatever the tithe-land produces is subject to the tithe, though it be a bundle of vegetables. The same view is held by Zufar. But according to the view of Malik, ibn-abi-Dhi'b and Ya'kub, vegetables and the like are not subject to *sadakah*. Nor is there *sadakah* on what is less than five *wasks* of wheat, barley, maize, husked barley, tare, dates, raisins, rice, sesame, peas and the grains that can be measured and stored, including lentils, beans, Indian peas and millet. If any of these measure five *wasks*, then it is subject to *sadakah*. The same view, according to al-Wakidi, is held by Rabi'ah

ibn-abi-'Abd-ar-Rahman. According to az-Zuhri all spices and pulse is subject to *zakat*. Malik holds that no *sadakah* is due on pears, plums, pomegranates or the rest of the fresh fruits. The same view is held by ibn-abi-Laila. According to abu-Yusuf, there is no *sadakah* except on what can be measured by *al-kafiz*. Abu-az-Zinad ibn-abi-Dhi'b and ibn-abi-Sabrah hold that no *sadakah* is taken on vegetables and fruits, but there is *sadakah* on their prices the moment they are sold.

From al-Muhassan ibn Ali. C. 991. *The Table-Talk of a Mesopotamian Judge*. Translated by David Samuel Margoliouth. 1922. London: The Royal Asiatic Society.

The author of the text generally known as The Table-Talk of a Mesopotamian Judge, *al-Muhassan ibn Ali (ca. 940–944), is attempting at one point to estimate the size of Baghdad during its greatest period, and one measurement he employs, as described in the excerpt below, is the amount of lettuce farmed in its vicinity and sold in the city.*

We were discussing the vastness of Baghdad and the number of its inhabitants in the days of Muqtadir, as well as its buildings, streets, lanes, the size of the place, and the multitudinous classes of the inhabitants. I happened to mention a book which I had seen by a man named Yazdajird b. Mahbindān al-Kisrawī (who lived in the time of Muqtadir) at the court of Abū Mohammed Muhallabi, of which some sheets had been handed to me and to other courtiers to copy and send to the Prince Rukn al-daulah, he having asked for it, containing a description of Baghdad, and an enumeration of its public baths, which were ten thousand—a number which some writers actually name—and the number of the population contained in the place, and of the vessels and sailors, and the wheat, barley and other comestibles which it requires and how the money which came from the ice-merchants every day to the ferrymen was thirty or forty thousand dirhems. Some one else mentioned a book composed by Ahmad b. Tayyib on the same subject. The *qādī* Abu'l-Hasan said to me: That is indeed an enormous amount, of whose truth I have no knowledge; still I have witnessed facts therein in connexion wherewith the statements of Yazdajird and Ahmad b. Tayyib are not improbable, though we have not counted so as to be able to attest their accuracy. Only, a short time ago, in the year 345 [begun, April 15, 956] when Mohammed b. Ahmad known as Turrah, farmed Bādūrayā, he took great pains with its cultivation. Once we made a calculation of the number of *jarībs* [about 70 feet by 70 feet] of lettuce sown there in this year, and computed roughly how much lettuce was brought into Baghdad from Kalwādhā, Qutrabull and other places in the neighbourhood. It came to two thousand *jarībs*. Now we found that on every *jarīb* six sorts were sown, and that of each sort so many roots were plucked—this I do not remember. On each *jarīb* then there were so many roots. The average price of lettuce at the time was twenty stalks for a dirhem. The average amount earned by a *jarīb*, produce and price being both considered, was 350 dirhems, valued at twenty-five dinars. Two thousand *jarībs* then gave fifty thousand dinars. All of this was consumed in Baghdad. What then must be the size of a city wherein in one season of the year one sort of vegetable was consumed to the value of fifty thousand dinars!

Hunters

Hunting was an important activity in the early Islamic world for several reasons. For everyday citizens living in regions where agriculture might be difficult or impossible, it was essential to hunt and kill animals to provide needed food and hides. For soldiers, hunting was regularly required both to provide exercise and practice in using their weapons and to supplement their diets while on campaigns. For caliphs and other wealthy people without mundane concerns, hunting became a favorite sporting activity, and it thus became a source of income for those individuals employed to assist their wealthy patrons in tending to the animals trained to track prey, maintaining the necessary equipment, and accompanying them during each hunt. Others earned a living by selling weapons and hunting animals to royal hunters. It is not surprising, then, that there were numerous manuals written about this valued skill, though only a few representative examples have been preserved.

We have little information about the hunting habits of poor people. Certainly, they lacked the resources

to engage in the lengthy, elaborate hunting expeditions enjoyed by their caliphs, and many suspect that hunting was generally a part-time profession; farmers hunted whenever they had no other tasks to perform, and craftsmen would occasionally hunt to obtain extra food for their families. Still, those who were especially effective in this art undoubtedly found that they could largely support themselves by selling the animals they killed or captured, and they may have preferred to engage in this active and adventurous profession as an alternative to more sedentary labors.

A typical Islamic hunting party, with men on horseback pursuing animals, is shown in this seventeenth-century illustration for a book of poems by the thirteenth-century Islamic poet, Jalal al-Din Rumi (1207–1293). (The Walters Art Museum)

Hunters could employ two strategies: using weapons to kill animals, or catching them with nets and traps. The most common weapon was the bow and arrow; archers typically aimed between the shoulders in order to strike the heart, though arrows that struck the face or neck could also be damaging. To train archers to strike animals, a large animal hide filled with straw was attached to the front of a chariot, representing the animal to be hunted, and a smaller hide was placed at the rear, representing the hunter's dog chasing the animal. The chariot was then rolled downhill and archers aimed at the front hide. If they struck the other hide instead, they needed additional practice, because it meant that they might accidentally kill their own dog in an actual hunt. Birds were killed with another weapon, a crossbow that shot small metallic pellets, and spears might also be employed to kill larger animals.

To trap animals, one common method was to dig a ditch, place iron rods over the top, and cover the opening with dirt; then, animals would be chased out of hiding so they would step on and fall into the ditch. Smaller animals could be caught by extending large nets across a pathway and getting animals to run into them. Some sources indicate that the animals were sometimes chased into these traps by starting fires or ringing bells. Animals like camels and horses might be captured with a lariat or a tool called a *hibāla*, a snare attached to a rope with a wooden handle, and one writer describes a man who killed lions by luring them into the water and drowning them. A variety of techniques were employed to capture birds: a net would be hung between tree branches and a small decoy, like a sparrow, would attract birds into the net. A similar decoy could be placed inside a pot with a narrow opening, and after birds flew in, they could not get out. A sticky wood called *dihq* or some lime might be placed on a branch and when birds landed on the branch, their feet would adhere to it. By one report, hunters would also mix some grain with special herbs that made birds fall asleep when they ate the grain.

When ordinary men went hunting, they may have gone out by themselves with a bow and arrow, or tools and equipment to set up traps; at times, they probably brought their sons along, or worked with a few other hunters as a team. The hunts of a caliph were more complex affairs. An official called the Master of the Chase would first advise the caliph's archers, trappers, animal trainers, and servants to ready themselves for the hunt, and he would arrange for all of the needed supplies, such as food, beverages, cooking utensils, tents, and medicines. Caliphs would also be accompanied by friends and family members, guides who knew where to find prey, soldiers, and experienced physicians. Once they had reached the area where they would be hunting, the caliph's entourage would set up their tents for a stay that might last for several days. Local hunters may have been invited to join the party, to lend their skill and expertise to the challenge of killing as many animals as possible. Hunters would focus their attention on a wide variety of animals, ranging from lions and wild boars to deer, rabbits, wolves, and foxes.

A special feature of royal hunts was the use of exotic animals to assist in tracking down and killing the prey. One popular choice was the cheetah; after being captured and trained by a worker called a cheetah-master, the hooded animal would be taken to a field, unhooded, and released to chase down prey. Once successful, however, the cheetah would have to be quickly hooded again, or it might attack one of the caliph's own animals. Cheetahs could also be used for only ten captures in one day, or the animals could become too tired or lose interest in the hunt. Another large cat, the caracal, was similarly used in hunting; trained weasels were helpful in chasing large birds and foxes out of hiding; hunters might ride on horses to chase down their prey; and dogs were commonly assigned to retrieve the carcasses of dead animals. There are a few accounts of wealthy hunters using trained panthers, wolves, and lions, but such instances were undoubtedly rare. Wealthy hunters were also fond of employing trained birds to attack smaller animals; the most common choices were goshawks, saker falcons, peregrine falcons, and eagles. After a long period of training, these birds would be hooded and brought to the edge of a lake or river; by beating drums, the hunters could frighten water fowl into flight, so the birds could be unhooded and released to capture and retrieve them.

Caliphs would typically spend vast amounts of money on their hunting and provide employment for numerous people. Some hunting animals had to be imported from other regions and were very expensive, and each variety required at least one full-time employee to train and take care of them. Large numbers of archers and trappers were paid to be constantly available for hunts, while artisans were on hand to build and maintain a large supply of weapons and equipment. Also, since Islamic law sanctioned hunting primarily as a way for hunters to sustain themselves, it was considered important to cook and eat the animals, requiring cooks who specialized in broiling meat and preparing soups and stews. Even poets and singers might earn some extra money by accompanying hunting expeditions for the express purpose of composing and performing poems and songs to celebrate the caliph's successes at the end of each day's hunt, and farmers could benefit from royal hunting, as they could demand generous payments if any of their crops were damaged or destroyed by hunters. Clearly, caliphs must have devoted a large portion of their annual budgets to this favorite leisure activity.

It is difficult to assess the overall impact of hunting on the early Islamic world. Certainly, it provided many citizens with needed food, and even caliphs may have benefited from the physical and intellectual exercise that the activity provided. On the other hand, several large animals became less and less common in the Middle East due to constant hunting, and several caliphs were so fond of frequent hunting expeditions that they undoubtedly neglected their other duties. Still, like modern U.S. presidents criticized for playing too much golf, the caliphs might have responded that their hunting represented an essential respite from the heavy responsibilities of governing a large and powerful nation.

LEADERS AND HUNTERS

The Islamic caliphs were avid hunters, as were many British kings, suggesting to some that the activity is especially appealing to people who are skillful leaders. It is certainly interesting to note that while only about six percent of Americans engage in hunting, five of the ten most recent former presidents—Dwight Eisenhower, Lyndon Johnson, Jimmy Carter, George H. W. Bush, and George W. Bush—were all avid hunters, and even current President Barack Obama has stated that he enjoys the form of hunting known as skeet shooting, where the targets are clay objects instead of animals.

A ROYAL HUNTING ANIMAL

Although cheetahs have great strength and speed and are easily trained to hunt, the great expense of purchasing and feeding this animal meant that, in the Islamic world, only caliphs could afford to use such animals in their hunts. Surprisingly, even in the twentieth century, some Asian noblemen continued to hunt with cheetahs. There is a film from 1939, which can now be found on the Internet, showing an Indian prince hunting with a cheetah, providing an image of what it was like to track down and kill an animal with the assistance of this speedy feline.

Further Reading

Allsen, Thomas T. 2011. *The Royal Hunt in Eurasian History*. Philadelphia: University of Pennsylvania Press.

Goodman, Lenn E., and Richard McGregor, translators. 2012. *The Case of the Animals Versus Man Before the King of the Jinn*. Oxford and New York: Oxford University Press.

Harper, Prudence Oliver. 1978. *The Royal Hunter: Art of the Sasanian Empire*. New York: Asia Society.

ibn-Munqidh, Usamah. 2000. *An Arab-Syrian Gentleman and Warrior in the Period of the Crusades: Memoirs of Usāmah ibn-Munqidh*. Translated by Philip K. Hitti. New York: Columbia University Press.

Shatzmiller, Maya. 1993. *Labour in the Medieval Islamic World*. Leiden, The Netherlands, and Boston: Brill.

Shehada, Housni Alkhateeb. 2012. *Mamluks and Animals: Veterinary Medicine in Medieval Islam*. Leiden, The Netherlands, and Boston: Brill.

Document

From al-Muhassan ibn Ali. C. 991. *The Table-Talk of a Mesopotamian Judge*. Translated by David Samuel Margoliouth. 1922. London: The Royal Asiatic Society.

Al-Muhassan ibn Ali (ca. 940–944) worked for many years as a judge in the area now known as Iraq. His eccentric book, usually referred to in English as

The Table-Talk of a Mesopotamian Judge, *represented his effort to present all of the unusual information he was aware of that not had been recorded in other books. The passage below provides a report of one man's unique way to hunt lions.*

I was told by the *qāḍī* Abū Bakr Ahmad b. Sayyār how a certain traveller was benighted and had to pass the night in a deserted *khān* [inn] near a thicket where there was stagnant water. It was a moonlit night, and the place a haunt of lions. The traveller being aware of this mounted the roof of the *khān*, and getting some bricks laid them in the doorway of the staircase; he then sat and watched. Presently a naked man came and sat on the brink of the pool. I asked him—said the traveller—what he was doing. Lion-hunting, he replied. I told him in God's name to consider what he was about. He told me I should see in a moment. After a very short interval a lion appeared, who when he saw the man, roared and made for him. When he came near, the man flung himself into the pool, and the lion dashed in after him. Both dived and presently the man emerged behind the lion, into whose body he presently forced a strong sharp hollow Persian reed a yard in length; he then proceeded to pump the water with one of his hands into this reed, and as it entered the animal's body the latter became weighted and his force decreased, till finally he drowned the beast, then dragged him in the water and finally landed him, when he removed the skin, the brow, the claws, the fat, and certain valuable parts with which he was acquainted; and then called out to me: Sheikh, that is the way to hunt lions. He then left me and disappeared.

Imams

The term "imam" has very different meanings for believers in the two major sects of Islam. For Shi'ite Muslims, who thought that only the son-in-law of the prophet Muhammad (570–632), Ali ibn Abi Talib (ca. 600–661), and his descendants should govern Islam, only twelve men were true Imams—Ali and eleven of his direct descendants—and they are revered for their special relationship with Allah and their role in establishing the major doctrines of their sect. The twelfth of these men, Muhammad ibn Hasan al-Mahdī (ca.

789–unknown), is said to be still alive, though in hiding, waiting for the end of the world to return. However, for Sunni Muslims, who accepted the notion that a religious leader could be any qualified man chosen by his peers, an imam is simply the man who leads prayers and delivers sermons at the mosque, a figure somewhat comparable to the priests of the Roman Catholic Church.

Of the twelve Imams of the Shi'ites, only Ali actually held political power as the fourth caliph, although his oldest son, Hasan ibn Ali (ca. 624–670), was briefly recognized as caliph by his followers until he officially ceded the title to his rival, Muawiyah I (602–680), who later arranged for him to be poisoned so he could not threaten his son and designated successor, Yazid I (647–683). But Hasan's younger brother Husayn ibn Ali (626–680) did challenge Yazid's rule and was subsequently killed, making him one of the Shi'ites' most venerated martyrs. Subsequent Imams, beginning with Husayn's son Ali ibn Husayn (ca. 658–712), focused their energies on engaging in Islamic scholarship and leading members of the Shi'ite community, who were frequently persecuted by the caliphs; indeed, Shi'ite historians report that Ali ibn Husayn and the next seven Imams all were eventually poisoned by reigning caliphs. Ali ibn Husayn is best known as the reputed author of a revered book of Islamic prayers, the *Al-Sahifa al-Sajjadiyya*, though its actual authorship and date of composition are fiercely disputed, while Muhammad ibn Ali al-Baqir (676–733) and his son Ja'far ibn Muhammad al-Sādiq (702–765) were renowned for their scholarly achievements. As part of their religion, Shi'ite Muslims were expected to make pilgrimages to the tombs of their venerated Imams, often engaging in elaborate ceremonies in their honor, since they were regarded as men who, like Christianity's Jesus Christ, had suffered in order to benefit others.

Not surprisingly, there are even matters of controversy regarding the Imams within the Shi'ite sect. The sixth Imam, Ja'far, was officially succeeded by his younger son Musa ibn Ja'far al-Kadhim (745–799) because his older son Isma'il ibn Ja'far (719–?) had already died; however, a branch of Shi'ite Islam arose, the Ismailites, claiming that Isma'il was actually still alive at the time of his father's death and hence should be recognized as the seventh, and final, Imam. Another branch of the Shi'ites, the Zaidiyyah, established a tradition of later Imams in Yemen who exercised both religious and political authority: any man who could claim descent from the prophet Muhammad was eligible to be chosen for the position. There are other disparate beliefs within Shi'ite Islam, which often confuse nonbelievers who are unfamiliar with the many disputes that have characterized the history of the sect.

The humbler imams who preside over prayers in the mosques claim no special authority over religious matters, and in fact are not required to undergo any formal training. Any man who has intently studied the Koran and other Islamic texts, and is respected as a scholar in his community, may assume this role. Whenever governments build mosques, they may appoint the imams who serve there, but in mosques financed by private individuals, imams are typically elected to the position by their congregations. A typical mosque may have several imams, who are supported by its founder and ongoing donations, and they work alongside other members of the staff, including the muezzin who calls believers to their prayers, doorkeepers, and servants.

The major responsibilities of imams occur on every Friday, the day when Muslims traditionally gather in mosques for their prayers. The meeting place is a large hall without furniture, only carpets for the praying attendees. They line up in rows facing Mecca—the men stand in front, while the women stand in the rear or in an adjoining room—and the imam leads them in the prayers from a pulpit. Afterward, it is traditional for imams to deliver a Friday sermon about the Islamic faith. They are never upset by behavior that other religions might regard as disrespectful—believers who fail to attend, or believers who fall asleep during the sermon—since any Muslim is always allowed to perform their Friday prayers at home, and it is understood that hard-working people on hot days may naturally grow tired by the time the sermon begins, usually around noon. More broadly, the mosque is not considered sacred ground—it is only a convenient meeting place for believers—and imams do not assert that they have any special relationship with Allah—they are merely more learned than other believers—so nodding off in a mosque can be readily excused. If an imam is

not available to lead the prayers, the most educated man in the group can perform that duty, but women can only lead prayers if everyone present is a woman; this is a task usually performed by an imam's wife.

Imams are rarely idle on the other days of the week. They are expected to hold classes for young people, to teach them the tenets of Islam, recognizing that their brightest and most enthusiastic students are likely to someday become imams themselves. Some mosques developed into major educational institutions, attracting students from many regions. Imams are expected to regularly engage in ongoing study of their religion, and some become the authors of theological texts. Mosques are also kept open, from sunrise until the day's final prayers after sunset, and any believer may enter to simply rest after traveling, or to receive assistance for physical ailments or personal problems. The imams, then, should be available to any Muslim who needs their services, though their usual role is to provide guidance in resolving religious issues, based on their superior knowledge of Islam. As with any institution, there are matters of daily business to tend to in a mosque—supervising staff members, handling the budget, and so on—though these tasks may be performed by an administrator sometimes referred to as an intendant. Imams had special duties to perform during Muslim holidays and festivals; during the month of Ramadan, for example, imams would lead many believers in special prayers on every day of the month. During major religious ceremonies in the Islamic empire, however, the imams would defer to the caliph, who would personally lead the public prayers as a sign of his piety and religious authority.

Unlike priests in other religions, imams were not required to meet any special requirements in their daily behavior, other than the general expectation that they would lead exemplary lives to serve as role models for other Muslims. It is generally expected that they will have long beards, though some Muslims would regard a clean-shaven imam as more undesirable than sinful. Since "imam" is a title of respect as well as a description of a job, it is usually not a position that ends with a formal retirement, though aging imams will naturally become less active and increasingly shift their responsibilities to younger colleagues. It should be noted that outside of the Arab world, the man performing

PRAYERS AND THE FAIRER SEX

Traditionally, only men were allowed to serve as imams and lead public prayers, although some sects of Islam recognized a few exceptional cases—when all the people praying are women, when everyone present is part of one family, and when there are absolutely no qualified men available. However, like the Catholic Church's insistence on male priests, this rule is now being challenged by some progressive Muslims, though they are being met with fierce resistance. Thus, in 2004, when a woman in Bahrain disguised herself as a man and started to lead prayers, worshippers were not fooled, and the woman was arrested and taken away.

AN ELUSIVE IMAM

Shi'ite Muslims believe that their twelfth Imam, Muhammad ibn Hasan al-Mahdī, is still alive and will emerge from hiding when the world is about to end. However, there have been reports of his brief reappearances, usually to advise or assist believers. In the 1950s, for example, a pharmacist had to bring needed medicine from Baghdad to his hometown Karbala, in Pakistan, but had no way to transport them. Suddenly, a stranger riding a jeep appeared and offered to give him a ride to Karbala; but as soon as they arrived, the man and his jeep vanished. The pharmacist concluded that the Imam himself must have come to his aid.

the duties of an imam in a mosque is often called a mullah, while especially distinguished imams in some cultures came to be granted another title, ayatollah.

Despite the important role they played in the daily lives of believers, imams often receive little attention in the writings of contemporaries or historical surveys, and in a sense, this is a reflection of one distinctive feature of Islam: that every believer necessarily maintains a personal relationship with Allah and his faith. This means that the thoughts and actions of the religious figures around a Muslim may not have as much of an impact as those of leaders in other faiths. One might say that in Islam, each individual is supposed to function as his or her own personal imam, so that the public figures with that title are only of secondary importance.

Further Reading

Cooperson, Michael. 2000. *Classical Arabic Biography: The Heirs of the Prophets in the Age of Al-Ma'mun.* Cambridge and New York: Cambridge University Press.

Gaiser, Adam. *Muslims, Scholars, Soldiers: The Origin and Elaboration of the Ibadi Imamate Traditions.* Oxford and New York: Oxford University Press.

Lassner, Jacob, and Michael Bonner. 2009. *Islam in the Middle Ages: The Origins and Shaping of Classical Islamic Civilization.* Santa Barbara, CA: ABC-CLIO.

Madelung, Wilferd. 1985. *Religious Schools and Sects in Medieval Islam.* London: Variorum Reprints.

Talmon-Heller, Daniella. 2007. *Islamic Piety in Medieval Syria: Mosques, Cemeteries and Sermons under the Zangids and Ayyūbids (1146–1260).* Leiden, The Netherlands, and Boston: Brill.

Virani, Shafique N. 2007. *The Ismailis in the Middle Ages: A History of Survival, a Search for Salvation.* Oxford and New York: Oxford University Press.

Document

From George Percy Badger. 1871. *History of the Ima^ms and Seyyids of 'Oma^n.* By Salil ibn Razik, translated with notes by George Percy Badger. London: Printed for the Hakluyt Society.

In an appendix to his translation of a nineteenth-century historical work, Badger, a British Anglican missionary and scholar, attempts to explain the various meanings of term "imam" in the Islamic world.

The word "Imam"' comes from an Arabic root signifying to aim at, to follow after, most of the derivatives of which partake, more or less, of that idea. Thus *Imam* means, primarily, an exemplar, or one whose example ought to be imitated. It is applied in that sense. . . to Muhammad, as being the leader and head of the Muslims in civil and religious matters, and also to the Khalifahs, or legitimate *Successors*, as his representatives in both capacities. It is also given—in its religious import only—to the heads of the four orthodox sects, namely, the el-Hánafy, esh-Shâfa'iy, el-Mâliky, and el-Hánbaly; and, in a more restricted sense still, to the ordinary functionary of a mosque who leads in the daily prayers of the congregation—an office usually conferred on individuals of reported piety, who are removable by the *Nâzirs*, or wardens, and who, with their employment and salary, lose the title also.

The term is used in the Koran to indicate the Book, or Scriptures, or record of a people; also, to designate a teacher of religion. Hence, most probably, its adoption by the Muslims in the latter sense. "When the Lord tried Abraham with certain words, which he fulfilled, He said, I have made thee an Imam to the people." Again, referring to Abraham, Isaac, and Jacob, "We have made them Imams that they may direct others at our command." And, again, "We delivered to Moses the Book, therefore be not in doubt of his reception thereof, and we ordained it to be a guide unto the children of Israel. And we appointed some of them to be Imams to direct the people according to our command."

It is not clear whether Muhammad himself adopted or received the title; but he never omitted performing the ordinary functions of an Imam until his last illness, when, finding himself unable to leave his house, which communicated with the mosque, he directed that Abu-Bekr should be sent for to lead the prayers of the people. It is certain, however, that the title was assumed by his immediate Successors who regarded the duty associated with it of leading in public worship as their special prerogative, and as involving their supremacy "in all matters of religion and of the world." It is recorded of the Khalifah el-Maimûn (a. h. 198–218 = A.D. 813–833), that on entering the mosque at Baghdad one day, and finding a private individual conducting the prayers, he regarded the act as one of high treason.

"The Muhammadans," writes D'Herbelot, "are not agreed among themselves respecting the Imamate, that is, the dignity of Imam. Some regard it to be of divine right and restricted to a single family, like the Aaronic pontificate; others, whilst admitting it to be of divine right, nevertheless, do not believe it to be so limited to one family that it may not pass over to another. Moreover, according to these latter, the Imam must not only be exempt from great sins, such as infidelity, but also from lesser sins; he may be deposed, if he fall into such, and his dignity transferred to another." To these may be added the opinions of the sects called *en-Nujdât* who held it to be "unnecessary that the people should have an Imam at all; but it behooves them to settle all questions equitably amongst themselves, and if they are unable to do so without the cooperation of an Imam, then they are at liberty to appoint one."

Mathematicians

The mathematicians of the early Islamic world were in an ideal position to advance their discipline, because their empire's conquests had brought them into contact with two valuable bodies of work: ancient Greek mathematics, with its fully developed geometry, and Indian mathematics, which offered important concepts unknown to the Greeks, such as the number zero. Not only were they able to synthesize these two traditions, but they made many breakthroughs on their own, which were eventually conveyed to the Europeans to serve as the basis of their own achievements in mathematics during the Renaissance and thereafter. The very name of our modern number system—the Arabic numbers—and the many mathematical terms that begin with "al," the Arabic definite article, like algebra and algorithm, testify to the key role they played in the development of modern mathematics.

Islamic mathematics began in the eighth century with the caliphs of the Abbasid Dynasty, founded by Abul 'Abbas al-Saffaḥ (ca. 721–754), since they regarded the pursuit of knowledge as a central requirement of Islam and encouraged scholars to translate the major works of other cultures. The most energetic supporter of these efforts was the caliph al-Ma'mūn ibn Harūn (786–833), who had encountered an astronomer named Musa bin Shakir (ca. eighth century) and brought his three talented sons to Baghdad and provided them with a generous budget. Known collectively as the Banū Mūsā, or sons of Moses, the brothers—Abū Ja'far Muḥammad ibn Mūsā (ca. 800–873), Abū al-Qāsim Aḥmad ibn Mūsa (died ninth century), and Al-Ḥasan ibn Mūsā (died ninth century)—imported texts from the Byzantine Empire and hired men to translate them from Greek to Arabic. As they and their employees learned more and more from the earlier scholars, they also began to engage in original research.

One distinguished member of the Banū Mūsā team, Thābit ibn Qurra (826–901), was recruited by a brother while visiting Turkey and returned with him to Baghdad, where he specialized in translating mathematical and scientific treatises, including the works of Euclid, Archimedes, and Ptolemy. He went on to make new contributions to mathematics involving conic sections and number theory; most interestingly, he was first to identify and examine a category of numbers created by the equation $(3 \times 2^n) - 1$, now known as Thabit numbers in his honor. One of Thābit's students was Muḥammad ibn Mūsā (ca. ninth century), the son of Abū Ja'far Muḥammad ibn Mūsā, who was assigned by al-Ma'mūn to write a book on mathematics that could be understood by lay readers; while it contained no original work, its later French translation effectively introduced algebra to the Europeans.

However, the most talented mathematician to work as part of the Banū Mūsā was probably Muḥammad ibn Mūsā al-Khwārizmī (ca. 780–850), sometimes regarded as the true father of algebra because of his groundbreaking *Compendious Book on Calculation by Completion and Balancing* (ca. 820), which presented a systematic approach to the solution of quadratic equations and also discussed the computation of areas and volumes. He also promoted the use of the decimal number system of the Indians, including the number zero, in a work called *On the Calculation with Hindu Numerals* (ca. 825); its popularity explains why these numbers came to called Arabic numbers. He demonstrated their value by showing how they could be used to precisely calculate square roots. Al-Khwārizmī also participated in an impressive effort to confirm the finding of the Greek mathematician Eratosthenes that the circumference of the Earth was about 25,000 miles, using an alternate method. In response to a personal request from al-Ma'mūn, who was curious about Eratosthenes's accuracy, he and other members of the Banū Mūsā traveled to an absolutely flat plain in northern Iraq and stopped in one location to determine the altitude of Polaris, the North Star. Then, repeatedly extending a long rope to measure the distance that they traveled, the men walked directly north, constantly checking the altitude of Polaris, until they reached a place where it was precisely one degree higher. Having traveled about 66-2/3 miles, they established that it was the length of one degree of Earth's circumference. To make sure that they had not made a mistake, they

returned to their starting point, walked 66-2/3 miles directly south, and found that the altitude of Polaris was precisely one degree lower. Multiplying 66-2/3 miles by 360 degrees showed that the circumference of the Earth was about 24,000 miles, proving that Eratosthenes had been roughly correct.

Other practical work assigned to court mathematicians involved astronomy, an important subject for Muslims for two reasons: they practiced astrology, and so needed accurate records of the movements of planets and stars to make their predictions, and residents of every town had to determine the exact direction of Mecca so they could say their prayers facing the holy city. For that reason, Al-Khwārizmī was asked to prepare a compilation of astronomical data from Indian astronomers, and a later mathematician, al-Ḥarrānī al-Battānī (ca. 858–929), endeavored to reconcile the findings of Greek, Persian, and Indian astronomers to produce more accurate records of the movements of the Sun, Moon, and planets.

The Abbasid caliphs gradually lost their power as former provinces asserted their independence, though they retained control over Baghdad and its environs and continued to support the work of scientists and mathematicians. But some of the Islamic world's new rulers valued mathematicians as well. For example, one of the sultans of the Seljug Empire that took over Persia and other regions, Malik-Shah I (1055–1092), employed the noted mathematician Omar Khayyám (1048–1131) as an adviser. While today he is better known as a poet, thanks to the translations of his quatrains by the English poet Edward FitzGerald, he devoted most of his energies to science and mathematics, achieving particular success in methods of solving cubic equations and explorations of Euclid's parallel postulate. He was also asked to devise a more accurate calendar, which remained in use until the twentieth century.

Omar Khayyám's life story—which is better known than that of other Islamic mathematicians—also illustrates the various ways that mathematicians of that era were able to support themselves. An aristocratic background was not required, for despite a humble background—his father made tents—the young Khayyám was so obviously gifted that he was able to study under two distinguished scholars and eventually

Though Omar Khayyám is now esteemed as a poet, this drawing shows him devoting his energies to his true avocation, mathematics, as evidenced by the ruler and compass beside him. (Bettmann/Corbis)

CARRYING ON A TRADITION

The mathematicians of the Islamic world were long the finest in the world, but they were eventually eclipsed by the talented mathematicians of Europe who began moving beyond their achievements during the Renaissance. Yet some residents of the Middle East continued to excel in mathematics. A twentieth-century example is Waleed Al-Salam (1926–1996), who earned two degrees in his native Baghdad before immigrating to the United States to earn his PhD and become a mathematics professor. Among his many achievements, he and a U.S. colleague, Leonard Carlitz, developed a new sort of polynomials now known as the Al-Salam-Carlitz polynomials, adding yet another term beginning with the Arabic article "al" to the field's vocabulary.

MANDATED MATHEMATICS

The government of the Islamic world sometimes asked its mathematicians to do practical work for their benefit, such as preparing astronomical tables and devising a more accurate calendar. In the twentieth century, the American and British governments recruited several hundred mathematicians to provide assistance during World War II. Their work in cryptography, helping to break the codes used by the Germans and Japanese, is most renowned, but they solved many other problems as well, such as calculating how far rockets would travel and advising gun-wielding soldiers in aircraft how to aim accurately at the moving targets of enemy planes.

come to the attention of the sultan. During his years at the royal court, he typically devoted most of the day to teaching students, who undoubtedly paid handsome fees to be educated in mathematics by such a renowned scholar. In the early evening, he would visit with Malik-Shah I to apply his wisdom to whatever matters were concerning the sultan. When it was dark, he would have time to devote to his own work in astronomy and mathematics. Later in his life, after Malik-Shah I died and his services were no longer valued by the new sultans, Khayyám primarily made his living as an astrologer, an easy and profitable activity for anyone learned in mathematics and astronomy, though he probably continued to do some teaching as well. In fact, as traditions of royal patronage dimin-

ished, teaching students was undoubtedly the major way that later mathematicians earned their living; for example, the Persian mathematician Sharaf al-Dīn al-Ṭūsī (died ca. 1214) may be best known today for his skills in solving cubic equations, but he was one of the most famous teachers of his day, attracting interested students from faraway regions.

In addition to other noteworthy mathematicians who lived in Persia, we know that many were active in Spain and northern Africa as well; unfortunately, few of their manuscripts have survived, so we generally have little information about their accomplishments. Perhaps, as scholars continue to search for texts, new data will come to light about other mathematical discoveries that first occurred in the medieval Islamic world. However, during the fifteenth and sixteenth centuries, a new culture was rising to dominate the Western world—Europe—and it is there that the next breakthroughs in mathematics would come, including the invention of calculus and new forms of mathematics like statistics and topology. Still, the European mathematicians who pioneered in those areas regularly made use of the work of the Islamic mathematicians, who effectively reinvigorated and sustained a field that had remained stagnant since the days of the ancient Greeks, and students today can still benefit from the study of their finest treatises.

Further Reading

Al-Kahlili, Jim. 2010. *Pathfinders: The Golden Age of Arabic Science.* London: Allen Lane.

Katz, Victor J., editor. 2007. *The Mathematics of Egypt, Mesopotamia, China, India, and Islam: A Sourcebook.* Princeton, NJ: Princeton University Press.

Mohamed, Mohaini. 2000. *Great Muslim Mathematicians.* Johor Darul Ta'zim: Universiti Teknologi Malaysia.

Rashed, Roshdi, editor. 1996. *Encyclopedia of the History of Arabic Science: Volume 2: Mathematics and the Physical Sciences.* London and New York: Routledge.

Rashed, Roshdi, and B. Vahabzadeh. 2000. *Omar Khayyám, the Mathematician.* New York: Bibliotheca Persica Press.

Rosenfeld, Boris A., and Ekmeleddin Ihsanoğlu. 2003. *Mathematicians, Astronomers and Other Scholars of Islamic Civilisation and Their Works (7th-19th C.).* Istanbul: Research Centre for Islamic History, Art, and Culture.

Documents

From Muḥammad ibn Mūsā al-Khwārizmī. C. 820 CE. *The Algebra of Mohammed Ben Musa.* Edited and Translated by Frederic Rosen. 1831. London: Oriental Translation Fund.

As noted, Muḥammad ibn Mūsā al-Khwārizmī was one of the greatest mathematicians of the medieval Islamic world. Below is a passage from the opening of his greatest work, Compendious Book on Calculation by Completion and Balancing, *sometimes referred to simply as his* Algebra.

When I considered what people generally want in calculating, I found that it always is a number.

I also observed that every number is composed of units, and that any number may be divided into units.

Moreover, I found that every number, which may be expressed from one to ten, surpasses the preceding by one unit: afterwards the ten is doubled or tripled, just as before the units were: thus arise twenty, thirty, etc., until a hundred; then the hundred is doubled and tripled in the same manner as the units and the tens, up to a thousand; then the thousand can be thus repeated at any complex number; and so forth to the utmost limit of numeration.

I observed that the numbers which are required in calculating by Completion and Reduction are of three kinds, namely, roots, squares, and simple numbers relative to neither root nor square.

A root is any quantity which is to be multiplied by itself, consisting of units, or numbers ascending, or fractions descending.

A square is the whole amount of the root multiplied by itself.

A simple number is any number which may be pronounced without reference to root or square.

From William Edward Story. 1919. *Omar Khayyám as a Mathematician.* Worcester, MA: Rosemary Press.

In this passage, a noted college professor discusses the mathematical work of Omar Khayyám (1048–1131).

Omar's greatest original contribution to algebra is the complete classification of the cubic equation, a classification that he recognizes as applicable to equations of every degree. He believed that cubic equations could not be solved by calculation, but that one must be satisfied with the construction of solutions by intersecting conics. In the discussion of the several classes he sometimes overlooks particular cases. Thus, he fails to see that an equation of the form $x^3 + bx = ax^2 + c$ may have three positive real roots. Again, he lost many roots by using only one branch of an hyperbola in his construction. And he was not very exact in the investigation of the numerical values that the several coefficients must have in order that the equation of one or other type should give real intersections of the conics. He considered biquadratic equations to be unsolvable by geometric constructions.

But these faults are of little consequence in comparison with the remarkably great advance Omar made in algebra by treating equations of degree higher than the second, and by having classified them. He was the only mathematician of any nation before 1,100 who distinguished trinomial cubic equations from tetranomial, forming two groups of the former according as the term of the 2nd or 1st degree was wanting, and two groups of the latter according as the sum of 3 terms was equal to one term or the sum of 2 terms equal to the sum of two others.

Apparently, also, he considered the binomial theorem for positive integral exponents. He says: "I have taught how to find the sides of the square-square, of the square-cube, of the cube-cube, etc. to any extent, which no one had previously done." This theorem he used, apparently, for the purpose of extracting roots after the manner of the Hindus. Omar incidentally solved the geometrical problem: to construct an equilateral trapezoid whose base and sides are of the same given length and whose area is given,—a problem that he reduced to the solution of the equation $x^4 + bx = ax^3 + c$.

Merchants

From one perspective, it may seem strange that the early Islamic world became a center of commerce and trade, since Islam forbade usury (charging a high amount of interest for loaning money)—which was usually necessary for businessmen seeking loans—and believers tended to frown upon speculative investments and an obsessive focus on making profits. Yet as in the past, farmers and artisans had to sell their goods to survive, so they either had to become merchants themselves or use the services of professional marketers. To meet their needs, the government was required to sanction and regulate marketplaces in all of its expanding cities. As for the large-scale enterprise of importing and exporting goods throughout the known world, this was largely managed by Jews and Christian Armenians, unhampered by religious restrictions and happily tolerated by Muslims who recognized the value of their labors.

The earliest marketplaces of the Arab world were merely conveniently located meeting places where farmers and craftspersons from nearby areas could periodically gather to sell their products out of temporary

This painting from a manuscript shows Islamic merchants selling their goods in the city of Constantinople during the early days of the Ottoman Empire. (UIG via Getty Images)

stalls. Over time, these evolved in small towns where several hundred artisans and merchants could permanently live to carry on with their business every day. Since their work was essential, members of feuding tribes or factions were required to interact peacefully while visiting these settlements. As these towns grew larger, they evolved in response to specific circumstances: if the surrounding farmers were providing quantities of flax and timber, for example, weavers and carpenters would be attracted to the town as an ideal locale to set up their shops and make use of the readily available materials they required. If the town was near a river or sea, it would naturally become a place where local goods would be packaged for export by boat and the imported goods that arrived on return voyages could be sold.

The markets that primarily served local consumers were similar to those in other regions of the world. One master artisan would own a small workshop that employed a handful of assistants and apprentices to produce items to be sold on the premises; as he aged, he would train his son or sons in the trade, and they would gradually take over the business and inherit the workshop when their father died. In this way, shops offering the same products might endure for centuries in the same location. Certain professions, such as metalworking and the production of paper and perfume, were considered very respectable, while others, like butchering and tanning, were looked down upon. At the very bottom of the hierarchy were the peddlers who walked through the streets or nearby neighborhood pushing carts filled with goods.

A key figure in the lives of these small-scale merchants was the government's market inspector, or *muhtasib*. Since most goods were priced according to their weight, his most important task was to regularly inspect the scales and weights used by merchants to ensure that they were accurate. Another priority was to keep the narrow streets clear, so that pedestrians and people riding horses or camels could easily pass through. While problems caused by inclement weather could not be controlled, the market inspector often had to deal with aggressive merchants who placed their goods far out into the streets to make them more conspicuous. Disorderly people who disrupted the marketplace were supposed to be disciplined as well: there is one story of a general who had too much to drink and was advised to stay indoors instead of walking through the marketplace because a displeased market inspector might arrest him. Assuming that his status would protect him from any punishment, he staggered out anyway, but he was spotted by an elderly inspector who promptly ordered his subordinates to seize and severely beat the miscreant. In fact, to make sure that rules like these were vigilantly enforced, it was common to appoint a wealthy noble to the position who would not be tempted to succumb to corruption.

The merchants and artisans who lived and worked in these marketplaces often made only enough money to keep themselves alive, though there is one story of a merchant who prospered by going to work for a wealthy man. The usual pathway to riches, however, involved obtaining and selling large amounts of valued goods from distant lands. As noted, while some good Muslims specialized in this business, most of its

practitioners were citizens of the empire who practiced other religions, especially Jews and Armenians, although traders from Venice and other western European cities eventually became key figures as well. Many imported items could prove highly profitable: to provide only a few examples, sub-Saharan Africa provided gold, lions, and ivory; Europe offered amber, tin, and animal furs; India was famous for its fine textiles and spices; China was noted for its silk garments and tea; and all regions could provide distinctively crafted artworks and vessels. In exchange, these areas could be sold fabrics, carpets, agricultural products, precious stones, weapons, and many other items found or manufactured in the Islamic world.

Of course, a merchant who engaged in trade had to make certain investments and face certain risks. To transport goods by sea, one would have to purchase a sturdy ship, recruit an experienced crew of sailors, and provide them with the guidebooks and instruments they would need to navigate their way to the proper destination. The increasing construction of lighthouses helped to reduce the number of shipwrecks, but storms remained a hazard, as did the pirates who preyed upon ships laden with valuable goods. Using the overland routes took considerably more time but was usually considered safer; in this case, merchants would need a large number of camels, ample weapons and supplies, and reliable riders who had the knowledge to keep their camels healthy. To provide assistance, governments erected fortified structures called caravanserais, where caravans could stay every night and enjoy protection from thieves and raiders; some places also offered hospitals for ailing travelers, bridges, and wells.

Despite the challenges involved, merchants eagerly engaged in trade because of the huge amounts of money to be made; according to one estimate, they typically earned a profit of fifty percent from each item that they imported and exported. As one example of how rewarding this profession could be, one scholar has studied the life of one wealthy merchant named Rāmisht (died 1140), a Persian who lived and operated his business in the port city of Sīrāf. He was renowned for his enormous earnings: one author reports that his sons used silver plates, and even his clerks had become rich. He appears in the historical records as an enormous

BENEVOLENT BUSINESSMEN

The Persian merchant Rāmisht, having made a fortune, donated large sums of money to religious institutions in the city of Mecca. More recently, U.S. businessmen who have earned millions of dollars also choose to give away much of their fortunes to worthwhile projects, although instead of providing money directly to recipients, they tend to set up foundations with generous endowments to distribute the funds. In the early twentieth century, steelmaker Andrew Carnegie established his Carnegie Corporation for this purpose; more recently, Microsoft founder Bill Gates established the Bill and Melinda Gates Foundation, with current assets of almost $40 million.

THE SCALES OF JUSTICE

In the marketplaces of the Islamic world, government inspectors regularly examined the merchants' scales to ensure that they were accurate, and this has remained a concern of consumers in contemporary times. However, in the United States it is a private nonprofit corporation, the National Conference on Weights and Measures, that guarantees the accuracy of the scales used in the produce sections of grocery stores. For food products that are sold in cans or cardboard packages, the Fair Packaging and Labeling Act, passed in 1966, requires the label to provide the total weight of the products.

benefactor to Mecca's sacred building, the Kaaba, providing it with a waterspout made of gold and a covering made of expensive fabric from China. He also financed the construction of a hospice in Mecca for visiting believers in the Islamic sect known as Sufism. We are not sure precisely what products Rāmisht purchased and sold, but he and his ships made regular trips to India, which were sometimes perilous; at one time, two of his ships were almost captured during a battle in the Persian Gulf, but they managed to make it to the safety of the port, where troops came to protect them.

Rāmisht evidently preferred to devote his excess income to charitable acts, but others came to exert political power over the government, as the declining Abbasid Dynasty grew dependent upon money borrowed from these very successful businessmen. Yet their ascendancy was short-lived: in the eleventh century, political turmoil in Russia and Asia disrupted trade with those regions, while merchants from Venice and other European cities took over most of the Islamic world's trade with Europe. Eventually, the only Islamic merchants who were playing an important role in international business were those of the expanding Ottoman Empire in Turkey. As wealthy traders declined, however, the humbler merchants of north African and Middle Eastern cities carried on as they had before, unaffected by the shifting political currents. As one sign of continuity in their affairs, a historian surveyed the twentieth-century marketplace of the Moroccan city of Fez and concluded that, in its nature and dimensions, it was largely identical to the city's sixteenth-century marketplace. Even today, one can visit cities in the Middle East and experience marketplaces that in many ways are very similar to those that flourished a thousand years ago.

Further Reading

Çizakça, Murat. 1996. *Comparative Evolution of Business Partnerships: The Islamic World and Europe, With Specific Reference to the Ottoman Archives.* Leiden, The Netherlands, and Boston: Brill.

Çizakça, Murat. 2011. *Islamic Capitalism and Finance: Origins, Evolution and the Future.* Cheltenham, England, and Northampton, MA: Edward Elgar Publishing.

Ghazanfar, S. M., editor. 2003. *Medieval Islamic Economic Thought: Filling the Great Gap in European Economics.* London and New York: Routledge.

Goldberg, Jessica. 2012. *Trade and Institutions in the Medieval Mediterranean: The Geniza Merchants and Their Business World.* Cambridge and New York: Cambridge University Press.

Shatzmiller, Maya. 1993. *Labour in the Medieval Islamic World.* Leiden, The Netherlands, and Boston: Brill.

Udovitch, Abraham L. 2011. *Partnership and Profit in Medieval Islam.* Princeton, NJ: Princeton University Press.

Document

From al-Muhassan ibn Ali. C. 991. *The Table-Talk of a Mesopotamian Judge.* Translated by David Samuel Margoliouth. 1922. London: The Royal Asiatic Society.

One of the many anecdotes related by al-Muhassan ibn Ali (ca. 940–944) in his book, usually called The Table-Talk of a Mesopotamian Judge, *involves an ice merchant who achieved a comfortable position by shrewdly adjusting the price of his product.*

I was informed by Abu Ahmad al-Fadl b. ‘Abd al-Rahman b. Ja’far of Shiraz, secretary of state, who said he had heard the following from the son of Sulaimān the Ice-merchant. He said: My father told me that the source of his wealth was five *ratls* [pounds] of ice. One year, he said, ice was scarce in Baghdad; I had a supply of which I had sold all but five *ratls*. Shājī, slave-girl of ‘Ubaidallah b. Tahir at that time prefect of Baghdad fell ill, and asked for ice. I was the only person who had any. When they applied to me, I told them I had only one *ratl*, which I declined to sell for less than 5000 dirhems. Of course I was acquainted with the situation. The steward, not venturing to pay that price, returned for instructions to ‘Ubaidallah at his slave-girl’s residence. She was crying for ice and urgently demanding it. ‘Ubaidallah abusively bade him go back and buy the ice at any price without further consultation. He came and offering 5000 dirhems demanded the *ratl*; but I refused to let him have it for less than 10,000, and he, not venturing to return without it, gave me the sum I asked and took the rail. The invalid improved somewhat and then demanded another *ratl*. The steward then brought another 10,000 dirhems and asked for another *ratl* if I had it. I sold him it, and when the invalid had consumed it, she showed signs of convalescence, sat up, and asked for more. They applied to me again. I assured them that I had only one *ratl* left, and that I would only sell it for a larger sum than the others. However he cajoled me into letting him have it for ten thousand. Then the desire seized me to consume some myself, in order to be able to say that I had consumed ice worth ten thousand dirhems the *ratl*. And when I had consumed one, near dawn I received a visit from the steward, saying that the invalid was now nearly well, and that if she could consume one more *ratl*, she would be completely restored. If then I had any left, I might make my own terms. I replied that I had only one *ratl* left, for which I demanded thirty thousand dirhems. He offered me the sum; but I felt shame before Allah

at taking thirty thousand for one *ratl* of ice, and said I would take twenty thousand, but that after that, were he to bring me "an earthful of gold," he could get none from me, since all I had was now gone. He gave me the twenty thousand, and took the *ratl*; and when Shaji had consumed it, she became herself again, and asked for solid food. ‘Ubaidallah gave away a large sum as a thankoffering, and summoning me the next day, told me that after Allah I was the person who had restored his life by giving life to his slave-girl, and bade me name my own terms. I replied that I was the humble servant of the governor. So I was appointed to look after the ice and drinks, and many of the affairs of his household, and so the dirhems which had come to me in this lump sum were the foundation of my fortune, which was increased by what I continued to earn from ‘Ubaidallah during my career with him.

Poets

Poetry had been an important element in Arabic culture long before the coming of the prophet Muhammad (570–632), as nomadic tribesmen maintained an oral tradition of poems that celebrated chivalrous warriors and their adventures, described men’s romantic and erotic longings, and at times conveyed the fatalistic outlook of people who lived in a harsh, unforgiving environment. Poets regularly engaged in contests for the honor of having their names engraved in gold in Mecca’s Kaaba. While Muhammad disapproved of such poetry as frivolous and immoral, he could not suppress this beloved means of expression, and as poetry went on to become popular in the courts of the caliphs, it uniquely retained a secular character, in contrast to the religiosity that is so prominent in other aspects of Islamic culture.

Even a man from a humble background could prosper as a poet during the early centuries of the Islamic empire, as long as they could contrive to attract the attention of a wealthy patron, perhaps even the caliph himself, who would support the poet in order to be entertained by poetry that was often devoted to effusive praise of the patron and his family—the so-called "praise poetry" that was characteristic of the era. Such poems were preferred because not only did they flatter their immediate listeners, but they could be written down and widely circulated to enhance the reputation of the noble or official being praised. As long as one composed and performed many poems of this type, however, poets could also deal with other subjects, such as romantic love and satirical attacks. Poets would typically chant their poems with a musical accompaniment provided by a few musicians playing a lute, a stringed instrument called a *tunbūr*, a wind instrument called a *mizmār*, a drum called a *tabl*, and a tambourine called a *duff*. Performances were private affairs, attended only by the caliph and a few family members and friends, since some Muslims disapproved of all forms of music. Sometimes the caliph and his party would remain behind a curtain, so the poet could not be sure precisely who was listening, but some poets were allowed to relax and socialize with an unconcealed caliph. Boldness and originality were prized in their poems, though there was always the danger of going too far and offending members of the court.

One of the earliest of these court poets, Ghiyath ibn Ghawth al-Taghlibi al-Akhtal (ca. 640–710), first encountered members of the family of Muawiyah I (602–680) and was later a favorite by the caliph Abd al-Malik ibn Marwan (646–705), even though he unusually remained a Christian, purportedly because of his love of wine. When he was not focused on the virtues of the Umayyad family, al-Akhtal would praise his own tribe and savagely criticize other tribes, especially those of other poets. One of his rivals, Jarir ibn 'Atiyah al-Khatfi Al-Tamimi (ca. 650–728), also performed for al-Malik, though he was more popular with a later caliph, Umar ibn Abd al-Aziz (682–720). Jarir also feuded with the poet al-Farazdaq (ca. 641–728), who fell in and out of favor due to his controversially erotic poems. However, poets of the time did not have to move to the capital city of Damascus, since many rich men in the cities of Mecca and Medina were happy to support talented poets, and those poets may have enjoyed less stressful lives, far from the intrigues and shifting loyalties of the caliph's court. Two of these specialized in the love poem called a *ghazal*: Jamīl ibn 'Abd Allāh ibn Ma'mar al-'Udhrī (died 701) described the poet's thwarted love for an unavailable woman, while Umar Ibn Abi Rabi'ah (ca. 644–712) was renowned for both his love poetry and his licentious lifestyle.

If anything, poetry was even more popular during the Abbasid Dynasty, as an interest in poetry came to be regarded as a key trait of any educated and sophisticated person. Praise poetry remained the most common form—it is estimated about ninety percent of the poems written by Ibn al-Rumi (836–896) were of this type—but these poets' other works have better stood the test of time. One poet of this period, Bashār ibn Burd (714–784) demonstrates that virtually any man with talent could achieve great success, since he was a blind, and notoriously ugly, former slave, but his mastery of language could not be denied. He had the peculiar habit of beginning each performance by clapping and spitting into his hands, and he was so daring in his verses that he once attacked the caliph Muhammad ibn Mansur al-Mahdi (ca. 744–785). It is not surprising, then, that he was eventually murdered by one of his enemies. Another noted poet, Abu'l Atāhiyya (748–828), was the son of a potter who reached the caliph's court by means of his praise poetry and love poems, but his later works more somberly lament how transitory the joys of life really are. A third poet, Abū Nuwās (756–814), was a friend of the caliph Muhammad ibn Harun al-Amin (787–813) who unabashedly celebrated the pleasures of hunting, drinking wine, and amorous encounters with attractive young boys. As his real-life adventures of this nature grew more and more outrageous, even his patron al-Amin was finally driven to imprison the witty and impudent poet.

During this period, the further development of poetry was hindered by the growing influence of Arabic philologists, whose dictates led to awkward and artificial manners of expression. Only a few poets, like Abu'l Atāhiyya, resisted their rules and continued to employ more natural language. By the time of the tenth century, when the Abbasid Dynasty was losing its power, the best Islamic poetry was being written far from Baghdad in the city of Aleppo in present-day Syria. One poet who flourished there was al-Mutanabbi (915–965), who devoted all of his energies to poetry only after failed efforts to establish himself as a prophet and a politician. While he wrote much praise poetry to please patrons, he also, like other poets, was often in trouble because of his sharply worded criticisms of major figures, and his purported death at the hands of robbers while fleeing to Persia

POETIC LICENSE

Since Hollywood long sought to profit from producing "biopics" about the lives of famous historical characters, it is not surprising that, in 1957, Paramount Pictures offered viewers *Omar Khayyám*, featuring Cornel Wilde as Persia's most famous poet. Its story was not completely inaccurate, as it initially depicted Khayyám as a mathematician preparing a revised calendar for his sultan, but matters grew more and more absurd as the poet went on to romance a beautiful woman in the sultan's harem and picked up a sword to thwart a plot against the sultan's life—both activities that the sedate scholar surely did not actually experience.

THE LANGUAGE OF LAMENTATION

The early female poets of the Islamic world specialized in lamentations of the deaths of male relatives, and other cultures have traditions of poems, called elegies, that similarly discuss a deceased person. In eighteenth-century England, there emerged a school of so-called "graveyard poets" who would literally visit graveyards to inspire thoughts about the tragedy of death, though these rarely focus on one individual. But poets have continued to write about the deaths of famous people as well; examples include Walt Whitman's "O Captain! O Captain," about the death of Abraham Lincoln, and W. H. Auden's "In Memory of W. B. Yeats," about the death of the Irish poet.

may have been arranged by his foes. Talented poets also emerged in the caliphate governing present-day Spain. Persia continued to produce poets as well, but its most famous poet, Omar Khayyám (1048–1131), primarily worked as a mathematician and astronomer; yet like many educated men, he also dabbled in poetry, and his occasional quatrains, loosely translated by Edward FitzGerald in the nineteenth century, have garnered much praise.

Poetry was also one of the few artistic activities open to women, though they were initially restricted to composing poetic laments for deceased male relatives. One highly regarded female poet, usually known as al-Khansa (ca. 575–645), wrote celebrated poems in honor of two of her dead brothers. Women could not recite poetry in the courts of the Abbasids, but there

were slaves who entertained audiences by writing and singing original songs; the sister of the caliph Harun al-Rashid (ca. 763–809) was also a respected poet. There were talented female poets in Spain as well, such as Wallada bint al-Mustakfi (1001–1091), noted for her passionate poems about her secret romance with another poet, Ibn Zaydún (1003–1071). However, female poets were often disparaged by their male counterparts, and their works were often not preserved, so that some of these poets are only known by their reputations and a handful of surviving poems.

Overall, it seems that Islamic poets often had quite enjoyable lives, as their royal patrons provided them with a comfortable lifestyle and stimulating opportunities to compose poems for distinguished listeners and, later, a broad audience of readers. But they were also in a constantly precarious situation: if they limited themselves to bland and safe sentiments, they risked boring their royal supporters, yet if they went too far in expressing their true feelings, they might offend powerful people and consequently face death or imprisonment. Still, since poetry represented one of the few ways that an ordinary man could become a wealthy celebrity, it is not surprising that many were willing to accept the risks involved in pursuing such a career.

Further Reading

Gruendler, Beatrice. 2003. *Medieval Arabic Praise Poetry: Ibn Al-Rūmī and the Patron's Redemption*. London and New York: RoutledgeCurzon.

Jones, Alan, editor. 2003. *Early Arabic Poetry: Select Poems*. Second edition. Reading, England: Ithaca Press.

Meisami, Julie. 2013. *Structure and Meaning in Medieval Arabic and Persian Lyric Poetry: Orient Pearls*. London and New York: Routledge.

Sharlet, Jocelyn. 2011. *Patronage and Poetry in the Islamic World: Social Mobility and Status in the Medieval Middle East and Central Asia*. London and New York: I. B. Tauris & Co.

Speri, Stefan. 2004. *Mannerism in Arabic Poetry: A Structural Analysis of Selected Texts (3rd Century AH / 9th Century AD—5th Century AH/11th Century AD)*. Cambridge and New York: Cambridge University Press.

Tobi, Yosef. 2004. *Proximity and Distance: Medieval Hebrew and Arabic Poetry*. Leiden, The Netherlands, and Boston: Brill.

Documents

From al-Khansa and Fari'a Bint Tarif. C. seventh century. *Translations of Eastern Poetry and Prose.* Translated by Reynold A. Nicholson. 1922. Cambridge: Cambridge University Press.

The women poets of the Islamic world initially specialized in writing laments for their male relatives who had died in battle. Below are three examples: the first two are by the famous poet usually called al-Khansa; the third is by a less renowned woman known only Fari'a Bint Tarif (ca. seventh century), or Fari'a the Daughter of Tarif.

Tears, ere thy death, for many a one I shed,
But thine are all my tears since thou art dead.
To comforters I lend my ear apart,
While pain sits ever closer to my heart.

*****

When night draws on, remembering keeps me
    wakeful
And hinders my rest with grief upon grief
    returning
For Sakhr. What a man was he on the day of
    battle,
When, snatching their chance, they swiftly
    exchange the spear-thrusts!
Ah, never of woe like this in the world of spirits
I heard, or of loss like mine in the heart of
    woman.
What Fortune might send, none stronger than he
    to bear it;
None better to meet the trouble with mind
    unshaken;
The kindest to help, wherever the need was
    sorest:
They all had of him a boon—wife, friend, and
    suitor.
O Sakhr! I will ne'er forget thee until in dying
I part from my soul, and earth for my tomb is
    cloven.
The rise of the sun recalls to me Sakhr my
    brother,
And him I remember also at every sunset.

*****

For aye was Wali'd, till Death drew right forth
    the soul of him,
A grief to the foeman or a home to the friendless.
Come weep, O my kin, the doom of death and
    the woeful change
And earth trembling after him and quaking
    beneath us!
Come weep, O my kin, the turns of fortune, the
    perishings,
And pitiless Fate that dogs the noble with ruin!
Alas for the perfect moon fall'n low from
    amongst the stars,
Alas for the sun when toward eclipse was his
    journey!
Alas for the lion, yea, the lion without reproach,
What time to a hollowed grave, roofed over, they
    bore him!
Oh, God curse the mounded stones that covered
    him out of sight,
A man that was never tired of doing a kindness!
If he by Yazid the son of Mazyad was done to death,
Yet many a host he led of warriors to combat.
Upon him the peace of God abide evermore !
    Meseems
That fast fall the strokes of Death on all who are
    noble.

From Omar Khayyám. C. 1100 CE. *The Rubáiyát of Omar Khayyám.* Translated by Edward FitzGerald. 1859. London: B. Quaritch.

The Persian mathematician and poet Omar Khayyám wrote about 1,000 quatrains during his lifetime. There have been many English translations, but the most famous one is that of Edward FitzGerald, who first published a translation of selected quatrains under the title The Rubáiyát of Omar Khayyám *in 1859. His translations, though admired as poetry, have been criticized as inaccurate; below are the first twenty-three quatrains from FitzGerald's first edition, including the often-quoted eleventh quatrain.*

I

Awake! for Morning in the Bowl of Night
Has flung the Stone that puts the Stars to Flight;
And Lo! the Hunter of the East has caught
The Sultan's Turret in a Noose of Light.

II

Dreaming when Dawn's Left Hand was in
  the Sky
I heard a Voice within the Tavern cry,
"Awake, my Little ones, and fill the Cup
Before Life's Liquor in its Cup be dry."

III

And, as the Cock crew, those who stood before
The Tavern shouted—"Open then the Door,
You know how little while we have to stay,
And, once departed, may return no more."

IV

Now the New Year reviving old Desires,
The thoughtful Soul to Solitude retires,
Where the WHITE HAND OF MOSES on the Bough
Puts out, and Jesus from the Ground suspires.

V

Irám indeed is gone with all its Rose,
And Jamshýd's Sev'n-ring'd Cup where no one
  knows;
But still the Vine her ancient Ruby yields,
And still a Garden by the Water blows.

VI

And David's Lips are lock't; but in divine
High piping Péleyi, with "Wine! Wine! Wine!
Red Wine!"—the Nightingale cries to the Rose
That yellow Cheek of hers to'incarnadine.

VII

Come, fill the Cup, and in the Fire of Spring
The Winter Garment of Repentance fling:
The Bird of Time has but a little way
To fly—and Lo! the Bird is on the Wing.

VIII

And look—a thousand Blossoms with the Day
Woke—and a thousand scatter'd into Clay:
And this first Summer Month that brings
  the Rose
Shall take Jamshýd and Kaikobád away.

IX

But come with old Khayyám, and leave the Lot
Of Kaikobád and Kaikhosrú forgot:
Let Rustum lay about him as he will,
Or Hátim Tai cry Supper—heed them not.

X

With me along some Strip of Herbage strown
That just divides the desert from the sown,
Where name of Slave and Sultan scarce is
  known,
And pity Sultán Máhmúd on his Throne.

XI

Here with a Loaf of Bread beneath the Bough,
A Flask of Wine, a Book of Verse—and Thou
Beside me singing in the Wilderness—
And Wilderness is Paradise enow.

XII

"How sweet is mortal Sovranty!"—think
  some:
Others—"How blest the Paradise to come!"
Ah, take the Cash in hand and waive the Rest:
Oh, the brave Music of a *distant* Drum!

XIII

Look to the Rose that blows about us—"Lo,
Laughing," she says, "into the World I blow:
At once the silken Tassel of my Purse
Tear, and its Treasure on the Garden throw."

XIV

The Worldly Hope men set their Hearts upon
Turns Ashes—or it prospers; and anon,
Like Snow upon the Desert's dusty Face
Lighting a little Hour or two—is gone.

XV

And those who husbanded the Golden Grain,
And those who flung it to the Winds
  like Rain,
Alike to no such aureate Earth are turn'd
As, buried once, Men want dug up again.

XVI

Think, in this batter'd Caravanserai
Whose Doorways are alternate Night and Day,
How Sultán after Sultán with his Pomp
Abode his Hour or two, and went his way.

XVII

They say the Lion and the Lizard keep
The Courts where Jamshýd gloried and
  drank deep:
And Bahrám, that great Hunter—the Wild Ass
Stamps o'er his Head, and he lies fast asleep.

XVIII

I sometimes think that never blows so red
The Rose as where some buried Caesar bled;
That every Hyacinth the Garden wears
Dropt in its Lap from some once lovely Head.

XIX

And this delightful Herb whose tender Green
Fledges the River's Lip on which we lean—
Ah, lean upon it lightly! for who knows
From what once lovely Lip it springs unseen!

XX

Ah! my Belovéd, fill the Cup that clears
To-day of past Regrets and future Fears—
To-morrow?—Why, To-morrow I may be
Myself with Yesterday's Sev'n Thousand Years.

XXI

Lo! some we loved, the loveliest and the best
That Time and Fate of all their Vintage prest,
Have drunk their Cup a Round or two before,
And one by one crept silently to Rest.

XXII

And we, that now make merry in the Room
They left, and Summer dresses in new Bloom,
Ourselves must we beneath the Couch
  of Earth
Descend, ourselves to make a
  Couch—for whom?

XXIII

Ah, make the most of what we yet may spend,
Before we too into the Dust Descend;
Dust into Dust, and under Dust, to lie,
Sans Wine, sans Song, sans Singer
  and—sans End!

Soldiers

While Roman armies had long held sway over the Mediterranean world, the most feared soldiers in medieval times were those of the Islamic world, as they marched outward from Arabia to conquer vast territories in Central Asia, the Middle East, northern Africa, and Europe's Iberian Peninsula. While fervent devotion to their faith undoubtedly contributed to their many victories, their success also stemmed from their unusual willingness to constantly alter and improve their technology and tactics in response to new enemies and new challenges. In particular, the entire character of their military forces changed, as they stopped relying upon their own citizens and instead forged a professional army of enslaved foreigners, called *mamluks*.

Any discussion of Islamic soldiers must address the belief that motivated many of them, the complicated concept of *jihad*. The term literally means "struggle," and many scholars have regarded this imperative primarily in spiritual terms, the responsibility of all believers to be devout and pure in all of their thoughts and actions. Yet passages in the Koran also suggest that it describes the necessity of achieving military victories over nonbelievers, which is how it was usually interpreted in medieval times. Despite popular beliefs, however, there is little evidence of soldiers forcing people to convert by threatening them with death, or deliberately endeavoring to slaughter nonbelievers, and Islamic governments were often tolerant toward religious minorities.

Before the rise of Islam, warfare in Arabia was largely nonviolent, as nomadic tribes would periodically engage in an attack called a *razzia*; mounted warriors would rush into another tribe's camp or small village, seize whatever valuables were available—like animals, precious metals, or fine clothing—and flee with their booty. There was an unstated understanding that the raiders would generally avoid harming anyone so they would be treated with similar mercy when they were similarly raided. But fierce disputes sometimes led to genuine battles in which soldiers would endeavor to kill hated enemies. There was also a tradition of resolving disputes in the manner celebrated in Homer's *Iliad* by having representatives of each side engage in single combat. For example, when the prophet Muhammad (570–632) was attempting to gain control of the city of Mecca, the conflict began with Muhammad and his foes sending out three soldiers to fight three soldiers from Mecca; illustrating the sort of chivalric code that governed such encounters, the forces of Mecca rejected the first three soldiers sent by Muhammad on the grounds that they were not sufficiently worthy foes. In the end, although Muhammad's men were victorious, his triumph over Mecca also required a full-scale battle.

An unusual characteristic of early Islamic combat was that women were regularly present on the battlefield. However, they generally did not carry weapons or fight, but rather shouted encouragement to the troops and beat percussion instruments to inspire them. One of Muhammad's wives, Aisha bint Abi Bakr (ca. 613–678), played such a role in the so-called "Battle of the Camel" in 656 against the new caliph ibn Abi Talib (ca. 600–661). When the fighting was over, women might also participate in mutilating enemy bodies or tending to the wounds of their soldiers.

As Islamic soldiers quickly conquered territories to the west and east of Arabia, they had the advantage of using camels, which had recently emerged as an efficient way to transport men and supplies over long distances. The weapons they brought with them, initially, were mostly imported from India or the west, and since each man had to purchase his own equipment, the number and quality of these items varied tremendously. Every soldier had a large straight sword, which he carried on his person, and many used bows and arrows as well; men might also hurdle spears at distant foes, wield axes or maces, and pull out small knives for hand-to-hand combat. To protect themselves, some soldiers held shields or wore helmets and coats of mail. As the Islamic empire developed more

This illustration from a sixteenth-century book about the prophet Muhammad shows his wife Aisha bint Abi Bakr alongside Islamic soldiers and fighting the fourth caliph ibn Abi Talib in the "Battle of the Camel." Women were often present on the battlefield of early Islamic combat. (Universal Images Group/Art Resource, NY)

resources, it created and manufactured its own distinctive type of sword, the scimitar, with a long, slightly curved blade that could inflict grievous wounds. Emulating rivals, Islamic soldiers also mastered the art of defeating enemies by means of sieges, and after being devastated by the Byzantine Empire's "Greek Fire" in 672, the Islamic government devised its own version of the petroleum-based incendiary weapon.

As the expanding empire made more and more horses available, archers on horseback became its most common and effective soldiers. Though there are records of bamboo arrows, the most effective arrow, called the *nushshāba*, was wooden, with feathers attached to guide its flight. Bowstrings were made out of leather or silk; bows often had two strings that could be used alternatively. Later, Islamic archers employed a form of the crossbow, called a *bunduq*, that propelled tiny metallic pellets at enemies; sometimes they were first placed in a fire so that, when heated to a high temperature, they could start fires. For the same purpose, archers could also use *bunduqs* to launch the petroleum-based liquid called naphtha at their foes.

Like other growing empires, the Islamic forces felt an increasing need to recruit soldiers from distant lands, but these did not merely augment, but eventually replaced, their native warriors. The caliph al-Mu'tasim (795–842) recruited the first army of such soldiers, called *mamluks*, by buying large numbers of suitable male slaves, mostly from present-day Turkey. Later

WOMEN WARRIORS

In the early battles that established the Islamic state, women were regularly present on the battlefield, though they contributed by encouraging the male soldiers instead of taking up arms themselves. Later traditions, however, dictated that Islamic women should not involve themselves in combat. Still, in recent years, Islamic women have begun to participate in the terrorist attacks of Islamic extremists by becoming suicide bombers. They are especially effective because few people expect that a woman might be a terrorist, so they are not subjected to the sort of scrutiny directed toward suspicious-looking men.

HEROES ON HORSEBACK

Soldiers in Islamic armies came to rely on horses, which were long a part of many nation's armies, including the U.S. Army, which maintained stables of horses at every base. In the twentieth century, as soldiers came to travel in jeeps and tanks, horses were phased out of service, but they dramatically returned to the frontline in late 2001, when U.S. soldiers fighting in northern Afghanistan successfully used horses to traverse the region's rugged terrain. By one report, renowned Hollywood producer Jerry Bruckheimer planned to make a film about these soldiers' achievements. And in 2014, marines were still training men, women, horses, and mules for service in Afghanistan.

mamluks also came from Africa, Central Asia, eastern Europe, and India, and since *mamluks* could not pass their positions on to their sons, armies always needed new members. These soldiers offered a number of advantages to their overseers: they could be purchased at a young age and intensely trained to become skilled professional soldiers, and lacking ties to local communities, they remained loyal to their commanders. They also enjoyed far more rewarding careers than their officially enslaved status might suggest; indeed, some actually earned their freedom but continued to serve as soldiers. *Mamluks* might be entrusted with important responsibilities, such as tending to the horses of the ruler or working as aides to commanders; a few were even appointed to govern provinces. In later centuries, *mamluk* generals had great influence on their societies, sometimes determining who would serve as caliphs, and they were the outright rulers of Syria, Palestine, and Egypt for three centuries.

The equipment used by the *mamluks* resembled that of their predecessors, but since their lives were devoted to combat, they preferred weapons and armor that were elaborately decorated with words and images. Slogans on shields would boast of their carrier's altruism and ferocity in battle, and images of both real and imaginary animals, like leopards, elephants, unicorns, and sphinxes, were observed as well. Later, upon coming into contact with the heavily armored soldiers of medieval Europe, many of the *mamluks* improved the strength and extent of their armor as well. Horses were also central to the careers of the average *mamluks*: they lived in permanent garrisons alongside their steeds, and manuals prepared for their study suggest that large portions of their training were dedicated to teaching them the proper care and treatment of horses. Even their leisure activities were designed to improve their skills in handling horses: they played polo, which provided practice in maneuvering horses; while riding horses, they engaged in archery contests; and they staged formal battles between mounted soldiers that resembled the jousts of medieval Europe.

Although the *mamluks* came to do most of the fighting on behalf of Islam, others sometimes contributed to their campaigns. Though not part of the regular army, some men might volunteer for temporary service in exchange for a portion of the wealth to be seized from enemies. In hazardous regions along the frontier, different sorts of volunteers emerged, groups of independent warriors known as the *ghāzis*, or "campaigners." Tolerated by the authorities, these bands attacked and harassed nonbelievers as they chose, living off the property looted from them, though they might also profit from engaging in trade.

The initial strength of the Islamic soldiers, as noted, stemmed from their tendency to adapt the strategies and technologies of others, but their decline can be attributed to their general disinclination to adopt a new weapon: firearms. In the fifteenth century, the Ottoman Empire came to rely upon guns and cannons, and the archers and foot soldiers of the *mamluk* dynasties were no match for its artillery. Still, the effective fighters of the Islamic world left a legacy of fierce, single-minded dedication to their cause that has continued to inspire later generations of like-minded combatants who have remained a force to be reckoned with in the global arena.

Further Reading

Amitai-Preiss, Reuven. 1996. *Mongols and Mamluks: The Mamluk-Īlkhānid war, 1260–1281.* Cambridge and New York: Cambridge University Press.

Kennedy, Hugh. 2013. *The Armies of the Caliphs: Military and Society in the Early Islamic State.* London and New York: Routledge.

Lev, Yaacov, editor. 1996. *War and Society in the Eastern Mediterranean, 7th–15th Centuries.* Leiden, The Netherlands, and Boston: Brill.

Nicolle, David. 2009. *The Great Islamic Conquests AD 632–750.* Oxford: Osprey Publishing.

Nicolle, David. 1994. *Mamluk: The Muslim Conquest of Syria.* Oxford: Osprey Publishing.

Zakeri, Mohsen. 1995. *Sāsānid Soldiers in Early Muslim Society: The Origins of 'Ayyārān and Futuwwa.* Wiesbaden, Germany: Harrassowitz Verlag.

Documents

From 'Aḥmad Ibn Yaḥyā al-Balādhurī. C. ninth century. *The Origins of the Islamic State: Being a Translation from the Arabic.* Volume I. Translated by Philip Khūri Hitti. 1916. New York: Columbia University Press.

'Aḥmad Ibn Yaḥyā al-Balādhurī (died 892) was an Islamic scholar who lived in Persia. His major work, Kitab Futuh al-Buldan, *translated as* The Origins of the Islamic State, *describes the many battles of the prophet Muhammad (570–632) and his early successors. In this passage, he describes a key battle in the conquest of Persia.*

The Battle of Jalula'

A description of the battle. After spending several days in al-Mada'in, the Moslems received word that Yazdajird had massed a great host, which was then at Jalula', and had directed it against them. Sa'd ibn-abi-Wakkas thereupon dispatched Hashim ibn-'Utbah ibn-abi-Wakkas at the head of 12,000 men to meet them. The Moslems found that the Persians, having left their families and heavy baggage at Khanikin, had dug trenches and fortified themselves, binding themselves with a pledge never to flee. Reinforcements were coming to them all the time from Hulwan and al-Jibal [the mountains, *i.e.,* Media]. The Moslems, thinking it best to hasten the attack before the reinforcements became too strong, met them with Hujr ibn-'Adi-l-Kindi commanding the right wing, 'Amr ibn-Ma'dikarib commanding the cavalry and Tulaihah ibn-Khuwailid commanding the infantry. The Persians were on this occasion led by Khurrazad, a brother of Rustam. The fight that ensued was the fiercest they ever had, in which arrows and lances were used until broken to pieces, and swords were applied until they were bent. Finally the Moslems altogether made one onslaught and drove the Persians from their position, putting them to flight. The Persians fled away and the Moslems kept pursuing them at their very heels with fearful slaughter until darkness intervened and they had to return to their camp.

Hashim ibn-'Utbah left Jarir ibn-'Abdallah in Jalula' with a heavy force of cavalry to act as a check between the Moslems and their enemy. Yazdajird thereupon left Hulwan.

Mahrudh. The Moslems carried on many raids in the regions of as-Sawad on the east bank of the Tigris. Coming to Mahrudh, Hashim made terms with its *dihkan*, stipulating that the latter should pay a *jarib* of dirhams [?] and the former should not kill any of the men.

Ad-Daskarah. On a charge of treachery, against the Moslems, Hashim put the *dihkan* of ad-Daskarah to death.

Al-Bandanijain. Hashim then proceeded to al-Bandanijain, whose inhabitants sued for peace, agreeing to pay tax and *kharaj*. Consequently, Hashim promised them security.

Khanikin. At Khanikin there was a small remnant of the Persians against whom Jarir ibn-'Abdallah now marched and whom he put to death. Thus was no region of the Sawad Dijlah left unconquered by the Moslems or unpossessed by them.

According to Hisham ibn-al-Kalbi, the leader of the army in the battle of Jalula' in behalf of Sa'd was 'Amr ibn-'Utbah ibn-Naufal ibn-Uhaib ibn-'Abd-Manaf ibn-Zuhrah whose mother was 'Atikah, daughter of abu-Wak-kas.

After the battle of Jalula', Sa'd left for al-Mada'in where he gathered a host of men, and then kept on his way to the region of al-Hirah.

The battle of Jalula' took place at the close of the year 16 [c. 638].

From Benton, Kate A. 1900. *Geber: A Tale of the Reign of Harun al Raschid, Khalif of Baghdad.* New York: Frederick A. Stokes Company.

In this passage from a posthumously published historical novel about alchemist Abu Mūsā Jābir ibn Hayyān (ca. 721–815), the author describes the harsh sentence imposed upon a misbehaving soldier. The book's Introduction explains that the "story grew out of a poem that Mrs. Benton had planned to write. But as her researches brought forth a wealth of material. . . she took the character of Geber and, around it as a central figure, constructed her plot." One might assume, then, that this fictional account is based on accurate information.

[T]hrough the door way crowded an excited old woman and cast herself at Harun's feet, while behind her appeared two of the police with a soldier in arrest between them. The soldier's face was evil and sullen, and he cast a malignant glance at the prostrate woman.

"Oh, most merciful Prince!" she cried breathlessly, "I pray thee, give me justice on this man! He hath bought milk of me, and now having drunk it he refuseth to pay me, and for loss of both the milk and the money my babes must go supperless to bed to-night!"

"Hast thou bought milk of this woman?" Harun demanded of the man.

"Nay, gracious King!" replied the man with contempt. "I bought naught of the old hag, who seeketh but to rob me. She spilled the milk and seeing me passing her stall, she accused me of having drunk it that she might force me to make good her loss."

"Canst thou bring witnesses to prove the truth of thine accusation?" Harun turned again to the woman, who began to sob in despair.

"I cannot, alas! There were none to witness it save the man and myself, who for that reason took the advantage of me."

The khalif looked grave and the soldier boldly triumphant. Suddenly Jaafar stepped forward and confronted him.

"Thou art the man whom I saw but yesterday at muezzin in the Street of the Minarets. Thou didst cruelly beat and abuse thy noble mare, which reared and plunged in her terror and pain until I wondered that she did not throw thee and break thy worthless neck. Before I could reach thee thou hadst vented thy drunken rage and ridden away like a monsoon."

The soldier's face had lost some of its unhealthy colour and he tried feebly to deny Jaafar's charge. Harun's lips were tightened to a narrow thread, for nothing enraged him like abuse of a horse or a helpless woman.

Jaafar's voice continued relentlessly:

"Once before also I saw thee, if I mistake not, for I never forget faces. The first time I saw thine it was convulsed with an evil rage, much as it was but now when thou didst enter the khalif's gracious presence. Then too thy rage was concerning a woman, but this time a young and helpless girl, heavy with thy child, though she was not thy wife. She clung despairingly to thine arm and pled with thee passionately, and thou didst raise thy clenched fist and strike her tear-wet blossom of a face to the earth. Then too thou didst escape me by flight, and the girl, with a woman's foolish loyalty, refused me thy name, else had I sought thee out long since and punished thee."

The soldier's face was now a ghastly yellow as he looked at the khalif. Harun had risen and towered in all his kingly height above the accused man. His fine brows met in an ominous embrace, his thin arched nostrils quivered, his lips were white and his deep eyes flamed like fire striking the blade of his own famous sword, "The Piercer."

"Woman, how long since thou didst sell the milk to this man?"

"He hath but swallowed the last from his throat, Illustrious." She trembled, affrighted at the cold and fearful anger in Harun's face. He tossed her a gold dinar. "There is the price of the milk. Abdallah!" A gigantic Nubian clothed in scarlet came forward from his place behind Harun's judgment chair. In his hand he carried a heavy and short two-edged sword, and in his girdle was a dagger of Damascus steel, also with two edges to its blade. At sight of him the wretched soldier shrieked and threw himself at Harun's feet while the woman hid her face in her mantle in pallid fright.

"There is one way in which to learn the truth." Harun's voice was terrible in the quiet of its intensity. Even Jaafar shivered as he looked upon that face.

"Abdallah, take thy dagger and with it search the man's belly, till we find if the milk indeed be there."

. . . . [T]here was something in this sudden tipping of the scales of blinded Justice that sent a thrill of horror through the crowded hall, but the murmur was drowned in the curdling shriek of the victim. Then Abdallah arose with his usual immovable countenance and saluted the khalif.

"He hath drunken the milk, Commander of the Faithful," he said. Harun's face relaxed, and he turned quietly from the Thing at his feet.

"Take the dinar and go thy way," he said to the woman, whose face was grey and her eyes starting. "And tell my people that Aaron the Just hath ever an ear and an arm for their needs."

Weavers

Weaving is an ancient art, and it is not surprising that the women of the emerging Islamic world, along with some male professionals, continued longstanding traditions of using looms and thread to make fabrics for clothing and other purposes. But the expansion of their empire, and vigorous trade with other nations in Asia and Africa, introduced new materials, which were enthusiastically adopted, such as hemp, cotton, and silk. The fine textiles produced by Middle Eastern weavers became an important part of the trade between the Islamic empire and other regions. Many weavers of the Middle East also specialized in one particular product—rich, colorful carpets—and their work was especially coveted throughout the Western world. Indeed, while much about the Muslim and their societies long seemed strange and mysterious to Europeans, they admired and regularly walked on the rugs that decoratively represented their culture.

A number of important innovations in weaving can be traced to the Middle East, including the foot-pedaled loom that later became standard throughout the world. Middle Eastern weavers were also the first to employ a spinning wheel to produce their thread, and in the thirteenth century, they originated the art of macramé, or making fabrics with knots, when they learned that instead of cutting off the excess thread on the edges of fabrics, they could be tied together to provide an attractive border. The most common materials used to produce their fabrics were originally wool from sheep or goats and linen from flax, but the weavers who were employed by caliphs and other wealthy men were asked to adapt their techniques to make silk fabrics, which aristocrats came to prefer for their clothing despite the fact that the prophet Muhammad (570–632) had forbidden his followers to wear silk clothing. The mulberry bushes needed to feed the silkworms were imported from China and planted wherever they would flourish, especially in Central Asia and Spain, which became centers for silk production. Even though everyday people were rarely able to afford silk, weavers outside of court circles began producing silk fabrics to be exported, and they became especially skilled at producing silk brocade fabrics, with colorful, complex patterns that often included silver and gold thread. Moving beyond traditional images of animals and polygonal shapes and stripes, weavers provided fabrics with complex geometric patterns or fabrics featuring written phrases in Arabic letters, termed tirāz. The letters of these inscriptions might be woven into the fabric, embroidered, or painted or printed onto the fabric.

Weaving was done in three locations. Poor women typically owned their own small loom and would produce fabrics and items of clothing for themselves and their families, perhaps earning a little extra money by doing work for others. They were not constantly busy because everyday people typically wore their clothing until it was literally falling apart. Bedouin women faced the additional challenges of making and repairing the tents that their people lived in, as well as curtains to separate men's and women's living quarters and saddles for horses, and they had to use special looms that could be taken apart for easy transportation and reassembled later. Second, in cities, there were large workshops called *al-tirāz al-'āmma*, owned by businessmen, which sold fabrics and clothing to local customers or exported them to other regions. In one center of silk production, the city of Cordoba in Spain, one scholar estimates that the workshops had over 13,000 working looms. Finally, the caliph would have his own workshop, called *al-tirāz al-khāssa*, to make cloth for his palace and family members. These establishments were large and busy enterprises in themselves, since caliphs typically liked to have enormous wardrobes. One caliph, according to a report, owned 8,000 tunics with gold thread or fur linings, 10,000 shirts, 11,000 robes, 2,000 pairs of pants, 1,000 cloaks, 1,000 girdles covered with pieces of gold, and 5,000 handkerchiefs. Caliphs might also order their weavers to make expensive items of clothing to be given as gifts to friends, foreign dignitaries, and even ordinary citizens. For example, the caliph Muhammad ibn Mansur al-Mahdi (ca. 744–785) sent thousands of attractive robes to be distributed to the residents of Mecca to ensure their loyalty in an age when rebellions were commonplace. The caliph's many pillows and cushions also required fine woven covers.

Islamic weavers, having completed their fabrics, often were not required to do any sewing, for two reasons. First, some common items of clothing were simply large pieces of fabric that people draped over their bodies in various ways. For example, the *izār* was a large fabric that both men and women would wrap around their waists to cover their lower bodies and legs; some women also wore an *izār* on their heads, kept in place by a small belt. In Arabia, an *izār* might be the only item of clothing that a man wore. The *mi'zar* was a smaller piece of cloth that men wrapped around their waist as a sort of loincloth in warm weather or when they visited the public baths. For protection against

inclement weather, men and women could don a large cloak, called a *ridā'*, or a piece of woolen fabric also used as a blanket called a *kisā*. A similar item made of silk, the *mitraf*, was donned solely for ceremonial occasions and was often embroidered. Simple strips of fabrics were wrapped around a conical cap to provide Middle Eastern men with their distinctive turbans. Second, in addition to items of clothing, unsewn fabrics with elaborate designs were made to be used as household decorations, hung on walls to provide otherwise bare rooms with some color. When these fabrics became faded or torn, people would commonly leave them in place and cover them with new fabrics. In the sacred building of Kaaba in Mecca, the walls had been covered with so many layers of fabric that their combined weight was starting to cause structural damage until the caliph Muhammad ibn Mansur al-Mahdi ordered all of them removed.

Along with fabrics on their walls, Islamic families of all social classes also enjoyed having attractive carpets on their floors—or on the ground, in the case of the tents of the nomadic Bedouins, who made and transported carpets as their sole pieces of furniture. Individual believers also tended to own their own small carpets for their daily prayers. The process of weaving such carpets has also been described as "knotting," since weavers had to tie small knots around the threads. To produce thick carpets with bright colors, it was important to make the knots as small as possible; in some cases, a fine carpet might have up to 8,000 knots per foot. The wool used to make carpets was dyed with readily available materials: indigo leaves provided blue, henna leaves yielded orange, the bark of nuts offered light and dark browns, the insects called cochineals created red colors, saffron flowers produced yellow, and the berries of buckthorn trees produced green. To preserve precious water, indigo dye could be pressed into the fabric without soaking it. The carpet designs would range from geometric patterns to images of flowers and trees. Understandably, while everyday people were happy to own one or two carpets, used for years and years and even passed on from generation to generation, caliphs kept their weavers busy with their constant requests for new carpets; the caliph Harun al-Rashid (ca. 763–809) reportedly had over 22,000 expensive carpets in his palace.

CLOTHING FOR WALLS

Islamic weavers sometimes produced attractive pieces of fabric to hang on walls as decorations. In the modern United States, as an alternative to painting or applying wallpaper, which can be expensive and time consuming, some designers also advise people to place fabric on their walls. One can cover the walls of an entire room in one day by carefully cutting lengths of fabric to match the walls' height and stapling each piece of fabric to the wall, keeping staples about one inch part. One advantage of this method is that, if the fabric is no longer deemed desirable, it is easier to remove staples than to paint over paint or remove wallpaper.

COSTLY CARPETS

One of the most popular products made by medieval Persian weavers was their intricately designed and colorful carpets, which were widely exported to Europe and other regions. Even today, most of the carpets made in Iraq are still handmade, using the traditional method of dyeing natural fibers and individually tying each knot. However, since a great deal of time is required to make a single carpet, these have become very expensive items. Fortunately, consumers on a budget can also purchase similar-looking rugs that are made by machines and employ synthetic fibers.

While they were often impressive works of art, few fabrics from the medieval Islamic world have survived, since they are by nature very fragile, and since old fabrics were often torn apart to be reused. Some items were preserved inside arid Egyptian tombs, and carpets that made their way to Europe may have been carefully saved as antiques. More often, though, the work of the Middle Eastern weavers is available now only in the form of fragments, often found and cut up to be sold to several buyers by opportunistic scavengers, and their current owners may not know where they came from or whether they were part of a cloak, tunic, or wall hanging. But the techniques of these weavers were passed on to descendants who continued to produce similar items, commonly available today, which aptly convey just how skillful and creative they were.

Further Reading

Baker, Patricia L. 1995. *Islamic Textiles*. London: British Museum Press.
Balfour-Paul, Jenny. *Indigo in the Arab World*. London and New York: Routledge.
Ecker, Heather. 2004. *Caliphs and Kings: The Art and Influence of Islamic Spain*. Washington, DC: Arthur M. Sackler Gallery.
Pinner, Robert, and Walter B. Denny, editors. 1985. *Oriental Carpet and Textile Studies*. Volume 1. London: Published in Association with *HALI* Magazine.
Shatzmiller, Maya. 1993. *Labour in the Medieval Islamic World*. Leiden, The Netherlands, and Boston: Brill.
Sinclair, Susan, editor. 2012. *Bibliography of Art and Architecture in the Islamic World*. Two volumes. Leiden, The Netherlands, and Boston: Brill.

Document

From al-Muhassan ibn Ali. C. 991. *The Table-Talk of a Mesopotamian Judge*. Translated by David Samuel Margoliouth. 1922. London: The Royal Asiatic Society.

al-Muhassan ibn Ali (ca. 940–944), the judge who wrote the text generally known as The Table-Talk of a Mesopotamian Judge, *here describes a man's desire for a magnificent carpet, and he mentions a carpet-merchant who was one of Baghdad's most prominent citizens.*

This Abū Makhlad was a man of great liberality and cupidity such as is found only among the Persians. One day he entered the presence of the Caliph Mufi', and saw in the room a vast rug of yellow poplin and embroidery, fit for a Caliph. When he saw it, he was amazed, and said to his secretary Abu Ahmad Shirāzī: I should like to do with this as I did with the seat of Mu'izz al-daulah; for the story of his carrying it off on his back was by this time celebrated. Abu Ahmad told him that a trick of that sort could not be played in the Caliph's court; for with the Caliphs jesting might only be practised in private, whereas that was a public audience. But, he said, as I see how much you admire it, I will procure it for you as a present. When the function was over, Abu Ahmad, as he went out, found the man sitting in the vestibule. What is this, Sheikh, he asked.—You had better go back, he replied, and tell your master that I shall not go away without that rug; had it not been for my respect for your advice, I should have taken it as I took the seat. Abu Ahmad went back and told the whole story to the Caliph, who ordered it to be taken to the man's boat, and he went off with it accordingly.

I was told this by Abū Ahmad al-Fadl b. 'Abd al-Rahman b. Ja'far of Shiraz and I heard Ibn Diyah the carpet-merchant, who was head of the trade in Baghdad and had greater experience of furniture there than anyone else, narrate in a large assembly how he had seen furniture belonging to Abu Makhlad brought out by the latter for him to value; I valued it, he said, and though I put it at the lowest figure, the price came to two hundred thousand dinars, and even so I do not know whether that represented the whole of his furniture, or whether he had more besides.